# Thoroughbred Racing's Greatest Day

# Thoroughbred Racing's Greatest Day

*The Breeders' Cup
20th Anniversary Celebration*

Perry Lefko

TAYLOR TRADE PUBLISHING
*Dallas • Lanham • Boulder • New York • Toronto • Oxford*

First Taylor Trade Publishing edition 2003

This Taylor Trade Publishing hardcover edition of *Thoroughbred Racing's Greatest Day* is an original publication. It is published by arrangement with the author.

Published by Taylor Trade Publishing
An imprint of the Rowman & Littlefield Publishing Group, Inc.
4501 Forbes Boulevard, Suite 200
Lanham, Maryland 20706

Distributed by National Book Network

Library of Congress Cataloging-in-Publication Data

Lefko, Perry.
  Thoroughbred racing's greatest day : the Breeders' Cup 20th
anniversary celebration / Perry Lefko.— 1st Taylor Trade Pub. ed.
    p.   cm.
  ISBN 1-58979-013-8 (cloth : alk. paper)
  1. Breeders' Cup Championship Day races.   2. Lefko, Perry.   I. Title.
SF357.B74 L45   2003
798.4'00973—dc22                                        2003015705

∞ ™ The paper used in this publication meets the minimum requirements of American National Standard for Information Sciences—Permanence of Paper for Printed Library Materials, ANSI/NISO Z39.48–1992. Manufactured in the United States of America.

*To Charles Taylor for supporting me as a writer and having the vision to be a founding member of the Breeders' Cup and playing a significant role in bringing it to Canada in 1996.*

# Contents

*Preface*          *ix*

*Acknowledgments*          *xiii*

1   How It All Began: The Birth of the Breeders' Cup      *1*

2   California Dreamin': The First-Ever Breeders' Cup      *13*

3   Blowing into the Windy City: The 2002 Breeders' Cup      *23*

4   A World of Difference: The 2001 Breeders' Cup      *49*

5   Coming to a New Country: The 1996 Breeders' Cup      *59*

6   The Maple Leaf Forever: Canadian Horses      *79*

7   The Drought Is Over: Bobby Frankel      *93*

8   Cool Hand Lukas: D. Wayne Lukas      *113*

9   The Kentucky Kid: Shug McGaughey      *139*

10   The Classic Trainer: Jack Van Berg      *149*

11   The Lord of the Longshots: Andre Fabre      *159*

12   Flying High: Frankie Dettori      *169*

13   Divine Intervention: Pat Day      *193*

14   The Showman Must Go On: Angel Cordero      *209*

15   Oh, Brother: Budroyale and Tiznow      *219*

16   From Triumph to Tragedy: Go for Wand      *239*

17   Fleet Feet: Arazi      *249*

18   Smokin': Cigar      *259*

19   The Blunder Horse: Ricks Natural Star      *273*

20   That's the Ticket: The Pick 6 Score      *299*

21   The Fix Six: The Pick 6 Scandal                              317

22   The First Family of Racing: The Paulsons                      337

23   Heard around the Rail: Twenty Interesting Stories             349

24   The Best of the Best: The Greatest Races                      363

# Preface

The Breeders' Cup has had a profound impact on my life and my career.

In 1996, after almost 10 years of writing and reporting about horse racing, I wrote a book called *The Greatest Show on Turf: A History of the Breeders' Cup*. It was the first-ever book written about the sport's annual year-end championship. The amount of time and research it took me to write the book was enormous and, at times, emotionally draining, but it was something I felt needed to be done to provide a history of one of the greatest annual events in horse racing. That's why I decided to name the book *The Greatest Show on Turf*.

There were many great stories from the origin of the Cup to the time I completed my writing. Working as the full-time beat writer for the *Toronto Sun*, I happened to attend every Cup from 1987–94, witnessing some thrilling finishes, amazing upsets and, sadly, some tragic endings. Through it all, the Breeders' Cup endured as an international sporting event, kind of like the Super Bowl of horse racing.

I stopped writing full-time about horse racing after 1994, choosing to move on to other sports. But I was drawn back to the Breeders' Cup because it was scheduled to come to Canada's Woodbine Racetrack in 1996, the first time the event would be held outside of the U.S. It seemed apropos to use that benchmark as a reason to write about the championship day.

I went to the 1995 Breeders' Cup in New York and began interviewing anyone and everyone I thought had a connection to the event. It took me nine months to complete the book, and in the end I felt like I had delivered a baby. There is no greater satisfaction than to see your first published book, even more so when you truly believe and care about the work you've done. For me, writing about the Breeders' Cup meant everything.

I subsequently wrote biographies about football star Doug Flutie, wrestler Bret Hart and an Olympic gold-medalist, Sandra Schmirler, the curler whose heartbreaking story became a national best-seller in Canada. The Canadian Broadcasting Corporation bought the rights to the book for the purposes of developing it into a television movie, and hopefully that will come to fruition sometime in the future. But the Breeders' Cup book, perhaps because it was my first, held a special place in my heart.

After my literary agent Arnold Gosewich talked to me, I considered doing an update of *The Greatest Show on Turf* to coincide with the 20th edition of the Breeders' Cup in 2003. Numerous stories had evolved since the original book was published, so there was no shortage of material. We approached Rowman & Littlefield about acquiring the book and they agreed, but sought a name change. We agreed on *Thoroughbred Racing's Greatest Day*.

I had some reservations when I went to Chicago last year to do research for the new book, having essentially departed the racing scene. Many people I knew had gone on to other endeavors and some, sadly, had died. Going back in time would not be easy.

I hitched a ride with Glenn Crouter, vice-president of media and community relations with Woodbine Entertainment Group (formerly the Ontario Jockey Club), and his trusty assistant, Darryl Kaplan. I barely knew Glenn and didn't know Darryl at all. After a week with them, they probably regretted meeting me at all. I drove them crazy—all in good fun—and they were great sports. I roomed with John Siscos, the manager of media and corporate communications for the Woodbine Entertainment Group, for a couple of days and with Tom Cosgrove, the company's director of backstretch operations, the other two days. I met many industry colleagues, including Suneet Singh, who is now Suneet Ashburn. She reminded me—rightfully so—I had neglected to include her in the original book. In addition to Suneet, it was great seeing again the likes of Larry Bortstein, Steve Haskin, Mike Kane, Mark Simon, Pohla Smith, Neil Milbert, Dave Joseph and Dave Surico, all outstanding writers and equally great people. As a whole, the people who write about racing are quality individuals and sometimes don't receive the recognition they should because horse racing isn't the top "beat" on most daily newspapers.

And, along with the aforementioned people I hooked up with my longtime friend, Ted Labanowich, the king of handicapping in Ontario and possibly the king of the world. This guy literally wears a gold-papered crown. He provided me with emotional relief and, more importantly, some cassette tapes. "Ted, thanks as always. You're a big man with a big heart. I only wish our good buddy George Williams could have joined us." He is busy these days in other aspects of his life, although he's still hoping to write the definitive biography on his favorite trainer, H. Allen Jerkens.

The whole experience of being back at the Breeders' Cup after all those years felt strange and surreal, like walking back in time and seeing how things had changed.

And how much they hadn't changed at all. On Breeders' Cup day, once again it was some of the same people winning races: trainers D. Wayne Lukas and Shug McGaughey and jockey Jerry Bailey.

After a long drive back with Glenn and Darryl, who thought they'd have to make an extended stay at the border because of my shenanigans, the process of transcribing, writing and interviewing began again. It took forever to pin down Frankie Dettori for an interview—he didn't ride in the Breeders' Cup but we had prearranged to talk on the phone after meeting at Woodbine—and he provided me with some great material. After I hung up the phone, I listened to the tape and heard my voice and nary a word from Frankie. Technology had reared its ugly head, a common occurrence in my career, but a few weeks later, after he had concluded a hectic schedule of riding and vacationing, Frankie made himself available. He was just as fascinating the second time.

Much has happened to the Breeders' Cup since I wrote my book, including a name change in 2001. The Breeders' Cup is now known as the World Thorough-bred Championships to make it more identifiable.

It now has a new book to reflect that. The new name reflects the greatness of the event and should make it more identifiable to sports fans, even if they don't specifically follow horse racing. I believe the book can be used as a tool to learn what drives the people in the game to do what they do. In essence, this is a hand-book for the sports fan in general.

Enjoy.

# Acknowledgments

$\mathcal{A}$ heartfelt thanks to The Rowman & Littlefield Publishing Group—in particular editor Jill Langford and production editors Janice Braunstein and Alden Perkins—for believing in this project and to my agent, Arnold Gosewich, for providing the push.

Thanks to Dirk Pfenning, Richard Blais and Tristan Caray for their technical computer support.

A collective thanks to the following companies, organizations or individuals for supplying much-needed material, phone numbers or contacts:

The *Toronto Sun* library/research staff, especially Jillian Goddard, and imaging department, in particular Joe Duffy. Keeneland's award-winning library and director of broadcast services G.D. Hieronymus.

James Fry of the International Racing Bureau.

Jim Gluckson, Joan Lawrence and Eric Wing of the National Thoroughbred Racing Association. D.G. Van Clief, Damon Thayer and Pam Blatz-Murff of Breeders' Cup Ltd. Steve Sexton and Karl Schmitt of Churchill Downs Inc. Dan Leary and Dave Zenner of Arlington Park. The Ontario Racing Commission and the New Mexico Racing Commission.

Glenn Crouter, John Siscos, Darryl Kaplan, Tom Cosgrove, John Whitson, Steve and Jennifer Lym and Lou Cauz of the Woodbine Entertainment Group.

Terry Meyocks, Bill Nader, John Tierney and Fran LaBelle Jr. of the New York Racing Association. Remington Park's Dale Day. Emerald Downs' Susie Sourwine. Rockingham Park's Lynne Snierson.

Matt Hegarty, Brad Free, Steve Andersen and Irwin Cohen of the *Daily Racing Form*.

The *New York Times*' Joe Drape. Scott Finley and Bill Finley. The *Dallas Morning News*' Gary West. The *Las Vegas Review Journal*'s Richard Eng.

Jockey agent Ray Cochrane and trainer Luca Cumani.

Teddy Beckett and Sandra Gray Volpe of Juddmonte Farms. John Sikura Jr. of Hill 'N Dale Farm.

Cindy Pierson Dulay of Horse-Races-net. *The Racing Post*. Hammond Communications. *Thoroughbred Times*. Neil Milbert and Dave Surico of the *Chicago Tribune*.

Ed Musselman, a.k.a. Indian Charlie.

Joltin' Joe Peisich and Stormin' Norman Rumack.

Public relations guru Phil Levine.

Tommy Wolski and Kent Gilchrist.

Larry Bortstein of the *Orange Country Register*. Steve Haskin of *The Blood-Horse*. Robbie Henwood, Richard Mauntah, Jamie Macdonald, Ted Labanowich, George Williams and Paul Wiecek.

To the countless people who availed themselves for interviews, no matter how trivial, a collective thanks. In particular I want to single out jockeys Frankie Dettori, Pat Day and John Velazquez and trainers D. Wayne Lukas and Bobby Frankel for their unlimited time.

To John R. Gaines, thank you for having the inspiration to create the Breeders' Cup.

To my longtime friend, trainer Peter Ron Walder, and his wife/assistant Francine, thanks for your insights and guidance. May you both find that one special horse—and may Sol and Bessie be there for the ride.

To my family—Jane, Ben, Shayna and the world's greatest dog Bandit—a heartfelt thank you for allowing me the time to work on this.

Lastly, to my sister—Robyn—thanks for being my greatest inspiration and my guiding light.

# How It All Began

## The Birth of the Breeders' Cup

*In* the late 1970s, Kentucky horseman John R. Gaines had an inspiration that would forever change horse racing.

Concerned about negative publicity aimed at thoroughbred racing—in particular a segment on the CBS-TV show *60 Minutes* that he viewed as inflammatory and biased—Gaines wanted a promotional vehicle for the sport. He envisioned a championship event day in October that would bring together the best horses from around the world for a single afternoon of competition.

Gaines' idea, the Breeders' Cup, has become the major international event in horse racing since its inception in 1984, and is referred to by many as "the greatest show on turf."

Gaines, who owned and operated Gainesway Farm, one of the leading stallion and breeding operations in the world, kept his idea mostly to himself during the embryonic stages. In December 1980, he quietly formed a corporation called Breeding Incentives Ltd., the forerunner of Breeders' Cup Ltd.

One of the few people who knew about the idea was Nelson Bunker Hunt, at the time one of the world's top breeders and owners and someone with whom Gaines regularly did business. Gaines considered him a combination friend, partner and confidant. One day while sitting in his office talking, Gaines told Hunt about his "crazy" idea and how he planned to finance it, using annual nomination payments from owners of stallions and foals. Hunt thought it a great concept and urged Gaines to pursue it. In 1981, Gaines put his plan into serious motion for its unveiling a year later, but told only a few people in the industry about it.

"I didn't want to piecemeal it out," Gaines said in explaining his tactics. "I understood because of experiences I had it's almost impossible to create a consensus, that it's something that had to sort of happen, had to be imposed on the industry in a way. That's why I elected to announce it when I did, to hopefully generate tremendous press that would excite people in the industry and create sort of a bandwagon situation, which indeed it did."

Joe Hirsch, executive columnist of the *Daily Racing Form* and arguably the most influential journalist in the sport, had advance knowledge of the idea. Hirsch had a reputation for writing fairly and honestly, and Gaines wanted him to have the story first. Gaines called Hirsch on April 20, 1982, three days before publicly announcing the Breeders' Cup plan, and asked him to come to his office. Hirsch politely declined because he said he was too busy writing about the forthcoming Kentucky Derby. But when Gaines told him he was about to give him the most important story he'd ever written, Hirsch arranged to meet the following morning for breakfast.

Hirsch listened to Gaines' idea, but reacted with uncertainty because he felt the Breeders' Cup would clash with football, which ruled sports during the fall. Gaines told him that it wouldn't matter because if the purses were large enough, the horsemen would come and make the event big enough to garner major media and fan attention. Hirsch wrote the exclusive story, which appeared in the *Daily Racing Form* on April 23, the day Gaines publicly announced his plan.

He made the announcement at the annual Kentucky Derby Festival "They're Off" luncheon in Louisville, Kentucky, where Gaines received an award of merit for service to horse racing. He called his plan the Parade of Champions, a one-day racing spectacular with seven races, including one for steeplechasers, totaling $11.5 million in purses. A $5 million weight-for-age race at the classic distance of a mile and a quarter highlighted the day. In theory, it was five times greater than the richest purse at the time, the Arlington Million.

Gaines planned to hold the event annually at the end of October, starting as early as 1984. He announced Belmont Park in New York as the logical inaugural site because of its size. The plan also called for $3 million in breeders' prizes and awards, and $100,000 to be added to 10 select races in the U.S. and 10 in Europe.

Gaines planned to generate purse money from two sources: stud fees and yearling and weanling payments. He said a "conservative estimate" of $5 million would be generated from stallion owners, who would make annual payments each year equal to one half of one stud fee (it would eventually be one full stud fee). The other $6 million would come from a series of eligibility payments when the horses were weanlings and yearlings.

Gaines also talked about showcasing his championship day on television and broadcasting it to tracks around the continent, in essence to let all the world see the greatest single day of racing.

"We're only looking at a single person and that's the racing fan, the bettor," Gaines said in his speech. "He is the person we are trying to reach and whose imagination we are trying to excite. This might help him become a true racing fan instead of going to stock-car races or other sporting events."

Among the few print journalists in attendance was Billy Reed, sports editor of the *Louisville Courier-Journal* and a correspondent for *Sports Illustrated*. Reed had been to the Derby kickoff luncheon before and had not considered it a major newsworthy event, but Gaines' idea gave him an excellent story that appeared the following day on the front page of the *Courier-Journal* sports section. Later that day, when he arrived at the press box of Churchill Downs, Reed encountered Andy Beyer, the racing writer for the *Washington Post*, who was totally skeptical of the concept and was not afraid to say so. Beyer may have been the most outspoken of the journalists who discussed it with Reed that day, but he was not the only doubter. Most of the journalists at Churchill Downs had what Reed described as "healthy skepticism."

"It sounded like a good idea to me; it's something worth thinking about and exploring," Reed said. "Mr. Gaines certainly had the clout and the connections with his fellow breeders and other horsemen to get something done. I thought it was a good idea from day one. We all wondered if all the mechanics would be worked out."

Gaines wanted to influence the trade journals, knowing that was where he had to market the concept, and received positive editorial support from the *Daily Racing Form*, the *Thoroughbred Record* and *The Blood-Horse*. Gaines was off and running with his idea.

"I established an agenda of what I wanted to accomplish and a detailed timetable for executing those goals," Gaines said. "I developed a blitzkrieg attitude and a SWAT team mentality because I knew that momentum was everything. I realized before the idea was ever launched that the two problem areas would be what I called the Kentucky hardboot mentality and the eastern racing establishment mentality. I anticipated many of the hardboots would want to use the money strictly for the premium awards program without having a championship day. This of course would end up being no more than a welfare program for the nation's breeders and owners, similar to the restrictive state breeding programs that accomplish nothing for the public image of racing."

Gaines sent out texts of his speech to people he planned to conscript for his executive committee. He wanted a group that comprised the top stallion managers and commercial breeders in the business. He chose John Nerud (Tartan Farm); Brownell Combs (Spendthrift Farm); Seth Hancock (Claiborne Farm); Brereton Jones (Airdrie Stud); Charles Taylor (Windfields Farm); Will Farish (Lane's End Farm); Bert Firestone; John Mabee; and Nelson Bunker Hunt. Gaines chose them on the basis of their ability, character, intelligence and credibility in the industry. He considered them a "new, fresh group of experienced faces." Each of the founding members put up $10,000 as operating capital and the Breeders' Cup Ltd., a non-profit organization for the event, which officially became known as Breeders' Cup Day, was announced on May 3.

Three months after his announcement, Gaines revealed the full Breeders' Cup Ltd.'s board of directors, 30 of the most prominent people worldwide in racing. In addition to the executive committee, he had some of the top breeders, owners, trainers and stallion operators in the world, people such as Robert Sangster, Vincent O'Brien, Daniel Wildenstein, Stavros Niarchos and Alec Head.

The executive committee agreed to solicit proposals from every racetrack in North America, although some tracks were immediately disqualified from the running because they lacked the qualifications outlined in a two-page list. Churchill Downs, for instance, was eliminated because it did not have a turf course. The track eventually built one, which led to it hosting the event in later years.

At this point in the project, Gaines' plan looked healthy and strong. In addition to requesting seed money from each of the executive members, he asked them to choose a specific committee to head. Nerud, the Hall of Fame former horse trainer who built Tartan into a leading stallion operation, chose marketing and then chuckled aloud: "This old country boy just stole the Breeders' Cup and you don't even know it." In Nerud's opinion, marketing meant everything and, in the overall scheme of things, he was probably right.

Following a recommendation by sportsmen Marvin Warner and George Steinbrenner, Nerud and Gaines approached New York's Robert Landau Associates, which had won television contracts for the upstart United States Football League well before it began play and the U.S. Olympic Committee. Landau's group was a promotional consulting company which had a fast-growing sports marketing and television division headed by Mike Letis and Mike Trager. The two were proven executives who were well-known in the communications industry. They later became co-owners of Sports Marketing and Television International Inc., which became the official Breeders' Cup marketing agency in 1985 following the demise of Landau's company.

Nerud arranged for the executives to make a presentation to himself, Gaines and a trio of businessmen with ties to horse racing: Johnson & Johnson chief executive officer Phil Hofmann; *Florida Horse* magazine publisher Fern Audette, and Madison Square Garden chairman Sonny Werblin. The meeting took place at the Garden and when it was over, Werblin declared his support for Letis and Trager. Nerud respected Werblin's judgment and hired the two men as consultants.

In September, the executive committee and Letis and Trager convened in Lexington to hear proposals from representatives of eight North American tracks— Belmont Park, Santa Anita Park, Hollywood Park, the Meadowlands, Atlantic City, Hawthorne, Arlington Park and Woodbine—which made pitches to play host to the inaugural event.

The New York Racing Association, which operated Belmont Park, Aqueduct and Saratoga, ruled the fall season with its races and, in some respects, ran the equivalent of the Breeders' Cup over a six-week period. NYRA had been considered the early front-runner, but there had been rumblings it did not favor the Breeders' Cup. Steven Crist, the *New York Times'* racing writer who in later years became an executive with NYRA, alluded to it in an article earlier that year. He wrote: "According to industry sources, New York racing officials have been decidedly unenthusiastic about the idea, saying that they already stage several series of races in each major division each fall. These officials say privately that they are reluctant to take the championship edge off these races in favor of a one-shot weekend that would move from track to track each year. Nonetheless, if the series is to happen, they want it in New York."

Gaines said NYRA proposed adding the Breeders' Cup money to the existing New York stakes schedule, thereby making it significantly more important from a financial aspect. Gaines said NYRA had made a similar pitch at an earlier meeting which included NBC Sports president Arthur Watson, who said NBC would have no interest in the Breeders' Cup without the championship day.

What would eventually be the winning bid came from Hollywood Park, spearheaded by its controversial vice-chairman of the board and chief operating officer, Marje Everett. She had been involved in racing for more than 40 years and had the largest financial interest in the publicly traded company. Everett believed in Gaines' concept from the moment she heard about it and impressed upon the Breeders' Cup selection committee how Hollywood Park would bring an aura of glamour and attractiveness to the event. Hollywood Park had celebrities such as Cary Grant and John Forsythe on its board of directors and planned to incorporate them and other popular figures from the entertainment industry into the Cup festivities.

"She was very effective in person, very effective. I'd never seen her in action before and basically she wanted it and she made that clear," Charles Taylor said of the presentation.

Everett considered New York the frontrunner because in addition to the size of the track, it also wielded influence and power in the industry with its chairman, Ogden Mills (Dinny) Phipps, who a year later would become chairman of The Jockey Club. The Phipps family had a long and celebrated history in racing and had connections to the Kentucky power brokers in the sport.

Following the presentations, Letis and Trager retreated to Gaines' house and impressed upon him the need for the event to be conducted on one day and to be televised live in its entirety. At this point, the directors considered various possibilities for the Cup, everything from running it on one day, to running it on three separate weekends, to running the seven races at seven separate tracks.

Letis and Trager thought the Meadowlands had made the best presentation, but that would not necessarily be the sole criterion for choosing it as the host track. The two executives understood the importance of television and marketing and for those reasons, plus weather, the Los Angeles tracks made the most sense as the inaugural host track. They outdrew the New York tracks at that time of the year and the directors, who were hopeful of showing the event on worldwide television, were acutely aware of the benefits of a favorable broadcast, time slot and packed grandstand on a presumably sunny day.

Later that day, at a dinner meeting Gaines convened at a country club, the board discussed the various proposals. It made three critical decisions: to conduct the event on one day; to begin it in California; and to take the Cup to the East Coast the following year, with New York the likely place.

The board planned to announce its inaugural site in November, after receiving contract submissions from Hollywood and Santa Anita. Hollywood proposed November 10, while Santa Anita picked October 27, during its Oak Tree meeting.

"We hope we can convince the committee that Hollywood Park would be the perfect site, and that we can do as well as anyone in the country in presenting it," Everett told the *Daily Racing Form*.

"To present the Breeders' Cup as the climax of the Oak Tree meeting would be highly appropriate, and the worldwide attention that will be focused on Santa Anita during the Olympic Equestrian events would be a natural carryover to the Breeders' Cup," said Jimmy Kilroe, the senior vice-president of racing for Santa Anita and director of racing of the Oak Tree meet.

On the surface, everything looked great for the future of the Cup. But it wasn't. While there had been tremendous support for Gaines' concept, the actual implementation of the plan highlighted differences in philosophies and egos among the directors. A split developed between two camps with opposing views in allocating the purses. One side, led by Gaines and Nerud, wanted it spent on Breeders' Cup races; the other favored spreading money out over a year-long series of stakes races. The division became so great it led to the resignation of Seth Hancock, Brereton Jones and William duPont III of Pillar Stud. All three operated major stallion operations in Kentucky and the Breeders' Cup needed their support—and the influence they carried—to financially sustain the program.

In an article in the *Daily Racing Form*, Jones described the format as "unfair and unworkable." Hancock cited "opinion differences with controlling parties." DuPont said he was resigning because of "philosophical differences."

"There are too many loose ends, too many unanswered questions, too many egos and too much money," duPont told Maryjean Wall of the *Lexington Herald-Leader*. "If it had not started out on such a grandiose scale, it might have had a better shot."

In his letter to Gaines, Jones, who in later years became governor of Kentucky, said he did not believe the Breeders' Cup in its present form would be acceptable to the vast majority of the industry. In his view, it was "unhealthy" to collect all the money and give nearly 75% of it to a handful of people on one day.

"It has been my desire to match at least every dollar that is given away on the big day with a dollar that will go to stakes races at every track in America, from the first of January to the last of December," Jones wrote. "This would help upgrade racing all over America, not just at one track on one day. If this equality of matching funds could be coupled with a substantial nominations awards program, I think that the majority of our industry would feel that they were getting a fair break and would be far more inclined to participate."

Gaines defended his Super Bowl concept as the reason for putting the majority of the purse money into one day of racing and added that smaller breeders could share in the year-round stakes program. "The smaller breeder would have an excellent chance of winning races conducted at Latonia and smaller tracks as well as lesser stakes at bigger tracks," he told Wall. "So, it's a positive thing for the smaller breeder."

"I talked with more individuals in the industry at every level than Mr. Gaines did and it's not going to work," Jones told Wall. "The basic concept was a wonderful thing and at first we all said, 'sure,' but as time went on we recalled the board of governors didn't have much say. The average guy is not going to benefit from this."

In Nerud's opinion, Gaines had difficulty gaining full support because he was never popular with the Kentucky horsemen. Gaines came from New York and started out in standardbred racing, in which he enjoyed success as the owner of two horses, Kerry Way and Speedy Streak, who won the prestigious Hambletonian in 1966–67. At the same time, he was also involved in thoroughbred racing and was about to branch into breeding, too. By 1984, his operation stood 47 stallions, which he valued then at about $400 million.

Gaines thought there was a lot of paranoia among some of his fellow stallion managers who seemed to feel he had a hidden agenda that somehow benefited him and disadvantaged them. Gaines said there were some stallion managers, both in Kentucky and elsewhere, who refused to nominate their stallions at the current market stud fee. Moreover, there was little the Breeders' Cup could do about this, although Gaines said "it was widely recognized as being unfair."

Taylor, for one, felt it was Gaines' warp-like speed that also may have played a factor. "For some people he was going too fast and encompassing too much," Taylor said. "Not everybody is initially open to bold new ideas, especially when it's going to cost them money. We were pledging our stallions and some of us put up money to pay the bills."

The concept came at an interesting time in the breeding industry. Buyers spent freely at sales, engaging in frantic bidding that pushed up bloodstock sales to incredible heights. Commercial breeders started realizing multimillion returns on their yearlings, allowing them to operate at a profit. Six-figure stud fees became a common thing. There was a $1 million no-guarantee in private deals for Northern Dancer, the hottest sire of the decade and the greatest influence of the modern generation.

But according to Nerud, the breeders overall didn't understand the benefit of the multimillion marketing concept, thinking selfishly instead of about the overall good of the industry. Not only did the Breeders' Cup Ltd. have dissension among its board members, it also had rapidly diminishing funds that actually shut down operations for a while. A total of $300,000 was raised by six members who agreed to each sign a $50,000 guarantee to borrow money from the bank.

"The place was dead," Nerud said. "We had a business and no money. And you had no guarantee you were ever going to get it back. If it doesn't run, you're dead and even if it does run you might not get it back."

Gaines did not have any worries that the Cup might not happen, but he realized that it was in everyone's best interest, including his own, to step down and let someone else take over as president. In October that year he approached C. Gibson Downing about replacing him. Gaines felt Downing had credibility and would be acceptable to everyone, including the important Kentucky–New York faction that had power and influence in the breeding industry. Downing had served three terms in the Kentucky senate before returning to his law practice. He owned mares and stood stallions at his Winfield Farm and had done business with all the directors in one way or another. He was not heavily involved in the Breeders' Cup executive at the time, but told Gaines he would accept the position if the executive supported the move. After Gaines called some directors and told them of his decision to step down and to consider Downing as the successor, the board had a new interim leader.

"Everyone wanted this to succeed and to work and my style in the past in other things I had done was to get something started, implement it so that it's a going concern and then step aside and let others run it," Gaines said.

Nerud said after Downing's appointment, "everybody got back on the same page again."

Shortly after the change in the presidency, the board hired D. G. Van Clief as its new executive director, replacing John Hardy. Van Clief grew up on a breeding farm in Virginia and knew many of the directors. He had worked for the Fasig-Tipton Sales Agency in Lexington before going to California, where he had been employed at Hollywood Park as one of the assistants to the chief executive officer. When he joined the Breeders' Cup Ltd., it had a secretary, a publicity director and a modest office. The Cup had roughly $75,000 in early nominations in the bank and some $300,000 in unpaid advertising bills.

"My job was to tidy things up in terms of operations policy and the rules for Breeders' Cup, and then to go out and sell the concept to the industry, which would hopefully fund the first championship," Van Clief said. "Had we not done that by the late spring of '83, it's very likely the Breeders' Cup would not go forward."

In a January 1983 *Thoroughbred Record* article written by executive editor Mark Simon, Downing said he recognized the concerns of the reluctant stallion operators, but believed they were based on a desire to see the program laid out in detail before making a decision. Downing noted a committee had been appointed to study and develop a year-round premium awards program and a committee had been established to put a financial plan in place for the Breeders' Cup. "What we're trying to do is to proceed with the raising of the money and taking advantage of the momentum that was generated in the spring and summer and fall of 1982 and then develop through the use of the best brains in the industry the best plan for how that money will be distributed," Downing said. "I think we're approaching it the right way now."

After much debate the Breeders' Cup settled on nomination payments: $500 for foals of 1981 and '82, $3,000 for foals of 1980 or older.

"We started off and made these decisions and it's stayed," Nerud said. "We had no precedents. We had no way of knowing what the hell we were doing."

Among the other financial decisions was allocating 50 cents of every dollar for the championship day purses while giving the remaining half for stakes races throughout the year. "That was an important compromise because it gave us the wherewithal to go out and sell the program to the breeders who felt they would have a chance of receiving a return on their nomination investment even if they didn't get a horse to the championship," Van Clief said. "In many ways the alleged controversy between championship day and the premium awards program was a totally manufactured issue," Gaines said. "From the very beginning they were both an integral and synergistic part of the Breeders' Cup."

Little by little the Breeders' Cup program started taking shape in 1983. In February, Hollywood Park received the nod over Santa Anita as the inaugural host track. Nelson Bunker Hunt, the chairman of the selection committee, said in an article written by Tony Chamblin in the official 1984 Breeders' Cup program that it was the most difficult decision he ever had to make as a horseman.

Nerud said he and other directors influenced the decision. While Oak Tree's Clement Hirsch made an impressive financial presentation, Everett won over the board with her gung-ho attitude and the promise to use her entertainment contacts to have the event televised. Every couple of months thereafter announcements were made indicating the progress of the Breeders' Cup Ltd. By mid-March, roughly one-fifth of the registered 5,393 stallions in North America had been nominated, contributing more than $10.5 million in funds. Chamblin reported that 47 of America's 52 stallions with fees of at least $50,000 were nominated to the program. The list included the 20 top sires of two-year-olds in 1982.

"There was an overwhelming response from stallion owners," Downing told Chamblin. "Based on our original projections, we expected to receive $7.5 million."

An additional $10 million came from the nomination of 18,000 foals. In June, Breeders' Cup Ltd. announced a $10 million Premium Awards Program, allocating funds for 90 racing associations in 22 states and five Canadian provinces. Nominators of stallions and foals would receive awards equal to 5% of the purses, a concept that also applied to the championship day.

While all this was happening, Gaines talked either in person or by telephone to prominent owners, breeders and trainers of European horses to convince them to participate in the program. The European participation became another topic that produced heated discussion. Some of the directors did not feel the need to incorporate the foreign representation, while others felt it crucial to the turf races. Taylor, who chaired the European Liaison Committee, felt the foreign contingent was needed to make the event truly international. He also recognized that many of the top buyers during the '80s raced horses in Europe.

The Europeans had adopted a breeders fund financed by the nomination of stallions only and designed to augment purses. This diametrically differed from the Breeders' Cup philosophy, which Gaines and his executive created as a mass marketing tool. To bring the Europeans back on board, the Breeders' Cup Ltd. subsidized the European Breeders' Fund in the first year by $600,000, using a formula of stallion nomination fees from the EBF to the Breeders' Cup and vice versa. A cross-registration agreement was also established, providing a mechanism for allowing Breeders' Cup horses to participate in the European Breeders' Fund. In the second year the subsidy escalated to $800,000, the highest level in Breeders' Cup history. Eventually, Breeders' Cup Ltd. worked it out so it did not have to subsidize the Europeans at all. Early in 1984, the graded stakes panel of the Thoroughbred Owners and Breeders' Association announced its decision to award Grade One status to all seven Breeders' Cup races. Normally, it took a minimum of two years before a race earned graded status and even longer to become a Grade One.

The office staff of Combs' Spendthrift Farm, in conjunction with Gaines and Brereton Jones, devised rules for entry and nomination to the races. It would cost 1% of the purse for pre-entry fees 12 days before the race and another 1% to enter. Only through an illness or disability certified by the track or state veterinarian acceptable to the Breeders' Cup Ltd. could the money be refunded.

It would cost 12% of the gross purse to supplement a horse if the sire was not nominated to the Breeders' Cup program when the foal was nominated or 20% if both the sire and foal were not nominated. The huge supplementary fees were intended to encourage breeders and owners to nominate to the program.

The supplementary fees led to a public outcry when John Henry, the top horse in North America, would have to be supplemented because neither he nor his sire,

Ole Bob Bowers, were nominated by the April 1983 deadline. It all became moot when John Henry failed to make it to the Breeders' Cup because of a leg injury.

Breeders' Cup Ltd. rules limited each race to 14 starters. The top nine point-earners from the Breeders' Cup North American graded stakes program received starting preference. A panel of racing experts determined the other five, based on European horses and horses who did not have enough graded stakes points (for example late-developing stars).

The winner of each race received 45% of the total purse, followed by 22.5% for second, 10.8% for third, 7% for fourth, 5% for fifth and 1% for sixth. Stallion and foal-nominator awards consisted of $25,000 for first, $12,500 for second and $6,000 for third. All unpaid nominator awards reverted to Breeders' Cup Ltd.

After Breeders' Cup Ltd. raised sufficient starting funds and had its racing program in place, it had to work on its next project: securing a television deal.

"There was a huge amount of skepticism and doubt whether this event would ever work because people thought there would never be enough unity within the industry," Van Clief said. "Also, they thought the industry would never be able to go outside to attract television to this event."

"Right from the beginning television was the critical thing," Letis said. "In horse racing, it was proven that except for the (Kentucky) Derby, which was in a time frame where there was little or no sports competition, that horse racing could not produce good numbers on television. It was not profitable for television. Their big races in the fall were not on the air. Football ruled the fall and here we were saying we want to be on live, in the middle of football, with four hours of horse racing."

Letis and Trager approached NBC, ABC and CBS, seeking a live presentation of all seven races. CBS had minimal interest. ABC mostly wanted to show the Classic, but NBC embraced the entire package. Arthur Watson had given Nerud and Gaines a feeling of hope when they talked to him in 1982.

"We knew we couldn't do it without one of the three major networks, so we were nervous," Gaines said in an article written by *Boston Globe* television writer Jack Craig. "But, then I saw Arthur's Irish face, that cherubic look, eyes lit up, and at the end he said, 'I just want you to know that NBC is going to find some way to do this, John.'"

Watson delivered on his promise the following year after some strong selling by Letis and Trager. Letis guaranteed that any race sponsors had to also buy television commercial time, which would diminish NBC's cost.

On Sept. 13, 1984, NBC and the Breeders' Cup announced an exclusive multiyear agreement for a reported $5 million to broadcast all seven races worldwide in a five-hour telecast.

"It will carry the impact of the Super Bowl and World Series for those involved in the sport of thoroughbred racing," Watson said in a press release. "We're extremely confident that Super Saturday—the Championship Series—will immediately be recognized as one of sports television's biggest attractions."

Letis and Trager then took their packages to corporations to seek sponsorship. It would prove to be the hardest sales pitch of all.

"In the beginning it was a tough, tough sell," Letis said. "No one knew what Breeders' Cup was. Breeders is a funny word—gambling, horse racing, things that people in the corporate world didn't know anything about. We went out to see them all, including places like IBM. We did a lot specialized work in terms of presentations and graphics and logo treatments, etc., in order to show these companies what the hell they would get, what it would look like to be a sponsor of a race."

Sponsors were assigned races based on how much money they committed and what seemed like the best fit. The sponsorship fee ranged from $250,000 to $750,000, depending on the magnitude of the race. The Classic, which would have a $3 million purse, was billed as the most important from a marketing standpoint, followed by the $2 million Turf. The sponsors paid the race sponsorship fee to the Breeders' Cup Ltd. and also agreed to buy the required commercial time from NBC. In addition, money was accrued from secondary sponsors, whose products were advertised as the official product of the Breeders' Cup.

In May, the Breeders' Cup announced the official names of the seven Breeders' Cup races totaling $10 million in purses and nominator awards: The $1 million Juvenile (for two-year-old colts and geldings at a distance of one mile on the dirt); the $1 million Juvenile Fillies (for two-year-old fillies, also one mile on the dirt); the $1 million Sprint (six furlongs for three-year-olds and up); the $1 million Mile (a one-mile grass race for males and females three and up); the $1 million Distaff (a mile and a quarter dirt race for fillies and mares); the $2 million Turf (a mile and a half grass race for males and females); and the $3 million Classic (a mile and a quarter race on the dirt for males and females).

In August, the Breeders' Cup announced its race sponsors: the Chrysler Corporation (Chrysler-Plymouth Division) for the Classic; De Beers Consolidated Mines Ltd. for the Turf; and Mobil Oil Corporation for the Distaff. By race day, First Jersey Securities signed on for the Juvenile and Michelob (Anheuser-Busch, Inc.) for the Mile.

On October 30, the Breeders' Cup received 77 entries from North America and Europe for the seven races.

On November 10, almost 19 months after John R. Gaines' original announcement, the Breeders' Cup had finally arrived.

# 2

# California Dreamin'

## The First-Ever Breeders' Cup

*L*ate in the fall of 1984, an aspiring young California writer quit his job as a deskman and assistant editor at the *Daily Racing Form* to embark on a freelance career that would one day earn him the reputation as the Hemingway of the Horse Set. Jay Hovdey had a lot of reasons for making the career switch, not the least of which was his employers' wish to have him work on November 10. Not only was it his birthday, it also happened to be the date of the inaugural running of the Breeders' Cup. Hovdey just had to be there, both to write about it and to witness a piece of racing history. He was not alone. The Cup had finally arrived, but like the first walk on the moon, nobody knew exactly what they were about to see.

Marje Everett, vice-chairman and chief operating officer of Hollywood Park, spared no expense. Well before the announcement of the Breeders' Cup, the board of directors of Hollywood Park had planned to upgrade the facility, which had opened in 1938, with a four-step improvement program. Acquiring the inaugural Cup expedited the process. Building the $30 million Cary Grant Pavilion—named after the movie star who was on the track's board of directors—topped the priority list. It was to be a five-story turf club, located close to the clubhouse end of the existing stands and adjacent to the new finish line. Everett also renovated the main track, extending it from one mile to a mile and an eighth, providing one of the longest stretch runs on the continent. The extension of the main track allowed the inner turf course to become a one-mile oval, perfect for the $1 million Mile race on the turf.

Everett unveiled the pavilion, which could accommodate 30,000 people, the day before the Cup with Grant and several other movie stars in attendance.

Everett had promised the executive of the Breeders' Cup she would add glamour and glitz to the event and she did not disappoint. She provided a party atmosphere that had stars galore from Hollywood. Two days before the Cup, she staged a black-tie affair at Paramount Studios, attended by such Hollywood icons as Grant, Jimmy Stewart, Joan Collins and Frank Sinatra. In the words of Charles Taylor, one of the Breeders' Cup directors, "that was pretty damn impressive." The night before the Cup, Everett had a bash at her house, where the guest list included Elizabeth Taylor. In the midst of it all, a man who would emerge as one of the stars of the Breeders' Cup arrived in town from New York with little fanfare but with the difficult assignment of calling the races. Tom Durkin, then 32, had worked as the harness racing announcer at the Meadowlands and had backed up Dave Johnson for thoroughbred racing. He also had done some thoroughbred announcing in Florida for a couple of months and had just begun to call the occasional race on television. Durkin couldn't believe it when he was chosen to call the Breeders' Cup races. It literally changed his life, from a professional and financial standpoint.

The late Arthur Watson, president of NBC Sports and executive producer of the Breeders' Cup in the early years, took a liking to Durkin when he attended the races at the Meadowlands. His decision to hire the relatively unknown announcer for the Cup proved a shrewd move. Like many people, Durkin had no idea whether the Breeders' Cup would be a one-shot deal or stand the test of time, but he committed himself to do the best job he could. Beginning in the fall, he underwent a radical change in his diet, eating healthy foods and abstaining from alcohol (a regimen he has followed every year since on the road to the Cup). In addition, he traveled to Belmont Park every race day and, standing in the teletimers' booth, made mock race calls into a tape recorder, trying to come up with new ways to describe the action.

He also started stockpiling information on horses who might be Breeders' Cup bound, although he had little material with which to work. After all, this was well before the era of the internet and the simulcasting boom, the combination of which made it easier to access racing data. In later years, he compiled a notebook that included pages on the horses in each of the races, but for his first assignment Durkin had to wing it. Durkin was not the only one experiencing something new. The journalists who had come to Hollywood from various parts of North America and Europe found themselves in the midst of an unbelievable situation. The late Dale Austin, who had been covering racing for 22 years for the *Baltimore Sun*, arrived toward the end of the week, his first occasion reporting on a race on the West Coast. He had covered major international races, most of them in Maryland, but never before had had access to so many top European trainers in one place at one time. Normally, the owner of a European starter would be on hand days before the race but rarely the trainers. This time they were all there, Austin said. "All those guys you had always heard about but had never seen."

On the day of the Cup, the area around Hollywood Park saw a traffic jam not seen before. "It wasn't even Kentucky Derby traffic, it was Rose (Bowl) parade traffic," Hovdey recalled. A crowd of 64,254 crammed into the track to watch the historic event and they bet $11,466,941, only about $20,000 less than had been bet on the Kentucky Derby that year. The people came eager to watch and wager. And they were treated to beautiful weather: clear and sunny with a temperature of 70 degrees—exactly the kind of day Breeders' Cup Ltd. wanted to showcase its new event around the world.

Before the first race, the stewards addressed the jockeys and told them that the image of racing would be closely scrutinized because of the scope of the day.

They emphasized that regardless of the large purses, any form of rough or careless riding would result in a disqualification. It proved a prophetic speech.

As the first race neared, Durkin felt "absolutely apoplectic, as nervous as anybody could be." He could barely hold on to his binoculars. Durkin suffered then from nervousness when calling races and later almost quit because of that. It took hypnosis, before the 1988 Breeders' Cup, to help him relax, something he is able to do now when calling races. In anticipation of the stress of the first Cup, Durkin had a gooseneck harness built that would support his binoculars. He still uses it.

The Juvenile, for two-year-old colts and geldings, started the day. In years to come, the race would be recognized as the major preview for the Derby the following year. The Juvenile had 10 starters, featuring the best of the east, the west and all the rest, including one, Concert Hall, owned by British soccer pools magnate Robert Sangster, from Ireland. Star Crown Racing Stable's Chief's Crown, who had five wins in eight starts, headed the group. He had run in New York, where he had won the Saratoga Special, the Hopeful and Cowdin Stakes, and had finished second by a length in the Futurity, at Belmont, the first time in his career he had run in the slop. He was then shipped to California, where he won the Norfolk Stakes, his third Grade One victory.

Trained by Roger Laurin, whose father, Lucien, conditioned the likes of Riva Ridge and Secretariat, Chief's Crown was sired by Danzig, a son of Northern Dancer, out of the Secretariat mare Six Crowns. His breeder, Carl Rosen, who was known as the Chief, died in August 1983. Rosen had campaigned the 1974 champion three-year-old filly Chris Evert. Her first foal was Six Crowns. Rosen's son Andrew, the president of Calvin Klein Women's Jeans, owned Chief's Crown in partnership with his brother Douglas.

The principal opponents figured to be Spectacular Love, who had beaten Chief's Crown in the slop in the Futurity, and Spend a Buck, second at the Meadowlands in his previous race. Spend a Buck led from the start to the stretch, but was overtaken by Chief's Crown who outlasted 25-1 shot Tank's Prospect in the final sixteenth of a mile to win by three-quarters of a length. Spend a Buck finished another three-quarters of a length back in third.

Chief's Crown, the 7-10 favorite, provided Durkin with the first of what would be many well-worded calls in the event. When Chief's Crown crossed the wire, Durkin said "a champion is crowned." In Durkin's opinion, the Breeders' Cup was defined at that moment. No longer could there be much debate among voters about the best horse in a specific division. The answer would now be provided on the track.

Laurin brought Chief's Crown to California specifically to run against Saratoga Six to prove he had the best juvenile colt in the country. Early in the race Chief's Crown appeared vulnerable. He did not display his early willingness and his jockey, the late Don MacBeth, took the colt back after attempts to focus his attention. It wasn't until midway down the backstretch that MacBeth felt confident, after his horse began gobbling up ground en route to his victory in a time of 1:36 1/5 for the mile.

The victory by Chief's Crown earned him the year-end championship and favorite status for the 1988 Derby, in which he ran third to Spend a Buck.

While the Juvenile ran to form, the Juvenile Fillies proved the opposite and provided the first example of the rough riding the stewards had warned the jockeys about before the races began. The field featured 11 runners from across North America, including the 8-5 favorite, Bessarabian, who came from Canada on a four-race win streak and then upped it to five with a victory in the Gardenia Stakes at the Meadowlands. But Bessarabian never figured in the finish, when she was bumped by Pirate's Glow, who was knocked off stride by Fran's Valentine, who finished first by a half-length at odds of more than 74-1. But the stewards deemed her jockey, Pat Valenzuela, had caused interference and disqualified Fran's Valentine and placed her 10th. The DQ cost the owners $450,000 in first-place prize money.

Valenzuela received a tongue-lashing from veteran Fernando Toro, whose mount, Pirate's Glow, was only three lengths back after three-quarters of a mile, before losing all hope in the bumping. Toro's horse nearly fell because of the collision. The incident of the veteran Toro scolding the young Valenzuela in Spanish was caught live by NBC in a brilliant piece of news footage.

"I had no room to race," Valenzuela told reporters after the race. "The horses in front of me were stopping. I had to come out. Fernando was there at the time and I bothered him."

"I yelled at him, 'watch out,' but it was too late," Toro told reporters. "I could have gone down. It's not only money, it's our lives. I had just gotten in the clear when that happened. I think I would have been in the first four and I wouldn't be surprised if I would have won. After it happened, I tapped (Pirate's Glow) a couple of times on the shoulder, but she was out. She lost her action and her coordination."

Outstandingly, ridden by Walter Guerra, finished second after avoiding traffic problems and was elevated to first, returning a generous $47.60. Dusty Heart, the longest-priced runner in the field at more than 77-1, was placed second. Fine Spirit, second choice in the wagering at just over 7-2, was moved up to third.

Years later Durkin said that was his worst call in Breeders' Cup history because he missed the bumping and picked up Fran's Valentine too late. But hardly anyone was critical of Durkin; the action in the race far overshadowed the call.

Outstandingly carried the famous pink and black silks of Louis and Patrice Wolfson's Harbor View Farm, which had swept the Triple Crown with Affirmed in 1978. Outstandingly had only one win and a second in three starts heading into the race. Her prerace earnings of $31,470 multiplied by almost 15 times with the win.

The Sprint was next and it had 11 runners—nine from North America and two from Europe—slugging it out at six furlongs. Eillo, the 13-10 favorite, won by a diminishing nose over a fast-closing Commemorate. The tiring racetrack proved unkind to front-runners all day and it took every ounce of courage and heart for Eillo to overcome the bias. Four days before the race, Eillo had rattled off a half mile from the gate in a blistering 45 seconds, indicating his readiness, but trainer

Budd Lepman expressed concern about the long stretch, worrying that it could be Eillo's undoing. It almost was.

Eillo entered the gate last and misbehaved once inside, but finally settled down. Starter Tucker Slender sprung the latch and the Mr. Prospector colt, running in four yellow bandages, zoomed to the lead. Jockey Craig Perret guided him through fractions of :22 4/5 for the opening quarter of a mile and :45 3/5 for the half. Eillo appeared to be comfortably in front, leading by 2½ lengths at the top of the stretch. But he started to tire in the lane and required prompting from Perret to overcome the fatigue factor. Eillo held on over Commemorate, who was given an aggressive ride by Chris McCarron. Running in the silks of Windfields Farm, which had just bought him as a stallion prospect, Commemorate earned $225,000. Fighting Fit, the second choice in the betting at 27-10, rallied strongly under Eddie Delahoussaye to be third a length and a half farther back. Eillo collected $450,000, plus $25,000 in breeder awards for owner/breeder Ollie Cohen. Eillo's victory had been somewhat apropos because he had been named the first Breeders' Cup horse of the month in February of 1984. Tragically, Eillo died a month after the final race of his career and before he could begin a stallion career.

Royal Heroine continued the procession of favorites, winning at odds of 17-10 in the Mile. The only filly in the field of 10, she was coupled in the wagering with Prego, who had come from England. Sangster owned both horses. Royal Heroine and Sabin starred in the female turf division that season. The day before the Breeders' Cup, Sabin won a stakes at Hollywood Park in 1:33 2/5, eclipsing the course record by a fifth of a second. Sabin's owner, Henryk de Kwiatkowski, missed a payment leading up to the Breeders' Cup and opted not to supplement her.

Royal Heroine's victory followed a season-long series of problems. She fell in her seasonal debut, the Grade One Santa Ana Handicap, in which two starters died. Royal Heroine injured a stifle and didn't return for three months, but won her comeback race, the Inglewood Handicap, and then the Beverly Hills Handicap. She followed that with a first in the Palomar Handicap, but was disqualified and placed third. She then ran second to John Henry, the venerable gelding who would win Horse of the Year honors at season's end, in the Arlington Million in Chicago. In her next race in California, she ran second in the Ramona Stakes.

Trainer John Gosden, a classy Englishman based in California, pointed Royal Heroine for the Yellow Ribbon, but she suffered a foot injury. It forced her to miss the prep, but she was ready for the Breeders' Cup. Toro rode the winner, who was never more than 4½ lengths back at any time in the race. Royal Heroine benefited from a quick pace set by Smart and Sharp and Tsunami Slew. At the top of the stretch, Cozzene, owned by John Nerud, one of the executive directors of the Breeders' Cup, and trained by his son, Jan, inherited the lead. Royal Heroine kicked into overdrive at this point and Toro steered her down the middle of the stretch, finishing a length and a half ahead of Star Choice, the long shot in the field at 69-1. Royal Heroine bettered Sabin's mark set the day before by winning in 1:32 3/5, which also represented a North American record for the distance on grass.

Sangster had conominated the filly's sire, Lypheor, to the Breeders' Cup program. Sangster did not own the stallion, but was moved to nominate the stud to the Breeders' Cup program after another son of Lypheor, Tolomeo, won the 1983 Arlington Million.

One fabulous filly followed another. Princess Rooney, who like Royal Heroine had a season of problems, prevailed by an authoritative seven lengths in the Distaff. Not that it was much of a surprise. Princess Rooney, a strapping grey, drew the public's support as the 7-10 favorite after winning her previous start, the Spinster Stakes at Keeneland in Kentucky, by six lengths.

Princess Rooney, owned by Jim and Paula Tucker, starred as a two-year-old and three-year-old, winning multiple stakes races, including the Kentucky Oaks. A stress fracture of the left knee interrupted her three-year-old season and kept her out of action until December. She ran disappointing races in New Jersey and Florida before the Tuckers opted to send her to California and trainer Neil Drysdale with one goal in mind: the Breeders' Cup.

The patient Drysdale waited 10 weeks before running her and she prevailed by a nose in a minor stakes race. Her next two starts featured third- and second-place finishes to Adored, whom she would beat in the Breeders' Cup. She then rattled off four wins, three of them Grade One, en route to the Cup. Drysdale had her in peak condition. Lucky Lucky Lucky had led for three-quarters of a mile, when Princess Rooney, under Eddie Delahoussaye, pounced on the lead and cruised home in the final half mile. She won in a time of 2:02 2/5.

Following the Distaff came the Turf, the other grass race designed to attract Europeans. This one drew 11 starters, but noticeably absent was the venerable John Henry, who had won Horse of the Year honors in 1981 and would duplicate that in 1984. John Henry represented one of the most remarkable stories in racing history. His sire, Ole Bob Bowers, sold for $900 and stood for $1,000 at the time of John Henry's conception. John Henry's dam, Once Double, sold for $5,000 after his birth. He was, as the expression goes, by nothing out of nobody. Owner Sam Rubin bought him for $25,000 and ran him for tags of $25,000 and $35,000 with no takers. At the age of nine, when most horses are retired, the marvelous gelding kept displaying class and talent.

In 1984, John Henry had won nine races, four of them Grade One, and only lost one of seven grass starts. Moreover, he banked more than $2.3 million, an unbelievable sum at that time.

John Henry equaled the course record for a mile and three-eighths at the Meadowlands in the Ballantine's Scotch Classic on Oct. 13, in what was to be his final prep for the Breeders' Cup. By this time, Breeders' Cup Ltd. had been assailed by the press when it was feared John Henry would not run because of the $400,000 supplementary fee. The Breeders' Cup Ltd. had tried its hardest to have Ole Bob Bowers nominated to the program by the April 1993 deadline, knowing that would assure John Henry's eligibility.

"The stallion was being sold by his current owners to new owners and somewhere along the line we couldn't get consent of the new owners to make the commitment," said D. G. Van Clief, who began as the Breeders' Cup executive director and took over as president in 1996. "We took quite a bit of heat in the press because it was feared John Henry would not run (because of the cost). The Breeders' Cup was urged publicly to bend the rules, which we ultimately could not do." Rubin agreed to run his great horse, considering it a sporting gesture. Ten days before the race, he paid the first installment of $200,000. The day after the payment, John Henry developed a strained ligament in the left front ankle, although he continued to train. McAnally wanted to give his horse a serious workout six days before the race, but the swelling had not subsided sufficiently despite extensive treatment and the decision was made not to race. The money was refunded to Rubin, and the inaugural Breeders' Cup had lost its most important horse.

Seattle Song, winner of the Grade One Washington, D.C. International, fractured the cannon bone of his left front leg in a workout three days before the race and also had to be scratched from the list of starters. The field did have a big name with the presence of All Along, the five-year-old mare who had won Horse of the Year honors the year before and the unofficial title of "horse of the world." But she had not won in three starts in 1984. Walter Swinburn, the young English jockey who rode her to victory in 1983, found himself replaced by American-based Angel Cordero Jr. for the Breeders' Cup, the final race of the brilliant mare's career. Cordero had always wanted to ride All Along and had even had a dream about being aboard her in the Breeders' Cup.

Strawberry Road, ridden for the first time by Bill Shoemaker after trainer John Nicholls blamed jockey error for some of the colt's losses, led for the opening mile in a pedestrian 1:37 4/5. But All Along, tugging at the bridle, was given the go-ahead by Cordero rounding the turn. She fought off the challenge of third-place finisher Raami, but could not repel Lashkari, who grabbed the lead in the final stages and won by a head. It was a heartbreaking loss for All Along, who gave her all in a gutsy defeat. The race featured a typical European-style development: slow in the beginning and a quick run to the wire. The final quarter of a mile was covered in 24 seconds. The top five finishers had all trained in Europe in 1984. Lashkari, ridden by French champion Yves Saint-Martin, did not start as a two-year-old and came into the race off only seven career starts, the last two victories. In fact, he had won his last race, the Group Two Prix du Conseil de Paris, regarded as a second-tier contest for horses not good enough for the more prestigious Prix de l'Arc de Triomphe. Lashkari had won the race by five lengths, but Breeders' Cup bettors gave him little credit and dismissed him at odds of 53-1.

Saint-Martin settled Lashkari in midpack, but never more than four lengths back of the lead. He gradually inched forward and was only a length and a half back at the top of the stretch. In motoring down the lane, he finished in a respectable time of 2:25 1/5.

Lashkari represented the first North American starter for trainer Alain de Royer Dupre, who had taken over training the Aga Khan's horses in 1983 following the death of Francois Mathet. Royer Dupre had saddled the winners of the French Derby and French One Thousand Guineas, but commanded little respect among the bettors. Using a strategy that would become commonplace in later years for European trainers running horses in North America, Royer Dupre shipped the colt late, arriving three days before the race and clearing quarantine the day before.

The world's richest race, the $3 million Classic, followed and, befitting the Hollywood background, featured an unbelievable ending. The race drew eight starters, but Slew o' Gold figured to be the main protagonist. He came into the race undefeated in five 1984 starts and had a chance to cap off the season with a victory that could possibly make him Horse of the Year.

Slew o' Gold was a three-year-old star who matured into a four-year-old sensation. A son of 1977 Triple Crown winner Seattle Slew out of Alluvial, which made him a half brother to 1979 Belmont winner Coastal, Slew o' Gold had magnificent bloodlines. He also had owners—Jim Hill and Mickey Taylor and the Equusequity Syndicate they managed—who were equally spectacular. Hill and Taylor had campaigned Seattle Slew and put together the syndicate that owned Slew o' Gold. They also made the decision to fire trainer Sid Watters early in the season after the horse injured his hind end and legs in a fall in late May on a rain-slicked road alongside the conditioner's barn at Belmont Park. The owners and trainer had squabbled before and this was the last incident en route to the dismissal. John Hertler, a 33-year-old native New Yorker, received the horse and several others in the transfer.

Slew o' Gold bounced back from his mishap and won his season opener in a blistering time of 1:34 2/5 for the mile. He rattled off wins in the Whitney, Woodward, Marlboro Cup and Jockey Club Gold Cup thereafter, earning a $1 million bonus for sweeping the latter three races which comprised the New York Fall Championship Series.

Yet Slew o' Gold had problems with his front feet throughout his campaign. He sheered off the entire frog (the v-shaped pliable support structure) on the bottom of the left front foot in the Whitney, but it grew back before the Woodward. However, he developed problems in the frog of the right forefoot. After winning the Whitney, he required a special bar shoe with a thin metal plate for protection. He also wore a special bar shoe on the left forefoot for the Marlboro Cup. He left New York after a victory by almost 10 lengths in the Gold Cup.

The field featured some other noteworthy horses. Gate Dancer, a curious three-year-old who had won the Preakness Stakes and the Super Derby and wore ear muffs to block out the crowd noise, represented one talented opponent. Desert Wine, who had beaten John Henry earlier in the year, starred on the west coast, as did Precisionist. Wild Again, the eventual winner, had run 14 times, winning four, including the Meadowlands Handicap and the Oaklawn Handicap. Track Barron had shown his versatility as a sprinter and distance specialist. Canadian Factor starred in Canada. Mugatea, a rabbit who had been entered to ensure a rapid pace for entrymate Slew o' Gold, rounded out the lineup.

"Cecil B. DeMille would have been hard-pressed to fashion a more appealing cast," *Daily Racing Form* executive columnist Joe Hirsch wrote in his year-end synopsis.

Wild Again's owners, Bill Allen, Ron Volkman and Terry Beall, who collectively ran as the Black Chip Stable, supplemented their colt for $360,000, or 12% of the purse. The group had formed in 1980 and took its name from a black poker chip discovered in a coat pocket by a friend of one of the owners. The trio paid

$35,000 for the colt as a yearling. He won two of seven starts as a two-year-old and only $33,700, and started only once as a three-year-old and finished out of the money. A chipped bone in his left foreleg left him sidelined until the following February. He won two of his first three starts at his home base in California before trainer Vincent Timphony took him on the road, beginning with the trainer's hometown of New Orleans. Wild Again won the Grade Two New Orleans Handicap at the Fair Grounds. After a lackluster effort in the Grade Two Razorback Handicap at Oaklawn Park, he rebounded to win the Oaklawn Handicap 13 days later in track-record time. He lost his next six before winning the Grade One Meadowlands Cup Handicap by six lengths, only a fifth of a second off the track record for the mile and a quarter. He did not race for almost two months afterward as Timphony searched for a prep race. He found one 12 days before the Cup, a mile race on the grass at Belmont. The colt finished third. When he worked out in the week leading up to the race, his exercise rider misjudged the finish line, standing up at the 16th pole. Making matters worse, the horse did not have a rider when entered. Pat Day, the leading race-winning rider in North America at the time, received the mount. Day saw the horse did not have a listed rider on the entry sheet and called Timphony, who just happened to be heading to the jockeys' quarters to ask him if he wanted to ride the horse. Day had ridden Wild Again before and jumped at the chance, regardless of the odds. He just wanted to be a part of the world's richest race.

Slew o' Gold's foot problems recurred at Hollywood, which necessitated applying a fiberglass patch the day before the race and extending it further the day of the race. He was also treated with the analgesic phenylbutazone, which was legal under California rules.

The speedy Mugatea and Precisionist quickly engaged in a heated duel, but Wild Again, under Day, wanted to run and wanted the lead, which he had after a brisk half mile in :45 3/5. He kept on top without much difficulty through a mile in a decent 1:37. The final quarter of a mile, run in a crawling 26 2/5 seconds, proved to be the most interesting. Wild Again began to feel serious heat from Slew o' Gold heading into the stretch. "I just knew at the top of the stretch this was going to be a great stretch drive and I said to myself, 'Okay, take it easy and just go. Don't go nuts,'" Durkin recalled.

Gate Dancer joined the mix in the lane, and from the eighth pole to the wire the three horses engaged in bumping and brushing. Wild Again started to come out, while Gate Dancer leaned in, sandwiching Slew o' Gold in the process. Wild Again won by a head over Gate Dancer, who had a half-length lead over Slew o' Gold, whose rider, Angel Cordero Jr., was taking a hard hold of his horse to avoid clipping heels and falling. No sooner had the horses crossed the wire than the stewards lit up the inquiry sign and the richest race in the world was under close scrutiny. The stewards analyzed and reanalyzed the race. One of the judges, Pete Pederson, said years later that some stewards decisions are "slam dunks," but this one wasn't quite that easy.

"It was kind of a landmark decision, you could have argued it in another direction," Pederson said.

Clearly, Wild Again had veered out from the rail, but exactly why became the question that would influence the decision. The stewards felt Wild Again had been "tipped out" when hit in the rear quarters by Slew o' Gold.

"You might look at it and say he's coming out and getting into the other horse, or you'd say the other horse was lugging in and initiated it and caused him to come out," Pederson said. "That was our determination." It was also determined that Gate Dancer had triggered the bumping with Slew o' Gold in the final sixteenth of a mile to the wire and he was disqualified and placed third.

The winning result stood "after eight minutes that seemed like a long weekend" wrote Tim Capps, editor of the *Thoroughbred Record*. Wild Again, an unlikely victor at 31-1, claimed first prize in the richest race of his life and justified the faith of his owners, who almost quadrupled their supplementary payment. It was a wild ending to a wild day.

Exhilarated and exhausted from his first Breeders' Cup, Durkin had to unwind. He worked his way down to the nearest place serving beer and came upon a party. He approached two men who looked like security guards because they were wearing earplugs. Durkin asked if they wouldn't mind looking after his binoculars while he headed over to the bar for a beer. They obliged, but told him when the person they were guarding had to leave, they would have to accompany him. Durkin asked who they were guarding and it happened to be Gerald Ford, former President of the United States.

"I looked around the room and there was Frank Sinatra, Fred Astaire, Cary Grant," Durkin recalled years later. "I was walking over to the bar and Arthur Watson was there and he just grabbed hold of me and gave me a bear hug. I had only met him once before very briefly. He told me I had done a good job. I was just on cloud nine. I was just floating."

In Beverly Hills, Breeders' Cup founder John R. Gaines rented the Bistro Garden, a famous local eatery, and celebrated with a group of friends and associates who had made the Breeders' Cup a reality. The day had been a resounding success in every possible way. Gaines felt great relief that no one could question that it was a championship event. It had been obvious to everyone who attended and the millions watching worldwide on television. Gaines had the look of a proud father. His baby had been delivered and it was healthy and strong. He had brought the racing industry together and showed what could be accomplished by virtue of cooperation. In Gaines' words: "It established racing's value system in a very dramatic way and answered the question of who has the best horse."

# 3

# Blowing into the Windy City

## The 2002 Breeders' Cup

$\mathscr{A}$nyone who has ever been to Arlington Park can't help but be impressed by its beauty and its opulence. It just might be the Taj Mahal of all racetracks in North America and truly one of the most magnificent in the world. Beyond just its elegance, the place is rich in history, one that goes back to the 1920s and has maintained its presence throughout the years because of horsemen with passion and vision. These were horsemen willing to take risks no matter the costs—literally—allowing Arlington to one day play host to the greatest annual horse racing showdown in the world, the Breeders' Cup.

In August 1983, the Madison Square Garden Corporation sold Arlington to a group headed by Richard (Dick) Duchossois, a Chicago native who had served in World War II and earned the Bronze Star and Purple Heart. He made his fortune in an industrial company that manufactured automatic garage door openers, munitions and electronics, and performed railroad car building and repair. Duchossois ventured into owning and racing horses in the 60s, which later spawned his interest in racetrack ownership. He gave Sheldon Robbins and Joe Joyce 5% ownership for $100 apiece. Duchossois wanted them to run the racetrack, make it profitable and make sure nothing went wrong. Above all, he wanted to be kept out of it.

In 1985, a fire gutted the grandstand at Arlington Park, a month before the running of the Million. A massive cleanup of the rubble occurred and tents were erected. The Million took place, witnessed by an on-track crowd of more than 35,000, and the experience earned the track an Eclipse Award. A statue at the track with the words "against all odds" commemorates the '85 Million.

In 1986, Duchossois bought out his partners and began an annual international festival of racing. In 1988, while Arlington would undergo some $200 million in renovations, the Million shifted to Woodbine in Canada. Arlington reopened for business in 1989, featuring a pristine plant with state-of-the-art equipment and a scenic paddock. Arlington continued as the site for wonderful racing, but less than 10 years later it closed for two years because of antiquated state taxation, while riverboat gambling, which penetrated the market, received substantial concessions by comparison. A new administration ushered in following an election helped the racing industry—and Arlington, in particular, as the largest stakeholder—by reducing the state's takeout on pari-mutuel wagering by some 4½%.

"It wasn't for Arlington. It was for the entire racing industry in Illinois," Duchossois said in an interview for this book. "Sometimes we get labeled the Arlington bill, but that's only because we're the largest and we were leading the charge. The pari-mutuel tax, which was a major thing, was brought down so it would become competitive. The riverboat gambling that we competed against had no real estate taxes. The real estate taxes at Arlington when we burned were $1.25 million. When we rebuilt, they promised us they wouldn't raise the real estate taxes, except when other taxes went up, but as soon as we got up they went to $5.2 million. That was a big part. In that same legislation, there was another riverboat to be added to the group and that would have seriously affected all of the tracks. An equity fund was set up and a part of the earnings of that riverboat and the taxes would go to the horse racing industry, which would be sort of a supplement to pick up the difference for the amount of money we would have lost on that.

"They were basically destroying the thoroughbred industry. We had a number of different rules and regulations that helped us operate on more of a competitive basis. These things were all put into the new law. A lot of people said the economics shut us down. The economics were very bad, but that didn't shut us down. The riverboats didn't shut us down. We were trying to prove a point that there had to be racing reform in Illinois if we were going to be a strong, viable industry. The industry was going down. Once it starts down, it keeps going down. There had to be something to reverse it. The only thing we could think of is shutting our place down to call to the attention of the public and the legislators that they were destroying an industry. That's the reason we shut down. I didn't have other stockholders to say yes or no. We could make our own decision. We control our own destiny.

"We always knew these racing reforms would come about. They were so logical. Things just had to be done if we were going to save this industry that common sense would have said 'Hey, we have to make these changes.' We knew that with the wisdom of the legislators, with the wisdom of the new governors, sooner or later this would happen. We didn't know how soon or how late. But we knew it would happen."

Arlington reopened in 2000. During this time, Duchossois and Churchill Downs president and chief executive officer Tom Meeker had been dialoguing about the racing industry, which had been moving more towards simulcasting than the live on-track product. While Churchill Downs Inc., the parent company of venerable Churchill Downs, had purchased Hollywood Park and Calder and some other less notable plants, Duchossois had no intentions to sell his company. However, a merger appealed to him because it allowed Arlington to maintain its independence while joining an expanding operation, so the merger took place in 2000.

Arlington had been mentioned numerous times when talks surfaced about future sites for the Breeders' Cup, but it didn't really become serious until an alternate location was required for 2002. Santa Anita couldn't play host to the site as scheduled because of capital improvement plans, preempting the event until 2003.

In the absence of Santa Anita, members of the Breeders' Cup management team huddled together and considered alternatives. The discussions pointed to one place: Arlington Park.

"It's always been looked at as a likely venue for the Breeders' Cup and people have been openly curious as to why it hadn't gone to Chicago in the first 18 years," Breeders' Cup Ltd. president D. G. Van Clief said. "The fact of the matter is that first you had the reconstruction of the track after the fire, then you had the closure of the track for two years pending the passage of favorable legislation to reopening it. Dick Duchossois obviously had other priorities he was dealing with, and although he has been a huge supporter of the Breeders' Cup, we had never talked seriously with Dick about having the event there. He just had a lot on his plate during those years."

When it was decided to look at Arlington, Van Clief telephoned Tom Meeker and told him of the snag at Santa Anita and the consideration of Arlington as an alternate venue. Van Clief asked Meeker if he considered it a good idea and whether he wanted the Breeders' Cup to consider Arlington Park and would the corporation support the move. Meeker answered positively and then called Duchossois.

"We all agreed it would likely have several types of benefits," Van Clief said. "From the Breeders' Cup perspective, we were excited to go into the nation's third largest marketplace. From the standpoint of the Breeders' Cup mission we've always hoped and tried to position the event in a way that it would stimulate the sport of thoroughbred horse racing in whatever market it entered. We felt the midwestern market could use some stimulation, that this would be a great way to profile racing in the Chicago marketplace soon on the heels of the reopening of Arlington Park. We all agreed it was a great opportunity. From the Breeders' Cup standpoint as well, we are always identifying potential new host-track candidates because we liked to keep as much flexibility at our fingertips as we can in making selections. If for some reason one of the regular venues is precluded—for example construction projects at Santa Anita and Churchill Downs in different years—it's always nice to know you've got other venues that work well for the event. All this being said it was kind of a logical choice."

In May, the Breeders' Cup sent three key executives—Ferguson Taylor, treasurer and chief financial officer; Debbie Blair, vice-president, customer service; and Damon Thayer, event marketing—to do an on-site inspection. The Breeders' Cup Ltd. knew it would have a major challenge because of Arlington's seating capacity, which is roughly 10,000, although it can comfortably house more than 25,000. So, there were temporary seating issues and customer service facilities to be considered.

The Breeders' Cup management told Arlington's management it wanted to accommodate a crowd of 45,000 or close to it to make the event economically worthwhile.

The cost of the added infrastructure would likely amount to more than $3 million, an investment the Breeders' Cup did not want to undertake on its own, so if Arlington wanted the Cup it would have to secure funding. Aside from financial issues, other things had to be considered. Most Breeders' Cups had commenced at the start of a season for a racetrack or at the end of a short season, and some of the tracks already had had the infrastructure in place. In this case, the Breeders' Cup would be coming into a new venue concluding its meet, but which would require physical changes impacting on the customers. Arlington had to work out the financial and physical feasibility and viability, which basically took about three months from the time of the original on-site inspection by the Breeders' Cup executives and a subsequent visit by Van Clief.

While maintaining regular dialogue with the Breeders' Cup, Arlington worked diligently on receiving state grant monies from the Department of Commerce and Community Affairs. Arlington sought $2 million to help pay for seats, bathrooms, temporary wagering windows, tents and other requirements. To help secure the grant money, Arlington had to educate the government on the Breeders' Cup, which was renamed the World Thoroughbred Championships in 2001 to make it more understandable to the public and sponsors.

"Chicago is a very popular tourism destination, but some of the leading tourism officials weren't altogether familiar with the Breeders' Cup and the economic impact it could have," former Arlington Park president Steve Sexton, who now works for Churchill Downs, said.

Arlington approached the local convention and visitors bureau in the suburb near Arlington and asked if it could assist in commissioning an economic impact study to determine the value of the Breeders' Cup coming to Chicago. Armed with that information, Arlington could then talk to political and tourism officials. The study determined the Breeders' Cup could generate $54 million for Chicago.

By late October, Breeders' Cup officials publicly stated they were running out of time to conclude an agreement with Arlington Park. Van Clief said Churchill Downs remained a possibility as a host site for 2002 if Arlington failed to receive necessary financing from the state.

At the ESPN zone in downtown Chicago on December 5, 2001, about the time the state came through with funding, Arlington announced plans to stage the Breeders' on October 26, 2002. The economic impact study was distributed to the assembled audience.

In early February, Arlington officials announced the ticketing process, with a June 16 purchasing deadline. In addition, a series of different marketing initiatives were unveiled to educate and inform people in the marketplace who didn't understand the Breeders' Cup. Internally, Arlington worked on security and traffic plans, staffing the event and communicating to employees what was going on and the importance of the Cup to the track.

The track opened for live racing on June 5, and the task of operating a live meet on the 75th anniversary season, coupled with that of building a temporary infrastructure, commenced. The Arlington Million took place on August 17 and two days after that the building of the temporary seating began. An Alabama-based company that does PGA tournaments and other major events started erecting what were called seating envelopes.

"We treated each area separately because we knew we couldn't accommodate 40,000–50,000 people inside the grandstand (due to) space and the corresponding traffic plan that had to go with it," Sexton said. "With the magnitude we had it was going to take somewhere in the area of 15,000 spots. It took a lot of summer nights, which during that time the mosquito population escalates in Chicago. There were a lot of (tough) factors: the heat, the humidity, the mosquitoes and adapting to a different work schedule. When any human being shifts a schedule from what is normally an eight-to-five schedule and starts working from six p.m. to three a.m. or four a.m., sleep becomes a little bit of a challenge sometimes."

From October 1 to the Breeders' Cup day, Arlington's management spent inordinate amounts of time on putting everything and everybody in place. The executives literally sat in every seat to make sure it provided a sight line of the entire track. At one point, Duchossois sat in a high-level grandstand seat and watched a race and then walked down to a wagering window to make sure he could make a bet and return to his place before the commencement of the next race. Two trees located near the gap in the track were removed because they were blocking about three rows of seats on the clubhouse turn.

"We broke each seating area down to kind of a mini grandstand," Sexton said. "If you had a ticket there that was your infrastructure. If you had a tent, you had heating, mutuel windows, televisions, restrooms and concessions. And we had a manager and an assistant manager in each of those areas. That last three-week process leading up to the Breeders' Cup there was just a massive amount of details to make sure we were prepared for the actual event day because a lot of it was just temporary in nature. There were a lot of things that had changed. As we went through and started putting up temporary seats, keep in mind we had already sold tickets for around the venue. Any time you go into a first-time event, there are a lot of ramifications and adjustments you have to make and when you're working to put them up at night it becomes even more of a challenge. You have to give a tremendous amount of applause to the group that put up the seating combined with the staff that we have here that spent their lives for six to nine months just making this event happen."

Weather became an overriding concern. Sexton personally watched the weather for three weeks leading up to the event. Arlington asked the president of a local television station for a 10-day forecast, but he replied they didn't have that predictability.

"He said they'd be looking into it for years, but there isn't just a solid enough forecast to put on the air," Sexton said. "It was a big consideration for us. We talked about whether we should buy weather insurance but it was too expensive. Weather insurance guarantees you a certain amount of revenues if it rains or snows, but it's obviously very expensive because nobody can predict whether that's going to happen or not. We opted not to buy it. The premium is about 70% of revenues."

On Wednesday morning, three days before the Cup, Duchossois made the morning rounds on the backstretch and the apron overlooking the track. Dressed in a fedora and overcoat, the bespectacled racetrack owner resembled legendary football coach Vince Lombardi in one of those shots on the sidelines of chilly Lambeau Field.

"I jokingly say I've got 187 vice-presidents in charge of the weather and one of them will come through," he said. "Weather is always a concern (in the Cup). It's been a concern down in Kentucky, wherever it's been. I also tell the British that they've been praying for rain and cold weather and they have their weather. This is British weather. We do feel that by Saturday afternoon it will be fine. I think we'll get it. But rain or shine, it's going to be some of the best racing in the world. A lot of people don't understand that we run rain or shine. It might be a little chilly, but all the tents are heated. Everybody can get inside. They don't have to sit outside all of the time. The rain and the weather is something that is beyond our control. We're going to do everything up to that point that we can and just pray that we have good weather."

Duchossois said the whole process of preparing for the Breeders' Cup had been interesting.

"We had not built it for the one day, every six years or so, to hold the Breeders' Cup, but we were not at that time anxious to get it," he said. "After being down for two years, we had basically all new people coming in and those people have to be built back into the culture of Arlington. The Breeders' Cup is the Super Bowl of all racing, that's the biggest thing we have. It's worldwide. It's the biggest thing there is."

On Wednesday evening, Isobel Cunningham, a reporter from Scotland and European contributor for the annual publication *Crushing The Cup*, which provides analysis on the various races, chatted about the event and her own background. Cunningham formerly worked full-time for the *Scotsman*, the prominent broadsheet in her country, handicapping (or touting as they say across the pond) and reporting the race meetings in the United Kingdom. She began handicapping in 1977 at small meets before graduating to the bigger ones in 1985. How it all evolved is quite fascinating, the classic story of a junior reporter.

"I went to work in London and part of my work was going to Paris to phone back the fashion notes for the fashion writer for the *Daily Sketch* newspaper in London," she said. "I was the only one who could read her handwriting after two or three glasses of champagne. She would hand this notebook to me and go on to the next fashion show and I was left, with no glasses of champagne, to phone in the notes to London. When I'm done doing that, I'd beat it to Longchamp and there I saw flat racing—real flat racing—and I thought this is something different. Then you come back to England and Scotland and you're left with this junk racing again."

In between court reporting, crime reporting and helping out on the fashion beat, she wrote about the races for the sports department on her time off. In the intervening years, she married, had a family and began doing more race writing, principally the amateurs national hunt variety for the *Scotsman* and a trade magazine in England, *Horse and Hound*. The *Scotsman* sports editor asked her if she'd mind covering thoroughbred racing at the race meetings at Edinborough and she obliged. Her reputation as something of a sharp-eyed sleuth grew when she picked Secreto to win the Epsom Derby one year, while almost all the noted public handicappers picked El Gran Senor. Both were Northern Dancer colts out of unraced mares. She preferred Secreto because the dam was sired by Secretariat, whom she considered a solid sire of mares. In her opinion, Secreto had a "little jump" in the pedigree. Her knowledge paid off.

Isobel had been "angling" to get to the Breeders' Cup for several years but couldn't convince the *Scotsman* to send her. At the time the Breeders' Cup didn't have the presence or magnitude in Europe, probably because the European horses had been routinely doing poorly. But some improving results in the '90s, particularly in dirt races with the likes of Sheikh Albadou in the '91 Sprint and Arazi in the '91 Juvenile, started to change the attitudes of the racing public and the media.

"It was becoming more a thing in Europe, instead of something eccentric, like (trainer) Clive Brittain with Pebbles (in the Turf in 1985)," Isobel said. "That was seen as something flying a kite at the moon kind of thing. It began to be seen as something that counted in racing and it was taking that long actually in European racing, but it was beginning to filter down from trade papers to the actual daily papers. Until then you wouldn't get a pick for every Breeders' Cup race. You would only get a pick for whatever race there was a European entry and you had to pick a European, otherwise they wouldn't print it. If you had a European running say in the Breeders' Cup Mile and you didn't pick it as the winner, well, they didn't bother to print it. They wouldn't print the Breeders' Cup card. Good gracious. That was the beginning of the changing. Now they print the cards. They didn't then. You made a pick but you didn't know who the other runners were. Your service to your readers was appalling because they didn't really understand the concept of what the Breeders' Cup was. You couldn't see it on television. How you were going to get the card in the morning newspaper was something else again.

"All the time I kept saying this is the Olympic Games of racing. You've got every discipline and they would say, 'Oh, well, what's going to win the 2:30 at Edinborough tomorrow?'"

It wasn't until 1993 that Isobel made it to the Cup after paying her own way to Santa Anita.

"It was the 10th anniversary of Breeders' Cup and I thought I've got to get there, but this race meeting was like this unachievable aim in the distance," she said. "I wanted to get there. Until I decided I'd pay my own ticket, nobody was interested. I thought I'd have to get there somehow or another. I'll admit I paid my ticket, but I don't think many of the other European writers at the time might. I think perhaps they had to (pay for their trips). I don't think you'd ever get the honest analysis of that, but I would like to know how many of them got frustrated like I did."

Isobel liked a European horse, Arcangues, who had run fourth in the 1993 Prix de l'Arc de Triomphe and had been shipped by trainer Andre Fabre to run in the Classic at Santa Anita.

"He looked like me when I've fallen in love with a pair of shoes that are a half a size too small and I wouldn't give up. I'll get them and wear them," she said. "He always looked uncomfortable in Europe. I thought this will be interesting because that horse is a beautiful, big, strong horse, but he'd never run on dirt. It was just the sort of feeling of the thing that this was a horse that just needed a chance."

She had been sitting in the press box in front of Jim Mazur and Peter Mallett, authors of *Crushing The Cup*, and they asked her who she liked in the Classic. She said Arcangues. They noted he hadn't run on the dirt and had been winless in five races. A few minutes later Arcangues snapped his losing skid, scoring at odds of more than 133-1, the highest odds for a winning horse in Breeders' Cup history. Sadly for Isobel, she hadn't bet the horse whom she had selected for the *Scotsman*.

"It was the biggest mistake of my life, absolutely," she recalled, albeit with less anguish than at the time. "It was a success, an achievement, to have got to the Breeders' Cup and to have to pay my own ticket to get there. In the midst of it all I just forgot to bet (the race)."

Some five years later at a corporate function at Edinborough Racetrack, she encountered a well-known solicitor who wanted to shake her hand after betting her selections, including Arcangues. He had been sick in bed with the flu and when he saw the results coming and Arcangues' payoff, he jumped out of bed, got dressed and told his wife they were going for dinner to the most expensive restaurant in Edinborough.

"I thought he might have offered me a cut of his winnings. He didn't even do that," Isobel lamented. "It was the greatest moment of my life and it was the worst moment of my life."

It was at her inaugural Breeders' Cup that Isobel found a connection to the event and her country. In reading the racing program she discovered the Breeders' Cup trophy had been designed after the Ecorche statue at the Edinborough Museum, only three blocks from her office. She phoned the office and told them to send a reporter to the museum but found little interest on the other end. The following year while at the Breeders' Cup, she was able to contact Breeders' Cup founder John R. Gaines, who informed her that before he became a racehorse breeder and owner he was an art connoisseur. He knew about the Ecorche statue, the finest equine bronze in the history of art. He told her he wanted the winning trophy to symbolize something of artistic value and excellence.

"I think it must be fate that the trophy was already there in Edinborough," Isobel said. "I had this absolute target to get to the Breeders' Cup and maybe that was the horse that was inspiring me, although I didn't know about it then."

On Thursday morning, two days before the Cup, Ed Musselman, a.k.a. Indian Charlie, walked around handing out his newsletter/tip sheet to the media and horsemen. Liberally sprinkled with biting commentary about the horse racing business on one side, and tips and advertising on the other side, the paper's motto is: "We never let the truth get in the way of a good story." In this edition, he targeted trainers Murray Johnson, Dallas Stewart, John Shirreffs, D. Wayne Lukas, Bob Baffert and Bobby Frankel. He also took a good-natured dig at John McCririck, the English broadcaster who routinely wears outlandish clothes: "Halloween ain't till next week!" He also took a swipe at his favorite target, Churchill Downs Inc. president/chief executive officer Tom Meeker.

Following training on Thursday morning, trainers Aidan O'Brien, Bob Baffert, Patrick Biancone, Donna Ward and Patrick Kelly participated in a media conference. Kelly arrived first and fielded questions about his horses, long shot Riskaverse in the Filly & Mare Turf, and 8-1 shot Evening Attire in the Classic.

Evening Attire had won his last two races and four of seven overall on the season, principally racing in New York. Kelly trained the horse for his father, a longtime trainer on the New York circuit and an inductee in the Hall of Fame. Thomas Kelly bred and co-owned the four-year-old gelding with Joseph and Mary Grant, natives and residents of Boston. The Grants had never had a Breeders' Cup horse before and approached the first experience with excitement. "It's almost just not real," Mary said in a quote in the biographies of the owners and trainers. "It hasn't sunk in yet. It's the experience of a lifetime." Patrick Kelly had run four other Breeders' Cup starters, but had had miserable luck, his best result a fifth. Two horses finished last and the other failed to finish. Kelly had not had a horse in the Breeders' in nine years.

Ward talked about her two-year-old colt, Sky Mesa, whom she trained with her husband John. They had won the Breeders' Cup Distaff in 1999 with Beautiful Pleasure and the Kentucky Derby in 2001 with Monarchos, both horses owned by John Oxley. Sky Mesa had won all three of his career starts and had been installed as the favorite for the Juvenile.

Biancone had been one of Europe's most celebrated trainers, winning the Prix de l'Arc de Triomphe in 1983 and '84 and losing the '85 edition on a disqualification. Biancone had run seven Breeders' Cup starters without a win, but he'd been second by a neck twice. Biancone shifted his operation to Hong Kong in the '90s but left in 1999 after he had his license suspended for 10 months when three of his horses tested positive for prohibited substances. He came to the U.S., where the Florida Racing and Wagering Board waived his suspension because the prohibited substances were deemed "class three drugs" in America. He worked full-time in 1999 as an advisor in California to the Stronach Stables before embarking on his own with a public training stable beginning late in 2000 at Santa Anita. He had two 2002 starters: Whywhywhy and Zavata in the Juvenile. Whywhywhy appeared to be the better of the two with three wins in four career starts.

Clearly, the three trainers took a backseat to Baffert and O'Brien when they arrived and were peppered with a variety of questions. O'Brien, the Irish wunderkind who had a set a European record the year before for Group One wins and celebrated his first Breeders' Cup victory when Johannesburg romped in the Juvenile, was asked about the program of preparing for the year-end championship day of racing.

"It's the Olympics of thoroughbred racing, so we look forward to this every year," he said. "We just hope that when you compete earlier in the year in the classics and try to get them through to meet the older horses in the middle of the season they last this far. I think you always have to forgive them if they're gone a little bit at this time of the year. It's the day we look forward to all year. I think this brings the whole world together if the European horses come and obviously race against the American horses. Anybody who has good horses and they're healthy and well is looking forward to coming."

Baffert was asked about the form of War Emblem. He won the Kentucky Derby and Preakness Stakes in the spring, then flopped in the Belmont. After winning the Haskell, War Emblem finished sixth by 4¼ lengths in the Pacific Classic

Stakes. He had not run in two months and this would be his last start before heading off to Japan to begin a career as a stallion.

"It's very natural in our business if the horse runs a bad race, everybody jumps off (the bandwagon)," Baffert said. "We were hoping to sneak in here like we did in the Derby, but we really don't worry about that. I feel he's ready to run. He's doing great. He's training well, so we're just glad to make it here after running in the classics."

Baffert also took the opportunity to use O'Brien's expression "high-cruiser" when describing his horse.

"He's a super high-cruiser," Baffert said. "He just needs to get out of the gate. I think he's a very fast horse and I think he likes the lead. He likes to get out there and lead, that's his race style. I told (jockey) Victor (Espinoza) that 'we need the lead. No matter how you break, just send him out there and put him on the lead and see what happens.' We know taking a hold of him is disastrous. He'll just have to get out there and get on the lead. We'll probably go pretty quick early. I really at this point don't try to handicap or anything. There's so many little things that people don't realize you have to worry about. When that gate comes open, there's a lot of pressure on everybody. I think that we're here with a really strong hand, we feel good that we made it this far. With War Emblem, there's a lot of buzz. I think a lot of people want to come out and watch him run. It's his last race in the States. It's quite interesting. They're all tough races. There's no margin for error in these races. You can't break bad, you can't go too wide. You've got to be good on that one day. You're just hoping for racing luck and that's all we can hope for right now."

Baffert was asked about the death of Prince Ahmed bin Salman, a member of the ruling family of Saudi Arabia. The Prince gave Baffert $900,000 to purchase a 90% interest in War Emblem from Russell Reineman three weeks before the Kentucky Derby. Baffert took a shot on the colt who had romped in two races in Illinois, including the Illinois Derby, even though War Emblem had well-documented problems with his knees. The colt's subsequent wins gave the Prince a thrill, although the joy was literally short-lived when he died of a heart attack later in the year at age 43.

"I think it's had an impact on thoroughbred racing in general," Baffert said. "They were missing him at the sales. He was very aggressive. Not having him there, it's huge. It's going to be a big impact. It's a ripple effect. You're going to feel it. It hasn't affected our racing, but we'll probably feel it next year."

It was at that point that the press conference turned into a spectacle. Flamboyant English racing journalist John McCririck, dressed in a long fleece jacket decorated with bison figures and sitting beside his wife who was wearing matching garb, asked O'Brien for a tip on one of his horses to "sort of pay the expenses."

"Just give us, one. It's not asking much, old chap," McCririck asked, eliciting hearty laughs from the assembled audience.

"I'm the worst tipster in the world," O'Brien said sheepishly.

"No, you're not," McCririck said.

"I hope that they run good races, the whole lot of them," O'Brien said, trying to squirm out of the inquisition.

"Just give us one," McCririck continued.

"Come on," Baffert said playfully. "(Just) don't make it the two-year-old race." Baffert had three horses in the race: Vindication, Kafwain and Bull Market. O'Brien had Hold That Tiger, Van Nistelrooy and Tomahawk.

"We always thought (Turf favorite) High Chaparral would come on from the Arc and we think he's in good form," O'Brien began. "We always thought (Mile favorite) Rock of Gibraltar was a serious miler and he's traveled well. It would be real (great) if some of them could win. Sorry, that's as close as I can give you. The horses had been very sick in the middle of the season, so really we're lucky to be here at all. Rock of Gibraltar and Van Nistelrooy are the only two that didn't cough."

McCririck asked which horse he would tip to owner Michael Tabor, who made his fortune in betting shops and had many horses trained by O'Brien.

"Tell the truth, what are you going to tell Michael?" McCririck wondered.

"Should I go through all the races with ya, John?" O'Brien replied. "In the Mile, I think the two horses (Rock of Gibraltar and Landseer) have drawn well. I think both are going to drop back. I'd say whichever gets loose is going to be thereabouts."

"He can't have bets at half way, can he?" McCririck joked.

"High Chaparral is in good form," O'Brien replied. "He's come forward since the Arc and he'll be there, thereabouts. I think in the Juvenile if Tomahawk hadn't run in the (Darley) Dewhurst (Stakes) last week he'd be very sweet. He's a very good horse, very high-cruisin' pace. I'd say he's made for the dirt, but you have a question mark when he ran in the Dewhurst. Van Nistelrooy will run a good race and it will depend on how much the dirt will step him up. I think Hold That Tiger, if he gets luck and running, he'll be coming home well."

"So we know the whole secrets now of Ballydoyle now, do we?" McCririck said in reference to the world-famous training center where O'Brien's stock is conditioned. "I don't think we do."

"What's Patrick Biancone going to do?" Baffert asked playfully.

Tabor had an ownership interest in Whywhywhy.

Later that day, David Hood, head of public relations for the English-based William Hill bookmaking agency, one of the oldest established bookmakers in the world, perused the internet. His company had just issued a press release indicating it had placed odds of 5-2 that Irish trainer Aidan O'Brien would not win at least one race.

Asked if he expected the O'Brien-trained Rock of Gibraltar to be the heaviest-backed European horse in the Cup, Hood could not be sure. Rock of Gibraltar had been listed as the even-money favorite in the morning line.

"I can see Rock of Gibraltar, even though he'd be a short-priced favorite, being one of the most heavily backed Europeans ever, in terms of takeout, in terms of his liability," Hood said. "Because he's only an even-money shot, he's going to do less damage than say Sakhee (in the 2001 Classic) or Giant's Causeway (in the

2000 Classic). Giant's Causeway was 11-4 or 3-1. Sakhee was 5-2, so you've got 2½ times the damage. If you had a million pounds wagered on Rock of Gibraltar at even odds, he cost you a million pounds. If you've got a million pounds wagered on Sakhee at 5-2, it cost you 2.5 million pounds. The wagering would be the same, but the takeout is significantly more."

Knowing a win by Rock of Gibraltar would be great for European racing but bad for his company's business, Hood indicated bookmakers have to take occasional hits so the bettors will hopefully come back and play again.

"These types of races don't generate much new business," he said. "You don't convert people to be bettors on these types of races. Anyone who is going to have a bet on Saturday is a pretty regular punter. Everybody needs to win every now and then to keep playing. If you don't have the encouragement, they won't play. We'd happily lose a million on an even-money shot than $10 million on a 10-1 shot because it takes an awful lot longer to get it back."

Neil Morrice, who works for Britain's National Press Association and the American publication *Backstretch Magazine*, joined in the conversation and offered a perspective on Rock of Gibraltar, or the Rock as he came to be known. Morrice said the horse, who is co-owned by Sir Alec Ferguson, the manager of the Manchester United soccer team, is a "lovely story. It sells newspapers."

Morrice was attending his 14th Breeders' Cup, 12 on his own ticket. "I think every paper nationally sends one guy and *The Racing Post*, the national racing paper, usually would send two or three," he said. "The rest have to forage around for whatever freelance work they could get if they wanted to get paid for coming here. It took a few years for the whole thing to kick in. If you went back to the first Breeders' Cup, you'd find there were probably only four or five British journalists covering that. Year by year as the event grew in stature the need for having a guy out here for your paper also increased. Now we have about 30 people out here at any one time. There are basically two ethics of work regarding racing journalism: one is that you're salaried for one paper, in which case your chance of coming out here depends on your ranking amongst a racing staff and usually only one person would be sent. If you're a freelancer, it depends on how good you are at getting hold of sufficient work from different people to justify the trip. That's what I do. I work for a U.S.-based magazine at big events and I also try to get work for any national papers back home which don't have a man out here for any reason. In this instance, I'm working for the national news agency as a backup.

"It's important for me to be here. It's the highlight of the year. I would come here even it was down to my last red cent. I'd get here somehow. I just love the whole buildup to the day. The Americans are very good at doing that: getting the excitement and the attention to that one day. By the time it comes around, you're absolutely thirsting for the action to start. Being a bettor, it's also a very good meeting to go and bet and actually have a chance of winning some serious money.

"In the early days, sports editors had an indifferent attitude to the Breeders' Cup and wondered why there was any need to send their racing writers to America for the event.

"As the profile of the event has raised and as European success has increased, it has become more acceptable for sports editors to find space for it, so it has been a snowball effect and consequently the media presence has increased. I can't think of one daily paper in England that isn't represented with a journalist here. Actually there is one, but they're taking a feed from the Press Association. Racing in England has dedicated pages daily. I would say every single racing paper in the U.K. this week has carried stories about the Breeders' Cup."

The event attracted journalist Michael Ingram, who was born in the U.S. but now lives in Canada. He works for the *Afro News*—"The Voice Of The Black Community"—in Aldergrove, British Columbia, the most western province in Canada. Ingram had impressed upon his boss how horse racing fits into the overall black culture, pinpointing the success of some top North American jockeys.

"When I told her about the Breeders' Cup, I said there was this kid from New York, Shaun Bridgmohan, who is Jamaican, who would start to raise some feathers because he's starting to really get some better horses and ride well," Ingram said. "I said if he gets a shot to go, I want to be there."

Bridgmohan received the call to ride Evening Attire, whom he had steered to victory four times in seven races in 2002, including the Grade One, $1 million Jockey Club Gold Cup.

"This is like the World Series, the Super Bowl, everything," Ingram said. "Horse racing really doesn't get a lot of ink if you look at every paper and how they divide their space. There's got to be an outlet for this, especially if you want to see a sport where you want to see black athletes excel. This is on my own ticket and I'm hoping to get an exclusive with Shaun Bridgmohan and ask him how he feels (about being in the Breeders' Cup). I've always been passionate about horse racing. I've been a 'hoss' player for 25 years, so this gives me an opportunity to do the best of both worlds.

Ingram came with a "budget" of $400 to play on the Breeders' Cup and planned to "skill out each race" and decide on his plays, using all kinds of exotic wagers.

"The races with smaller fields obviously afford me a chance to catch something, so I'll likely try the exotics where there's small fields," he said. "Because it is the Breeders' Cup, there's going to be huge pools, not just here but simulcasting everywhere. In Vancouver last year at Hastings Park, it was unbelievable the amount of money that was generated through those turnstiles. One woman, this old black woman in her mid-60s who is like a steady $2 horse player, made $91,000 on a straight triacta/superfecta combination in the Juvenile. She just knew something about Johannesburg, for whatever her reason was, and he came through like a noble beast should.

"I was in another part of the track area and the word came down and everybody was just going crazy, genuinely happy for her because this is like the punter's dream come true. God bless her. That was like Merry Christmas, Happy New Year. They never declared who she was but word got around later on that it was one of the locals. There's a certain bunch of folks who play over in a certain section and we found who it was afterwards. She gave everybody a $100 bill for good luck and I got one. I know who she is but I can't say who she is. I respect her."

On Thursday night, the Breeders' Cup had its annual press party, usually at a renowned place in the city in which the event is being hosted. This one took place at Chicago's Field Museum, about an hour away from the principal media hotel in Arlington Heights. Two guys dressed in Chicago Bears jerseys and pretended to be characters from a *Saturday Night Live* skit, doing their best to entertain the audience. At one point, Francis LaBelle, Jr., the New York Racing Association's assistant director of communications, joined the band and belted out a damn good version of "Kansas City." LaBelle routinely sings at these types of events, usually performing a rock 'n roll or blues tune because it is easy for the band to play along without complicated chords.

On Friday morning, Indian Charlie passed out his latest sheet, and this one is surprising because there's actually something benign—mostly—in his commentary. He congratulated "two oldtimers" making their fifth consecutive start in the Breeders' Cup Sprint: trainer Bruce Headley and his horse, Kona Gold. "Especially in this day and age, this is one hell of an accomplishment by both horse and horseman!" He also thanks (in giant black type) Mr. D.—Dick Duchossois—"from a whole lot of people!" He offers a friendly message to *Washington Post* writer (and renowned handicapper) Andy Beyer: "Halloween ain't till next week." He provides a "horriblescope" for Breeders' Cup Day and underneath each zodiac sign are bon mots about a variety of subjects, except trainer D. Wayne Lukas. And of course there's the obligatory shot at Captain Tom Meeker, this one totally in jest about an announcement that Churchill Downs will have a quarantine barn up and running prior to the 2012 Kentucky Derby.

In the afternoon at Barn 1A, trainer Howard Zucker sipped on coffee to warm up from the dampness and chill while tending to his horse, Crafty C.T. The four-year-old colt is entered in the Sprint and rated 15-1 in the morning line. Virtually no one in the media has noticed Zucker or his horse next to the powerful contingent in the same shedrow trained by Bob Baffert, who has long since gone to get ready for the annual Breeders' Cup black-tie charity gala while his help takes care of business. Zucker has trained for some 30 years and this is his first Breeders' Cup starter.

"I never really had a horse that deserved to come," he said. "Jerry Hollendorfer has 150 in training in California and had a full barn here of 65 horses all summer and he doesn't have one in the Breeders' Cup. It's not easy to have one. I've got a small barn ranging anywhere from eight to eighteen horses depending on how my clientele is doing and we don't spend gazillions of money for horses generally speaking. We're very happy to have one that can go to the Cup."

Zucker said his day routinely begins when the alarm clock rings at 3:30, seven days a week, 365 days a year, and that little would change if he won the Sprint.

"It ain't going to mean a vacation in Hawaii or anything like that," he said. "Maybe it will mean a down payment on a house, something more earthy. My biggest thing would be just the personal satisfaction of having been able to do it. Even just being here gives me a lot of satisfaction to know that I started off with a few that weren't maybe the highest-priced horses at any auctions, although this horse that I'm running was not cheap. We paid quite a bit of money for him,

$240,000. It's just nice to know I was able to manage him in his career to get to this point and I'm looking ahead with his career to a better year next year. I just need to get lucky here. I think he can run with these.

"My owners have gotten fairly serious about this game the last four or five years. Everybody likes to run in the Breeders' Cup. You go into it knowing that the owners would love to run a horse in the Breeders' Cup. The question is, can you get 'em there and in good enough shape to warrant being there? I told them early in the year that I thought our plan was more to run in the Breeders' Cup next year in Santa Anita because he'd be at his home track, where he's done a lot of good. This horse is maybe a little better at a mile on the dirt. We're really here just through circumstances because there really weren't any good mile dirt races for him. He's a very good sprinter. I think he's a superior miler, but he's a very good sprinter and when he's right like he is right now I think he can run with anything in the country, short or long.

"We're kind of letting this horse pull us into it rather than pushing him into it. There's a big difference there. It's always easier on the horse and better to let the horse kind of make you train 'em and take you to the races and pull you along rather than you pushing on 'em.

"When you stay behind the horse a little bit in your training, they go forward on their own. When you start getting ahead of them and pulling on them, they keep backing up. You'll find when you lead one down the shedrow if you're pulling on their head, they always drag it back. As soon as you stop pulling, they start pulling you. That's just like an analogy but it holds true as far as racing goes. When one's doing well on their own and they're dragging you towards a date like this, you've got to kind of go along with them. You're just the horse's connections. You're not really the horse. You're not going to go out there and run yourself. There's probably a couple of trainers that can outrun me, but I don't think they've got too many horses around there that can outrun mine. We'll find out certainly tomorrow."

Donna Brothers, a jockey-turned-broadcaster, walked up to the barn. The following day she would be on horseback, following the Breeders' Cup starters from the time they stepped on to the racetrack leading up to the races and interviewing the winning jockeys afterwards. This is her third year working on the broadcasts for NBC after replacing Gregg McCarron, another former rider.

Brothers rode for the first time in the Cup in 1994. Her mount, Cat Appeal, ran a well-beaten 12th in the 13-horse field of the Juvenile Fillies. She rode Hennessy in the 1995 Breeders' Cup Juvenile, picking up the mount because Gary Stevens committed to riding Honour and Glory. The decision to hire Brothers—who was known as Barton then before she changed her last name after marrying prominent trainer Frank Brothers—became a controversy, particularly when trainer Wayne Lukas had a chance to hire Pat Day, the top-winning rider at that time in Breeders' Cup history. Brothers had ridden the colt to an impressive 9¾-length score in the Sapling Stakes three races before.

"A guy like (*Washington Post/Daily Racing Form* columnist) Andy Beyer knocked the fact that Wayne chose me to ride the horse while Pat Day sat in the room," she said. "Wayne knew better than anyone that I had a really good connection with Hennessy. He and I just had a really good connection. To me, it wouldn't have made any sense to ride another rider on him because Hennessy was a horse that ran well for me. It just never made sense. The first time Pat Day won a Breeders' Cup race was the first time he won a Breeders' Cup race. I just didn't understand why people would question it.

"Earlier in the day Julie Krone had run second on Mr. Greeley in the Sprint at a bit of a price (31-1 odds) and just got beat a neck. I was really happy for Julie because the horse ran a big race on a big day. When she came back to the jocks room she was terribly disappointed and I said, 'You should be happy, that horse ran a super race.' She said, 'I'm not (happy). I got beat.' Nobody expected Hennessy to run one-two-three-four. None of the other jockeys expected Hennessy to run one-two-three-four, but I knew he could win that race. I knew he could beat all those horses. I just knew it. I knew I'd win that race."

She was almost right. Hennessy placed second by a neck to Unbridled's Song, who would go on to become a major horse the following year on the road to the Kentucky Derby.

"When I got beat there was nobody more disappointed than me," Brothers said. "When I walked back to the jocks room Julie said, 'So, tell me, are you happy that you ran second?' I said, 'No, I'm not.' The loss didn't stick with me too long once Unbridled's Song turned out to be a really good horse. At the time nobody knew how good of a horse Unbridled's Song was. Afterwards I didn't feel too bad because I knew I rode the horse very, very well. I knew the horse ran his eyeballs out for me. I couldn't second-guess any decision I made during the race, postparade, gate, nothing. So then what do you do? You just got beat. That's all."

Brothers lamented the withdrawal of Sky Mesa from the Juvenile. He's a son of Pulpit, whom Frank Brothers trained and who developed into a decent three-year-old and made some noise going into the 1997 Kentucky Derby. Sky Mesa, the morning-line favorite, developed an ankle injury that had been detected earlier that day, forcing his withdrawal after deliberations between trainer John Ward, his wife/assistant Donna and owner John Oxley, who hadn't yet arrived in Chicago. The connection had won the 1999 Breeders' Cup Distaff with Beautiful Pleasure and the 2001 Derby with Monarchos.

Back at the Wards' barn, assistant trainer Patrick Gallagher leaned against a wall talking on his cell phone, his mood understandably subdued.

"There's obvious disappointment, but at the same time relief that it's not something that happened in the race and it's not something that's catastrophic," he said. "He seems to be fine as far as that goes. Certainly we felt good about him and he's been doing great all week, so it's a difficult thing but it's something that just goes with horse racing and just in the interest of taking care of the animal. We're just glad it appears to be something that's not more serious. It should be something he'll definitely recover from. It was pretty obvious from overnight he'd swelled up and something wasn't right and it seemed at that point right away pretty unlikely that he'd be able to run tomorrow. It's unfortunate because it might be something that's just a few days in getting over or just a couple weeks. If it had happened three weeks ago, some time after his last race, it might be something that nobody ever would have heard about. He could have just gotten over it and come on, but that's not the way the timing turned out. I guess it would be disappointing at any point but there's bigger races next year. I think we're looking forward to those right now."

Heading back to their hotel on Friday following their first day at Arlington Park, Mike and Janet Hominda had a few minutes to catch their breath. The couple had arrived the previous night from Seattle, Washington, winners of a handicapping contest sponsored by Emerald Downs and a sports radio station, KGR-AM. The contest required picking the winner of every Sunday's stakes race throughout the Emerald Downs season. Points were awarded based on the payoffs of each winner (for example a $10.80 mutual equaled 10.8 points).

"The reason I entered the contest wasn't because there was a Breeders' Cup," Mike said. "I just wanted to enter the contest to test my handicapping skills more than anything else. Knowing it was in Arlington at the beginning was a bit of a disappointment because I was saying to Janet, 'Why couldn't it be at Churchill Downs or Belmont?' because in my mind I think of Churchill and Belmont and Del Mar and Saratoga as a step up from Arlington."

"People I know and work with know nothing about horse racing, so trying to explain to them what we were going to, they just didn't quite get it," Janet said. "I'd tell them it's kind of as if you were a women's figure skating fanatic and you had tickets to the finals in the Olympics. It's kind of on that scale. In fact, my neighbor said yesterday, 'If I knew where to tune in I'd look for you guys on Saturday on TV.' I said, 'It's going to be on NBC for five hours of coverage' and she said, 'It is?' People who don't know about horse racing are kind of clueless."

The Homindas arrived at the track early in the morning and spent about an hour and a half walking around, then took a train to see downtown Chicago and toured for about four hours before arriving back to the track. They never saw a race.

"We just couldn't see going to Chicago without going into the city," Mike said. "We just felt like we had to do that. My sister lived in Madison, Wisconsin, and we always planned to come to Arlington Park because she told us how beautiful it was. I didn't think it was as big as it was. I never envisioned the architecture and the atmosphere. We don't have paddock privileges tomorrow, so we wanted to walk around the paddock this morning and check out the grandstand and all that kind of stuff. I'm really sorry I didn't take my sister up on the offers (to come to Chicago years ago). I really would have loved to see Arlington eight or nine years ago because when we were going on the train today women were talking and oohing and ahing saying, 'Look at all those seats they've put up for this event.' It's like they couldn't imagine why there'd be that many seats and how could there be that many people going to a horse race? I was thinking people would be in the infields. I had no idea what Arlington was like."

"One of our friends at Emerald Downs said, 'Do you realize you'll be seeing the greatest racehorses in the world right now?'" Janet added.

"I don't think it's hit me yet," Mike said. "I think tomorrow when we wake up and finally get a good night's sleep, we're going to be pumped."

At the media hotel, the annual Breeders' Cup media rotisserie took place. The rotisserie has been going on for years among a small group of print and electronic media, public handicappers, industry types and wise guys. All of the Breeders' Cup horses in that particular year are auctioned off among teams, which can be individuals or partnerships. The teams are identified by the name of the person making the selections or in some cases pseudonyms. For example, The Maven is prominent American-based public handicapper Dave Gutfreund, while Sheikh Robert is Italian journalist Franco Raimondi, who is partnered with French-based journalist Emmanuel Roussel.

"We don't have a name for (the auction)," noted longtime player Scott Finley, who works as the North American Development Manager for the interactive betting service Attheraces.co.uk, said. "It's been called the Breeders' Cup Rotisserie, the Breeders' Cup Auction, the Breeders' Cup Calcutta. A good friend of mine, Graham Rock, a racing journalist from England, who loved to play (in the annual lottery), died last year. We're thinking of calling it The Rocky Pool."

Teams are given a budget of either $150 or $200 depending on how many participants are involved. Usually it's limited to 10 or 12 teams, no more than 14. This year there are only eight teams involved.

The top bid is $64 for Storm Flag Flying, whom English-based journalist Neil Morrice considers a lock in the Juvenile Fillies. He also shelled out $54 for Azeri, the heavy favorite in the Distaff. He's also purchased defending Filly & Mare Turf champion Banks Hill for $16 and stablemate Starine for only $7. Geoff Sotman of *HorsePlayer Magazine*, who annually runs the National Handicapping Championship for the *Daily Racing Form*, paid the second-most money of all teams for Rock of Gibraltar, the favorite in the Mile. It cost him $62. Overall he picked 15 horses, compared to only 10 for Morrice. The third-highest-priced horse is High Chaparral, the favorite in the Turf, who brought the gavel down at $50 for the team known as The French. The entry only has eight horses, including Medaglia d'Oro, one of the solid contenders for the Classic, who cost $40. The cheapest horses, at $2 apiece, are sprinters Thunderello and Wake At Noon, both purchased by English journalist Paul Haigh. Overall, he has 11 horses, his most expensive being Take Charge Lady, who cost him $44. She is rated second in the morning line in the Distaff.

On the day of the races, Liam Durbin, a 37-year-old whose computer-based handicapping program E-ponies.com is carried in several daily newspapers, including the *Chicago Sun-Times*, awoke early. He had arrived from Kentucky the night before, poised for the battle for top public-handicapping honors in the Arlington meet with Joe Kristufek of the *Chicago Daily Herald*. Heading into the final two days, Kristufek led by $20 and Durbin admitted there's pride on the line. He went down to the gift shop in the hotel to buy a *Daily Herald*, but the store hadn't opened yet, so he stuffed a dollar in the stack of newspapers and grabbed a copy.

"It's really cool (being at the Cup), plus I love horse racing," Durbin said. "Any day I go to the races I get excited. I've got four kids at home. I leave the wife and kids at home and come here to Chicago for a weekend and just play the horses and just be part of the element and that's why I couldn't sleep. It's a chance to step out and do something really fun. All I could think about was getting up, running down to buy a *Daily Herald*, opening it up and seeing who he picked, so I can line 'em up against who I picked and see how the day would unfold. I was hoping he would pick a different horse in each race, so somebody would win and somebody would lose. Any day where we picked the same horse, there's not much chance for me to gain ground on him, so I had to run down and grab a paper and see whom he picked differently. It's a great day. We only agreed on one horse all day long."

Durbin's full-time job is as a senior IT manager with General Electric, while his handicapping is something of a hobby. At his workplace, his fellow employees and his boss are aware of his other gig and don't consider it a conflict in any way.

"They think it's fantastic," he said. "The guys are always asking who I like when the big races come out. Plus I work for GE in Louisville, so horse racing is part of the culture there. It's okay to be into horses in Louisville."

While his computer programming is picking up in business, it hasn't grown to the point where he can give up his day job.

Indian Charlie has come out with his sheet indicating his choices for the Breeders' Cup races. There's little in the way of fun and frivolity in his comments because this is serious business, picking horses. He likes Farda Amiga over Starrer in the Distaff but he's put heavy favorite Azeri on his loser's list because he doesn't think her California form will hold. His advice is to "play the race like she ain't in there and if she beats you, turn the page." He favors long shot Ruby's Reception in the Juvenile Fillies over favorite Storm Flag Flying because she is lightly raced and yet to run around two turns: "You can't leave her out, but she's definitely no cinch." In the Mile, he's taken another flier, Domedriver, whose form in 2002 he said is "stronger than lye soap and his last-to-first move in his last start was better than it appears." He picked Rock of Gibraltar second, even though he noted "according to our informants there has not been a horse like this to race across the big pond in a long, long time." Next is the Sprint and he has touted Kona Gold over Bona-paw over Xtra Heat. He has selected Orientate on the loser's list: "Darnell Wayne Lukas has had him good all summer, but never matched him against the likes of these. He's a 12-1 or 15-1 shot against this bunch but you're probably gonna get less than 5-1." In the Filly & Mare Turf, his choice is Islington, who is racing against her own sex after tackling males in the Prix de l'Arc de Triomphe and only losing by two lengths, over defending champion Banks Hill. In the Juvenile, he has Toccet, "even though he's halfway to the parking lot from the flag fall," but "he's got Breeders' Cup breeding on top and bottom and very good form." European invader Hold That Tiger is second. He's tossed out Vindication, whom he said is coming out of a "Grade Three pony race at Turfway Park. He looked good winning, but it took him a long time to do it." In the Turf, he's picked heavy favorite High Chaparral over Perfect Soul and tossed American stars Denon and With Anticipation. Finally, in the Classic he's taken another outsider, Perfect Drift, who he said is all racehorse and will be completely overlooked at the mutuel windows. His second choice is Evening Attire, whose recent form he said is an indication he is going to run a powerful race. On his loser's list he's indicated War Emblem, whose chances of stealing an easy lead "do not look too promising," and Medaglia d'Oro, whose wins "have come at the expense of horses far inferior to these. He's in good hands, but his odds on the tote board will not be enough."

By the time of the first Breeders' Cup, there's no sign of dampness from the previous days but there's a Windy City chill. The main track is almost completely dry following exhaustive work by the crew of track superintendent Javier Barajas and the wind effect. Barajas' team packed the track down the night before by sealing it. The following morning, after the completion of training by horses, Barajas' crew sealed the track again and floated it to allow the excess water to rise to the surface. The results yielded lightning-quick races on the first two undercard races. Hero's Tribute, the stablemate of Sky Mesa, who had to be scratched out of the Juvenile the day before because of a leg injury, won the second race as a measure of some consolation for owner John Oxley and trainer John Ward. By the first Breeders' Cup race, the main track had been upgraded to fast.

The first race, the Distaff, opened with a facile victory by 9-5 favorite Azeri, who romped to a five-length tally under jockey Mike Smith. She recorded her eighth win in nine starts on the season. Laura de Seroux made history by becoming the first woman to saddle a Breeders' Cup winner with her first starter and immediately Azeri became a contender for Horse Of The Year honors. In the second race, Storm Flag Flying continued the procession of favorites, winning the Juvenile Fillies at 4-1 odds. But unlike Azeri, she had to work hard, claiming the lead with about three-sixteenths to the wire, giving way to Composure a few strides later and reclaiming it by digging in gamely and winning by a half-length. In many ways she resembled her maternal grandmother Personal Ensign in her epic win in the 1988 Breeders' Cup Distaff.

The results of the first two races had Neil Morrice in first in the Breeders' Cup rotisserie pool.

In the third race, Domedriver wins the Mile, scoring a three-quarter-length decision over Rock of Gibraltar, the 4-5 favorite who broke tardily and had to overcome some traffic problems after one of the other horses, Landseer, broke down at the top of the stretch. At least two people are rejoicing over the amazing upset by Domedriver, who went off at 26-1. Indian Charlie bet $40 to win and place, pocketing the princely sum of $1440.40. The tipster also touted the exacta, which paid $152.60, and he had it 10 times. Overall, he totaled $2996.40 on his $100 investment. Meanwhile in the rotisserie, Paul Haigh is on the board with his first winner after buying Domedriver for $20. Reigning champion Geoff Sotman not only had Rock of Gibraltar as his top-priced horse, he also invested $18 on Landseer.

Domedriver's trainer Pascal Bary missed the race while stuck in an elevator along with a group that included Maria Niarchos-Gouce, who manages the horse for her late father's racing operation. They had gone to the paddock to see the saddling of the horse. Fortunately, they made it out of the elevator in time for the victory presentation.

Following the Mile, David Hood, head of public relations for the William Hill bookmaking agency, opined that The Rock should have won.

"At the end of the day you can make excuses for him because of the draw but he's always going to ride a waiting race, but the bottom line was he was given too much to do," Hood said. "He wasn't really inconvenienced by the mishap in the turn into the straight with Landseer. He (swerved) left-handed. It didn't stop his run at all. He was bearing down that straight, absolutely, it was just a case whether or not he'd get to the winning line or the winning line would come too soon and it did."

The Juvenile followed and it featured Orientate, the 27-10 favorite, wearing down long shot Thunderello in deep stretch to win by a half-length. Crafty C.T., trained by Howard Zucker, who ran his first starter in Breeders' Cup history, made a gallant run from far back but ran out of racetrack and finished third by only a length. Orientate's victory gave trainer D. Wayne Lukas his unparalleled 17th Breeders' Cup win and once again put his critics, including Indian Charlie, in their place. The Filly & Mare Turf race came up next and it produced a stunning result: trainer Bobby Frankel won with his own horse, Starine, beating Banks Hill, who is owned by Frankel's top client, Juddmonte Farms. Neil Morrice had the top two finishers after purchasing Banks Hill for $16 and Starine for only $7. Starine went postward at more than 13-1.

The Juvenile followed the Filly & Mare Turf and featured a trio of runners trained by Bob Baffert: Vindication, Kafwain and Bull Market, and three from the barn of trainer Aidan O'Brien: Hold That Tiger, Van Nistelrooy and Tomahawk. Baffert prevailed with Vindication, who basically led from start to finish en route to a 2¾-length victory. Another Baffert runner, Kafwain, placed second, followed by Hold That Tiger. Bull Market ran fourth, followed by Van Nistelrooy, while Tomahawk came eighth. Scott Finley recorded his first win in the rotisserie with his $25 purchase of Vindication, while Haigh added some more points with Hold That Tiger, a $16 purchase.

David Hood of William Hill bookmakers immediately issued odds on the Kentucky Derby, making Vindicate and Hold That Tiger joint favorites at 8-1. Kafwain is priced at 12-1. All other horses are 40-1. The only other horse is Frankel's highly rated runner Empire Maker, who has only raced once at that point, at 20-1.

In The Turf, High Chaparral, the 9-10 favorite, unleashed a lethal kick in the stretch and won by 1¼ lengths. The team known as The French scored with its $50 buy, while Bill Finley placed second with With Anticipation, grabbed for $14.

Inside the media interview room located in the executive office area of Arlington, there is a break. John Magnier and his wife Susan, who collectively own Turf winner High Chaparral with Michael Tabor, are unavailable for comment because Hawk Wing is running in the next race, the Classic. The fact John Magnier rarely does interviews will likely preclude him from talking to the media anyway. Trainer Aidan O'Brien can't deputize for him because he had to saddle Hawk Wing. The absence of any people associated with the winning horse gives Peter Paul Balestrieri and his assistant, Kristen Cawley, a breather following a hectic schedule. Balestrieri is the president of ASAP Sports, which provides transcripts of the questions and answers between the media and athletes at major sports events. ASAP Sports has been employed for the World Series, NBA Finals, tennis' U.S. Open and the Kentucky Derby. Overall, the company has worked about 130 events and has satellite offices situated throughout the U.S.

"This is a nicely unanticipated break," he said. "I don't know what to say right now. There's like a thousand words in my head and I'm just ready to hit the pillow. So many events and so many words have gone through my head today, it's difficult to even know what I ate this morning. It's sort of like the conveyor belt with the Lucy Show. Here if you've got a little pitfall you've got to know how to get out of it and not lose your rhythm and your momentum. That's the key thing. You sit around and watch the World Series and all of a sudden the game ends and it's boom, boom, boom: coach, player, coach, player, and that's what we're trying to do, stay on our toes. It's the terminology (that's difficult to understand). Sometimes we're taken for a loop with some strange names and strange accents. That can bite you. It's pretty much what I had anticipated."

On the table beside one of his computers is a Chakra book about unlocking body energy.

"It keeps you sane," he said.

Prior to the final race, the $4 million Classic, Michael Ingram, the writer from the *Afro News*, "The Voice of the Black Community" in Aldergrove, British Columbia, Canada, placed his bets down—$10 across the board on Evening Attire and a box with Hawk Wing, Medaglia d'Oro and War Emblem. Beyond just the financial gain, Ingram wanted the horse to win because it could really make for a great story on Bridgmohan.

"It's always good to see new talent, no matter what they are—age, gender, ethnic background," Ingram said. "I'm a horse man, first and foremost. I appreciate the skill that the men and women utilize in this sport. To see new talent, like a Shawn Bridgmohan, is encouraging. Hopefully in future Breeders' Cups we'll see more of the Patrick Husbands and Marlin St. Juliens, not just because they're black but because they can ride. That's always the reason. When someone loses a race—and that includes the brothers as well—the last thing I care about is the color of the jockey. He's earned the right to be here, so hopefully with a little bit of racing luck he'll give a good account of himself."

The Classic shaped up perfectly for Medaglia d'Oro, the 27-10 favorite, who had the lead with a quarter mile to go, but Volponi, dismissed at 43.50-1 odds, rambled past him and posted a 6½-length win. Trainer P. G. Johnson, a Hall of Famer, bred and co-owned the winner in partnership with his wife, Mary Kay, with whom he would be celebrating their 57th wedding anniversary the following day. The Johnsons' two children, Kathy and Karen, the latter a *Daily Racing Form* reporter, were involved in the partnership along with Edward Baier.

The irony of the win, at least for Ingram, was that Bridgmohan had been riding the four-year-old colt for most of the year, but jumped off him to steer Evening Attire. Jose Santos, who had ridden the colt twice in 2002, picked up the mount, the jockey's share $208,000. Bridgmohan placed fourth on Evening Attire, collecting $22,400 for his efforts, but clearly had he won the race with Volponi it could have been a major boost for his career, not to mention a wonderful story for black athletes.

"It was the right move, but he outsmarted himself," Ingram said. "I can't fault what he did. He had a good horse to ride. He maybe should have taken the horse midpack and tried to keep him interested before sending him like he did, but the horse did what he was supposed to do. He closed. His problem was he didn't have enough ground. He got going too late. He was full of run in the end there. It's going to be ironic now. I wonder how long Bridgmohan will think about the fact he got off the Classic winner who's going to bomb the tote now at 45-1. That's unbelievable. That's horse racing."

While most of the grandstand emptied out, some people remained for the final non-Breeders' race of the day. Sandra Gray Volpe and one of her daughters, Pamela Volpe Jelaca, were among the hearty faithful. They had been seated outside near the clubhouse turn on the third level.

"I should have bet Volponi because it's similar to my maiden name," Pamela said. "I almost did and I didn't. It was a great day. The weather was an issue because it was very chilly outside with the wind and people were going in and out all day rather than sitting in their seats. What I was surprised about was this was completely sold and it has been for a long time and you could never tell. It was so cold, so many people stayed inside, except for the big races. As a native Chicagoan it was great to see the Breeders' Cup here. It was pretty exciting to have such a huge thing finally come to Chicago. It's nice to have international attention on Chicago for something other than pizzas and mobsters."

"Arlington did a fantastic job hosting the Breeders' Cup here. They always do a marvelous job," Sandra added. "It's a first-class organization and I think they've kept it throughout the Breeders' Cup. I think what Pamela said was very interesting. At one point you sat here and said, 'For a place that's sold out, there's nobody around, at all. The seats are empty.' People would come out when the race was on and they'd go back in because of the weather."

Sandra had moved a few years before to Lexington, Kentucky, to work on a horse farm. She didn't have a job, a place to live or any friends to contact. She simply decided at age 61 she didn't want a stressful job anymore after working 15 years in the admissions office of Lake Forest College.

She found a job working as the secretary for Juddmonte Farm.

Pamela said her mother was nervous watching Juddmonte's runners in the Mile and Filly & Mare Turf. Banks Hill did the best of the bunch, running second in the Filly & Mare race.

"It was like having her kids out there running," Pamela said.

"You always get very nervous when you have your horses from the farm running like that," Sandra replied.

About that time, the sun peeked through the clouds, offering some warmth.

"Typical Chicago weather," Pamela said. "The thing they say about Chicago is if you don't like the weather, hang around 10 minutes and it will always change. The sun was supposed to come out sooner, it was supposed to be 50 degrees."

When the final race ended, Trevor Loftus and some of his buddies, who had stuck around to make one last bet, made their way out of the racetrack. The following day they would be returning to Ireland. Loftus, a 28-year-old construction worker, lives about 15 minutes away from noted horse owner J. P. McManus.

"He's a cool guy," Loftus said. "His nickname is The Sundance Kid. All the bookmakers in Ireland and England are afraid of him."

Loftus had been to five other Breeders' Cups, more so for the prospect of making money than watching the best horses in the world.

"You've got to go," he said. "It's the money that attracts. You can make a small fortune in minutes here."

He had awoken earlier in the day to peruse the newspapers for information. He also had some jockey friends in Kentucky who had provided him and his contingent with some other useful tidbits. Beyond his wool jacket—and ample quantities of ale he'd consumed by that point—Loftus hadn't bundled up to brave the cold.

"That's all that came in the bag," he said. "Clean socks, clean jocks. We go back tomorrow."

Loftus' gang came to play the Irish horses, specifically Rock of Gibraltar and High Chaparral. He bet about $1,800 on The Rock and about $2,000 on High Chaparral. Because the last race had an Irish horse in it, Loftus' group decided to play it. Appropriately, the horse they fancied was named One More Round. When the race concluded, One More Round placed second and the Irishmen had him backed across the board, saving the day from a financial standpoint.

Later that evening, when the rotisserie results had been tabulated, Neil Morrice collected first-place prize money, while Haigh, who had purchased Volponi for only $5, took the runner-up loot. Morrice credited his "partner-in-crime" Angus Hamilton for the win.

"He's a bookmaker and he's a great mathematical brain, which I'm not," Morrice said. "When you're bidding for those horses, he's very, very good at knowing how to play your $200 to your best strength. It's the first year we teamed together. We have linked now to do betting in Las Vegas and things. I'm based in England, he's based in an island off South America, an offshore betting haven. I do the groundwork. I go and check and make sure that certain horses are going to run in races and I inform him and he does the betting."

But Morrice said his advance bets in Vegas didn't do well.

"All the bets in Vegas were win only and I do like betting each way, but I can't in Vegas, and the Rock was the big one," he said. "But I won the competition and I won money betting with a British bookmaking organization. It wasn't that bad. The day kind of evened itself out."

William Hill publicist David Hood said the day started off "badly" for his company with some short-priced horses winning but business got a "whole lot better" afterward.

Isobel Cunningham, the sleuth from Scotland, was asked if she had a good day gambling.

"Yes, but that's not what is important," she said. "What is important is being here."

Liam Durbin, the computer handicapper, had three winners on the Breeders'

Cup card, basically finishing even on the day with his rival Joe Kristufec, who would go into the following day's card with a slight advantage. Either way, Durbin figured he'd made Kristufec take notice.

The following morning, Dick Duchossois walked the backstretch to congratulate the winning connections. D. G. Van Clief, the president of the Breeders' Cup, announced a few hours later that Arlington had done such a terrific job that it would now be considered for future editions of the World Thoroughbred Championships.

By all accounts it had been a great day all around at the races at Arlington.

# 4

# A World of Difference

## The 2001 Breeders' Cup

*H*eading into the year 2001, the management of the Breeders' Cup Ltd. realized the event lacked recognition and understanding by sports fans around the world. Even some people who followed the sport didn't truly understand what the Breeders' Cup meant or signified. Something needed to be done to clarify the event for the public and to make it resonate in the future.

The Breeders' Cup Ltd. huddled with the management of the National Thoroughbred Racing Association to formulate a strategy. The NTRA had been created in April 1998 as a national body to promote the sport, complete with a commissioner, Tim Smith, who had an impressive history with the Professional Golf Association and later formed a company specializing in sports and entertainment marketing. The Breeders' Cup Ltd. contributed $3.5 million to the NTRA. In December 1999, the executive committee for the Breeders' Cup Ltd. and the board of directors of the NTRA approved in principle a strategic alliance between the two organizations. In January 2001, the operational merger between Breeders' Cup Ltd. and the NTRA became effective.

To help facilitate the rebranding of the Breeders' Cup, the Breeders' Cup Ltd./NTRA contacted Jim Host of Host Communications. Host's company is a well-known sports-marketing firm based in Lexington, Kentucky, but with offices in New York and Dallas. Host is best known within the sports community for developing the National Collegiate Athletic Association Final Four, an event that is an institution in U.S. college basketball and the American sports public. With Host's help, the Breeders' Cup Ltd./NTRA looked to strategize its corporate sales effort and to rebrand its signature event in a much clearer and descriptive way.

Many names were considered and put forward in focus groups, but ultimately World Thoroughbred Championships resonated in the surveying. National Thoroughbred Championships also received some consideration, but using the word "world" carried much more meaning in the global sports landscape.

On June 26, the NTRA and Breeders' Cup Ltd. launched a new brand—the World Thoroughbred Championships. In addition, Bessemer Trust, a private banking and wealth management company headed by prominent New York breeder/owner Ogden Mills (Dinny) Phipps, was announced as a new sponsor of the event, in particular the Juvenile race. Furthermore, NBC announced an increase in its broadcast of the annual event, allowing for more time between each of the eight races.

Collectively, all three announcements signaled a major change in the Breeders' Cup. Little did officials know how much the name, in particular the word "world," would mean in the months to come.

On September 11, 2001, the world stopped and stared, and it ultimately mourned one of the most significant and shocking events in history. Osama bin Laden's al-Qaeda network launched a series of attacks on the United States, including flying two hijacked planes into the World Trade Center. The two buildings, part of the cultural landscape of the New York skyline, imploded, killing thousands of people trapped inside.

Immediately after the attacks, most major North American sports events shut down to pay respect to the victims and to give people a chance to come to grips with the chaos. The New York Racing Association, which had just commenced its Belmont fall meeting, had some important decisions to make, including whether or not to continue with the Breeders' Cup World Thoroughbred Championships, October 27 at Belmont Park. NYRA chairman Barry K. Schwartz, president/chief executive officer Terry Meyocks and vice-president Bill Nader huddled together to formulate a plan.

"At first we didn't know how to react," Nader recalled. "There was a sense in New York that you didn't know what you were supposed to do. That was the overriding sentiment at the time. We looked at other sports and what they were doing. We looked at what Broadway was doing. We looked at getting some sense of direction from the mayor and the governor. The theme at that time was 'Go on with your daily lives,' almost try to operate in a sense of business as usual. But that was very, very difficult to do at the time. It was hard for people to kick back up and go on with their daily routine, especially with horse racing, which really wasn't important in the whole scheme of things."

The New York Racing Association management decided to suspend racing for at least a week, scrapping some key races a few days later on the road to the Breeders' Cup. Coincidentally, one of those races happened to be included in Bessemer Trust's overall Breeders' Cup sponsorship package announced back in June. Breeders' Cup president D. G. Van Clief called NYRA president/CEO Terry Meyocks and talked about the prospects of the weeks to come. They agreed NYRA should contact the relevant political and law-enforcement authorities—the Nassau County Police Force, New York Police Department, State Police, Governor's Office, Mayor's Office, Federal Bureau of Investigation and the Federal Joint Task Force on Terrorism—to make sure they all understood what the Breeders' Cup was and who was likely to participate in it. The Breeders' Cup Ltd. and NYRA needed to know if these organizations still wanted the event to come to New York, taking into account security and safety issues. It took maybe two days for NYRA to contact all the necessary authorities, which collectively gave their blessing to go ahead with the event, which would be the first major international sporting event to take place in New York following the terrorist attacks.

On September 14, the Breeders' Cup Ltd., NTRA and NYRA announced the 2001 Breeders' Cup would be dedicated to the families of New York firefighters, police officers, emergency services personnel and other victims in the surrounding communities who lost their lives in the search and recovery process. The three racing authorities created the New York Heroes Fund to financially assist the families of the workers. Monies would come from a portion of each paid admission on Breeders' Cup day, along with a percentage of all other revenues in connection with the event, such as the Charity Gala the night before the races. Officials encouraged owners, trainers, jockeys, racetracks, simulcast partners, corporate sponsors and the media to join in the cause and raise a minimum of $1 million.

"We want this year's Breeders' Cup in New York to have special meaning by honoring these true heroes and innocent victims, and by helping their families cope with this tragedy in some tangible fashion," Breeders' Cup president D. G. Van Clief said in a press release.

"Our sport works every day with emergency personnel like the brave men and women who gave their lives this week," NYRA president/CEO Terry Meyocks said. "In our particular case at NYRA, they and other victims are literally also our neighbors and, in many cases, our relatives or friends. It is entirely appropriate to dedicate racing's biggest day—held this year in New York—to their memories and to their families."

Meanwhile, in a separate but noteworthy move, Sheikh Mohammed bin Rashid al Maktoum pledged $5 million to a campaign set up by Keeneland Racecourse's management to raise money for the American Red Cross Disaster Relief Fund. A member of the ruling family of Dubai and also its defense minister, Sheikh Mohammed had been in Lexington for horse sales during the terrorist attacks and publicly condemned the actions.

It did not take long for horsemen to show their financial support for the Heroes Fund. Coolmore Stud, the major commercial breeding/racing operation based in Ireland but with divisions in Australia and the U.S., announced plans to earmark 10% of its earnings from Breeders' Cup day. Coolmore's exclusive trainer Aidan O'Brien and stable jockey Michael Kinane also pledged 10% of their winnings. Breeder/owner Harry T. Mangurian of Florida pledged $1 million. Prince Ahmed bin Salman, the Saudi Arabian who runs horses under the stable name Thoroughbred Corporation, donated a 2002 breeding season to Preakness and Belmont Stakes winner Point Given.

Ernie Paragallo, a Brooklyn native, pledged $1 million through breeding seasons from 2000 to 2004 to two of his stars: Artax, who won the 1999 Sprint, and Unbridled's Song, who won the 1995 Juvenile. Owner Tracy Farmer pledged 5% of the potential winnings by Albert the Great in the Jockey Club Gold Cup Stakes and the Breeders' Cup Classic. Organizations also made pledges, including The Meadowlands/New Jersey Sports & Exposition Authority; Thoroughbred Charities of America; Los Alamitos Racecourse; Fasig-Tipton (one of the leading horse auction companies in the world); and the National Turf Writers Association.

Within a couple weeks of its announcement of the Heroes Fund, the Breeders' Cup Ltd./NTRA had doubled its minimum financial goal to $2 million.

While the Breeders' Cup Ltd. and the NTRA worked on the Heroes Fund, the New York Racing Association spent countless hours on safety and security issues leading up to the Cup.

"Once we decided to have the event, we just went full throttle with every level of protection and aspect of security that you could imagine," NYRA's director of security John Tierney said. "We reached out to every law-enforcement branch we could in regards to what we could do to make the environment (safe and secure) for our patrons, for our facility, for our horsemen, for everyone, to make sure that the event went free of incident. There were so many different avenues we were pursuing. We were trying to encompass it all into one comprehensive plan. It was absolutely incredible the effort and the work that was put into that Breeders' Cup in that six-week period. Based upon the events of 9-11, it was the most amazing amount of pressure that I've ever faced in my life, just trying put together a plan for the protection of everyone. Emotions were high at the time. There was so much new information coming in every day. It was very difficult to make certain you had all aspects of everything covered in your own mind because you always have to wonder about what you don't know, the possibilities of what could happen because you don't have that information."

About a month before the event, the Breeders' Cup Ltd./NTRA began setting up temporary offices at Belmont Park. The majority of the employees were in place two weeks before race day. With the threat of additional terrorist attacks and an anthrax outbreak, concerns and anxieties reached additional heights.

"It's the first time in 18 runnings that I've actually noticed our staff making sure their wills and estate plans were in order," Breeders' Cup president D. G. Van Clief recalled. "There was a great deal of concern that the initial attack was not the only one, that New York would continue to be a target area. They were flying combat air patrol when we got there. The anthrax mailings were taking place while we were in New York. One of them arrived in the governor's Manhattan office the day they were shipping us some material to our temporary offices at Belmont. We actually had people sort of walking around with FedEx envelopes held by two fingers wondering what to do."

In the week leading up to the event, the NYRA investigative unit did background checks on every person coming into the track, including horsemen and their employees, media and Breeders' Cup representatives. NYRA routinely does background checks on new owners or employees coming into the track, but never to this extreme.

Concern about the Muslim involvement in the Cup, normally a nonissue, became a major topic in the trade publications and the major dailies. Questions began to arise whether or not the Arab principals would be in New York. It had not been uncommon for some of those owners to skip an event, for one reason or another, but the issue became more focused this time. The Breeders' Cup annually had strong Arab representation, but in this case Sheikh Mohammed bin Rashid al Maktoum planned to send his largest contingent ever to the event. And he would not be the only representative of Muslim descent. Prince Khalid Abdullah, a member of the Saudi Arabian royal family, and his son-in-law, Ahmed Salman, would also have multiple runners in the event.

"It was actually a delicate situation," Breeders' Cup president D.G. Van Clief said. "There was a lot of sentiment following 9-11 and not all of it was pro-Arab. There was some very aggressive positions taken by certain writers as to whether or not the middle-Eastern-based owners ought to even come to the event. Those sentiments were kind of reactionary and unfortunate, but nonetheless they did occur. We were questioned almost daily in the week leading up to it as to which Arab owners might be coming and if so where would they be staying and so forth. People in the media were just curious and presumably they were reacting as they saw to their viewership and readership."

Four days before the Cup at a major news conference, Sheikh Mohammed pledged all of the earnings from Godolphin Stable, his international racing operation, to the New York Heroes Fund. Some of the Sheikh's prominent runners included Fantastic Light and Sakhee, both pre-entered in the Turf and the Classic. The decision in which race they would run would be made the following day. Other Godolphin runners pre-entered included Imperial Gesture and Tempera in the Juvenile Fillies; Noverre and Express Tour in the Mile; and Essence of Dubai and Ibn Al Haitham in the Juvenile.

On race day, NYRA's security plan went into effect. Bomb-sniffing dogs were employed well before the track opened for early-morning training. Anybody entering the track had to pass a full inspection. Policemen in vehicles, on horses and in stationary positions were noticeably visible. A bomb-squad truck scanned vehicles coming into the tunnel of the track. The Bureau of Special Operations, a division of the Nassau County Police, had sharpshooters strategically positioned in various areas to quickly squelch anything that might happen, assisted by specialized investigative units. They did several dry runs in and outside the plant to critique the most important areas they would cover. Provisions were made for specialized emergency vehicles to enter the premises in the event of a tragedy or calamity. Commercial or domestic flights were banned from flying above as part of the Federal Aviation Act, while police also monitored the air site.

With American flags prominently displayed on the backs of cars, in the front of homes and storefront windows, a renewed sense of patriotism arose out of the 9-11 tragedy, particularly in New York, and the New York Racing Association and the Breeders' Cup Ltd. wanted to embrace that. NYRA vice-president Bill Nader had an idea to celebrate this patriotism on race day with a prominent flag display. He contacted Breeders' Cup/NTRA executives Chip Tuttle and Damon Thayer to bounce around some ideas and they wholeheartedly supported the plan. In fact, Chip Tuttle suggested unfurling a large American flag in the infield. After contacting some of the New York-based jockeys, including Jerry Bailey, John Velazquez and Richard Migliore, who pledged their support and assistance, Nader conceived an idea to involve the Breeders' Cup in a ceremony before the first race. Each of the riders would run in alphabetical order onto the infield turf course carrying a U.S. flag and the flag of their respective country of birth. In addition, the jockeys would wear baseball caps with logos of either the New York Police Department or the Fire Department.

An announced crowd of 52,987, a record audience in New York for the Breeders' Cup, filled the venerable track. At about 11:05 a.m., one hour before the first race on the card, the jockeys commenced their procession. Robby Albarado, slated to ride Sam-Son Farms' Quiet Resolve in the penultimate Breeders' Cup race, began the parade wearing the yellow and orange silks of an owner whose horse he was slated to ride on the undercard. Albarado had been used to such proceedings, having participated in similar festivities in the Jockey Challenge at Lone Star Park in Texas, but this was different, more emotional. Jerry Bailey, dressed in the famous red, white and blue silks of the Paulson family for whom he had ridden the great Cigar, followed Albarado. Pat Day wore the colors of W. T. Young's Overbrook Farm. Frankie Dettori dressed in the blue silks of Sheikh Mohammed's Godolphin Stable. Chris McCarron wore the pink and blue colors of the Cee's Stable, bidding for a second consecutive win in the Classic. Corey Nakatani had on the white, red and green silks with the prominent apple of Arthur Appleton. John Velazquez had royal blue and gold silks of Canadians Eugene and Laura Melnyk and Iris Bristow. Collectively, it represented a beautiful display of color and pageantry among people from various regions of the world.

The jockeys assembled together for a picture and were joined by representatives from the New York firemen and policemen nattily attired in their uniforms. New York police officer Carl Dixon, a member of the ceremonial unit in addition to his patrol duties, sang the national anthem. He had been singing the anthem or God Bless America for about a year with the ceremonial unit. Dixon had been en route to his precinct, about 10–15 minutes away from the World Trade Center, when the attacks happened. He had been scheduled to do ceremonial work that day but was reassigned to do patrol work in or around Ground Zero.

"After 9-11, every ceremony was different, it just had a different tone," Dixon said. "The spirit was very apparent. You just tend to do the ceremony with that in mind. I didn't have any adverse effects from 9-11, but it was something to remember—a solemn memory. It's just something that I will always remember, from the time it happened and having to work in Ground Zero and having a mask on."

A plan to unfurl a $40 \times 80$–foot American flag as part of the proceedings had to be scrapped because of high winds, the only disappointment in what was otherwise an emotionally moving display.

"I think it was pretty good," Albarado said. "It was emotional, for sure. I felt for the people of New York."

"It was a good scene, a great scene," Nader said. "I thought it went really well. It certainly drew on the fact that the Breeders' Cup World Thoroughbred Championships really is an international sporting event. For us it was more to showcase New York than horse racing. It was to show that New York was strong, that New York was unified—not only within our own state boundaries. I think a lot of the foreign jockeys were touched to be part of that ceremony because they were showing support for New York. Everybody reaches out at a time like that and wants to demonstrate some show of support and that was a nice way to do it. I think it was more about New York at that point than it was about horse racing."

NBC's Breeders' Cup producer David Michaels and host Tom Hammond discussed before the event the Arab factor and how it played out in various races and overall on the day. It was left up to Hammond to decide what he would say and how much he would delve into the topic. Hammond, who had talked to various people connected with the Arab-owned horses, viewed it from the perspective that while there may have been a backlash against Arabs because of the actions of a few, in the horse-racing community there had been some wonderful displays of goodwill. Owners of Arabic background didn't attend the event—either because of health issues, business, civic duty or simply to avoid becoming the story.

"I thought they thought it was in better taste not be there, not to put anyone in an awkward position and not to subject themselves to maybe verbal abuse, but also not to embarrass the Breeders' Cup or the NYRA or those kind of people," Hammond said. "They're pretty sensitive to that."

For Hammond, who had been with NBC for every one of its Breeders' Cup telecasts, either as a reporter or host, this particular occasion had a different feel to it, a somewhat somber side to it.

"You couldn't help but reflect a bit because there was an Arab influence and presence there and because if you looked out from the top of the grandstand you could see the Empire State Building and the skyline of New York," he said.

Sadly and unfortunately, the Breeders' Cup began ominously. Just before the first race, the Distaff, Exogenous, one of the favorites, spooked en route to the track. She reared up and hit her head upon landing and also caught her leg in a railing. The filly thrashed around trying to extricate her leg, while millions of people watching the event live witnessed the heartbreaking sight. Even when the limb was freed Exogenous had a hard time regaining her balance and repeatedly hit her head, causing some trauma. Coupled with the palpable tension because of the 9-11 tragedy and its impact on the event, the newly named Breeders' Cup World Thoroughbred Championships appeared destined for an awful beginning.

"The problem of Exogenous sort of added that there was a somber side to this occasion," Hammond added. "It wasn't festive and joyous as it normally is. Normally it's a celebration of the horse really. It's like the year-end championship. It's celebrating all the good things about thoroughbred racing."

Various horse people and security rushed to the fallen horse, creating an unexpected security problem.

"I'm in the paddock and I hear this huge roar, thinking the first horse has just gone on to the track and everyone is excited, only to find out the horses are coming back," NYRA's director of security, John Tierney, said.

He was informed a horse had fallen down and immediately figured a tragedy had occurred, possibly because of a shooting. He ran to the front of the track and witnessed the fallen horse and was apprised on the events leading up to it.

"It was a frightening moment for the fans," Tierney said. "If you've been in racing as long as I've been it and so many other people, these things happen before; you've seen them before and they're all tragedies. Based upon the events of 9-11 and what people had gone through it was gut-wrenching to me that they had to witness something like this in the first race. If you're here as long as I've been, you've got tremendous sentiment for the animals, too."

Once emergency personnel were able to load Exogenous into a horse ambulance, the card continued without incident. The Arabian storyline played out like never before, but more because of the horses. Flute, owned by Prince Khalid Abdullah's Juddmonte Farms, went postward as the favorite in the Distaff, but ran out of the money, continuing a lengthy losing streak for the Prince in the Breeders' Cup. Defending champion Spain, owned by Prince Ahmed bin Salman, ran a close second. In the second race, Sheikh Mohammed's two horses, Tempera and Imperial Gesture, ran one-two in a stunning upset. Tempera was almost a 12-1 long shot, while Imperial Gesture was more than 50-1. It was the first tangible sign of a plan begun the year before by Sheikh Mohammed, one of the leading owners in Europe, to race some of his two-year-olds in the U.S.

Three races later in the Filly & Mare Turf, Juddmonte Farms' Banks Hill scored a mild upset at 6-1 odds, giving Prince Khalid Abdullah his first Breeders' Cup win in more than 30 starts.

In the seventh race, the Turf, Sheikh Mohammed's Fantastic Light won, while in the eighth and final Breeders' Cup race, the Classic, stablemate Sakhee finished second by a nose to American-owned Tiznow, the defending champion who prevailed with a gutsy effort. Overall, the Godolphin horses collected more than $2.7 million for the New York Heroes Fund.

Purely from a patriotic perspective, the victory in the Classic by an American horse, particularly one with a history in the Breeders' Cup, punctuated the day perfectly. However, politics aside, the result had been everything that symbolized the glory of horse racing—a fight to the finish among two horses giving everything they had.

"I didn't put much political significance into that," Hammond said. "You could, I guess, with the American beating the Arab-owned horse, but by then I'd sort of forgotten about that side of events and had gone on to competition on the racetrack and it was such a tremendous race. Tiznow had such a courageous performance that the political ramifications or any kind of metaphors that you could make from a finish of that race were mostly forgotten. I just saw it as a hell of a horse race. The horses didn't know who owned them and to me that was the focus rather than any sort of political statement or impact or inference you could make from it. By that time we had gone past that and were celebrating the greatest horses in the world and the Classic was just the epitome of that. By then, that somber note had largely been forgotten and we were back to celebrating the horse again."

Breeders' Cup president D. G. Van Clief said it was "very fortuitous" that the organization had decided that year to emphasize the global branding of the event, thus adding more stature and impact to the New York marketplace.

"We were put in a position, by luck really, to be able to be of some tangible benefit to a region in the community that so badly needed it," he said. "We created the NTRA New York Heroes Fund and raised about $5 million for the families of the victims of 9-11, and although that's a goodly amount of money it's not much compared to the need, but we were able to do something. We felt also that this was a way to provide a moral boost for the community to show that there were others who were supportive and despite the fact there may have been some misgivings we were determined to bring a very high quality event to New York. New York turned out and supported the event like they never have before.

"The fact Godolphin sent its largest contingent was again another irony given that it could have just as easily decided to bypass the event with their horses and personnel for security purposes. It was a wonderfully talented group of horses and of course they performed as well as they ever have. The European-based contingent took home more prize money and won more races in 2001 than they ever have before. It was a tremendously dramatic event for all of the obvious reasons. I don't want to overstate the importance of our being there. It was an opportunity for us to serve in many ways that we don't get an opportunity to serve every year. It was immensely gratifying in that regard. We were able to provide some tangible support for the people of New York who had been so hurt and I would imagine when it's all over and done with that may personally be the one Breeders' Cup I'll be the most proud of being involved in."

# 5

# Coming to a New Country

## The 1996 Breeders' Cup

*In* 1956, E. P. Taylor opened Woodbine Racetrack in the west end of Toronto with the idea of bringing together the best horses at one modern site. It is likely that not even Taylor, a man of great foresight, could ever have anticipated his track would one day play host to the world's biggest day of thoroughbred racing. Or that problems would conspire to almost scratch the event before it made it to the starting gate. In fact, the history of how Woodbine became the host track of the 13th edition of the Breeders' Cup has a little bit of everything: family ties, politics, luck and heroism. But, above all else, it proved the old adage that the show—or in this case the Greatest Show on Turf—must go on.

Principally through the persistence of E. P. Taylor's son, Charles, Breeders' Cup Ltd. chose Woodbine in 1993 as the first track outside the U.S. to host the event. An esteemed journalist who had worked in some 50 countries as a war correspondent and authored five books, Charles Taylor's ascension as a prominent figure in the racing and breeding world began when he was named a trustee of the Ontario Jockey Club in 1969. In the next decade he became provincial and national director of the Canadian Thoroughbred Horse Society, but Taylor's biggest appointment came in the fall of 1980 when he succeeded his father, who had suffered a debilitating stroke, as president of Windfields Farm.

Charles Taylor did not have an easy task. He had to manage an international business and continue the family tradition of excellence. Windfields had developed into one of the premier commercial nurseries in the world and the home to the hottest stallion in the world in Northern Dancer, who in 1964 had become the first Canadian-bred to win the Kentucky Derby. The Dancer's stud prowess had exceeded his talents on the track.

On the strength of Windfields' reputation, John R. Gaines contacted Charles Taylor about becoming a member of the Breeders' Cup steering committee when he unveiled the idea of the championship day of racing in 1982. Taylor supported the concept from the outset and nominated Northern Dancer, which in many ways was like a new league signing a marquee player. Northern Dancer commanded a breeding fee of $500,000 with no guarantee in 1984, but in some private deals buyers were willing to pay $1 million with no guarantee.

When tracks were asked in 1982 to submit proposals for the first Breeders' Cup in 1984, Taylor urged the OJC to step up to the plate.

"The concept (of the Breeders' Cup) was always to travel as much as possible around North American racetracks that were capable of putting on such a big day," Taylor said. "I say North American and here I won't be modest. For the first four or five years, at least in our discussions at the executive committee level in particular, my colleagues who were all American, would say things like 'America' or 'this country' and I would very politely but firmly keep saying, 'Please, for the record and the minutes, it's North America and this is a North American phenomenon and I do hope we will at some point be moving to Woodbine.'"

For its presentation to the Breeders' Cup management in 1982, the OJC prepared a video assembled by publicist Bruce Walker in cooperation with Angelo Kosmidis, the director of television and broadcasting. The video recapped great moments in Woodbine's history for Breeders' Cup officials. Shepherded by OJC chairman Charles Baker and accompanied by president Jack Kenney and other executives from the company, the OJC made its presentation. Realistically the Canadian contingent had little chance of bringing the Cup home for the first running because there were too many obstacles, principally the limited size of the track and concerns about the weather. Breeders' Cup Ltd. management wanted to stage the first running at a track that had a sizeable grandstand and was in a hot climate, and subsequently chose Hollywood Park in California. Image meant everything for the inaugural event, which would be telecast by NBC and shown worldwide. With its unpredictable weather, Canada did not appeal to the Breeders' Cup Ltd. executive, regardless of the OJC's good reputation and its presentation.

"We got our feet wet," Taylor said. "We showed we were serious and we made a very professional pitch. I know this impressed some of my colleagues."

In 1991, Major League Baseball showcased its all-star game at the SkyDome in Toronto and showed how successful an American event could be when played in another country. OJC officials believe it helped bring the Cup to Canada. Baker traveled to the Canadian capital of Ottawa to visit Ed Ney, U.S. ambassador to Canada, and explained what a great idea it would be for the Breeders' Cup to come to Canada. Ney relayed that message to Nick Brady, secretary of the treasury for the U.S. and a horse owner who raced under the nom-du-course Millhouse Stable.

Baker is convinced the message to let Canada host the Breeders' Cup came from the White House to the Breeders' Cup management through Will Farish Jr., who worked for President George Bush as his administrative assistant. Farish's father, Will Sr., carried tremendous clout as vice-chairman of The Jockey Club, chairman of Churchill Downs and head of the prestigious Lane's End Farm stallion operation. Baker traveled to Lexington to meet with the senior Farish, whom he described as the "key to the whole thing."

"Over the years it was us pressuring the Breeders' Cup, finally getting to the U.S. ambassador and finally getting to Will Farish (Sr.) through the White House, that I managed to influence them that they should come here," Baker said.

Late in the summer of 1992, the OJC sent a letter to Breeders' Cup management expressing interest in hosting the event that year if Gulfstream Park couldn't honor its commitment because of political problems in the Miami area.

"There wasn't a great deal of time between when we heard about the possibility Gulfstream might not hold it and the time of the Breeders' Cup," said Rick Cowan, the OJC's executive vice-president at the time. "We thought we could get our act together in a hurry because we had been thinking of the Breeders' Cup for a number of years, not officially but certainly assessing the prospect of Woodbine staging it. At the time we thought with our facilities and with our experience running the Rothmans International we could make a quick move and one that might be accepted a lot more quickly than going through the process of formal hearings."

The OJC was not the only organization seeking to pinch-hit; others came forth, including the New York Racing Association, which carried more clout because it had played host to the event twice at Aqueduct and Belmont. NYRA would have been the site based on its track record in the Cup.

"We were not going to take a chance of moving that quickly into a host track that never had the experience of putting it on," former Breeders' Cup Ltd. president James E. (Ted) Bassett III said. "Their gesture was certainly well-received and that was important to us for future consideration."

In September of 1992, the OJC began the long process of gathering material and manpower to make its case to Breeders' Cup management in December. The task was broken down into five categories: the operational components of the day itself, including everything from ticket sales to seating allocation; food and beverage; television and audio/video and publicity; stabling, access to the training facilities and accreditation; and support from politicians representing the municipal, provincial and federal levels of government.

The province assured funding of $1.5 million to help pay for costs—including construction of a new press box—which the OJC outlined for the event. Never before had an organization seeking the Breeders' Cup secured funding up front from a political source. Frank Drea, then the high-profile chairman of the Ontario Racing Commission, worked as a serious lobbyist, assisting with the key people in the government to make them aware of how important the event would be. Rod Seiling, then the OJC's vice-president of industry relations, worked on the provincial network with Marilyn Churley, the minister of consumer and commercial relations.

Federal support came from Tom Hockin, the minister of small business, through OJC trustee David Weldon. Hockin met with OJC president Jack Kenney, chairman George Hendrie and Cowan at his home. Hockin had some interest in racing, but the OJC impressed on him the positive impact the Breeders' Cup would have on Canada and Canadian racing and assured him financial assistance would be required more from the provincial level than the federal level. The OJC used the figures from the all-star game to show the impact on Toronto and stressed that the Breeders' Cup was more of a weeklong event than just a day of racing. Hockin initially offered his support with a letter or a phone call to the Breeders' Cup executive, but took it one step further when he joined the Canadian contingent in Lexington for its presentation. Municipal support came from Dennis Flynn, the mayor of Etobicoke and subsequently the Metro Chairman of Toronto.

Collectively then, the OJC had at least one representative from all three levels of government.

The OJC videotaped an endorsement by Ontario Premier Bob Rae, who read a prepared script. One of Rae's assistants told Kosmidis, who drove to the provincial legislature to videotape Rae, that he would not have much time because of the Premier's busy schedule.

"It was all very hurried and he came in and sat down and I went over the script with him," Kosmidis recalled. "We had about a two-minute chat and he just banged it off. I asked him if he wanted to do it again and he said he was happy with it and that was it. Poof, he was gone. He didn't give us any kind of feeling either way. It was probably the 40th thing he had done that day and he probably had another 40 things to do. I just think it was a poof, poof, let's get it over with."

Rae talked about horse racing's importance to the province because it employed more than 50,000 people and had millions of fans, and added the bid had the full "financial, moral and political support" of the Ontario government.

"We have a tradition of over 100 years of wonderful horse racing in this province and this country," he said. "We very much feel we can add something to the Breeders' Cup and we would be delighted to be the host for the Breeders' Cup."

The OJC, which had been sending key representatives more frequently to the Breeders' Cup in the late '80s, sent additional representatives that year to Gulfstream to gather important information. The OJC wanted to know about physical changes that had to be made to Woodbine to accommodate the crowd and the media, plus the logistics of staging parties for officials before the event. The OJC acted like tourists, filming everything in sight.

"It was our first serious visit to see how things were done and sort of get a feel for what would be involved. It was mind-blowing," Kosmidis said. "It's a huge undertaking. NBC rolled in nine trailers parked behind the grandstand. That's unbelievable. We're talking Super Bowl type of proportions. It was really something."

To put its package together, the OJC worked with two specialists in advertising and presentation. Joe Warwick, executive vice-president of the advertising firm Vickers & Benson, assisted in the glitzy brochure and video that were presented to the Breeders' Cup Ltd. executive. Bill Duron, head of the Metropolitan Toronto Convention and Visitors Association, which claimed the Breeders' Cup would provide $50 million to the local economy, worked on strategy. Duron identified the "hot points" that could appeal to the Breeders' Cup management and how the message would be delivered. Regular meetings were convened to put it all together.

On December 8, 1992, the Canadian contingent traveled to Lexington to make its presentation the following day. Before he left, Taylor told the *Toronto Sun*: "We will have a strong case. I'm very confident it will pay off in terms of the Breeders' Cup coming here, whether it is '94 or '96, I don't know."

The night before the presentation, the members who had already gathered had dinner and then broke into groups for final discussions. Taylor, who was assigned the opening monologue and whom Duron identified as the "point man" because of his connections to the OJC and Breeders' Cup executives, excused himself afterward to go over the proposal.

The following morning the group assembled early and was joined by the political officials and Larry Regan, president of the Toronto division of the Horsemen's Benevolent and Protective Association. Each of the assigned speakers delivered his or her speech to the group. After a few formal runs, the group broke off and prepared for the meeting. Cowan said it was one of the few times in his career at the OJC where all facets of the industry were excited and positive about working together.

The Canadians had a key document with them: a letter of support from Prime Minister Brian Mulroney. It had taken four weeks and two calls a day to obtain that piece of paper, but the letter added one more dazzling item to the entire package.

Warwick said the Canadians felt upbeat, believing they had a "great story to tell and the team to back it up. We thought we were going to knock them on their ass and we did." Taylor began with a compelling pitch, one that inspired both the OJC and the Breeders' Cup. "From an emotional side, I know how badly Charles wanted it and how committed he had been," Cowan said. "He was just outstanding on his feet. He just had so much emotion built up within him and so much pride in Woodbine. It was certainly an obsession that he had had for a number of years. On a scale of one to 10, he was a 12 in terms of his presentation and his conviction."

Following Taylor, the other speakers took their turns, offering political and economic reasons for running the Cup in Canada. Duron, a Philadelphia native, offered some of his experiences going to the Derby while studying at Murray State University in northern Kentucky.

"The only reason I did that was so (the Breeders' Cup management) would be more predisposed to listen to what I was saying," he said.

"That was a plus we hadn't planned on and I think it worked well at the time," Cowan said.

Of all the Breeders' Cup executive directors in attendance the one who most concerned the OJC was John Nerud, who had played a key role in the original marketing of the event. Baker said he never found Nerud "effusive" or friendly toward the OJC cause.

The OJC spent considerable time trying to ease his reservations. Influential Canadian owners and breeders such as Taylor and Jean-Louis Levesque were dispatched to talk to Nerud, who had concerns about the currency exchange, passports, importing of horses and the limited size of Woodbine. Nerud thought the Breeders' Cup should have a west coast site and an east coast site and a place in between. He considered moving to Woodbine at that point premature, but after the presentation he refused to stand in the Canadians' way.

"The only reason I didn't raise hell is because when we started this, the Canadians put up their money and put their horses up and acted like gentlemen," Nerud said.

As late as the day of the presentation, the OJC officials still felt the need to satisfy Nerud, who was admittedly impressed by the presentation.

"They came down there loaded for bear," Nerud said.

Warwick said judging by the reaction of Breeders' Cup management, "We blew them away."

"Everything fell into place beautifully, nobody tried to outdo anybody else in terms of what they were saying," Cowan said. "Anybody who had a question directed to him or her answered the question specifically. You can always tell by facial expressions and we knew we were making progress, especially with Ted Bassett. He had what I would say was sort of a contented look on his face. All the other people, some of whom you know might be somewhat skeptical, seemed to be turning the corner and were nodding when we gave them answers such as our dining capacity and our training facilities and proximity to the airport and some quotes we received from some of the major horsemen in the world."

In particular, a climatological study, showing the temperature in Toronto relative to other eastern sites on the days of the Breeders' Cups up to that point, played a significant role. The OJC demonstrated the difference between temperatures at Toronto compared to New York and Kentucky on Breeders' Cup day was only a few degrees. The OJC also showed evidence of the temperature the day before the event compared to the day of it to demonstrate there were no significant aberrations. The Breeders' Cup management had done its own climatological study, but not to the extent of the OJC. Bassett called the OJC's work "outstanding."

Overall, Bassett described the presentation as "very concise, very professional, very persuasive. It was a terribly impressive presentation, the most impressive of any one I've seen in the eight or nine Breeders' Cup site meetings I've been involved in."

After the presentation Taylor stayed behind and talked to his fellow Breeders' Cup executives for a few minutes. He received a favorable impression. The Canadians had exceeded the executive's expectations with the enthusiasm and sincerity of their representatives.

"I'm not saying we thought we had it in the bag, but I think we were pretty confident after the December meeting," Taylor said.

There were some minor issues on which the Breeders' Cup management wanted further information, including dining-room seating, the press box and the stakes scheduled for that weekend, but overall the Canadians left feeling good about their chances.

In the intervening weeks Taylor spoke on and off to Bassett, with whom he regularly worked on other areas of the business, and other board members, accentuating all the positives, such as the government funding. There were still some lingering doubts according to Bassett among some members over whether the event could be financially successful because of the size of the track relative to other sites, the past history of the pari-mutuel handle and the weather. Moreover, Bassett said many of the board members had never run a horse at Woodbine and were unfamiliar with the place.

Bassett said if the Breeders' Cup wanted to take a "safe harbor" it could have chosen past sites, but the management felt the need to overlook the risks and move into uncharted territory.

"There was a strong feeling of obligation to the Canadian breeders and the Canadian owners, that plus the enthusiasm of the people showing they really wanted it and that they would roll up their sleeves and make the maximum effort to make it work," Bassett said.

On February 25, 1993, Taylor left word for Cowan, who was in Las Vegas with other OJC officials and horsemen for meetings, to call him at home. Taylor said it was not official, but that Woodbine would be selected as the site for 1996 and that the announcement would be made the following day.

"I was just so happy for Charles, it was so important to him," Cowan said. "I'm glad he got the news first to tell us."

The following day in Florida, where the executive board members convened for their annual meetings, the Breeders' Cup disclosed its plans for the next three years. Woodbine, Belmont Park in New York and Churchill Downs in Kentucky would be the sites for the next three years. Kentucky would go first, followed by New York, then Canada. It meant waiting a little longer, but the Canadians didn't mind. It gave them more time to prepare and, most importantly, they had achieved their goal.

"The underlying strength about Canada, more than the proposal, was that the Canadian breeders had supported the Breeders' Cup since day one by nominating their foals and nominating their stallions," Bassett said. "And equally important was the support the Canadian owners gave us. They ran their champions in the Breeders' Cup. So, the combination of the breeders nominating foals and stallions, the owners sending their horses to compete in the Breeders' Cup, the leadership of Charles Taylor and the cooperation and enthusiasm shown by the provincial and national governments were all contributory toward making the decision. There was a strong feeling Canada had earned its place in the rotation."

Cowan called it a "shot in our arm and for the industry in general."

Although it was not part of the original presentation, the OJC opted to make several changes to the Woodbine track. In 1994, a harness racing course replaced the seven-furlong inner turf course, a move some thoroughbred purists considered blasphemous but which the OJC deemed necessary once it closed Greenwood for live racing at the end of 1993 to restructure the struggling operation. The OJC also opted to rebuild the grass course, extending it completely around the dirt track to make it an uninterrupted mile and a half, with European-style undulations and the longest stretch in North America. Fans standing on the apron could almost reach out and touch the horses as they passed by the wire. The OJC appropriately named it the E. P. Taylor Turf Course. Charles Taylor joined in the ribbon-cutting ceremony when it opened for racing on Sept. 10, 1994. The winning breeder/owner of the first grass race was David Willmot, who became president of the OJC in 1996 and a central figure in Woodbine almost losing the Breeders' Cup.

In an interview in the *Thoroughbred Times* in January 1996, Willmot talked about the Breeders' Cup and how important it would be for Woodbine and for the OJC, which was suffering from financial problems brought on by the free fall of horse racing economics. Willmot said whatever happened in the past should have no bearing on the OJC's ability to host the event.

"For anyone to say they don't think it's a good idea for the OJC to host the Breeders' Cup, you've lost your senses," Willmot said. "It will be absolutely the greatest opportunity to show horse racing fans throughout the world the quality of our facilities and the quality of our racing."

No one could have ever predicted at that point the impending problems down the stretch for the OJC and the Breeders' Cup Ltd. The OJC and its 700 pari-mutuel clerks began the year without a contract, but the matter received scant attention at the time. The OJC made an offer giving the clerks $20 an hour, four dollars less than they were seeking. The clerks turned it down, to which the OJC responded with an offer of $16 an hour in its next proposal. The battle lines had been drawn. The clerks charged the OJC with negotiating in bad faith. On February 26, the OJC exercised its right to lock out the employees and hired replacement workers to operate the mutuels.

On March 23, opening day of the Woodbine thoroughbred season, the clerks set up pickets at each of the entrances to the OJC tracks and the teletheaters they managed. It caused delays of almost three hours at Woodbine and, in some cases, violent confrontations that sent a few people to hospital. No serious injuries were ever reported, however, nor were any people charged by police.

The first significant happening, beyond the events on the picket lines, came on April 8. The OJC announced it had changed the date of the Queen's Plate—the premier horse race in Canada—to July 13 from July 6 and recommended to Princess Margaret of England that she not attend the race as the representative of the Royal Family. The Royal Family has a standing rule of not attending an event in which there is any labor conflict and the OJC expected the lockout to continue by that date.

On April 12, the OJC received a court injunction limiting the picketers to only four per entrance, preventing them from coming closer than two feet of incoming traffic, and limiting their communication to people coming in to only one minute.

Hopes of a settlement in May were dashed when the union rejected the OJC's latest offer due in part to the firing of three mutuel clerks for alleged malicious behavior. There were also alleged threats to Willmot.

While the OJC maintained its resolve, the mutuel clerks stubbornly dug in their heels and received important support. The Ontario Federation of Labor, which represents all unions in the province, backed the clerks, accusing the OJC of bargaining in bad faith. OFL president Gord Wilson sent a letter dated May 23 to Bassett indicating that despite limitations imposed on the union by the court, it had the ability and determination "to put maximum pressure" upon the OJC to resolve the dispute and attain a "reasonable" collective agreement. Moreover, Wilson said if the dispute continued, "the occasion of the Breeders' Cup and other major events will provide an opportunity and focus for demonstrations."

The OFL had planned to protest the provincial Progressive Conservative party on the weekend of the Breeders' Cup, scheduled for Oct. 26, over its policies.

Supposedly the PCs had a convention in Toronto the weekend of the Cup, but even if they didn't, Breeders' Cup Ltd. could not afford to have its biggest day affected by labor disruptions. As many as 10,000 hotel rooms had been booked, and Bassett worried about the effects of labor strife on essential services such as accommodation and transportation.

A day after Wilson's memorandum, Andrew Stern, president of the Service Employees International Union, which includes the mutuel clerks, sent Bassett a similar letter. He said "we do not want to use the Breeders' Cup as a vehicle to demonstrate our labor dispute with the OJC, but we will use the full power of our union to get these members back to work and to win them a contract that ensures dignity and respect."

Collectively, it was enough to worry Bassett and Breeders' Cup Ltd. management, which at that point had been convinced the labor dispute would be resolved. The letters offered the first example of a threat of disruption of public services, hotels and restaurants in downtown Toronto.

"We were not going to subject our visitors who were coming in to that sort of action," Bassett said. "It never crossed our mind we'd do that. There was an unwelcome sign being hung out."

Bassett notified Willmot that in light of the threat by the OFL, the Breeders' Cup planned to pull out of Woodbine unless the matter was straightened out. Bassett said the Breeders' Cup Ltd. was "not going to let grass grow under our feet" while the dispute dragged on indefinitely. The matter crossed over into the public domain when the OJC issued a press release indicating the concern of Breeders' Cup Ltd. The release offered a comment by Bassett, who said: "Our primary and major responsibility is to ensure that the Breeders' Cup is put on under the most advantageous conditions. The event is conducted but once a year; therefore we would be acting irresponsibly if we exposed it to any unnecessary risk or disruption."

The OJC conducted a press conference indicating its concern the event might be moved. It cancelled a scheduled lottery for the 3,500 reserved tickets for Breeders' Cup day. Willmot stated emphatically that as important as the Breeders' Cup is, the OJC did not need to buy it by giving in to the clerks. He sounded hopeful that the Breeders' Cup management would give the OJC some time to follow through on what he believed was movement in the right direction.

Willmot suffered the first of several criticisms the next day in the media by some members who did not believe him or, more importantly, found it difficult to fathom he would allow the Breeders' Cup to be lost.

Wilson reaffirmed the OFL's hard-line position and called OJC officials "arrogant, snotty bluebloods. We'll take their bluebloods and blue noses and turn it red. By the time organizers of the Breeders' Cup see what's going on, they won't want to come anywhere near Toronto."

Nerud, who had been cautious about the Cup coming to Canada in the first place, told the *Toronto Sun*'s Rob Longley the OJC should scrap plans for the Cup, straighten out its affairs and then reapply in later years.

"The Breeders' Cup doesn't make a whole lot of money for the (host) track, but it does bring a great deal of prestige," he said. "Right now they don't need prestige, they need harmony. . . . I have nothing against Toronto or Canada, but the timing is all wrong. We have to get our money that day. It is our only chance. We can't afford to have anything disrupt it."

On June 3, Breeders' Cup executive director D. G. Van Clief said he expected the Woodbine matter to be decided in the next 72 hours after the union vote. The OJC accepted a deal proposed by provincial mediator Robert Pryor, who laid out terms of $18 an hour for the first year, $18.25 the second year and $18.50 the third year, plus a four-hour work day and maximum 35-hour week. The union wanted $20 an hour, five hours a day and 30 hours a week, thereby giving more work to more people. Brett Goodall, the chairman of the mutuel clerks, said his association discussed the mediated offer and considered it "ridiculous."

"I really don't think the OJC gives a hoot about the Breeders' Cup," Goodall insisted. "If it did, it would make us a serious offer. It seems to have total disregard for everybody but itself." The next day, Wilson indicated that if the dispute was settled, the OFL would not disrupt the event.

On June 6, a dark, overcast day, more than 320 members gathered at a teamsters hall about a 15-minute drive from Woodbine and voted overwhelmingly against the mediator's proposal. Goodall said the lockout had resulted in some members losing their homes or going to food banks. He added a representative of the workers contacted Willmot with the result and urged him to make another offer. He said the "magic date" had been extended by one day, but that the mutuel clerks planned to remain at the hall for another vote if it was forthcoming. The union believed that if the OJC really wanted to save the Cup, it would have a backup plan, possibly even ask for another 24-hour extension.

Willmot refused to comment until after an announcement by the Breeders' Cup Ltd. At about 5 p.m., the Breeders' Cup Ltd. issued a press release indicating the event had been cancelled at Woodbine and that a new site would be announced within the month. The union could not believe it.

"We guessed all along the company was prepared or even wanted to lose the Cup, but the media did such a powerful job of putting pressure on the Jockey Club to save the damn thing, we were shocked they fumbled the ball at the last minute," recalled Brian Henderson, the mutuel clerks' chief negotiator. "That was absolutely shocking to us."

The media criticized Willmot heavily. *Toronto Sun* columnist Ken Fidlin wrote that if the Cup is lost, Willmot must resign or be dismissed if he is too arrogant to do it himself. *Toronto Globe and Mail* columnist Neil Campbell wrote a few days later that "losing the Breeders' Cup will be a deep wound from which Ontario racing will never fully recover and the blood will be on the hands of David Willmot."

Within 36 hours of its announcement, the Breeders' Cup Ltd. received expressions of interest from nine American tracks seeking to become alternative sites. The Breeders' Cup had considered two locations: California or Kentucky, both of which had staged the event before. Santa Anita would have been the preferred California site because Hollywood Park was scheduled to be the host track in 1997. Most people assumed Churchill Downs would be the choice. Bassett admitted after the whole controversy had been settled that logistically going to Kentucky would have been the most efficient move because of the past experiences there and the hope the last contract could be rolled over with some minor revisions. The Breeders' Cup Ltd. even began booking rooms in Louisville.

Willmot figured that after the Cup had been lost and the union no longer had that leverage, it would bring a "new sense of reality" to the situation that was necessary to have "meaningful" negotiations. And, unbelievably for those viewing the situation from the outside, that's exactly what happened in the 72 hours after the Breeders' Cup pulled the Cup. On the morning of June 7, Carmen DiPaola, president of the Ontario division of the Horsemen's Benevolent and Protective Association, read the newspaper reports that the Breeders' Cup planned to consider other locations and immediately began making calls. He phoned his standardbred counterpart, Malcolm MacPhail, and received his assistance to negotiate a settlement, thereby consolidating all the horsemen for one common goal. DiPaola then phoned Wilson to ask him for a letter of support ensuring no problems from labor if a settlement could be reached. After that DiPaola phoned Henderson and told him there was still a chance to get the Breeders' Cup, but it was important for their members to negotiate a settlement because he didn't think the OJC would improve on its offer.

DiPaola had been in horse racing for some 25 years and head of the HBPA for a year after a dramatic split with the previous administration. DiPaola was a realtor who understood negotiating and he quickly set out a game plan. He asked for a copy of the union's demands excluding wages and, after looking at it, phoned Henderson back and told him his committee should concentrate on four items instead of a dozen or so. After the two parties worked out a memorandum of agreement, they huddled with the union's negotiating committee in the evening and refined the agreement. It meant a 25 percent cut in pay for the full-time employees, which Henderson considered a significant loss, but DiPaola promised to fight for job security.

DiPaola then called Willmot at his home at about 11:30 p.m., after the two had tried unsuccessfully to reach one another during the day. DiPaola told him he had the memorandum of agreement and wanted to reach a settlement and needed to meet Willmot immediately. Willmot knew at that point DiPaola had been talking to the union negotiating committee and welcomed the help. DiPaola had offered his assistance from the outset of the dispute, but the OJC had rebuffed him because the gulf between itself and the union had been so wide OJC management figured it did not make any sense to involve him in the negotiating process. When DiPaola called, Willmot was "pleasantly surprised" figuring the two sides had something with which to work.

Willmot called some of his negotiating team and they met DiPaola at midnight at Woodbine. It took until 3 a.m. before an agreement could be reached, in which the OJC made an irrevocable offer for midnight Saturday and a vote on Sunday.

DiPaola contacted Henderson at about 7 a.m., apprised him of the OJC deal and asked to meet with the union's negotiating committee. In between, Henderson received a call from the provincial Minister of Labor, who had been authorized by Premier Mike Harris to convene at the provincial legislature that day to work out an agreement between the clerks and the OJC. Harris had been strangely silent during the controversy, considering the importance of the event and the money it meant to the local economy and the exposure to the province and the country.

Moreover, Harris' government had just given track operators in Ontario a major concession by slicing 5 percent off the tax on pari-mutuel betting, a move that could amount to $50 million in savings based on figures from the previous year. The OJC, the largest pari-mutuel operator in the province with 80 percent of the money wagered on its products, would be the greatest beneficiary.

Harris, who had been in New York on business matters the previous day, called Bassett, who was in New York for the Belmont Stakes the following day. Bassett said the Breeders' Cup had been 95 percent sure of a move to an alternative site and he had contacted NBC earlier in the day to discuss the likely switch. Bassett and Harris had a constructive conversation, in which the Ontario premier asked about the necessary steps required for the Breeders' Cup Ltd. to return to Toronto. Bassett outlined four requirements: a letter from Wilson indicating assurances of no labor action or work stoppage in the city of Toronto on October 25–27; a letter from Harris indicating his support and his assurance the Breeders' Cup would proceed without any impediments or disruptions; a letter from Fred Sykes, the president of the mutuel clerks local; and a letter from the OJC indicating its continued commitment and enthusiasm to play host to the event.

The following morning Ontario deputy prime minister Ernie Eves called Bassett to reassure the Breeders' Cup about the interest of the provincial government and the premier's office in ensuring the event would go on unimpeded. Bassett said the assurances given by Harris and Eves gave the Breeders' Cup Ltd. the impression the authority and the power of the government had been exercised. He had no idea about DiPaola's involvement at that point because in the U.S. the horsemen's groups are usually not involved in disputes between management and mutuel clerks.

DiPaola, meanwhile, urged Henderson to postpone the meeting with the provincial minister and the OJC, feeling he would be "hammered" by the two sides. DiPaola would continue to be the intermediary and, as it turned out, the savior. At about 11:30 a.m., DiPaola and the union's negotiating committee met and an hour later the members initialed an agreement. At about 1 p.m., DiPaola met with Willmot's group, but the OJC wanted to make a change.

"I said, 'Fine, you want to make a change, you go and negotiate with the union because I will not go back. I believe you've got everything there and I want you to sign it because we've got to save the Breeders' Cup,'" DiPaola said later.

At 2 p.m., the OJC agreed. The multifaceted three-year agreement had the wages outlined by the mediator and the 30-hour maximum workweek. The two sides agreed on a shift of 4½ hours a day and first crack at jobs created by the introduction of video lottery terminals, which Harris' government planned to introduce throughout the province later that year, mainly at racetracks.

The union gathered Sunday, June 9, and heard from its bargaining committee, which recommended taking the package. Although there had been speculation that if the workers rejected the offer they would never be rehired, Henderson claimed labor laws prevented that. Quite simply, the workers felt they had no other choice but to take the deal.

"If the Cup is saved it will be our Cup, not the OJC's," Henderson told his constituents. "This may be our last opportunity to go back to work with dignity, with our pockets empty but our heads high, with our union intact and the respect of the entire racing world."

After the union voted overwhelmingly to accept the package and the results were announced, the clerks broke into a chant of "We saved the Cup."

The following day after he returned home, Bassett had a message from Willmot on his answering machine that the union had voted to accept the offer. DiPaola called Bassett that night to advise him of the vote and stressed the local thoroughbred association's strong commitment and interest in support of the Breeders' Cup and urged the management to reconsider.

The next day, June 10, at his office, Bassett received a fax from Harris, Wilson and the OJC. All that was required was the letter from Sykes. Bassett told Willmot a decision would not be made until the Breeders' Cup Ltd. received all four letters. About noon the letter from Sykes arrived, after which the Breeders' Cup management committee faxed the executive committee with the recommendation to return to Woodbine. If any members of the executive committee had any questions or objections, Bassett urged them to call in the next two hours. When that expired, Bassett called Willmot and told him the Cup had come back to Woodbine.

Ironically, the controversy shed attention in Canada on an event that few people outside of horse racing knew anything about. It was a classic example of bad publicity turning into good promotion. Almost six months before it would reach the starting gate, the first-ever Breeders' Cup outside the U.S. had already become the talk of the town, and even the country.

Three days after the agreement, the *Toronto Star* ran a front-page story headlined: "How Harris Helped Save The Cup." To be sure, Harris played a significant role, but clearly DiPaola had been the unexpected hero, even though he shifted the praise to the clerks. DiPaola received several congratulatory messages and letters for his work, including one from Charles Taylor, who had been an interested observer throughout.

"I praise Charles Taylor for bringing the Breeders' Cup to Toronto in the first place," DiPaola said. "If it wasn't for his efforts and that of his family and father and what he did for our industry and for horse racing around the world, Canada would never have been given, in my opinion, the opportunity to host the Breeders' Cup."

Now that the Breeders' Cup had come back to Canada—did it ever really leave?—some important logistical issues had to be addressed. NBC came up to do a site inspection and had two important concerns: the harness track adjacent to the main track and the flow of airplanes flying above the track. One was hard on the eyes, the other on the ears—at least from a television perspective—so OJC officials had to work on some solutions. Both matters fell into the bailiwick of Dave Gorman, the OJC's senior vice-president of corporate affairs. The lanky and bespectacled Gorman, who cast a tall and calming figure, addressed both of the television issues with relative ease.

"To deal with the racetrack issue we looked at a number of options; one of them was to try to use plants and trees, similar to what is employed at the Canadian Royal Winter (agricultural) Fair," Gorman recalled. "But putting them on the standardbred track just made them look small and insignificant, so that idea was scrapped. Then someone suggested painting the track green, but that posed an even bigger problem of how to do that. We came up with a dye that was sprayed on. It wasn't going to last forever and a heavy rain would wipe it away in a hurry. The airplane problem, God, I remember it so well. I raised it at a board of directors meeting and said one of the things we were going to get the airport to do was use alternate runways instead of flying (over the facility), which of course is totally dependent on the wind. One of our board members, who shall remain nameless, said 'You haven't got a snowball's chance in hell of getting them to do that.' I made one phone call to the top dog at the airport because I didn't want to fool around with the ramp guys and he said, 'Sure, we can do that.' And that was the end of it—after I'd been told (by the anonymous board member) that there was no chance."

That matter resolved, another problem still loomed in the distance, one which the OJC could not influence: the protest against Ontario premier Mike Harris, scheduled the day before and the day of the Cup. Ten days before the Cup, the issue of the labor protest loomed like a dark cloud, threatening to rain on the greatest day of horse racing in Canada and in its biggest market. Tourism officials had serious concerns.

"We've all spent, collectively, millions of dollars to promote tourism and, in one afternoon, there's the potential to destroy that," said Rod Seiling, the president of the Hotel Association of Metro Toronto and, coincidentally, a former OJC executive.

Kirk Shearer, the president and chief executive officer of Tourism Toronto, added: "We're in the most competitive business in the world—tourism. Imagine bringing the whole world to this city on those days. It'll be a distorted picture, but the bad news gets more play than the good."

Following the pre-entries 10 days before, the Breeders' Cup had the makings of a great field for the Classic, headed by Cigar, running in perhaps his final career race. He had lost his last race and two of his last three, but hopes were still high among his handlers and fans. Three-year-old sensation Skip Away, who had beaten Cigar in their last race, did not make it into the pre-entries because his trainer, Sonny Hine, who ran the horse in his wife Carolyn's name, had taken ill with gallstones. Still, the field looked strong overall.

Media came from various parts of the world to chronicle the first Cup outside of the U.S. One trainer, Reade Baker, went out of his way to welcome the outside media with coffee and donuts as a symbol of Canadian goodwill. But another trainer, Jim Day, who had won the first Breeders' Cup for Canada in 1991 with

Dance Smartly in the Distaff, distinguished himself for an infamous act. Two Kentucky-based writers, Jennie Rees of the *Louisville Courier-Journal* and Deirdre Biles of the *Blood-Horse*, who had parked their cars at Day's barn, returned to their vehicles to find the hoods and windshields smeared with dirty, damp wood shavings that reportedly included horse manure. When the manure hit the fan, so to speak, the OJC addressed the matter, even though Day defended his actions by saying the contents he dumped on the cars were horse shavings and not droppings. Moreover, he claimed he had the right to do it because the parking spots were reserved for his clients. That didn't sit well with the OJC. The management wanted to do everything it could to put on a good show for its visitors to send a positive message about Canadian racing and hospitality. The OJC exacted punishment on Day by restricting his stall allocation in the future.

Ricks Natural Star, a cheap claimer who hadn't run in more than a year and had been pre-entered for $20,000 in the Turf even though he had never run on the grass, arrived after a long journey from New Mexico. The media came to the barn of the horse's owner/trainer Dr. William Livingston to talk to him about his reasons for taking a shot in the Turf. By this time, the horse had already qualified because the overfilled race had lost two horses that had been pre-entered. Livingston anted up $20,000 the next day to enter the horse.

Later that day, Cigar arrived at Woodbine from the airport, escorted by a Royal Canadian Mounted Police cruiser. A crowd of reporters and photographers crowded around the barn to see the star, the greatest thoroughbred to grace the Woodbine backstretch since Secretariat took up residence for his final career race 23 years before.

The next night, a day and a half before the Breeders' Cup, the annual press party took place at the SkyDome, a landmark in downtown Toronto and about 40 minutes away from Woodbine. A few years earlier, the Toronto Blue Jays had won back-to-back World Series and the SkyDome, with its retractable roof, became famous around the sporting world. And with the world press gathered for the biggest annual horse-racing event, the Ontario Jockey Club wanted to put on a spectacular show. The OJC picked specific high-profile sites for parties or dinners—such as the annual Turf Writers Association Awards Dinner, the Press Party, the Charity Gala and Post-Race Reception Party—to give visitors a glimpse of the culture and surroundings of Metro Toronto.

The day before the races, the weather turned pleasant, as cold and rain gave way to sunshine and warmth. On the Woodbine backstretch, a jockey named Jack Lauzon basked in the glow of the day and the moment. He had returned to Ontario, where he had established himself as a top rider, from Macao following a debilitating injury two months before. He broke his neck in a racing spill and required two operations that confined him to a bed wearing a halo brace. He still had marks in his forehead from the attachment. Lauzon still had numbness from the waist down, but was otherwise in great spirits. Seven years before, he rode Regal Intention in the Breeders' Cup Sprint. The horse finished 11th in the field of 14, eliminated at the break.

"I had a lot of good feelings back then . . . until I left the starting gate and I got wiped out and that was the end of my race," Lauzon recalled. "I wish I was in better shape to ride (in the Breeders' Cup) again. What is really good here is that it seems like there's more coverage than back in '89. You have this nice horse Cigar and I did my best to get out there and watch him train today because he's probably the legend of my lifetime. It's good to be back and be around this Breeders' Cup scene. History is in the making having the Breeders' Cup come to Canada. It's a really, really good feeling being Canadian and being a Canadian jockey and being around the Canadian scene and seeing the Cup come here. I hope it boosts racing even more than what's taking place now."

The irony of the weather change is that Breeders' Cup officials had already shipped some rain suits contained in a storage facility at the U.S. border. Because of trade laws, merchandise produced outside of the U.S. could not be shipped back once it crossed the border without being subject to duty tariffs. The rain suits weren't the only merchandise affected by the duty regulations, nor was that the only problem officials had to deal with because of the change from one country to another. Complications with jockey visas and licenses to ride also became logistical issues. Eventually, it all worked out.

As people started pouring into the track for the races on Friday, Woodbine boss David Willmot started walking through the grandstand. By the third or fourth race, the grandstand had an excitement level that made Willmot emotional, tears welling up, as he soaked up the experience. The following morning on the day of the big event, Willmot had full confidence in Woodbine's operational staff, having seen the employees conduct their business without any panic, taking every little detail into consideration. Willmot had been to numerous Breeders' Cups and had a pretty good feel about the day ahead, but he prayed there would be no incidents of horse breakdowns. He had been thinking of the 1990 Cup in which Go For Wand suffered a fatal injury.

The racing gods smiled brightly on the Breeders' Cup and Toronto. Spring-like weather, with a temperature in the mid-50s and brilliant sunshine, provided unseasonably warm conditions. Willmot recalled days of horse racing glory back in the '60s and '70s.

"It was a rush," he recalled. "It was a terrific feeling."

Storm Song, the 8-5 favorite in the opening race, the Juvenile Fillies, won easily. It gave trainer Nick Zito, one of the forces on the Triple Crown trail, his first Cup winner in 10 starters.

"What can I say? It's a great feeling," he said.

Lit de Justice, the 4-1 favorite in the next race, the Sprint, prevailed by 1¼ lengths, making history when trainer Jenine Sahadi became the first woman to saddle a winner.

"It's nice to be the first, but it has nothing to do with gender," she said. "It just shows you that if you work hard and take care of your horses, you can do well."

Jockey Corey Nakatani, still grieving following the loss of his sister Dawn, who was murdered earlier in the month, recorded the win with a stunning rail-skimming ride.

"I know Dawn got me there," an emotional Nakatani said.

A secondary story line had emerged in the race, albeit one which didn't receive much coverage. The horses had been loaded in the gate by saddlecloth number instead of by post position.

"The lowest, lowest low point of the event was the stewards calling me about half an hour after the Sprint and telling me the horses had broken from the wrong stalls," recalled John Whitson, Woodbine's general manager of thoroughbred racing at the time. "There were several entries, so somehow the gate crew loaded them all (without checking). It's something the gate crew check every day of the year and it had likely never happened before. Nobody noticed it until it was too late. None of the jockeys said anything. It was incredible that nobody would have noticed it. After the race was over and official, somebody had realized what had happened. That was the low point of the day for me. The reaction among people was pretty good. People just shrugged their shoulders. Nobody lodged an appeal. The starter reported to me. Nobody could have felt worse than he did and I did and all the guys on the gate. We were very fortunate that there was as little fallout as there was. It was a very embarrassing mistake. Post positions are probably more important in the Sprint than any other race and everybody kind of accepted the outcome as official. There were no appeals or anything, it was just a very embarrassing chapter in my career, that's for sure."

Jewel Princess, the 24-10 second choice in the third race, the Distaff, won by 1½ lengths. It gave Nakatani back-to-back wins.

"I've got an angel on my side and her name was Dawn," he said. "This is for her. This is for everyone, my family, my mother and my dad. This is for them."

Da Hoss, ridden by Gary Stevens, won the fourth race, the Mile. The official prices weren't available because of a problem with the tote board. It was caused by a bettor who plunked down $20,000 U.S. on Urgent Request, a California invader, who went postward at 12.50-1. The bettor's name was never revealed, but it turned out to be Stewart Aitken, the owner of the horse. His son called Whitson in advance of the bet to cash a check. Whitson okayed it and escorted Aitken's son to the pari-mutuel department, whereupon a voucher was issued. But the tote equipment hadn't been set up to handle more than $5,000 in U.S. currency.

"It didn't totally crash the system, but the tote board and some betting lines, both ontrack and offtrack, were temporarily lost," recalled Woodbine official Dave Gorman. "I remember running in the tote room the minute the board went dark and the fellas told me they thought they could solve it sometime in the next hour. I remember saying, 'We don't have an hour. The next race goes in 30 minutes or so. We're on national television. They have no leeway here. We've got to get it fixed.' Then I left the room. I'd learned long ago that when something goes wrong in the tote room, the only thing you can do is go in, find out what the problem is, tell 'em what your problem is and get the hell out of the way and let them solve it."

It took some 40 minutes before the prices were officially listed.

The fifth race saw Boston Harbor, the second choice at just under 5-2, lead all the way under jockey Jerry Bailey. It gave trainer D. Wayne Lukas his first win at Woodbine, which he'd managed to avoid in his many forays across the continent.

In the sixth race, much of the attention focused on Ricks Natural Star, who broke sharply for the first quarter of a mile and had the lead for about an eighth of a mile after that before beginning his retreat. He finished well behind the rest of the horses, well after they had crossed the line.

Pilsudski, a long shot at more than 13-1, prevailed over stablemate Singspiel, giving trainer Michael Stoute a one-two finish. For jockey Walter Swinburn, it capped off an emotional year. He had suffered several injuries, including multiple skull fractures, earlier in the year in a racing mishap in Hong Kong.

"It's been a pretty rough year, not just for me personally but my family," Swinburn said. "Since I started back riding on August 11, the whole idea was just to get back riding and do what I like doing best. What's happened since August 11 and especially today is wild. I'm just waiting for someone to wake me up and tell me it's not true."

That led to the seventh and final Breeders' Cup race, the Classic, featuring Cigar. All eyes had been focused on the superstar, who would likely be running in his final race, even though rumors had been rampant about one more start, possibly in California, maybe even a match race with Prix de l'Arc de Triomphe winner Hellisio. Cigar went postward at .65-1, slightly more than 3-5, despite losing two of his last three races. Jockey Jerry Bailey tracked the pace and made a five-wide move heading into the stretch, about two lengths back of Canadian star Mt. Sassafras, who had a half-length lead over five-year-old California invader Alphabet Soup, with New York invader Louis Quatorze a head back in forth. The stage had been set for a thrilling stretch duel and for Cigar to unleash his customary finish, but as gamely as he tried he found his opponents unyielding. In a blanket finish that resembled the inaugural Classic, albeit without all the bumping, the three horses finished virtually even, but Alphabet Soup, almost a 20-1 shot, claimed the win by a nose over Louis Quatorze, an 18-1 shot, who finished a head in front of Cigar.

Alphabet Soup, a five-year-old ridden by Chris McCarron, had won his previous race but had been disqualified and placed third. In winning the Classic he set a Woodbine track record for the 1¼-mile race by stopping the clock in 2:01, a fifth of a second faster than the 24-year-old mark.

"I thought the track record here would be broken but I thought Cigar would do it," winning trainer David Hofmans said. "This is a thrill because he beat the champion on the level. He's the best horse in the world and we beat him. He's heavier than we are, bigger than we are and sometimes faster, but not today."

The final figures showed 41,250 crammed into the track, 2,000 more than the previous record set in 1973 when Queen Elizabeth II attended the Queen's Plate. The ontrack handle totaled almost $12 million, twice as much as the previous Woodbine record set on the day of the 1994 Rothmans International.

Canadian broadcaster Terry Leibel, an Olympic equestrian rider at one point in her life, offered a summation of seeing Cigar make his way from the backstretch for the Classic and of the day itself.

"One of the things about racing that truly is remarkable is the fact that everybody that works here at Woodbine works to try and have a horse of greatness," she said as the Canadian Broadcasting Corporation wrapped up its simulcast coverage.

"Sure they have their claimers and their so-called cheap horses, but they all regard and respect a great one, so when Cigar made his way along this road to the track, that is a sight I will never forget, pure elegance, pure champion. Toronto, Woodbine, Canada should be very proud of hosting a great Breeders' Cup."

CBC host Brian Williams, who has covered many of the biggest sporting events in the world, and analyst Jim Bannon offered their own musings on the day from their broadcast location overlooking the picturesque walking ring, framed by willows.

"It's the 13th year we've covered the Breeders' Cup together and little did we think at the beginning the event would come to Canada," Williams said. "I can remember Jim campaigning in Gulfstream, talking to Breeders' Cup president Ted Bassett (that the event should come to Woodbine). The weather's been great, the crowd's been great, the labor protest did not affect the Breeders' Cup."

"Well, Brian, we watched from the back here on a monitor and I must say anyone that watched it from the huge television audience, maybe 30 million people, has to go away with great thoughts of Woodbine," Bannon said. "The pictures were outstanding, the trees around Woodbine, the landscape around Woodbine. There's been a lot of people who have contributed to make Woodbine and Canadian racing great. . . . I think our hats are off to them today."

Among the viewing audience had been the person most important in the history of the Breeders' Cup from a Canadian perspective. Charles Taylor, undergoing chemotherapy treatment to battle cancer, stayed at home watching the event he had lobbied so hard from the outset to bring to Canada. His father had built Woodbine and clearly this was a crowning achievement for Charles.

"I'm not feeling great," Taylor told *Toronto Sun* corporate sports editor George Gross, who wrote a touching column that appeared the following day. "I don't like to go into details about my problem, but it had something to do with reaction to chemotherapy. I just wasn't well enough to make the trip to Woodbine and spend the day there. I'm, of course, very disappointed. But from what I can gather, according to reports from Woodbine, it is a great day at the racetrack. The weather has held up and the people seem to be enjoying the races very much. . . . What we'll have to do is take a look at all angles of today's operation and learn from our mistakes. Then, we'll sit down and start making plans to bring the Breeders' Cup back to Toronto. They usually award the event to a city four-to-five years in advance, so there's a possibility that Woodbine may host the big event again after the turn of the millennium."

On Sunday morning, Woodbine's chief executive, David Willmot, walked the backstretch, smiling proudly. All things considered, it had been a great day of racing, the weather playing a big role. Willmot knew he and everyone associated with the Breeders' had been lucky. The week before and the week after the Breeders' the weather had been lousy.

When trainer D. Wayne Lukas attended the breakfast to salute the winning connections, he made an interesting remark. Stunning, in fact, to the Canadian horsemen and media.

"I'll be honest with you, I said in the past the Breeders' Cup was an American institution and that it shouldn't leave the country," he said. "If you asked me last week what the chances of having the Breeders' Cup come back here were, I would have told you it was zilch. Now I would say it should get serious consideration. Of the 13 Breeders' Cups, I would say none were run better than this. I would come back in a heartbeat. I would never hesitate to bring a horse up here."

Almost nine months after the Breeders' Cup at Woodbine, Charles Taylor lost his battle with cancer at the age of 62. Were it not for Taylor's persistence and insistence, the Breeders' Cup would have never come to Canada.

There is no guarantee it will ever come back, although there have been some discussions along those lines. Breeders' Cup president D. G. Van Clief toured Woodbine in 2001 as part of National Thoroughbred Racing Association business, seeing many of the changes that had occurred since the event in 1996. Massive changes to the plant, including the implementation of slot machines, had changed the look of the historic track. While Van Clief mentioned to Willmot that Woodbine should try to bring the Cup back, Willmot noted the absence of general admission and the likelihood slot-machine players, who don't necessarily come to the track to play the horses, wouldn't want to pay a fee to play.

Beyond just that, Woodbine still has major capitol expenditures planned and Willmot, for one, is not keen to bring the Cup back again until the track is fully finished. There are also some financial issues, such as a onetime government loan of $1 million and the possibility that might not be available again. And local racing fans grumble about ticket access and price hikes.

"There's all those issues floating around," Willmot said. "Personally I think I am moving back into a space where if we could work out any kind of a reasonable deal with the Breeders' Cup that we might want to have it again. I'm a bit concerned that we could never duplicate the weather. The memories of that day are so terrific in the international racing community's minds, how could we ever repeat that? Sure as shoot if we had it again, it would snow six inches on the day. Having said that, that was a pretty miserable day at Arlington (in 2002). And there's been some pretty miserable days at Belmont and Churchill.

"How serious is weather if you're having it at a northern racetrack? Weather is always an issue and sometimes you get lucky and sometimes you don't. Never say never, that's probably the best way to put it. I jokingly said to someone that maybe I'll do it as bookends, that the first year I was CEO we had the Breeders' Cup and maybe I'll work towards my last year—I'm not going to be here forever—and have it then, too. Try and do it like a bookend. That's probably the way the timing is working out as you look forward. You're probably looking at least some time near the end of the decade before we would have it again. But I really want to emphasize that apart from general discussions, I really haven't gone to D.G. and said, 'Okay, look, it's time to sit down and talk about a specific year we should point for to try and do it again.'"

# 6

# The Maple Leaf Forever

## Canadian Horses

*W*hen the Breeders' Cup first began, Canadian horsemen showed no fear of crossing the border to take on the best horses in the world. And why not? In 1964, E. P. Taylor, one of the forefathers of Canadian racing, came to Kentucky and beat the American breeders at their own game with a pint-sized colt called Northern Dancer. Nineteen years later, another Canadian colt, Sunny's Halo, repeated the feat. So there was absolutely no reason for Canadian horsemen not to try the Breeders' Cup, which offered more opportunities for Canadian-bred and Canadian-owned horses than just one race on the first Saturday in May.

The first year, Canada sent a complement that included Bessarabian, a talented two-year-old bred and owned by Eaton Hall Farm and trained by the lanky Irishman Mike Doyle. Sent postward as the 8-5 favorite in the Juvenile Fillies and ridden by Canadian jockey Gary Stahlbaum, Bessarabian disappointed her backers, finishing sixth by seven lengths. It would be an indication that as good as the Canadian horses were, they were now facing the best of the best from around the world.

And they would not have it easy.

Each year from that point forward, Canadian horses came and went, returning home with little to show. In 1985, Imperial Choice, bred and owned by Ernie Samuel's Sam-Son Farm and trained by Jim Day, had the lead in the Classic with a quarter of a mile to the wire, but faded badly in the stretch, presumably wilting in the pressure. In reality, the horse broke a leg, explaining his sudden retreat when the real running began, but otherwise it just amounted to another loss for Canada.

Samuel and Day came back the following year with another star runner, Ruling Angel, who finished fifth in the Juvenile Fillies.

In 1987, Canada sent arguably its best contingent since the Cup began, but at least one critic had his doubts. Andy Beyer, the opinionated columnist from the *Washington Post*, criticized the Canadian contingent, having seen numerous horses come to the Cup with glorious reputations and return home with their heads handed to them. And yet, Beyer still had an interest in this edition. Regal Classic loomed as an interesting possibility in the Juvenile, but it was Afleet, in particular, whom Beyer—and many other people who based their opinions and their bets primarily on figures that matched speed to distance—planned to back. Regal Classic, the second choice in his race, ran a solid second, beaten only 1¾ lengths by the front-running Success Express. Afleet, sent postward at more than 9-1 odds, failed to flash his speed and finished a distant 10th in the field of 12. To many people, including Beyer, the ride of jockey Gary Stahlbaum was to blame, but the horse had probably ruined any chance of doing well when he stopped eating in the days leading up to the race.

Canadian horsemen were starting to wonder what it would take to win. They were tinkering with different ways of shipping, either a month in advance or in the days leading up to the race, to account for the travel from cool to warm climates. And, there was the idea of sticking with the jockeys from Canada or going with international riders with big reputations. The delicate balance of loyalty versus business was becoming a significant issue.

In 1988, Afleet, who had been cut back from distance races to sprints and had posted some exceptional results in the U.S., lined up in the Sprint. Once again, the "wise-guy" bettors jumped all over the horse, although they were critical of the decision by the owner and trainer to stick with Stahlbaum, who had been battling some personal demons. Afleet struggled in the sloppy going and ran third, beaten 1¾ lengths, and once again Stahlbaum felt the sting of the bettors, who blasted his ride. Yet Canadians basked in the second-place finish of Play The King, who ran second, beaten only three-quarters of a length at odds of more than 49-1, the longest shot in the field of 13.

After an inconsequential result in 1989, the Canadian contingent in 1990 flirted with success again. Dance Smartly ran third in the Juvenile Fillies, while With Approval, who had swept the Canadian Triple Crown the year before and emerged as a major grass star in the U.S., placed second in the Turf. The connections of both horses were critical of the rides. Trainer Jim Day found fault with jockey Sandy Hawley, whom he felt foolishly engaged in a front-end speed duel with stablemate Wilderness Song. Owner David Willmot blamed jockey Craig Perret for making a premature move, in his opinion, in the Turf aboard With Approval.

All of the excuses, legitimate or otherwise, led to a watershed year in 1991. Dance Smartly, the queen of Canadian racing, was shipped to Kentucky to run in the Breeders' Cup Distaff, after sweeping the Canadian Triple Crown and beating male horses in the Molson Million, almost seven weeks before. Only a victory by the big bay daughter of Danzig would stop the snide remarks from critics of the Canadian-based horses.

The filly was infinitely stronger and more talented heading into the '91 Cup than she had been the year before. Woodbine-based jockey Brian Swatuk had ridden Dance Smartly in the first two races, both wins, of her three-year-old season, but Day became concerned about the rider's dependability after he missed some morning work and opted to change riders. He enlisted American-based Pat Day, no relation to the trainer but held in high regard by him. Pat Day had been the regular rider of Dance Smartly's stablemate Sky Classic.

The Day-and-Day connection first developed when Jim hired Pat to replace Canadian-based Dave Penna on Samuel's Regal Classic following the colt's second-place finish in the '87 Juvenile. Samuel and Day secured Pat Day's services several times in the following seasons. Jim Day jokingly referred to him as "Brother Pat." Pat Day had what Jim Day liked: patience and the ability to save something for the end.

Day demonstrated those qualities in the Grade One Spinster Stakes, a major prep for the Breeders' Cup Distaff, under Pat Day. He allowed the filly to be overtaken in the stretch, then called on her, and she responded by regaining the lead to win.

While Dance Smartly developed soundness problems in her left front foot and Jim Day became worried about her fitness, she worked well in her last major tuneup for the Cup. A week after the Spinster, the Sam-Son juggernaut continued when Sky Classic recorded his sixth consecutive victory, winning the Grade One Rothmans International at Woodbine. Sky Classic became the first Canadian horse to win the race—the most prestigious grass event in the country—since 1967, doing so in course-record time.

In Las Vegas, where the racebooks take advance bets on the Breeders' Cup, Dance Smartly commanded serious attention. At Bally's and Caesars, Dance Smartly was 4-5 to win the Distaff two weeks before the race. Only Housebuster, everyone's favorite to win the Sprint, had a lower price.

In addition to Dance Smartly and Wilderness Song for the Distaff and Sky Classic for the Turf, Canada sent one other representative to the 1991 Cup: Key Spirit for the Sprint. A claimer turned stakes winner for flashy owner Mike Singh, Key Spirit looked out of place among the more celebrated runners from the U.S. Steve Barnes, the 34-year-old conditioner of Key Spirit, acted like Alice in Wonderland.

Day, by contrast, took the event in stride. He had run at least one horse in six of the previous seven editions of the Breeders' Cup, although none as highly regarded. The media flocked to Day's barn frequently in the days leading up to the Cup, eagerly asking him about his horses and his background. Day accommodated everyone with courtesy, humor and honesty. He answered the same questions as often as a politician repeating a campaign promise.

Two of the most widely known handicappers had different opinions. Steven Crist, the opinionated editor of the *Racing Times* and a New Yorker, said more than one Canadian horse with a big reputation had come to the U.S. and failed. He pegged Dance Smartly as one of the most vulnerable favorites on the card and picked Queena. Andy Beyer, the racing writer for the *Washington Post* and creator of the Beyer Speed Figures that equated a horse's finishing time in a race to a number, liked Dance Smartly. He told Ted Labanowich, a freelance writer for the *Hamilton Spectator*, he thought Dance Smartly "had the goods" and he planned to single her in his Pick 7 tickets.

Canadian-based jockey Francine Villeneuve, who had ridden Wilderness Song well in Canada, received the call for the Breeders' Cup, while another Canadian rider, Mickey Walls, stayed on Key Spirit. Neither had ridden in the Cup before.

The emotion on race day was the highest ever among Canadian supporters, some of whom lined the paddock area and held up a six-foot-wide sign which read: "Breeders' Cup 1991, Go Canada." The left part of the sign had the words Sam-Son Farm and a drawing of its red and gold silks and cap. The right side had a drawing of Singh's Big Bux Stable and its green, yellow and red silks that featured a dollar sign. Singh looked at the sign with pride and said: "That is really good."

As Barnes prepared to saddle his horse, he uttered a statement that forever will remain a Breeders' Cup classic quote for the few that heard it. He turned to Lukas and said brazenly: "Who the hell is D. Wayne Lukas?"

Lukas looked at him with disgust. Key Spirit ran last in the Sprint and it was the last of Barnes in the Breeders' Cup.

The Distaff came two races later and Dance Smartly and entrymate Wilderness Song went off at odds of 1-2. Dan Kenny, an owner and blood-stock agent who worked as a racing analyst for the Canadian Broadcasting Corporation, offered the Canadian perspective on NBC's telecast. "The Canadian horses brought the Canadian air with them here, so they should be very comfortable. I've seen some great champions (from Canada), but they've not yet won a Breeders' Cup event. Like the Toronto Blue Jays in baseball, they've come tantalizingly close, but our neighbors to the north want to see if their horses Dance Smartly and Sky Classic can get the job done today. The Kentucky hardboots still need convincing, however, that these two are for real."

In a taped interview with the CBC, which cut in between NBC breaks, Samuel told Ontario Jockey Club handicapper Jim Bannon about the honor of competing in the Breeders' Cup and representing Canada. "There's always that little extra notch any time you're carrying the flag—and we do that when we come away," Samuel said. "Having a Canadian-bred win these important races raises our profile and is extra exciting as well."

NBC analyst John Veitch, trainer of the great Alydar and 1985 Breeders' Cup Classic winner Proud Truth, remarked that Dance Smartly probably was the best Canadian filly North American racing fans had ever seen. "She has the opportunity today to become the best in the world," he said.

Prior to the race, Bannon added: "This is the race that many Canadian fans have been waiting for. Will Dance Smartly, the first lady of Canadian racing, be able to drink from the coveted Cup? We've been waiting a long time for a Canadian-bred to win and I think this is our best chance. She'll win if she runs with the same power and precision that she has competed with in her seven wins."

The scene shifted back to the paddock, where NBC's Jenny Ornsteen interviewed Shug McGaughey, trainer of Queena and Versailles Treaty.

"How do you beat Dance Smartly?" she asked.

"I don't know whether we can beat Dance Smartly or not," McGaughey responded honestly. "I don't have anything to judge her by off her previous form, except an exceptional record. We'll just have to see if her Canadian form travels to here."

At 1:21 p.m, on Nov. 2, 1991, at Churchill Downs, they were off in the Distaff. Day rode patiently on Dance Smartly, nursing her well off the rail, while never more than five and a half lengths off the lead. At one point, he inched up on the outside of Villeneuve and told her to sit tight. If Villeneuve could win the race with her mount that was fine, but the primary objective was to be a team player and not cause any mistakes that would compromise Dance Smartly's chances. Villeneuve knew her role and avoided doing anything to adversely affect Day's job.

Three-quarters of a mile into the race, Day had Dance Smartly in third, only two and a half lengths behind the leader, Brought to Mind. With a subtle turn of his hands, Day sent the message to his willing mount to power forward and she accelerated into another gear. She took the lead in midstretch and, for the first time since he had ridden her, Pat Day took out the whip and gave her a left-handed crack. Day then kept both hands on the reins for about six more jumps before he gave Dance Smartly three quick left-handed whips. An attempt by jockey Angel Cordero Jr. to catch up to Dance Smartly with Versailles Treaty proved fruitless.

"It's too late and not enough and it is Dance Smartly who strides under the line, undefeated this year and the undisputed queen of racing on this continent," announcer Tom Durkin said.

Dance Smartly prevailed by a length and a half in a time of 1:50 4/5, the second-slowest running since the race was switched from 1¼ miles to 1 1/8 miles in 1988. It mattered little. Dance Smartly had a lot to live up to in the Breeders' Cup and she handled it like a champion. With her victory, she became the all-time money-winning distaffer in racing history.

NBC's replay of Samuel's nervous reaction watching Dance Smartly in the stretch drive became a classic tape for Canadian racing fans. "Hurry up, hurry up, you're gonna get caught," he said in the stretch drive. As the filly neared the wire, Samuel's wife, Liza, confident the horse had the race won, turned to her husband to hug him, but he pushed her away, still unsure of the outcome. "Hurry up. Hurry up." A few strides from the finish line, Samuel relaxed and let out a huge victory cheer. "Yeeeyawhooo," he said, raising his left arm, then his right, hands clenched, looking somewhat like a referee signaling a successful field goal.

In an interview with Pat Day, Kenny wondered if Dance Smartly needed everything to win.

"Well, not really, the jock probably got a little excited inside the eighth pole," Day said with a smile. "I went to my left hand and asked her to run on just a little bit—probably more than what was really necessary—but a million dollars, Horse of the Year, all-time top-earning mare, it was a lot on the line and I certainly didn't want to get caught sleeping at the switch."

Before the winner's circle presentation, CBC's Brian Williams trumpeted the Canadian triumph. "Well, it's a proud day for Canadian racing," Williams said. "If you listen carefully you can hear the fans cheering at Canadian tracks from coast to coast. Let me put it into perspective for you: the three greatest performances in Canadian racing have all occurred at this track: Bill Hartack riding Northern Dancer in 1964 in the Kentucky Derby; Eddie Delahoussaye for David (Pud) Foster on Sunny's Halo in 1983, also in the Kentucky Derby; and today, Pat Day riding for Ernie Samuel. Certainly a day to remember in Canadian racing."

In the winner's circle, NBC's Bob Neumeier talked to Samuel while pointing to a monitor of his reaction to Dance Smartly roaring down the lane.

"Oh, darn," Samuel said smiling. "I don't know what I was doing, but she's something special."

"You see what she's doing, your heart's going a little pitter patter there," Neumeier said.

"Well, I got a workout out of that one," Samuel said.

"This is the Breeders' Cup, after all," Neumeier said. "To breed a champion like this . . . "

"We bred her, of course, a wonderful filly and the first daughter (of an Oaks winner) and here we are," Samuel said. "She's never been tried before and I'll have to watch the replays because I could hardly see whether she had to work at it today. But, she's just had it all her own way up till now and what a wonderful feeling. We're just in heaven. And Jimmy Day did a wonderful job nursing her along. And well, just magic. Just magic."

While Pat Day raced to the jockeys' room to change silks for the next race, Jim Day and Samuel headed to the interview room to answer questions from the media. One of the inquirers wanted to know about Samuel's thoughts on Dance Smartly becoming the first Canadian-bred to win a Breeders' Cup race and what that meant to him and the breeding programs in Canada.

"We're proud she carries (the Canadian flag) the way she does," he said. "It's a big boost, I think, for Canadian-breds. You saw Wilderness Song come down and win the Spinster. I think that probably caught people's eye how good Dance Smartly might be because Wilderness Song normally can't get close to her. Thank goodness we haven't reached the bottom with her, she's wonderful. The Canadian thing is there. With our great relations with these two great countries, I'm sure it's well received here."

The press conference concluded and Samuel and Day headed back to their seats. At that point, Dance Smartly had to be considered a serious candidate for North American Horse of the Year. She had come to the U.S. and proven her ability and finished the season with an unblemished record, and had vaulted to the top as the leading money-winning filly or mare of all time, surpassing Lady's Secret.

For Samuel and the two Days and all of Canada, there still remained Sky Classic's race in the Turf. The bettors made Sky Classic the second choice at post time at 3.30-1, with European invader Pistolet Bleu the favorite. Unlike Dance Smartly, Sky Classic had been rushed into action on only 13 days' rest and had a tough task ahead. He led for a mile and a quarter, but tired in the final quarter of a mile and finished fourth behind 42-1 shot Miss Alleged. Pat Day said he never wanted to be on the lead from the start, but unexpectedly found himself in that position and just couldn't sustain it on the soft footing, which proved to be too tiring. All and all, it had been a good day for Samuel and Jim Day and all of Canada. The Canadian winless streak had finally ended.

However, later in the day an interesting detail surfaced about Dance Smartly. She had returned to her stall bleeding on the inside of her right hind foot after being nicked by another horse in the race. A heel patch, in place for more than two months as protection for a quarter crack, prevented a possible tendon injury that would have forced her retirement. Jim Day called it "dumb luck."

At the year-end Canadian awards, Dance Smartly was named Horse of the Year in Canada and top three-year-old filly. The North American Eclipse Awards loomed as another source of trophies. In the December 4 issue of the now-defunct *Racing Action, Los Angeles Times* racing writer Bill Christine voiced his support for Dance Smartly.

"I have a month or so to change my mind, but I've already listed Dance Smartly on top in the Thoroughbred Racing Communications poll, and it looks as though she's going to lead my Horse of the Year ballot, too," Christine wrote. "I won't quit speaking to those who vote for Black Tie Affair or Arazi or even In Excess. A qualified case can be made for all three, but I'm making the case for the Canadian filly. She didn't lose in eight races, from six furlongs to 1½ miles, on grass, within her own division or against the boys. All of her wins came in Canada until the Distaff, which amounts to a stigma, but she forged a perfect record nonetheless. Dance Smartly won her last race, her first race and all of those in between."

Dance Smartly finished second to Black Tie Affair, the Breeders' Cup Classic winner, in Horse of the Year voting, but won honors as top three-year-old filly. Samuel won the outstanding owner award—the first time for a Canadian—while Walls earned the Eclipse as top apprentice. Collectively, it represented Canada's greatest year overall on the North American front.

Dance Smartly ran only four times as a four-year-old before a leg injury ended her outstanding career, but the Samuel-Day-Day partnership did not end. Sky Classic continued to carry the Canadian flag with aplomb. He won five of eight races heading into the 1992 Breeders' Cup Turf, including setting a new course record in the Grade One Turf Classic at Belmont in New York. Samuel and Jim Day chose the Turf Classic rather than the Rothmans Ltd. International at Woodbine because it gave them more time between races. Shortly after the Turf Classic, Day shipped the horse to Samuel's farm in Ocala, Florida—five hours away from the Breeders' Cup site at Gulfstream Park—to acclimatize to the weather. Day had tried shipping south within a week or so of a Breeders' Cup with horses he considered competitive and well-prepared, only to see them wilt due to the change in climate and what he perceived to be the equivalent of equine jet lag. He figured horses should be sent within a couple days of the race, as the Europeans did, so they didn't need to adapt to the change in environment. The alternative was shipping a month in advance to have plenty of time to adapt.

Day vanned Sky Classic from Samuel's farm to Gulfstream two days before the race. He had done that all year when shipping from Woodbine to the U.S.

"Whether it's luck, management or superstition, there's no sense changing the program now," he said.

Sky Classic had shown marked improvement in each of his two previous races in the Breeders' Cup Turf. Whether the third time would indeed be the charm became the key question. Like Dance Smartly a year before, he had a chance at an Eclipse Award as top male turf horse. As was the case a year before, the public back home gave the horse plenty of respect. The Canadian shutout was no longer an issue. Now it was a question of whether Sky Classic could put together some kind of streak for Canada.

The public sent him off at odds of 9-10, lowest of any favorite in all seven races. Sky Classic wanted to run early and Pat Day had his hands full harnessing the horse's energy for the long journey on the hot day. They advanced from fifth after a quarter of a mile to the lead at the top of the stretch, appearing like winners until 14-1, Fraise, ridden brilliantly by Pat Valenzuela, scooted through up the inside. Sky Classic spotted the horse late and fought back gamely, but ran out of ground and lost by a nose in course-record time.

Once again Samuel displayed his anxiety, particularly when it became apparent that this year his horse would be caught. When it happened, Samuel said: ". . . Rats."

While the majority of his friends and family sympathized with Samuel, two Ontario Jockey Club employees seated in his box cheered gleefully. They had boxed Fraise and Sky Classic in the exacta.

"I tried to finesse my way down in there, but I couldn't close the door," Pat Day lamented. "He was much more anxious than I anticipated. My horse never settled. He was pulling me out of the saddle the first time around. Wrestling with him early on could have been the difference in the race."

"He wanted to be aggressive, which isn't good running a mile and a half," Jim Day said of Sky Classic. "He was too sharp, that rascal. He thought the race was over once around instead of twice. It's hard to say (why he was so rank). We kept the program exactly as the other races. He just wasn't willing to be settled."

However, there had been one slight switch to the program. The horse had never been vanned from the farm to the track before a race. It had always been from one racetrack barn to another. Some people pointed to this as a possible flaw in the plan. Day doubted that it impacted the outcome, wondering instead if he had left the horse too long on the farm instead of shipping much earlier in the week.

Whatever the reason, Sky Classic had lost another tough one, just like in September in the Arlington Million, the other major international grass race in North America. The only question was what effect the loss would have on the Eclipse Awards. The answer was none: Sky Classic won the title as top male turf horse.

In the next three years, seven more Canadian-based horses shipped south to the Breeders' Cup without success. In fact, they weren't even close. A combination of racing luck, injuries and lack of ability collectively led to their poor outings. The best placing came in 1995 from Peaks and Valleys, trained by Day for American owner Josephine Abercrombie. Peaks and Valleys split his season between Canada and the U.S., winning the Molson Export Million at Woodbine and the Meadowlands Cup in New Jersey. But he ran sixth by 12 lengths in the Classic and broke a bone in his left front foot in the process.

He was named Canadian horse of the year six weeks later, and a week after that Abercrombie fired Day as her Canadian-based trainer. Jim Day said Abercrombie offered no reason except to "think about the Breeders' Cup." Had Jim Day run the horse, who had chronic foot problems, against Abercrombie's wishes or was there more to the story? Her farm manager, Clifford Barry, insisted that the Breeders' Cup result had nothing to do with it, that Abercrombie simply was taking a different direction in her racing operation.

At the 1996 Breeders' Cup at Woodbine, Canadian-based horses had the home-court advantage.

"OK, so the United States got lucky and beat us at our own game (of hockey) in the World Cup," wrote Bill Tallon, the Canadian editor of the *Daily Racing Form*. "But it's not hockey were talking about now—it's horse racing and the Cup is the Breeders'. A formidable team of Woodbine-based runners is onside and are ready to do some serious stickhandling in their own arena."

It turned out to be a marvelous day in defeat for the Canadians, highlighted by two thrilling finishes by horses trained by Barb Minshall. Kiridashi, with Woodbine-based rider Mickey Walls aboard, led for three-quarters of a mile, only to finish fourth by 4½ lengths. Stablemate Mt. Sassafras, also ridden by Walls, moved up from the middle of the pack early in the race to grab the lead heading into the stretch before succumbing late to finish fourth, but only less than a length back. It was a marvelous effort and a great training job by Minshall, in only her second season of conditioning horses after principally working with the yearlings on the farm for her late husband, Aubrey.

The following year at Hollywood Park, Canada came armed with another big contingent and this time the Maple Leaf banner flew proudly—both in victory and defeat. It began in the opening race, the Juvenile Fillies, when David Willmot's Primarily ran third, followed in fifth by another Canadian-owned and -bred horse, Kirby's Song. In the Juvenile, Joe Stritzl's Dawson's Legacy, trained by Rita Schnitzel in partnership with Norm McKnight Jr., tracked the early pace through taxing fractions for the first half mile. But the colt didn't fade under Woodbine-based rider Todd Kabel, carrying on instead to finish second, albeit by 5½ lengths to Favorite Trick, who came into the race undefeated in six previous races and was the overwhelming favorite. Dawson's Legacy overexceeded the expectations of his owner and handlers, who thought the horse might be good enough to finish fourth or possibly third. At more than 78-1 odds, Dawson's Legacy went postward as the longest shot in the board, so running second, particularly to a monster such as Favorite Trick, represented a moral victory, not to mention a juicy consolation prize of $200,000. Stritzl celebrated by telephoning Woodbine Racetrack and ordering drinks for all the patrons at the bar where he usually congregated for the races.

That set the stage for Chief Bearhart, who went into the Turf as the 19-10 favorite following the defection of European invader Singspiel, who was pre-entered and then scratched after breaking a leg. By Chief's Crown, the first winner of a Breeders' Cup race when the event began in 1984 out of the mare Amelia Bearhart, Chief Bearhart had been acquired as a yearling by owner Ernie Samuel in a horse trade on the advice of Lexington bloodstock agent Robert Falk. The Chief, as Chief Bearhart was known, had a three-race win streak going into the Breeders'. Jose Santos had been aboard for all of the horse's races after three separate jockeys had ridden him the year before.

The race had some drama even before the Chief made it to the paddock. The stewards determined he had been fitted with illegal shoes, which necessitated a blacksmith filing them down. Because of a pattern of bad behavior in the saddling enclosure, he was taken to the tunnel, away from the other runners. The Chief jumped in the air and slammed into a wall. Only when Santos was on the horse's back did the horse settle.

Buck's Boy, a 35-1 outsider, charged to the front and led for the opening 1¼ miles, but the final quarter of a mile is where the race is regularly won, particularly among the Europeans charging from far back. In this case, the rush from behind came from the Chief, who had raced in eighth for the opening mile, about five lengths back of the lead. Santos, who had his mount reserved towards the inside, angled out for running room going around the turn for home. Trailing by a length at the top of the stretch, Santos worked furiously and Chief Bearhart responded, wearing down leader Flag Down and runner-up Buck's Boy in midstretch en route to a three-quarter-length win. European runner Borgia, who came into the race off a third-place finish in the Prix de l'Arc de Triomphe, ran second.

"I wasn't worried," Santos said. "Horses were coming strong, but he would have been able to give me more."

"This is such a great thrill, the same as when Dance Smartly (won)," trainer Mark Frostad's assistant Malcolm Pierce, who had been assistant to Jim Day when he saddled Dance Smartly to her historic Breeders' Cup win in 1991, said.

Frostad not only had his first Breeders' Cup triumph, but had topped more than $4.8 million in earnings.

"We're going to party somewhere," he said.

Samuel, known for his demonstrative reactions watching his horses run, did not attend the event. He had suffered a subdural hematoma—bleeding between the brain and the skull—the year before and had been confined to a wheelchair. He watched the race at home with his wife, Liza, and members of his family.

His daughter, Tammy, had kept in regular contact with him from California.

"It killed Dad not being here," she told *Toronto Sun* reporter Rob Longley. "When I spoke with him right after the race, we were both laughing and crying and screaming."

The following day, he talked about his latest Breeders' Cup triumph in an interview with Longley.

"Dance Smartly was the first one and that's always pretty special, but the Chief is one exciting horse to watch," he said. "It shows that we are right there with the best. I hope he will be even bigger and stronger and, who knows, maybe we can do this all again."

Samuel had received a great honor that same year by being named to the Order of Canada, an award presented by the Governor-General of Canada for contribution to the country, for his philanthropic work. A couple of months after the Breeders' Cup, Samuel celebrated another Eclipse Award when Chief Bearhart was voted top male turf horse in North America.

Canada's success in 1997 carried over the following year, albeit with a new hero. After a last-place finish by Kirby Canada's Kirby's Song in the Distaff, Chief Bearhart made his way to the paddock to defend his win. Frostad had followed a fall campaign similar to the year before, although The Chief ran second in his last start before heading off to the Breeders' Cup. After some traffic problems going into the first turn, Chief Bearhart trailed the field. Although he began to make a wide move into the turn for home, he could not close as strongly and placed fourth by more than three lengths. That left the Classic, which featured Awesome Again, who had won the Queen's Plate, Canada's equivalent of the Kentucky Derby, the year before. While he had been raced exclusively in the U.S. afterward, the fact he had been foaled in Canada classified him as a Canadian-bred. And for Canadian racing fans—and the Canadian Broadcasting Corporation, simulcasting the event and with a crew on hand to play up the national angles—that was good enough.

Awesome Again was bred and owned by auto parts industrialist Frank Stronach, who also had representation in the race as a co-owner of Touch Gold. Awesome Again lived up to his name, scoring a stunning three-quarter-length win over American superstar Silver Charm in what was arguably the deepest collection of talent ever assembled for the Classic.

"In the stretch run of a race that lived up to its hype as one of the greatest assemblies of horses ever, Awesome Again stole the show," wrote Jennie Rees in the *Louisville Courier-Journal*.

"Awesome Again won not only the laurels and the loot but also his sixth straight start in a perfect year at the races," wrote Joseph Durso in the *New York Times*.

"One gray horse (Skip Away), the one who had dominated the racing season with an iron fist until the very end, had fallen apart without so much as breathing hard upon the history of which he had been sent in pursuit," wrote *Newsday*'s Paul Moran. "The other gray (Silver Charm), the one who had stood draped in roses last year after the Kentucky Derby and was seen as the most formidable threat to upset the floundering favorite, fell apart in the shadow of the wire. At the end . . . the richest race of all time fell apart at the feet of Awesome Again."

Trainer Pat Byrne credited the horse's maturity as a big reason for the victory.

"He gained a great deal of confidence," Byrne said. "It was something you could see in him. He kept improving with each race. With each race, he kept winning. With each win, he got more and more confident. He thinks he's King Kong. He acted like a horse that wanted to go to the racetrack."

In the Kentucky Derby Room, where many of the horsemen had gathered after the day's racing, Silver Charm's trainer Bob Baffert was encountered by Canadian-based writer Ted Labanowich. He had been invited into the exclusive Derby Room by a representative of Stronach's racing team. Labanowich asked Baffert how he felt about being beaten in another big race by a Canadian horse. The high-profile American trainer looked at Labanowich incredulously, pointing out the horses are all Americans or Kentucky-breds. Labanowich noted that while Touch Gold had been an American-bred, he had strong Canadian roots, sired by Canadian star Deputy Minister, who also fathered Awesome Again. In addition, Touch Gold had been out of a mare, Passing Mood, who had produced some quality Canadian horses, notably With Approval. He swept the 1989 Canadian Triple Crown and the following year rattled off some major wins in the U.S. and placed second in the Breeders' Cup Turf. Passing Mood changed ownership in later years in a dispersal sale.

For Labanowich, literally and figuratively a big Canadian supporter, this was a chance to tout the Maple Leaf roots.

In 1999, Canada's success came to an end. David Willmot's Talk Back ran seventh in the Juvenile Fillies. Samuel's Quiet Resolve ran last in the Mile, John and Glenn Sikura's Anglia ran second-last in the Filly & Mare Turf, Eugene and Laura Melnyk's Graeme Hall ran 12th among a field of 14 in the Juvenile and Steve Stavro's Thornfield ran second-last in the Turf. Stronach's Golden Missile, who had been campaigned in the U.S. and was only considered a Canadian because of the connection to Stronach, ran a surprising third in the Classic at odds of more than 75-1.

In 2000, Canada's horse racing industry mourned the loss of Samuel, the first Canadian to win a Breeders' Cup race, when he died in May at age 69. Coincidentally, a month later Samuel's operation celebrated a victory in the Queen's Plate with Scatter the Gold, a son of Mr. Prospector out of 1991 Breeders' Cup Distaff winner Dance Smartly. The colt came into the race as a maiden. Scatter the Gold followed up the Plate win by notching the Prince of Wales Stakes, but his bid to duplicate his mother's Canadian Triple Crown sweep came up short when he ran third in the Breeders' Stakes. It was an emotional time for the family, who reveled in the sensational season of the colt but mourned the man who had founded the operation and developed it into one of the best in the world.

"He was a fiercely proud Canadian," Tammy Samuel-Balaz, who manages the operation now, said of her father in an article written by George Williams in the 2000 Breeders' Cup magazine. "Whenever we raced in the Breeders' Cup he would look in the crowd and see the Canadian flags waving and get choked up. It wasn't like (Dance Smartly) was our filly, we were just honored to own her. She was Canada's filly. That's the way Dad thought about her. It was never about Dad as far as he was concerned. He was always a team player. It was never 'I,' it was always 'We,' as in the family or the farm managers and the exercise riders and the grooms and the trainers. He was a team player. I can't tell you how proud I am to have had Dad for a dad. He's still here with us in spirit. The world has lost an incredible guy."

"It wasn't all about racing and winning for Ernie," Frostad said. "It was all about the horses. He always wanted what was best for them. He loved the animals. He would visit with them for hours on the farm. He was very competitive, but also very patient and that contributed to his success. And it was a family affair for him. It was always a lot of fun. He was a terrific guy."

As if to underscore Ernie Samuel's mark on thoroughbred racing, his color-bearer Quiet Resolve nearly pulled off an amazing upset in the 2000 Breeders' Cup. Under jockey Shane Sellers, Quiet Resolve, dismissed at more than 41-1, finished second by a half-length in the Turf. The five-year-old horse had the lead in the stretch and was only overtaken late in the run to the wire by European invader Kalanisi.

"This feels like a win for us," Tammy Samuel-Balaz said afterward.

Quiet Resolve's result added some heartfelt sentiment to the day which saw Stronach win the Filly & Mare Turf with Perfect Sting and the Juvenile with Macho Uno, both trained by New York–based Joe Orseno. Both horses were foaled in the U.S., although Macho Uno had prepped for his race at Woodbine. Jerry Bailey was aboard for both wins, neither of which caused shockwaves among the bettors. Perfect Sting was the second choice overall in her race at 5-1—European invader Petrushka went postward as the 7-5 favorite but failed to hit the board—while Macho Uno went off at 6.30-1.

Canadian-bred Fly For Avie, owned by Ivan Dalos, finished sixth to Perfect Sting, while Pico Teneriffe, owned by Eugene and Laura Melnyk, ran 12th. Stronach had another starter, Collect The Cash, who ran 11th. His final representative on the day, Golden Missile, ran last in the Classic.

In 2001, Quiet Resolve returned to run in the Turf, but placed second-last. Overall, Canadian-based horses did not fare well. Jealous Forum, trained by Mark Casse for Floridian Harry Mangurian, ran second-last in the Juvenile Fillies. Lodge Hill, trained by Phil England for Eugene and Laura Melnyk, ran eighth in the Turf, and A Fleets Dancer, trained by Roger Attfield for Cam Allard, ran 12th in the Classic. Neither of the horses were rated as contenders in their respective races.

In 2002, Scatter the Gold's full sister, Dancethruthedawn, had emerged as a solid four-year-old filly and had been pointed to the Distaff, but she was sidelined before making it to the Cup. That was a disappointment not only to her handlers, but to a publicist who had been following the horse. Lynne Snierson, the director of communications and marketing for Rockingham Park in New Hampshire, had been assigned by the Breeders' Cup to do biographies of horses that were potentially running in the Distaff.

"I was always such a great admirer of Dance Smartly," Snierson said. "I just thought that she was just a beautiful, professional filly. I've always followed her offspring just because I held her in such high esteem. I was really wanting to see Dancethruthedawn and see her in person and watch her run and hope that she had a chance."

Snierson worked as the director of communications and on-air racing analyst for Arlington Park back when Dance Smartly ran there in 1992. The great Canadian filly concluded her career by running in the Arlington Budweiser Breeders' Cup Handicap and then the Beverly D. She ran third by two lengths as the 2-10 favorite in the first race and third by 1¾ lengths in the second race in which she and an entrymate were the 8-5 favorite. Snierson will never forget the hostile reaction Dance Smartly received from the angry bettors after she was unsaddled following the second defeat.

"People should have reveled in the fact that they were witnessing the horse who at that time was the all-time leading distaffer in the history of racing and a horse who was exquisite to look at and was such a beautiful, wonderful champion in her own right," Snierson said. "That they would boo her and scream horrible names and throw things, to me it was so disgusting. It's a moment throughout my career that I'll always remember because it was one of the low points in being around racing. It's bad enough to boo the trainer or boo the jockey, but to boo a horse who just went out on the racetrack and gave her all and tried as hard as she could to win, to me I thought it was the antithesis of what sportsmanship is. You'd hope people come to the racetrack because they love the animals and they appreciate the animals and they recognize what incredible athletes and beautiful creatures these horses are. But just to have somebody who had to tear up a ticket disrespect and dishonor a champion like that was heartbreaking to me."

Canada did not field a particularly strong lot in 2002 and the results showed it, without any of the horses doing anything of significance.

Overall, there have been three Canadian-bred winners—Dance Smartly, Chief Bearhart and Awesome Again—and some close finishes by others. Given the Canadian foal population, which is one-tenth of the U.S. crop, and the fact Canada has only one major track, Woodbine, the overall results are not bad.

# 7

# The Drought Is Over

## Bobby Frankel

$\mathcal{I}$t's been a long time since Bobby Frankel was known as the king of the claimers, some three decades to be precise. Now he's a conditioner of quality blue-blooded stock, capable of winning the most prestigious races in the world and winning Eclipse Awards as the top trainer in North America. But for all he had done—and will continue to do—it took Bobby Frankel a long time to lay claim to his first Breeders' Cup win.

"I wish you were doing a book on my career rather than just the Breeders' Cup because then I've got good stats," he said in the days leading up to the 2002 edition. "My batting average is over 20% for my life and I don't even know how many Group Ones I've won. When you want to do something on the Breeders' Cup that's not my fondest memories."

Robert (Bobby) Frankel was born July 9, 1941 in Brooklyn, New York, and could best be described as your typical wise guy growing up. To make a buck he'd work assorted jobs—construction, parking cars, a lot of little things like that. His life changed when he was introduced to the races and the lure of laying down a bet to make a big score—and he had his fair share. His entrance into the sport came in his teens when his parents took him to the harness races at Roosevelt Raceway. At first he didn't like it but then he started becoming more enthusiastic, handicapping the races and trying his hand at gambling.

He had little interest in school, and his homeroom teacher failed him one semester, making him ineligible for playing the sports he loved. In the mornings he'd caddy at golf courses, giving advice on a game he'd never played, and receiving $7 a round. He used his earnings at the racetrack.

"The homeroom teacher, it's his fault I ended up at the racetrack," Frankel said in the 1995 Breeders' Cup issue of *The Horseplayer Magazine*.

When introduced to thoroughbred racing at Belmont Park, he'd buy the *Daily Racing Form*, which had information that looked like Chinese to him. With the harness program, the races all had the same fixed distance—one mile—but now he was reading different distances on different surfaces and it confused him until he started picking up on the handicapping. He started studying and made some "good scores" in the process. In fact, that became his education, far more than the lure of school. He spent all of two days in college.

"I was supposed to go for the year but I said 'The hell with it. I'm not going through with this' and went back to the races," he recalled with a big grin.

He was living at home then and his parents never really bothered him too much about working. But he really didn't have any reason to seek traditional employment, not when he could make a living gambling. One day he went to the races with $40 and two days later he had $43,000. He bet on his favorite jockey—and in later years a good friend—Bobby Ussery, who had a good day winning a handful or so of races. The next day Ussery again crossed the finish line with several winning mounts and that contributed to Frankel's betting bounty. Another time, Frankel borrowed $20 from a jockey agent and parlayed that loan into $5,000 in a single card.

Inasmuch as he liked gambling he became attracted to the game in another way when he went to a party and talked to a guy who worked at the track ponying horses. Frankel asked to go along with him and the following morning he went to the track. He met a trainer, Joe Williams, who had a couple of horses and put Frankel down on his list as a hot walker, just to give him a free pass into the races and free parking. Frankel started hanging around the backside, where he gained a reputation for his gambling prowess, and when the racing scene shifted to Florida when New York shut down for the winter he went to work as a hot walker for a trainer named Buddy Bellue. When he returned to New York and made another gambling score he met a guy named Tony Vittereti who wanted to hook him up with an owner, John Petrosi, who had a farm up in the Finger Lakes. By this time Frankel was hanging around John Campo, who was an assistant to Eddie Neloy. Campo owned a filly who had a bowed tendon and didn't figure she'd make it to the races. Campo couldn't take care of the filly because of his obligations to Neloy, so he worked out an arrangement with Frankel to look after her. Accompanied by Campo, Frankel went in and took his trainer's license. He bought a horse named Pink Rose from Allen Jerkens for $8,500. Petrosi gave Frankel $3,500 and he went to Saratoga and bought another horse from Jerkens, a filly called Taint Funny. Petrosi also sent him a horse called Double Dash. Frankel ran Pink Rose for a $12,500 claiming tag first time out and she got beat by a half-length. She ran two more times but didn't do anything meaningful. He ran Double Dash twice, the first time losing in a sprint race, then sent him long and he won with Ussery aboard. It happened at Aqueduct on November 29, 1966, and whatever the horse paid to win, Frankel has long since forgotten. It's the winning feeling that he savored from that experience.

The first time he ran Taint Funny she won. Then he won with Pink Rose, who followed up with two more victories.

He won a handful of races that year with about 15 or so starters and started attracting attention en route to becoming known as The Boy Wonder, a name given to him by prominent jockey agent Lenny Goodman.

Frankel began an association with owner Bill Frankel, no relation, who operated a brokerage house and ran horses under the name of his wife, Marion. The trainer had instant success with his new owner, who decided he needed more action and had his young conditioner claim some horses. After racing in California in the winter meet when he couldn't receive stalls at Hialeah, the young trainer returned to New York and won the spring meet with his 14-horse stable of claimers. As he continued to win, Frankel's stock started to improve as his reputation as the King of the Claimers started to soar. His prize halters included Baitman, Pataha Prince, Barometer and Lakeside Trail, meat-and-potatoes horses turned into stakes winners.

When Bill Frankel decided to move full-time to California in 1972 because of the warmer climate—the three-hour time difference in the West allowed him to conduct business back east via the phone—Bobby Frankel shifted his shingle to Hollywood Park. He had instant success, winning a record 60 races in 75 days. Of the 60 tallies, 55 were owned by Bill and Marion Frankel.

In his first 11 years in California, Frankel won 25 of a possible 44 training titles, nine at Hollywood Park, six at Oak Tree and five apiece at Del Mar and Santa Anita. His success earned him additional clients, including Jerry Moss, chief executive officer of A&M Records; Edmund Gann, a successful tuna fish operator, who later parlayed his fortune into other businesses; and Greek shipping magnate Stavros Niarchos.

In 1984, the first year of the Breeders' Cup, Frankel had two Moss starters in separate races—Fighting Fit in the Sprint and Night Mover in the Mile. With purses of $1 million apiece, Frankel looked to make a score, but it didn't happen and to this day Frankel blames himself for not entering both horses in the Sprint. Fighting Fit, sent off at odds of just under 3-1, rallied from last under jockey Eddie Delahoussaye and finished third, beaten less than two lengths to the frontrunning race favorite Eillo. Night Mover ran eighth in the field of 10, beaten more than seven lengths with Laffit Pincay Jr. aboard. Unlike Fighting Fit, Night Mover failed to threaten at any point in the race, which Royal Heroine won by 1½ lengths.

"I got greedy," Frankel said. "I probably should have run Night Mover in the Sprint, too. If I had have run Night Mover in the Sprint I would have won the race with him. I was so mad at myself because I ran him in the Mile race on the grass. It was probably too far for him, but I got greedy. I'm trying to win both races, wasn't happy just to win one Breeders' Cup. I didn't realize at the time that I'd go 0-for-30 or 40. I thought I was in my backyard and I could do whatever I wanted to do."

Frankel had a bigger contingent in the Breeders' Cup the following year. He ran Fighting Fit in the Sprint and once again he rallied from the back of the field, this time finishing fourth, beaten 2¾ lengths to Precisionist, a distance horse cutting back for the first time in almost a year and who narrowly missed the track record for six furlongs. Fighting Fit was the only runner among the top four finishers to rally from well off the pace.

Frankel also sent out Bert Firestone's Al Mamoon in the Mile, and the four-year-old ran third under Angel Cordero Jr. but was advanced to second when runner-up Palace Music was disqualified and placed ninth for interference early in the race. Frankel's last starter on the card, Moss' Sharannpour, ran in the $2 million

Turf, the second-richest race on the card, but the five-year-old never made it further than ninth in the field of 14 and finished last, beaten more than 16 lengths with Chris McCarron in the irons.

In 1986, Frankel came armed with Al Mamoon in the Mile and Theatrical in the Turf. Al Mamoon, the second betting favorite at just under 5-2 in the full field of 14, ran fifth, slightly more than three lengths back of European invader Last Tycoon, who lit up the board at just under 36-1 odds. Theatrical went postward as the favorite at 27-10 odds with Estrapade. Allen Paulson, who owned Estrapade, had a financial interest in Theatrical, hence the coupling of the two in the wagering. Theatrical, ridden by Gary Stevens, tracked Estrapade for the opening mile of the mile and a half grass race before taking over going into the stretch. Manila overcame a troubled journey to overtake Theatrical about 40 yards from the finish.

"Gary Stevens was sitting there turning for home and if he had just sat a 16th of a mile further—because he had the race—he would have won," Frankel said. "He got excited and he let the horse really run and opens up two lengths or a length and a half and Manila, who was trapped, finally got out and came to me right on the money. If it was the Stevens 10 years later, I never would have got beat. He wouldn't have moved that fast."

It was a tough loss for Frankel, not made any easier despite winning two stakes later in the card after the Breeders' Cup races had concluded. But the defeat would also be a harbinger of some frustrations for Stevens, who would go through his own lengthy drought in the Breeders'.

The following year, Firestone presented Frankel with an opportunity to become his private trainer. Frankel rejected it because it would mean having to return to live and work in New York and he had been doing too well in California to up and leave. The decision cost Frankel some quality horses, including Theatrical, who would be switched to a young up-and-coming trainer named Bill Mott, the future conditioner of the great Cigar. Theatrical would be pointed to the Turf again, but not before a public squabble between Paulson and Firestone over ownership of the horse heading into the race. Theatrical prevailed by a half-length over Prix de l'Arc de Triomphe winner Trempolino under a heady ride by Pat Day.

In April 1988, Frankel celebrated a major feat when his horse Simply Majestic set a world record for a mile and one eighth race at Golden Gate Fields in California. The horse ran 12 times that season, posting five wins, two seconds and two thirds and earnings of more than $667,000. He did not run in the Breeders' Cup that year. In fact, Frankel saddled only one starter, Ruhlmann in the Sprint. Stevens was aboard the three-year-old, who was dismissed at odds of more than 22-1. Ruhlmann ran ninth by 7½ lengths to Gulch, who ran a gritty race under an aggressive ride by Angel Cordero Jr. to prevail by three-quarters of a length in the slop.

In 1989, Simply Majestic ran 14 times, winning eight and recording $729,968 in earnings. He didn't run in the Breeders' Cup and Frankel did not have a starter that year, nor the next year. But his success with grass horses did not go unnoticed. In 1990, Prince Khalid Abdullah, a member of the Saudi Arabian royal family and a prominent international breeder/owner who runs horses under the stable name

Juddmonte Farms, wanted to expand his operation, which had been thriving in Europe. The Prince set his sights on the U.S., and his racing management did a computer analysis of Southern California trainers and picked Frankel and Ron McAnally to send horses to based on their success with European runners. Juddmonte already had some horses with Eddie Gregson, a friend of Frankel's. The story goes that when Dr. John Chandler, the American racing manager for Juddmonte, called up Frankel to ask if he'd be interested in training horses for the Prince's operation, Frankel told him he'd think about it and call back with an answer. Apparently, Frankel wanted to consult first with Eddie Gregson, who advised Frankel to take the horses. Frankel called back agreeing to work for Juddmonte.

Given four horses, Frankel won with three of them, but it would be his success with a runner called Exbourne that proved instrumental. Frankel rejuvenated Exbourne, who had placed second in the Two Thousand Guineas and a Group Three race in England as a three-year-old, but whose career was limited by an injury. Shifted to the U.S. as a five-year-old in 1991, Exbourne ran eight times, winning five and placing in the other three. Exbourne would win almost a million, the overwhelming majority in Frankel's care.

"I handled Exbourne with enormous confidence," jockey Gary Stevens wrote in his autobiography *The Perfect Ride*. "We could be fifty yards from the finish line, three lengths behind whichever horses were in front of, but if any daylight opened up ahead of us, I knew we could win by a length and a half. Exbourne would do that."

The highlight victory came in the Grade One Hollywood Turf Handicap, in which he beat Prized, the 1989 Breeders' Cup Turf winner, and Itsallgreektome, who would go on to finish second in the 1991 Turf.

"The record speaks for itself what Bobby did with Exbourne," Chandler said. "That firmly established Bobby (with Juddmonte) and he started getting better horses. It's paid off handsomely."

Exbourne never made it to the Breeders' Cup that year and almost died because of colic. He ran only once as a six-year-old and won, but he came perilously close to dying again that year because of a severe injury.

"Nobody thought he had a chance to be saved and we saved him," Frankel said. "That's the most emotional I ever got with a good horse."

In 1991, Frankel returned to the Cup with Edmund Gann's Val De Bois in the Mile, Filago in the Turf, and Juddmonte Farms' Marquetry in the Classic. Val des Bois was given little hope by the morning-line handicapper, who coupled the horse with Jolie's Halo and Sultry Song in a three-horse mutuel field. Because the betting board could accommodate only 12 betting interests, Val des Bois and the other two were included as a three-for-one betting proposition that went postward at more than 16-1 odds. Anyone who took a shot on the trio was rewarded when Val des Bois stormed from almost dead last in the field to rush up for second, only a length and a quarter back of Opening Verse, who pulled off a stunning upset at 26-1 odds. The exacta paid a whopping $834.20.

Filago, who came into his race off a victory a month before, drew decent support from the bettors at just under 8-1 odds. Ridden by Pat Valenzuela, who was aboard Opening Verse and who stunned the racing world on the same card with his victory aboard Arazi in the Juvenile, Filago was never prominent in his outing. The horse pulled up lame heading into the stretch.

Marquetry ran seventh in the field of 11 for the Classic, trailing winner Black Tie Affair by more than eight lengths. Black Tie Affair led from the outset under Jerry Bailey en route to a 1¼-length victory that solidified his bid for horse-of-the-year honors. But it was just another day at the Breeders' Cup races for Frankel.

In 1992, Frankel had Luthier Enchanteur and Val des Bois in the Mile, Quest For Fame in the Turf, and Defensive Play and Marquetry in the Classic. Luthier Enchanteur and Val des Bois, coupled as an entry because they were both owned by Edmund Gann, were dismissed by the bettors at odds of more than 14-1. Val des Bois made a spirited run for the second time in two years in the Mile but finished fourth by almost five lengths to Lure, who led all the way in setting a course record in his second career try on the lawn. Luthier Enchanteur tracked the early pace of Lure but couldn't sustain his position and faded to sixth. Much of the focus in the race centered on Arazi, who went into the race with a big reputation from his stunning win the year before in the Juvenile but never recaptured the same consistent form. He finished a distant 11th in the field of 14 as the 3-2 favorite.

Quest For Fame, third the year before while running for English trainer Roger Charlton and shifted by Juddmonte to Frankel's barn the next year, had run almost two months before in the Arlington Million and placed sixth, but Frankel had pointed him for the Turf. The night before the race at a dinner attended by several people from Juddmonte Farms, Frankel told jockey Pat Eddery Quest For Fame had changed from the horse he knew the year before. Eddery had ridden the five-year-old regularly the year before. Frankel said he explicitly instructed Eddery to keep his mount running along the rail. While Eddery followed the prerace instructions for the first part of the race, he opted to shift Quest For Fame outside down the backside. Fraise started creeping up along the inside and eventually made a winning move along the hedge to beat 9-10 favorite Sky Classic by a nose. Quest For Fame ran another two lengths back in third, much to Frankel's chagrin.

"If I stay on the rail, (Fraise) has no place to go and I might have run by Sky Classic," Frankel said in his racetrack parlance. "If I'm in the race, I get through and he don't get through. That's one time I was pissed off and everybody (who was at the dinner) knew it."

Defensive Play and Marquetry, both five-year-old male horses, were coupled as an entry with the three-year-old French filly Jolypha, trained by Andre Fabre, because Juddmonte owned an interest in all or part of the trio. Frankel had an ownership interest in Marquetry. Defensive Play tracked the early pace, and advanced along the inside and took a short lead at the top of the stretch but faded to sixth. Marquetry tired while racing wide and only made it as close as eighth before finishing 11th. It wasn't all bad news for Juddmonte, however, as Jolypha ran a credible third, beaten less than three lengths. She had shown little in her last race back home, while also trying the main dirt track for the first time.

In 1993 at Santa Anita, Frankel entered an army in his biggest assault on the

Breeders' Cup: Now Listen in the Sprint, Toussaud in the Mile, Luazur in the Turf and the combination of Bertrando, Marquetry and Missionary Ridge in the Classic. Now Listen, sent off at more than 28-1 odds, made a run from the back of the pack but could only advance as far as eighth. Toussaud was maintained well off the pace by jockey Kent Desormeaux, saving his late-charging mount for the final run. The four-year-old filly advanced to fourth, slightly more than four lengths back of Lure, who defended his victory of a year before. Luazur led from the start under Pat Day but surrendered his diminishing advantage in the final quarter of a mile, although he held well to place third.

That led to the Classic and the potential that Frankel would finally win a Breeders' race. Bertrando had quality speed he liked to flash on the front end. Marquetry had the ability to be placed near the lead while Missionary Ridge preferred an off-the-pace style. Bertrando and Marquetry had come into the race off wins in their last starts, the former in New York, the latter at the Meadowlands. However, Bertrando had not run in 48 days. Because Frankel trained all three, the rules forced them to be coupled as an entry and the betting public backed them at 6-5 odds. Frankel figured Marquetry, in whom he had an ownership interest, could probably win the race on the lead, but had to keep him slightly back of Bertrando, lest the two wilt one another in a front-end battle.

Gary Stevens liked his chances aboard Bertrando.

"I thought (he) would bring me my first win in the Breeders' Cup Classic," Stevens wrote in his autobiography. "Bertrando was a massive black animal with a great temperament. He was a true racehorse and gorgeous. Bertrando had what I can only describe as a John Wayne swagger. When he was walking to the starting gate, it was like 'I'm the daddy, I own this racetrack. The rest of you running against me have no chance.' That was the feeling he gave me. I really loved riding that horse. He had versatility as well as great speed. He could run six furlongs in a minute eight seconds, or a mile and a quarter in two minutes flat. His performance was push-button easy, for he could really carry his speed. I could use him hard out of the gate to establish the lead, then take hold of him to slow down the pace. When the other jockeys figured out that the pace had been slowed, they would press their mounts up to about his shoulder and I would let him pick up his speed a notch. With Bertrando I could play cat and mouse throughout a race—right up to the quarter pole. Then I would ask him for his best and he always gave it to me. He was fun to ride."

Stevens seized the lead early, tracked by Marquetry, who had Kent Desormeaux aboard. Heading into the stretch, Bertrando led by 1½ lengths and appeared to be heading to victory. But a funny thing happened on the way to the finish line. Seemingly out of nowhere, a European invader named Arcanques, who had been sent postward at more than 133-1 odds, bested Bertrando en route to a two-length victory. It proved to the biggest upset—at least from a $2 payoff point of view—in Breeders' Cup history.

"When Bertrando finally got the lead, I felt confident that he had put away every other horse that I had been concerned about and had a clear shot to win the big purse," Stevens wrote in his book. "Then about fifty yards from the finish along came a horse with Jerry Bailey onboard wearing silks I didn't even recognize. His horse flashed by and beat us. I was stunned. Riding back after the race I didn't even know the horse's name, only that the tote board said that he had gone off at 99-1. His actual odds (were) 133-1. No wonder I felt doomed never to win a Breeders' Cup Classic."

But at least Stevens had won a Breeders' Cup race, snapping out of a 0-for-36 shutout in the series piloting In The Wings to victory in the 1990 Turf. This was just another tough loss for Frankel.

"Bertrando would go as fast as he could, so I put him on the lead and all of a sudden I see some horse go by me and I said, 'Who the fuck was that?' I couldn't believe it, it was Arcanques," Stevens wrote in his book.. "I thought the race was over (going into the stretch) because all the competition ran up to him and they all spit it out and all of a sudden here comes Arcangues."

Marquetry faded to fourth and Missionary Ridge ran 11th in the field of 13.

In the year-end statistics, Frankel led all trainers in money won by his horses with more than $8.9 million and received his first Eclipse Award as America's leading trainer. Bertrando became his first Eclipse Award champion, winning the older horse division.

Frankel and Bertrando's owners had a falling out in 1994 because of their decision to send the horse to stud while recovering from knee surgery. Frankel disagreed with the move and when the owners wanted to race the horse later in the year, Frankel said he wouldn't train him.

"I just think I could have done a better job than they did," he said in the 1995 *HorsePlayer Magazine* article. "I said, 'If you don't do what you're doing, I'll make another $2 million.'" That was Frankel's way then and little has changed.

"I really don't get swayed by owners too much about what to do," he said. "I'm lucky that way. The owners usually let me call all the shots."

Owner David Lanzman, who won a Breeders' Cup in 2001 with the Frankel-trained Squirtle Squirt, said it's hard to argue with Frankel.

"He obviously does well," Lanzman said. "He's not the trainer you'd want if you want a phone call at 10 in the morning to know how your horse breezed or things like that. You're not going to get the day-to-day information, but you can't really expect it. He's got too many horses to watch over."

Added Chandler: "People have said to the Prince that Bobby's a strange fellow and what does the Prince think of him. The Prince says Bobby's a trainer. That's what we hired him for, to train horses. What people perceive his personality quirks to be is absolutely irrelevant. He wants to train horses and win races, to which extent he has succeeded admirably."

In 1994 and '95, Frankel continued his Breeders' Cup losing streak, this time without even a sniff. Raintrap, the lone entrant in 1994, ran 13th in the '94 Turf.

In 1995, Frankel received induction in the National Museum of Racing's Hall of Fame. He expressed disappointment and bitterness that the plaque he received referred to him as Bobby instead of Robert and listed several owners and horses that he felt were not as important as some left off the plaque.

Frankel had already developed a reputation for speaking his mind, regardless of the offending target, be it stewards, track management, jockeys or just about anybody. Gary Stevens wrote in his book about his rocky relationship with Frankel.

"I have done a lot of business with Frankel and have always considered him one of racing's great trainers, but he is a difficult man to ride for. For one thing, he's a poor loser. Yes, it's true, if you show me a good loser, I'll show you a loser. Even so, he's not a gracious winner either. After all the races I have won for him over the years, he has never once said 'nice ride' or 'thank you' afterward. But if I got beaten, it was a damn sure bet that he would berate me. Frankel has always loved to own his riders. He loves to have one or two jockeys riding all of his horses so he can control them completely. Control means it's so well known that you're riding for him that no other mounts are offered to you. The result is that if and when he fires you, you're left out in the cold with no clients to ride for because he has so completely dominated your racing schedule. . . . I am always happy to ride some of Frankel's horses, but I won't commit to riding his whole stable."

Less than a week after his induction, Frankel won the Pacific Classic with Tinners Way. That made Frankel the first-ever trainer to win the same $1 million race four consecutive years.

In the '95 Breeders' Cup, Frankel's charges did little. You And I placed 10th in the Sprint, while stablemates Winter Quarters finished sixth in the Juvenile and Tinners Way placed seventh in the Classic.

In the next two years, Frankel did not send out any runners in the Cup, and the litany of losses continued upon his return in 1998, although he did pick up some checks. The Exeter Man, a 57-1 shot, ran second-last in the Sprint. Keeper Hill brought some relief finishing third in the Distaff, albeit five lengths back of runner-up Banshee Breeze, the 4-5 favorite who was nosed out by the front-running Escena, ridden by Stevens. Stablemates Dushyantor and River Bay, both five-year-olds, ran as separate entries in the Turf, with River Bay rated as the better of the two in the betting at just under 9-1 and Dushyantor at more than 58-1. Dushyantor ran third by only three lengths under Kent Desormeaux, who rallied from almost last in the final third of the race. River Bay ran a distant 11th in the field of 13.

In 1999, Frankel's entrants included Keeper Hill in the Distaff, Kirkwall in the Mile, Spanish Fern in the Filly & Mare Turf, and Chester House in the Classic. Keeper Hill, owned by Chandler, came into her race off a win in the Grade One Spinster Stakes three weeks before. She ended up placing fourth behind the front-running Beautiful Pleasure, who rattled off her third consecutive Grade One win en route to year-end honors as the champion older filly or mare. Kirkwall, a winner of his last race but dismissed in the wagering at more than 26-1 in the Mile, ran eighth by about four lengths. Spanish Fern, who won the Grade One Yellow Ribbon Stakes in her previous race, went postward as the co-second choice at 4-1, but ran last. Chester House, who had been running in England for Juddmonte and was transferred to Frankel's barn for the Classic, ran fourth by almost 3½ lengths at more than 63-1 odds.

The new millennium would prove to be a major turning point in Frankel's overall career and certainly his Breeders' Cup drought, largely due to the increasing confidence shown in him by Juddmonte.

"When you train for somebody like Juddmonte and you do well, it's all of a sudden you've got the stamp of approval, that you're a stakes kind of trainer," he said. "Now, people start giving you horses. Now they have the confidence in you, so they start looking for you."

In the 2000 Cup, Frankel had only two runners: Honest Lady in the Sprint and Spanish Fern in the Filly & Mare Turf. The results of the two fillies, both owned by Juddmonte, could not have been more extreme. Honest Lady, a four-year-old filly, had not raced in almost two months and had run dismally in that outing, the Atto Mile at Woodbine. But Frankel had her ready for redemption in the Sprint, although the public didn't think so and let her go at more than 31-1. She ran from far back under Kent Desormeaux, charging hard down the line and placing second by only a half-length to 17-10 favorite Kona Gold, a six-year-old gelding who won in track-record time. Frankel thought the filly could have won had the race gone another two jumps.

But the bittersweet feelings Frankel had about the near miss were completely obliterated by the abject sorrow resulting from the tragic fate of Spanish Fern. A winner of six races in 20 career starts and earnings of almost $750,000, Spanish Fern had run second in her last outing, the Grade One Yellow Ribbon Stakes. Coincidentally, she had won the race the year before. Spanish Fern had never shown any soundness problems, but she injured her left hind leg shortly after the start of the Filly & Mare Turf race and was pulled up by jockey Victor Espinoza and vanned off with a suspected broken pelvis. She was treated for signs of shock and later transported to Rood and Riddle Equine Hospital in Lexington. A veterinarian did a follow-up examination, which confirmed the break. The filly was given intravenous fluid, blood volume replacement and drugs, which collectively helped to stabilize her. However, she began hemorrhaging again in the evening and died later that night from internal bleeding.

"Fractures of the pelvis are occasionally seen in the horse as the result of trauma or muscular exertion during exercise," veterinarian Dr. Larry Bramlage said in a report issued to the media. "Fractures of the pelvis are seen in horses while racing, training, or while turned out in a field. The pelvis serves as the anchorage for all of the major musculature of the hind limb.

"As the gate opened . . . we could see Spanish Fern accelerate and then immediately become lame on the left hind limb. She created the fracture with the force of her own musculature acceleration. The immediate swelling indicated that she lacerated one of the large blood vessels, which lie within the pelvis, when the fracture occurred. The first aid and care of this filly stabilized the situation. Unfortunately, she began to hemorrhage again. . . . Fatal hemorrhage is a rare, but well-documented sequel of fracture of the pelvis in the horse. This is one of the situations where absolute bed rest is the prescription for stabilizing the hemorrhage and allowing the vessels to clot. Unfortunately this is not possible in the horse and they become victims of their innate desire to remain mobile and unrestrained in times of stress. In this instance that instinct re-initiated the hemorrhaging and proved fatal to Spanish Fern."

At year's end, Frankel won his second Eclipse as trainer of the year. It all seemed to be going Frankel's way, but he still didn't have his first Cup win.

The Breeders' Cup came to New York in 2001, the first major international sporting event since the terrorist attacks leveled the World Trade Center less than two months before. In fact, the attacks occurred early in the week of some key Breeders' Cup prep races scheduled to be run at Belmont that weekend but cancelled and never rescheduled. Some of these races Frankel had intended to run with his horses. The native New Yorker had started to run a string of horses again in the state where he launched his career back in the '60s.

Frankel brought his best collection of talent to the Breeders' Cup. And the media had its fare share of stories documenting Frankel's national success but winless skein in the Breeders'. Ed Musselman, the acerbic former horseman known as Indian Charlie who writes a Kentucky-based tip sheet sprinkled with caustic comments, most of them tongue-in-cheek, took a few shots at Frankel's streak in the days leading up to, and including, the race. It began on Wednesday, when he wrote: "Terry Meyocks (the chief executive officer of the New York Racing Association) announces that if Bobby Frankel goes into the Breeders' Cup Classic winless on the day, half of Governor George Pataki's and Mayor Rudolph Giuliani's security force will be switched over to Frankel in case Aptitude gets beat." On Thursday, Indian Charlie wrote: "Do you know why Bobby Frankel is 0-for-36 in the Breeders' Cup? Because Juddmonte is 0-for-29 in the Breeders' Cup! If Bobby Frankel wants to win any Breeders' Cup races, he better ditch that bad outfit." On Friday, Indian Charlie wrote: "Bobby Frankel called a news conference to announce he would pledge 10% of all his winnings from Breeders' Cup Day to the National Thoroughbred Racing Association's New York Hero Fund or he would just give that organization a check for $1,000 up front. Officials from the New York Hero's Fund carefully looked over all the past performances of all Cup starters and informed Mr. Frankel that if it were all the same to him they would just go ahead and take the grand up front."

When he offered his selections for race day, the honest Indian did not pick any of Frankel's horses to win.

*New York Post* horse racing writer Ed Fountaine, in his race-day preview, posed the question: will trainer Bobby Frankel be a dud or a stud? Fountaine noted Frankel had been having an MVP season with 13 Grade One victories "and he comes to bat swinging some heavy lumber." He added Frankel had a shot to surpass Lukas' 1988 record of three winners on a single Breeders' card, but noted Frankel's winless streak. Fountaine wondered if it would have special meaning for Frankel to snap his winless streak in his hometown, a question that undoubtedly had been asked leading up to race day. But Frankel responded: "I'd like to be a romantic and tell you all that stuff about New York, but just winning a race would be good enough. I'd take a Breeders' Cup win anywhere."

The Distaff commenced the first of the eight Breeders' races and Frankel had the post-time favorite with Juddmonte's Flute. Flute had four victories and two seconds on the season. She had placed second in the Grade One Beldame Stakes at Belmont three weeks before, her first start since winning the Group One Alabama Stakes at Saratoga some seven weeks before. Her principal opposition appeared to be Exogenous, who had bested her by 1¼ lengths in the Beldame following a victory a month before in the Group One Gazelle Handicap Stakes at Belmont. She had placed second before that to Flute in the Alabama.

Exogenous, a lovely gray filly, spooked coming on to the track and flipped, hitting her head on the ground and catching a leg in a railing. The horrific scene started off the Breeders' on a bad note and it took the work of veteran horsemen to load the stunned filly into an ambulance and hopefully save her life (although tragically she had to be humanely destroyed six days later). Flute, who had already been on the racetrack, expended needless energy because of the added time needed to address the Exogenous situation. With Exogenous scratched, Flute became the overwhelming favorite in the field of 11 at 13-10 odds. Flute had a troubled trip early in the race but advanced up to fourth, a length and a bit behind pacesetter Pompeii after three-quarters of a mile. As jockey Jerry Bailey angled out Flute for running room leaving the turn for home, Flute failed to fire down the lane, finishing seventh by 7¼ lengths.

Unbridled Elaine, touted by Indian Charlie, won by a head over Spain. Unbridled Elaine went off at more than 12-1 and combined with Spain for an exacta payoff of $133.50. Indian Charlie picked the winner and the exacta. Not that that mattered to Frankel. He had lost another race and didn't like the ride of jockey Jerry Bailey.

"I don't want to take anything away from Jerry, but I think the track played with his mind a little bit," he said after the race. "I'm not saying she would have won, but she might done more. He was fighting her and she was trying to go."

A year later, Frankel would point to the Exogenous mishap as a contributing factor for Flute's failure. "People don't realize this—and I'm not making excuses—but she was on the racetrack for 10 minutes and everybody else's (horse in the race) is in the paddock without a rider and I've got my filly on the track and she got all nervous and everything and she didn't run her race," Frankel said.

Next on the Frankel list came Edmund Gann's You in the Juvenile Fillies. A romping winner of the Grade One Frizette Stakes three weeks before at Belmont after winning the Grade Two Adirondack Stakes at Saratoga on the same day Flute won the Alabama, You was rated the 8-5 morning-line favorite. She went postward under jockey Edgar Prado at just under even money, the lowest-priced horse of the six Frankel would send out on the card. Prado placed You in midpack in the field of nine for the opening three quarters, less than two lengths off the lead. Angled out for running room heading into the stretch, You offered no response when roused and finished fourth by 5½ lengths to 11-1 outsider Tempera.

Squirtle Squirt followed two races later in the Sprint, but Frankel's spirits had been lessened by the results of Flute and You. As he put the saddle on Squirtle Squirt the Hall of Fame trainer wondered if fate would deal him another disappointment. When he assessed his horse's chances at the beginning of the day, Frankel did not fancy Squirtle Squirt with the same enthusiasm as the likes of Flute, You or Aptitude, who would be running in the Classic. He considered Squirtle Squirt his fourth-best shot.

Owner David Lanzman, a 44-year-old Los Angeles mortgage broker, paid a mere $25,000 for the colt at a two-year-old in-training sale, unaware he had a floating chip in his right knee. The colt had been sold with the name Marque the Code, a combination of his sire Marquetry and his dam Lost the Code. Lanzman wanted to rename the colt using his 10-year-old son Blair's favorite Pokemon character Squirtle. That name had already been registered with the Jockey Club, so Lanzman submitted Squirtle Squirtle, but the last two letters in the second name failed to make it through on the fax. When notified by the Jockey Club that no one else had used the name Squirtle Squirt, Lanzman opted to keep it.

Lanzman turned the colt over to trainer Joe Garcia Jr., and the two had great success. Squirtle Squirt won five of eight races and almost $250,000 and appeared headed for the Breeders' Cup Juvenile, but surgery on both knees forced him to the sidelines in October. At that point Lanzman made the decision to turn over his horses to separate trainers, specifically Squirtle Squirt to Frankel because he had trained the colt's sire, Marquetry. Lanzman's girlfriend knew somebody who worked for Frankel, so a connection was made, and Lanzman brought along all the reports about the surgery.

"He knew how good the horse was before he ever got him and I figured this horse is going to be travelling all over the country and I wanted to give him to somebody who knew what he was doing and had people at those places," Lanzman said.

While there had been thoughts of possibly making it to the Kentucky Derby the following May, the horse took longer to recover from the surgery and didn't make it to the races until the day before Derby. He ran and won in a six-furlong allowance race at Hollywood Park and that convinced Frankel that the colt's best chances to succeed would come in sprints. The Breeders' Cup became the long-range goal.

Squirtle Squirt ran seven furlongs in his next start, but came up short, finishing second by three-quarters of a length after leading for most of the way and fighting back gamely in defeat. A dearth of sprints for three-year-olds made it difficult to find races for the colt in his own age group and ideal distance of six furlongs. His third race off the layoff came against horses aged three and up and Squirtle Squirt ran solidly again, finishing a close second in a seven-furlong race. Some seven weeks later, he ran another seven-furlong race, this time in his own age group, and prevailed easily in the Grade One King's Bishop Stakes at Saratoga. A month later the colt ran in the Grade One Vosburgh Stakes at Belmont, going postward as the 3-4 favorite. He ran second by a half-length in the seven-furlong test against older horses but once again showed his gameness in defeat. Now it was on to the Breeders', and Lanzman liked his chances and had absolutely no fear of Frankel's drought.

"That was one of the reasons I picked him," he said. "I knew he was one of the greatest trainers of all time. It was so ludicrous that a guy that was great as he was as a trainer hadn't won a Breeders' Cup. I figured the odds were he'd have to break it."

The field of 14 had been so competitive that the lowest-priced horse was Kona

Gold, the defending champion, at 7-2 odds, while Squirtle Squirt went postward at more than 9-1. Even though the colt showed a fondness for rushing to the front after breaking from the gate, Frankel and jockey Jerry Bailey, who was aboard for the second consecutive time, hoped Squirtle Squirt would relax and settle in behind the frontrunners. And that's exactly the way it unfolded. Speedy filly Xtra Heat took control early and zipped a half mile in 44 3/5 seconds. That had been the kind of torrid pace Squirtle Squirt had clicked off in his previous races, but this time he had to come from behind in a much bigger field with better competition. Bailey was able to split horses in midstretch with his mount, who dug in strongly and went on to win by a half-length over Xtra Heat.

Finally, the streak had ended for Frankel at 39, while it only took Lanzman one shot. Moreover, Lanzman had beaten some of the biggest owners in the world in that race and, overall, he had posted a win while many top outfits would be shut out on the card.

"It's Cinderella, man," Lanzman said in retrospect.

Lanzman watched the race from the grandstand, while Frankel viewed the race on television in the racing secretary's office. It's a superstitious habit Frankel had developed a long time before with his horses and rarely veered from it. He had watched the Vosburgh in a separate box in the grandstand and after losing vowed never to do it again.

After the Sprint, Lanzman and Frankel encountered one another moving in different directions. Lanzman attempted to shake Frankel's hand, but the trainer pushed it aside and hugged him. Lanzman did not say a word about the end of the streak but sensed Frankel's relief.

"There has to be," Lanzman said. "He never said anything, but for him to hug somebody first of all (that said a lot). I can't imagine what it would be like to have accomplished almost everything and be as good at something as he has and all anybody would talk about was how many of his horses got beat (in the Breeders' Cup)."

Frankel's enthusiasm had been tempered by the losses early in the card with Flute and You. He also had been thinking about the races ahead, including running Starine, whom he owned and supplemented for 9% of the $1 million Filly & Mare Turf race immediately after the Sprint. Purchased privately by Frankel for $150,000 earlier in the year after an undistinguished career in France, Starine developed into a stakes-caliber runner in the U.S., particularly on giving ground. She rattled off two consecutive victories at Saratoga, including a smashing 5¼-length tally in the Grade Two Diana Handicap, winning $300,000. She followed that up with a third-place finish in the Grade One $750,000 Flower Bowl Handicap at Belmont. Both races were run on turf listed as good, so Frankel decided to pony up the $90,000 supplemental fee, although the fact that the turf was firm didn't help Starine's cause. She showed some early run but faded to finish a well-beaten 10th in the field of 12. She clearly did not favor the footing, over which French invader Banks Hill, bred and owned by Juddmonte, skipped along sensationally to win by 5½ lengths in her first try beyond a mile. But Banks Hill would figure prominently in the future for Frankel.

Timboroa followed the Frankel procession two races later in the Turf. Supplemented by Gann for 9% of the $2 million purse after winning the Grade One Turf Classic Invitational in his last start and the Grade II Del Mar Invitational Handicap before that, Timboroa drew some serious consideration, the 5-1 second choice in the morning line behind 8-5 favorite Fantastic Light. Timboroa ran credibly, assuming the lead after half a mile and enjoying a two-length cushion with a quarter mile to go. Fantastic Light, the 7-5 post-time favorite who finished fifth the year before but had come back strongly the following season in a global campaign, charged to the front nearing the final furlong and went on to win by three-quarters of a length. Timboroa placed third by 6½ lengths.

All that was left now for Frankel was the $4 million Classic and his final representative, Aptitude. He had won by 10 widening lengths in his previous race, the Grade One Jockey Club Gold Cup, and by 4¼ lengths before that in the Grade Two Saratoga Breeders' Cup Handicap. The dark bay son of 1992 Classic winner A.P. Indy had a record of a win and a second in two lifetime races over the Belmont strip. The International Ratings, a theoretical weight handicap comprised by the North American Racing Committee and representatives of the International Classification Committee, had Aptitude on top by a clear margin in his division. The morning line had him favored at 2-1, but by post time the odds were closer to 5-2. Aptitude had shown an ability to be placed in midpack and kick in strongly in the run through the stretch. After a quarter of a mile he lay seventh by only four lengths, albeit after running extremely wide for most of the trip. At the point where he would normally unleash his kick, Aptitude failed to fire, finishing eighth by 9½ lengths. He became nothing more than a postscript mention in one of the greatest finishes in Breeders' Cup history as reigning champion Tiznow engaged in an epic battle with Prix de l'Arc de Triomphe winner Sakhee and prevailed by a nose.

The end result for Frankel: one win, one third and three beaten favorites who finished out of the money. And the following morning when the winners convened at a breakfast to rehash the races, he still harbored the bitterness of defeat more than the joy of winning.

"I wasn't happy because the two fillies got beat and I felt terrible about it," he said. "There was relief but I couldn't really enjoy the Squirtle Squirt win as much as I should have. I never got the enjoyment of winning, but I was glad (the losing streak) was over with."

Squirtle Squirt won the Eclipse Award as the championship sprinter in 2001 and Frankel won another Eclipse as the top trainer. He finished as the second-leading money-winning trainer with a personal best of $14,727,446 and won 101 of 392 starts. He won 49 stakes, 36 of them graded and half of those Grade Ones.

Frankel carried over his torrid season from 2001 into 2002. In August at Arlington Park, the site of the Breeders' Cup two months later, Frankel won the Arlington Million and Secretariat Stakes, both Grade Ones.

In late September, Lanzman received an offer from a Japanese interest seeking to buy Squirtle Squirt and offering an "outrageous" seven-figure sum. Frankel advised Lanzman to sell and Lanzman agreed, but he wanted to run in the Breeders' Cup again, this time with his new partner, who would be given 100% of the race earnings. The buyer wanted no part of that deal, seeking the colt purely as a stallion and concerned about diminishing his value with an off performance. So Lanzman sold the colt.

While Frankel lost one Breeders' Cup winner, he picked up another. Banks Hill was sent to Frankel from France, where she had been trained by Andre Fabre for Juddmonte. Banks Hill's final race in Europe featured a runner-up finish to European superhorse Rock of Gibraltar in the Group One Prix Du Moulin De Longchamp. A plan to run in New York went awry because the turf came up soft, so the four-year-old filly was sent to California to run in the Grade One Yellow Ribbon Stakes. Banks Hill ran third as the even-money favorite but lacked running room for a portion of the race.

Frankel came to the 2002 Breeders' Cup with his winless streak now a distant memory. But trainer D. Wayne Lukas, the top-winning trainer in Breeders' Cup history, opined a few days before the races that Frankel needed that win from the previous year in the world-championship showdown.

"He's done so well and he's an excellent horseman and it was mindboggling to me that he wouldn't get one of these," Lukas said. "I think he probably made some adjustments and so forth. It's amazing that he could run 42 of them and only win one. Actually he won with a horse he least expected. I don't know if that's the olive-out-of-the-jar theory, that once you get the first one, the next ones come easy. It will be interesting to see how he does the next few years."

Besides wanting to win at the Breeders' Cup, Frankel also had another goal: to collect as much as possible with his horses in his pursuit of Lukas' 1988 record of $17,842,358. With a win or two, notably in the $4 million Classic, Frankel had a shot and would still have almost five weeks remaining. He had been leading the nation in money won by trainers with more than $13.9 million. His Cup contingent included Beat Hollow and Aldebaran in the Mile; Banks Hill and Starine in the Filly & Mare Turf; Denon in the Turf; and Milwaukee Brew and Medaglia d'Oro in the Classic. Overall, he appeared to have almost as good a shot as the year before, the only distinction being that he didn't have as many perceived favorites. Medaglia d'Oro, who had run in all three legs of the Triple Crown and finished second by a half-length in the Belmont Stakes in his best result, had been pointed to the Classic after winning the Grade One Travers Stakes two months before. He had preceded that win with a 13¾-length win in the Grade Two Jim Dandy Stakes three weeks before. He was installed as the 7-2 second choice in the morning line behind the 3-1 odds of War Emblem, winner of the Kentucky Derby, Preakness Stakes and Haskell Invitational. In Frankel's opinion, his horse deserved to be the favorite in the wagering and he'd be proven right by the bettors. Frankel had a second runner in the Classic, Milwaukee Brew, winner of the Grade One Santa Anita Handicap and Grade Two Californian Stakes in the spring. He hadn't done much in the interim to command anything more than 15-1 odds in the morning line. Denon, rated at 5-1 for the Turf, had posted a win in the Grade One Turf Classic Invitational in his last race and had two wins and two close seconds in his four races leading up to the Breeders'. Banks Hill was listed as the 3-1 second choice in the Filly & Mare Turf behind Golden Apples, who beat her in the Yellow

Ribbon Stakes and had won the Beverly D. Stakes at Arlington in August. Starine, who had run only three times on the season and had two seconds, was deemed a 12-1 shot. Frankel felt she might benefit from the turf course that had been softened up by days of rain leading up to the race. In the Mile, Frankel had Beat Hollow, winner of the Arlington Million and third in the Grade Two Shadwell Keeneland Turf Mile Stakes earlier in the month, and Aldebaran, who had placed second in the Grade One Vosburgh Stakes and Grade One Forego Handicap in his last two races. Beat Hollow was listed at 6-1 and Aldebaran at 15-1.

Frankel had mixed emotions running his own horse Starine against one of his client's, in this case his biggest, but believed Starine belonged.

"I know it would be better professionally to win with Banks Hill because it's them and, listen, I don't need the money," Frankel said a few days before the race. "I'd like my filly to run good. If Banks Hill beats me and I was second I'd be over the moon."

His comments would be stunningly prophetic. Beat Hollow placed sixth by five lengths in the Mile, while Aldebaran ran 11th by 12 lengths in the field of 14 but experienced severe traffic problems.

Two races later in the Filly & Mare Turf, Frankel's pre-race comments came true. Starine took kindly to the give in the ground and posted a 1½-length victory at 13-1 odds. Banks Hill placed second on a surface she clearly did not relish but displayed her class in the process. Frankel accepted the win with some resignation having beaten Juddmonte's runner, but managed a laugh after addressing the media when told he was the recipient of leather bags given to the winning trainer and owner. He joked that he could use them for his laundry.

Teddy Beckett, the European racing manager for Juddmonte, said there was little reason for Frankel to feel badly about winning.

"For one, Starine had been with Bobby for quite a long time and she was always being aimed at that race," Beckett said. "It wasn't as if Banks Hill was with Bobby for the whole year. She'd been with Bobby only three weeks. From that point of view, she might have run in Fabre's name anyway. It was just that Bobby had her. What else could Bobby have done? I think Banks Hill proved she liked a firm turf and the going at Chicago was perfectly good going, but she had always shown her best form on good, fast ground. But it's the same for everybody. I hate sort of making excuses for horses because on the whole it's the humans who make mistakes rather than the horses. It was still an excellent run, but it wasn't quite the explosive quality of the previous year."

Two races later, Denon ran fifth in the Turf, almost six lengths in arrears of 9-10 favorite High Chaparral, who kicked into another gear in the stretch when cleared for running room. Then came the Classic and the potential for Frankel to close out the day with another winner. Medaglia d'Oro went postward as the favorite at 27-10 odds, followed by War Emblem at 4-1. Milwaukee Brew drew considerably less support at more than 24-1 odds. Jockey Jerry Bailey had Medaglia d'Oro track the early pace while positioned about four wide on the backstretch. War Emblem, who many people figured could win only if he inherited a quick lead, was outgunned to the front by E. Dubai. Bailey crept closer to the lead and seized it with a quarter of mile to the wire, but Volponi, a 43-1 long shot, scooted through on the inside and motored down the lane to win by 6½ lengths over Medaglia d'Oro. Surprisingly, Milwaukee Brew ran third, only a neck back of his stablemate.

Volponi, the longest-priced horse in the field of 12, pulled off the stunning upset of the day. It was not entirely like Arcangues' win in the 1993 Classic, which Frankel lost with Bertrando in deep stretch, but it was yet another interesting result. In this case he simply felt Medaglia d'Oro ran on a racing strip he didn't appreciate.

"He doesn't like a drying-out racetrack," Frankel said. "His two worst races were on a drying-out racetrack. I didn't think he liked it, but he was still leading turning for home. I think it was a thing of him not really caring for the track that much and the winner really liking it."

Much like the year before, the racing gods had been both cruel and kind to Frankel. Overall his horses posted more than $2.3 million on the card, giving him more than $16.2 million on the season. With a little luck, he might break Lukas' record. He thought Starine had a shot to win the $500,000 Matriarch Stakes at Hollywood Park a month later and be voted the female champion turf winner at season's end, but he decided to offer her up for sale two weeks after the Breeders' in the Keeneland November Breeding Stock sale. He originally put her in the sale, then took her out, but her value had been at its peak off her win and he decided he'd be taking a risk waiting to run in the Matriarch. He put a reserve on her of $990,000 and when the gavel came down she fetched a bid of $1 million from Klaus Jacobs' Newsells Park Stud in England. Frankel had paid $150,000 for her and she earned 10 times that amount, winning four of 11 starts in a year and a half. Add in the $1 million sale price and Frankel turned over a solid profit on his investment. It may have been the greatest score of his career.

By season's end, Frankel's horses had won $17,748,340, missing Lukas' mark by only $94,018, but he had finished with another personal best. He won 117 of 478 starts and posted 43 victories in graded stakes, 13 of them Grade Ones, four of which had purses of $1 million. And he received the Eclipse Award for the third consecutive year.

As he looked ahead to the future, Frankel expected to be back in the Breeders' Cup in 2003, maybe even with a three-year-old called Empire Maker.

"It's going to win the Derby," he told me confidently in the days leading up to the 2002 Breeders.

The word had been out on the well-bred colt bred and owned by Juddmonte for some time. When Frankel worked the colt once with Medaglia d'Oro and another time with Milwaukee Brew and the young colt held his own with the older, established runners, it became apparent Empire Maker had the racing talent to match his exquisite breeding. Rather than rush his campaign to have him ready for the Breeders' Cup, Frankel and Juddmonte decided on taking a patient and pragmatic approach.

"This is a natural mile and a quarter horse and I didn't want to rush him," he said. "He's such a good horse. He's by far the best two-year-old I've ever trained. The farm manager at Juddmonte said a year and a half ago, 'I've got your Derby horse, 2003.' This was when he was a weanling. He told me this was the one, so we've been anticipating. You hate to get too high on a horse, things happen, but I've been in the business a long time and I want one of those superstars—Secretariat, Seattle Slew, Affirmed, Spectacular Bid, they don't come around that often. I'm talking about those real elite ones. I'm hoping, I'm dreaming, that he's the one. So far people haven't been wrong about him from the day he was born to the day I got him to his first race. You learn over the years nothing's a cinch and you can't get too high or too excited about these horses because they disappoint you. There's always time to talk about them after they win."

Empire Maker made it to the 2003 Derby, after romping by 9¾ lengths in the Florida Derby, then following up his facile victory with a three-quarter-length victory in the Wood Memorial. Empire Maker beat an unheralded, modestly bred gelding called Funny Cide in the Wood, although little was thought of the second-place finisher at the time. Besides Empire Maker, Frankel brought a decent backup for the Run for the Roses in Edmund Gann's Peace Rules, who had developed into a pleasant surprise on the Triple Crown trail, winning the Blue Grass Stakes at Keeneland. Empire Maker developed a bruised front foot heading into the Derby, but Frankel still thought his colt would win and the public liked his chances, sending the multiple winner postward as the 5-2 favorite. Frankel won three stakes races on the Derby undercard, continuing a string of successes in what was shaping up to be his best-ever year. But Frankel's dream of winning his first Derby came up short. Funny Cide, a 12-1 long shot ridden by Jose Santos, won the race, 1¾ lengths in front of Empire Maker. Peace Rules finished a head behind of his stablemate in third. Winning trainer Barclay Tagg, a 65-year-old veteran, won the Derby with his first starter. Santos, who scored the stunning upset in the 2002 Breeders' Cup Classic with 43-1 outsider Volponi, won the Derby for the first time in six tries.

For Frankel, the Derby would have to wait at least one more year, along with obligatory questions about being jinxed in the race he hadn't won in his illustrious career—kind of like the questions he annually had to face in the Breeders' Cup until Squirtle Squirt won the Sprint in 2001.

Frankel passed on the Preakness Stakes with Empire Maker to point him to the Belmont Stakes five weeks later, but saddled Peace Rules in the second leg. Peace Rules was no match for Funny Cide, who romped by 9¾ lengths. With Funny Cide fever sweeping the racing industry and a Triple Crown sweep dancing in people's heads, Frankel came to the Belmont to play the role of the spoiler. The native New Yorker liked his chances with Empire Maker, whom he felt may have been undertrained going into the Derby. Similar to Derby day, Frankel had success on the undercard, but this time it proved to be an all-around good day. Empire Maker avenged his Derby loss, winning the Belmont by three-quarters of a length over Ten Most Wanted, who had flopped in the Derby but developed a back problem, while Funny Cide finished third by five lengths.

Frankel had finally won the Belmont after placing second in two of the last three editions. It was his first win in a Triple Crown race in his hallowed career—a career that has included some Breeders' Cup memories he'd just as soon forget.

# ·8·

# Cool Hand Lukas

## D. Wayne Lukas

*W*hen word filtered out about the Breeders' Cup, a California-based trainer named D. Wayne Lukas grinned with anticipation. Lukas approached racing like a baseball player standing at the plate thinking of the fences instead of first base. Lukas viewed everything with greatness in mind, and in his opinion the Breeders' Cup had great possibilities. He could swing for the fences in seven different races on one card. Not even Babe Ruth had that many cuts in one game. Sitting down with a couple of assistants, including his son Jeff, Lukas emphasized the importance of the Breeders' Cup. "Let's point for it," he said, "let's look at it like the Triple Crown or the (Kentucky) Derby and make it something big." And he truly has.

A onetime high school and university teacher and basketball coach in his native Wisconsin, Lukas spent his summers training horses and racing at a small track in South Dakota. Lukas abandoned academia in 1972 at the age of 37 in favor of a full-time training career. He moved to California and quickly dominated the quarter horse circuit, where his horses topped every division with average earnings of $1 million each year. Once he conquered the quarter horse circuit, Lukas set his sights on the thoroughbred world. In 1978, he switched breeds and two years later won his first Triple Crown race with Codex in the Preakness Stakes at Pimlico. In 1982, Lukas trained his first national champion, the two-year-old filly Landaluce, who died before her three-year old season. A year later, he conditioned another two-year-old filly champion, Althea, and Lukas continued to celebrate at least one championship award each year for the remainder of the decade.

Lukas operated various divisions across the country with assistants, whom he directed by phone or with routine visits, with the outfit eventually gaining recognition as "Team Lukas." In New York, Jeff personally guided Winning Colors' career, which included the first Kentucky Derby victory for his father in 1988. Lukas aggressively campaigned his horses, searching for spots and shipping with regularity, which prompted the expression "D. Wayne Off The Plane."

"He was the first trainer to approach the business on a truly national scope," *Washington Post* racing writer and noted handicapper Andy Beyer said in an interview prior to the 1995 Preakness Stakes. "Even the good trainers—Charlie Whittingham, Woody Stephens—operated in a particular area. Sure, they shipped here and there for a race, but here's a guy who saw the country as his chess board. He finds opportunities and moves horses into them like nobody else has."

Image is everything to Lukas. Neatly groomed lawns surrounded by exquisite floral arrangements that could easily grace the cover of a horticulture magazine adorn his barn area. Green and white signs in bold Gothic lettering read "D. Wayne Lukas Racing Stables." Inside, the barns look equally immaculate as grooms take painstaking care to rake the dirt in a neat herringbone pattern. Everything has to be spotless and perfect. Lukas likes to tell a story about how he once rebuked one of his assistants because the stable pony was not perfectly turned out. And, of course, there are the trademark white bridles that easily distinguish his horses from the pack.

Lukas added a certain style to the game not only with his stable look, but with his personal wardrobe, wearing designer suits and tinted glasses—even on overcast days. And in the mornings for regular training hours, he wears custom-made monogrammed sweaters.

Even his pearly white teeth, which look like Chiclets stacked perfectly in rows, are part of his image. It has long been speculated the teeth are as manufactured as his suits, but even if the rumor is untrue the myth is more exciting. "Mr. Toothpaste I call him," said Janet Slade, a writer with the French-based racing newspaper *Paris-Turf*. "I don't know if they're false or not, but my goodness he's got an awful lot of teeth; shiny white teeth."

Lukas likes to talk, making himself available to the media to chat about his horses, the sport or just about any subject. A reporter once jokingly said if you asked Lukas about nuclear disarmament, he'd probably have an answer.

"D. Wayne Lukas (is) the best salesman in racing and of racing," *Daily Racing Form* executive columnist Joe Hirsch wrote in a column the week after the 1995 Breeders' Cup. "Lukas has projected a positive outlook through his career and has brought giants into the sport. . . . His contributions toward racing's health and success are often overlooked."

Trainer and racing analyst John Veitch offered a more interesting description of Lukas during NBC's telecast of the 1995 Breeders' Cup. "He talks with the fire of a Baptist preacher and is as mesmerizing as P. T. Barnum, and when you walk away you wonder if you stepped in something," he said.

Lukas' success in the '80s—and his entry into the Breeders' Cup—came in concert with the emergence of his main client, Gene Klein, as the dominant owner of the decade. In the '60s, Klein bought the San Diego Chargers of the National Football League and sold out in 1984 for some $50 million after a much-publicized heart attack and a growing appreciation for owning horses, spawned by the interest of his wife Joyce. Klein became a horse owner in 1982, choosing the Chargers' colors as his silks: gold and blue with a lightning bolt.

Klein and Lukas hooked up that year and they had a lot in common: they liked the action and they liked to win. By January of 1983, Lukas had saddled his first winner for Klein, a filly named Cassie's Prospect. Lukas, who has a sharp eye for young horses, used Klein's money to buy top yearlings for big bucks. Lukas also dipped into his own pockets to buy horses in partnership with other clients. With a stable full of the best horses money could buy, the Breeders' Cup became his showcase.

Lukas saddled Klein's Tank's Prospect in the first Breeders' Cup race ever run, the 1984 Juvenile. Chief's Crown, the 7-10 favorite in the field of 10, won by three-quarters of a length over Tank's Prospect, who went postward at 25-1 odds.

Lukas' two starters in the Juvenile Fillies—Fiesta Lady and Tiltalating, both owned by the Kleins—ran eighth and ninth, respectively. Life's Magic, partly owned by Klein, ran second to heavy favorite Princess Rooney in the Distaff while another Lukas runner, Lucky Lucky Lucky, ran sixth.

Overall, Lukas ran five horses in the inaugural Breeders' Cup (in later years he would saddle that many in one race alone) who collectively earned $450,000. Not bad for a start, but peanuts in comparison to what was to come.

"When you go into it, you can hope you're contentious, but if you don't have the livestock you're not going to be contentious," Lukas said. "Even though we pointed and put the emphasis on it, we just weren't probably strong enough. We came very close to beating Chief's Crown and it kind of stamped Tank's Prospect. The second year I think we had a little better feel for it, but much better livestock, too."

Lukas ran 10 runners in four races in the 1985 Breeders' Cup at Aqueduct and this time he had infinitely better results. Klein's Twilight Ridge and Family Style ran first and second, respectively, in the Juvenile Fillies. Klein's Life's Magic and Lady's Secret posted a one-two finish in the Distaff. Overall, the Lukas brigade collected $903,000. Family Style earned the Eclipse Award as the champion two-year-old filly, while Life's Magic received older female honors. Klein, who won 30 stakes that year and set a single-season earnings record at the time of $5,446,401, won the Eclipse as top owner. Lukas won the trainer Eclipse, boosted by a record 70 stakes victories.

In 1986, the Lukas-Klein juggernaut continued as they again won the top trainer and owner awards. Lukas started seven horses in the Cup at Santa Anita and they collected $1.195 million. Capote won the Juvenile en route to capturing two-year-old colt divisional honors and setting himself up as the early Derby favorite. Lady's Secret, known as the "Iron Lady" because of her rugged constitution and competitiveness, won the Distaff and later gave Lukas his first Horse of the Year title on the strength of 10 wins, eight of them Grade Ones, in 15 starts. Pine Tree Lane's second-place finish in the Sprint behind Smile represented Lukas' other top-three finish on the card.

Klein proudly displayed that Horse of the Year award, along with his other Breeders' Cup awards and trophies, on a massive mahogany desk in his office. The effect was as impressive as it was gaudy. Lukas said when you walked into the office it "hit you right between the eyes."

In the 1987 Breeders' Cup, Lukas sent out a total of 16 runners—including five of the 12 starters in the Juvenile Fillies—who combined for $1.566 million in purse earnings. Success Express won the Juvenile and Sacahuista the Distaff (and subsequently the Eclipse as top older filly or mare). Lukas' success came in a year in which the media's love affair with him soured. Capote had bombed in the Derby, eased in the stretch by Angel Cordero Jr. Lady's Secret, meanwhile, had numerous humbling outings and never even made it to the Cup. Some members of the media, including Beyer, who would become one of Lukas' biggest critics, attacked him for his handling of the mare. When a horse ran poorly, the critics said Lukas "Dwayned" another one.

At the annual post–Breeders' Cup breakfast, where the connections of the winning horses appear to answer questions, Lukas took his turn at the microphone. Yet a funny—and quite unexpected—thing happened that caught Lukas and everyone else in attendance off guard. An English journalist named John McCririck stood up and asked Lukas if he would criticize the "American hacks" when he won the Kentucky Derby "as he someday surely would." Lukas had no idea who McCririck was. Anyone who sees the London-based TV turf commentator once won't forget him. McCririck is an incredibly huge man with large sideburns and is fond of wearing a Sherlock Holmes detective-style hat and brightly colored suits. He talks rapidly and is quite opinionated, particularly on the subject of Lukas, whom he thinks American journalists have totally misread.

"I just looked at his record," McCririck said of his soliloquy in 1987. "You look around the Wayne Lukas barn and everything is spotless. You go to the other barns and they're a bit rough and shoddy. His are immaculate. The staff are immaculate, the horses look magnificent, the place is turned out to perfection and he gets champion trainer year in and year out and the American journalists accuse him of running his horses too hard and have smear campaigns against him.

"I was there when Winning Colors won, the only Kentucky Derby I've ever seen, and I was delighted. You recognize somebody who is a pathfinder, somebody who is knocking down the barriers. We've got them over in Britain, like Martin Pipe and in the old days Henry Cecil, who absolutely changed the way it was done. I've been a Lukas fan just looking at the man's record. Just seeing the horses."

Lukas eclipsed his 1985 single-season record for stakes wins by collecting 92 in 1987, leading to another Eclipse award. But the best was yet to come.

In 1988, Lukas enjoyed his greatest tour de force. He not only won the Derby for the first time—after years of sending out multiple entries and not even getting a sniff of the roses—with Winning Colors, but registered his best Breeders' Cup performance at the same track six months later. On a damp, dark day at Churchill Downs, Lukas lit up the Twin Spires by saddling 12 starters and posting three victories, three seconds and one third for purse earnings of $2,183,000. Lukas' horses made more money in a few hours that day than many top trainers made all year.

Team Lukas kicked off the day when Cordero rallied Peter Brant's Gulch from off the pace for a three-quarter length win in the Sprint. Cordero then completed a daily double for himself and Lukas by guiding Klein's Open Mind to victory in the Juvenile Fillies. What made the race so special was the fact that Lukas saddled the top three finishers—Darby Shuffle ran second and Lea Lucinda third. All three horses ran for different owners, but were coupled as an entry. Two other

Klein horses, Some Romance and One Of A Klein, also part of the Lukas entry, ran sixth and 11th, respectively, in the field of 12.

"I could see that happening again, although I think that's quite a feat," Lukas said. "It's one thing to enter five, it's another to run one, two, three. That is domination. I ran three horses in the Kentucky Derby (in 1995) and luckily we won it, but you could run three and not win it, too. I think the fact we came one, two, three is the significant thing there."

The Distaff came next on the Lukas agenda and it featured a battle between the Derby winner, Winning Colors, and the undefeated Personal Ensign—two splendid fillies who embodied the spirit of excellence. It ended with Personal Ensign, seemingly hopelessly beaten at the top of the stretch, courageously running down the front-running Winning Colors, who surrendered her lead only in the final jump while exerting every ounce of ability she could muster.

"That was the best race I've ever seen in horse racing because of the magnitude of the day and the fact one of them was going for a completely undefeated career," Lukas said. "I would say that was the best race I've ever been involved in a losing effort. That hurt. You wanted to bring the wire up a foot closer. You wanted to run it one more time. You wanted to make sure that in the replay that it did turn out that way. On the other hand, I could see the greatness of that race, too. I appreciated it. In the winner's circle after I'd gotten to Winning Colors and unsaddled her, I walked back in and I told the (Ogden) Phipps family who was standing there, 'When they bred these things 300 years ago this is what they had in mind.' I mean that was one of the hardest losses but one of the most appreciative efforts I had from a horse."

Lukas ran second with the 37-1 Steinlen in the Mile but returned to the winner's circle a race later when Is It True posted a victory in the Juvenile at 9-1. Lukas reversed the tough loss two races before in the Distaff by beating a Phipps-owned, Shug McGaughey–trained horse. Yet this was no ordinary horse. This was the great Easy Goer. New York's Easy Goer. The next Secretariat, according to the East Coast scribes. Easy Goer left the gate that day at odds of 3-10, one of the lowest prices in Breeders' Cup history. He clearly didn't handle the going on the Churchill Downs track (it would happen again the following May in the Derby) but it was a loss nonetheless.

"That to me was the biggest upset in the 20th century, that to me was maybe my best training job ever," Lukas said with nary a glance at hyperbole. "To put that thing in perspective, we had run in the Cowdin at Belmont and were beaten soundly (by Easy Goer). We came back in the Champagne and were beaten soundly and then went to the Breeders' Cup, again pointing our horse, thinking positively, getting set up so that we were going to look good on that day. I don't think there was one turf writer, one handicapper, one person in the grandstand that thought, in his heart, that Easy Goer could get beat. He was so dominant that year. I don't think in any of the handicapping sheets or any of the papers was any other horse even picked. I told Laffit Pincay in the paddock that 'Easy Goer has run by you twice but he won't run by you today.'"

The following year marked a pivotal time in Lukas' Breeders' Cup story and his career. After only seven years in the game, the 68-year-old Klein announced his departure. He planned to sell every horse he owned—yearlings, broodmares, racehorses and stallions—to travel and devote more time to his children and grandchildren. After three Eclipse Awards as top owner, one Horse of the Year award, seven Breeders' Cup victories, more than 400 stakes wins and purse earnings in excess of $26 million from over 2,000 runners, Klein planned to leave the sport he had single-handedly dominated in the '80s.

Klein officially made the declaration in June 1989, although it had been building for some two years.

"It was almost as though I woke up one day and I suddenly realized I had over 200 horses," he said the day before the 1989 Breeders' Cup. "It just got too big. I had to get a hold of it."

Standing outside Lukas' barn that day wearing jeans, a T-shirt and running shoes, Klein looked as comfortable in his decision as he did in his relaxed attire. He came, he saw, he conquered. And, now he planned to leave for good.

"I never live at the temple of regret," he said, yet allowed himself the opportunity to possibly return to the game. "That's me now, I can get bored. I'm totally confident with my decision. I never get back to anything I've sold. Whether that holds true for racing, I don't know. I'm leaving the door open."

Behind-the-scenes whispers surfaced of problems between Klein and Lukas. Klein denied them, calling Lukas his "guru."

"Wayne and I have spoken almost every day and we still do," Klein said. "I can tell you quite truthfully we have never had one argument. We have never had any cross words. We have had a wonderful relationship."

"We have a great relationship, we're close friends," Lukas insisted. "I will replace the clients, but I don't know if I will ever find another with a feel for the game."

Years later, Lukas said Klein did not leave for the reasons he had stated publicly. The decision had to do with his health.

"He said he didn't want to discuss his health, he didn't want his health to be the reason he was dispersing his stable," Lukas said. "Here you've got a guy that's dominated North American racing and all of a sudden he's dispersing overnight. He just wakes up and said, 'I'm outta here.' He asked me not to ever discuss it and I never did, but a lot of people said, 'Are they getting along? What's the reason behind this?' Gene just said he wanted to travel and spend time with his grandchildren. In reality, his health was bad.

"It was more deep-seated than that. He had other problems, too. I don't know which complicated what."

Klein had five horses in the 1989 Breeders' Cup and failed to come close. In fact, his first runner, On the Line, ran last in the Sprint and suffered what became a fatal leg injury after Sam Who wiped out half the field at the start of the race. Open Mind, who swept the Triple Crown for three-year-old fillies, finished third in the Distaff that saw Winning Colors, the Derby winner of a year before but badly off form at that point, run second-last. Wonders Delight, another Klein representative, trailed the field.

Lukas recorded his 10th Breeders' Cup victory when Steinlen won the Mile with a brazen ride by Jose Santos, who darted through a narrow opening along the hedge. Steinlen subsequently earned the Eclipse Award as the top male turf horse.

Two days after the Breeders' Cup, the Klein dispersal headlined the Keeneland Mixed Sales. Some agents estimated the stock would fetch $40 million. Lukas, who had financial interests in several horses in the dispersal, pegged it at between $32 and $34 million. "Anything over $30 million will be an excellent sale," Lukas said.

The late John Sikura said at the time: "I hope he gets all his money and a huge profit. If he does it will confirm one thing: You can get results and get out with your pants on."

The sale of 114 horses grossed $29,623,000. Overall, Klein broke even with his investments in horses. In a sport where the overwhelming majority of owners lose money but write it off against the vicarious thrills they receive from watching their horses race, Klein had done well. He did not lose his shirt and he had trophies and awards to attest to his domination.

Klein missed the game and the action and started feeling the itch again to return the following spring. He called Lukas in March of 1990 to talk about doing it all over again and prove it was not a fluke. They planned to meet March 12 at Remingtons, Klein's favorite restaurant in Del Mar. The meeting never happened. Klein had died the day before at age 69, ending a brilliant chapter in horse racing.

"He loved the fact that a used-car salesman from New York could rise to prominence financially and then go into a tradition-bound, hardboot-mentality sport and dominate it like he did," Lukas said. "And I don't think thoroughbred racing ever gave Gene Klein a lot of credit for that. He was very lucky, they said, and that was b.s. He stepped up. He had the balls of an elephant. He put up his money. He believed in what I wanted to do.

He gave me carte-blanche, but he used to always say, 'Big boy, just roll to 'em. Do what you want as long as you're making money, but if you start losing money I'll jerk the rug out from underneath you.' He loved the competition. He loved to take on those people and that didn't always set good with a lot of people in thoroughbred racing. That run may never be equaled. You can take these old, traditional families—the Whitneys, the Phippses, the Combses—I don't care who you take and put all the records up there and you're going to say that guy right there in San Diego had the best run of everyone. I don't think anyone ever had a six-year run like Gene Klein. I know they didn't. Not even close."

In the '90s, Lukas found several clients to replace Klein, headed by W. T. (Bill) Young, a wealthy Kentuckian who made his fortune manufacturing peanut butter, then branched out into the warehouse and trucking industry. Young's involvement in horse racing began in the '70s, but it grew significantly in the mid-'80s with the development of Overbrook Farm, which acquired top broodmares, some of whom had been racehorses trained by Lukas originally, and grew into one of the top breeding operations in the country.

Young ran his first Breeders' Cup horse in 1985, when Storm Cat, trained by Jonathan Sheppard, was beaten by a nose in the Juvenile. Two years later, he had his next Breeders' Cup starter in Pine Tree Lane, who ran 10th in the Sprint, saddled by Lukas. In 1989, he had a third starter, Grand Canyon, whom he owned with Lukas, and who finished second in the Juvenile. Grand Canyon won the Hollywood Futurity in his next start after the Breeders' Cup with the fastest mile ever for a two-year-old (1:33), but tragically died a month later.

Lukas saddled only six horses, three of them for Young, in the 1990 Breeders' Cup. His best finish, a fourth, came with Steinlen in the Mile. Overall, his runners had total earnings of $120,000. For a guy like Lukas, whose horses had collected almost 20 times that much only two years earlier on Breeders' Cup Day, it was a bad day at the races.

Overall, though, it was a good year. He still led the nation in purse earnings (more than $16 million) and conditioned his second Horse of the Year, Criminal Type, for the legendary Calumet Farms, which collapsed the next year in a maelstrom of financial mismanagement. Lukas felt the financial pain of the Calumet tumble, personally losing more than $3 million.

In 1991, Lukas returned to Churchill Downs, the scene of his greatest Breeders' Cup achievement, but the familiar surroundings did little to help what was turning into a slump. Farma Way, who finished the year on top in the inaugural American Championship Racing Series and earned a $750,000 bonus, injured an ankle five days before the Classic.

Lukas entered eight horses—ironically none of them in the Juvenile Fillies, in which he had run five three years before and had had the top three finishers—but his chances did not look good.

"I don't feel any pressure to win," he said two days before the Cup. "I think we're going to win more (money) than anybody else this year. I'd be disappointed as hell (getting shut out), but I could live with it because of the quality of the horses."

Lukas' horses collectively earned $740,000. Twilight Agenda ran second in the Classic to the front-running Black Tie Affair and received $600,000 for his efforts.

One of the horses Lukas saddled that year was Media Plan, who ran fifth in the Sprint for the Oaktown Stable, the nom de course of rapper MC Hammer—Stanley Burrell—and his brothers. The Burrells hired Lukas to train some of their horses, including the filly Lite Light, who campaigned brilliantly all year for trainer Jerry Hollendorfer but who had not made it to the Breeders' Cup. Many people attributed it to a questionable decision by the Burrells to run Lite Light against male horses in the Super Derby in Louisiana. She never was the same after wilting in the heat of the day and the heat of battle.

The Burrells did not last long in the sport, but made their presence felt. Hammer made outrageous bets with Carl Icahn, whose horse, Meadow Star, engaged in classic battles with Lite Light, and the rapper dispensed with his shirt in the Belmont clubhouse, much to the disgust of the New York racing establishment. In 1992 at the Preakness Stakes in Baltimore, one of Hammer's brothers said racism was a reason the family's horses drew poor post positions. In actuality, it just came down to luck of the draw—or in their case, bad luck. Amazingly, the Burrells received the Big Sport of Turfdom award for their contributions to the game, but they lasted as long in racing as Hammer did on the rap scene.

"The Hammers of the world usually burn their flame pretty bright and then it flickers quick," Lukas said. "Gene Klein didn't do that. Gene jumped up and had a bright flame but he held it there for six years without any drop in quality or production. I never thought that Hammer had his heart in it. He had too many other things going on. His family was more interested in racing than Hammer himself was. Hammer was a very small part of our program. We only trained a few horses for him, Lite Light and Media Plan and Dance Floor. It was a very, very select, small group. Hammer never made much impact on our program. I will say this: the little time he jumped in and wanted to play, we were successful. Dance Floor was successful. Lite Light obviously was very successful, but you have to go to guys like Bill Young and Bob Lewis in order to sustain any kind of program."

In 1992, Lukas returned to Gulfstream Park, where three years earlier he and Klein had had their last hurrah. But this time it was more a whimper than a bang. Lukas' Breeders' Cup shutout continued for a third year. If anything, this may have been the low point for Cool Hand Lukas, who saddled four starters and netted only $20,000 from Mountain Cat's fifth-place finish in the Juvenile. Twilight Agenda fell off form from the year before and ran ninth in the Classic.

The bright note was Mountain Cat, who rebounded to win a race in Kentucky, which earned him a $1 million bonus for sweeping the four major juvenile races in that state. The bonus made him the all-time leading money-winning juvenile, with more than $1.4 million in the bank.

In 1993, Lukas experienced a year of hell, both in his professional and his personal life. In the Preakness Stakes, Union City broke a leg and had to be destroyed. The critics came out in full force, launching the most vicious attacks ever on Lukas. Some trainers even criticized him, claiming he ran an unsound horse who had missed a day of training during the week.

Lukas said the horse had been physically sound. Privately, though, he was emotionally crushed and required the support of many of his clients, associates and friends to help him through the rough period.

Major fires in the Los Angeles area literally put a cloud over the proceedings in the week leading up to the 1993 Breeders' Cup at Santa Anita, and an inflammatory article in *Sports Illustrated* created an inferno all its own. The controversial piece, penned by the award-winning Bill Nack who had reported on racing for some 30 years, documented the breakdown of horses. The article incensed Lukas, who believed the piece had been timed to coincide with the Breeders' Cup, which had been besieged by a series of breakdowns or mishaps—particularly in the Sprint—dating back to 1989.

"Their article wasn't just coincidental and maybe they've served a purpose as self-serving as it is, but I think the sport's bigger than anything and it's certainly bigger than Bill Nack," spat Lukas.

His Breeders' Cup dry spell, meanwhile, continued. He started only two horses—Stellar Cat who ran fifth in the Juvenile Fillies and collected $20,000, and Tabasco Cat, who ran third in the Juvenile and netted $120,000.

Lukas' stable had fallen from first overall to ninth in purse earnings, the first time since 1983 he did not claim the title. It appeared Lukas' domination had finally ended, but that would be secondary compared to what lay ahead as he was about to experience the lowest point of his life. Tabasco Cat, a high-strung son of Storm Cat, ran over Jeff Lukas the morning of December 15 in the stable area at Santa Anita. Jeff's head smacked the hard-packed dirt as he fell to the ground. He suffered massive injuries and lapsed into a coma. He nearly died from intracranial swelling and pneumonia. The elder Lukas kept a daily vigil at his son's bedside and tended to the horses at the same time. Miraculously, Jeff recovered, and Tabasco Cat began maturing into a professional racehorse under Lukas' personal tutelage. He demanded that no one in the barn make the horse a scapegoat for what had happened to his son.

After running sixth in the Kentucky Derby, in which he sat down in his stall in the starting gate after some rough handling by the assistant starters, Tabasco Cat put it all together two weeks later in the Preakness Stakes. A year earlier at the same track in the same race, Lukas had a horse break down. On this day, he broke down—with emotion. He attempted to call Jeff back home in California after the race, saying "It's more important than (the victory)," but his son had taken his children to a carnival after watching the race on TV.

The win gave Lukas his first Grade One victory in 19 months. For someone who once collected Grade One victories as easily as picking apples in an orchard, it became a sidebar to his rise from the ashes.

"Any time you win one of these classics, it's special," he said. "This one probably means a little bit more for a number of reasons, Jeff being the obvious one."

He had broken out of his deep slumber and Team Lukas climbed up on its high horse again. Tabasco Cat won the Belmont Stakes, defying the doubts about his ability to go the mile and a half. Jockey Pat Day said Lukas did some "very unorthodox things" with the horse—such as letting him roll around in the sand—which kept the high-spirited Cat happy and able to conserve all his energies for the marathon race.

At the 1994 Breeders' Cup, NBC's coverage focused on Lukas, who dressed in an expensive suit and his trademark shades and looked entirely in his element. Proud. Confident.

The Lukas machine had grown back to its old self—even with the criticism— and, back at Churchill Downs, he simply dominated the Breeders' Cup as he had six years before. He sent out eight runners and posted two wins and a second and purse earnings of $2.98 million, the best in Cup history. Lukas' success came early in the card as 2-5 favorite Flanders and stablemate Serena's Song engaged in a ding-dong battle down the stretch, each filly digging in, each jockey doing everything he could to win. In the end, Flanders, pinned on the rail with Pat Day, just headed Serena's Song and Corey Nakatani. Next to the 1988 Distaff, it ranked as one of the best slugfests in Breeders' history. Unfortunately, Flanders suffered a badly injured leg in the race and never ran again.

"Flanders was good, Serena's Song started getting good at the right time, that's what happened, and I told a lot of my close friends this is going to be a hell of a horse race," Lukas said. "And they said, 'How are they going to beat Flanders?' I said Serena's Song is going to give Flanders all she can handle. And, I knew that. In fact, I told Paul Hornung and some of those guys that bet, 'Boy, if you bet, don't bet that exacta one way. Box it because you're going to get into trouble.' The amazing thing about that race was that they pulled even at the five-eighths pole. You'd have thought that one of them would have had to cave in and it just didn't happen. Throw in that Flanders somewhere in that race injured herself and it was an incredible run."

Some critics attacked Lukas for not showing more compassion for his injured horse, who had to be vanned off, choosing instead to engage in a television interview. At the time, he did not realize the gravity of the injury and, when asked about it, didn't think it was too serious. Even the day after he believed there was a chance she could return to the races, but most people considered that a long shot at best. Flanders had showcased her class and courage in the most trying circumstance; what more could she prove? Better yet, what more did she have to prove? As far as Young was concerned the answer to both questions was nothing.

Timber Country won the Juvenile, giving Lukas the favorite for the Derby the following year, but it was the Classic that really meant something special to him. He had never won the race and continued that streak that day, but not before a gritty effort by Tabasco Cat, who was collared by Concern in the late stages of the stretch drive.

"It was a huge race, more than people could possibly realize," Lukas said. "Jeff was there for the first time at any major race since his accident. We now felt his physical recovery would be strong. If not 100% at least close. We knew we were in the zone in those earlier races. I went on national television before the Classic and said, 'Tabasco Cat will not disappoint you.' I felt he was going to be there. It was tough, but it was an emotional day. Had we pulled that one off, I don't know if '94 could have gotten any better." As it was, Lukas had risen to the top again and would continue his roll in '95. Michael Tabor's Thunder Gulch, the gutsy, overachieving little horse Lukas had virtually ignored in his daily discussions with the media, won the Derby in a storybook finish. Jockey Gary Stevens dedicated the win to a friend, Mark Kaufman, who had died earlier in the week.

Lukas saddled the winners of the Preakness and Belmont Stakes with Timber Country and Thunder Gulch, respectively. Turf writers were urged by their editors to write Lukas comeback stories. In an interview with the *Toronto Sun*, Beyer balanced his praise for Lukas by badmouthing him for his handling of horses.

"Some of his faults have been gross and palpable, like the way he handled Lady's Secret in the twilight of her career and the number of horses that have been casualties in his desire to win Triple Crown races," Beyer said. Lukas told reporters at the Preakness it is "human nature to care" about criticism, but "you have to put it into perspective. I think some of the members of the media got a little carried away and got a little personal." Lukas came to the 1995 Breeders' Cup five days beforehand via plane from Kentucky, escorting his equine entourage, all of whom looked like winners to the man.

Even minus Thunder Gulch and Timber Country, who had been retired with injuries, Lukas' confidence could not be diminished. Some of Lukas' critics pointed to the loss of the two colts as another example of his reckless training, but he stood behind what he had done.

"All of them are subject to injuries," he said. "These things are bred to run, you put them out there, you know those things can happen, but the ultimate is you have to look at the big picture and say, 'what did they accomplish?' Well, some of these horses accomplished unbelievable things. And, the other thing is that the greater the racehorse—the more brilliance they show—the more susceptible they are to injury. And, that's true in athletics, too. You find very few Serena's Songs in athletes. Horses that can run as fast as Ruffian, God didn't put them together to let them do that. I don't have any problem with that. My job is to get maximum effort per race out of them. I know they say, 'He's raced Serena's Song 13 times.' Well, I think that's a tribute to me, not a knock. Jesus Christ, I've taken her over there and she's done everything a person can ask. I can run her three times and who's to say that on the fourth time she doesn't take the bad step. So, I don't have any trouble with that."

Lukas also came under some scrutiny over a supposed problem with his top two-year-old Hennessy, who had run sixth in the Grade One Champagne Stakes three weeks before won by Maria's Mon. Gary Stevens jumped off the horse in favor of another Lukas runner, Honour and Glory. Editor's Note, the third member of the Lukas troika in the Juvenile, was to be ridden by Jerry Bailey. Surprisingly, Pat Day, who had ridden many Lukas horses in the past and who was available, did not get the call on Hennessy. Instead, Donna Barton, who rode regularly for Lukas in Kentucky but who had only ridden once before in the Breeders' Cup, drew the assignment.

Lukas liked his chances and some of the more astute handicappers gave Hennessy a chance to improve on his last race after deciding he had run on the worst part of the track and tired.

In rating the two-year olds, Lukas scoffed at Maria's Mon, who had suffered a season-ending injury training for the Breeders' Cup, and dismissed the lightly raced Unbridled's Song, who many handicappers figured had a big chance to win the race. Unbridled's Song had opened up a six-length lead in the Champagne and faded to fourth.

Lukas also suggested Serena's Song should be Horse of the Year and added—partly tongue-in-cheek—that he wished the top-rated candidate for the award, Cigar, was racing in the Distaff—which is restricted to females—because he would have a hard time beating her.

Two days before the Cup, Richard Schosberg, the trainer of Maria's Mon, fired back at Lukas for the comments about his horse. "I understand Lukas is trying to do the right thing and campaign his horses, but to say Maria's Mon isn't in the hunt for the championship is just ridiculous," he said.

Schosberg was not the first horseman Lukas insulted, nor would he be the last. In a business where it is sometimes okay to knock a man but not his horse, Lukas often crossed the line. During the Triple Crown, he missed a dinner where several trainers took some liberties at his expense. Lukas, in turn, replied by good-naturedly renaming some of their horses, calling Talkin Man, "Walkin Man"; Star Standard, "Substandard"; and Tejano Run, "Tejano Done." One of the offended trainers thought it was classless and later made fun of Lukas' handling of horses by saying: "Someone asked Lukas about his four-year-olds and he said, 'What's a four-year-old?'" Nick Zito, who had become Lukas' arch-rival in the Triple Crown, needled him by telling the media Lukas' three horses in the Derby were "Me, Myself and I."

History repeated at the 1995 Breeders' Cup. Just like five years earlier at Belmont Park, Lukas failed to win a race, although this time he came close. Hennessy came within a neck of winning the Juvenile, losing a battle royal in deep stretch to Unbridled's Song—the horse Lukas figured had no shot. Second-guessers said if a jockey such as Day had been on the horse instead of Barton, Hennessy might have won. Owner Bob Lewis gave no indication in an interview with NBC after the race that he had been dissatisfied with Barton's ride. Editor's Note ran third in the Juvenile and Honour and Glory, the post-time favorite, fourth. Cara Rafaela and Golden Attraction ran second and third, respectively, for Lukas in the Juvenile Fillies. Serena's Song finished a dull fifth in the Distaff. Lukas' horses collected $716,000.

"We thought we could win a couple of them, but we didn't win any," he said. "On the other hand, it wasn't all that bad. A lot of guys would trade places."

Two writers wagered that night whether Lukas would show the following morning at the post–Breeders' Cup breakfast. One of them said Lukas had no reason to attend if he hadn't won a race. Sure enough, he didn't show. Lukas had no time to dwell on yesterday's losses, when he could be planning tomorrow's victories.

Lukas noted earlier in the week he planned to be even bigger in '96 and each year after that due to a string of committed owners with big bankrolls and an even bigger belief in the man who conditioned their horses.

"We've got three of the strongest breeding farms in the world behind us, plus we've got the cash flow of the Lewises and Tabors and so forth," Lukas said. "We should be double tough. I can see us—and I don't say this obnoxiously—running three and four in the Fillies (and) three and four in the Juvenile every year the next couple years. You know what I think? We just won five Triple Crown races, which everybody is saying is a hell of an achievement. I'm not sure six, seven and eight won't be easier than three, four or five, in light of what I see eating grass in front of me out there on the lawn and what I haven't started."

In 1996, Lukas had an interesting—and controversial—year. He entered a record five horses in the Kentucky Derby—Editor's Note, Grindstone, Honour and Glory, Prince of Thieves and Victory Speech—which prompted some media criticism. The Lukas bashers wondered about his tactics and his ego. He had the last word, registering a record sixth consecutive Triple Crown win when Grindstone ground out a nose victory over Cavonnier largely due to a masterful ride by Jerry Bailey. Prince of Thieves ran third. Cavonnier's trainer, Bob Baffert, winner of the 1992 Breeders' Cup Sprint with long shot Thirty Slews, had also come from the quarter horse circuit. Some of Baffert's first thoroughbred clients happened to be Bob and Beverly Lewis, and when the couple wanted to expand their stable and sought an additional trainer, Baffert recommended Lukas. The similarities between Lukas and Baffert, coupled with the close finish in the Derby, would become highlighted often in the ensuing years on the Triple Crown trail. And a misinterpreted remark the quick-witted Baffert made about Lukas to a reporter during Derby week sparked the beginning of a public hissing match between the two trainers.

Grindstone suffered a career-ending knee injury in victory, leaving Lukas with backups to try and continue his Triple Crown streak in the Preakness. He entered Prince of Thieves, the second choice in the morning line behind 9-5 favorite Cavonnier, Editor's Note, who placed sixth in the Derby, and Victory Speech, who had placed 10th. Lukas replaced Pat Day with Bailey aboard Prince of Thieves, but Day turned around and rode Louis Quatorze, who would up winning the Preakness. Editor's Note ran third, while Prince of Thieves ran seventh. Lukas' streak was over, but his luck was not about to end. Editor's Note was about to emerge, although not entirely surprisingly to jockey Gary Stevens, who had ridden him regularly, albeit with frustration.

"He was a big, strong horse with a mind of his own, and most of the time his mind was telling him to play around," Stevens wrote in his autobiography *The Perfect Ride*.

"We entered the Kentucky Derby certain we were going to win, but didn't. We were favored to win the Preakness . . . but once again the horse failed to fire."

Stevens suffered a shoulder injury in the interval between the Preakness and Belmont Stakes and was sidelined. Rene Douglas picked up the mount and won by a length, the third consecutive Belmont victory for Lukas. Stevens was at the Belmont doing color commentary for ABC, and even though disappointed about missing the riding opportunity he felt good for the horse.

"People in racing had been saying that Lukas and I were too high on Editor's Note, that he wasn't nearly the horse we believed he was," Stevens wrote in his book. "We both had continued to have faith that Editor's Note would win big races, so I felt vindicated even though I was not riding him in the Belmont."

In the fall, Lukas readied for the Breeders' Cup, which would be held in Canada, the first time the event had gone outside of the U.S. Lukas had been critical of that, believing the Breeders' had established itself on American soil and didn't need to expand to a new country. This would be his first foray into Canada. After years of hinting he might run a string of horses at Woodbine, following conquests at just about every other major track in North America, D. Wayne would finally come off the plane to Canada, if only for an instant.

Lukas arrived a couple of days before the race, maintaining a practice he had done with most tracks, regardless of the race. By contrast, Nick Zito, trainer of Preakness winner Louis Quatorze, had shipped his horses the week before to acclimate to the track. In Lukas' mind, a work over the track wouldn't matter, regardless of whether or not he had even run a horse over the strip to learn about its nuances. Lukas brought 10 horses and was stabled on the opposite side of the barn that housed Sam-Son Farm, one of the powerhouses of Canadian racing and winner of the 1991 Breeders' Cup Distaff with Dance Smartly, the Eclipse winner as the champion older filly or mare. There had been many instances in which Sam-Son runners trained by Jim Day had battled Lukas runners in the Triple Crown and Breeders' Cup.

Lukas began his initial assault on Canada with Cheyenne City, Sharp Cat and

City Band in the Juvenile Fillies. Cheyenne City, who won the Grade One Alcibiades Stakes at Keeneland in her last start, and City Band, who had won the Grade One Oak Leaf Stakes at Santa Anita in her previous outing, were owned by William T. Young. He had celebrated wins in the Derby and Belmont earlier in the year with Grindstone and Editor's Note, respectively. Sharp Cat, owned by The Thoroughbred Corporation, the nom de course of Prince Ahmed Salman, had placed second in the Grade One Frizette Stakes to Dogwood Stable's Storm Song. The Dogwood representative went postward as the 8-5 favorite in the field of 12. Lukas felt good about Sharp Cat, who went off as the third choice in the field at 4-1 odds. Cheyenne City and City Band were coupled as an entry at just under 10-1. Lukas and jockey Jerry Bailey wanted to put Sharp Cat on the lead, but had to accede to the wishes of the owner.

"The Prince had this theory you couldn't win on the lead at Woodbine, so he wanted us to take her back," Lukas said. "Jerry Bailey and I said, 'No, she can win anywhere you take her.'"

Sharp Cat advanced to second after half a mile, then began to retreat and finished ninth by 18½ lengths. Storm Song rallied from well off the pace to secure the lead heading into the stretch and won by 4½ lengths under Craig Perret. Cheyenne City ran eighth and stablemate City Band 10th.

Next came the Sprint with Michael Tabor's Honour and Glory and David P. Reynolds' Lord Carson, who had run first and second, respectively, in the same race in their last starts. They each garnered some interest in the wagering at slightly more than 5-1 and ran third and fourth, respectively, behind Lit de Justice, the 4-1 favorite.

Lukas was represented by the Lewises' Serena's Song in the Distaff, which only had six starters although three of them looked tough. Jewel Princess, who would go on to be named champion older filly that year, and Different, the latest in a series of transplanted Argentina-breds trained by Ron McAnally, both had solid records. Serena's Song, bidding for her first Breeders' Cup win in three consecutive years, tracked the pace and had the lead heading into the stretch, but couldn't repel the run of Jewel Princess. She prevailed inside the final furlong to win by 1½ lengths.

One of Lukas' best shots on the day appeared to be Young's homebred Boston Harbor in the Juvenile. He had won a $1 million bonus heading into the race by capturing all four races in a series of Kentucky stakes races. His ability to win those four races at four different distances over four different tracks had proved his versatility. As Lukas would later say, "That's a hell of a parlay."

Overall, Boston Harbor had come into the Breeders' with a three-race win streak and five victories in six career starts. On the basis of those wins, in particular the last one in the Kentucky Futurity at Keeneland, Lukas felt confident he had a solid contender. He also had Gold Tribute, owned by a partnership of the Lewises, Mrs. John Magnier and Michael Tabor. Boston Harbor, who was second in the wagering at just under 5-2 odds behind 7-5 favorite Ordway, grabbed the lead with Bailey and held stubbornly by a neck over the fast-charging Acceptable, a long shot at more than 12-1. Ordway, the 7-5 favorite, ran third. Gold Tribute, Lukas' other runner in the race, had a rough trip going into the first turn under Stevens and finished sixth by slightly more than five lengths. Boston Harbor's victory, combined with his earlier wins, set a Juvenile earnings record with $1,928,605 and he won the Eclipse Award winner in his division and subsequent favorite status for the Kentucky Derby.

Lukas later ran Tabor's Marlin in the Mile, but the 43-1 outsider in the field of 14 ran second-last. The trainer's day concluded with Editor's Note, who had won the Louisiana Super Derby with Stevens in the fall and then tackled salty older horses for the first time in the Grade One Jockey Club Gold Cup and ran fourth to Skip Away. Editor's Note had little left for the Classic, featuring an equally tough field, and ran second-last.

"I thought we could have a hell of a day," Lukas said. "You go into the Breeders' Cup loaded up . . . but they're difficult to win. We changed the strategy on Sharp Cap and that nullified her. I felt we were going to run the best horse in that particular race. When you run the best horse I think you should always run to your strengths. It's like any athletic event: when you change up in the championship, you usually get beat. You need to run to your strength and we have always done that. We have always never worried about the opposition. We've always wanted to run to what our horses do best. If we have a horse that makes the lead or comes from out of it or whatever, we play to those strengths. I didn't think the track was any different than probably Belmont or some of the other tracks we've been to. It was a deep, tiring track, obviously, but not any different than what we'd been running that summer at Belmont. The other horses I thought ran well. I was a little disappointed, but I think you always have to feel a certain amount of gratification winning one."

Lukas finished the year first in earnings among trainers with almost $16 million, the most in five years, although Bill Mott, who conditioned Cigar among others, won the Eclipse Award.

The following year, the Breeders' Cup Juvenile jinx caught up with Boston Harbor, who ran only one time, suffered a leg injury and had to be retired. Heading into the Derby, Lukas appeared to be without a representative for the first time in 16 years. Deeds Not Words, the last of his apparent Derby hopefuls, ran third in the Lexington Stakes two weeks before, but Lukas publicly said the horse was not ready for the Roses. Lukas tried to buy a horse, Concerto, owned by New York Yankees' boss George Steinbrenner, but the deal fell through. Lukas began eyeing his top three-year-old filly Sharp Cat as a possible Derby runner, but couldn't persuade her connections, who wanted to run in the Kentucky Oaks the day before. Two days before the deadline for the Derby entries, Lukas worked Deeds Not Words, liked what he had done and the decision was made to run in the Derby. It provided the latest fodder for another Lukas lynching by the media, although this one was arguably the ugliest, prompting a volley of verbal attacks. A Louisville columnist called him D. (elusional) Lukas, which really irked the trainer. The horse was rated at 50-1 in the morning line, and no amount of convincing by Lukas could persuade people to think he was running the horse for anything more than personal vanity. When Deeds Not Words ran last it exacerbated the controversy.

It also sparked the first tangible shift in popularity toward trainer Bob Baffert, who won the Derby with Silver Charm, a colt who at one point in his career had lost a race won by Deeds Not Words. Baffert's Derby win coincided with his rising popularity, as he became the media darling, while Lukas' reputation waned. Silver Charm won the Preakness but was denied a sweep of the Triple Crown in the final leg. Lukas did not enter a horse in either race.

In the '97 Cup at Hollywood Park, Lukas ran Love Lock and Bay Harbor in the Juvenile Fillies; Trafalger in the Sprint; Sharp Cat in the Distaff; Fantastic Fellow in the Mile; and Double Honor, Time Limit and Grand Slam in the Juvenile. On paper, it appeared his best chances were with Sharp Cat and Grand Slam, both of whom were highly regarded in the morning lines for their respective races and in the wagering. Love Lock and Bay Harbor finished well back in their race, which 2-1 favorite Countess Diana won in a romp. Trafalger also finished up the track. Sharp Cat, a winner of her last race, grabbed the early lead but was overtaken by Allen Paulson's Ajina heading into the stretch and placed second by two lengths. Grand Slam, the second choice in his race at 2-1, never factored in the finish, placing last by more than $11\frac{1}{4}$ lengths to 6-5 favorite Favorite Track, who romped by $5\frac{1}{2}$ lengths. But Grand Slam had a rough journey. He clipped heels entering the first turn and after going four wide nearing the second turn was eased in the stretch by jockey Gary Stevens. Grand Slam returned bleeding from a cut on the left hind leg but was able to walk off.

"He ran an unbelievable race," Lukas said. "That was one of the worst injuries I've ever seen on a racetrack. One of the horses in behind him cut him above the hock and just stripped all the tendons and skin down to the ankle. They sewed on it for hours and hours into the night and we thought we'd never save his life."

He survived the surgery and the postrecovery and developed into a top sire.

In 1998, Lukas entered into two interesting partnerships: a business arrangement with a thoroughbred owner and a new marriage. The business arrangement involved Satish Sanan, a native of India who migrated to Great Britain when he was 16 and, among other things, developed an interest in horses. In later years, Sanan founded—and made his financial wealth with—IMR Global Inc., a company that supplies computer outsourcing and software services worldwide. He made the decision in 1997 to win classic races around the world by investing heavily in the yearling and breeding-stock sales around the world. According to Lukas, Sanan chose him as his general manager and minority shareholder in his Padua Stables after interviewing almost a dozen trainers from coast to coast in the U.S. Sanan had had horses with Lukas beginning in 1995, but it was nothing in comparison to what they were about to do.

"We hit it off, we had a great rapport, the charisma and the karma and the chemistry was good right from get-go with him," Lukas said. "He wanted me to be a partner and we did that."

Lukas sold his training center in Santa Barbara, California, and moved his headquarters to Ocala, Florida, where Sanan purchased the 586-acre Silverleaf Stud Farm and developed it into a state-of-the-art facility. Lukas' son, Jeff, became a component in the operation in an administrative capacity. Lukas and Sanan attended the prestigious Keeneland yearling sales and doled out millions without a blink of an eye.

Lukas remarried in June, the fourth time for both him and his new wife, Laura Pinelli. She worked as a quarter horse trainer and had had some success in five years. Together, the Lukases set up a quarter horse division at Los Alamitos and charted a course for success, breeding to quality stallions and buying quality yearlings, the objectives being to race and sell when possible.

Lukas came to the 1998 Cup armed and ready, pointing five horses to the Juvenile: William T. Young's Cat Thief, Tactical Cat and Mountain Range, and Yes It's True and Time Bandit, owned by Sanan. Of the five horses, Cat Thief did the best, placing third by less than a length. Grand Slam ran in the Sprint and, although he was dismissed at more than 32-1 odds, placed a solid second, rallying from far off the pace to finish two lengths back of the frontrunning Reraise. Partner's Hero, also sent out by Lukas, placed eighth by almost six lengths.

Sanan's Unbridled Delight, dismissed at more than 58-1 odds, ran eighth in the Juvenile Fillies.

Lukas did not have a banner year by his standards in 1998, his horses winning some $7.2 million in purses, almost $3 million behind his total from the year before. He also had his string of four consecutive earnings titles snapped by Baffert, whose stable banked more than $15 million. But Lukas more than made up for it in 1999, in which he was elected to the Racing Hall of Fame and won his fourth Eclipse Award, highlighted by victories in the Kentucky Derby and Preakness Stakes and the Juvenile Fillies and Classic in the Breeders' Cup. The Hall of Fame honor was announced during Derby week. There had been a time when Lukas had been angry that he had been passed over by the selection committee in favor of people with lesser records and had threatened he'd boycott the event if ever elected. His absence had been a product of not meeting the requirement of training thoroughbreds for 25 consecutive years, and when the honor finally came he had softened his boycott stance.

Lukas came to the Derby with Bob Lewis' Charismatic and William T. Young's Cat Thief, expected to be the stronger half of the two. Cat Thief came into the race with a lengthy winless streak, but he had consistently finished in the money and had raced against solid competition. In contrast, Charismatic had been a classic underachiever. Lewis paid $210,000 for the colt as a yearling, but he did little at two and had plummeted to the $62,500 claiming ranks twice in his sophomore season in attempts by Lukas to raise his confidence. Charismatic scored a smashing win in the Coolmore Lexington Stakes a couple of weeks before the Derby, setting a stakes record by more than a full second, although critics suggested he beat a weak field. Jerry Bailey was aboard for the victory, but he had a commitment to ride Worldly Manner for Sheikh Mohammed bin Rashid al Maktoum. He had bought the colt the previous fall for a whopping $5 million and shipped him to Dubai to gear him up for the Derby. Lukas contacted several high-profile jockeys to ride Charismatic but received little interest. He settled on Chris Antley, who was the winner of the 1991 Derby with Strike the Gold, but whose career had gone through various peaks and valleys because of drug and weight problems. He had just returned to riding following a lengthy retirement and seized the opportunity to ride Charismatic. Lukas told Antley to sit chilly in the second pack of the bulky field until the midway point on the backside, then begin to turn the colt loose. Lukas believed if the colt had the lead with an eighth of a mile to the wire he'd win. Cat Thief, ridden by Mike Smith, ran solidly and had the lead in the stretch, but Charismatic had crept up to him with an eighth of a mile to the wire and surged ahead in the final jumps to the wire, holding off a fast-charging Menifee. Cat Thief finished third.

Lukas had pulled off another minor miracle—and he profited after betting $2,000 to win on the colt, pocketing some $60,000 in the process—and it didn't end there. Charismatic won the Preakness and it was on to New York for the Belmont Stakes and the latest bid to sweep the Triple Crown. Trainer Bob Baffert wasn't about to yield to the competition, sending out Mike Pegram's fleet filly Silverbulletday. Bob Lewis did not consider it a sporting gesture and the media played up the controversy, suddenly painting Baffert as the guy in the black hat instead of Lukas. Pegram ran to his trainer's defense, claiming his filly belonged in the race because of her solid record and earnings. Silverbulletday shot to the lead in the 1½-mile race and Charismatic followed suit under Antley. With a quarter of a mile to the wire, Antley pressed forward and appeared headed for the historic win. In deep stretch, with the finish line some 60 yards away, Charismatic lost his momentum, taking a bad step. His bid for a Triple Crown came up short when he placed third, behind Lemon Drop Kid and Vision and Verse. Antley dismounted shortly after the wire when he realized the colt had suffered an injury to his left front leg. The picture of the ailing horse and the heartbroken rider, clinging to Charismatic to prevent further damage to the fractured limb, would become etched in the annals of thoroughbred racing. It was a sad end all-around for Lukas, Antley, Charismatic and the sport.

But the game would go on, and in the fall Lukas had the Breeders' Cup on his radar. He brought six runners to the Cup: Cash Run and Surfside in the Juvenile Fillies; Natalie Too in the Filly & Mare Turf; High Yield and Millencolin in the Juvenile; and Cat Thief in the Classic. Cash Run appeared to be the weaker half of the two Lukas entrants in the Juvenile Fillies. She had run third in her last start and had won two of five overall, but none of her victories had come in stakes. Surfside had won her last start and was considered the second-best runner in the field of nine behind the undefeated Chilukki, sent out by Baffert. Cash Run, ridden by Jerry Bailey, went postward at 32.50-1 odds, the third-highest price in the field. Chilukki headed the field at 3-2, followed by Surfside at 5-2. Cash Run grabbed the lead and owned it for the opening half-mile but was headed by Chilukki just before three-quarters of a mile. She regained the lead with about a quarter of a mile to the wire, then responded strongly to Bailey's left-handed urging and prevailed by 1¼ lengths over Chilukki. Surfside finished third by 1¾ lengths.

Regally bred by Seeking the Gold out of the Pleasant Colony mare Shared Interest, Cash Run cost $1.2 million as a yearling. She provided Sanan with his first major return on investment in the two years since his grand entrance into the sport and only a year and a half since hooking up with Lukas.

"We didn't think we could do it in our second year," Sanan was quoted in the *Daily Racing Form* a few days later. "We would have been happy if she won on the board." That would not be the only story line resulting from the victory. A novel piece of equine equipment provided an interesting sidebar. Many athletes, including jockeys, had started wearing a brand name of nasal strips as part of their equipment. The strips had become popular because of their aid in helping to improve breathing, and Lukas seized the opportunity to take advantage of the strips, placing an equine version over the bridge of his horses' snouts. As odd as the patches looked, it only took one example by the top-winning trainer in Breeders' Cup history to prove their worth.

Sanan's Natalie Too ran 10th in the inaugural running of the Filly & Mare Turf, while another representative, Millencolin, placed 10th in the Juvenile. High Yield, owned by Bob and Beverly Lewis and Mrs. John Magnier, ran a respectable third by 3¼ lengths in the Juvenile. He appeared to be in a strong position to win at the head of the stretch, trailing the leader Chief Seattle by only a head, but flattened out in the lane. Anees, a late-running son of Unbridled, resembled his father in the 1990 Classic, running from last to first.

Lukas' final runner on the card, Cat Thief, came into the race with only one win in 11 starts on the season, although his record also showed three seconds and four thirds. Overall, he had three wins, six seconds and five thirds in his career and earnings of about $1.3 million. He had run in some of the biggest Grade One races on the season, distinguishing himself as a hard-knocking colt characteristic of his sire Storm Cat. At best he appeared to be the kind of horse worth throwing in exacta or trifecta tickets. In his last start, he had run third in the Kentucky Cup Classic at Turfway Park. The brain trust at William T. Young's Overbrook Farm debated at length in advance of the Breeders' Cup whether or not to enter Cat Thief, assessing the relative merits strictly from a business/breeding perspective. Lukas said only he and Young among the group of seven wanted to take a shot in the race. The naysayers thought the colt had no chance to win and the debate, which took place over lunch, escalated in emotion as various thoughts were thrown into the mix.

"Those meetings at Overbrook are very open, nobody holds back," Lukas said. "We use a lot of four-letter words and everybody gets into it. I remember distinctly Bill Young was sitting at the head of the table eating salad and it got a little bit heated and he just suddenly looked up at said: 'Boys, I think we've talked about this enough. We're going to do what Wayne wants to do. We're going to run the horse.'"

Lukas liked the way Cat Thief had flourished in the weeks since his last race and imparted that to jockey Pat Day the morning of the race.

"You will not sit on the same horse you got off a month ago," he said. "You are going to be unbelievably surprised."

Cat Thief tracked the lead of pacesetter Old Trieste for the opening three-quarters of a mile, then responded willingly when Day called on him approaching the stretch and gained a narrow lead. Under left-handed and right-handed urging from Day, Cat Thief extended his lead to finish first by 1¼ lengths over Budroyale, who had been bumped twice by the winner in the drive to the wire. Cat Thief came close to matching the course record time in the 1¼-mile race, running it in 1:59.52.

For his handlers, the winner's purse of the $3.6 million race amounted to more than $2 million, boosting the win-shy colt's career earnings to more than $3.3 million.

"Cat Thief had a reputation of never quite getting the job done. He was in contention from the start and, this time, he was in first place at the wire," summed up the story of the race in ESPN.com.

Lukas, who had won his first Classic, shrugged off a reporter's query that Cat Thief's breathing apparatus aided his victory.

"I don't think those nose strips beat the other horses," he said. "Cat Thief beat the other horses."

For Lukas it added another laurel to his career.

"It was great year, in fact in looking back I don't think I had a better year with the material I had in front of me," he said. "A couple of those were some of my best training jobs ever, I believe. Winning the Classic with Cat Thief was not only one of the highlights of my training career but also one of the highlights emotionally for me. It was not only the Classic and the Breeders' Cup but the whole W. T. Young family was there and nobody expected us to win. We felt good about it. That horse touted us. When we won the Classic, we went to the press conference and one of the media members asked about the heated discussion (at Overbrook Farm whether or not to run the horse). Bill Young looked out very calmly (at the assembled gathering) and said, 'Yes, at Overbrook we thoroughly discuss these things among all of the people who are involved and in the end we voted and it was unanimous, two to five.' That was a great line, I thought."

Charismatic's success earned him horse-of-the-year honors, the third time Lukas had accomplished that feat with one of his steeds.

Lukas ran horses in the Kentucky Derby and Preakness Stakes, but came up empty; however he rebounded in the Belmont, the site of his tough loss the year before, and won with Commendable, dismissed at almost 19-1 odds. It represented his ninth Triple Crown win in six years. Coincidentally, it finally gave the Lewises the win in the last leg of the Triple Crown, albeit in a year in which they didn't have a shot to sweep the series. In fact, neither the Derby winner nor the Preakness winner ran in the race, which belittled Commendable's accomplishment in the viewpoint of some critics.

A few months later Lukas came to the Cup with a six-pack: Spain and Surfside in the Distaff; Cash Deal in the Juvenile Fillies; Scorpion and Yonaguska in the Juvenile; and Cat Thief in the Classic. The Lukas camp liked Young's Surfside's chances. The big, robust daughter of Seattle Slew out of 1994 Juvenile Fillies winner Flanders dominated the three-year-old filly ranks in California early in the season. She faltered against male horses in the Santa Anita Derby and required time off afterward because of surgery to remove bone chips in both of her front ankles. She returned to racing in the fall and placed second in her only start leading up to the Cup, and Lukas figured she had all the ingredients to be a Breeders' Cup winner. Her entrymate Spain, owned by Prince Ahmed Salman's Thoroughbred Corporation, had shown positive signs in training. Lukas received the three-year-old filly, who had begun the year in the care of another trainer and hadn't done anything of consequence, in May. He guided her to three wins, including two stakes, in five starts. Her two losses, in which she placed second and third, occurred in tough Grade One races.

"Every day that we took her out, we said, 'Watch out for this little gal because she is going to make some noise,'" Lukas recalled.

Riboletta, a winner of six consecutive races on both coasts, came into the Distaff as the heavy favorite, bet down to 2-5, the lowest-priced runner in the eight Breeders' Cup races. Surfside, under Pat Day, led for three-quarters of a mile, but Spain, ridden by Victor Espinoza, kept in close pursuit and slipped through along the rail to take the lead going into the stretch. She prevailed by 1½ lengths over Surfside. She returned a whopping $113.80 on a $2 ticket. Once again Lukas bombed the tote board, this time with the second-highest payoff in Breeders' Cup history to that point.

Three weeks later, Surfside raced in the $400,000 Clark Handicap at Churchill Downs and soundly beat male horses en route to being named the champion three-year-old filly that year.

"We were one race off with Surfside and Spain had her day," Lukas said. "In all fairness it was not a one-day deal or 15 minutes of fame for Spain. She just got good and stayed good. She just kept on rolling."

Cash Deal, let go at slightly more than 9-1 odds in her highly competitive race, went down to her knees at the start, struck her nose on the ground and lost all hope thereafter, finishing last in the field of 12.

A few races later Lukas saddled Scorpion and Yonaguska in the Juvenile. Yonaguska, owned by Michael Tabor, was deemed to be the stronger half of the two by the bettors, who sent him postward at just under 10-1 odds. Scorpion, owned by the partnership of Baker, Cornstein and Mack, was one of the outsiders at more than 45-1 odds. Scorpion ran ninth and Yonaguska 12th.

Cat Thief, who went postward at more than 11-1, did not fare well defending his championship, running seventh by almost 10 lengths to winner Tiznow, who would become a Breeders' Cup legend.

In a story headlined Duke of Fluke in the *Backstretch Magazine*, writer Andy Plattner highlighted Lukas' success with long shot winners in the Triple Crown and Breeders' Cup.

"Lukas' horses have been regarded as unwelcome poachers. During the year and a half prior to the 2000 edition of the Breeders' Cup at Churchill Downs, Lukas saddled a total of 15 Triple Crown and/or Breeders' Cup starters. The average odds of each horse were higher than 13-1. Two of them, Charismatic in the 1999 Kentucky Derby and Cash Run in the Breeders' Cup Juvenile Fillies later that year, actually went to post at odds higher than 30-1. We know the punch line: Both Charismatic and Cash Run were victorious, as were three others from those 15 starters. Overall, the record of these 15 horses was 5-0-4, a 60% ratio of in-the-money finishes. Average winning payoff? More than 20-1. This includes Cat Thief's 1999 swipe of the Classic, Charismatic's Preakness, and Commendable's mind-bending win in the 2000 Belmont. When did Lukas become so out-of-style with bettors, the people who are supposed to know horse racing the best? Why the yawns when horse racing's all-time, leading money-winning trainer enters a horse in a major event? This year's Breeders' Cup brought the same questions.

"Spain's victory meant that Lukas' Breeders' Cup and Triple Crown race winners now have paid greater than 28-1 in the past two years. There's another word for long-shot winners in this business: flukes. And that is what most of these Lukas long shots have been called. . . . Most people, however, would likely agree on one thing: that Lukas is a world-class envelope-pusher. He has trained some great horses—Lady's Secret, Breeders' Cup Distaff winner of 1986, might have been his best—and won some great races with them. But his new feat is winning great races with less-than-great horses.

"If you are Lukas, you might see just the big-daddy races—the Derby and the Breeders' Cup—as, more than anything else, the most likely spots for an upset. In short, the racing gods giveth and the racing gods taketh away. And when they taketh, there needs to be someone there to picketh up the pieces. And that someone is Lukas. . . . Nobody is throwing any parades for Lukas these days, and perhaps no one connected with the sport ever will. Handicappers can continue to insist Lukas' horses don't belong, but they are forgetting the adage that says the only truth is the tote board. And the truth of late seems to be that Lukas understands horse racing better than just about anyone."

In 2001, Lukas had another controversial year. He didn't run a horse in the Kentucky Derby for the first time in 20 years, but caused a stir when he made critical remarks about the commitment of Chris Antley during Charismatic's bittersweet run in the Triple Crown. Antley had died of a drug overdose the previous December and the fact that Lukas badmouthed him months later did not sit well with many people in the industry, the media, the rider's family and his widow. But *Daily Racing Form* editor-in-chief Steve Crist wrote a column in which he said Lukas should not be castigated for telling the other side of the story, which had been overlooked amid the homages and remembrance stories devoted to Antley and Charismatic. In August 2001, Lukas' business relationship with Satish Sanan ended amicably. Randy Bradshaw, who apprenticed under Lukas, remained with Sanan's operation in a management capacity, while Jeff Lukas stayed in an administrative capacity. Sanan split his stock of more than 30 horses principally with Todd Pletcher, Bill Mott and Bob Baffert, and gave a few each to Steve Asmussen and Dallas Stewart. Pletcher and Stewart both apprenticed under Lukas.

"I have no regrets, I love the guy," Lukas said of Sanan. "We still have a great relationship, we just don't have a partnership anymore. What he wanted to do and what I was doing with my public stable would not blend. My loyalty to the Bob Lewises and W. T. Youngs—clients that I had had for so long—was just too much of a conflict of interest."

Lukas brought only three horses to the 2001 Breeders', one of his smallest contingents ever: Spain in the Distaff, Jump Start in the Juvenile and Orientate in the Classic. Spain, winner of only one of seven starts on the season and third in her last two races, merited second status in the wagering in the Distaff at just under

5-1 odds. It might have been higher, but Exogenous, who had won her last two starts, was scratched after a horrific spill en route to the track. Flute, second to Exogenous in her last race after winning three in a row, became the post-time favorite at just under 6-5 odds. Spain, ridden by Victor Espinoza, stalked the leaders and took a commanding two-length lead going into the stretch. She opened up a clear advantage in midstretch, but a fast-closing Unbridled Elaine, who had broken in the air and had had a miserable trip thereafter, won by a head over Spain. Trainer Dallas Stewart, one of Lukas' many proteges, had pinned the loss on his former boss. Lukas said the defeat represented the biggest personal disappointment in all of his Breeders' Cup experiences.

"She ran as well as a horse could run and did not get the garland of flowers. Unbelievable," Lukas said. "I talked to Victor Espinoza at length. I told him that he can't ride a mile and a half at Belmont like you could ride a mile oval, that when you're on the far turn it's not the three-eighths pole, it's the five-eighths pole, and that you've got a long drive to the wire. He had ridden her in the Beldame prior and he had made the same mistake. He had sent her from the five-eighths pole in a drive and she had run her eyeballs out and lost. He comes back in the Breeders' Cup and rides her exactly the same way."

Jump Start ran a non-menacing 11th in a field of 12 in the Juvenile and Orientate placed 12th in the field of 13 in the Classic.

Spain started out the 2002 season and Lukas had hoped to have her run one more time in the Breeders'. She was bred to Storm Cat during the year and continued to race and win, but a decision was made to retire her well before the completion of the season and she finished as the all-time money-winning filly or mare with more than $3.5 million. Other potential runners such as Snow Ridge and Proud Citizen were lost to injury.

He came to the Breeders' with just two starters, Orientate and Day Trader, both in the Sprint. Orientate, owned by Bob and Beverly Lewis, had not run in almost two months, but he'd won the Grade One Forego Handicap, his fourth consecutive victory. All five of his wins came at distances under a mile on the dirt. Orientate had shown the classic profile of a former distance runner cut back and pointed specifically for the Breeders' Cup Sprint. A year earlier he had run in the Classic, flashed early speed for half a mile and then fizzled out, finishing second-last. Based on his record and freshness, he became the morning-line favorite at 5-2. Day Trader, owned by William T. Young, had won three of nine on the season but clearly lacked the profile and class of his stablemate. He was 20-1 in the morning line, but Lukas thought he at least had a shot after securing Pat Day to ride. Day had ridden the three-year-old colt off and on during the season and had recorded two wins with him.

Indian Charlie, the Kentucky-based former horseman who writes a daily tip sheet, referred to the Hall of Famer as Darnell in his latest bit of caustic prose.

"It's sad what has happened to Dead Duck Darnell," Indian Charlie wrote. "We knew he'd been having a subpar year, but when we saw his gold cufflinks in the window at Uncle Miltie's pawn shop just before we left Louisville, we knew come Breeders' Cup day Orientate and Day Trader (Lukas' only two runners in the Cup) would be running the longest six furlongs of their lives."

Lukas laughed it off.

"It's all satire," he said. "Some guys can't handle it. I tell him if I'm not in there every three days I'm offended. He likes to take the little shots, but if you ask Indian Charlie is he a Wayne Lukas fan, he is a 100% Wayne Lukas fan. We have a great exchange. I laugh. You've got to laugh with him, because if you don't laugh with him tomorrow's will be scorching. You have to take it in the spirit in the way it's written. He knocks everybody. You've got to take it in the right spirit. The ones that I make accountable are the guys in the media. I don't think (they) have any privilege or any special right to pick up that pen and write scorching articles, especially with the lack of knowledge that some of these guys have and the irresponsibility of doing damage to some people's career. I can name a few. Those guys make my short list and I have no use for them.

"I used to tell my students when I was teaching, 'How many of you had a teacher that you didn't like?,' and half the class would raise their hand. I always looked them right in the eye and said, 'We don't like all you little bastards, either.' That's the nature of the game. But I don't have any problem with (Indian Charlie's) comments. I laugh at that. He's got a cartoon where every time I win a big race I'm coming out of a casket and it always says 'I ain't dead yet.'"

Lukas said he could have had many more runners in the Cup were it not for a cautious approach he took with his young horses. Rather than drive on them for the Cup's two-year-old races, which were extended a sixteenth of a mile to a mile and an eighth, he opted to look ahead to the Triple Crown the following spring. It was, if nothing else, uncharacteristic for a trainer who routinely grabbed the money and ran without looking too far into the future.

"I've got some two-year-olds that I think are really special," he said. "They're all bred for and act like classic route horses. I'm thinking grandiose ideas here because I've got some good ones. If we ever brought anything to the table, we've been innovative. Years ago everybody would have not come into the Breeders' Cup three days before the races. We did that for years in the Triple Crown races and the Breeders' Cup, now that's the mode. We got criticized for that 10 years ago. People said, 'Why would he come in so late and not work over the racetrack?' Now, hell, everybody does it. It's the way to go. But I think you've got to keep adjusting. Thoroughbred racing is so stereotyped and so tradition-bound that people bury their heads in the sands. I like to see if I can experiment a little bit. There's a reason why we haven't had a Triple Crown winner in 25 years and it isn't all pedigrees. We're matching them up better than we ever did."

Orientate went postward as the 27-10 favorite, while Day Trader was dismissed at almost 30-1. Jockey Jerry Bailey had Orientate close to the pace and only a length back of 48-1 outsider Thunderello heading into the stretch. In deep stretch, Orientate overtook the pacesetter and won by a half-length. Day Trader placed 11th by almost eight lengths. It didn't turn out to be Day's day, but it marked another Lukas triumph.

"If you go back, you members of the press, you know so well the number of horses and great horses that Wayne has brought Beverly and I," Bob Lewis said in the media room after the win. "I could just go on and on and on with all of them. . . . The list is just endless. What he's done for racing is just absolutely incredible."

*Daily Racing Form* writer Mike Welsch summed it up best in his post-race story: "D. Wayne Lukas took an uncharacteristic backseat coming into the 2002 World Thoroughbred Championships, with starters in only one of the eight races on the card. What Lukas lacked in quantity he made up for in quality, though."

Like him or loathe him—and there are a great many people in both camps—Lukas is a winner. He has taken the Breeders' Cup and orchestrated it like a conductor, attaining personal levels of glory unheard of in the sport—at least in the modern era. He has done things that have boggled the mind like running multiple horse entries, and outfitting his horses with nasal bands and his jockeys with form-fitting silks. And he's won more races and more money than anyone else. He has made numerous comebacks after losing high-profile owners, a prolonged personal slump that saw him go 19 months without winning a Grade One race and the near-loss of his son Jeff. He has repelled the criticism of trainers and the media for his handling of horses and his off-hand remarks. Throughout his career, Lukas has been able to answer back with results where it has mattered the most—on the track.

"What have I left to prove?" he asked. "No matter what page you turn in the record book, we're there somewhere. I don't feel compelled or a need to go out every Breeders' Cup or every Triple Crown or every major stake and try to prove I can do it again and again. We are at a position—and I feel comfortable—of just doing a good job and letting happen what happens. I don't fight the awards banquet. I don't fight the media. How can you knock a guy that's won 17 Breeders' Cups?"

# ·9·

# The Kentucky Kid

## Shug McGaughey

*Y*ou could feel the excitement in the cool November air in 1988 as Kentucky geared up for its first Breeders' Cup. Churchill Downs is home to the Kentucky Derby, the most famous horse race in North America, yet the Breeders' Cup was different. It represented a totally new experience, a racing extravaganza on the first Saturday in November instead of the first Saturday in May. The setting couldn't have been more perfect for trainer Claude R. (Shug) McGaughey III, a native Kentuckian coming home with a group of horses that would start his incredible run in the Breeders' Cup.

McGaughey was born in Lexington in 1951, the son of a real estate agent. His grandmother endearingly called him "Sugar," which was later shortened to Shug. McGaughey developed a love for horses going to the races at Keeneland and later began working with them. He left university after two years to keep his groom's job with David Carr, whom he later assisted. He then apprenticed for Frank Whiteley, the trainer of such champions as Forego, Ruffian and Damascus. After six months in South Carolina with Frank, McGaughey moved to New York to work for Whiteley's son, David, who had become a successful trainer in his own right. Shug worked there for five years before taking out his own license in 1979.

In 1982, McGaughey received his first big break when he was hired by John Ed Anthony to train Loblolly Stable. A year later, McGaughey won his first Grade One race when Try Something New scored in the Spinster at Keeneland. Two years later, 1985, McGaughey ran his first horse in the Breeders' Cup, saddling Vanlandingham in the Classic. The four-year-old ran seventh and failed to collect a check, but was named champion older horse that year.

Nine days after the 1985 Breeders' Cup, McGaughey received his second big break when Ogden Phipps and his son Ogden Mills, better known as "Dinny," hired him as their private trainer. Training the Phippses' horses represented a dream come true, not unlike managing the New York Yankees, albeit with considerably more stability. McGaughey might have been from Kentucky, but he trained enough in New York to appreciate the significance of working for the Phippses: prestige and horse power. Ogden Phipps' mother and uncle started the family's involvement in the sport in the 1920s with the Wheatley Stable, which bred 1938

Horse of the Year Seabiscuit and bred and raced 1957 Horse of the Year Bold Ruler. Taking his grandfather's colors of black silks and cherry red cap, Ogden Phipps bred and raced several champions, including Buckpasser, the 1966 Horse of the Year. While not as successful as his father, Dinny Phipps had a solid string of horses. He also had political clout as the chairman of the New York Racing Association and chairman of The Jockey Club, which is dedicated to improving thoroughbred breeding and racing.

The Phippses, who breed rather than buy horses, had a barn full of older stock with some running ability and younger ones with loads of potential. In 1987, McGaughey led all New York trainers in win percentage, a distinction he would hold for the next two years. In his third full term, the now-defunct publication *Racing Action* did a cover story on McGaughey and his stars under the headline "Murderers' Row," borrowed from the famed 1927 Yankees' team. McGaughey brought five Phipps runners to Kentucky for the 1988 Breeders' Cup: Personal Ensign for the Distaff; Easy Goer for the Juvenile; Mining for the Sprint; and the entry of Personal Flag and Seeking the Gold for the Classic. Among them they had 10 Grade One victories and all but Personal Flag had won their preceding starts. Collectively, they represented an awesome talent.

From the moment they touched down by plane from New York, McGaughey's Fab Five had the media buzzing around them. It made for a wonderful Kentucky story; not only were the horses bred in the Bluegrass State, but so was the trainer.

"I was excited, I loved Churchill, I loved Louisville," McGaughey said. "Being from Lexington, it meant a lot to come back home holding that strong of a hand."

The actual Breeders' Cup Day had less pressure for McGaughey than the weeks leading up to it. As far back as the summer McGaughey had had the Breeders' Cup as his goal, but getting there had been the hard part. McGaughey had shipped in earlier than normal to Churchill because he knew the track well and how tricky it could be.

"This racetrack can be different in the fall than in the spring," he told *Newsday*'s Paul Moran five days before race day. "They all got over the track good today. Everyone's going along good."

But on race day, not all of his horses handled the quirky course made even more difficult by rain. Mining, ridden by Randy Romero, became the first victim in the Sprint. Owned by Dinny Phipps, Mining had won all six career races, including the Vosburgh Stakes about a month before. But his racing life, which was to end after the Sprint, had been plagued by unsoundness problems. Sent off as the 17-10 favorite, the four-year-old son of Mr. Prospector had good position early but faltered on the greasy footing and finished 10th. Gulch, trained by D. Wayne Lukas, won under a brilliantly aggressive ride by Angel Cordero Jr.

Two races later came the Distaff, featuring Ogden Phipps' Personal Ensign, whom history will recall as one of the greatest and grittiest racemares of all time. She was by Private Account, whose dam, Numbered Account, won the 1971 Eclipse Award for Phipps as champion two-year-old filly in North America. Personal Ensign boasted a record of 12 wins in 12 starts coming into the race. She had won her first two starts as a two-year-old—including a debut score by nearly 13 lengths—but had her season abruptly halted when she broke her left hind leg in two places following her last major workout before the 1986 Breeders' Cup. Five screws were used to hold the bone in place. When the vets told him after the operation she could race again, McGaughey thought they were nuts.

McGaughey patiently brought her back to the races in September of 1987. She rattled off four consecutive wins in less than six weeks, the last victory coming in a key Breeders' Cup prep, the Beldame Stakes. But with the Distaff only 16 days away and in California, McGaughey and the Phippses opted to retire her for the season. Personal Ensign returned in July of 1988 to win the Molly Pitcher Stakes at Monmouth Park in New Jersey. She then won the prestigious Whitney Stakes in the slop at Saratoga against male horses, including eventual Breeders' Cup Sprint winner Gulch. She won two more times, including a repeat in the Beldame, before making her long-awaited debut in the Breeders' Cup, which would conclude her career. Personal Ensign had a chance to become the first horse in 80 years to retire undefeated.

Gene Klein's 1988 Kentucky Derby winner Winning Colors, a Wayne Lukas–trained filly built like a colt, represented Personal Ensign's principal opponent in the field of nine. Though a Kentucky Derby winner commands attention, she had lost to Personal Ensign in the Maskette and did not have the same overwhelming credentials. Winning Colors had won the Derby in front-running fashion under a heady ride by Gary Stevens and six months later it appeared as if that same tactic would work in the Distaff. Stevens nursed his filly on a comfortable lead, setting a moderate pace for horses of that caliber. After a slow three-quarters, Winning Colors had a two-length lead, while Personal Ensign was eight lengths back in fifth. Normally with three-eighths of a mile to the wire, Personal Ensign would have been in full flight, but this time she looked vulnerable. McGaughey, standing next to a friend at that point in the race said, "Not today."

Romero, who knew from the outset Personal Ensign was uncomfortable on the off-going, also had his doubts. Romero came into the race figuring Personal Ensign was "the best filly that ever lived, a push-button machine," but clearly this would require an effort for the ages to prove that. And that's what she gave.

At the top of the lane, Romero angled his mount out wide for better footing and she began her memorable run down the long stretch at Churchill. Stevens had Winning Colors running closest to the rail and gave her several left-handed cracks with the whip to keep her focused. Midway in the stretch, Personal Ensign was almost stopped by Goodbye Halo, who was running second and veering into her path. With a sixteenth of a mile to the wire, Stevens started nonstop, rapid-fire left-handed whipping. Romero used a combination of right-handed whips and rhythmic pumping on the reins in the final few strides to the wire. Romero said Personal Ensign could see Winning Colors and instinctively kept fighting, refusing to be beaten. In the final stride, Personal Ensign prevailed by a nose. As they galloped out past the wire, race announcer Tom Durkin, who sounded exhausted from the battle, said: "A very close finish. At the sixteenth pole, it looked like Personal Ensign was facing her first defeat, but in those final 110 yards she certainly proved herself a champion this afternoon."

As Romero returned back to the winner's enclosure, he held up an index finger to signal his filly was No. 1, knowing she was the best and deserved to be recognized as such.

"She was one in a million," Romero said. "I really think if ever there was a miracle that was one because she wasn't handling the racecourse at all. She wasn't comfortable. But all the determination and guts, the desire and the fight made her that one in a million and made her a winner. She didn't want to get beat."

"It might have been the best race I ever saw," Dinny Phipps said.

Seven years after that Distaff, a daughter of Personal Ensign named My Flag revived memories of her mother by winning the Juvenile Fillies with a similar determined rally.

Angel Cordero Jr., who finished fifth in the '88 Distaff aboard Classic Crown, said Personal Ensign's undefeated career combined with her comeback from a broken leg and the marvelous job McGaughey did with her made it a memorable moment.

"It was wild to see something like that happen," he said. "It was something that I said, 'If I can't win I want to see her win.' It got to the point where she had grabbed everybody's heart and everybody was rooting for her." In McGaughey's mind, Personal Ensign overcame both himself and Romero, beating good horses on a track she didn't like. He did not think Personal Ensign would win until the last jump and immediately felt a great sense of relief. He walked to the winner's circle exhausted and emotionally drained. The pressure had been building as her winning streak grew and it wasn't until well after that Breeders' Cup that McGaughey could savor the overall experience, both for the filly and for himself. "Her last start, in the Beldame, was the first time I ever really was able to sit back and just enjoy watching her run," McGaughey told Moran a few days before the race. "Before that, I was always too nervous because of her undefeated record. I wish I could have enjoyed those races because she really is a treat to watch. I have all the tapes of her races, but I've never watched them. This winter, I'm going to pull them out and watch them over and over."

Clearly the Distaff would be the one he would watch the most.

Two races after the Distaff, McGaughey returned to the paddock with Easy Goer for the Juvenile, a race many consider the best preview to the Kentucky Derby. In many minds, Easy Goer had the Derby already won and this was but a stepping stone. By Alydar out of Relaxing, the champion older mare in North America in 1981, Easy Goer certainly had the bloodlines. His maternal grandsire was Buckpasser, the best horse Ogden Phipps ever bred and raced. He won champion two-year-old colt honors in 1965, Horse of the Year honors in '66 and handicap horse in '67. If ever there appeared to be a reincarnation of Buckpasser, Easy Goer was it. He had magnificent looks, the kind that could win a beauty contest, and the conformation breeders desire.

Leaving postward the 3-10 favorite—lowest odds for any horse in Breeders' Cup history at that point—Easy Goer, ridden by regular jockey Pat Day, started second widest in the field of 10. The Lukas-trained Is It True, who had run second to Easy Goer in their last race, had the two hole and inherited the lead after a half mile. He never surrendered it, winning by a length and a quarter over Easy Goer. Like Personal Ensign, Easy Goer did not handle the track, but unlike the filly could not overcome it. Lukas later called the victory one of the biggest upsets in the history of racing and his greatest training job. McGaughey scoffed at that, saying Easy Goer could "pull a wagon and beat that horse. He just didn't handle the racetrack."

With the Juvenile still fresh in his mind, McGaughey prepared for the Classic. The entry of Seeking the Gold and Personal Flag represented McGaughey's weakest offering of the day if the odds were any indication. The public sent them postward at just under 6-1, fourth choice behind 3-2 favorite Alysheba. The year before, Alysheba had won the Kentucky Derby but lost the Classic by a nose to 1986 Derby winner Ferdinand. In the interim, he had become the top horse in America and had a chance to set an all-time career earnings record with a victory. Seeking the Gold had posted a gutsy win over Forty Niner in the Super Derby in his last race and while McGaughey liked his chances, he also knew the three-year-old was facing tough older horses for the first time. The five-year-old Personal Flag represented a solid entrymate, and McGaughey liked him as the better part of the entry because of the age factor. In near darkness, Alysheba closed out the dramatic day winning by a half-length over Seeking the Gold, who rallied from far back. Personal Flag finished sixth. It had been an incredibly emotional day for the young Kentucky trainer, and it continued on a walk back to the barn with veteran trainer Charlie Whittingham, who had finished a distant eighth in the Classic with Lively One and had only a third-place finish from among the three horses he saddled on the day. McGaughey lamented about winning only one and posting two seconds, to which Whittingham, almost 40 years his senior and with a world of experience behind him, replied: "Boy, you had a big day, didn't you?"

The Bald Eagle, as Whittingham was known, had put it all into perspective and years later McGaughey could appreciate his achievement. "I was disappointed, but I was a pretty young trainer, and now I realize it was a good day," McGaughey said. "To be able to compete in those kind of races and have legitimate chances means a lot."

McGaughey won the Eclipse Award as the top trainer in North America that year. He tied Lukas nationally with 15 Grade One winners and Personal Ensign and Easy Goer were named champions. Ogden Phipps won the Eclipse Award as the top owner and breeder and led all owners in earnings with a then-record $5,858,168.

McGaughey and Whittingham became the two principal figures among trainers the following year in the Triple Crown. Easy Goer, as expected, made it to Louisville as the favorite. Whittingham brought along a horse named Sunday Silence, a virtual unknown at two but considered a freak runner at three. He had almost died at one point in his life after a van accident and had passed through the sales ring twice without finding a buyer who was willing to meet breeder Arthur Hancock's price. Hancock later sold an interest to the horse to Whittingham, who in turn sold a share to his longtime friend Ernest Gaillard. Sunday Silence won the Derby, when once again Easy Goer found the slippery footing at Churchill not to his liking. Sunday Silence then beat his rival by a nose in the Preakness. Many people called it the race of the year after the two horses engaged in an eye-to-eye stretch battle. Easy Goer trounced Sunday Silence by eight lengths in the Belmont Stakes in a time that was second only to the immortal Secretariat, much to the delight of the partisan New York crowd. That led to a rematch in the 1989 Breeders' Cup Classic at Gulfstream Park in Florida. Easy Goer took the New York route to the Cup, beating the competition in four races by a combined 13½ lengths. He won so easily in one race that track announcer Marshall Cassidy exuberantly proclaimed him "horse of the year." Whittingham prepped his horse in Louisiana, winning the Super Derby almost six weeks before the Classic. Besides Easy Goer, McGaughey brought Dancing Spree for the Sprint, Adjudicating and Rhythm for the Juvenile and In Full Cry for the Juvenile Fillies. This handful didn't have the same magnitude on paper as the five McGaughey had brought to the Cup a year before, but they were talented. Dancing Spree won the Sprint at 16-1 odds by a neck over pacesetter Safely Kept after a furious finish under Angel Cordero Jr. The five-year-old, owned by Ogden Phipps, had been a long-term project for McGaughey, who practically gave up on him in the winter of his three-year-old year. Although Dancing Spree won his first career outing on the dirt, McGaughey moved the horse to the grass to capitalize on his turf breeding. Dancing Spree never won on the lawn in seven career starts. At the suggestion of his then wife, Mary-Jean, McGaughey switched Dancing Spree to sprint racing on the dirt late in his four-year-old year, setting the stage for his future career highlight.

Dinny Phipps' In Full Cry finished a well-beaten 10th to Go for Wand in the Juvenile Fillies, but three races later the owner celebrated victory in the Juvenile with Rhythm, ridden by Craig Perret. Rhythm tallied by two lengths, while entry-mate Adjudicating, who had beaten him in their previous race, ran 11th by more than 15 lengths. Adjudicating had appeared the stronger of the pair, but McGaughey loved Rhythm, figuring he had had some trouble in his last race and had trained spectacularly at Gulfstream for the Breeders' Cup. Rhythm, who won champion two-year-old honors that year, did in fact develop into the better of the two.

The Juvenile set up McGaughey for the Classic and the rematch with Sunday Silence. The public liked Easy Goer, making him the 1-2 favorite over Sunday Silence at 2-1. Easy Goer had some ankle problems that required work going into the race, but not enough that McGaughey felt compromised his chances. Sunday Silence, ridden by Chris McCarron after regular jockey Pat Valenzuela was fired for missing a workout aboard the horse, always had the upper hand on Easy Goer in the race. Sunday Silence won by a neck, after a strong rally by Easy Goer, whose rider, Pat Day, came under heavy criticism from some media people but not from McGaughey. Easy Goer lost position early in the race trying to head towards the gap between the chute and the main track. McGaughey also thought Sunday Silence had better ability on turns and had the edge turning for home, where he led by four lengths. Once again, McGaughey felt dejected despite the victories and it required a pep talk of sorts, this time by Dinny Phipps, to again make him appreciate the overall day.

"I was disappointed," McGaughey said. "I was sitting back (in the barn) and

I remember my boss came back and said, 'No matter what happened, you had a great day today.' You put it in perspective, we did have a great day." Ogden Phipps won the Eclipse Award as the top owner and again led the continent in purse earnings with $5.4 million.

A leg injury midway through 1990 ended Easy Goer's career and typified McGaughey's year, which paled in comparison to his big runs late in the '80s. He ran only one horse in the 1990 Breeders' Cup, Travers Stakes winner Rhythm, who ran in the Classic as the favorite. He trained well but ran poorly, finishing eighth, almost 20 lengths behind Kentucky Derby winner Unbridled.

McGaughey ran five horses in four races in the 1991 Breeders' Cup at Churchill Downs, but this time he didn't have the Kentucky luck. His best finish came with Versailles Treaty, who ran second in the Distaff for owner Cynthia Phipps, daughter of Ogden Phipps.

In 1992, McGaughey brought six horses to the Breeders' Cup at Gulfstream: Furiously for the Sprint; Educated Risk for the Juvenile Fillies; Versailles Treaty for the Distaff; Lure for the Mile; and Living Vicariously and Strolling Along for the Juvenile. By day's end, he would post only one victory, but it would be one of the biggest of his career. Lure was bred and owned by Claiborne Farm, one of the most prestigious stallion operations in the world and the place where the Phippses foal their horses. Claiborne's president, Seth Hancock, had recommended McGaughey for the job when the Phippses sought a replacement for Angel Penna. Lure blasted out of the one hole under Mike Smith and led all the way in winning by three lengths in course-record time.

A star was born, but McGaughey wasn't the least bit surprised. He had transformed the well-bred horse from a disappointment on the dirt to a star on the grass. In his eighth career start and first on the grass, Lure won a mile and a six-teenth grass race by $10\frac{1}{4}$ lengths in a time of 1:41. Even though he finished second on soft ground against older horses in the Kelso Stakes next time out, McGaughey felt confident. Lure trained well in New York and continued to improve each day in Florida.

"I don't think I've ever run a horse as good as he was that day," McGaughey said. "Everything he did, he was going in the right direction."

"We all felt he had a great chance in the race and to go on and become what he turned out to be," Lure's regular rider Mike Smith said. "Of course I got to go on him a lot and knew what he was capable of."

Smith exhibited unbridled enthusiasm when he won, waving his whip like he had taken a course from Angel Cordero on how to celebrate. It would become a trademark reaction for Smith in the big races.

In 1993, McGaughey won an unprecedented five consecutive stakes at Belmont Park on Breeders' Cup Preview Day and six of 10 races on the card. Lure headed McGaughey's Breeders' Cup contingent, which included Heavenly Prize in the Juvenile Fillies, Dispute in the Distaff and Miner's Mark, a son of Personal Ensign, in the Classic.

Seth Hancock marveled about Lure's ability following his victory in the Kelso Stakes. "I may be prejudiced, but it's been a long time since we've seen a horse that can do the kinds of things he can," Hancock was quoted as saying in *The Blood-Horse.*

Once again, Lure proved to be McGaughey's only winner, but this time it was more dramatic. He had to overcome his post—second-widest in the field of 13—and avoid traffic problems created by runner-up Ski Paradise heading into the first turn. Lure became only the second runner in Breeders' Cup history to record back-to-back victories.

"There was a crucial moment there going into the first turn, where we were going to be hung out 15 wide if we didn't make a move and when I asked him, man, he just accelerated and kind of beat all the traffic over and didn't lose as much ground as he would have (had he been affected by Ski Paradise)," Smith said.

The race was one of a record 62 stakes wins by Smith that year in which his mounts won more than $14 million. That helped earn him the Eclipse Award as the top rider.

Smith and McGaughey failed in their attempt to record a triple with Lure in the 1994 Mile at Churchill. Lure suffered a stunning nose defeat to long shot Nijinsky's Gold in the Kelso, the race preceding the Breeders' Cup. Moreover, before leaving for Kentucky, Lure rapped a leg that hemorrhaged and swelled. Once in Louisville, he developed a quarter crack that became an even bigger concern.

"We were working on that the whole time. Had we had another two weeks it would have been perfect," McGaughey said. "I think we were hoping against hope in that respect, but he wasn't the same horse."

At 9-10 odds, Lure finished ninth, beaten by more than nine lengths. He never displayed any of the ability he had shown in the previous two Breeders' Cup races. Ironically, the winner, European invader Barathea, had run in the Mile the previous year, but lost all chance when involved in the interference by Ski Paradise.

"I would have liked to have won three because no horse had ever done that before but that wasn't the way it was," McGaughey said.

The race prior to the Mile, McGaughey ran Heavenly Prize, who the year before was third in the Juvenile Fillies. In the Distaff, jockey Gary Stevens, a master at controlling the pace, took the lead early on the 47-1 One Dreamer and kept her going, staving off Heavenly Prize, who made a menacing rush under Pat Day but finished second by a neck.

In 1995, at Belmont Park—his home court—McGaughey had one of his most emotional Breeders' Cups. He ran four horses—all for the Phippses—including My Flag, the improving daughter of Easy Goer out of Personal Ensign. On the first race of the card, My Flag, under Jerry Bailey, rallied like her mother and ran down a pair of Lukas trainees, Cara Rafaela and Golden Attraction. McGaughey then saddled Ogden Phipps' Our Emblem to a sixth-place finish in the Sprint. In the next race, the Distaff, McGaughey recorded a one-two finish with the entry of Inside Information, ridden by Smith, and Heavenly Prize. Inside Information won by a whopping 13½ lengths, the largest winning margin in Breeders' Cup history, easily eclipsing the previous mark of seven lengths set by Princess Rooney in the inaugural Distaff in 1984. Inside Information liked the muddy track, which Heavenly Prize didn't, and the Belmont configuration.

After the Distaff, a rainbow appeared over Belmont. But McGaughey, with his best-ever day at the Breeders' Cup in hand, already had his pot of gold.

It would prove to be a while again before McGaughey savored success at the Breeders' Cup. In 1996, he came to the Cup with My Flag in the Distaff and Hidden Reserve in the Juvenile Fillies. My Flag ran fourth by 8½ lengths in her race and wasn't given much of a shot by the bettors, who dismissed her at more than 7-1, the fourth choice overall in the field of six. Hidden Reserve preceded her and placed seventh by 18 lengths in her race.

In 1997, McGaughey did not run a horse in the Breeders', ending a streak of running at least one horse since 1988. In 1998, he brought three starters: Emanating in the Juvenile Fillies; Furlough in the Sprint; and Coronado's Quest in the Classic. Emanating ran fifth by more than eight lengths, Furlough placed 10th by some seven lengths and Coronado's Quest ran fifth by about two lengths. Neither of the horses came into their respective races with the kind of form to make them appealing from a betting standpoint. Furlough represented McGaughey's only horse in 1999 and he ran 10th in the Sprint. In 2000, McGaughey again did not have a runner. In 2001, McGaughey had Atelier in the Distaff and Saarland in the Juvenile. Atelier ran fourth and Saarland eighth.

In 2002, McGaughey experienced professional and personnel changes. Earlier in the year, Ogden Phipps, the patriarch of the Phipps family and the man who shaped McGaughey's career when he hired him in 1985, died at the age of 93. On June 13, McGaughey underwent a triple bypass after a routine physical revealed some blockages. He returned to work almost six weeks later.

"I hated not being at the barn," he told the *Albany Times-Union*. "Just sitting at home was hard, and I had to do a little more of that than I wanted to. I think I am getting better now, and I feel good. My biggest problem is trying to do too much. They warn you, warn you, warn you not to do that, and it has kind of knocked me in the head a couple of times, but I think I've learned my lesson."

A two-year-old filly with impeccable breeding made her debut on August 18 at Saratoga and by year's end she would provide the Phipps family and McGaughey with the latest star in their galaxy of great racehorses. Storm Flag Flying, a daughter of Storm Cat and My Flag, had Breeders' Cup bloodlines. Her sire ran second in the 1995 Breeders' Cup Juvenile, then became a prominent stallion, whose progeny included 1999 Breeders' Cup Classic winner Cat Thief. Storm Flag Flying's dam won the 1995 Breeders' Cup Juvenile Fillies and had been a daughter of the great Personal Ensign, who culminated her undefeated career with a breathtaking win in the 1988 Breeders' Cup Distaff. Storm Flag Flying debuted on August 18 at Saratoga in a six-furlong race and came from off the pace to win by a length under John Velazquez. She raced again on September 15 at Belmont in the Grade One Matron Stakes and demolished the field well with a smashing 12¾-length score. She followed that up with a two-length win in the Grade One Frizette Stakes on October 5 at Belmont as her final race before the Breeders' Cup. She was rated one of the heaviest favorites on the card and went postward at 4-5. She tracked the front-runners and took the lead midway in the stretch from Composure, then surrendered briefly but dug in with determination in the final strides to the wire to prevail by half a length.

More than a few people remarked she displayed the gameness of her maternal grandmother Personal Ensign in her valiant victory in the 1988 Distaff.

"In Personal Ensign's race she's hopelessly beaten and came on and won, so I think that's the bloodlines and the breed and it's jumping out at them to give them the class," McGaughey said. "My Flag was a great racehorse, her family was great and then you get Storm Cat on top of it as a sire. If they can run they're going to show some class. When she made the lead I wasn't surprised that she tried to pull herself up. I mean, I just know her with us being around her every day and how she acts and what she sees. When she's doing that she's all ears. It all happened so quick. I don't think it ever went through my head, 'Well, she's beat.' I was watching her come and I was a little concerned around the turn whether she was going to get by the filly on the lead or not. When she did I saw her kind of brace herself just a little bit and then when that filly came by us it was the best thing that could have happened and she got back into the race so quick. You know, I thought it was a pretty handy win.

"To get Personal Ensign and to get My Flag and then to get this one, I think is extraordinary. To have them all run the races they ran in the Breeders' Cup, all three of them, made it exciting. We all remember Personal Ensign and My Flag got up three jumps to win and this filly comes back and wins today, so they kind of keep your heart in the game.

"Personal Ensign was a different thing because she had won 12 in a row when she won (the Breeders' Cup) as a four-year-old. We had never won a Breeders' Cup, so not only was that at stake but an unbeaten streak was at stake. I think the races were different because until the last jump you didn't think Personal Ensign was going to win and today where she was, Storm Flag Flying was in tracking position at all times. Johnny said she was pretty green running today. Going down the backside I can't see that. I thought she was laying good and laying where I wanted her to be. That was sort of my concern coming into the race."

Dinny Phipps used the occasion to make a comment about McGaughey's staff.

"As great a trainer as Shug is—and he's in my mind extraordinary—he's also got a wonderful organization behind him. . . . They are first-rate horsemen and I think that is also a credit to Shug."

# 10

# The Classic Trainer

## Jack Van Berg

*W*hen he won the 1995 Breeders' Cup Classic with Cigar, trainer Bill Mott received a congratulatory call from his former boss, Jack Van Berg. Besides having a soft spot for Mott, his top protégé, Van Berg had a keen appreciation for the Classic. It is the richest of the seven Breeders' Cup races and the most prestigious, one in which victory plays an influential role in the vote for Horse of the Year honors. But beyond all that, Van Berg knew more than any other trainer just how difficult it is to win the Classic. He is one of the top-winning trainers in history, but it took him four tries before he was able to shrug off the frustration of Classic defeats that deflated his spirits and dented his finances. As he is fond of saying with his wry humor: "I was three noses away from being out of debt."

Born in Nebraska in 1936, Jack is a Hall of Famer who followed in the footsteps of his Hall of Fame father, Marion Van Berg, a master trainer who owned most of his stock. He led the annual owners' category in wins 14 times and in purse earnings four times. Jack started working for his father—known to everybody as Mr. Van—at the tender age of eight and had his trainer's license by his mid-teens. He won his first race at age 16 and his first stakes three years after that. His career took a major turn when he took over the family business after his father's death in 1971. From 1968 to 1976, Jack Van Berg led the nation's trainers in wins six times.

Van Berg ground it out the hard way—through the claiming game—haltering someone else's discarded goods and turning them around with good old-fashioned horsemanship learned from his father, whom he described as the greatest teacher in the world. Van Berg became the first trainer to win 5,000 career races and he remains second only to Dale Baird as the top-winning trainer in history.

While trainer D. Wayne Lukas has capitalized on running multiple divisions across the country with assistants, Van Berg pioneered the idea long before. He had an incredible seven outfits running at one time before scaling back in 1977, but he has not reduced his overall operation. He has training centers in California and Kentucky that are also used for his other occupation—breeding for personal and commercial purposes. The collective costs of phone bills—he is the only trainer to have an 800 number—airplane tickets, motel rooms and car rentals now annually exceed the six-figure mark. Van Berg figuratively stands taller than just his 6-foot-

2 frame. He is one of the sport's most innovative trainers and one of its greatest characters, a combination cowboy, entrepreneur and raconteur. He tells stories with a generous supply of similes and metaphors, the best of which are about his Breeders' Cup Classic experiences.

Gate Dancer thrust Van Berg into the limelight as his first Classic contender. Purchased as a yearling in 1982 for $62,500 by Nebraska insurance executive Ken Opstein, a longtime client of Van Berg's, Gate Dancer ran four times as a two-year-old, winning twice and placing in the other two. He also showed the first signs of reckless racing behavior, which subsequently earned him the reputation of a rogue. Van Berg used a special bit to correct the horse's habit of lugging in. He added assorted other equipment, including a shadow roll to prevent him from looking down, but by far Gate Dancer's most unusual attire was a purple hood with ear muffs. Gate Dancer, according to Opstein, was "super-sensitive and aware" of everything more than most horses. When he heard the crowd noise he would look and be distracted from giving his best effort in the stretch drive. To silence the crowd sounds, Van Berg stuffed sponge in the horse's ears and covered them up with the hooded muffs attached to a mask normally used for blinkers. It was not unusual in other countries for horsemen to cover up racehorses' ears—sometimes to keep bugs out—but in the U.S., Gate Dancer's hood was an original. Not that this was the first time Van Berg contrived some unique equipment. He once bought a pair of falsies at a lingerie shop to place on the back ankles of a horse called Summertime Promise, who scraped herself while running. The newspapers had fun with the story.

Gate Dancer wore his contraption for the first time in the 1984 Kentucky Derby, drawing guffaws and derision from the crowd. "I'll have to admit he looked like he was dressed to lead the Easter parade," Van Berg told the *Los Angeles Times'* Bill Christine in an interview the following year. "He needed the earmuffs so he couldn't hear all the terrible things people were saying about him."

"He became probably the most recognizable horse in America because of the hood over his ears," Opstein said.

Gate Dancer finished a respectable fourth in the Derby after trailing the field at the start, but the stewards disqualified the colt and placed him fifth for causing interference with Fali Time in the stretch drive. It marked the first disqualification in Kentucky Derby history for a foul during the running of the race. Opstein believed Gate Dancer had been primed for that race more than any he'd ever been in, but broke last because he'd been held up by the assistant starter and subsequently banged his head on both sides of his stall leaving the gate.

Under Angel Cordero Jr. in place of Eddie Delahoussaye, Gate Dancer rebounded by winning the Preakness Stakes in course-record time. He then ran a distant sixth in the Belmont Stakes to Derby winner Swale. In the fall, he registered victories in the Omaha Gold Cup and the Super Derby in course-record time in Louisiana. In the latter race, he felt the smack of Bill Shoemaker's whip squarely in the face after the veteran rider threw his crop while riding runner-up Precisionist.

Gate Dancer rose to the top of three-year-old ranks, setting himself up as one of the contenders in the first-ever Breeders' Cup Classic, the world's richest race at the time. Opstein, a onetime sportswriter, couldn't have dreamed up a better story: prestige and money and a talented horse with a hood.

"It wasn't just the money, but the idea of having a horse good enough to race in such company that was really the exciting part," Opstein said. "Inasmuch as there had been no race anywhere for that amount of money, you were facing the very best competition that there could be in the world. Those kinds of horses don't come along every day where you could put them in such an elite race."

The race produced high drama as Wild Again, Gate Dancer and Slew o' Gold, the 3-5 favorite from New York ridden by Cordero, bumped and brushed repeatedly in the stretch as if they were on a crowded dance floor. For 10 minutes the stewards viewed the films, but Wild Again's first-place finish by a head stood, while Gate Dancer, the runner-up, was disqualified and placed third for causing severe interference. In Van Berg's opinion, his horse would have won the race had Laffit Pincay ridden him as he did in the Super Derby. Moreover, he believed the other horses caused the interference, specifically Wild Again, who he believed shied away from the fence while being crowded by Slew o' Gold. Van Berg believed Gate Dancer's reputation for erratic stretch runs led to the disqualification; in other words, he was the usual suspect.

"His number was taken down because he was the bad kid on the block," Opstein said. "NBC, in fact, told my farm manager that Wild Again's number was going to be taken down and we'd be elevated to first. To this day, people see Van Berg and myself and say, 'I still think you were the winner of that race.'"

The following morning, a crowd of reporters viewed films of the race with Van Berg, who claimed the pictures bore out his horse's innocence. "I kid the stewards to this day (that) I saved them from being lynched," Van Berg said.

Van Berg never appealed the stewards' decision as a matter of principle.

"If you're going to race somewhere, you should race by their rules," he said. "That's the decision they made. I may not agree with it, but I'm racing under their rules, so that's what you're supposed to do. I think there's too much nowadays every time something happens, some lawyer comes along and wants to sue somebody. I don't believe in that kind of stuff."

"The officials chose to say the bumping in the upper stretch was incidental and it was more important farther in the stretch," Opstein said. "Our contention was had they not bothered Gate Dancer he would have gone by on the outside and won by a couple lengths. But it's like an umpire's decision in baseball: you don't argue over balls and strikes and that was their decision. How do you say one's incidental and the other's more important? That's their decision."

Hall of Fame trainer Charlie Whittingham sided with the stewards, telling Christine that Gate Dancer was the best in the race "if he hadn't squeezed the other horse (Slew o' Gold)."

Van Berg led the nation with 250 wins in 1984 and became the first trainer to win that title and the Eclipse Award in the same year. Previously, voters had chosen the trainer whose horses won the most money. Van Berg felt the award made up for his disappointment in 1976 when he broke the record for wins and purse earnings. Laz Barrera won the Eclipse that year on the strength of his work with Kentucky Derby and Belmont Stakes winner Bold Forbes. Gate Dancer tried again in the 1985 Classic, going off the second choice in the wagering to 1984 Breeders' Cup Juvenile winner Chief's Crown. Gate Dancer had been second in the Jockey Club Gold Cup to Vanlandingham and Van Berg liked his chances in the Classic. Chris McCarron rode him that day and had a clear lead in the stretch but Florida Derby winner Proud Truth, recording his third consecutive win after a four-month layoff caused by an injury, ran him down to win by a head.

"To this day I say Gate Dancer should have won both his Breeders' Cups," Van Berg said. "He was the best horse on both days. After Chris knew him better he knew he made his move too quick. That horse wanted to run no farther than the last five-sixteenths of a mile. That's all the move he wanted to make. When Leroy Jolley's horse (Track Barron) made his move up around the turn, Chris went with him. Gate Dancer had such a strong move he just blowed by them horses. When you let that horse run, he could catch horses like a roping horse catching a calf. It was just one of those things that I thought he made his move too quick and Gate Dancer, when he got to the lead, lost interest."

McCarron said the horse inherited the lead earlier than he had hoped and Gate Dancer had a tendency to pull himself up when he made it to the top. "He would wait on the other horses, he just wouldn't draw off and leave them," McCarron said. "That was one of his habits. He was not an easy horse to ride by any means. He had a lot of talent. He had a tremendous amount of ability, but he was probably a very difficult horse for Jack to train and I know that he was a difficult horse to ride as well. I was in a position where I had a lot of horse. When I started gaining on the horses turning for home, I didn't want to take hold of him and slow him down at that point and encourage him to further decelerate when he hit the front, so I went ahead and asked him to run and he blew by the horses very quickly but it was premature. Once he opened up, he started looking around and pulling himself up and he allowed Proud Truth to run by him in the very late stages. From the eighth pole to the wire I was just relying on my ability to keep him running and relying on his talent and his ability to get to the wire first, but I know he could have beaten Proud Truth that day if the race had turned out just a little bit differently and I could have waited a little longer. I know he was the best horse in the race that day."

Gate Dancer ran only three more times as a five-year-old before an ankle injury incurred in a workout in Omaha ended his career. He retired to stud in Florida, where he was born, with more than $2.5 million earned. "He was two heads away from being a legend," Opstein said. "He had a length and a quarter lead in the early stretch and Chris McCarron moved too soon on him and got caught at the wire by Proud Truth and one step past the finish line he was in the lead again. There were a lot of of people who thought Gate Dancer never put out his very best because his ears weren't pinned back which a horse's are when he's giving his very best. Whether they were that way or they weren't, you don't know because maybe the mask prevented him from laying his ears right back. But he was an interesting horse and an exciting horse because he could come from 10 lengths behind and pick up lengths in a flash. That was the trouble Van Berg had with the jockeys. They were afraid the field was getting away too far and they'd move too soon. We certainly didn't want to take the lead in the upper stretch in '85, but jockeys are human beings. They make mistakes. It's a judgment call and those things happen. But, we lost another $1.675 million with those two heads."

The same year Gate Dancer retired, Van Berg found an heir apparent in Alysheba, owned by Texas cattle ranchers Clarence and Dorothy Scharbauer and their daughter Pamela. The Scharbauers, new to the thoroughbred game after a long involvement in quarter horse racing, hooked up with Van Berg through a mutual contact, Dr. Bill Lockridge. The Scharbauers came to the Kentucky summer yearling sales in 1985 looking to buy quality. Alysheba had the bloodlines: by the great Alydar out of the mare Bel Sheba, whose mother Belthazar produced the Group One–winning colt Lear Fan. Alysheba cost $500,000, the seventh-most expensive Alydar yearling of the 23 sold that year. The Scharbauers also bought three other prospects for a total of $1.2 million. Van Berg trained all of them to win, but Alysheba became the best of the bunch. When he retired after winning the Classic, he stood alone as the top money-winning horse of all time.

Alysheba impressed Van Berg from the time he was broken to saddle to his gallops, in which he outdistanced other horses with ease. He had abundant natural talent, but it took him three starts before he won his first career race by eight lengths with Don Brumfield aboard at Turfway Park. He ran two more times, losing both by a total of a length and a quarter, which Van Berg attributed at the time to a lack of fitness. Unbeknownst to Van Berg, the horse had an entrapped epiglottis, which was affecting the air passage. The stress incurred by the problem also caused blood buildup in the trachea.

Going into the 1986 Breeders' Cup, jockey Bill Shoemaker received the call on Alysheba because he had ridden Tomy Lee to victory for Dorothy Scharbauer's father (Fred Turner Jr.) in the 1959 Kentucky Derby. But Shoemaker didn't know about Alysheba's tendency to relax coming out of the gate and that he needed an encouraging tap with the whip to get his mind on business. After a quarter of a mile, Shoemaker found himself last in the 13-horse field. "I forgot to tell Bill in the paddock to slap him on the neck when he left the gate," Van Berg said. "He just let him settle down. Well, hell, that horse got so far back he galloped around like he was in another race. But, he came flying and ran a very credible race."

Alysheba ran third, 2½ lengths behind Capote. He closed out the year running second by a neck to Temperate Syl in the Hollywood Futurity, and posted earnings of $358,486 on the season.

Alysheba ran fourth by five lengths as the 7-10 favorite in his 1987 debut at Hollywood Park. Afterward, Van Berg had him checked internally with an endoscope, and that revealed the entrapped epiglottis and traces of blood. Van Berg ran him with the diuretic Lasix, which helps to control internal bleeding, in his next start. Alysheba finished second by three-quarters of a length in the San Felipe Stakes, but threw his head up at the top of the stretch, giving Van Berg cause for concern. After a subsequent scope, it was decided to operate on Alysheba to correct the epiglottis problem. Chris McCarron, who had only been back a month after a five-month layoff with a badly broken left leg, took over as the horse's rider and immediately benefited from a new and vastly improved Alysheba. The colt finished first in the Blue Grass Stakes but was disqualified and placed third for interfering with War at the eighth pole. Nine days later, however, Alysheba won the Kentucky Derby, giving Van Berg his first and only victory in the Run for the Roses. Alysheba followed that with a score in the Preakness Stakes, but faltered in his bid to sweep the Triple Crown in the Belmont Stakes, finishing fourth to rival Bet Twice. Alysheba returned from a little break and ran second by a neck in the Haskell Stakes, then threw in the worst race of his career, running last in the slop in the Travers. He rebounded to win the Super Derby, which set up a showdown in the Classic with 1986 Derby winner Ferdinand, ridden by Shoemaker.

On a clear day at Hollywood Park, enlivened by the presence of stars such as Linda Evans, Merv Griffin and John Forsythe, the Breeders' Cup had a warm and electric air about it. The rare confrontation between two Derby winners in the richest race on the card served as a marvelous punctuation to the day. Van Berg had Alysheba on his game and loved his chances of winning. Would this be the end of Van Berg's drought in the Classic? It took slightly more than two minutes to add another chapter to Van Berg's frustration. Ferdinand, who left the gate as the even-money favorite, prevailed by a nose, staving off a late bid by Alysheba. It appeared Alysheba had the race won when he hooked up with Ferdinand nearing the sixteenth pole, only to see the patient Shoemaker call on his horse for the finishing kick. It was a textbook ride by Shoemaker, using his head to escape being trapped along the rail nearing the far turn, and his hands to draw on something extra from his willing mount.

"I had so much confidence going into that race," Van Berg said. "Ferdinand was a good horse and Alysheba was just a three-year-old going up against him but he ran a super race and I think when McCarron came up to Shoemaker, he thought he had him. I don't think Shoemaker had enough saved there for another sudden little spurt. Two jumps past the wire we were back in front again. It was just one of those things. It wasn't supposed to happen. I'd run three horses in the $3 million races, the richest races ever run, and got beat by about a nose three times. You think something is riding on your shoulders that isn't good. But you've got to just keep trying. It's like when you walk out of a bar and somebody knocks you down and you've got to get back up and go in again."

McCarron said Alysheba was a difficult horse to ride, and as a three-year-old he was still relatively immature.

"When he was a two- and three-year-old, he was kind of a playboy, he was out there goofing around half the time," McCarron said. "He was so much better than a lot of the horses he ran against he was able to goof around and still win. In the Breeders' Cup Classic he kind of ran in stop-and-go fashion. He would move up a little bit and then he would decelerate and lose his momentum and then he'd move up again and decelerate. I think he was the best horse in that race and if he had just gotten down on his belly and run hard from the middle of the turn on to the wire, I think he would have gotten there first. I shouldn't take anything away from Ferdinand or Shoe. I had the good fortune of riding with Shoe for 15 years and saw two of his greatest rides. Unfortunately, I finished second in both of them. They were both on Ferdinand: one in the Kentucky Derby and one in the Breeders' Cup Classic. Alysheba was a victim of Shoe's excellent ride in the Breeders' Cup Classic and that was just a case of (Alysheba) being a little bit immature mentally. But, I tell you what, he turned the tables when he was four."

Four months later in the Santa Anita Handicap, Alysheba beat Ferdinand by a half-length. Almost six weeks later, they clashed again in the San Bernardino Handicap and Alysheba prevailed again, this time by a nose. He raced five more times before the Breeders' Cup, losing the Pimlico Special and Hollywood Gold Cup, but winning the Iselin, Woodward and Meadowlands Cup. Collectively, he won the three by about a length.

His next—and what would be his last—start came in the 1988 Breeders' Cup, an edition which history will recall as the greatest ever for sheer drama and emotion. Each race provided an interesting story: Angel Cordero sweeping the first two races, the first time that had ever happened in Breeders' Cup history; Personal Ensign courageously overcoming the off track to win the Distaff by a nose and concluding her brilliant career undefeated in 13 races; Miesque prevailing in the Mile to become the first back-to-back winner in Breeders' Cup history; and Easy Goer losing the Juvenile in a stunning upset.

By post time for the Classic, the crowd had been whipped into an emotional frenzy. A lot rode on the race: the chance for Alysheba to surpass the immortal John Henry as the all-time money-winning horse with a victory; Horse of the Year honors; and, for Van Berg, the opportunity to finally break his Classic losing streak. The public backed him as the 3-2 favorite, but Alysheba had to prove he could handle an off track.

"Churchill Downs is, I think, one of the best racetracks there is to race over in the country and so I was very confident in him, even though everyone else thought the mud would stop him," Van Berg said.

Darkness had descended on the Downs by post time for the race, which became known as the Midnight Classic. The high stakes, coupled with the fact that a Derby winner was returning home to close out his career, gave the Classic everything but a classic ending. Alysheba provided that. McCarron positioned him perfectly and had the lead in the stretch, but a gritty three-year-old named Seeking the Gold, trained by Shug McGaughey, made a furious run at his older and more celebrated opponent. At that point, Van Berg, who had trouble following his horse through the eerie darkness, felt "damned nervous" wondering if he again would come up short in the Classic. But Alysheba prevailed by a half-length. "America's Horse," as race announcer Tom Durkin proudly proclaimed, won the richest race in the world in the state where he was born.

"The horse just absolutely ran the race of his life," McCarron said. "He beat, I think, a very solid field of horses and he came through at the right time. When the race started and as it unfolded, my confidence grew because he was handling the track. I wasn't concerned after the gates opened. He got himself a very forwardly placed position compared to some of the other races he had run in the past. The farther he went in the race the more confident I got because he was really moving forward the whole time. Seeking the Gold got head and head with us but he never got past us. I can't say that I knew I was going to win it the whole way, but I wasn't concerned that he was going to pass me, either. I had a lot of confidence that Alysheba was going to run his guts out because he was a very competitive colt. He had a tendency to wait a little bit when he got in front but he also responded when a horse would come back at him. He always seemed to be able to find a little bit more. It was a great relief. There was a tremendous amount of pressure involved. He had to show he could beat a field like that and do it under adverse conditions. If he could, he would virtually be assured of Horse of the Year."

As McCarron returned to the winner's circle, the crowd roared in approval. Someone held up a sign which read: "Alysheba For President."

"It was fun," McCarron said. "Any adjective you could think of, that's what it was."

Van Berg said winning the richest race in the world was a "heck of a deal." To this day he is convinced that nobody fully appreciated Alysheba's talents because he didn't win by widening margins.

"He did just enough to win," Van Berg said, before beginning an analogy of his own life to put the subject into a human context. "I was kind of short and fat when I was little. And my buddies could outrun me. You'd run like the devil and get up to them and pass them and they'd run right by you. You'd be going 90 miles an hour and they'd jog by you again. Alysheba was like that. He just broke horses' hearts."

Alysheba, similar to many great horses, liked the limelight, kicking his back end up when the people cheered and called for him in the paddock. He loved the attention and the people loved him. Van Berg figured he probably sent out 2,000 pictures of the horse to children, who would send a quarter or 50 cents to buy Alysheba carrots. Such was the allure of America's horse.

The Scharbauers retired Alysheba after the Classic, much to the chagrin of his adoring public and his trainer, who said the horse was physically sound when his career ended.

"The crowds love him so much he would have attracted people like the Barnum and Bailey Circus did," Van Berg said. "You're just so fortunate and lucky when you get a horse with that much talent. There've been horses with maybe more talent, but they didn't stay sound."

Blumin Affair, the next young prospect for Van Berg, was a case in point. The $20,000 yearling purchase, owned by the partnership of Iowa residents Art Vogel and Leroy Bowman, won his two-year-old debut in July of 1993 by 7½ lengths and finished second nine days later. Vogel and Bowman shipped their prospect to Van Berg, with whom they had previously had horses. The colt had some ankle problems but also tremendous talent. Van Berg couldn't believe what he saw when the colt burned up the track in his first few workouts. Blumin Affair showed his ability after a three-month layoff, winning a six-furlong race in a time of 1:09 4/5, which is fast for a horse of any age, let alone a two-year-old. Van Berg wanted to run in the Breeders' Cup Juvenile, which at that point was only 16 days away. It meant having to cram foundation work into the horse who would be stretching out to a mile and sixteenth and stepping up in class.

Van Berg consulted with Vogel and Bowman, who were told it would cost $10,000 to pre-enter and another $10,000 to run. They decided to take the $20,000 they had earned from the horse's recent win and parlay it on the Cup. It proved a solid investment. At odds of 42-1, Blumin Affair ran second by five lengths to Brocco, the top-rated horse in California at the time.

"If I'd had about two more weeks to the Breeders' Cup, there was nobody that would beat him," Van Berg said.

Vogel and Bowman couldn't believe their good fortune. Their $20,000 investment had turned into a $200,000 return. The whole experience happened so fast, they didn't have time to appreciate their horse's ability.

"Jack Van Berg, though, when he said 'You've got a good horse here we better try to get him in the Breeders' Cup,' we kind of realized well maybe we had a better horse than we thought we had," Vogel said. "And then when he ran in the Breeders' Cup, we knew we had a good horse. The horse did very well and we've got to give Jack credit for it."

Blumin Affair closed out the year with a fourth-place finish in the Hollywood Futurity. He posted second in the Remington Park Derby and Arkansas Derby the following year, then ran third behind Go for Gin in the Kentucky Derby. He was sixth in the Preakness after swallowing his tongue. Soundness problems plagued him thereafter and he never made it back to the Breeders' Cup.

But Van Berg will make it back to the Breeders' Cup. When you've been training as long as he has, there's always hope for tomorrow—and another chance in the Classic.

# 11

# The Lord of the Longshots

## Andre Fabre

$\mathscr{I}$n 1993, a horse with an unusual name crossed the finish line first in the Classic at odds of 133-1, a Breeders' Cup record. The horse had never run in the U.S. before and had never raced on the dirt. His American jockey had never even seen the horse in the flesh until he jumped aboard him before the race. The whole scenario seemed a tad baffling. Yet, it didn't take long to solve the mystery; the answer could be found merely by looking at the name of his trainer, Andre Fabre, The Lord of the Longshots.

Fabre has been the top trainer in France since 1987—and one of the best in the world—but he remains somewhat of an enigma. Although he tries to avoid the limelight and does his best to shield himself from the media, particularly in his own country, Fabre is constantly bringing attention to himself with his uncanny ability to train horses to win major international races, no matter what the odds.

Andre Fabre is not your typical horseman. He did not grow up as the son of a famous trainer or owner. In fact, he did not really discover horses until the age of 23. Fabre was born in France in 1945, but spent much of his youth in Germany where his father was a diplomat. He returned to France in 1968 to study law, something he is still qualified to practice. During his schooling, he began riding in the mornings at Maisons-Laffitte and his experiences provided the impetus for what has become a brilliant equine career.

Fabre apprenticed as a groom for leading steeplechase trainer Andre Adele in the early '70s, then became an exercise rider and eventually rode in amateur races. He turned professional because of his success and won more than 250 races, including the Grand Steeplechase de Paris in 1977. Adele died that year and Fabre had an opportunity to train. He did well as a steeplechase trainer and extended his scope to the flat circuit, to which he would gravitate full-time by the end of 1983.

Fabre made his first impact that year winning the Grade One Oak Tree Invitational at Santa Anita at odds of more than 10-1 with French invader Zalataia. The runner-up in that race happened to be the legendary John Henry, U.S. Horse of the Year in 1981 and 1984.

Fabre posted his first major victory in his native country when he won the 1987 Arc de Triomphe—the most prestigious race in France and one of the most coveted in the world—with Trempolino. Co-owned by France's Paul deMoussac and American Bruce McNall, Trempolino received scant attention from the bettors. They let him go at 20-1 in the field of 11, despite his victory three weeks before in a prep for the Arc. Fabre liked his chances off the prep win and conveyed that confidence to jockey Pat Eddery, who asked him if Trempolino was feeling and doing as well as before the prep race.

Fabre told him the horse was doing even better. That was all Eddery, one of the best in the world, needed to hear. He felt confident, telling Fabre they were going to win.

"He was overconfident, just as I was," Fabre recalled.

Trempolino not only won, he did so in course-record time.

Fabre did not react with any great emotion to what was the first of his five Arc wins. He savored it, but not like an American who had won the Kentucky Derby for the first time after dreaming of winning it all his life.

"For me it was just another work day, a good one, but a work day," he insisted. "I didn't celebrate. I was very happy, I was proud of my horse. I considered it my job. I see no reason to be over happy. It is just as difficult to win some small races with bad horses as it is to win the Arc."

Fabre did not indulge the French press before or after the Arc. In fact, he did not even waste a word on them. By that time, Fabre had developed an intense dislike for the French press—and little has softened that enmity. Stung by an article early in his career alleging he had drugged his steeplechase horses, Fabre will not talk to French journalists. He will talk to members of the media from outside his country, but guardedly. In England, he views some of the tabloid writers as boors, and in the U.S. he finds some journalists too aggressive and difficult to accept. Fabre is an extremely private person—maybe even shy, according to some who know him closely—who prefers to keep his thoughts to himself.

"I'm not a great believer in communication," Fabre said. "Communication is the same as propoganda. I don't want to discuss my personality or things I'm doing. I just do what I want to do. If it had been a condition to be successful to communicate with the press every day, I wouldn't be successful. I wouldn't do it."

In 1996, Janet Slade, a journalist who regularly rode against Fabre in their steeplechase days, said Fabre was extremely pleased to be interviewed when he first became a trainer, but he isolated himself more as his success became greater.

"I know people who've known him for years who think he's the greatest guy on earth," Slade said. "He's very, very loyal to his friends. He's just a bit of a nutcase really. He's a bit of a megalomaniac. He thinks he's god. We call him god anyway. We used to say in racing there were two gods in France: the (late) president, Francois Mitterand, and Andre Fabre. . . . He just doesn't want to be bothered (with the press). I think that's the whole thing, which doesn't take anything away from his ability as an exceptional trainer."

Beginning in 1987, Fabre started running horses regularly in the Breeders' Cup. Prior to that, he didn't have horses good enough and did not feel the need to show up just to be noticed. That year, Fabre brought over Trempolino for the $2 million Turf and also saddled A. J. Richards' Village Star, who had been based in

California. Trempolino faced a major opponent in Theatrical, the top distance grass horse in North America, who also had a shot at Horse of the Year honors in the U.S. Trempolino came into the Turf off a seven-week layoff and the public backed him as the 13-5 second choice behind the 9-5 favorite Theatrical.

The two warriors ran to their odds. Theatrical, a former European runner making his third Breeders' Cup start, prevailed along the rail by a half-length over Trempolino. Village Star ran third at 26-1. To this day, Fabre ranks the race as the toughest defeat in his Breeders' Cup experiences.

"The problem was that the interval between the Arc and the Breeders' Cup that year was too long," he said. "He would have done well with a prep race. Nowadays, I would say the opposite. Perhaps the Breeders' Cup is a bit too close to the Arc, so I would say it's probably one of the problems faced by the Arc winner. And the Arc is always a very difficult race. I think Trempolino was a bit unlucky not to win. He was a bit fresh. Pat Eddery had made his move too soon and couldn't settle him anymore. There was a horse that made a move in front of him and he had to go with him and it was too soon for him."

It did not take long for Fabre's long shot wizardry to strike again. In 1988 at Canada's Woodbine Racetrack, he saddled C. N. Ray's Mill Native in the Grade One Arlington Million, temporarily moved from Arlington Park, which was being rebuilt. Mill Native had run solidly in mile races, but was viewed by the bettors as suspect going a mile and a quarter.

How wrong they were. Under Cash Asmussen, Mill Native won at 42-1.

Because of an abundance of stock, Fabre said he doesn't have to risk running horses where they don't belong.

"I try to go always to the easiest (spot), I don't want to complicate things," he said. "I try to give the horses a nice life, a happy one, treat them as though they were friends or children, and that's it."

Fabre only had one Breeders' Cup horse in 1988, Sarhoob, who ran eighth, more than 40 lengths behind Great Communicator in the Turf. Sarhoob had been the weaker half of the 6-5 favorite entry with Indian Skimmer, conditioned by England's top trainer Henry Cecil, who was starting his first horse in the U.S. Both horses were owned by Sheikh Mohammed bin Rashid al Maktoum of the United Arab Emirates. Cecil's personality is the exact opposite of Fabre's: flamboyant and flashy. He came to the track in a stretch limousine and had the European media all over him. He accommodated them with witty remarks. Cecil might have won the race were it not for a questionable ride by Michael Roberts, who was soundly criticized by the media for restraining the mare too much. It had been just that kind of criticism that turned Fabre off on the media in the first place.

Fabre brought two horses, Star Lift and Sierra Roberta, to the $2 million Turf at the 1989 Breeders' Cup at Gulfstream Park in Florida. Sierra Roberta, a three-year-old filly who had placed fifth in the Arc, ran second by a head to Prized. Star Lift, 19th in the Arc, finished a length farther behind in third. Fabre had lost the race but flaunted his long shot prowess in the process. Sierra Roberta went post-ward at 25-1, while Star Lift was 51-1, longest shot in the field.

Fabre's horses proved that Europeans could run in hot-weather conditions, despite major failures by other higher-profile runners in previous editions and complaints by the losing connections.

"They were blaming the course, blaming the heat, blaming everything," Fabre said. "The conditions were the same for everybody. You just have to adapt and travel your horses early enough. I've seen some European horses who haven't even been clipped going to Florida. They couldn't be feeling well. It's just like you're sitting in the sun wearing a heavy jacket. You have to adapt your horse to the conditions."

Fabre recorded his first Breeders' Cup victory in 1990 at Belmont Park in New York, when he connected with Sheikh Mohammed's In The Wings, who had finished fourth as the favorite in the Arc in only his second race back after a knee operation. With that hard race behind him and a few more weeks to get fit, In The Wings ran down world-record holder With Approval by a half-length in the Turf. In the Wings was coupled with Prince Khalid Abdullah's French Glory, who had won the Grade One Rothmans Ltd. International at Woodbine the week after the Arc. In the Wings' jockey, Gary Stevens, had never won a Breeders' Cup race in 22 previous mounts, but it didn't worry Fabre. He's not superstitious and he specifically wanted an American rider.

"I thought at the time French jockeys were not good enough to ride in those races in America," he said. "I've changed my mind since and have ridden (Thierry) Jarnet and (Olivier) Peslier. I always try to get the best Americans and I think Gary is a top-class jockey. I was very pleased. I thought his coolness and his style of riding would suit my horses very well. It's a real achievement for a European trainer to win a big race in America, so I was very happy. In one sense it's more fun because it's abroad. It's different. When you're in another country it's always more difficult.

"I like the American racing system," he added. "I put aside the drug problem, which is complicated to understand for us Europeans. Every horse has a really good chance (racing in the U.S.). There are no tactical problems. There are very good jockeys. The surface is very sound. The races are fairer than in Europe."

In 1991 at Churchill Downs in Kentucky, Fabre ran only one horse, Pigeon Voyageur, who finished sixth in the Turf at 19-1.

The following year Fabre recorded his second Arc win (Subotica) and continued his Breeders' Cup evolution. Fabre ran two horses—Subotica in the Turf and Jolypha in the Classic—and the decision to run on dirt had been made by owner Prince Khalid Abdullah.

"He thought he had a good chance with his filly, and the closer I was coming to the race the more interesting it seemed to me," Fabre said.

Subotica ran fifth in the Turf after threatening at the top of the stretch. Then came the Classic. Jolypha had never run on the dirt and faced 13 male rivals. Coupled with two other Khalid Abdullah horses trained by American Bobby Frankel, Jolypha went postward at 15-1. By herself, she likely would have gone at three times those odds. Jolypha closed well to be third, beaten only 2½ lengths by A. P. Indy, who was later named Horse of the Year in the U.S.

"Jolypha showed me it was not as difficult as people thought to win those races," Fabre said. "I think Jolypha should have won on that day. She had an unlucky race. I suddenly realized those dirt races weren't that difficult to win, but obviously you need a good horse."

Fabre had many of those in 1993, collecting classic victories in various countries, yet the most shocking came in the Breeders' Cup Classic. Although Arcangues had won the Group One Prix d'Ispahan in May for the second year in a row, he had run only once in the interval, finishing fourth by 10 lengths in the Group Two Prix Dollar. Fabre said he couldn't find suitable races for Arcangues after the Prix d'Ispahan because of few opportunities in France for Group One horses. Moreover, Fabre did not want to run the horse in England. While it was reported after the Breeders' Cup that Arcangues had had back problems, which he did, Fabre said the poor showing in the Prix Dollar was more a case of the horse not liking the downhill course at Longchamp. Fabre had one goal in mind—the Classic—and merely used the Prix Dollar as a prep race.

Some two months before the Classic, Fabre worked Arcangues in company with multiple group winners. In a mile exercise over owner Daniel Wildenstein's dirt course named after the great mare All Along, Arcangues beat his rivals. That prompted Fabre to call Wildenstein and tell him about the plan to run in the Classic. Wildenstein trusted his trainer and gave him the go-ahead.

Fabre enlisted the services of American jockey Jerry Bailey, who had never seen the horse and had no idea how to pronounce his name.

"I didn't know if he was bay or gray when I walked into the paddock," Bailey said. "I knew who Mr. Fabre was, but I had never met him and I didn't know what he looked like. It was a very crowded paddock so I just went to the horse's (postposition) number. I found the horse and I couldn't find the trainer and it was time to mount. The assistant trainer was there but he spoke nothing but French. And the groom spoke nothing but French. And I spoke nothing but English. Whatever they told me I just nodded in affirmation but I didn't understand a single word they said."

As the horses headed to the track, Fabre caught up with Bailey and told him only that Arcangues liked to come from far back. Given Bailey's total unfamiliarity with the horse, this seemed like too little, too late. Some trainers will give jockeys race tapes days in advance of horses they are riding for the first time. Not Fabre. He is not a great believer in giving orders to riders. More importantly, he had confidence in his horse, regardless of what anyone thought.

The attention focused on the Bobby Frankel–trained entry of Bertrando, Marquetry and Missionary Ridge, all running for different owners. The crowd made the trio 6-5.

Bertrando had early speed and looked to be the strongest of the trio, followed by Marquetry, who also liked the front end. Missionary Ridge had the perfect come-from-behind style to complement the others. Arcangues received scant attention, but Fabre did not feel Arcangues' odds accurately reflected the true ability of the horse. Had the race happened in France, Fabre believes Arcangues would have been no higher than 10-1.

"He was a Group One winner and placed in a lot of group races in France and they are not easy races to win," Fabre said. "He was a very good horse. The problem is his consistency wasn't as good because he had back troubles. On his good day, he was a very good horse."

Bertrando predictably took the lead, followed closely by Marquetry, whose rider, Kent Desormeaux, did not engage in a foolhardy front-end battle. Bertrando led all the way into the stretch and looked like a winner until Arcangues, who had improved almost unnoticed from seventh to second, gained on him midway in the stretch and drew away to win by two lengths.

The infield board flashed the winning price of $269.20 for a $2 ticket. No winning horse in Breeders' Cup history had even come close to that pari-mutuel price. Lashkari—another French invader—had provided the previous highest price, winning the inaugural Turf at 53-1. Fran's Valentine had been first in the Juvenile Fillies' race that year at 74-1, but was disqualified for causing interference.

"If you expect me to say I was enthusiastic or things like that—the American style of reaction—you won't get it," Fabre said.

What Fabre acknowledged, however, is that Bailey rode him perfectly, allowing the horse to settle into stride and slowly angling him over to the rail rather than rushing him from the 12-post.

"The horse needed a bit of time to get his legs (underneath him), more like the European horses," Fabre said. "Bailey didn't rush him. When everything is done well it seems easy. What can I say? It's good for the jockey, for the horse, everybody. That's my job. I wasn't surprised at all. You don't travel so far for races like that if you don't think you've got a good chance."

In 1994, Fabre won the Arc for the third time and scored stakes victories in other countries, including ringing up another long shot win in the Rothmans International at Woodbine with the 18-1 Raintrap. His Breeders' Cup horses did little, however, as Ski Paradise ran 10th in the Mile and Intrepidity ran fourth in the Classic, while stablemate Dernier Empereur finished 14th.

An interesting social development occured that year. Fabre started appearing more regularly for victory presentations in France after years of avoiding them because of a strained relationship with France-Galop. He had been unhappy with the way French racing was run, believing it had been managed by aging people with a lack of efficiency and democracy. The situation changed in 1994 under the direction of France-Galop's new chairman, Jean-Luc Lagardere, the top breeder in the country. Fabre began training for him that year and he supported the new chairman's work in improving French racing.

In 1995, Fabre won the English 2,000 Guineas for the second time and almost won the Arc a fourth time when Freedom Cry ran second by only three-quarters of a length to the undefeated Lammtarra. While Sheikh Mohammed retired the battle-fatigued Lammtarra afterward amid some criticism, Wildenstein opted to go to the Breeders' Cup with Freedom Cry.

Fabre and Wildenstein debated over whether to run Freedom Cry in the Turf or Classic. The undefeated Cigar, one of the strongest American horses in years, headed the Classic. Fabre preferred the Classic because he thought the mile and a half distance in the Turf would be too far for Freedom Cry. He had never won a race longer than a mile and a quarter. But the opposition looked weaker in the Turf so Freedom Cry was pointed to that race.

"It was a difficult decision," Fabre said. "The fact that Cigar seemed to dominate by far the rest of the field was part of the decision. It made me think we were running for second place. It was the conservative decision."

Besides Freedom Cry, Fabre also had Carnegie in the Turf. Freedom Cry ran courageously, but finished second by a neck to an improving American horse, Northern Spur. Carnegie ran two lengths farther back in third. Even though Fabre didn't win, he still put his imprint on the race. He had trained Northern Spur before the colt was sold in March of that year for $1.2 million to American Charles Celia. Winning trainer Ron McAnally almost had Freedom Cry, too, but a purchase for $2.5 million fell through because of concerns about the horse's wear and tear.

In 1996, Fabre had only one starter in the Cup, Jean-Luc Legardere's Luna Wells, a three-year-old filly entered in the Turf after placing fifth in the Arc de Triomphe. Ridden by Thierry Jarnet, Luna Wells ran fairly close to the pace early in the Turf and was only about four lengths back of the leaders with a quarter of a mile to go but faded in the stretch and placed a distant 10th.

In 1997 and '98, Fabre did not have any representatives in the Breeders' Cup, but these proved to be pivotal years in Fabre's career, as he won the Arc back to back. In 1997, he won it with Peintre Celebre, a three-year-old Nureyev colt owned by Daniel Wildenstein. Peintre Celebre beat a field that included defending champion Helissio and five of the first six finishers from the previous year's race: Pilsudski, Oscar Schindler, Swain and Le Destinx. Peintre Celebre won three of four races going into the race, his lone loss by a neck after experiencing traffic problems, and drew the public's fancy as the 22-10 favorite. He won by a stunning five lengths.

The colt was retired for the season with the intention of running as a four-year-old and pointing towards the Breeders' Cup, but he never made it to the races after suffering a bowed tendon and was retired to stud. Fabre won the Arc a record fifth time in '98 with Sagamix, a three-year-old colt bred and owned by Legardere. He became only the third horse in the last 50 runnings of the Arc to win with an undefeated record. The colt was later sold to Darley Stud but ran only twice in 1999 and only three times the following year, failing to win in all five races before he was retired.

Fabre returned to the Cup in 1999 with four starters: Louve Mysterieuse (Distaff); Borgia and Louve (Filly & Mare Turf); and First Magnitude (Turf). It would not be a memorable outing, however, for Fabre because neither of his starters placed in the top three and only Borgia collected a check, by placing fifth in her race.

It would be a much different story in 2000. Fabre saddled only one starter, Juddmonte Farms' Dansil, a four-year-old who had run second at Longchamp in his last start. Fabre liked his chances but had concerns about his horse's ability to handle the tight turns at Churchill Downs. Dansil, ridden by American-based jockey John Velazquez, settled well back of the pack, the intention being to save the colt for a spirited run in the stretch. Dansil exploded from virtually last with a quarter of a mile to the wire and accelerated quickly down the lane while moved to the inside and simply ran out of ground, placing third by a neck and a nose.

"He was a horse with a turn of foot and it's always a problem on the tight course like that with a short straight," Fabre said. "On those type of courses it's better to race closer to the pace, but Dansil needed to be covered up behind horses. He'd been a shade unlucky, but you cannot call it lack of luck if that's your horse's way of racing. When you want to come from behind on those tight courses, you always get into trouble."

In 2001, Fabre brought Banks Hill and Spring Oak for the Filly & Mare Turf, and Slew The Red for the Turf. He had tremendous confidence in Banks Hill, whom he considered the best filly he had ever trained. The three-year-old, bred and owned by Prince Khalid Abdullah's Juddmonte Farms, had had an interesting year. She proved her class against her own age and sex, in which she posted back-to-back victories, first in the Prix de Sandringham Stakes at Chantilly in France and then in the Group One Coronation Stakes at Ascot in England. She raced against open company and older horses in her next two starts, both Group One races in France, and finished third and second, respectively. She had been sched-uled to race one more time in France, in the Prix de l'Opera, but that plan was aborted because of soft turf. Because she had been untried beyond a mile and had had two consecutive losses, she did not look appealing to the bettors.

"I think mainly American punters probably didn't fully appreciate two things," Juddmonte's European racing manager Teddy Beckett said. "Most of her races in the second half of that year were against colts and also everyone felt she was untested at a mile and a quarter. She won the Coronation Stakes at Ascot, which is a mile but it's a big mile. It takes some kind of staying. And a two-turn mile and a quarter was never a great worry. On pedigree she's out of a mare whose father, Kahyasi, stayed a mile and a half. From that angle, we had no real concerns she wouldn't handle a mile and a quarter."

And Beckett said the filly looked fantastic, even in her winter coat that Fabre had clipped.

"It wasn't just a slight winter coat. It was a wooly winter coat," Beckett said. "Sometimes they get a winter coat and they look a bit dead in themselves, like they're gone. She didn't. She had a great sheen to herself and she was in very good form."

Olivier Peslier, who had steered her in the two victories earlier in the season, was hired for what would become the biggest race of her life. Peslier settled the filly in close to the lead and inched up to second, by only a head, with a quarter of a mile to go. Then he called on the filly, who absolutely exploded en route to a 5½-length score. Stablemate Spring Oak, ridden by Frankie Dettori, ran third.

"She looked really well and the way she just exploded was a fantastic perform-ance," Beckett said.

Banks Hill broke Juddmonte's winless streak of 33 previous Breeders' Cup races, thrilling her breeder/owner.

"He's one of the world's leading breeders, if not the world's leading breeder, and to win at a major meeting was a tremendous thrill," Beckett said. "And not only that, the real exciting added thing was he bred the sire, Danehill, and her mother, Hasili."

The following October, Juddmonte sent Banks Hill to the U.S. to train under Bobby Frankel, who conditions many of the operation's runners in the U.S. Originally Fabre was going to saddle her in the Grade One Flower Bowl at Belmont, then turn her over to Frankel. Rains softened up the course, which didn't favor Banks Hill, who favors a firm surface, so she was kept out of that race and turned over to Frankel at his California base. She ran third in the Grade One Yellow Ribbon in her American debut. She followed it up with a second-place finish by 1½ lengths to Starine. Even in Fabre's absence, he still had an impact on the horse.

"Andre has been the leading trainer in France since 1987 and it's unbroken," Beckett said. "That alone speaks more words than I can say. There's no question he's the master of his profession, at every level. He's a superb horseman, a tremendous eye for detail and has a tremendous confidence, which transposes itself not only to his staff but his horses as well."

Fabre wants to be a regular presence in the Breeders' Cup as long as he has horses good enough to run in it.

"I would like to run as many horses as I can in these races," he said. "They're prestigious races and the purses are good. I feel the American trainers are giving the Breeders' Cup a lot of importance, keeping fresh horses for it. We're really competing against good horses. I have the feeling that in the first Breeders' Cup, the American trainers took it (lightly). They were concentrating more on the summer races and then said, 'Let's try the Breeders' Cup.' A lot of horses might have been a bit tired or over the top. Now, I feel it's a major goal for the trainers."

Which means it will become increasingly harder for Fabre to pull off another 133-1 heist. The Lord of the Longshots knows it is only a matter of time before he blows his cover—if he hasn't already.

# 12

# Flying High

## Frankie Dettori

*M*eet the man known in racing circles as Frankie, popular for his ability to win races—and infamous for a loss he'd just as soon forget—followed by his patented leap out of the saddle. Lanfranco (Frankie) Dettori is the most recognized jockey in Europe, possibly even the world if you take into account his global feats. He's won many of the premier races and his successes have basically allowed him to parlay his fame into fortune beyond the racetrack. He has had endorsement deals with Yves St. Laurent, McDonald's, and Alfa-Romeo and has begun his own food company, which has products in major supermarket chains in London, England. That's his adopted home, where he regularly appears on television and radio shows and is considered among the top athletes in popularity and marketability. It's all pretty amazing, really, more so when you consider he is lucky to be alive following a plane crash that nearly claimed his life and, for all intents and purposes, reshaped his career.

Born Dec. 15, 1970 in Milan, Italy, and christened with the given name Lanfranco, Dettori had the pedigree to become a championship rider. His father, Gianfranco, won 13 titles in Italy and posted back-to-back victories in the English Two Thousand Guineas in 1975 and '76. His parents divorced when he was only six months old and he lived with his mother until the age of five. Then it was time for him to go to school and his mother thought her ex-husband, who had remarried by then, had the money to help finance his son's education, so young Lanfranco went to live with his dad. He endured a strict upbringing, but in later years would credit his stepmother's toughness for preparing him for living away from home at age 14. His father starting him riding at age six, and two years later he took him to a horse farm to buy him his own pony. They were shown three ponies—two bays and a palomino—and the youngster was allowed to make his own decision.

"At my age it was like taking an adult to the Ferrari shop and asking, 'which car do you like?'" he wrote in his autobiography, *A Year In The Life of Frankie Dettori*, published in 1996.

He chose the palomino, who had four white socks, white tail, mane and face. She was a filly named Sylvia. The elder Dettori made sure his son looked after the horse, so every day after school the youngster headed home, dressed in jodhpurs and the jockey silks in the colours of famed Italian horseman Carlo d'Allessio, and ran to the horse farm where Sylvia was stabled about a quarter of a mile away. His father taught him how to muck out a stall, place fresh bedding down and clean the horse's feet with a hoof pick. The impetuous youngster couldn't wait to ride her, so he'd hide the droppings in a corner of the stall and then put the saddle on his horse and "go straight out and gallop for the hell of it" around the outside of the farm. About a year later, he rode his horse in the local Pony Derby at the San Siro racecourse. He had prepared for his big moment by galloping his horse each day, only to discover the other horses and riders were gigantic compared to him and his mount. He was so nervous before the race, he missed the dropping of the flag to signal the start and finished last in the three-furlong dash run on the jumping course between the last two fences. To add embarrassment to the result, his horse dug in her heels at the finish line and he fell head over heels straight into a water jump. Clearly, a star was not born.

The young rider lost interest in caring for his pony about a year later, so the elder Dettori sold the pony and his son quit riding for several months, then rediscovered his interest. His equine apprenticeship continued when his father attached reins to a well at home and instructed the youngster how to switch sticks, enabling him to become proficient with both his right hand and left hand, requisite skills in the all-important drive to the wire. For half an hour almost every night for a year when the weather permitted, the youngster worked on the skill that would eventually make him one of the more accomplished riders of his generation.

"He pushed me hard, but he's the person most responsible for where I am today," Dettori told journalist Robert Henwood in a profile for the 1998 Breeders' Cup magazine.

Growing up wild and unbridled, the young Dettori had designs on following his father's career. He worked for the d'Allessio stable at the age of 12 and then continued his equine education living with a friend of his father in Pisa, which had milder winters. He returned home in April and impressed his father with his riding skills, and plans were made to send the jockey-in-training to trainer Luca Camani in England for six months. The elder Dettori had ridden for Cumani's father Sergio, an accomplished trainer in his time. He saddled the winners of the 2000 Guineas the senior Dettori rode in back-to-back years. Young Lanfranco left in July to join the Cumani stable, and the stablehands quickly took a shining to the effervescent Italian who spoke limited English and nicknamed him Frankie. It stuck forevermore and regularly flowed off the tongues of racing fans worldwide.

He returned home in November for 10 days, but instead of heading off to go to trainer Patrick Biancone's yard in Chantilly, France, which had been part of the original plan, Frankie stayed in Italy to begin his riding career. The rules in his country differed from those in England, where jockeys couldn't ride professionally until age 16, so he got a leg up on his career in Turin in late November, a month before turning 16. He rode 15 winners that first season, his initial victory aboard a horse called Billy Pitt. Occasionally he competed in races against his father, including one time when the elder Dettori helped his son win by whipping his horse to the wire. It proved to be a funny moment, albeit illegal.

His first mount in England came aboard a horse called Mustakbil for owner Sheikh Hamdan bin Rashid al Maktoum, a member of the ruling family of Dubai and one of the foremost racing owners in Europe. Dettori finished second by a head at odds of 33-1. His first English victory came on June 9, 1987, aboard a horse called Lizzy Hare at Goodwood. The horse had been named after Cumani's secretary, who drove the 16-year-old rider to and from the races that day in the trainer's car. Dettori won on the 12-1 shot, beating the favorite Interlacing, ridden by legendary American jockey Steve Cauthen, who was headed for his third English riding title that season.

"He was obviously elated coming home because when I got into my car the next morning he had written on the bottom of a box of Kleenex that I keep there 'Frankie goes to Hollywood,'" Cumani recalled in 1998 in Henwood's Breeders' Cup article. "We teased him about it afterwards, but he wasn't embarrassed. Frankie doesn't get embarrassed about anything."

His English racing career began incrementally, starting with eight victories in 1987, but his talent as a horseman did not go unnoticed. Veteran jockey Ray Cochrane, the senior stable jockey for Cumani at the time, noticed the teenager's talents during the morning gallops.

"He seemed to have a natural ability on horses and he had all the background knowledge," Cochrane recalled. "He just seemed to know all about it. Sometimes you get young kids coming along and you're trying to educate them and get the job done properly, but he was like a very, very seasoned head on a very young body."

From eight victories in his first year, Dettori almost trebled his total with 22 in his second season. In his third year, he had 75 victories and was named champion apprentice. It was during these years that Dettori spent winters in California to hone his skills on the advice of Cumani, who had him work for several transplanted English trainers. It was a practice Cumani had done with other riders to improve their horsemanship.

"When he went to America the only thing I impressed on him was to learn about pace because it's just about the only place where trackwork is timed against the clock," Cumani said. "His actual style was adapted from Steve Cauthen, who was the best rider in Europe while Frankie was growing up. We made a conscious decision that he should model himself after Steve."

It was during these years that Angel Cordero Jr. happened to be riding in California fairly regularly and Dettori used the opportunities to learn from the Puerto Rican great. Dettori looked up to him as an idol. In particular, Dettori started emulating Cordero's famous flying dismount, which he routinely did after winning a race.

"Like any other teenager I found it pretty amazing," Dettori said. "I used to work for Richard Cross, Chris Speckert and in between sets when the grooms used to come to get the horse, I used to jump off like Cordero. It was a little bit of fun there in the stable."

He worked on his riding style in the U.S., combining it with what he had learned in Europe.

When Dettori graduated to the journeyman level after that, it became apparent to Cochrane he was going to lose his job as the senior rider in Cumani's stable to the young phenom. Cochrane took advantage of an opportunity with trainer Guy Harwood, but the two riders maintained their relationship and over some 20 years it developed into a working partnership, preceded by a plane accident in which the two came perilously close to losing their lives.

In 1990, his first year as a journeyman, Dettori recorded 141 victories, the first teenager to record 100 winners in a season since the great Lester Piggott in 1955. He also registered his first Group One win that year in the Queen Elizabeth II Stakes at Ascot with Markofdistinction. The next year he won 94 races in England. The following year he improved upon his win total, the highlight victories including the French Derby and Ascot Gold Cup. After the racing season ended, he rode in Hong Kong. He made the decision to ride there on an extended basis, taking advantage of an opportunity to make more money. Cumani advised him to stay put, but the headstrong Dettori, who in later years would admit he had become too big for his own britches, didn't heed the helpful words.

"I thought it was crazy because he was on the verge of becoming one of the very best in Europe and there was no need to go into a backwater like Hong Kong," Cumani said. "He was taken in by the glitz and the money and the easy life of Hong Kong. I basically told him if you go to Hong Kong, I'll never talk to you again or something like that. You go there over my dead body. He was sort of stubborn and decided he was going to do it anyway."

So the two parted company. The Hong Kong experience never materialized after an incident in which London police picked up Dettori for possession of a small amount of cocaine he had purchased at a club. While the police slapped him only with a caution, the Hong Kong racing association abruptly cancelled his application. Without Cumani's backing, Dettori had to go back to England and freelance for whomever would hire him to ride.

"That made a man of him, the fact he had no (contract) job in England and nowhere to go in Hong Kong," Cumani said. "Up to then it had been easy because all he had to do was get on my horses and pilot them. He started again basically from scratch because he didn't have my horses to ride and gradually worked his way up again. He was a new Frankie then. He was no longer Frankie the Kid, but Frankie the New Man."

Dettori posted his best season in England, finishing second to Pat Eddery in victories with 149 winners. Later that year he was hired to ride first call for Sheikh Mohammed bin Rashid al Maktoum, the brother of Sheikh Hamden, for whom Dettori rode his first horse in England. The Maktoums operated the premier racing/breeding operations in the world. Sheikh Mohammed had some 450 horses at the time, including some who wintered in Dubai, where the warm climate helped keep the stock in shape for racing in other parts of the world. In fact, by 1995 the Dubai operation, which became known as the Godolphin Stable, became the full-time off-season training site for Sheikh Mohammed's horses, who became prominent worldwide in their owner's blue silks.

In 1993, Dettori came to the Breeders' Cup at Santa Anita to ride for the first time. He had only one mount, Wolfhound, owned by Sheikh Mohammed and breeder Gerald Leigh, in the Mile grass race. Sheikh Mohammed also had two other runners in the race, Barathea, trained by Cumani, and Catrail, trained by John Gosden. European horses had done dreadfully poorly in the Breeders' Cup up to that point, and the betting public gave the troika little chance at the windows, sending the entry postward at greater than 9-1 odds. Lure, the defending winner of the race, went in as the heavy favorite and ran to his backing by winning easily. Wolfhound was forced wide into the first turn when Barathea bore out badly and finished 10th by 14½ lengths in the 13-horse field. Barathea, ridden by California-based Gary Stevens, ran fifth, slightly more than four lengths behind Lure, after doing his best to recover from his erratic start.

In 1994, Dettori recorded his first English riding title, winning 233 races, only the third rider in 42 years to surpass the 200-mark in a season. But the biggest victory, certainly on a world stage, would come later in the season aboard Barathea in the Breeders' Cup. Cumani learned something from the horse's erratic experience the year before to help his horse adapt to the course at Churchill Downs, site of the 1994 Breeders'. He acquired the measurements of the sharp clubhouse turn at the venerable Kentucky oval and built a bend at his yard to educate his colt. Because the colt's regular jockey Mick Kinane had been under contract to ride in Hong Kong and couldn't break free from his obligation to ride in the Breeders', Cumani employed Dettori. By that time the two had already begun working together following their parting a few years earlier. In the colt's final tune-up before shipping to America, he worked exceptionally well under Dettori, who thought he had the horse to win the Mile.

"I said to the (groom), 'If we get a bit of luck, we'll be close,'" Dettori recalled. "The horse was four. I raced against him so many times. Even if I didn't ride him that many times, I knew exactly what he was like. The key thing was the draw. On a two-bend, if you've drawn too wide, you've got no chance. Lure (the winner of the Mile the last two years) had done it because he was a front-runner, very quick, managed to get out of trouble. If you ride a normal horse and you're drawn too wide, it's almost impossible to win."

Dettori remarked to Cumani after the final workout that if he won he would do a flying dismount. Cumani had reservations, fearing Dettori might break a leg. It would lead to an interesting moment for Dettori in his career, albeit something controversial in the beginning.

Barathea drew the inside post in the field of 14 and the European media considered it bad luck.

"What are you talking about bad luck? It's the best seat in the house." Dettori told them. "I'd rather be one than fourteen."

Dettori had a mount in the first race, the Sprint, aboard the fleet six-year-old mare Lochsong, winner of her last race, the prestigious Prix de l'Abbaye in France. She prepped for the race by zipping off three furlongs in 33 seconds, stunning the clockers in the process, but the combination of her age and, more importantly, the distance and having to run around a turn instead of a straight course, made her vulnerable. The mare had an awkward beginning and after showing some early run faded to last and suffered a knee injury. Dettori's next mount, Belle Genius in the

Juvenile Fillies, placed fourth, well back of the D. Wayne Lukas duo Flanders and Serena's Song. The two engaged in a brilliant battle that Flanders won by a head. Two races later came the Mile. Lure, seeking his third consecutive win in the race, had the outside post, but the bettors ignored that and made him the 9-10 favorite. Barathea went postward at more than 10-1 odds. Dettori reserved Barathea behind the early pace and had no trouble negotiating the first turn. Inching up closer, Dettori angled out for running room nearing the stretch, by which point he had inherited the lead and drew away to win by three lengths in track-record time.

In the excitement of the moment, Dettori vaulted from Barathea like Cordero in one of his classic flying dismounts.

"I thought it was a bit of fun," Dettori said. "Angel used to do it, so I did it."

Dettori capped off his day riding 26-1 outsider Only Royale, who had run seventh in the Prix de l'Arc de Triomphe, to a fifth-place finish in the Turf.

Dettori headed off to Hong Kong for a week before returning home to England, whereupon he found himself in the center of a controversy for his leap, something that didn't appeal to the racing establishment and critics. There were debates about the potential of injury to the horse and the rider for dismounting so dramatically.

"When I went back I couldn't believe they were still talking about it in the newspaper about my flying dismount," he recalled. "It was a debate in the newspaper, there were hundreds of letters. People were having a dispute about it. It really took the whole thing out of proportion and it didn't give Barathea the credit he deserved. They were more interested in talking about me leaping off the horse than the actual achievement of breaking the track record and winning the Breeders' Cup. I just did it because I thought it was a bit of fun. It just took me by surprise when I went back home and everybody was going mad."

In 1995, Dettori came up short in the Epsom Derby, a race that would prove elusive in his career, finishing second by a length aboard Tamure to Lammtarra. Dettori picked up the mount on Lammtarra for the prestigious King George VI and Queen Elizabeth Stakes and won in a thrilling finish over a game Pentire. Lammtarra's next—and final—race came in the Prix de l'Arc de Triomphe, Europe's most prestigious middle-distance race.

"When I was a little kid in Milan, I was going to the track to see my dad race every weekend and the only thing televised out of Italy was the Arc de Triomphe and the Epsom Derby," Dettori said. "I was thinking, 'Wow, I'd love to win the Arc one day.' When I actually did win it, it was something special. It was a dream come true, something special. There was a lot of pressure. To put that pressure into words, I took Catherine (his future wife) to Longchamp, where I rode the day before. On the day of the race, I got up at nine in the morning and my hair was standing up like Don King. About 10 o'clock I said to Catherine, 'Come on, quickly, come on. Let's go. There's traffic. We're late.' Catherine looked at me and said, 'Look, the first race is not till two o'clock. We're five minutes from the track.' Catherine said, 'I'm not going until late.' I left at 10, panicking. I was the first one at the jocks room. Not even the valets were there. That's how much I felt it. I settled down eventually, but (that's how it is when) you ride a special horse in a special race. Luckily for me, he wasn't a very complicated horse. He was quite straightforward. I sat second or third the whole way, kicked in at the quarter pole and went clear and he just kept on battling."

Lammtarra became the first horse since Ribot more than 40 years before to retire undefeated. Dettori celebrated by high-fiving fans in a jolly romp en route to the paddock for post-race interviews. Minus his brilliant mount, he headed to the 1995 Breeders' Cup, slated to ride Owington in the Sprint, Earl of Barking in the Mile and Tamure in the Turf. Owington, a four-year-old Green Dancer colt, had been winless in four starts on the season, finishing third three times. He had never run on the main track in 14 career starts in Europe and placed a nonthreatening seventh in the Sprint. Earl of Barking, a five-year-old Irish-bred trained by Richard Cross, a onetime assistant to Cumani, had nine wins and more than $1 million in 28 career races. He came into the Mile finishing out of the money in his last three races after winning the Grade One Hollywood Turf Cup in May at more than 24-1 odds. Given a two-month break from the races after running in the Grade One Eddie Read Handicap in August, he placed sixth in the Oak Tree Invitational 20 days before the Breeders' Cup. He was shortened up for the Mile, but placed 10th. Dettori's final mount was Tamure. Following the heartbreaking loss to Lammtarra in the Epsom Derby, Tamure won the Group Three Prix du Prince d'Orange at Longchamp more than three months later. He ran fourth in the Turf.

In 1996, Dettori scored another dramatic victory, this one in the 2000 Guineas, a race he had always wanted to win, aboard Mark of Esteem. It took several minutes for the victory to be announced while the stewards examined the photo of the finish, and when it was announced his horse had won Dettori sprang from the irons—and straight into the arms of Godolphin's travelling lad John Davies. Dettori had technically committed a foul because jockeys aren't allowed to come into contact with anyone before entering the unsaddling disclosure. But he was the only one still out on the track. He received a lecture from the stewards and a fine of 500 pounds. He also received an eight-day ban for excessive use of the whip. Two other jockeys were slapped with suspensions, albeit for fewer days. Dettori could not believe it. He had exceeded the maximum 10 strokes of the whip, but felt he deserved to be credited given the importance of the race instead of being punished. Moreover, the trainer of another horse accused him of unprofessional behavior for his leap. The stories in the paper focused on the fine and the trainer's comments about Dettori's unprofessional behavior.

"I thought it was a shame," he said. "Everybody was getting their knickers in a twist for nothing."

In June, Dettori broke his left elbow in a racing spill and missed two months of racing. Little would he realize that he'd return and etch his name in the record book with seven rides that became known as the Magnificent Seven. It happened in the British Festival of Racing at Ascot on Sept. 28. The key race happened to be the Queen Elizabeth II Stakes with Mark of Esteem, who faced a field loaded with Group One winners. Dettori began the sweep seven with 2-1 favorite Wall Street going wire to wire in the first race, the Cumberland Lodge Stakes. He followed up with 12-1 longshot Diffident in the second, the Diadem Stakes, by a head. Mark of Esteem, the 1-3 favorite in his race, won by 1¼ lengths. Decorated Hero, a 7-1 shot, won by 3½ in the fourth, the Tote Festival Handicap. Fatefully, the 7-4 favorite, kept the streak intact with a neck win in the fifth. Lochangel, the cofavorite in the sixth at 5-4 odds, prevailed by three-quarters of a length in the sixth, the Blue Seal Stakes. Dettori had tied a record with his six consecutive wins, matching a feat by the great Gordon Richards in 1933 and Alec Russell in 1957. His final mount Fujiyama Crest started the day at 12-1 odds but had been whittled down to 2-1 by post time. The horse prevailed in the two-mile race by a neck to give Dettori the record.

"I had such a great day but I couldn't see the horse winning," Dettori recalled. "He had won the race before but he was carrying a stone more (the equivalent of 14 pounds) this time. I thought 'I'm not going to make this horse spoil the day. I'm having the best day of my life.' I went out there. I was already floating on air. I was so overwhelmed by the whole thing. I even got standing ovations in front of the grandstand. It was unbelievable. He was a front-runner. When I turned for home, it was a long way. You had the screaming and from the corner of my eye I could see Pat Eddery on Northern Fleet coming and coming and my horse was tiring and he was slowing. I was just so eager to get to that winning post and when we got there, you don't know what to feel. I was tired. I was happy. I was everything. I was just numb. I didn't realize what I had really achieved. I thought I had done well. But by the time I had won the seventh race, it was like a three-day event."

The crowd of almost 21,000 gave him a hearty reception and in the winner's circle he joyously sprayed a bottle of champagne.

One woman won more than $1.5 million on an $8 win and show parlay. Numerous bettors won more than $500,000. The bookies reportedly lost more than $40 million.

"It is the worst day in bookmaking history," William Hill spokesman David Hood remarked that day in a Reuters story. "Our managers will be settling bets until midnight. The fifth winner was expensive, the sixth dismal and after the seventh it was time to put the lights out."

Fellow Hill employee Graham Sharpe added: "Frankie's seven winners have made this the blackest day in British bookmaking history. I shudder to think how much it's cost us. It's a disaster. We don't expect any sympathy but it's the worst day's business we've done since Lester Piggott was in his heyday and winning the Derby every year. It will cost us millions."

Call it serendipity, good luck or fate, but the timing couldn't have been more opportune for Dettori and his enterprising business manager Peter Burrell. He had entered into a contract with a publisher the previous fall to do an autobiography about Dettori. Because of the achievement of the Magnificent Seven, the presses had to be stopped to include the feat, which was positioned as the opening chapter.

Overnight, Dettori went from being a racing sensation to an all-around sports star. By year's end he would finish third in the BBC Sports Personality of the Year voting. He started receiving 40 to 50 letters a week and became regularly recognized wherever he went, even by people who didn't follow horse racing.

Dettori came to Woodbine in Canada a month later for the 1996 Breeders' Cup. He had three mounts: Mark of Esteem in the Mile; Shantou in the Turf and Tamayaz in the Classic. Hopes were extremely high for Mark of Esteem, the latest in a long line of super English milers, many of whom had failed to live up to their advance billings in Breeders' Cup history. Mark of Esteem went postward as the 5-4 favorite with lesser-known entrymate Charnwood Forest, but it would prove disappointing for the European faithful as Mark of Esteem ran seventh by almost nine lengths, showing a bit of run in the stretch but failing to sustain it.

"I think by the time he got there, he had done one too many (races)," Dettori said. "We started him off in the Guineas in May and then he kept on going throughout the season. He had a hard race in late September (the Queen Elizabeth II Stakes) and by the time we came to Canada the horse was a dying flame. The flame wasn't burning like he was early on. He traveled really, really good. When I pulled him out and asked him for run, the petrol was run out of him. I was disappointed because I thought the horse was probably the best miler I had ever ridden."

Shantou ran fourth in the Turf, while Tamayaz ran sixth in the Classic.

In July 1997, Dettori married Catherine, the daughter of a Cambridge University professor of equine reproduction.

Dettori had only one mount in the 1997 Breeders', the five-year-old gelding Decorated Hero, one of his winners from the Magnificent Seven, in the Mile. The experience leading up to the race proved quite interesting. After racing in Australia, Dettori flew directly to California, where the Breeders' would begin before noon to accommodate the Eastern time schedule. Dettori hooked up with some friends in Beverly Hills and planned to spend a relaxing night leading up to the next day's races. That changed when John Gosden, the trainer of Decorated Hero, called and offered him a chance to go to dinner at Rod Stewart's nearby home. Dettori was reluctant, wanting to ready himself for racing the following day, but Gosden persisted, telling him to "be a sport." Dettori relented and joined the trainer and several owners at the singer's home. After dinner and conversation, it had turned to 11 p.m., and even though Gosden was pushing him to stay Dettori begged off. Decorated Hero wasn't given much of a shot by the bettors, who let him go at more than 40-1 odds, the second-longest shot in the field of 12. Decorated Hero ran from almost dead last and made one run in the stretch, advancing to fourth at the top of the stretch, only 2½ lengths from the lead. French invader Spinning World, who had been racing near the lead, grabbed control in midstretch from pacesetter Lucky Coin and prevailed by two lengths over Geri, who held second by a neck over Decorated Hero.

"It was actually pretty amazing because up until that point, he had only won a Grade Two race," Dettori said. "For a Grade Two winner to finish third in the Breeders' Cup was a pretty amazing achievement."

The following year would prove to be one that impacted greatly on Dettori's career. He came to the Breeders' Cup with two mounts—Fly To The Stars in the Mile, and Swain in the Classic—both owned by Sheikh Mohammed. Fly To The Stars, coupled with Cape Cross, showed some early speed but couldn't repel the rush of the horses making a run from the back and finished fifth by 6¼ lengths.

Yet it was Swain, the battle-tested six-year-old, who would become the more memorable mount of the day for Dettori—for all the wrong reasons. Swain was a gallant warrior, who earlier in the season had run a close second to Silver Charm, the 1997 American Triple Crown star, in the Dubai World Cup. He suffered surprising defeats in his next two starts, but rebounded to win the King George Stakes against solid company and then won the Irish Champion Stakes, setting him up nicely for the Breeders' Cup. He had trained solidly at Newmarket before leaving for America and impressed his handlers acclimating himself to the tricky Churchill Downs racing strip.

The race was billed as the toughest ever for the Classic and, arguably, the best field assembled at any time for any race. Silver Charm, Skip Away and Gentlemen were each supplemented for varying amounts because they were not wholly nominated to the series, thereby increasing the overall purse to more than $5 million, making it the richest race of all time. Besides Swain, Skip Away, who had won the race the year before and was voted champion older horse in America, and Gentlemen, the field of 10 included several stars from the American Triple Crown series that year and the year before. The group included: Silver Charm, still solid after an arduous campaign, Awesome Again, Touch Gold, Victory Gallop, Coronado's Quest, Running Stag and Arch.

Swain drew post six and was sent postward at just under 7-1, fourth overall behind Skip Away at 19-10, Silver Charm at 5-2 and the entry of Touch Gold, Coronado's Quest and Awesome Again at 4.70-1. Dettori had Swain well placed early, never further back than about four lengths from the lead of pacesetter Coronado's Quest. With a quarter mile to go, Dettori had Swain moving well, poised to make a big move in the upper stretch. Silver Charm had the lead by a head over the faltering Coronado's Quest, who had a half-length lead over Swain. Dettori angled out his horse by repeatedly whipping his horse left-handed to try and get away from Silver Charm, who liked to view his opponents and was being steered toward Swain by rider Gary Stevens. As Dettori kept flailing away, the horse bolted to the right side of the track. It wasn't until Dettori had stopped flailing that Swain straightened out, but by that time Awesome Again, ridden by Pat Day, had split through a seam in midstretch and grabbed the lead. Awesome Again prevailed by three-quarters of a length over Silver Charm, who did not see him until too late. Swain finished another neck behind in third. Afterward, when questioned about the ride, Dettori claimed his horse may have shied away from the lights. In retrospect that had been only part of the problem. Dettori knew about Silver Charm's reputation as a fighter, and he had tried his best to remain clear of him at the top of the stretch. When Dettori asked his mount for more effort, he couldn't fight off Silver Charm. As they engaged in a duel, Dettori wanted to win so badly, he admittedly tried too much and hit his horse too hard.

"The first three smacks he went straight and the last two, because I probably hurt him, he ducked right," Dettori recalled. "Then I put my stick down, but I'd already swerved by then. I wasn't getting away from Silver Charm. I guess that's why I was trying too hard. The combination of me whacking him too hard and the horse seeing something on the left made him jink (swerve) even more."

Dettori flew by private plane from Louisville to New York—his head in the lap of his wife and practically crying—to catch a connecting flight back home.

"I said to her 'I really made a mistake this time. Ten years of my life destroyed in two minutes,'" he said. "I didn't even need to read what was written in the paper. I knew what they were going to do anyway. For 10 years my career has been all nice and rosy, so they couldn't wait to lay their hands on me."

In the *Racing Post*, arguably England's most influential newspaper for racing, David Ashforth and John Randall offered separate viewpoints in an article headlined: Would he have won? That's the big question the morning after Swain's agonizing near miss:

"What a moment to choose to blow it," Ashforth wrote. "And Frankie Dettori did blow it. The richest day's racing in the world and Dettori lost his head and, with it, Swain's chance of coronation. We don't know for sure that Swain would have won, although Dettori himself claimed that the unintended maneuver cost him victory. We do know that Swain's visit to the grandstand ruined the real chance he had a furlong from the wire. Not just because of the extra distance traveled but also because of the horse's loss of momentum and Dettori's loss of balance.

"When he arrived back in front of the grandstand fresh from self-inflicted defeat, he flung his arms out and told the Godolphin gaggle that it was all the fault of the lights. This is nonsense. And when (trainer) Saeed bin Suroor studied the replay, he knew it was nonsense. It would have been easier to forgive Dettori if he had put his hands up and admitted that it was his use/misuse of the whip that caused Swain to veer. . . . Swain did what he did because Dettori hit him and kept hitting him with his whip in his left hand when he should have switched it to his right. He hit him out of rhythm with Swain's stride and lost the quality of balance needed to ride his best possible finish.

"Dettori is one of the best riders in the world, but that was not the ride of a top international jockey. We all make mistakes, although the top jockeys make fewer than their rivals. Dettori made a mistake. It would be foolish to pretend he didn't, but unnecessary to hang it around his neck. Saeed bin Suroor put the position perfectly. Frankie made a mistake of a kind his trainer does not want to see, but he is a brilliant jockey, which Godolphin likes and admires. They have not lost faith. It is up to Dettori to justify it."

Countered Randall: "People always exaggerate the amount of ground a horse loses when, like Swain, he drifts across the course. It is common for estimates of several lengths to be made in such cases, but an elementary application of Pythagoras's theorem shows that the amount of ground lost is considerably less. Swain started to swerve early in the Churchill Downs straight and drifted steadily across the track until straightened about 100 yards later, so that he ended up about 10 yards further out than when he started. Yet the amount he forfeited was not several lengths, or even one length, but eighteen inches. This is because 100 squared plus 10 squared equals 10,100, which is the square of 100.5. Swain therefore ran only a yard—18 inches—further than he would have done had he kept straight. Since he was beaten a length, he can hardly be called unlucky on that score.

"Frankie Dettori is being criticized for not straightening Swain sooner, but it is often better for a jockey to let his mount drift rather than take corrective action and thus reduce his momentum. Pat Glennon allowed Sea-Bird to veer halfway across Longchamp in the 1965 Prix de l'Arc de Triomphe, but that didn't stop the colt putting up the best performance of the century. British journalists are very insular in their coverage of international races. When Dayjur threw away the Breeders' Cup by jumping a shadow in 1990, the British press gave blatant coverage to his mishap. Yet when Vincennes did the same thing in the 1971 Irish Oaks, there was hardly a mention of it. The attitude was that she was a French filly who lost to an English champion, so it didn't matter.

"Similarly, when Taufan's Melody won the Caulfield Cup last month, the fact that Jezabeel and Champagne were very unlucky losers were played down. The two New Zealand mares proved the point when finishing first and second in last week's Melbourne Cup. The reports of Swain's defeat should be viewed in light of that bias."

However, *New York Daily News* reporter Bill Finley interviewed George Pratt, a racing expert, horse owner and professor of electrical engineering at the Massachusetts Institute of Technology, who analyzed the finish. Pratt deduced Swain lost about eight feet of ground in his erratic stretch run. One horse length is about eight feet, so Swain lost the race based on Pratt's calculation. He determined Swain lugged out for 17 strides and that within each stride he went forward by 23 feet and sideways by two feet. By applying the Pythagorean theorem to these measurements, Pratt determined Swain lost six inches per stride, or a total of eight feet. Additionally, Pratt said Dettori's actions created the opening for Awesome Again to go through rather than around, which would have cost him some ground.

"I think what Dettori did very likely cost him the race," Pratt told Finley. "You can't say, though, it absolutely did. Everything broke right for Awesome Again and everything broke wrong for Swain. If not, they might have come to the wire in a dead heat."

Noted English broadcaster/writer Brough Scott wrote in the *Racing Post*: "Frankie's trouble was that he tried too hard. Picking up his whip with his left hand was correct. The one thing he didn't want was to lug in behind Silver Charm. . . . But as Swain began to close in on his rivals, even the experienced Dettori let the furies seize him. This won't be his favorite video.

"The lights may have been a factor. I believe that Awesome Again's amazing finishing sprint would have won anyway. Yet the facts are that with the greatest of all victories in sight, Frankie began to (whip) his partner so often and so hard that a gradual hanging to the left and then the final fateful swerve was not surprising. No one can truly say that Swain would have won or not, but he did throw away a winning chance."

The *Daily Telegraph*'s J. A. McGrath offered an opinion that deflected some of the blame away from the rider.

"Dettori's crtics will argue that he should have switched his whip from left hand to right when Swain began to run sideways 80 yards from the line. For a few seconds, the jockey seemed more intent on repeatedly hitting his mount than on correcting the waywardness. Also, Swain hung to his right, towards the lights instead of away from them. But if the lights were a distraction to the courageous Swain, there might also be other reasons. He is a seasoned performer who had only once failed to make the frame in 21 starts. Such is his experience, you would almost expect him to find the shortest way home despite anything his partner in the saddle might be thinking or doing. I suspect Swain gave a few hints when he swerved and unseated Dettori on the way to the post. Like some of the great heavyweight boxers, this warrior could just have had one journey and one fight too many. No matter what Dettori could or should have done, I doubt whether Swain would have beaten Awesome Again."

*Racing Post*'s Paul Haigh offered five separate versions of what happened: (1) "Frankie Dettori, with an inspired ride, almost lifted Swain to a memorable victory." (2) "Swain came to win immortality by dispatching what was supposedly the best Breeders' Cup Classic field ever assembled, only to allow himself to be distracted in the very moment of victory by the course floodlights. . . . One can only sympathize with his jockey, who tried valiantly to correct his self-destructive drift, but in vain." (3) "Frankie Dettori faced what was perhaps the most critical decision of his riding career when Swain began to veer right under pressure and away from the course floodlights. Should he risk losing momentum by stopping riding and trying to put his mount straight? Or should he continue to drive in the hope that Swain would correct himself, or at least not lose so much ground as to throw away all chance of what would have been an epic victory? Dettori had less than the time it takes to inhale to make up his mind, and with the benefit of hindsight we can all now say he probably chose wrongly. But, although it is for getting such decisions right that he earns the huge sums he does, no one is perpetually infallible and he scarcely deserves the scathing criticisms that have been heaped on him, particularly from the American media." (4) "Swain came to win the Breeders' Cup and for a stride or two seemed to have glory within his grasp, but when push came to shove on an unfamiliar surface and a distance short of his best, this ultra-brave hero of so many hard-fought campaigns could not quite find the speed to defeat the best the Americans had to offer. In the end, in spite of fierce driving from Frankie Dettori, this mighty horse just failed to round off his racing career with a triumph that would have staggered his hosts and, after wavering inside the final furlong, had to settle for an honorable third." (5) "Frankie Dettori delivered what may well have been the worst performance of his hitherto glittering career. . . . Dettori's persistence with a ferocious drive, even after his mount had begun to veer violently away from the whip, bordered on the downright incompetent. In an effort of which a raw apprentice would have been ashamed, the former champion made no attempt to correct the violent swerve that denied Swain, Godolphin and the rider himself what would arguably have been their triumph. On the contrary, the Italian continued to exacerbate the problem by thrashing his unfortunate partner's flank as they careered towards the stands. Whatever you think of extreme use of the whip, his failure even to try to change his whip hand was an embarrassment and a disgrace. Dettori has ridden brilliantly in the past and will no doubt ride brilliantly again, but this wild, head-down display can only lead even the most hero-worshipping observer to conclude that, for once, his nerve deserted him as a big race reached its climax."

American journalists lambasted Dettori without mercy.

"Dettori's excuse was a lot more creative than his ride," the *New York Daily News'* Vic Ziegel wrote. "Maybe he will have a better story by the time he gets home."

"Swain probably would have won the race if anybody but Frankie Dettori was on his back," Ziegel's colleague Bill Finley said.

David Scott of *Handicapper's Daily* wrote: "It looked to me like Frankie Dettori took Swain everywhere on the racetrack but the men's room. If he keeps the horse straight in the lane, they win it. It's the jockey, not the horse, who should have been whipped."

The website Handicappers.com offered this report: "Dettori blew the race. In fact, it was and is obvious that his ability to use the whip is excellent. The problem is he has no feel for the animal underneath him. The best horse lost the Classic due to the incompetence of the jockey."

"For a top rider, Dettori made an egregious error when he disdained to switch the whip to his right hand or choose to hand ride to the finish," Richard Eng wrote in the *Las Vegas Review-Journal.*

In an article in the *Racing Post,* trainer Saeed Bin Suroor offered his opinion about Dettori's excuse about the lights, his ride and Dettori's value to the stable: "I can't see that the grandstand lights were to blame. All the people watching the race there and on TV all over the world know he made a mistake. But that happens in a race. It's a shame. Frankie is a big name and he's our jockey. At the same time, I would like to see him ride better than this. I know he is a brilliant jockey. He is one of the best jockeys in Europe. It is normal to make a mistake. Frankie is our jockey. We like him. We love him. We need him to stay at the top all the time. At the same time, I understand Frankie can't do everything right all the time. This is racing. This was our best chance. It is very hard to find a horse like Swain and he was coming from behind to win. I am really sorry for Frankie. I am not upset. I understand in racing you can't win all the time, but I wish we'd done something better."

In Kentucky, Rick Nichols, the general manager of the Maktoums' Shadwell Farm, where Swain had been sent the day after the Breeders' Cup to prepare for a stud career, criticized the ride in a *Racing Post* article.

"It was a terrible ride," he said. "For a jockey of Frankie's experience, it was unbelievable. I was sitting in a position at the head of the stretch and I could see that aside from the lights that Frankie complained of, Swain was shying away from every stroke of the whip."

But Simon Crisford, racing manager for Godolphin, commented in a press release that he and Dettori had talked and the jockey received his full support.

"The main thing is he's one of us, very much a part of the team. Godolphin stands 100% behind him."

Upon returning home, Dettori called his business manager, Peter Burrell, and said four words: "Get me the tape." Together they watched the videotape of the race.

"I thought it was a combination of the lights and me hitting the horse too hard, but people did not believe me," Dettori recalled. "I wanted to see clear for myself. If you see the head-on shot, about 50 meters from the line you see him actually pricking his ears and looking at something on the left. Watching the replay was just to confirm to myself that I thought I was right."

"He was very, very sore about the whole thing," Burrell said. "It was as simple as that. Swain hurt him. It was a raw experience."

Sheikh Mohammed called Dettori soon after his return home and offered his full support, which gave the rider strength at a time when he needed it most.

Dettori could do nothing to redeem himself because the racing season in England did not begin for some four months.

"It's the price you have to pay," he said, recalling that time. "It wasn't fun at the time."

Burrell said the experience could have happened to any rider, but it became magnified because it happened in the Breeders' Cup Classic.

"Maybe he was a little hot in the head, as he would say now, but you have to take it in balance with all the rest of his rides," Burrell said.

Ray Cochrane, who would become Dettori's jockey agent a few years later, called the result a major mistake that was amplified because it happened in one of the biggest races and was televised all over the world.

"The criticism was well-founded," Cochrane said. "The horse should definitely have won, shouldn't he? Frankie knows that himself."

Cochrane thought Dettori had simply made a mistake born out of mental fatigue from a heavy schedule.

"When he went to ride Swain, I think he had been flying about all over the world," Cochrane said. "I think the traveling wiped him out. That's what I think. I knew he'd been all over the place and you do so much travelling in a short period of time in three or four different continents . . . you don't have a clue what day of the week it is. Your brain needs time to settle in and organize the time change. I think that was one of the main reasons, from my personal point of view, why Swain got beat. I think he went out there and rode a great race and then in the straight his mind wasn't really working. I think he was mentally knackered basically. You can try too hard to win the race, but I think if he had been a fresh jockey he'd have collected (the horse) very quickly. You've seen tired jocks ride and you've seen tired people. I just think he was very tired. It was a long season, a lot of travelling, and just basically he was worn out."

Dettori said he'd had a bad cough the day of the Breeders' Cup, but that type of thing had never stopped him in the past.

"Because everybody had built it up to be the best Breeders' Cup Classic of all time and the richest one as well, the whole thing just got big, big, big and I guess trying too hard to win it, that's the mistake I made," he said. "It's like when everybody has to fight Mike Tyson, they say 'I'm going to do this' and then they go in there and they freeze. They don't mean to freeze. You're faced with the reality and you're faced with the occasion. Turning for home in what they said was the best Breeders' Cup ever, almost in front, you're thinking, 'This is it, we've cracked it.' I wanted to win so bad. I was trying too hard and I just let the emotions take over. I didn't underestimate anybody. I went there and rode my race, but obviously I knew which horse was what and nobody was going better than me at that stage of the race. When we turned the last corner, there was only Silver Charm."

As the months progressed in 1999, Dettori enjoyed success with a five-year-old horse named Daylami, who had won a Group One race in England and a Grade One race in the U.S. the year before. By season's end in 1999, Daylami would become one of the most important mounts overall in Dettori's career, possibly the one horse who restored it to good standing, certainly in the Breeders' Cup. Daylami, who was entered in the Turf, was one of three mounts Dettori had in the Breeders', the others including Lend A Hand in the Mile and Zomaradah in the inaugural running of the Filly & Mare Turf.

The day before the race, Ed Musselman, who writes a cutting-edge tip sheet under the nom de plume Indian Charlie, took a shot at Dettori: "Gulfstream Park President Doug Donn has announced that in light of the fact Frankie Dettori will be riding in the Breeders' Cup races at Gulfstream Park, all photographers stationed at the finish line must be fitted with a helmet and safety vest."

The day of the races, Musselman had this item about Daylami: "If Frankie Dettori does not ride him down the outside fence, he'll have a tremendous chance to win." But Indian Charlie did not favor Daylami to win.

Dettori thought Lend A Hand would be his best chance of winning on the day figuring the two-turn course at Gulfstream Park and firm ground would suit the four-year-old. And Dettori was bang-on in his assessment because Lend A Hand chased the pace three wide and took over the lead at the top of the stretch but was overtaken about an eighth of a mile from the wire by Silic, who prevailed by a neck. Lend A Hand finished a head and a nose back in fourth.

Zomaradah put in a solid run in her race, placing third by less than a length. It was left up to Daylami at that point. Although he had run ninth by 23½ lengths in the Arc in his last start, he had won the Coronation Cup, King George VI and Queen Elizabeth Diamond Stakes and the Irish Champion Stakes leading up to that point. Dettori felt the Arc performance may have signaled the end of the season for the horse, but he had trained solidly in Florida and looked the part.

Dettori had reason to feel good about his chances in the Turf, coupled with the way Daylami had turned around. But the experience of the year before had taught him an important lesson of allowing his emotions to run rampant. He kept cool and focused and thought about the task at hand. Daylami went postward as the 8-5 favorite.

Dettori saved ground with Daylami, who was positioned about seven lengths back of pacesetter Buck's Boy, who had won the race the year before, for the first third of the race. Moving around the final turn, Dettori started getting his horse into top gear, knowing it routinely took Daylami about an eighth of a mile to find his best stride. Daylami was sitting second by only a head going into the stretch and overtook Buck's Boy just inside the eighth pole, drawing away to win by 2½ lengths.

Daylami's victory represented the first by a European runner in three runnings at Gulfstream Park. In the crowded winner's circle, Dettori shouted to the media: "What about Swain? What about Swain?" Then he took his helmet, tossed it in the air and then flew off of his horse.

Later on he uttered the immortal words: "They say revenge is a dish you eat cold. Mine is freezing."

"It took me six months to get over Swain," he added. "Everybody tried to bury me, but I'm back. It's been a long 12 months. My good friend Indian Charlie can kiss my backside."

He had finally put behind him the awful experience from the year before.

Around the winner's enclosure, English journalist/racing personality John McCririck celebrated unabashedly and commented to Dettori, "You showed America." Trainer Saeed bin Suroor remarked: "Frankie is a great jockey, the best jockey in the world. Last year he made a mistake on Swain, but he is only human. . . . Frankie is a little bit wild, a little bit emotional, but he loves the game. You don't get where he has without being able to horseback a little."

Veteran racing writer Bill Nack captured Dettori's emotion in his story for *Sports Illustrated*: "From the moment he swept to the wire in the Breeders' Cup Turf race until well after he skipped through the Gulfstream Park grandstand, stopping to gulp a beer a fan had given him, jockey Frankie Dettori looked and acted like a prisoner set suddenly free."

Marty McGee of the *Daily Racing Form* wrote: "No winner at the Breeders' Cup elicited more widespread emotion or was more impressive or carried a greater international impact than Daylami. With the weight of a sizable fraction of the racing world resting on his back, the gray superstar came through with one of the greater performances. He vindicated his beleaguered jockey and his innumerable supporters. . . . Daylami's emphatic triumph left some indelible images, most came from Frankie Dettori, who had been the object of derision since the Breeders' Cup last year when he permitted Swain to drift out badly in the stretch drive of the Classic. A long 12 months later, Dettori took great delight in bashing his critics just minutes after making his patented high-flying dismount in the winner's circle. . . . In direct contrast to the 1998 Classic, Dettori's ride was textbook."

Mike Phillips of the *Miami Herald* wrote: "Frankie sat on top of Daylami and the world. He tossed his head back and threw his arms in the air, shaking his fists toward heaven, shouting 'What about Swain? What about Swain?' He never heard an answer—only the long, loud shower of applause that came pouring down from the Gulfstream Park stands."

The website Race-horses.com also summed up the turnaround: "It had taken (Dettori) six months to get over the criticism he faced after Swain, but the dramatic win of the superb grey Daylami would have made up for a thousand disappointments."

The *Racing Post*'s David Ashforth, who had been critical of Dettori's ride the year before, commented on that in a postscript to the Daylami race.

"I rather thought Frankie Dettori missed the point in the moment of triumph because this talk about 'laying the ghost of Swain' is neither here nor there. Swain was then and Daylami is now. The meat of the moment should not have been (about the past) but about rejoicing in the extraordinary present and the seventh Group One notch on the belt. If any ghosts were exorcised it was the spirits of all those top-class horses we have sent to the Breeders' Cup, only for them to be blown away. For doing it perfectly, Frankie, many thanks. And if it has finally killed off something that has been preying in your mind for too long, then so much the better."

Patrick Jones, an Irish racing fan, took offence with Dettori's demonstrative reaction to his victory and offered his viewpoint in a letter published by the *Racing Post*.

"While I believe all racing fans were delighted and relieved that Daylami and Frankie Dettori were finally able to break the European duck at Gulfstream Park, I feel I must take issue with some of the comments made by the jockey in his interview afterwards. . . . Over whom does Dettori feel he has had revenge? Surely not the American and European racing correspondents who wrote objectively what they and many others had witnessed at Churchill Downs last year, namely the questionable ride given to Swain. Furthermore, if Dettori's own hysterical conspiracy theory is to be believed ('they tried to bury me, everyone tried to kill me', etc.), then how has he once again been able to ride over 130 winners worldwide this season; hardly the results of a jockey whom everyone is out to get. Part and parcel of being a top sportsman and ambassador for racing is that mistakes are made, and when criticized for these mistakes the criticism should be accepted in the same sporting fashion as one accepts the accolades."

Further to the topic, Thomas M. Miscannon of Orlando, Florida, offered his opinion in a letter to the *Racing Post*.

"I am tired of reading all the rubbish concerning Frankie Dettori's ride on Daylami. The fact is my grandmother (God rest her soul) could have won on Daylami. Simply put Daylami is the best grass horse in the world. To have a winning ride on him was no great accomplishment, and Dettori's win on Daylami, a very short-priced favorite, in no way absolves him of the substandard ride that he gave Swain in last year's Breeders' Cup. Dettori is a very good rider. In Europe he is a big fish in a medium-sized pond. The day he becomes a leading rider during one of the Southern California meetings or at Saratoga will be the day he is respected as a world-class rider. Dettori showed nothing. Come back next year and boot home a 19-1 shot and maybe we'll give you some consideration."

Well, Paul Loewenthal of Surrey, Australia, offered a counterpoint, pointing to Dettori's "awesome" ride aboard long shot Central Park in the Melbourne Cup.

"At least Frankie has silenced his Aussie critics and proved that no one rises better to the big occasion than he. I only wish Central Park had won so that we could have seen Dettori in all his glory at the scene of racing's most emotional moment. What a great prize, too. When did Frankie last ride a Godolphin first-string horse in a Group One (race) at 50-1?"

Breeders' Cup founding father John R. Gaines. (Breeders' Cup Ltd./NTRA)

Wild Again (closest to the rail), Slew o' Gold (center), and Gate Dancer finish bunched together in the inaugural Breeders' Cup Classic that featured bumping down the lane and produced a stewards' inquiry. After reviewing the film for ten minutes, the stewards kept Wild Again as the race winner, but disqualified Gate Dancer from second and placed him third. Slew o' Gold, who was sandwiched in between the other two and originally placed third, was elevated to second. (Breeders' Cup Ltd./NTRA)

Jockey Pat Day raises his whip to the heavens in a religious epiphany after winning the inaugural Breeders' Cup Classic. (Breeders' Cup Ltd./NTRA)

Randy Romero returns to the winner's circle signaling "number one" in recognition of his mount Personal Ensign, who won the 1988 Distaff to cap off her undefeated career. (Breeders' Cup Ltd./NTRA)

Jockey Angel Cordero reacts excitedly after winning the 1988 Sprint aboard Gulch. (Breeders' Cup Ltd./NTRA)

*Top:* Go For Wand (#4) is captured in the days leading up to the 1989 Juvenile Fillies, which she won to become the champion in her division. (Breeders' Cup Ltd./NTRA) *Bottom:* A year later she is seen in her battle in the Distaff with Bayakoa (#5). Go For Wand physically broke down in the stretch and had to be humanely destroyed, but she was posthumously recognized as the champion three-year-old. (Breeders' Cup Ltd./NTRA)

Arazi, with Pat Valenzuela in the irons, crosses the line first after his breathtaking run in the 1991 Juvenile. (Breeders' Cup Ltd./NTRA)

Dance Smartly, ridden by Pat Day, finishes first in the 1991 Distaff, becoming the first Canadian horse to a win a Breeders' Cup race. (Breeders' Cup Ltd./NTRA)

Arcangues, a European invader who had never raced on the dirt, scores a stunning upset in the 1993 Classic at odds of more than 133-1. It remains a Breeders' Cup record for the winning horse with the longest odds. (Breeders' Cup Ltd./NTRA)

David Willmot, chairman/chief executive officer of Woodbine Entertainment Group, formerly the Ontario Jockey Club, addresses the crowd before the commencement of the 1996 draw. (Michael Burns photography)

Personal Ensign's trainer Shug McGaughey, one of the top-winning trainers in Breeders' Cup history, addresses the media in later years. (Michael Burns photography)

Jenine Sahadi, right, is congratulated after saddling 1996 Sprint winner Lit de Justice. Sahadi made history by becoming the first woman to train a Breeders' Cup winner. (Michael Burns photography)

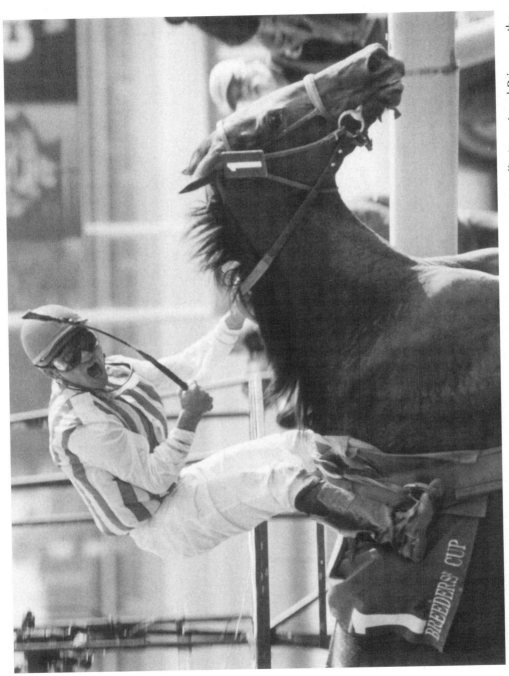

Jockey Corey Nakatani shows his jubilation after crossing the finish line aboard 1996 Distaff winner Jewel Princess—the second consecutive winner on the card for the rider, whose sister Dawn was murdered only a few weeks before. (Michael Burns photography)

*Left:* Trainer D. Wayne Lukas (in cowboy hat) escorts one of his horses on the track during the week of the 1996 Cup. (Michael Burns photography)

*Below:* Lukas, left, heads to the winner's circle, followed by his son, Jeff, after winning the 1996 Juvenile with Boston Harbor. (Michael Burns photography)

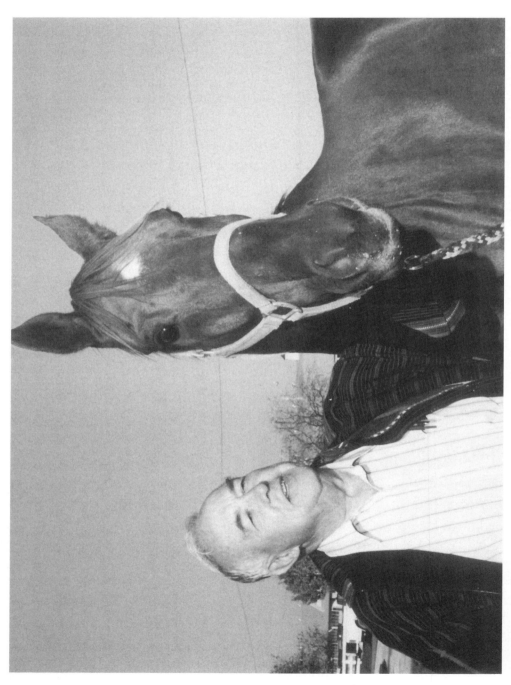

Controversial owner/trainer William Livingston poses with his long-shot horse, Ricks Natural Star, who was entered in the 1996 Turf against all odds and received an overwhelming amount of publicity—mostly negative. (Michael Burns photography)

Jockey Lisa McFarland makes her way to the track aboard the infamous Ricks Natural Star. (McFarland family photo)

Jockey Walter Swinburn reacts with astonishment after winning the 1996 Turf only months after suffering a severe head injury in a racing accident. (Michael Burns photography)

Swinburn poses with two Royal Canadian Mounted Police after winning the 1996 Turf with Pilsudski. (Michael Burns photography)

The great Cigar, led by trainer Bill Mott, is surrounded by a phalanx of photographers while heading out to the track for a gallop during the week of the 1996 Breeders' Cup. (Michael Burns photography)

Cigar's owners, Madeleine and Allen Paulson, pose with their beloved dog Oliver at the 1996 Cup. (Michael Burns photography)

Alphabet Soup (#10) scores an upset victory at more than 19-1 odds in the 1996 Classic. Louis Quatorze (#9) places second by a nose on the rail at 18-1 while heavy favorite Cigar is a head back in third in his final career race. (Michael Burns photography)

*Left:* G. D. Hieronymus put together the syndicate that won the 1999 Ultra Pick Six.

*Below:* Some of the winning members (and their relatives) pose for a group shot a few weeks later, after collecting their individual cuts. G. D. Hieronymus is shown in the center.

All of the jockeys in the 2001 Breeders' Cup, carrying the flags of their respective countries, congregate in the infield with members of the New York Fire Department and New York Police Department in a show of solidarity less than two months after the World Trade Center attacks. (NYRA/Adam Coglianese)

Jockey Jerry Bailey is captured in a solemn pose with other riders, who ran toward the infield from their quarters with their countries' flags before the start of the 2001 Breeders' Cup. (NYRA/Adam Coglianese)

*Left:* Jockey Jerry Bailey is all smiles aboard Squirtle Squirt as he is escorted to the winner's circle by owner David Lanzman following the 2001 Sprint. (NYRA/Adam Coglianese)

*Below:* Squirtle Squirt, with jockey Jerry Bailey aboard, poses in the winner's circle after the 2001 Sprint, a race that finally ended the lengthy Breeders' Cup losing streak for trainer Bobby Frankel. He is standing in the center casting a happy glance at his horse. (NYRA/Adam Coglianese)

Breeder/owner Cecilia Straub-Rubens, fifth from left, is flanked by co-owner Michael Cooper (on her left) and trainer Jay Robbins (on her right) after Tiznow won the 2000 Classic. Jockey Chris McCarron, who also rode Tiznow to win the Classic the following year, is at far right. Kentucky Governor Paul Patton is second from left. Straub-Rubens died just three days later. (Breeders' Cup Ltd./NTRA)

*Above:* Tiznow (#10) makes Breeders' Cup history in 2001 by becoming the first horse to win the Classic two years in a row, edging European star Sakhee (#6) following a thrilling stretch battle. (NYRA/Adam Coglianese)

*Left:* Jockey Chris McCarron, aboard Tiznow after the 2001 Classic, celebrates in what would be the final Breeders' Cup race for the veteran rider. He later had an acting role in the movie *Seabiscuit*. (NYRA/Adam Coglianese)

Trainers Bob Baffert, left, and Patrick Biancone share a few words during a media conference the week of the 2002 Breeders' Cup. (Arlington Park [Benoit & Associates])

Aidan O'Brien smiles while being pressed by English journalist John McCririck, who asked the celebrated Irish trainer about his horses' chances two days before the 2002 Breeders' Cup. (Arlington Park [Benoit & Associates])

John McCririck, who annually makes a fashion statement at the Breeders' Cup with his clothes and muttonchops, hams it up at Woodbine in 1996. (Michael Burns photography)

Arlington Park chairman Richard Duchossois, center, is flanked by NTRA commissioner Tim Smith, left, and Breeders' Cup president D. G. Van Clief in an address to the crowd before the start of the 2002 Bréeders' Cup. (Arlington Park [Benoit & Associates])

Trainer Bobby Frankel smiles proudly in the winner's circle after training 2002 Filly & Mare Turf victor Starine, whom he also owned. (Arlington Park [Benoit & Associates])

Trainer and part owner P. G. Johnson strikes a victory pose after his horse, Volponi, won the 2002 Classic at 43-1 odds. (Arlington Park [Benoit & Associates])

Jockey Jose Santos returns following his stunning upset aboard Volponi in the 2002 Classic. (Arlington Park [Benoit & Associates])

Chris Harn (top left), the mastermind of the Pick Six scandal following the 2002 Breeders' Cup, enters U.S. District Court in White Plains, N.Y., to plead guilty to the charges. Derrick Davis (top right) and Glen DaSilva (bottom left) also made separate appearances to plead guilty. (AP photos)

New York Racing Association vice-president Bill Nader (bottom right) made the initial calls that sparked the investigation in what became the 2002 Pick Six scandal. (NYRA)

The final word—and perhaps the most poignant—came from a 14-year-old racing fan, Victoria Parker, in a letter to the *Racing Post*.

"I wish that people would stop rubbishing Frankie Dettori over his emotional performances, particularly in Australia and America. He made a couple of mistakes last year on Annus Mirabilis and Swain, but I don't think he should be judged on those rides alone. He gave Central Park an amazing ride in this year's Melbourne Cup, adopting brave front-running tactics on a horse that had never run over the distance before. Daylami may have been the best horse in the Breeders' Cup Turf, but sometimes even the best horse will not win a race if it is not given a good ride. Frankie made sure he gave Daylami the best chance possible and redeemed his reputation by showing America that he is perfectly capable of a winning a championship race there. He must have been hurt more than some people think by the mindless insults thrown at him. He is one of the best riders in the world, if not the best, and would he be where he is now without being a great talent in the saddle? Why else would he be stable jockey to the most powerful team in the world?"

Cochrane offered an interesting overview of how Daylami's victory helped Dettori's confidence.

"To go back (to the Breeders' Cup) and win that race was very good," Cochrane said. "He would have wanted that horse to win that day. Daylami was a very good horse. It would have been his biggest chance to win. He wouldn't have been fancying the other two (mounts) too much, not from a jockey's point of view, anyway. They'll always look to have one banker which they think is their major chance and Daylami would have been the major chance that day."

Time and reflection allowed Dettori to look back on 1998 and '99 and put it into perspective a few years later.

"They tried to criticize me for one race in my career, which I thought was pretty unfair," he said. "So it was nice to put the record straight. I was lucky it only took me one year. Imagine if it took me five years? The problem is, if you keep on telling people the same thing all the time, eventually they tend to believe it. My record speaks to itself. Don't just criticize me because I'd done one thing wrong. So that's what I meant: 'Revenge is a plate you eat cold. Now eat it.' Obviously all those (critics) had to shut up. They only see in front of their noses. They don't see the whole picture. Sheikh Mohammed was 100% behind me from day one. When Daylami won obviously it was for him, too, but it was deeper and more personal than that for me."

If 1999 restored Dettori's career, 2000 became the year that shaped his life. It started off promisingly when he won the Dubai World Cup for the first time aboard Dubai Millennium, who scored a six-length decision. Dettori later posted Group One victories in England, Ireland and France. But on June 1, everything changed. He and Ray Cochrane came perilously close to losing their lives in a plane accident that claimed the life of the pilot. The trio had taken off from the ground-strip in Newmarket en route to racing in Goodwood. The flight was only supposed to take about 45 minutes, but trouble occurred on the takeoff and the pilot had to descend. The craft bounced on the ground but had enough momentum to take off again, albeit minus one of the engines which had been damaged. The plane started veering right and one of the wings clipped an embankment.

"You close your eyes," Dettori recalled. "I didn't even scream. I was just disappointed I was going to die, thinking 'This is it, you're finished.' I had a wife and a child and I was thinking 'Why? and why now?' You never think this is the end."

Then the plane crashed.

"Bang, mash, wallop, it was like being inside a washing machine," he said. "The first thing I recall is it was like when you open your eyes and you have 180 degrees vision and you can see everything, but you can't really focus on one point. I could see the two engines on fire, my pilot dead, and I couldn't move. I was just frozen. I don't know how long we were in that plane. It could have been one minute, five minutes, I don't know. It was like a disc that goes slow and all of a sudden it goes back to normal."

Cochrane urged Dettori to leave, sensing the airplane would explode, but the doorway beside him had been crushed in the collision. However, the luggage door that could only be opened from the outside had come undone during the collision, allowing the pair to leave. His face covered in blood from cuts and thinking he had lost an eye, Dettori could not see. And he was overcome by pain shooting through his right ankle, which had been broken. With a combination of his own strength and help from Cochrane, Dettori was able to escape. Cochrane dragged him some 20 yards and then turned around to retrieve the pilot whereupon the plane blew up.

"It would certainly seem to be a miracle that anyone got out of the crash," an inspector with the local police was quoted in a story carried by Associated Press. The story of the crash and the survival of the two jockeys and the unfortunate death of the pilot played out in all the major English dailies.

The near-brush with death and the two months he spent recovering from his injury gave Dettori a different perspective on his career. He basically decided to reduce his hectic globe-trotting schedule, becoming more selective with his mounts.

"I'll be honest, I was burning myself out really," he said. "Godolphin is a worldwide operation. It's become bigger and bigger and bigger. Basically I was pushing myself here, there and everywhere and getting to the end of the season when it really mattered. Mentally, I was tired; physically, I was tired. Where I thought I was able and doing a good job, I was actually wrong. I was feeling the pressure a bit more. That's probably why I made the mistake with Swain and stuff. I was a slave of my own job basically. Who cares if you ride 100 or 200 winners? Nobody cares. I wasn't making any more money. I was just traveling more and burning energy. I decided to cut down my workload in half, but concentrating more on the big day; on the good horses; on the track work in the mornings; on the things that are more important. Before the accident I had thought about it, but I didn't have an excuse to do it. I want to be in charge of my life. I want to do what I think is best. I don't need the newspapers to tell me what I have to do. So I decided to do it my way."

Dettori rode in the Breeders' Cup, but didn't have any success with his four mounts: Crimplene ran fourth by almost four lengths in the Distaff; Muhtathir ran fifth by almost two lengths in the Mile; Noverre ran 11th by 12½ lengths in the Juvenile; and Fantastic Light placed fifth by almost two lengths in the Turf. But for a little racing luck Dettori might have won on Fantastic Light, who was placed comfortably in sixth in a ground-saving trip. When Dettori made his move, he was caught in behind traffic and had to steady his mount in the final stages to the wire.

"I was so unlucky, I couldn't get out," Dettori said. "He should have won. I was so sick that I didn't win."

Fantastic Light overcame that loss to win the Hong Kong Cup.

In 2001, Dettori mourned the loss of his greatest personal mount, Dubai Millennium, who died in April after contracting grass sickness. The five-year-old had retired the year before with nine wins in 10 career starts by a combined 52 lengths. His only setback came in the 1999 Epsom Derby—the one major race Dettori had yet to win—in which he placed ninth. Dubai Millennium had been originally named Yaezer but was renamed by Sheikh Mohammed to celebrate the millennium, coincidentally during which he scored his smashing victory in the Dubai World Cup. Dettori lauded the horse, who he said showed his true class by winning at 10 furlongs—about a furlong beyond his optimum distance.

Dettori's racing season featured a string of key Group One victories, highlighted by his second Arc tally, this time aboard Sakhee, who won by six lengths. Dettori came to the Breeders' Cup with arguably his best array of horses: Imperial Gesture in the Juvenile Fillies; Noverre in the Mile; Spring Oak in the Filly & Mare Turf; Fantastic Light in the Turf; and Sakhee in the Classic. Imperial Gesture and Tempera were both trained by Eoin Harty, a longtime assistant for trainer Bob Baffert before breaking out on his own to work for Godolphin. Both horses had been racing in California, where Godolphin had set up an operation with Harty as part of a plan to succeed in the major American races. Neither of the two fillies had won their last races—Tempera hadn't run in two months—and they were given scant hope in the wagering. David Flores was aboard Tempera, who was considered the stronger of the two horses, and who prevailed by 1½ lengths, overtaking Imperial Gesture, who had tracked the pace and taken a short lead in the stretch but gave way in the final sixteenth of a mile in a game effort. Noverre, the betting favorite at just over 4-1 odds, ran seventh by four lengths, unable to quicken from the back of the pack. Spring Oak ran well to be third in her race, having to overcome a wide starting post in the field of 12. Stablemate Banks Hill—both horses were trained by Andre Fabre for different owners—thrived on the firm ground and won by 5½ lengths.

Riding Fantastic Light Dettori figured he was a certainty to win. The five-year-old horse had won the Irish Champion Stakes over the highly rated three-year-old Galileo six weeks before by a head in what was considered the race of the year in Europe. It reversed the two-length victory by Galileo in the King George VI and Queen Elizabeth Diamond Stakes. Dettori figured the presence of the front-running American With Anticipation would provide a more honest pace than the year before which featured dawdling fractions. And the longer stretch at Belmont compared to Churchill Downs would be in their favor. Dettori figured he merely needed the racing luck that had eluded the pair the year before in the stretch.

Fantastic Light drew the five hole in the field of 11 and went postward as the 7-5 favorite. Once again Dettori had Fantastic Light in good position and this time, unlike the year before, he didn't encounter any traffic problems. Midway around the turn for home Dettori began to make his move on the outside. With only a quarter of a mile to go, he had his horse in second, trailing the leader Timboroa by only two lengths. But Dettori had tons of confidence, taking repeated looks in behind, the sign of a sure rider. Heading toward the final furlong, Dettori shook off Timboroa and held off the challenge of Milan, who had come into the race off a fifth-place finish in the Arc, by three-quarters of a length.

"I was looking because I didn't want to let go too early," Dettori said. "As long as nobody was coming, I knew I could still afford to wait a bit longer because I know a mile and a half is just about his limit. I was not aware of Milan until after the race."

That left the final race, the $4 million Classic in which Arc winner Sakhee, who came into the race undefeated on the season in three races by a collective 16 lengths, would try dirt racing for the first time in his career. Sheikh Mohammed made the move to enter the horse in the Classic to prove he was the best in the world on any surface.

"It's a dream to have a horse like Fantastic Light in your life. I was so lucky to have two in the same year," Dettori said. "The worst thing for me would have been to have both running in the same race. If Sakhee would have run in the Turf he would have won. If Fantastic Light would have run in the Turf he would have won. If both would have run in the Classic and both got beat, you would have left empty-handed. I was just praying they would split them. I didn't care which one ran in what."

Aptitude, who had romped by 10 lengths in the Jockey Club Gold Cup at Belmont three weeks before, was installed as the 2-1 morning-line favorite, followed by Galileo, whose defeat to Sakhee had been his first loss in seven career starts, at 4-1. Defending champion Tiznow was rated third at 5-1, while Sakhee was rated at 8-1. Long shot Orientate, a horse who would make a name for himself winning the 2002 Sprint, led for more than a half mile, while Dettori had Sakhee in sixth by some 3½ lengths and well off the rail. With a quarter of a mile to go, Dettori had his horse in fourth but was gaining steadily moving seven wide. By the top of the stretch, Sakhee had the lead and maintained it in deep stretch before giving way to Tiznow by a nose.

"The track was quite biased in the middle," Dettori said. "Most of the horses that won that day were in the middle of the track. I was happy to run four or five off the rail. I wasn't actually following Tiznow as such because there was so many fancied horses in the race, so I was keeping my options open. One thing I knew about my horse is he stays (the distance). He wins a mile and a half on deep ground, so as I got to the three-eighths pole, I was rolling a bit more forward. By the time we got to the quarter pole, it was basically just me and Tiznow. Tiznow was just niggling along and I was going a little bit better than him. I thought, 'Right, I'll get him into the straight, I'm getting balanced, change leads and off we go.' He was half a length, three-quarters of a length clear and I'm thinking 'This is a dream come true, we're finally going to crack this.' The last 100 yards (Sakhee's) head was getting low and I could feel he was tiring and he gave Tiznow a chance to come back and beat us. It wasn't that Tiznow came and quickened past us. We actually slowed down and gave him a chance to come back and beat us. I think the horse hurt his knees again, that's why he slowed down at the end. When push came to shove and he had to go win the race and stretch for that extra effort, I think he started feeling his old injuries from his knees and the horse started to slow down. He was still a champion. The horse had never set foot on dirt and to do what he did was pretty amazing."

Dettori won his third Arc in 2002, scoring an upset victory with the five-year-old Marienbard, who had won two races in Germany and came into the Arc full of confidence but passed up at almost 16-1 odds.

"Dettori was seen at his absolute best and his decision to ride less and concentrate on the big events is paying off," the website Race-Horses.com wrote. "This is a different person to the over-stressed young man who beat up Swain both before and during the Breeders' Cup a few years back."

Marienbard did not run in the Breeders' Cup—and neither did Dettori, missing the series for the first time since 1993. Godolphin had him in Australia to ride Grandera in the Cox's Plate and there was no way he could make it back in time. Grandera ran a close third as the favorite, encountering traffic problems.

Fans of Dettori—and there are legions around the world—will be hoping to see him back in the Breeders' Cup, winning a race and punctuating it with his patented flying leap.

"Wherever I go in the world, it's become a bit of a trademark," Dettori said. "People want me to win and do it. If I don't do it, they boo."

# •13•

# Divine Intervention

## Pat Day

$\mathcal{A}$s soon as the stewards posted the official sign following the controversial running of the first Breeders' Cup Classic in 1984, a star jockey was born. His name is Pat Day and if you ask him what the Breeders' Cup means, he'll tell you it gave him recognition and exposure and the realization that any success he had in his career wasn't necessarily because of his own hands, but the hand of God. Day is the sinner-turned-winner.

Pat Day was born on a small farm in Brush, Colorado, in 1953 and fell in love with horses at a young age. In his late teens, he tried the amateur rodeo circuit, but had minimal success and gave it up after a couple of years to begin a career in thoroughbred racing. He started riding in 1972 in Arizona, moved to the Midwest and made a brief stop in New York in 1976. As his career escalated so did his skills. Day led all North American riders in wins in 1982 and held that title for the next two years.

His ability to ride was almost exceeded by his penchant for partying. He liked to drink and do drugs, including marijuana, cocaine and, by his own admissions, "ups, downs and everything in between." Riding high had a totally different connotation for Day during this turbulent time in his life.

"I can't give you a clear-cut reason why I got involved with that," he said. "Why does anybody get involved with something like that? I don't know. It was accessible. I was obviously open to it and thereby got involved. It's funny, (with) the negatives in our society you don't have to go looking for 'em. I was a pretty clean-cut individual, very athletic growing up. But, my senior year in high school and shortly after that, I got into drinking and partying, which I know a lot of kids do. I don't say that's right, wrong or indifferent. But I did it. I was trying to rodeo at the time and that's kind of a rough crowd. At that time it was. Today, they're a lot more professional and athletes in every sense of the word. At that time, we'd go to the rodeo and then drink and carry on and party. It was like a continual party. Then I got involved in racing. The racetrack crowd, they have their parties, too, so I went right into that crowd. That's where I was first exposed to marijuana, pills and eventually the cocaine."

Day wasn't the first high-profile rider to succumb to the problem, nor would he be the last. In a sport where money comes fast to young riders with an ability to steer 1,000-pound animals at speeds of 40 miles per hour, Day found himself wealthy and out of control. As fellow jockey Craig Perret said during the 1989 Kentucky Derby week: "He hadn't done anything that 85 percent of us haven't tried or done when were young and had money. I guess he's just got to be thankful he got out of it alive."

Day's wanton behavior reached a crisis point and it took a divine experience on Jan. 27, 1984, to save his career and his five-year marriage. The moment of awakening occurred in a hotel room in Florida, where he had come from Colorado to ride in a race the next day. Before going to sleep, Day turned on the television and saw evangelist Jimmy Swaggart preaching at one of his crusades. At the time, Day was searching for relief from his dependency problem, but did not think he wanted what Swaggart was offering. After flipping through the channels and failing to find anything that caught his attention, Day turned off the set and fell asleep. He had not taken any drugs or alcohol that day.

"I awoke some time later to the distinct feeling I was not by myself in that hotel room," he said. "Near the Miami International Airport is not the best side of town. If you go to bed and you're by yourself and wake up feeling like you're not alone, it's reason for concern. I sat up in bed and looked around. I didn't see anything but I did feel a definite presence there in the room with me at that point."

Day turned on the TV and saw Swaggart still preaching. Immediately, Day realized two things: he hadn't been sleeping for long and the presence in the room did not belong to a human being, but rather a spirit of a higher calling.

"That was the spirit of the living God there in the room with me and this was my opportunity to invite him into my heart," Day said. "I intuitively knew that's what I had been missing. I knew that's what I had been looking for. I think we all have a God-shaped void that only God is capable of filling. I knew that at that moment."

Day saw his life flashing before his eyes. He could clearly see the number of times he had come to the edge of ruining his career and how he had been saved by the hand of God. Day said he was given an option at that moment whether or not to open his heart and accept Christ in his life.

"For me there was no choice to be made," Day said. "I knew that's what I wanted and that's what I needed and I fell on my face on the floor of that hotel room and just cried out. I wept like a baby and cried out to God and asked him to forgive me of my sins and come into my life. I don't know how long I was on the floor. I vaguely remember getting back in bed and going to sleep."

When he awoke and headed off to the track, Day had no idea exactly what had happened the night before, only that he felt so different. He rode a horse called Eminency, finished third and headed off to the airport for his flight back home. The reality of what had happened to him in the hotel room hit him like a two-by-four when the stewardess offered him a drink. He declined, practically barking at the stewardess, surprising even himself.

"I didn't want to have anything to do with drugs and I realized at that point I had been delivered from the bondages of drugs and alcohol," he said. "I had been set free. That might have been what really confirmed for me that something truly had happened in that hotel room the night before, that it wasn't just a figment of my imagination, that there was a God that loved me."

In the ensuing weeks, Day faced another struggle. He wanted to quit racing, go into a seminary and become a minister. But then Day thought about his God-given ability, the relaxed style that earned him the nickname Patient Pat. At 4-foot-11, 110 pounds, Day is small even by jockey standards, yet his innate talent had helped him to win big races. As trainer Phil Hauswald said in 1989 about Day: "He has that little something extra that sets him apart (from other riders)." After much soul-searching and scripture reading, Day decided to stay in racing. He realized he had been given the talent to work within the sport and to use his success as a ministry to draw people's attention to Christ.

Later that same year, Day's career took a dramatic turn in the inaugural Breeders' Cup at Hollywood Park. Day had three mounts on the card: Proudest Hour in the Juvenile, Charging Falls in the Sprint, and Wild Again in the Classic. None was given much of a chance by the media or the public. By post time of their respective races, the horses had an average mutuel price of almost 35-1.

The manner in which Day gained the mount on Wild Again was the first sign of what amazing experiences awaited him by the end of the Breeders' Cup day. When the entries were drawn three days before the races, Day picked up the overnight sheet and noticed Wild Again did not have a rider named. The owners, who collectively called themselves the Black Chip Stable, had hoped to secure the services of Eddie Maple, but he committed himself to Track Barron, whom trainer Leroy Jolley had originally considered for the Sprint but then opted to run in the Classic. Day had ridden Wild Again before and, immediately upon seeing the open mount, headed for the phone in the jockeys' room to call the colt's trainer, Vincent Timphony. At that precise moment, Timphony and Bill Allen, one of the horse's owners, entered the jockeys' room to ask Day about riding Wild Again.

"It seemed all parties were on the same wavelength at that point," Day said.

Proudest Hour, sent off at 33-1 odds, ran ninth in the Juvenile by more than 24 lengths. Two races later, Charging Falls, at 40-1, ran sixth in the Sprint. Four races later came the Classic, at $3 million the richest race in the world. Most of the attention was focussed on 3-5 favorite Slew o' Gold, bidding for Horse of the Year honors, and Gate Dancer, a talented but erratic three-year-old colt who wore a hood that covered his ears to muffle the crowd sounds.

Wild Again had a season record of five wins (including one in course-record time), one second and four thirds in 15 starts leading up to the Breeders', but drew little respect. Allen and his partners thought highly enough of Wild Again to supplement him to the race for $360,000 (12 percent of the purse) because he had not been nominated to the Breeders' Cup program. The other six runners in the race were eligible and entering only cost their owners $60,000 each.

"It was the first race of that magnitude ever run in the world and just to be a part of it was a tremendous blessing," Day said. "It was a tremendous opportunity. I thought it was a stellar bunch of horses, an all-star lineup. I knew my horse was really up against it because it was such a competitive field, but I was just honored to be there and to be a part of the Breeders' Cup program, to be able to participate, and certainly to be in that race.

"We were a long shot, but with Mr. Timphony working on him and the owners extremely confident, that rubbed off and I was expecting a big effort out of him, although I would have been hard-pressed to say I could outrun them that afternoon."

Mugatea had been entered to ensure a fast pace for stablemate Slew o' Gold and, starting from the rail, he shot out quickly for the lead. Wild Again's connections had no desire to chase the rabbit, but Day found himself with little choice. When Mugatea ducked out from the rail crossing the wire the first time, Day had to grab a hard hold of his horse, who was racing alongside. Wild Again sensed the change in his jockey's hands and began to run off with him. All Day could do at that point was try to steer his horse in a straight course because Wild Again had a tendency to lug out. From the half-mile pole to the wire, Wild Again had the fight of his life. He faced competition at the top of the stretch from Slew o' Gold and Gate Dancer outside of him. By that point, Day expected his tired horse to throw in the towel.

But Wild Again refused to surrender.

"From the quarter pole to the wire, this horse finished on sheer intestinal fortitude and determination," Day said. "He ran the last quarter of a mile as if he knew that his people had so much confidence in him that they were willing to put $360,000 up to make him eligible and he wasn't about to let them down. I don't remember riding a horse that showed more determination than he did the last quarter of a mile that afternoon."

Wild Again prevailed by a head over Gate Dancer with Slew o' Gold a half-length back in third, but it took some 10 minutes to become official because of a stewards' inquiry. Day acknowledged his horse lugged out early and that there had been brushing in the stretch, but said he had done everything in his power to stay straight with his horse. The stewards also talked to Angel Cordero Jr., the rider of Slew o' Gold, and Laffit Pincay Jr., the jockey of Gate Dancer. While the racing world anxiously awaited the stewards' decision, Day said he felt remarkably calm despite so much being at stake. His trust in God had changed his disposition in life and given him more acceptance of things.

"I look back at it now and am amazed at how I calm I was, given what was on the line," Day said. "I knew that it was going to turn out the way it was supposed to. If it happened to be they took my horse's number down, so be it. I just knew he had run the race of his life, that he'd tried exceptionally hard and however it turned out I was extremely pleased to have been a part of it. I was extremely excited about my horse's effort. Certainly I was hoping the stewards wouldn't take the number down, but it was over, it was done and I just left it in their capable hands."

When the stewards posted the official sign (after disqualifying Gate Dancer from second) and declared Wild Again the winner, Day remounted. Just at the point he was about to take off his helmet to salute the crowd, Day had another religious experience.

"As my hand touched my helmet, the audible voice of God came to me and said, 'Not them but me,'" Day said. "At that moment I realized the whole thing had been ordained by God. And I realized it wasn't me but God. As the Bible said, 'Every good and perfect gift comes from God.'"

Day looked briefly at the crowd then looked to the sky and said, "Thank you, Jesus." The image became one of the most vivid in Breeders' Cup history. To anyone who has ever heard Day talk about his religious experiences, and he has recounted portions of them at various times in his career, it all seems like an amazing series of coincidences. Not to Day, however. Since he turned his life over to Christ, he has stopped believing in coincidences.

"As I have had occasion to reflect back over my entire life and my career as a jockey in particular, I know beyond a shadow of a doubt that it has all been from the hand of God," he said. "I know it has been directed divinely. It has been divine intervention. God has had me in the ideal spot. Just like when I ran to the front of the room to contact Mr. Timphony and he was coming in the door. I don't believe that was a coincidence. I believe it was divinely ordered. It was meant that I was to be a part of the team and that we were to win the race. I believe the Bible is the inspired word of God. God said it, I believe it, that settles it. In Romans 8:28, it said 'all things work together for the good of those who love the Lord and are called according to his purpose.'

"Early in the year in January, I had committed my life to Christ. I had struggled with whether I should stay involved in the racing industry. The Lord revealed to me that he had saved me to work within our industry, not to leave it; to take the obvious talent he had blessed me with and to do the very best that I could with that; and in the process to share the gospel of the good news of Jesus Christ; to be a walking, living testimony for the Lord Jesus. I had no idea how I would do that, but I just trusted that God would use me if I was willing. To be quite frank, at the moment I went under the wire in the Breeders' Cup, feelings toward God were basically nonexistent. I was caught up in the moment; I'm a very competitive individual. And it wasn't like I was saying, 'Thank you, Lord. Praise God.' It was nothing like the feelings I had 10 years later when I won the Kentucky Derby. I was still pretty caught up in myself."

Day received the Eclipse Award as outstanding jockey for the first of what would become four times between 1984 and 1991. In his acceptance speech, he praised God for helping him and then proceeded to thank everyone else who had played a role in his career.

Two years after that first Breeders' Cup, Day recorded his second victory, guiding favorite Lady's Secret to take the 1986 Distaff and Horse of the Year honors.

The following year at Hollywood Park in 1987, Day had his first multiple-win day on Breeders' Cup Day. Success followed another religious experience. This one occurred in his home in Kentucky, two days before he left for the Cup, while reading the Bible. He said God impressed upon him to lead the jockeys in prayer before the start of the Breeders' Cup, something usually reserved for the racetrack chaplain. Day had his doubts, wondering about the timing on race day and how the other riders would respond to his request. He received permission from the clerk of scales and support from everyone in the room, who joined him in prayer.

"At that point I realized everything that was going to happen to me that day was going to be second," Day said.

Day's first victory came in the second race on the card, the Juvenile Fillies', with the 30-1 Epitome, who won by a nose over Jeanne Jones, who had a six-length lead in the stretch. Four races later, Day guided 9-5 favorite Theatrical to victory in the $2 million Turf by a half-length over European star Trempolino. It was a patented patient Day ride, actually allowing the European horse to take a brief lead, before kicking into a another gear. Theatrical, a "borderline basket case" according to Day, had finally won a Breeders' Cup after three tries in the Turf.

It took three years and numerous disappointments before Day won another Breeders' Cup race. In between, he experienced the highs and lows of riding Easy Goer, a horse he still calls the best two-year-old he has ever steered. Easy Goer left the gate in the 1988 Juvenile race at 3-10, the lowest-priced horse at that time of any Breeders' Cup starter. But Easy Goer did not handle the sloppy track at Churchill Downs from the start and finished second to long shot Is It True. The following year, Easy Goer was the favorite for the Kentucky Derby, but ran second again on the greasy strip at Churchill. Sunday Silence, who beat him by a nose, again won by a nose two weeks later in the Preakness Stakes, in one of the most exciting races of the century. Some members of the media blamed Easy Goer's loss on the ride. Easy Goer rebounded to beat his rival convincingly in the Belmont Stakes and then won four subsequent races leading up to the Breeders' Cup Classic and a rematch with nemesis Sunday Silence.

Day liked his chances and so did the public, making him the favorite over Sunday Silence. But, as Day said, "Easy Goer didn't seem too interested in participating that day." Easy Goer tried to duck into the gap area leaving the chute. Day gathered Easy Goer together, but the colt did not show any run until midway on the backstretch when he pulled up to Sunday Silence. Race announcer Tom Durkin prefaced the battle when he said "Sunday Silence is bracing for the oncoming attack of Easy Goer, who is right at his neck."

Day was looking to play a "cat and mouse" game, but Sunday Silence exhibited his sudden acceleration and Easy Goer dropped the bit at that exact instant, as if he had just lost his confidence. Day started using his whip to get his colt's attention and although Easy Goer made a strong rally in the stretch, he finished a neck short, losing Horse of the Year honors to Sunday Silence. The two great horses never met again and, in fact, suffered career-ending injuries within a week of one another the following year.

There was some debate over Day's ride, including a blast from a radio personality in New York named Chris (Mad Dog) Russo, who severely criticized Day on a phone-in show. The *New York Daily News'* Bill Finley said Day became the "whipping boy" for Easy Goer, particularly after the ride in the Preakness. But Finley could not fault Day in the Classic. In his opinion, Easy Goer was goofing around from the outset of the race and Day had done everything possible to keep him going. Easy Goer had had some ankle trouble going into the race, but trainer

Shug McGaughey refused to use that as an excuse, nor would he find fault with Day's ride.

Day's next Breeders' Cup win came in the tragic 1990 running, which saw three horses die, including the brilliant champion filly Go for Wand. Day sensed trouble heading to the track that day.

"I could feel a cloud of oppression that seemed to be hovering over Belmont Park," he said. "It was just a feeling I had. It was nothing concrete. There was nothing you could hang your hat on, but in my spirit I felt uncomfortable, ill at ease."

A tragic accident marred the Sprint, which saw Mr. Nickerson collapse of a fatal heart attack and Shaker Knit fall over him, fatally injuring himself. Two races later, Go for Wand had to be humanely destroyed after breaking a leg while battling Bayakoa in a thrilling stretch duel in the Distaff. Day trailed the pack in the race aboard 74-1 shot Flags Waving and had a good look at the incident.

"I was watching from my vantage point—six or eight or 10 lengths, whatever it was behind them—this fierce battle between these two great fillies and saw (Go for Wand) snap her leg and fall," Day said. "It's all been played time and time again in my mind in slow motion."

As Day passed by fallen jockey Randy Romero and saw the "ghastly" look on his face, the whole thing "was like a mule kicked me in the belly." Immediately, he began praying.

"I was just appealing to God to be in the midst of that situation," he said. "And to be quite honest with you, when I got back to the jocks' room I was ready to take off and go home—like many people probably that were in attendance at the races that day. It was a very sad day in racing. I remember distinctly Angel Cordero came to me when I came back in the jocks' room and he said, 'Pat, I know we prayed earlier before the program started, but we need some help.' He said, 'Can we pray again?' I said, 'You better believe we can.'"

Collectively they prayed and Day said, "That turned the tide of the battle that was raging over Belmont Park that day. The end result was that God got the praise and the honor and the glory and Christ got the victory."

Day was aboard for the Classic victory with Unbridled, who had won the Kentucky Derby earlier that year for Craig Perret. But Perret had abandoned him in favor of race-favorite Rhythm. Day's original mount for the race, Summer Squall, never made it after a bad effort in his previous start. Unbridled had lost his last start in the Super Derby in Louisiana to unheralded stablemate Home at Last and drew the furthest post outside in the field of 14 for the Classic. He went postward as the fourth choice in the betting. It took a masterful ride by Day, weaving his way through traffic to win by a length.

"I think Unbridled was very well-conditioned, very well-prepared by (trainer) Carl Nafzger," Day said. "I think he ran a dynamite race. He ran to his full capabilities. He won the race but I don't think it was a fluke I was on him in that race. God being the Alpha Omega, he knew way before that particular Saturday afternoon what was going to transpire."

In 1991, Day rode Dance Smartly to victory in the Distaff, the first victory for a Canadian-based horse in the history of the Breeders' Cup. Moreover, it vaulted Dance Smartly to first overall as the top money-winning filly or mare in racing history, surpassing Lady's Secret, the Horse of the Year Day rode in 1986. Once again, Day had been the right person at the right time. Dance Smartly won her first two starts of the year, but her Canadian-based rider, Brian Swatuk, missed a morning assignment and Day took over the mount on the filly who had run third the year before in the Breeders' Cup Juvenile Fillies. Day kept her winning streak intact through six subsequent races.

In 1992, after numerous frustrations, Day finally won the Kentucky Derby aboard a horse called Lil E. Tee, a long shot at 16-1. All the hype had gone to European invader Arazi, a horse some called the next Secretariat, but it proved to be Pat's day. In the final strides to the wire, realizing he had the race won, Day started yelling, "Thank you, God." His prayers had finally been answered. He was also inducted into racing's Hall of Fame that year.

Day failed to win a race in the 1993 Breeders' Cup, but rebounded in 1994 with his second two-win day. Flanders kicked it off with a courageous nose victory over stablemate Serena's Song, but suffered a career-ending injury jogging past the wire. Timber Country won the Juvenile race with an explosive stretch run after lacking room at the top of the lane. Paradise Creek finished third as the heavy favorite in the Turf, which Day attributed to the horse experiencing a three-turn race for the first time and becoming overly aggressive. In the Classic, Day lost by a nose with Tabasco Cat, the high-strung horse whom he had guided to Preakness and Belmont victories that year.

Day suffered a shutout in 1995, although he did come close, posting two second-place finishes. But when he returned to the jockeys' room after it was all over, Day was philosophic.

"All of the participants returned safely and so from that standpoint it was a successful day," he said. "It was a great day. Personally, I didn't win any races and I'm a competitor. I like to win. Not because of myself but because of the power of the Holy Spirit working within me, I was able to put it all into perspective and I was able to openly thank God for just allowing me to be there.

"When I win I praise God and if I lose I praise God because I know, especially after what the Lord has seen me through, all things work together for my good in his glory as long as I allow him to work through me."

The 1996 season featured an interesting development for Day beginning in the spring. He rode Prince of Thieves to a third-place finish in the Kentucky Derby, then was replaced in the Preakness by Jerry Bailey, who had ridden long shot Grindstone masterfully to victory in the Derby. Grindstone was diagnosed with a career-ending knee injury a few days later, so trainer Wayne Lukas opted to employ Bailey aboard Prince of Thieves in the Preakness. Day picked up the mount on the Nick Zito–trained Louis Quatorze and took the lead from the get-go and never surrendered it in a brilliant performance. It was the third consecutive win for Day in the middle jewel of the Triple Crown, and Louis Quatorze would go on to become a major horse for Day the rest of the season, winning the Jim Dandy Stakes, then placing in the Grade One Travers Stakes to Skip Away. Louis Quatorze came to the Breeders' Cup after running third to Skip Away and Cigar in the Grade One Jockey Club Cup, but he still had something left for his final race of the season, the Classic.

Besides Louis Quatorze, Day's other mounts in the Cup included Minister's Melody in the Juvenile Fillies; Paying Dues in the Sprint; Volochine in the Mile; and Gun Fight in the Juvenile. Minister's Melody, who had run second in her last race, placed fourth in the Juvenile Fillies, well behind 8-5 favorite Storm Song. Paying Dues was given little hope in the race by the morning-line oddsmaker and was grouped with another outsider in the mutuel field because the tote board could accommodate only 12 betting interests and the race drew 13 starters. Sent off at more than 31-1 odds, Paying Dues ran an incredible race to finish second by 1¼ lengths to Lit de Justice, the 4-1 favorite in the competitive field. Lit de Justice had rallied from last under a heady ride by jockey Corey Nakatani, while Day had his horse rallying in the stretch and fighting courageously to hold second, a neck in front of Honour and Glory.

"We had a pretty good trip," Day recalled. "We got hung a little bit wide coming off the turn. But the horse ran a remarkable race."

Volochine, sent off at 23-1 in his race, ran eighth after showing some early run, while Gun Fight, dismissed at almost 13-1, also placed eighth.

Louis Quatorze was basically overlooked for the most part heading into his race because much of the attention focused on the great Cigar, while Skip Away had been retired for the season.

In the absence of Skip Away, Cigar's chances automatically improved.

"Cigar was obviously the favorite, but whenever you hang up $3 million, it's going to be a contentious and competitive race, which it was," Day said.

Alphabet Soup, a California shipper, scored a nose victory at almost 20-1 odds, followed by Louis Quatorze and Cigar in a blanket finish. Louis Quatorze had pressed pacesetter Atticus for the opening three-quarters of a mile, then made a strong bid between horses, narrowly missing winning the biggest race of his life.

"Louis Quatorze ran his eyeballs out," Day said. "He ran very hard, very game in the drive. It was a great stretch run. Alphabet Soup got a little bit in front of me, a little further than the margin of victory. We were coming back at him and fighting hard and got outnodded. But it was a great, great effort. He ran hard."

In 1997, Day had a mount for each of the seven races: Love Lock (Juvenile Fillies); Bet On Sunshine (Sprint); Clear Mandate (Distaff); Soviet Line (Mile); Favorite Trick (Juvenile); Awad (Turf); and Whiskey Whisdom (Classic). Bet On Sunshine, who placed third by less than a length, was the only one of Day's first four mounts to hit the board. Favorite Trick came into his race undefeated in seven starts and with a shot at horse-of-the-year honors, a rare feat for a two-year-old, although that didn't put any added pressure on Day.

"You might think about it prior to the race, just thinking about all that is in the balance, but when the doors open you're just concentrating on the job at hand," Day said. "It's not like 'Oh, I've got to do this or I've got to do that, the horse of the year is on the line.' You're not thinking about that. You're just doing the job at hand."

Day's mount went postward as the 6-5 favorite in the field of eight, but Grand Slam, one of three starters sent out by trainer D. Wayne Lukas, drew some support at 2-1. While Grand Slam suffered a nasty gash on his left hind leg after clipping heels with another horse in the first turn, Favorite Trick had a trouble-free journey. Day saved ground behind the leaders and basically took the lead going into the second turn. From that point forward, it took only one crack of the whip to keep the colt's mind on business as he drew away to win by 5½ lengths, ears pricked at the wire.

"I was very pleased with his effort," Day said.

While Awad ran seventh in the Turf, Whiskey Whisdom placed third in the Classic but was disqualified and dropped to fourth for interference in the stretch.

By year's end, Favorite Trick did indeed win horse-of-the-year honors, beating out hard-knocking champion older horse Skip Away, who had scored a smashing victory in the Classic to cap off his year.

Favorite Trick underwent a trainer change at the end of the year, when Pat Byrne and owner Joseph LaCombe parted ways. Bill Mott, trainer of the great Cigar, took over as Favorite Trick's conditioner and Day stayed aboard. But Favorite Trick did not escape the curse in which the winner of the Juvenile failed to win the Kentucky Derby the following year. After opening the season with a win in the Grade Three Swale Stakes at Gulfstream Park, he finished third by a neck in the Grade Two Arkansas Derby a month later. He ran a distant eighth in the Derby won by Real Quiet. He was given a break and brought back 10 weeks later, winning a non-graded stakes race, then won the Jim Dandy Stakes at Saratoga. He was shortened up from a mile and an eighth to seven eighths of a mile for the Grade Two King's Bishop Stakes, but encountered traffic problems and finished fifth by two lengths. The decision was made to give him time off again and prepare him for the Breeders' Cup and run him on the grass for the first time in his career. He scored a 3½-length win in the Grade Two Keeneland Breeders' Cup Mile, three weeks before the Breeders' Cup, and was immediately rated a solid contender for the Mile.

Besides Favorite Trick, Day's mounts included: Cat Thief (Juvenile); Wild Rush (Sprint); Tap To Music (Distaff); River Bay (Turf); and Awesome Again (Classic). *Louisville Courier-Journal* columnist Pat Forde touted a Pat Day kind of day in a story on the day of the Cup.

"Pat Day turned 45 last month. He'll be the second-oldest jockey riding in the Breeders' Cup, two years younger than Eddie Delahoussaye. He is, by general athletic standards, approaching fossilization. But even though he's a year older than Steve DeBerg, Day won't be a novelty act today at Churchill Downs. He'll be a major factor all day long. If John Glenn can do space at age 77, Pat Day certainly can do the Cup winner's circle at 45. This isn't a place to bet against the Chairman of Churchill, nor is this the afternoon to do it. Day being shut out of a Breeders' Cup in Louisville would be like Tim Couch throwing more incompletions than completions. . . . It sets up as a potential record afternoon for the Old Man. There is no better place and no better day for him to make another run to Daylight."

Cat Thief had been one of five Lukas starters and gave Day a decent run, finishing third, beaten a head and three-quarters of a length. Wild Rush went post-ward as the favorite at just under 3-1 odds but placed last in the field of 14, showing some early speed but backing up after three furlongs. Favorite Trick's previous race gave the bettors confidence and he was installed as the 26-10 favorite. He showed early speed and had a brief lead after dueling, but tired and ran eighth by more than seven lengths in what became the final race of his career.

Neither Tap To Music nor River Bay factored significantly for Day in his next two rides, but Awesome Again provided him with an incredible finish on the day. The Classic had been built up as one of the strongest ever, featuring Silver Charm, the 1997 Kentucky Derby winner who proved to be a rugged warhorse as a four-year-old. European invader Swain, who had battled in an equally hectic campaign, brought along strong credentials as well. Victory Gallop had finished second in the first two legs of the Triple Crown and then spoiled a sweep in the third leg. Coronado's Quest had won the Grade One Travers Stakes. And Skip Away, the defending champion in the race and headed for horse-of-the-year honors at the end of the season, represented another solid challenger.

"That was probably the most contentious and most competitive and deepest field quality wise of any races at any time I've had the opportunity to participate in," Day said. "It was a who's who of racing."

Awesome Again, a four-year-old colt by Deputy Minister, had drawn attention the year before when he won the Queen's Plate—Canada's version of the Kentucky Derby—in only his third lifetime start and without having run as a two-year-old. He won the Grade Two Jim Dandy Stakes at Saratoga, but finished third by seven lengths as the favorite in the Grade One Travers Stakes, then ran fifth by 7½ lengths in the Grade One Super Derby. He did not run again that season. He came into the Classic undefeated on the season in five races—his last the Grade Two Hawthorne Gold Cup in Chicago—following a patient training job by Pat Byrne, the former conditioner of Favorite Trick.

Awesome Again was somewhat overshadowed however because his victories had not come against the heavyweights of his division. Moreover, Day, who had ridden the colt in his last four races, had a decision whether to ride Awesome Again or stablemate Touch Gold, who had won the Grade One Belmont Stakes and Grade One Haskell Invitational the year before among his four victories in seven starts. Touch Gold had had only three races that year, his last start a month before in the Grade Three Fayette Stakes at Keeneland. He had placed second by a neck and in the interim had worked sensationally. When Day couldn't decide, Byrne made the decision for him, pointing to his unbeaten record on Awesome Again. Byrne enlisted Chris McCarron aboard Touch Gold. McCarron had ridden the colt in his major wins the year before.

Awesome Again and Touch Gold were coupled with Coronado's Quest because of ownership ties. Frank Stronach owned Awesome Again and had an interest in Touch Gold with Robert McNair, who had an interest in Coronado's Quest with Stuart Janney III. The bettors sent the trio postward at almost 5-1, but it's quite likely Awesome Again would have been a higher price if singled on his own.

"If Awesome Again was overlooked (by the bettors), he wasn't overlooked by me," Day said. "I was pleased to have the opportunity. What the gamblers do is what the gamblers do. That's the experts, and as the record shows the experts aren't always right."

The race featured a stunning finish in which Swain bore out badly in the stretch and Silver Charm also drifted out, allowing Day a clear run through the stretch. Awesome Again gobbled up ground from far back and under strong left-handed pressure by Day prevailed by three-quarters of a length.

"Pat rode him beautifully," Byrne said. "That's the advantage of having a top jockey like him, particularly at Churchill Downs. All he needs is a good horse and we gave him one this year."

Recalling that race, Day said it was "very gratifying" to record the win.

"He ran a marvelous race," Day said. "He was well back early, but there was a great pace in the race. I started making a move coming off the turn. I'd anticipated coming around Silver Charm. I was actually going to split Silver Charm and Swain, but Swain had drifted out and as I came to Silver Charm (jockey) Gary Stevens let him float out to Swain to try and keep his attention and I had a clear run up the middle of the racetrack. Awesome Again charged hard and got in front leaving the 16th pole and he was the kind of horse that when he got to the lead he'd wait on horses—kind of like Silver Charm—but obviously he was clear enough to get the job done. You can't count on something like (Swain and Silver Charm both drifting out), happening, so in that regard it was a little bit different. But to be honest with you, I don't think it had any bearing on the outcome. The way my horse was running and the way he won certainly leads me to believe if they'd had stayed down inside, my horse would have had a clear shot but it would have been on the outside. We might have lost a little bit more ground, but I don't think it had any bearing on the outcome. I think my horse was going to win anyway. I think Pat Byrne had done an awesome job of orchestrating the horse's season. He picked his spots well. His races, though not overpowering and not incredibly impressive in the fields that he was beating, certainly brought him to the Breeders' Cup in great shape and chock full of confidence and he responded."

The following spring, Day became a prime player in the Triple Crown with Menifee, who ran a close second in the Kentucky Derby to longshot Charismatic, trained by Lukas and ridden by Chris Antley. Cat Thief placed third. Day had ridden Cat Thief several times in the months leading up to the Derby, but had jumped off him three weeks before to ride Menifee in the Blue Grass Stakes, one of the major stepping stones to the Run for the Roses. Menifee won the Blue Grass, while Cat Thief placed second, the latest in a string of seconds and thirds for the colt. Two weeks after the Derby, Charismatic won the Preakness Stakes, with Day finishing second again on Menifee. Charismatic finished third in the Belmont Stakes, in which he suffered a career-ending leg injury. Cat Thief, meanwhile, continued to grind it out and emerged as an unexpected star for Lukas a few months later in the Breeders' Cup—and Day would be aboard for the ride. In fact, Lukas considered himself fortunate to have Day, both going into the race and certainly afterward.

Day had rides in all the Breeders' races but the Turf. He began with Banshee Breeze, who ran second in the Distaff by three-quarters of a length to the front-running Beautiful Pleasure, later to be named champion older filly or mare. Beautiful Pleasure was in an all-out drive at the wire under jockey Jorge (Chop Chop) Chavez because Banshee Breeze was cutting into her lead, which had been as much as three-quarters of a length with only a quarter mile to the wire. Banshee Breeze made a run at Beautiful Pleasure near the sixteenth pole, but hung in the final run to the wire. Day followed up that mount in the next race, the Juvenile Fillies, with Surfside, who raced wide for most of the trip but still finishing strongly, rallying from almost last at one point to grab third place by less than two lengths. His next mount, Hawksley Hill, the tepid 37-10 favorite in the Mile, had won the Grade One Atto Mile at Woodbine, but was disqualified for interference and placed fourth. This time he ran fifth by about a length, closing with a fury after running in the back of the pack for the first half of the race. Vicar followed in the Sprint but ran a nondescript 11th in the field of 14. Perfect Sting ran sixth in the inaugural running of the Filly & Mare Turf and Millencolin placed 10th in the Juvenile.

It was left up to Cat Thief to finish off the day for Day. The three-year-old colt had won the Grade One Swaps Stakes in July in California but had had a spotty record in the interim. Some six weeks before the Breeders' Cup, he had run third in the Grade Two Clark Handicap at Turfway Park, but Lukas felt Cat Thief had shown some positive signs in training leading up to the Classic.

"I went by the barn that morning and talked to Wayne and the horse looked great," Day said. "Wayne said 'I don't know if we can win but he's going to give you his best effort.'"

This Classic did not have nearly the same fanfare as the year before, but Cat Thief wasn't expected to do much by the bettors, who let him go at almost 20-1 odds. Starting from post six in the field of 14, Day's mount drifted in after the break and bumped with another horse. Day initially tracked pacesetter Old Trieste on the inside, then eased back and took him to the outside of the front-runner's flank. Cat Thief tugged on the bridle towards the end of the backstretch, giving Day some concern that the colt was expending too much energy at that point. But the colt eased his rider's worries just as quickly by relaxing again.

"I knew inside the quarter pole they were going to have to come running if they were going to beat him," Day said. "He was plum full of run at that point. I felt like I had plenty of horse left under me. He was ready to resist all challengers."

Cat Thief took the lead by a head in the stretch, and after his horse overcame some bumping Day kept busy switching his stick from his left hand to his right hand and prevailed by 1¼ lengths in a sizzling time of just under two minutes. He paid a juicy $41.20 to win and combined with 26-1 runnerup Budroyale for an exacta paying $1,209.60. The trifecta with 75-1 third-place finisher Golden Missile was worth more than $39,000. Chester House, a 63-1 shot, rounded out the superfecta that paid a whopping $692,907.

As his reward for winning, Day collected $208,000. Not bad for less than two minutes' work, but Lukas was effusive in his praise for the rider. Day, meanwhile, had top praise for the colt.

"He was really on top of his game and ready for a big effort and that's exactly what we got," Day said. "It was a great, great effort, probably the best race of his career—and he had a pretty stellar career."

At the 2000 Breeders' Cup, Day had six mounts: Surfside (Distaff); More Than Ready (Sprint); Snow Polina (Filly & Mare Turf); Yonaguska (Juvenile); Down the Aisle (Turf); and Cat Thief (Classic). His only top-three finish happened with Surfside, who placed second to stablemate Spain, both horses trained by Lukas. Surfside jumped to an early lead and increased it to 3½ lengths after half a mile but began to tire and relinquished control to Spain, who had been settled fairly close to the pace. Spain, who was let go at more than 55-1 in the latest in a series of Lukas shockers, prevailed by 1½ lengths over Surfside.

"Surfside was one race away from her best effort," Day said. "She got awfully tired and started hanging out just a little bit and Spain got through on the inside. We came back with Surfside and beat the boys in the Clark Handicap at Churchill Downs. In retrospect, we wished we could have got one more into her and I think she would have won the Distaff."

Cat Thief, who hadn't run in seven weeks and had placed sixth in his last start, was given mild support in the hype leading up to the race. Most of the attention focused on Fusaichi Pegasus, the Kentucky Derby winner. He had been pointed to the Classic by trainer Neil Drysdale, who is a master off the layoff, off a victory almost six weeks before at Belmont Park. Fusaichi Pegasus went postward in the Classic as the 6-5 favorite but didn't finish with his customary kick and placed sixth, two lengths ahead of Cat Thief in seventh by 9¼ lengths. The bettors sent Cat Thief off at 11-1 odds, but he never had a chance to show his true form when eliminated by Lemon Drop Kid going into the first turn and then bounced off the rail and pinched back.

"He found himself covered and surrounded by horses, which was an unusual position for him, and then really never got into the race," Day said.

Tiznow, a relatively unknown horse at the time but who would prove to be a legend in horse racing, in particular the Breeders' Cup, won by a neck over European sensation Giant's Causeway, who was making his first lifetime start on the dirt.

Day's 2001 Breeders' Cup started off strongly when he won the opening race, the Distaff, aboard Unbridled Elaine, who won by a head over defending champion Spain. It was one of Day's best rides in the Breeders Cup, as he rallied the daughter of Unbridled's Song from far off the pace and finished furiously down the middle of the track.

"I had a little traffic at the head of the stretch," Day said. "I went for a hole that closed and I had to alter course. It appeared that I left her with too much to do and not enough time to get it done but she really responded brilliantly in the last eighth of a mile and got Spain in the last couple of jumps. It was a big, big effort."

Day had five other mounts on the card, but none hit the board.

He failed to collect a win in the 2002 Breeders' Cup, but posted seconds with Farda Amiga in the Distaff and With Anticipation in the Turf and a third with

Good Journey in the Mile. Farda Amiga did well to rally for the place position, but couldn't match the favorite, the brilliant Azeri, who led from the outset and won by six lengths. Good Journey attacked the lead and had a one-length advantage in the stretch but yielded to third by less than a length. He subsequently came back a month later in his next race to win the Citation Handicap. With Anticipation did his best, but High Chaparral, the highly-rated European, unleashed an unbelievable kick to win by 1¼ lengths.

"We'd changed up tactics," Day said. "(Trainer) Jonathan Sheppard, being the awesome horseman that he is and understanding his horses, had drawn up a little different game plan. We couldn't run on the lead and repulse the bids by High Chaparral and the late closers. He suggested we take him back and try to make one run. We did that and were just second-best. With Anticipation certainly didn't lose any stature in defeat. He was brilliant all year. I think it was a masterful call by Jonathan and a great call in that particular race with regards to how to ride him. He came through for us and we were just second-best."

As he looked forward to the future of the Breeders' Cup, Day acknowledged the significance of the event on his career. Almost 20 years after he won the inaugural Classic with Wild Again in one of the signature races of the series, he is still riding strongly and battling jockey Jerry Bailey for most wins in the Breeders' Cup.

"I think the inaugural Breeders' Cup, when we were fortunate enough and blessed with the victory in the Classic, really took my career to the next level," Day said. "It made available opportunities to ride in major races around the country. I think it was singularly probably the most important victory in my career. I don't know where (almost) 20 years has gone. It's been a whirlwind to say the least, but I guess such is life. They say time flies when you're having fun, so obviously we're having a good time."

# 14

# The Showman Must Go On

## Angel Cordero

The morning after the 1995 Breeders' Cup, trainer Angel Cordero Jr. had a lot on his mind. His wife had been home sick, his son had lost his wallet and Cordero had horses that required his attention. Cordero had little time to reflect on his riding career, which had begun more than 30 years ago and ended abruptly the day before. Moreover, there was little time to dwell on how his dream to ride one last time in the Breeders' Cup, an event in which he'd had great success, never even made it to the starting gate when his mount, Classy Mirage, was scratched due to the sloppy track conditions.

"I planned to get a mount for the Breeders' Cup and I accomplished that," he said that morning, sounding more honest than bitter. "I got a mount for the Breeders' Cup but she didn't run. But I wasn't expecting anybody to support me because I don't want any pity from anybody. I rode for whoever wanted me to ride. I was very happy. Everybody that I rode for was very happy. That was the end of that. I'm not mad at anybody that didn't ride me. I did what I tried to do. It's whether Mother Nature or God cooperates. I can't be mad at them. It doesn't matter what happened in the Breeders' Cup. That's already forgotten. I'm more worried about my horses and my employees and the product that I'm putting out every day than I'm worried about the Breeders' Cup. That happened already. That's gone. I can't change the outcome of that. I've got to go to the next step and worry about my horses, my owners, my employees, my family. That's what I'm going to worry about. That's it. That's what I say and that's what it's going to be and that's the way it is."

Born Nov. 8, 1942, in Santurce, Puerto Rico, Cordero was literally born to be a horseman. His father, Angel Sr., rode horses and later trained them at El Comandante Racetrack in Puerto Rico. Angel began grooming horses as the first step toward becoming a rider. His riding career began in 1960, and he won his first race that year on June 15 with a horse named Celador at El Comandante. He won a race later on the card with an 80-1 shot named Jelly Debb trained by his father. A year later, Cordero led all El Comandante riders with 161 winners. In 1962, Cordero took his tack to the United States and began a brilliant career, although it was interrupted several times when he returned home while trying to overcome nagging doubts about his abilities in a foreign country.

In the U.S., Cordero became famous for his antics on and off a horse. He had an aggressive riding style, steering not only his own horse but doing his best to influence others'. His racing style was matched by his showmanship. In dismounting, he developed the habit of springing out of the saddle like an acrobat. In between dismounting and heading to the jockeys' room, Cordero hustled up future mounts by talking to the owners of losing horses. He turned his charm on owners and trainers and then displayed his riding talents on their horses. He talked the talk and then walked the walk.

By the mid-'60s, Cordero's star was on the rise. In 1967, he recorded the first of eight riding titles in New York. A year later, he topped all North American riders with 345 wins. In 1974, he won his first Kentucky Derby aboard Cannonade. Two years later, he recorded his second Derby victory, this time with Bold Forbes, who later won the Belmont Stakes, too, the third leg of the U.S. Triple Crown. Cordero led the nation in earnings that year with more than $4.7 million, then set a record by annually surpassing $5 million in earnings from 1977–91.

In the '80s, Cordero's star shone brighter than his smile. He won the Eclipse Award as the nation's leading jockey in 1982 and '83, seasons when he topped all jockeys in earnings with $9.7 million and $10.1 million, respectively.

By the time of the first Breeders' Cup in 1984, Cordero found himself in hot demand. He had six mounts in the seven races, headed by Slew o' Gold, who had a chance to win Horse of the Year honors with a victory in the Classic. Cordero's other prime mount included 1983 Horse of the Year All Along, who was running in the Turf.

"Like any major event you're performing in for the first time, you expect to win," Cordero said. "Those were probably the best mounts I could have had for one day. That was probably my best Breeders' Cup when it came to horses. It was a day we were hoping to get some good mounts first and we accomplished that. We had some very solid mounts. They were good horses before the Breeders' Cup and they all turned out to be good after. It just wasn't their day."

Cordero's first mount, Spend A Buck, ran in the Juvenile, the inaugural race of the Breeders' Cup. Sent postward as the third choice in the betting at 6-1, Spend A Buck led from the start into the stretch, before fading to third, a length and a half behind heavy favorite Chief's Crown. (The two met again the following year in the Kentucky Derby and Spend A Buck reversed the decision with Cordero aboard in one of the fastest runnings of the race.) His next mount, Tiltalating, ran ninth in the field of 11 in the Juvenile Fillies after leading for much of the race. Next came the Sprint and 28-1 shot Aras An Uachtarain, whose tongue-twisting name in Gaelic translated to "house of the president." He ran seventh in his first try on the dirt. Lucky Lucky Lucky, another outsider, ran a distant sixth to runaway winner Princess Rooney in the Distaff.

All Along, who had been referred to as the Horse of the World in 1983, fulfilled a dream for Cordero. He had wanted to ride the great mare for a year. All Along had only run three times leading up to the Breeders' Cup, including a fourth-place finish in the Rothmans Ltd. International, a race she had won the previous year, at Woodbine Racetrack in Canada. Britain's Walter Swinburn, who had steered her to victory in the '83 Rothmans, was judged by trainer Patrick Biancone to have given her a bad ride in the race a year later, which gave Cordero his long-awaited chance on the mare. Some people thought the jockey change would make a major difference.

Cordero had All Along perfectly positioned in the run up the backstretch, but was struggling to hold her back off a slow pace. He sprung her loose on the turn for home and did all he could to win, but All Along was beaten a neck by another French invader, Lashkari, the longest-priced horse in the field at 53-1. All Along may have lost the race, but not Cordero's admiration. In his opinion, she ran a "hell of a big race" and he had great pride in her.

Cordero had barely enough time to shake off the disappointment of that race before having to return for the Classic, which would indeed prove to be a classic. Slew o' Gold had not lost in six races that year, including a sweep of New York's fall championship series: the Woodward Stakes, Marlboro Cup and Jockey Club Gold Cup. But Slew o' Gold also had a history of foot problems and developed three quarter cracks in his left front foot, which required a major patch job the day before the race. A fibreglass patch fastened by sheet metal screws was affixed to the wall of the hoof.

Cordero thought the horse would be scratched to preserve his perfect record and a chance at Horse of the Year honors against John Henry, who had had to miss the Breeders' Cup because of a leg injury. But the horse had run and won in the past when he hadn't been 100%. Owners Jim and Sally Hill and Mickey and Karen Taylor—who collectively managed a syndicate known as Equusequity Stable—figured he could pull it off one more time in what would be his final career race.

The bettors jumped all over Slew o' Gold, making him the 3-5 favorite. As the late Pete Axthelm said on the broadcast: "They're betting not only on a great horse—a magnificent animal—but on an awful good blacksmith."

Mugatea, a speedball entered to ensure an honest pace for Slew o' Gold, did his job, but found a willing rival in Wild Again, who inherited the lead after a half mile. The race had been set up, however, for Slew o' Gold, who was on the attack after three-quarters of a mile, albeit reluctantly.

"He wasn't really trying in any part of the race," Cordero said. "I had to ride him to keep him in contention. When he got to the lead horse he wasn't himself. He was taking his time. He was very sluggish, with his ears pinned."

Cordero was using the whip by the top of the stretch to chase Wild Again, and had to contend with Gate Dancer, the erratic horse with the ear muffs, making a move outside of him. Down the stretch, the three horses brushed and bumped and Slew o' Gold took the worst of it physically and mentally.

"When they started touching him and pushing him from one side to the other, he was really in bad shape," Cordero said. "He really wasn't travelling the way he was used to." Wild Again prevailed by a head over Gate Dancer, with Slew o' Gold a half-length farther in arrears. A disqualification by the stewards reversed the order of Gate Dancer, who was deemed to be the culprit, and Slew o' Gold.

"He got bumped several times and he only got beat three-quarters of a length," Cordero said. "And he had all sorts of problems, more than the bumping. He was a beaten horse going into the race because he was in a lot of pain. I was more disappointed in the decision (to run) than I was (losing) the race. I thought he had a chance to get beat because he was hurting. He got bumped and that made it worse."

Cordero thought both Wild Again and Gate Dancer should have been disqualified because both bumped him.

"Fortunately for the winner and unfortunately for me, I was holding both bodies of resistance with my horse—one leaning out and the other leaning in," Cordero said. "It's like a guy fighting two guys. You can't win that way. But I was surprised the winner ran so big. We had a rabbit going with him to get tired. They were doing some decent fractions. We got to him and he hung in there tight. Pat (Day) put a perfect ride on him. He was a good horse that day."

Slew o' Gold lost Horse of the Year honors to John Henry, but was voted champion older horse. "Everything just went the other way," Cordero said of his fortunes in the initial Breeders' Cup.

The following year, Cordero won the Derby for a third time and a Breeders' Cup race for the first time as the scene shifted to New York, an appropriate setting for the rider to add another chapter to his great career. Cordero had mounts, many of them quality, for each race. Mogambo went postward as the even-money favorite in the Juvenile but ran sixth by about two lengths. Steal A Kiss, a 20-1 proposition, ran a distant third in the Juvenile Fillies. Ziggy's Boy, one of the favorites in the Sprint, finished sixth. Al Mamoon led into the stretch in the Mile but finished third. Then came Cordero's initial Breeders' Cup win, as he guided Life's Magic, one-third of a powerful Gene Klein–owned entry trained by D. Wayne Lukas, to an authoritative 6¼-length tally over stablemate Lady's Secret.

"Your first winner is like anything you do for the first time that you look forward to," Cordero said. "It's very hard to describe. You've just got to live the moment."

Cordero's next mount, Bob Back, coupled with Strawberry Road and Theatrical, ran a nonthreatening 12th in the Turf. His final 1985 Breeders' Cup mount, Track Barron, finished fifth after leading for three-quarters of a mile in the Classic.

In March 1986, Cordero had the second major injury of his career when he went down in New York. Cordero suffered a lacerated liver and a fractured tibia in the spill and required four and a half hours of surgery to repair the damage, which forced him to the sidelines for four months. During his recovery period, he helped out his fiancee and eventual wife, Marjorie, who trained horses on the New York circuit. When Cordero returned to the races, he won with his only two mounts in his first day back. One of the horses, Peter Brant's Gulch, represented Cordero's second Breeders' Cup victory two years later.

Cordero rode in six of the seven races in the 1986 Breeders' Cup, but had only long shots to steer. His best finish came in the Sprint, in which he guided 13-1 Pine Tree Lane to a second-place finish.

A year later, Cordero had much better stock to ride in the Breeders' Cup but still could not bag a winner. The much-heralded Groovy, whose owners gave out buttons that read "Feeling Groovy," ran second in the Sprint to the fleet filly Very Subtle, who led from start to finish. Groovy took the Eclipse Award as the top sprinter at year's end.

In 1988, Cordero came to Churchill Downs and lit up the track on the overcast day with some of the best riding in Breeders' Cup history. He started off the card winning the Sprint with Gulch, who was making his third consecutive start in the Breeders' Cup. Gulch, a solid middle-distance horse, had been cut back for the Sprint by Lukas, who had replaced Leroy Jolley as the horse's conditioner. Cordero brought Gulch from off the pace and, in typical Angel style, muscled his way through traffic to win by three-quarters of a length. Cordero added some excitement after the finish by celebrating wildly, punching the sky and smiling broadly at the crowd.

"I rode the horse as a two-year-old and the owner was a very good friend of mine," Cordero said. "I was riding a lot of horses for Wayne Lukas and he thought I didn't fit the horse and he was ready to take me off. When the horse won, I felt like I accomplished something. I proved something that I knew I could do."

Cordero became the first jockey to record back-to-back Breeders' Cup victories at the start of a card when he followed up his win on Gulch with a score on Open Mind, one of five horses trained by Lukas in the Juvenile Fillies.

"I was expecting to win, I really liked my chances and it was nice to win it for Mr. Klein again, the first owner I won a Breeders' Cup for," Cordero said. "He was happy. He was a very nice man, so it was nice, but Gulch really meant more to me personally."

Cordero rode in four of the five remaining races and came close in the Turf, finishing second by a half-length with Sunshine Forever to Great Communicator, a horse he had ridden the previous year in the same race. On the day, he earned $153,000 from his mounts. Gulch, Open Mind and Sunshine Forever won Eclipse Awards in their respective divisions, in no small way due to Cordero's riding talents.

In the 1989 Breeders' Cup, Cordero rode Ogden Phipps' Dancing Spree to victory in the Sprint. Like Gulch, Dancing Spree had been shortened up from longer races by trainer Shug McGaughey and had the stamina to finish strongly and run down the front-running filly Safely Kept by a neck. This was not an easy win, though. The crowd sent Dancing Spree off at 16-1 and it took all of Cordero's mastery to make him a winner.

"I think it was an extraordinary ride," Dinny Phipps, the son of owner Ogden Phipps, said. "For a horse to come from behind in a six-furlong sprint championship—and he came through the inside—it was an amazing ride."

Cordero rode in each race the rest of the card but couldn't find the winner's circle again, although he did post three third-place finishes and collected almost $100,000 as his percentage from his horses' earnings.

Cordero rode in five of the races in the 1990 Breeders' Cup, but only one of his mounts, El Senor, hit the board, running third in the Turf. In 1991, he again had five mounts and finished second with Versailles Treaty in the Distaff for his best finish.

That was the last time Cordero rode in the Breeders' Cup. Two months later, on January 12 at Aqueduct, Cordero fell hard to the track after his mount, Grey Tailwind, stumbled over a fallen horse as part of a chain-reaction spill. Cordero suffered a broken elbow, three broken ribs and multiple internal injuries that required the removal of his spleen. For 48 hours after the accident, doctors feared the worst. Cordero later indicated in articles he had nightmares about the spill for three nights in a row. He lost 16 pounds in 18 days, nine of those days spent in intensive care. Cordero recovered from what he calculated was the 24th injury of his career and, under advisement from his doctors, who worried that any further injury to his abdominal area could be fatal, retired from riding.

On May 6, 1992, at a downtown Manhattan club, Cordero tearfully announced his departure.

Cordero's beginnings in the sport in Puerto Rico and his years in the U.S. gave him the knowledge to prepare for a career training horses. Most everyone in the sport figured Cordero had the necessary credentials to be a good trainer. As Lukas told a *USA Today* reporter: "He's one of the few riders who could get off a horse and accurately tell you about the horse. That one ability will make him a successful trainer. He had a sixth sense about a horse."

Cordero also had the added quality of salesmanship, which some trainers will tell you is as important as a stopwatch. "He has great desire and a gift of the gab," Hall of Fame trainer Ron McAnally told *Los Angeles Times* writer Bill Christine about Cordero. "And let's face it, a gift of gab is an asset for a trainer."

On May 23 at Belmont Park in his first effort as a trainer, Angel saddled Empire Joy Stable's Puchinito to a dead-heat finish for fifth. On June 15 at Belmont, Cordero saddled his first winner when Puchinito won a $35,000 claiming race.

Cordero's training career did not take off with the same warp speed as his riding career. He struggled like an apprentice jockey trying to make an impression.

"This is hard, I'm telling you. Like everything else, you start at the bottom, that's the way it is," Cordero told the *Boston Globe*'s Michael Blowen in July 1995. "Getting up at five o'clock and spending all day with the horses and then doing the same thing the next day and the next day, it's not like it was when I was riding. I could stay out for a party and be at the track at 11 or so, that was fine. When I was riding, I really had no idea how hard the trainer's job was. When I lost a race as a rider, I just would wait for the next one. Now it's another week or two before I get another chance. I used to come (to Saratoga) trying to break the record for wins—40 wins I would aim for. Now, I just say, 'please, God, let me have one winner so I can make expenses.' I used to make my expenses in one week. Last year, I didn't make expenses. That's the way it is, no vacation."

Blowen raised the issue that many in the media had been suggesting for some time: Cordero's struggles as a trainer related to his skin color. While rich, influential owners gave Bill Shoemaker well-bred stock when he started out training, Cordero could only attract modest horses. The suggestion of prejudice rankled

Cordero when Blowen put the idea to him. "He just stares at you," Blowen wrote. "And stares. And stares. There is no answer to the question, just the silent, uncomfortable truth to the situation."

During this time, Cordero hinted of a return to riding, even though his doctor told him it could be fatal if he hurt himself. Like Steve Carlton of baseball, Guy Lafleur of hockey and Mark Spitz of swimming, Cordero had the need to finish unfinished business. Unlike the others who quit when their skills had diminished, Cordero had to exit the sport he dominated because of an injury. Cordero wanted to ride a few more times, to sit tall in the saddle once more and triumphantly jump out of the irons and then call it quits. He had seen the great Lester Piggott return from a five-year break in racing to win the Breeders' Cup Mile in 1990 and took it to heart.

"To me that was great, to see a man like him coming back at his age and win on a day like that," Cordero said. "That was an inspiration for me, to see if I could accomplish that, too."

On Oct. 1, 1995, at El Comandante Racetrack in Puerto Rico—the place where it all began—the 52-year-old Cordero returned to the saddle. Some three and a half years after he had hung up his tack, he put silks on once again to recapture the glory. A crowd of 12,000, four times the size of the normal Sunday crowd, attended the festive day. Cordero was paid an appearance fee, half of which he planned to donate to victims of a recent hurricane in the area.

Clearly, the day dripped with drama and it didn't take Cordero long to find the winner's circle. Riding Bandit Bomber, a winner of 28 races in 30 lifetime starts, Cordero scored a 12¼-length victory.

The return produced an interesting awakening. Despite the victory and the cheers that accompanied it, Cordero realized things had changed dramatically in the time between his retirement and return.

"I now realize that I have lost the love I always had for riding, which is very sad," he told Finley. "It was something that I loved so much and that was gone. I had that in mind throughout this."

But Cordero still had a desire to ride in the Breeders' Cup later that month at Belmont Park in New York. On October 14, Cordero rode in New York for the first time since his spill almost three years before at Aqueduct. For the first of his five mounts that day, two nine-year-old girls—Cordero's daughter, Julie, and granddaughter Amanda—escorted him to the paddock. Amanda wept, while Julie looked up anxiously at her father. The crowd lined up to get a close look at Cordero. One fan called out to Mike Smith, one of the top riders in the country: "The master is back, Mike." Cordero failed to win any of the races, but as *New York Daily News* sports columnist Vic Ziegel wrote: "The best news is he didn't get hurt."

Cordero took his shutout in hand. "Hey, I didn't get booed, so everything worked out," he told Finley.

But Cordero found few willing to put him on their horses for the Breeders' Cup. Early in the week, Cordero worked Northern Spur as a favor for trainer Ron McAnally, but the mount belonged to regular rider Chris McCarron, who later steered the horse to victory in the Turf. Cordero attended the midweek post-position draw, but it didn't help him to secure any more mounts, including one which was open at the time. Only one person came forward with an opportunity for Cordero to ride in the Breeders' Cup. Trainer H. Allen Jerkens gave him the call on Classy Mirage, a Grade One–winning mare with a record of 13 victories in 24 lifetime starts and earnings of $694,652. Jerkens had sought the services of several other riders but for various reasons came up empty. Classy Mirage, despite her record, was 12-1 on the morning line for the Sprint. But Cordero was willing and Jerkens knew he could still ride despite the long layoff. Some riders at Cordero's age just didn't have the style and grace anymore on a horse, but the veteran Puerto Rican still looked good on a horse according to Jerkens. He also hired him to ride a horse called Patysprospect in a stakes race on the grass after the Breeders' Cup races.

Heavy rains the night before the Breeders' Cup and early in the morning of the day waterlogged both courses and Jerkens scratched both horses. Classy Mirage had some physical problems that could have been compromised by the off going. There would be other races for the mare and other Breeders' Cups for Jerkens, but this had been the last shot for Cordero.

His missed opportunity registered a footnote in most stories recorded by the media. There were far too many compelling yarns to spin: the stakes-record victory by the undefeated Cigar in the Classic; the awesome stretch-run performance by Inside Information in the Distaff; and the heralding of a future star in Juvenile winner Unbridled's Song. On the Breeders' Cup telecast, contributing analyst and trainer John Veitch offered a personal message to his old friend Cordero, telling him to cheer up despite the bad luck. Cordero had been in transit at the time, picking up an owner to drive to the track and then heading home to watch the card on TV. He arrived just in time to see the horses step on to the track for the Sprint—minus him.

Had the 1995 Breeders' Cup had a perfect ending, Angel Cordero would have won the Sprint and performed one of his patented leaps from the saddle. It never happened. Angel did not ride off into the sunset in a blaze of glory. He drove home instead, his dream officially over.

Cordero's training career never really took off and in March 1998, after almost six years of conditioning horses, he retired to become an agent for jockey John Velazquez. Cordero's training stats did not jump off the page as prominently as he used to jump off horses: 88 winners from 687 starters, who collectively banked less than $2.3 million. He had only six horses at the time of his retirement and would leave only one with his wife, Marjorie, to continue training.

"I don't have the amount of horses to make money," he said in an interview with the *New York Post*'s David Grening. "I have three kids and they're going to be going to college pretty soon. It's gonna take me money to bring them up to be somebody. I'm not getting any younger and the only thing I know how to do is work around horses. I really love training and I think in the future I'll probably come back and train."

Velazquez came to New York in March 1990 from Puerto Rico, where he began jockey school in June 1988. About a year and a half later, he began riding professionally. He moved to the U.S. under the advisement of Cordero, who mentored him, and lived with the jockey and his family during his initial stages in New York. Beginning with his first full season in 1991, Velazquez placed in the top-10 annually in the New York riding colony. His achieved a personal best in 1996 when he won 212 races and $9.2 million in earnings. In 1997, his purse earnings dipped by some $2 million. The decision to switch to Cordero from Lee Taylor added a new layer to their relationship.

"To me, he's been more than a mentor," Velazquez said in the 1998 *New York Post* article. "He's been more like a father to me. He taught me almost everything I know. He's always been there for me."

"I'm disappointed but it's not devastating," Taylor said. "I understand the situation. They're really close. As the cliché goes, it was an amicable split. He's still a friend of mine."

Cordero predicted it would not be hard selling Velazquez' merits to trainers.

"I know he has the talent," he said. "Of all the people I ever helped, he's probably the one that's accomplished the most. I think he's a complete rider. A lot of people said to me, 'Johnny's turned out to be a real good rider.' There's no doubt about it that he's one of the best riders in the nation."

Those comments proved factually true in the first season Cordero and Velazquez worked together. The jockey ranked eighth in the nation with purse earnings of more than $10.7 million, including $600,000 winning the Breeders' Cup Mile aboard Da Hoss. Two years later he recorded his second Breeders' Cup win, this time with Caressing in the Juvenile Fillies. He added two more Cup wins to his collection in 2002 with Storm Flag Flying in the Juvenile Fillies and Starine in the Filly & Mare Turf. His four victories tied him with his mentor, who also had seven seconds and seven thirds and purse earnings of more than $6 million.

Velazquez was asked after his two victories in the 2002 Cup what it means having Cordero as his agent.

"He's been a great teacher for me, been a lot of help for me," Velazquez said. "I think all the things I've done it's because I learned quickly and I had a good teacher."

Velazquez also addressed the controversy that arose because Cordero exercised horses and some jockey agents felt that gave him an unfair advantage.

"You know, this is really funny because he was getting on a lot of horses that I never saw," Velazquez said. "A lot of people started saying that he was working the horses for me, which didn't make any sense. And then a lot of the agents complained and they made a rule that he couldn't get on horses anymore. That's in the past and I think he's been doing it for a little while now. I think he just loves it. He loves to be in the game. It keeps him fit and keeps his mind going. He was born to be a jockey and loves to be on a horse."

Sadly for Angel Cordero, his wife, Marjorie, died on January 22, 2001, from injuries in a hit-and-run accident. She was only 41. She had been jogging about half a mile from her home in Long Island, New York, when she was struck by a car. She had been working as an agent for jockey Hector Rosario at the time of her death. Almost five months after Marjorie Cordero died, police arrested a New York man, Robert Mikols, 61, and charged him with leaving the scene of a fatal accident. He faced a possible prison term of four years, but the judge gave Mickols a six-month sentence and five years probation.

"When you lose the best thing you have, it's difficult for anybody," Cordero told the *New York Post*. "She was a beautiful lady, young and full of life. She was killed by somebody who is going to get away with it. I just don't think it's fair that somebody kills somebody and gets six months maximum."

# 15

# Oh, Brother

## Budroyale and Tiznow

*If* you believe in fate, destiny, irony, coincidence and, perhaps, the racing gods, then you can't help but believe some kind of karma had to be happening with Budroyale and Tiznow. These two full brothers made for an interesting run in the Classic from 1999 to 2001 and gave their connections and all of racing a legacy of incredible memories.

Their story begins with the late California breeder Cecilia Straub-Rubens, who had an interesting background in racing. Her first husband, Arthur (Bud) Straub, a beer distributor who was also an avid bettor, began his own racing stable in the 60s after cashing a $10,000 daily-double ticket at Del Mar. He promptly went to Kentucky, stopped off at one of the commercial breeding farms and bought a young racing prospect. He'd owned quarter horses and harness horses, but this was his first thoroughbred racehorse. He named it Brewery Boy, and it had some success and was later retired to stallion duty in California.

In 1981 after Arthur Straub died, the executor of the estate, Mike Cooper, asked Cecilia, who was the major beneficiary, if she wanted to continue in the racing game. She had about 20 horses, including breeding stock, and liked the people in horse racing and considered the sport fun. She decided to remain active with Cooper as her managing partner. Four years after her husband's death, Cecilia married Roy Rubens.

In 1987, she purchased a yearling filly for slightly more than $40,000 and named it Cee's Song. She liked to be called Cee and named most of her horses after herself because it was easier to identify them. Cee's Song ran 18 times in three years, amassing $82,225. In 1988, she purchased a colt that she named Cee's Tizzy. He didn't make it to the races until his three-year-old year, winning three of six races and banking $173,150. Much of the earnings came with a third-place finish in the Louisiana Super Derby in which he fractured a knee and had to be retired. Straub-Rubens retained him as a stallion prospect and sent him to Lakeview Thoroughbred Farms in Southern California for commercial breeding.

In 1991, Straub-Rubens bred Cee's Tizzy to Cee's Song, the mating producing a colt named Ceebett. He amounted to nothing, collecting only $1,000-and-change in earnings.

The second foal, a full brother, appeared to be headed for only minimal success at the claiming level early in his career. Named Budroyale—a combination of the given names of the late Buddy Cruvant, who co-owned the mare, Roy Rubens and the suffix ale—the horse was gelded as a yearling because of his minimal value as a stallion prospect. After initial training at the farm, he was sent to the track to be trained by Jay Robbins, who had been working for the Straub-Rubens/Cooper partnership for two or three years, conditioning a handful of horses.

The veteran horseman came from a prominent California horse racing family headed by the patriarch Jack, a longtime equine practitioner who at one time or another had done veterinary work on the likes of legendary horses Citation, John Henry, Native Dancer and Ancient Title. He had also been instrumental in the formation of the Oak Tree Racing Association fall meet at Santa Anita in 1969. All of his four sons, beginning with Jay, followed him into the horse racing business, either in training, racetrack management or law.

Budroyale trained for about 100 days before he debuted in a maiden $32,000 claiming race. It was a spot in which he could win and, in turn, help market his stallion. Budroyale impressed Robbins as a sound horse with a good disposition and a nice way of moving. He almost won at first asking, placing second by a neck, and attracted a claim from another trainer. He was subsequently moved up to the $50,000 level for his next start and Robbins wanted to claim him back. Straub-Rubens and Cooper initially had no reservations, but then looked at the fact the dam had only won one career race and decided to take a pass on claiming him back.

Budroyale showed some talent henceforth, winning for $50,000 and then for $62,500, attracting a buyer afterward in a private sale. Suddenly, Budroyale was on the Triple Crown trail. He won an allowance race, then was tried in a stakes race in which he failed to finish in the top three. He placed second in the next one, after which he was entered primarily in claiming races. His future, however, was about to change in a big way as a five-year-old because of Jeff Sengara and the training tandem of Ted West and his son Ted Jr.

Sengara, a Canadian lumber businessman who followed his father in the racing game as an owner, had been looking to break into the southern California circuit in 1997 and wanted West to be his trainer. Sengara's father, who started in the racing game in the '50s, had told his son some 15 years before he'd never go wrong in the horse racing business with a trainer such as West. At that time, West had been training for some 20 years and had been doing well with a horse called Interco, who had reeled off a series of impressive stakes wins. West learned from his father, who trained for 50 years, and developed a successful career out of taking other people's horses via the claiming route and succeeding. Ted Jr. joined his father's stable operation in the mid-'90s and they became a true tandem. In fact, the elder West started making his son the trainer of record as a means to increase his public profile.

Sengara had never forgotten his father's sage remark about the elder West, so he went to California on the day of the California Cup, a kind of Breeders' Cup at Santa Anita in late October/early November. It took Sengara almost 45 minutes to introduce himself to West because he felt intimidated, but the trainer had been apprised by a track official that Sengara had been coming to see him. West immediately put Sengara at ease when they met. The first two horses the Wests claimed for Sengara won at first asking. With money in the account the ambitious, young owner decided to shell out $50,000 for his next claim, more than doubling the purchase price of each of the first two claims. Sengara and Ted West Sr. picked out a one-mile race on February 15, 1998, in which they planned to make their next claim and identified three possible choices. Sengara settled on the hard-knocking Budroyale. He indicated that to West, who had also fancied the horse. Budroyale was owned by Joe Scardino, for whom 15 years earlier West had trained, and West believed Scardino ran his horses at the appropriate levels. Budroyale won the race, increasing his career record at that point to nine wins, three seconds and one third in 25 starts.

He returned to West's barn and bled profusely from the nostrils. On a scale of five, Sengara gave it a four. Bleeding from the nostrils is the result of exercise-induced pulmonary hemorrhaging and can be alleviated, though not entirely prevented, individually or collectively with medication, rest, changing the bedding and changing the feed. Budroyale had been medicated in that race with the anti-bleeding diuretic Lasix.

West had success treating bleeders with his own "trade secret" and began a program to heal the horse and improve his physical condition. By about the third week, Budroyale started to show significant signs of physical improvement, in particular putting on weight.

West and Sengara decided to run him in an $80,000 optional claimer and Budroyale won, after which the decision was made to try him in a stakes.

"The first time you run a horse in a stake, it's about anticipation rather than solid planning," West said.

In his second start for West, Budroyale won the Grade Two San Bernardino Stakes by five lengths, stamping himself as a legitimate stakes horse. And he just continued to improve the rest of the way. He ran second in the Grade Two Mervyn LeRoy Handicap in his next race, then won the Super Diamond Handicap by a smashing nine lengths. He followed up with a fifth in the Hollywood Gold Cup, a key race on the road to the Breeders' Cup and featuring salty types such as Skip Away and Gentleman. Then he ran seventh in the Grade Three Longacres Mile, but rebounded in the Pomona Invitational. He finished off the year by winning the California Cup Classic, an irony of sorts given it was a year ago on the same day that Sengara first met Ted West.

"I never thought it could get much better, then '99 came around and it was like a fairytale," Sengara recalled.

In 1999 at the ripe age of six, Budroyale really rose to prominence, winning four of 11 races, finishing second five times and third in the other two, banking in excess of $1.7 million. It was an incredible journey, one that took them to the Breeders' Cup.

Budroyale failed to win in his first three starts of the season, though he posted two seconds and a third. After a runner-up finish in the San Bernardino, the race he won the year before to really catapult himself into the stakes ranks from the claiming company, Budroyale won the Mervyn LeRoy Handicap by a whopping eight lengths. He ran second next time out in the Grade One Californian Stakes to Old Trieste, who won by seven lengths, then Budroyale won the Super Diamond Handicap. His next start came in the Grade One Hollywood Gold Cup Stakes and he ran second by only half a length to Real Quiet, the Kentucky Derby winner from the previous year. He ran last in a field of four by 18 lengths in the Grade Three San Diego Handicap, but rebounded to win the Longacres Handicap.

The Breeders' Cup was about nine weeks away, and Sengara and the Wests started thinking about running in the Classic. Sengara had followed the Breeders' Cup since its outset in 1984 but never imagined he'd have a horse in it. Much to his surprise, the horse had been nominated to the Breeders'. Sengara said to Ted West Sr. that if Budroyale hit the board in the Breeders' Cup, he'd buy him a brand new Mercedes. But first Budroyale had to prove himself in the Grade Two Goodwood Handicap Stakes three weeks before racing's championship day. He faced five other challengers, including star three-year-olds General Challenge and Old Trieste. Budroyale showed an amazing display of courage and talent to win by a neck over General Challenge and earn a trip to the Cup to run in the $4 million Classic at Gulfstream Park.

West had been in the Breeders' Cup only once before, 11 years previously, to saddle Merrill Stables' Stocks Up in the Juvenile Fillies. She was one of the longer shots in the field at 22-1 odds and ran ninth by about 6½ lengths. He didn't know if he'd ever be back again.

"Most of our business is claiming," he said. "It's not often you'll claim a horse that goes on to the Breeders' Cup. The Breeders' Cup seems like a long ways away."

Budroyale blossomed when shipped from California to Florida and gave his owner tremendous confidence. Sengara, who came with family and friends, was already going through an "out-of-body experience" being in the Breeders'.

"We were just awestruck, and the day of the race the fairytale got even more magical," he said.

Ted West figured his horse could run third or fourth and couldn't believe it when the public dismissed him at more than 26-1 while giving more respect to General Challenge, whom he had just beaten fair and square. Budroyale, ridden by Garrett Gomez, was settled in close to the pace, never more than two lengths back of the lead. At the top of the stretch, Gomez had Budroyale in third, only two heads back of the leader Cat Thief, a three-year-old who had won the Grade One Swaps Stakes in July and had placed third in the Kentucky Derby earlier in the year, but whose overall form lacked any consistency. Cat Thief and Budroyale engaged in a bumping battle down the lane, but Cat Thief, a long shot at more than 19-1 odds, won by 1¼ lengths over Budroyale.

It wasn't until after he watched a replay of the race a half hour later that West realized how intense the bumping had been. Gomez hadn't said anything to him and the stewards didn't deem the bumping severe enough to lodge an inquiry, something that had happened in the inaugural Classic 15 years before. For the veteran West, it was kind of a bittersweet result because the horse had validated himself, but he was disappointed the controversial bumping had cost him a shot at winning.

As Sengara and his family exited the track to go back to the backstretch, they encountered Cecilia Straub-Rubens, who had traveled from California to watch the greatest horse she had bred. Sengara had never met the woman, but recognized her trademark big glasses. Sengara made a remark to his children that this was the woman who bred Budroyale. And then Sengara and the breeder engaged in a touching embrace, as if they had known one another for 20 years.

"I said to Cecilia, 'We may own this horse, but this day was made possible because you had such confidence to make him Breeders' Cup–eligible and by breeding such a great horse. This is very much your day.'"

Later that night, Sengara and his family had a celebratory dinner with the Wests. Sengara recalled the comment he made about the Mercedes and promised to deliver. A month later West bought a black Mercedes and had the abbreviated word "Budryle" printed on the plates.

"I never liked personally licensed plates, but I did it as a tribute to the horse," West said. "He paid for it."

Budroyale was subsequently named California horse of the year, winning the award on the same day he won a stakes race. Cecilia Straub-Rubens was named California Breeder of the Year for 1999.

Budroyale began the year with a second in the San Pasqual Stakes, but he won the San Antonio Handicap Stakes in his next race, soundly beating Cat Thief. It was a sense of redemption for Sengara, who had repeatedly watched the tape of the Classic and believed his horse would have been right there at the wire were it not for the bumping. Budroyale ran second in the Santa Anita Handicap and his form started to fade. He ran poorly in the Oaklawn Stakes and exceptionally poorly in the Pimlico Special. It was discovered afterward he had an injured shoulder, so he was given time off.

There had been three other foals produced by Cee's Song after Budroyale and neither of them—Balboa Betty, Tizso and Ceebett's Dancer—had distinguished themselves. The sixth foal would change that in a big way.

He was named Tiznow by Cooper, who wanted the colt to have a manly name. Cooper bought an interest in the colt and two other young horses when Buddy Cruvant died in 1998 and his widow wanted out of the business. The dark bay/brown colt had a distinguishing long, white blaze. He also had four white feet, which according to an old adage in horse breeding is not a good sign. But Cooper was not superstitious and trainer Jay Robbins didn't pay much heed to the white-stocking theory.

Because Budroyale had stated to show significant ability, the decision was made not to geld his full brother. It was one of many interesting decisions concerning the colt, who would become a hot commodity as a stallion prospect.

Tiznow had a larger body with more scope compared to Budroyale, who was more compact, and early in his career at the track he demonstrated more ability. Robbins thought the colt had a nice way of moving and worked well, showcasing his speed in his first workout two weeks after he had been brought to Robbins' barn and galloped on a daily basis. Sent out to breeze three-eighths of a mile, Tiznow clocked a sizzling time of 34 3/5 seconds.

As he watched Budroyale go on to a prosperous career, Robbins apologized to the octogenarian owner, but she said: "Dear, that will never change my lifestyle, don't worry about it."

Robbins knew a horse such as Budroyale could change his lifestyle, but when Tiznow came along Robbins knew Tiznow would develop into a better horse if he stayed sound.

Tiznow had an obstreperous streak, and Robbins had concerns about how the colt would handle the switch over to Del Mar, where the Southern California racing scene would be heading for the annual summer meet. Del Mar can have more ontrack traffic during training hours than the Santa Anita and Hollywood Park and can be tough on a young horse, particularly one that's unsettled. But the concerns that Robbins had were quickly alleviated when Tiznow "turned the corner and started behaving himself." After galloping for five or six days to get used to the track, Tiznow was set down for his second breeze. He worked in company with another two-year-old who had already made it to the races. Tiznow started three lengths in front for the other horse, but the jockey on the one in behind thought he would easily catch up. Robbins knew better. In fact, he thought the trailing horse wouldn't even warm up Tiznow. And he was right. Tiznow outworked the other horse easily.

That's when Robbins knew he had a special horse. He had had only one other two-year-old colt in his training career of that quality, a speedball called Stylish King. He won his initial lifetime start by five lengths in a six-furlong race run in 1:09 2/5. While the colt had tons of talent, he didn't have the strong mindset to go with it and never reached his potential.

Robbins planned to run Tiznow in his initial race in the first week in November, but within a couple weeks of the scheduled date the plan went awry. One day while approaching the gate, Tiznow started favoring his left hind leg. He had suffered a stress fracture of the tibia, an injury that usually heals well given time, so he was put away for slightly more than three months.

In the middle of February, he returned to Santa Anita to resume training and showed the same promise he did the year before. That's when Robbins, a low-key individual who is not prone to grand pronouncements, proclaimed to his wife Sandy that he thought they might have the best three-year-old in America and nobody knew it. Robbins had been training for more than 30 years, long enough to recognize talent. And it was becoming vastly apparent Tiznow had that ability.

"When he came back (off the layoff), he just did things so easily. It looked like he was never really extending himself," Robbins recalled. "He just loved what he did. He loved training. He really loved the racetrack."

Cooper considered Tiznow a special horse as far back as his unraced two-year-old year because he had a tremendous stride and incredible intelligence.

On April 22, 2000, at Hollywood Park, Tiznow made his debut in a six-furlong race and ran sixth by three lengths. Robbins said the colt appeared to go through the motions at the start, but finished up strongly and galloped out well.

He made his second start on May 11 at Hollywood Park going a mile and sixteenth and ran better, placing second by a neck, but Robbins said the horse was still immature and gangly and learning. On May 31 at Hollywood Park, Tiznow ran again going a mile and a sixteenth and trounced the field, winning by 8½ lengths.

Little was made of the performance across the nation, which was still in the midst of the Triple Crown and the euphoria of a colt called Fusaichi Pegasus, a $4 million yearling purchase who lived up to his breeding and billing by winning the Kentucky Derby and then finishing second in the Preakness Stakes. At that point, Tiznow was just a horse, as the expression goes, albeit one with potential.

With an eye toward key races down the road, the decision was made to pass up on condition races and point the colt immediately to stakes. The Affirmed Handicap, a Grade Three stakes five weeks later, loomed as a good spot. The mile and a sixteenth race appeared to be coming up with a relatively light field, with only Dixie Union, a stakes winner coming back off a long layoff, as the standout. Tiznow would be in receivership of 10 pounds, which is a significant weight break going a distance of ground.

"You knew Tiznow would run a route of ground, but we took a calculated chance going in the Affirmed rather than a non-winners of two race," Robbins said. "I wouldn't normally do that. But because of what he'd shown and what we thought he'd become we did it."

He won the Affirmed, and as a validation runner-up Dixie Union subsequently won the Grade One Haskell Invitational Stakes. Tiznow's next start came in the Grade One Swaps Stakes, a key mile and one-eighth race for three-year-olds in Southern California. He ran second by 2½ lengths to the more seasoned Captain Steve.

The race proved to be significant in many ways. Firstly, it would be the last time the horse would run in blinkers, which he'd worn all along but were making him upset and unmanageable. Blinkers are designed to narrow a horse's focus and keep its mind on the task at hand, but they can also increase adrenalin. Tiznow was becoming upset and unmanageable, something which surfaced in the Affirmed and then really evidenced itself in the Swaps. He became hot and bothered in the paddock and then tried to run over horses in front of him in the race. To make his horse more tractable, Robbins decided to remove the blinkers.

He also had to find another jockey. Alex Solis, who had ridden the colt, had a scheduling commitment to another horse in what was to be Tiznow's next start, the Grade One Pacific Stakes. Victor Espinoza, whom Robbins wanted to book to ride Tiznow, had an obligation to another horse.

Chris McCarron was available and subsequently hired. It would be one of the luckiest things to ever happen in his Hall of Fame career, in which he'd won a Kentucky Derby and two Breeders' Cup Classics, among his more notable achievements. The Massachusetts native who'd turned 45 earlier that year had been a teenage phenom, setting a single-season world record in 1974 in his first year of riding with 546 wins. It was a record that held up for 15 years. Coincidentally, the year it was eclipsed, McCarron won the Breeders' Cup Classic on Sunday Silence, a horse he also picked up by chance. The year before McCarron had won the Classic aboard Alysheba, his Derby winner from the previous year. McCarron had become the only rider to win back-to-back Classics. Both the wins were memorable—the first Classic because Alysheba, who'd lost by a nose the year before, won in near darkness and the following year because Sunday Silence staved off a challenge from his Triple Crown rival Easy Goer. Both horses had special places in the hearts of American race fans—in fact, Alysheba was known as America's horse—and, unbeknownst to anybody at that point, Tiznow was about to join the other two in the history annals.

Tiznow placed second by two lengths in the Pacific Classic, facing older horses for the first time, beaten by the four-year-old Skimming, who had proven himself to be a horse for the Del Mar course.

Tiznow's next start came in the Super Derby, the race in which his sire ran third and subsequently broke down. And that had Straub-Rubens worried. But it represented the last significant Grade One race for three-year-olds. Winning a Grade One could enhance his future stud potential and his sire's, so the decision was made to ship to Louisiana. The new experience of flying did not go initially well, however, because Tiznow became upset loading from the ramp onto the plane. He picked his head up, looked at some lights and kicked out at a sideboard. Robbins ran him up the ramp into the plane and Tiznow settled in for the flight in his box stall. Robbins spent the flight nervously hoping Tiznow didn't arrive in Louisiana off in his left hind leg. Robbins decided henceforth he'd tranquilize Tiznow when flying, which is not an uncommon practice.

Tiznow arrived safely and soundly, but then there was the concern about the possible weather implications. It can be incredibly hot and humid at that time of the year in Louisiana, with the thermometer hitting 90 degrees Fahrenheit (30 Celsius). Fortunately for the Tiznow connections, the weather concern did not become an issue. Tiznow looked great visually and ran equally impressively. He won by six lengths in a track-record/stakes-record time of 1:59.84.

"The Super Derby, in my opinion, was his most incredible performance in terms of his running," Cooper said. "He was totally awesome."

The Goodwood Stakes, which Budroyale had won the year before, loomed next on the schedule, which by that point included the Breeders' Cup three weeks after that. He won the Goodwood, beating Captain Steve, who had beaten him in the Swaps, after a great battle in the final quarter of a mile. Tiznow's time of 1:47 3/8 shaved almost a full second off the time of Budroyale's and was only about a fifth of a second slower than superstar Silver Charm two years before that. It was also only about three-fifths of a second slower than the stakes-record time set by Bertrando in 1994. Overall, then, Tiznow had stamped himself as a serious runner relative to some noteworthy horses of years past at that point in time.

The Breeders' Cup Classic at historic Churchill Downs in Kentucky was up next, and Tiznow clearly belonged, but it would cost quite a sum to do it. Straub-Rubens and Cooper had stopped nominating their foals to the Breeders' Cup program, even though it only cost $500 to do it at birth, because they had never had a horse that was any good. And that was before Budroyale established himself.

It would cost nine percent—a whopping $360,000—of the total purse to pay the supplementary fee to run in the Classic. Straub-Rubens, who had been battling liver and spleen cancer for 16 months, had health issues, but she and Cooper decided to take the sporting shot.

"I guess she thought she'd never get a chance to do it again," Robbins said, his voice cracking at the thought of that emotional period.

The conservative Robbins had some concerns about the plan because of the high cost of supplementing, but he had total confidence in his horse handling the rigors of racing three times within a five-week period.

"Physically, that horse had as tough a constitution as you'll ever see," Robbins said. "I thought he could handle it, but I was reluctant to have them put up $360,000. That's a big risk and you're racing over a surface he'd never been on. I didn't know if he was good enough to win, but I thought he could handle it."

Two weeks before the race, the partnership received interest from people seeking to buy the horse. A Florida-based agent, calling on behalf of an unnamed client, contacted Cooper to gauge his interest in selling.

The agent made an offer of between $3 million and $4 million, but the talk didn't go any further. The partners had focused on fulfilling a dream of running in the biggest race of the year and the biggest race of their lives.

"We thought we had the best horse in the race," Cooper said. "We were told many times of the fact that no California-bred had ever won a Breeders' Cup race. Of course, this was a thought that was most prevalent in the heart of the Blue Grass. By having to supplement to the race, if we didn't run well we were going to break even for the year on a horse that won multiple stakes, which would have been very embarrassing."

Nine days before the race, Tiznow worked a mile in 1:36 and change, a solid time that indicated he hadn't been drained from his earlier race.

As an oddity of sorts, Robbins would be running his fifth overall starter in the Cup, and each time he had been in the Classic. In 1986, he ran Nostalgia's Star, who was co-owned by his parents and two other couples, and he placed fourth. The following year, Nostalgia's Star placed seventh. In 1992, Robbins sent out Flying Continental, who finished 11th. Two years later, he saddled Reign Road, who ran fourth. That had been Robbins' last time at the Cup, and he had never given much thought in the intervening years whether he'd make it back to the Breeders'.

The Classic drew a field of 14, whittled down to 13 by the scratching of Euchre, who had placed third in the Goodwood. Fusaichi Pegasus drew much of the attention, particularly after he returned to his spring form with a victory at Belmont almost six weeks before the Classic. Trained by Neil Drysdale, who in years past had posted Breeders' Cup wins with A. P. Indy, Hollywood Wildcat, Princess Rooney, Tasso and Prized, there was plenty to like about the horse everyone called Pegasus. If there was any kind of sign about Drysdale's fortune, he won the Mile earlier in the card with War Chant.

European star Giant's Causeway, whose Irish connections wanted to try on the dirt for the first time, loomed as another serious contender. Cooper feared this horse after talking to a European horseman who told him if Giant's Causeway made the lead in the stretch he'd be tough to beat.

Tiznow drew some support, though not much, but Robbins believed his colt could win because Tiznow galloped strong and well over the track.

Fusaichi Pegasus went postward as the 6-5 favorite, followed by Giant's Causeway as the second choice at 7.60-1. Tiznow became the third overall choice at 9.20-1.

Cecilia Straub-Rubens, who had been instructed by her physician not to make the trip because of her health, had been confined to her room in the days leading up to the race. A $3,000 injection gave her energy to attend the most important race of her life. On race day she looked strong and healthy, smiling proudly.

Under McCarron, Tiznow led from the start through the first half mile in 47 2/4 seconds. He had been overtaken by a head by 9-1 choice Albert The Great after three-quarters in 1:12. After a mile, run in 1:36 flat, Tiznow led by a head over Albert The Great. At the top of the stretch, Giant's Causeway, who had never been far back in third, advanced to second by only a head. The battle followed with Irishman Mick Kinane on the outside and McCarron on the inside. The two jockeys demonstrated contrasting riding styles: McCarron crouching low on the withers and flashing a left-handed whip, and Kinane sitting further back in the saddle and cracking his colt on the right flank. This was the difference between the American's way of riding and, for the most part, the European's way. Under the backdrop of the Downs' famous Twin Spires, Tiznow prevailed by a neck in one of the Classic's best duels. He became the first California-bred from 48 starters to win a Breeders' Cup race.

On the way to the winner's circle, trainer Bob Baffert shouted: "Cooper, I sure wish you would have taken my offer." They never found out the client for whom Baffert was pursuing the horse.

"Giant's Causeway took the worst of it. He ran super," Robbins said. "From a realistic standpoint, he was probably the better horse, having to ship from Europe and running on the dirt for the first time. I was very impressed with Tiznow. He was down on the inside but it didn't bother him. Usually the outside horse has the advantage, but he was always game inside. A lot of his quality showed that way. He was good when on the inside of a horse. I was very happy for him that he was the first California-bred to win. I was very happy for California."

Only three days later, Cecilia Straub-Rubens died when she suffered a punctured aorta during exploratory surgery. She had been back only one day in California following the greatest triumph of her career in racing. Prior to surgery Straub-Rubens told Jay Robbins' wife Sandy: "You tell Jay to take care of my little boy."

"Those two minutes it took Tiznow to run that race were the best she had felt in a long time," Cooper said in a *Los Angeles Times* article. "I think it was Tiznow that kept her going. She went out in style, a true winner."

Tiznow's victory placed him into consideration for horse-of-the-year honors. Robbins liked his chances.

"My dad said they'd never give it to a Cal-bred," Robbins recalled. "I said, 'Who will they give it to?' He said, 'They'll figure out a way to give it to someone else.'"

Whatever prejudices may have existed, Tiznow won the award, although Robbins did not attend the Eclipse Awards. Tiznow had been back in training for his four-year-old campaign and had been having some problems with quarter cracks on the insides of his front feet. The problems may have resulted from the hard surface at Churchill Downs during the Breeders' Cup or from his current training back home. A blacksmith tried to apply patches, but the patches didn't adhere and Robbins didn't want to be away from his star horse for even one day. It was a tenuous time for the trainer, whose wife Sandy deputized for him at the Eclipse Awards. He played golf that afternoon and listened to the results of the awards when Sandy called him on her cell phone.

"It was a mild surprise, not shocking," Robbins said.

Coincidentally, Budroyale had stopped racing because of a shoulder ailment. Sengara believed it was a symbolic passing of the torch from Budroyale to Tiznow.

Pamela Ziebarth and Kevin Cochran took over from their mother as co-owners with Cooper in what became known as Cees Stable. Tiznow began his four-year-old season winning the Grade Two San Fernando Stakes after taking the lead in the last 150 yards of the mile and one-sixteenth race. Cooper talked to the media afterward about the plan to keep the horse in training as a four-year-old and spurn the decision to retire him.

"I got a degree in economics and so I'm trained to make smart business decisions," Cooper said. "I'm not saying this is one of them. This is (an act of) passion. I want to get through this season (before considering offers for Tiznow). I think this sport is in a bit of a crisis. I think racing is in need of a star. Tiznow isn't going to turn the sport around. But I think he can help."

Tiznow followed up his season-opening win with a disappointing second in the Grade Two Strub Stakes as the 3-10 favorite, beaten by Wooden Phone, who had finished third in the San Fernando.

"I have trouble explaining why he got beat," Robbins said. "Chris thought maybe in retrospect he should have let him run earlier. He couldn't get over to the rail. If Tiznow couldn't get over to the rail, he'd become lackadaisical."

Tiznow rebounded to win the Santa Anita Handicap by six lengths, turning back Wooden Phone.

Robbins figured he could give the colt some time off and let the feet grow out—because a quarter crack is like having a cracked fingernail or toenail—and eliminate the need for patches. The plan was to race him again in two months in the Grade One Pimlico Special in Maryland. The plan hit a major hitch one morning following a good workout. After the tack had been removed from his back, Tiznow did not want to walk off. Robbins thought his horse had cramped or "tied up" in his back. Tiznow appeared to have reinjured the left tibia he had fractured two years before, but a scan determined he had a problem with a vertebra in the lower back. He was going to need X-rays, which would have required laying him down. The vets were leery of doing that because of the possibility of aggravating the horse and doing further damage.

He was given a few days off, then had an additional scan. Tiznow was jogging stiffly and sorely. Robbins' personal vet, Dr. Rick Arthur, and Robbins' father both examined the colt, who didn't seem to be improving. The elder Robbins had never seen anything like it before in all his years of veterinary work.

Cooper told Robbins, who didn't want to hurt the horse, that if Tiznow didn't show signs of improvement by the third week in July for the start of the Del Mar meet, he'd be retired. Some three weeks before he was to be shipped to Del Mar, Tiznow showed signs of visible improvement. He breezed an easy three-eighths of a mile in 38 seconds, and while it was obvious Tiznow was not quite right, Robbins could see the improvement.

While the physical problem subsided, Tiznow started to exhibit personality quirks on the track that left his trainer and his exercise rider and jockey flustered. Tiznow would duck to the inside rail of his own volition or he'd suddenly stop and refuse to go.

"My first thought is he's protecting himself, then things got pretty trying at Del Mar," Robbins said.

Robbins became so frustrated he told the exercise rider one morning, "Take the stick to him and make him do what you want him to do. We're not going to pamper him."

While Tiznow was becoming dangerous to his exercise rider and jockey, the tough-love experiment lasted only one day. Tiznow didn't appreciate the rough treatment.

"He knew how far he could carry things," Robbins said. "For a horse he was pretty smart, but you couldn't get after him or things would get really nasty."

When the horse put his mind to work, he did well and it appeared he was back to his old self.

Though Robbins wanted to stay in California to race at Del Mar, Cooper wanted to go East to Belmont Park in New York. Cooper said he didn't want to hook defending race winner El Corredor in the Del Mar Breeders' Cup.

The media reported the differences between Cooper and Robbins.

"I didn't want the horse of the year beat intentionally," Cooper said. "It wasn't really as big a confrontation as the press made it to out to be. We didn't agree and it was my decision (where to run)."

Tiznow would run in the Woodward Stakes at Belmont, where about two months later the Breeders' Cup would take place. He placed third by 1½ lengths.

"We thought he got something out of it," Cooper said. "We weren't happy with the result, but he showed he could handle the track. Disappointing but encouraging is the right phrase."

"I was happy and pleased," Robbins said. "He'd got beaten, yet he'd come out of it fine. Chris was a little disappointed, but I thought Chris was maybe protecting the horse. Maybe he was holding him back a little bit because he felt it was the right thing to do. He may have compromised him."

Robbins and his wife headed home the next day, and two days after that the world came to a halt. It was September 11, a day in which Al Qaeda terrorists flew two planes into the World Trade Center buildings, killing thousands. The business of horse racing and, in particular a horse of the year on the comeback trail, mattered little to most people. Tiznow's return home with his groom and exercise rider had to be delayed, so he remained there to train for a few days. Robbins hadn't missed one day of the colt's training since Tiznow arrived at his barn.

A month later he ran in the Goodwood Stakes, the race he had won the year before and his brother had won the year before that, but Tiznow couldn't keep the family streak going, placing third by 1½ lengths.

"That was probably the most disappointing moment in his career," Robbins said. "I thought he was doing really well, but it looked like he was just going through the motions. Only in the last sixteenth did he look like he was interested and he galloped out strongly."

To most observers, the champ was simply not himself any more. Eleven days after his loss, Tiznow was sent to the track for a one-mile workout under McCarron. He galloped once around the track, then decided to stop. McCarron took him to the starting gate and put the blinkers on to try and get the colt to work, but Tiznow just froze. Finally, after some 35 minutes or so, Tiznow decided to get down to business. The exercise normally would begin from the front of the grandstand all the way around the track to the finish line, but commenced instead from the pole half a mile from the wire. Tiznow worked the mile in a snappy 1:35 2/5, much to the astonishment of Robbins, who had been totally frazzled up to that point while standing by the track apron with McCarron's agent Scotty McClellan.

Trainer Bob Baffert had been standing next to Cooper and told him it was the most incredible workout he'd ever seen from the half-mile pole. Normally, once a horse reaches the wire, it is conditioned to let up, but Tiznow kept going strongly.

"He was a very difficult horse mentally and it was a big concern for us," Cooper said. "This is a really smart horse. A lot of people think their horses are smart, but this horse was super smart. He got hurt at Santa Anita and I think he remembered it, and he was always unhappy at Santa Anita. The talent was there, but mentally he would be a monster. He was the type of horse that everything had to be done his way. You couldn't fight him."

So, it was decided to run Tiznow in the Breeders' again, although this time it wouldn't require another supplementary fee of $360,000. The payments for a previously supplemented horse would be the same henceforth as a horse already nominated at birth to the program following a rule change by the Breeders' Cup Ltd. In this case, it would amount to two percent of the purse or a cost of $80,000.

The day after the workout, Robbins had Tiznow shod. But Tiznow wouldn't allow his right front foot to be lifted by the blacksmith because he had been bothered by minor rashes on each elbow from a year before. To allow the blacksmith to do his job, Robbins had Tiznow tranquilized.

He was flown to New York for the Breeders' and sent to Shug McGaughey's barn, where he'd stayed in his previous trip to Belmont. He acted up his first time out on the track when Robbins attempted to have him jogged once around the track the wrong way. Tiznow ended up jogging twice as much as the original plan.

Robbins thought about tranquilizing the horse to settle him down, but with only six days to the race he ran the risk of possibly coming up with a positive drug test. Robbins considered going to the liquor store and buying some vodka and adding a few shots to Tiznow's feed. But it was Sunday and the liquor store was closed—at least at that time of the day—so Robbins passed on his idea, which is one of those old tricks of the horse racing trade.

The following day, Robbins allowed Tiznow to train at his own pace and he showed improvement.

But later that afternoon, when Robbins took the colt out for a walk, he emerged stiff and sore. There was no indication of anything serious when feet testers were applied, so Robbins applied a poultice to draw out inflammation and wrapped the knees and ankles. The next day Tiznow didn't have the problem, which was attributed to the shoeing.

In the days leading up to the race, Tiznow improved mentally in his training.

"We just let him do what he wanted to do," Robbins said. "When he decided to go, boom, he'd take off. I had a lot of confidence, maybe more than the year before. I could see that week that he was back to himself."

A field of 13 drew in for the race, but this time the public had no clear feel for the favorite. New Yorkers liked Aptitude, who'd romped in his last start at the same track. The Europeans liked both Irish invader Galileo and Sakhee, winner of the Prix de l'Arc de Triomphe, both of whom would be trying dirt for the first time. Galileo had six wins and a second in seven career starts. Sakhee had been one of two standouts owned by Sheikh Mohammed bin Rashid al Maktoum. He decided to run Fantastic Light in the Turf and point Sakhee to the Classic to further enhance his reputation. As for Tiznow, well, his reputation had been diminished by defeat. He had been the champion in name only. One of the Classic trainers did not respect Tiznow and had apparently called him Tiznever.

Robbins said he thought Tiznow could rise to the occasion and he perked up for the race. While in the receiving barn before heading over to the paddock, he let out a kick that came perilously close to nailing a security guard.

"It was almost like he could realize a special situation, like that day," Robbins said.

Aptitude went postward as the favorite at just under 5-2, followed by Galileo at just under 7-2 and Sakhee at just under 5-1. Tiznow went into the gate at just under 7-1.

Unlike the year before, he did not grab the lead, although McCarron had him running comfortably close to the pace, never more than two lengths back of pacesetter Orientate. After a mile, Orientate started to fade and Albert The Great took the lead, while Tiznow was second by a length. The pace was slightly quicker than the year before. Heading into the stretch Sakhee overtook the top two, leading by a half a length over Albert The Great, with Tiznow another head back and sandwiched in between the two. The defending champion looked hopelessly beaten, but he refused to be beaten, accelerating into another gear under McCarron, who waved his whip left-handed while furiously pumping on the reins. On his outside, Sakhee's jockey Frankie Dettori, who rode for a while in the U.S. and had a crouching style similar to the Americans', rode feverishly while sticking his colt on the right flank. Tiznow, the bigger and heavier of the two star runners, gained a slight lead in the final stages, literally gritting his teeth and holding on to win by a nose. So dramatic was the finish that the race would later be voted the National Thoroughbred Racing Association's Moment of the Year. As the television camera focused in on Robbins, he had a look of astonishment.

"That was because I thought he was beat and was going to finish second," he said.

Tiznow provided glory for Americans still aching from the terrorist attacks that altered the New York skyline by stripping away a landmark. You could say the horse displayed the heart of a champion and the sheer determination of a world-class athlete, but maybe, just maybe, the spirit of Cecilia Straub-Rubens willed this gallant horse home by the narrowest of margins.

In the winner's circle, Cooper looked up to the sky and said: "Cee, this is for you, babe, wish you were here."

In the interview room after the race, Robbins appeared with McCarron and Cooper, who was asked how often during the course of the year's races he was reminded of his onetime partner.

"She was such a special lady and a special friend of mine and, you know, I certainly wish she had been here," he said. "I think Tiz knew in spirit she was here, the way he came back in that race and gutted it out right down the line, kind of like the way she was, too. I thought about her immediately."

When the three were asked to comment about Tiznow for possible horse-of-the-year honors, Cooper said: "He's the horse of my life. I'm not going to worry about the year."

McCarron was asked about his horse's resolve.

"When I first pushed the button about the three-furlong pole, I did get a jump forward at first," he began. "I didn't get a feeling of acceleration that I'm used to with him. I didn't get that typical, nice burst that I got last year at Churchill Downs. Then when Sakhee got to my hip, Tiznow saw him before I did. And I felt an acceleration at that point and I said, 'Oh, good, I got the response' because when I first asked him to run . . . maybe he wasn't ready to go yet. He's always ready to go when the competition comes out. Sakhee had a great deal of momentum and a good head of steam up. Tiznow out-gamed him. He had more resolve."

McCarron was also asked to reflect on Tiznow in relation to the other great horses he had ridden.

"I just wish that Tiznow would go out there and run like he did in the Santa Anita Handicap and just get down and run as fast as he possibly can from the head of lane to the wire and show the world what he's capable of doing," he said. "He wins photos, but he obviously gives us all heart failure. But he's not quite putting out 100 percent in these races. I don't know if he's giving me 95 percent, 98 percent or 80 percent. But I know it's not 100. And I'm just longing for the day that he pulls a Secretariat and wins by 31."

There had been some consideration to running the colt in the Grade One Hollywood Turf Cup about a month later on the grass to enhance Tiznow's reputation for horse-of-the-year consideration. Tiznow hadn't run on the grass in any of his races. But Cooper changed his mind after reading about a star horse that had to be humanely destroyed after suffering an injury at the same track where Tiznow would be attempting his turf workout. He called Robbins and told him to take the colt out of training. It was time to retire him.

Tiznow finished with eight wins, four seconds and two thirds in only 15 starts in his illustrious career and earnings of $6,427,830.

Taylor Made Farms in conjunction with Bill Casnert and Kenny Troutt's WinStar Farms in Versailles, Kentucky, bought a half-interest in Tiznow as a stallion prospect and marketed him for a reasonable $30,000 service fee. The farm had some 300 applications from owners wanting to breed their mares to Tiznow, but the list was narrowed down to 124.

As part of the estate's liquidation of the stable, Tiznow's dam was sold in foal at the Keeneland sales less than a month after the Cup for $2 million, while a weanling full sister sold for $950,000.

Tiznow's reputation extended far beyond the racing industry. New England Patriots' star linebacker Bryan Cox, who is a big horse racing fan, took a copy of the Classic tape to show to coach Bill Belichick four games before the end of the 2001 season. The Patriots had a 7-5 record and were not assured of making the playoffs. Cox thought the tape of the race could be used to inspire the team, so Belichick played it for his squad. The Patriots were being led by a young, second-year quarterback named Tom Brady, who took over the team from injured veteran Drew Bledsoe and guided the Patriots to a storybook finish that ended with a win in the Super Bowl. It ended on a game-winning field goal. It was a finish not unlike the stunning end to the Classic.

Taylor Made and WinStar sent the Super Bowl–winning Patriots 100 hats featuring Tiznow's name/logo and the slogan: "To the Patriot in all of us." Belichick subsequently presented the trophy for the top older horse to the connections of Tiznow at the Eclipse Awards.

Tiznow was beaten for horse-of-the-year honors by Kentucky Derby and Preakness winner Point Given, who suffered a tendon injury after winning the Grade One Travers Stakes in August.

Tiznow attracted a following during and after his racing career. Co-owner Mike Cooper received a religious medal from a Catholic nun on behalf of Tiznow, but his favorite story about how Tiznow touched people's lives involves Eleanor Pittenger, a 90-year-old double amputee who lives in a small elder care home in Mission Viejo, California. She fell in love with Tiznow early on and began collecting stories about him and following his every race. When Cooper became aware of her interest, he began sending her various Tiznow items, such as T-shirts, hats and pictures. Cooper's wife visited the woman at her home and discovered that she had a shrine in her bedroom for Tiznow and that the other five elderly people in the home were kept aware of his every move by the loyal fan. She told Cooper's wife that Tiznow was the best thing that had happened to her in many years.

When stories surfaced about Tiznow's back problems, people wrote to Robbins with suggestions how to treat the problem. Some young kids sent little teddy bears; occasionally older people did, too. Some people wrote with suggestions about how McCarron should ride the horse. Robbins responded to the fans and sent them each a photo of Tiznow. When he retired, Winstar received letters addressed to Tiznow and occasionally packages with candy. Some people come to the farm to see Tiznow and are given peppermints to feed to him.

Budroyale and Tiznow, coupled with some other horses he sired, made Cee's Tizzy more fashionable to breeders. He had been moved about 250 miles north of Los Angeles a few years earlier to Harris Farms where he could receive access to better mares. He became the top-ranked sire in progeny earnings for the year 2000. In 2001, he ranked sixth overall from the lowest number of starters among the top-10 North American sires by progeny earnings. His onetime fee of $2,500 has escalated to $15,000. Instead of servicing a couple of dozen mares a year, his book has increased to 100 or so.

McCarron retired midway into the 2002 season and later became general manager of Santa Anita Park. He was also employed as a consultant and actor in the movie *Seabiscuit*. He played the role of the jockey who rode War Admiral in the historic match race against Seabiscuit. McCarron rode many outstanding horses in his career and said upon retirement that Tiznow was one of the best.

Trainer Jay Robbins and co-owner Mike Cooper, who had some philosophical differences in the management of Tiznow, subsequently parted company. Cooper has full or partial interests in 34 horses.

"I'm deeper than I've ever been and having a ball," he said.

Robbins still has a stable of 10 or so horses, the same amount he has routinely kept over the years. He has an annual breeding season to Tiznow.

"He was the greatest experience I've had in 35 years of training horses," Robbins said, his voice once again cracking with emotion. "I think he made me a better person having known him. He made me a lot more compassionate to animals and people. He did a lot of things to me. It wasn't so much that he was a talented racehorse. He was a really intelligent horse, really cognizant of everything that went on around him. He was an amazing animal to be around.

"He was a very good racehorse, but he was just so different than any horse I've been around by the way he reacted to things. He was amazing. He was more humanistic than other nice horses I had. This one was on a different plane, personality-wise, intelligence-wise."

But Robbins said part of his emotion for the horse is likely rooted in his relationship with Cecilia Straub-Rubens.

"She was always so nice, more than any other owner I've had," he said. "We went through some lean years, but she never complained to me. She'd say, 'Don't worry, dear, next time we'll get them.' She was always so optimistic. I always appreciated that. She comes into the whole thought process with him."

It's because of the relationship with his onetime partner that Mike Cooper said winning the Classic the first time has more personal meaning.

"The first time (winning the Classic) was everything because of Cee," Cooper said. "Anybody that's lucky to win a classic it's super special. I'm not belittling that. And it was a relief (to win a second time) because of all the stress and concern leading up to it. But the first time was more special because of what she meant to me and achieving the dream. That race was the most fulfilling thing that ever happened to me, with the exception of my wife and my family. That was a dream come true. Combining with the fact we had been together for 19 years with limited success, that was very special. I still get goosebumps thinking about it."

Budroyale's career came to an end at almost the same time as his brother's. Returned to the races 14 months after he was laid off, Budroyale ran a few more times but never came close to finding his form.

"The writing was on the wall to just wind him down," owner Jeff Sengara said.

Sengara, who lives in Vancouver, British Columbia, the westernmost province in Canada, retired the gallant gelding to a farm 45 minutes due east in Langley.

Budroyale finished with 17 wins, 12 seconds and two thirds in 52 races and earnings of $2,840,810. He was a true rags-to-riches horse and one of the greatest claims in the history of the game.

"Budroyale was a horse who touched the hearts of all the underdogs in the world," Sengara said. "Everyone loves heart. Everyone loves a Rocky. Everyone had a connection with Bud. He came up through the wrong side of the track and put all these silver-spoon horses on their ears."

Ted West Sr. said Budroyale is the best horse he has ever trained, and having the chance to achieve the success with his son added to the experience.

"If you can achieve something that good with someone that close and dear to you, it makes it that much more special," he said.

Sengara is convinced that the racing gods rewarded Cecilia Straub-Rubens with Tiznow for the classy way she handled the success of Budroyale, the greatest horse she had bred prior to Tiznow.

"The racing game is not about the guy with the biggest bankroll or the bloodstock agents working for them; there is magic in this game," Sengara said.

"That is the beauty of this game—the mystical part of it—that none of it makes sense," Mike Cooper said. "You can go to the sales with $5 million and buy five top yearlings and it doesn't mean you'll win anything. But then you can get a horse like Tiznow. The little guy has a chance. It's a mystical thing, completely mystical.

"Even the failures are mystical. It's humbling, but it's mystical. The racing gods, yeah, perhaps that's the answer."

Robbins said he'll likely never have another horse such as Tiznow. He doesn't train for big outfits who supply their trainers with blue-blooded prospects.

"Pedigrees make horses, trainers don't make horses," he said.

But reminded that Tiznow did not have a pedigree to suggest he would become great, Robbins said: "I don't like to use the word freak, but he was that good basically. You've got a lot better chance to succeed if you're Bobby Frankel training for Juddmonte Farms. Realistically, I'll never have a horse that approaches this horse. It's almost like he was born for me and I was born for him."

"Stylish King was the most talented horse I ever trained, maybe even more than Tiznow. I had really great aspirations for him and they weren't to be. He was being touted as a Kentucky Derby horse in the futurebook and then the wheels fell off. I never thought I'd get another horse like that. Lo and behold, Tiznow comes a decade later. The industry is fickle that way. Sometimes when you least expect it to happen or don't ever expect it to happen, it can happen again."

# 16

# From Triumph to Tragedy

## Go for Wand

*T*hey come along every so often, those horses who exhibit everything that is so special about the sport: the desire to win and the will to do everything to reach that goal. But in so doing, they sometimes push themselves too far and painfully show that they are as fragile as pieces of porcelain. Go for Wand gave evidence of that in a Breeders' Cup career that included a magnificent victory and a tragic defeat.

Bred and owned by Jane duPont Lunger's Christiana Stables, Go for Wand was a product of champion Deputy Minister out of the multiple-stakes-winning mare Obeah, whose mother was named Witching Hour. According to Jamaican ritual, witches could place a spell called an Obeah on bad people. From a list of some 50 names given to her by a friend for no specific horses, Mrs. Lunger chose Go for Wand for the daughter of Obeah. "If you have a spell thrown on you, you better find a way to get rid of it," Mrs. Lunger said. To her handlers, Go for Wand affectionately became known as "Wanda."

Trainer Bill Badgett Jr. and his fiancee Rosemary, who galloped Go for Wand, took their time with the filly, who early on displayed intelligence, the sign of a good horse.

"When you were breezing her, when you were in the gate, when you were walking her on the track, it seemed like she was eager to do it but she was always waiting for you to tell her when," Rosemary said. "She just seemed very smart to me. I've breezed so many horses that were real morning-glories—that could really run—but sometimes that's not enough. To me it's not always the fastest animal; it's the one that really wants to do it for you. I think that's how she was. Right from the beginning, she loved the whole scene. She loved the people. She loved the applause. She definitely gave you the impression she knew she was special. She was always the quietest, calmest thing to be around, but she knew she was special. And when you asked her, she was dying to show you what she could do." Go for Wand had tremendous size early in her two-year-old year, but needed time to grow into herself. She started "clicking in," according to Bill Badgett, about June or July as she caught up with her body. By August, she was training phenomenally. Jockey Randy Romero, who rode Go for Wand in all her races, worked her one morning and told Badgett the filly would win the Breeders' Cup. Romero had ridden champions Personal Ensign and Sacahuista, so he was in a perfect position to judge a horse's talents, particularly a young filly's. In his opinion, she had strength, intelligence and, in a word, the "feel."

Badgett, had been around some good horses, too, having been an assistant to Hall of Famer Woody Stephens, and he liked what he saw. "She was really breezing brilliantly and training great," Badgett said. "We elected to run her in the fall instead of August just to give her another couple weeks going into that (first) race."

Mrs. Lunger, whose principal occupation is breeding and racing, has been active in the sport for almost 60 years, and she does not as a rule like to run her two-year-olds. But Go for Wand had demonstrated such precocity, Mrs. Lunger acquiesced to her trainer. In the gate for her debut, Go for Wand grunted, a reaction Romero had never seen before in a horse. When he reflected on it later, he realized the filly had been psyching herself up. She had done it regularly in the mornings for Rosemary, who would often talk about that personality trait to Mrs. Lunger, who was eager to learn every detail about her horse.

Go for Wand made a successful debut at Belmont Park, winning a six-furlong race in 1:10 3/5, an impressive time for any juvenile, let alone one starting for the first time. Badgett described it as "incredible." A traffic jam en route to Belmont prevented Mrs. Lunger from witnessing Go for Wand's debut. Instead, she retreated to Brooklyn, had lunch and called Badgett for an account of the race. Less than three weeks later, Go for Wand won a one-mile race in the slop at Belmont by a whopping 18¼ lengths. As impressive as it was, her handlers felt she might not have gained enough work from it to advance her fitness. Twelve days later she tried stakes company for the first time, running in the Grade One Frizette Stakes in which the bettors made her the even-money favorite. Go for Wand's two-race win streak came to a sudden halt as she lost by a half-length to the D. Wayne Lukas–trained Stella Madrid. The running time was more than two seconds slower than Go for Wand's victory before. Badgett said if he had to make any excuses for Go for Wand that day it was the "loose, cuppy track," one of the few things the brilliant filly did not handle. Romero figured with more room he might have won the race and told Badgett when the two horses hooked up going longer in the 1989 Breeders' Cup, Go for Wand wouldn't lose.

In 1988, Open Mind, who was also a daughter of Deputy Minister and whose rise to glory in many ways resembled that of Go for Wand, won the Juvenile Fillies following a second in the Frizette. Like Romero, Badgett was encouraged, figuring the additional sixteenth of a mile could only help. The bettors had a hard time deciding between Go for Wand and Stella Madrid, but made the latter a slight favorite at 11-5, compared to 5-2 for the former.

Under Angel Cordero Jr., Stella Madrid tracked pacesetter Special Happening and took the lead at the head of the stretch. However, Romero had Go for Wand in full flight and she blasted by Stella Madrid and won going away by nearly three lengths.

"It was certainly a career boost for me because she was the first horse I had ever run in the Breeders' Cup," Badgett said. "For the owner, it was quite a thrill. It was a big deal all around."

On the strength of that victory, the Eclipse Award voters named Go for Wand the top two-year-old filly in North America in 1989.

Although Lunger had won many stakes in her career, including the Travers with Thinking Cap in 1955 and the Delaware Handicap four times between 1958 and 1970 (twice with Go for Wand's dam Obeah), she had never received an Eclipse Award before. But everything Go for Wand had done as a two-year-old paled in comparison to what she accomplished in her three-year-old season.

Go for Wand made tremendous strides physically from two to three. "I mean she just grew and filled out and did really, really well as far as that goes," Bill Badgett said.

Go for Wand picked up where she had left off upon her return to the races in the springtime. At Keeneland, she made her three-year-old debut in the mud in the Grade Three Beaumont Stakes, but it proved to be little more than a public workout as she romped by 8½ lengths. Eleven days later, she again had a muddy surface at Keeneland in the Grade One Ashland Stakes. This time she won by five lengths. Her third start came in Churchill Downs' Kentucky Oaks—called by some the Kentucky Derby for fillies—13 days later and for the third consecutive time she had to run over an off track. At odds of 3-10, Go for Wand lost the Oaks by three lengths to front-running Seaside Attraction.

She earned a break from racing and returned better and stronger than ever. She won the nine-furlong Grade One Mother Goose Stakes at Belmont on July 10 by a length and a quarter. Three weeks later at Saratoga, she dropped back to a sprint in the Grade One Test Stakes toting 124 pounds and won by two lengths. She stopped the clock in a sizzling 1:21 flat, equaling the stakes record. That race served as a tune-up for her third consecutive Grade One victory, the Alabama in August where she romped by seven lengths, running the mile and a quarter in a stakes-record time of 2:00 4/5. She became only the ninth horse to record the Test-Alabama double. "She threw a string of races that was incredible for a three-year-old filly and always ran really fast, which was quite amazing," Badgett said. She gave Romero the same feeling he had with Personal Ensign the year before at that stage.

"She was the real McCoy," Romero said. "She was sound, she was doing everything right. She could really, really run."

When September came around, Go for Wand returned to Belmont and readied for a fall campaign against older fillies and mares. Her first test came in the Grade One Maskette Stakes, and she had no trouble with the one-mile race, winning by 2½ lengths in a splendid time of 1:35 3/5. A month later she was sent off at 1-10 in the Grade One Beldame Stakes and won by nearly five lengths in a stakes-record time of 1:45 4/5, just two-fifths of a second off the track record held by the immortal Secretariat. The following day, Bill Badgett and Rosemary were married, but delayed their honeymoon until after the Breeders' Cup and the match-up against Bayakoa, the Best of the West.

Owned by Mr. and Mrs. Frank Whitham, Bayakoa was the complete opposite of Go for Wand in looks. A product of Argentina, where trainer Ron McAnally bought her in 1988 on behalf of the Whithams for $300,000, Bayakoa had what veterinarians call a "parrot-mouth," or what dentists would call an overbite. If Go for Wand was beauty, Bayakoa was the beast. But it was more than just her mouth that made Bayakoa a wallflower. Journalist Dean Iandoli described her perfectly in the 1995 Breeders' Cup issue of *HorsePlayer Magazine*: "Bayakoa would have never graced the cover of *Cosmo* or *Vogue*. Her looks were modest and her moods were not. She was from Argentina and some who knew her said she was a bit bitchy. Others thought she had something to prove. She had been plucked from her home in Buenos Aires and brought to the freak show in California. And she was no screwable starlet. There were occasional gasps when she was led onto the track, as if Cyrano de Bergerac had been saddled and paraded in front of the grandstand. But the five-year-old mare didn't have the nose. She had the bite. A ghastly over-bite which caused people to stare at her and point. And to make matters worse, when she ran, her tongue was tied down the side of her mouth to prevent the mare from swallowing it, causing it to flop wildly around, bringing only more attention to her bare-bucked teeth."

In eight starts in Argentina, Bayakoa won three starts and finished second three times, earning a paltry $87,735. In her final year of racing in her home country, she won the Argentine Champion Female Miler Award, her lone victory coming in the Premio Palermo. In her first year in the U.S. she won $73,200 with two wins and two seconds in seven starts, although McAnally was still trying to figure out whether she was better on the grass or the dirt.

In 1989, when Bayakoa turned five, McAnally ran her exclusively on the dirt and, like a horse named Cigar a few years later, she proved she would rather kick dirt than divots in her rivals' faces. She won nine races, seven of them Grade One, from 11 starts and earned more than $1.4 million. Her crowning achievement came in the Breeders' Cup Distaff, which she won. To run for a winner's prize of $450,000, the Whithams had to put up a supplemental fee of $200,000—the equivalent of 20% of the total purse—because neither Bayakoa nor her sire were nominated to the Breeders' Cup program.

The Whithams duplicated their sporting gesture in 1990 to race for the first and only time against Go for Wand.

Bayakoa came into the race off a tough campaign of nine races, two against male horses, and six wins, including a repeat victory in the Spinster Stakes at Keeneland in Lexington in her last start. Regardless of the Distaff outcome, both Bayakoa and Go for Wand were assured Eclipse Awards as the best of their respective divisions.

The 1990 Breeders' Cup Distaff drew only seven starters—Gorgeous was scratched the day before—but it really only mattered that Bayakoa and Go for Wand showed up for the dance. All the others were merely window dressing.

"I went into the race with a lot of confidence," Badgett said. "She had trained really well, she was doing good and I was looking forward to the challenge of running against Bayakoa. She was certainly the filly to beat, without a doubt."

Rosemary Badgett said this period marked the only time Go for Wand became difficult to gallop.

"She was just so full of herself, so good at that point," Rosemary said. "I knew she would always get strong around the breezing point, but she was getting really strong. I remember saying something like 'Wanda, Wanda calm down.' She would really start testing me and pulling me. There were a couple of days I remember pulling her up thinking, 'Oh my God when is this next breeze coming? When is this next race coming?' She was just so good at that point. I remember being really, really excited. I was worried, but anybody would be. Bayakoa was going to be one of her biggest challenges. I definitely wouldn't have traded places with anybody in the race." Talking to NBC contributing analyst Bob Neumeier before the race, McAnally brimmed with confidence. Six days before, Bayakoa had tuned up with a seven-furlong workout in a stunning 1:22 4/5. "I don't know about Go for Wand, they say she's something special, but at least we'll give her a run for the money," McAnally said.

The New York bettors, who support their racehorses more passionately than any other jurisdiction in the U.S., made Go for Wand the favorite at 7-10, compared to 11-10 for Bayakoa.

Romero's confidence had not wavered, but quietly he had one concern: the age gap between Go for Wand and the six-year-old Bayakoa. Never before in the history of the Distaff had there been such a spread in ages between two horses considered so similar in talent.

Bayakoa stumbled leaving the gate but recovered quickly and took the lead under Laffit Pincay Jr. However, Go for Wand wanted the lead and wrestled it from her rival after a quarter of a mile. Every time Romero tried to open some distance between himself and Pincay, he found the cagey Panamanian tracking his every move. As race announcer Tom Durkin said, it was a "chess game down the backstretch." The battle continued for three-quarters of a mile. Durkin called it a "cutthroat duel." The two horses gave everything they had, grittily accepting the challenge of the toughest race of their lives. Each had been used to winning with authority, but this was a match race and their hearts pumped in unison, unrelenting and unwavering. With each stride Go for Wand extended herself, responding to the right and left-handed urging of Romero's whip. Pincay maintained a steady right-handed whip on Bayakoa. Watching from the grandstand, Rosemary saw the familiar look of excitement in Go for Wand's eyes when she was in a tough battle and ready to draw off. It was, Rosemary said, the look of a horse "in it for herself" and loving the challenge.

But tragedy struck just inside the sixteenth pole. Go for Wand stumbled and fell forward, snapping her right front leg at the ankle and catapulting Romero to the ground. The sight stunned the crowd in attendance and millions more watching on TV. Standing next to Mrs. Lunger, Rosemary Badgett could not believe her eyes. In the worst scenario she could have imagined, Go for Wand would lose the stretch duel by a nose. But not this.

"That's why the whole tragedy was just that much harder to believe," she said. "That it was over at that instant. It's gone. That's what hits you. I couldn't believe it. It was probably just a matter of trying real hard, but I don't know if I completely believe in the trying-too-hard thing. I think she always tried 100 percent. I think it was just a matter of that foot stepping possibly an inch off and the way it hit the ground. It was a matter of her moving that quick, just like all those accidents are. It was just a misstep. When they write 'misstep,' that's sort of what I believe. Definitely there was this huge challenge going on, but I just thought she was going to surge on. And then this happened. It's something you could never ever figure, not with a horse like that. You could always understand in claiming horses that can have problems on and off, but this is a horse that never had a problem. Never."

Bayakoa won by nearly seven lengths over Colonial Waters. And yet the win by Bayakoa, who became only the second horse to score repeat Breeders' Cup victories, seemed unimportant. All that seemed to matter was Go for Wand.

Even the most hardened racetracker was saddened and shocked by the sight of the mangled leg dangling in the chilled October air. Unable to feel the pain because of a rush of endorphins—naturally produced substances that help the body cope with stress—Go for Wand hobbled forward on three legs. With each step she took, the crowd gasped in anguish and despair. Go for Wand collapsed by the outer rail near the winner's circle, a place she had visited often in victory but now where she would be humanely destroyed in the cruelest defeat of all.

Badgett, who had developed a routine of watching Go for Wand's races from trackside, rushed to his fallen horse and, after seeing the extent of the damage, knew there was no way to save her. Badgett then checked on Romero, who was later taken away by ambulance with undetermined injuries. When Badgett returned to his filly, he tried to comfort his wife, who had held Go for Wand's head in the final moments before she was put to death. Rosemary was six months pregnant at the time and about to quit galloping for a while, but she was looking forward to being aboard the filly the following year.

"I wanted to hold her and touch her and then people were pulling me away," she said. "I would halfway listen to them and then I'd go back. It was just kind of a blur. She seemed like she was her old self looking up at me, like, 'Help me, why did this happen?' She seemed as intelligent as ever, knew what was happening and was scared."

Bill Badgett said he felt like the captain of a sinking ship, just trying to hold everyone together as best he could.

The state veterinarian stopped Go for Wand's agony with a lethal injection that ended the life of one of the world's greatest racehorses and one of the best fillies ever. There are many people who say that it would be hard to separate her and Ruffian, who met a similar fate, as the greatest three-year-old fillies of all time.

Bill and Rosemary, unable to speak, walked in stunned silence back to their barn, surrounded by a crowd of people. They later returned home, mourning the filly who had been the center of their lives. In a moving interview with Bob Neumeier after the race, McAnally and his wife, Debbie, tearfully admitted they had mixed emotions about the victory. "I can't cope with something like this," McAnally said as his voice began to fall apart. "I feel good about our filly, but the other filly. . . ."

"They give their lives for our enjoyment and pleasure and to have something like this happen is such a tragedy," Debbie McAnally said.

Speaking to NBC's Jenny Ornsteen, Pincay said: "It is tough to win this way.

The other filly was putting (up) a tough fight and she's a great filly. I really feel for the owners and the jockey and everybody."

Winning owner Frank Whitham said: "Our heart goes out to the owner and all the public. . . . It's just a tough way to win."

Angel Cordero, who finished fifth aboard Luthier's Launch, returned weeping to the jockeys' room. He knew the filly and appreciated what she meant to racing. "People always complain about horses getting hurt, but athletes get hurt in any sport," he said. "They happened to watch that particular day a good horse got hurt. These horses run all year round. They put up a lot of work in between races. There are a lot of problems they run into. When Breeders' Cup time comes, they have to train real hard and anything can happen to them. It could happen to a sound horse. It could happen to a good horse. It could happen to a bad horse. These are just things that happen in sports and it's very sad. And when something like that happens, everybody is down, even the guy that wins the race. Everybody was really quiet."

Pat Day, who had finished last in the race and was praying for Romero's safety as he passed him by, felt like going home. An accident involving two horses had marred the Sprint earlier in the day, and the Distaff only reinforced a feeling of something bad happening that day that he had had as he came to the track. Day and his fellow jockeys joined in prayer immediately after the Distaff.

Romero had a slight red mark over one of his eyes, but had otherwise escaped unscathed from the fall. He rode Izvestia to a sixth-place finish in the Classic after pronouncing himself fit, or so it seemed. In retrospect, he had suffered numerous injuries, but his battered body had gone into shock and he was unable to feel the pain. A week later after a scan to determine what X-rays couldn't the day after the race, Romero discovered he had suffered hairline fractures of eight ribs and a hairline fracture of one of his shoulders.

Out of a sense of "duty," Mrs. Lunger remained at the track after the fateful race to congratulate others. "That's the way I've been brought up," she said.

The Breeders' Cup continued, albeit with much of the excitement gone and a sense of gloom hanging over the track.

"They ran four more races at Belmont yesterday after Dr. Neil Cleary administered the injection that would relieve Go for Wand of her misery," *Newsday*'s Paul Moran wrote in an article the following day that won him an Eclipse Award that year for the outstanding story in the newspaper division. "One was worth $3 million. But the seventh Breeders' Cup was over at the moment (Go for Wand) fell. Racing stopped, at least in spirit, as though it had been stabbed in the heart by a hot knife."

"Go for Wand was the worst," Tom Hammond, co-host of NBC's Breeders' Cup telecast, said three years later in an interview in the official Breeders' Cup souvenir magazine. "It happened right in front of me. I was almost physically sick. After what happened in the Sprint (when a fall led to the deaths of two horses), I was thinking something is drastically wrong, let's just call if off and go home. But we still had two and a half hours to go."

*Daily Racing Form* executive columnist Joe Hirsch wrote in the magazine:

"Many racegoers wept openly at the tragedy that had unfolded before them. If the remainder of the program had been called off, the crowd would have gone quietly. There was nothing to look forward to except more races and few were in the mood for that. But as in Munich, the Games continued so the horses went to the paddock for the Breeders' Cup Mile."

The morning after the worst tragedy of his life, Bill Badgett put on a brave face and returned to work. He had 30 horses that required his attention and a staff that needed to follow his orders. While everyone felt a collective hurt for Badgett, he could not allow the previous day's tragedy to take away from the tasks at hand.

"We've got to reach down and keep going," Badgett told a group of reporters who came to his barn to interview him and to offer their condolences. In tragedy as in triumph, Badgett handled himself with grace and dignity.

"There's not a whole lot to say, it's a tragedy," he said slowly while maintaining his composure. "It's a tough business. She dug down and gave a little bit extra and overextended herself. If she wasn't a special filly, it probably wouldn't have happened. She was determined not to let that mare get by her."

In 1984, Badgett watched as Swale, whom his boss, Woody Stephens, had trained to victory in the Kentucky Derby and Belmont Stakes, died of a heart attack while walking off the track. That had been traumatic, but it did little to prepare him for this tragedy. It only reminded him of how unforgiving the sport can be and how thin the line is between triumph and tragedy. "It's a tough game," Badgett said. "You never know (what will happen), that's why when anything good happens you'd better enjoy it." The tragedy had been so devastating that Rosemary Badgett did not come to work that Sunday.

Later that day, Mrs. Lunger had Go for Wand's head, heart and hooves—a time-old tradition for great racehorses—buried. It took place in a private ceremony at Saratoga. "It was the thing to do, where she had been so great, where people would always remember her," Mrs. Lunger said. "It was absolutely the thing to do."

The slow-motion tape of the breakdown by NBC sparked feelings of anger and bitterness among the horse racing community. Some felt NBC had overplayed the footage of the Go for Wand tragedy. To others, it was no different than a human tragedy, such as the destruction of the space shuttle Challenger. History had been made and, for better or worse, it had to be televised as such. That spring, television had captured remarkable footage of trainer Carl Nafzger describing the stretch run of the Kentucky Derby to the horse's owner, Frances Genter. That had been considered brilliant television. Some six months later, the picture of Mrs. Lunger, another grande dame of the sport, turning away from the sight of her fallen horse and then refocusing with a stonefaced look, was also an example of dramatic TV. The constant replays of Go for Wand falling, however, were deemed by some members of the sport's establishment to be morbid, sick and disrespectful.

"We couldn't ignore it and that alienated a lot of horse people," Hammond said in an interview.

The anger toward the media by the horse racing community intensified when

*Sports Illustrated* included several graphic photos, particularly of the shattered leg, in its Breeders' Cup follow-up story.

"I was a little disappointed with some of the media things that happened and I was a little pleased with others," Bill Badgett said. "It might have been a little overdrawn, but that's part of it."

For months after the tragedy, the Badgetts received thousands of letters, pictures, poems and records offering condolences. The outpouring of emotion proved that people cared, that an animal had touched their lives as much as it had impacted on the Badgetts. People who had lost family members in car accidents wrote to say they empathized with the Badgetts. "I had people writing me saying, 'I know how you feel, I lost a daughter,'" Rosemary said. "That's amazing. Usually when you lose an animal, no matter how big or small, you try to explain how important it was and people try to understand it. These people did understand. They said, 'I read about you. I saw your story. I saw the relationship. I know how hard this must be. I know this is going to be tough.' It helped a lot that people did understand, that she wasn't just a racehorse that made money. They really understood how special she was. It seemed like people loved her."

"You can't imagine in a million years, it was pretty incredible," Bill Badgett said. "It's absolutely unbelievable. Not one negative thing out of anybody."

Go for Wand posthumously received the Eclipse's champion three-year-old filly award and subsequently other awards, too. With each honor Mrs. Lunger impressed upon people to remember the joy Go for Wand gave everybody and not her demise. It's a message she still preaches. "She was such an enthusiastic mare and she was so kind and so wise. She was wonderful."

In the October 1995 issue of *Thoroughbred Champions*, journalist Sandra Boom wrote that to remember the filly only for her breakdown "does her a tremendous disservice, negating all that she was and all that she accomplished. . . . The memory of October 27, 1990, will always remain with those who watched the Breeders' Cup Distaff. But it's time to recall the other memories Go for Wand gave us. All who knew Wand know that she loved people and loved her racing. Rather than being remembered as the 'ill-fated Go for Wand,' the horse who broke down in the Breeders' Cup, she should be remembered as a beautiful filly and gifted athlete. She should be remembered as a champion."

Rosemary Badgett said she will never forget the final race, but that is only one fragment of the mosaic of memories she has of the filly. "It took me a while to try and forget the look in her eyes and that scared feeling upset me," Rosemary said. "And the reason is I just remember the grunting and the excitement and the galloping and the travelling and the planes. Just the talks and the carrots and the way she used to nudge me. I used to lay with her in the stall. She'd always reach over and bite Billy and he'd halfway laugh. And she'd just nuzzle me to death. We just got along so good."

It wasn't until 1995 that Bill Badgett started his first Breeders' Cup horse since the Go for Wand tragedy. Flitch did not approach the ability of Go for Wand and ran eighth in the Turf to Northern Spur. Ironically, Ron McAnally, who had saddled Bayakoa, trained the winning horse.

"I try to put the bad things of the Breeders' Cup behind me and just think of all the positive things leading into the race," Badgett said. "I kind of wipe out in my mind her breaking down. I'm very proud of everything that she accomplished and what we accomplished with her. I don't think I'll ever lose that memory. It made a harder person out of me, for sure. You try to handle things the best you can with a tragedy. I don't know if I've overcome it. I've kind of put it in the back of my head. It's just like any other tragedy. You deal with it the best way you can and go on with your life. It was a pretty amazing race, right up to the point she broke down. You still don't know who would have won."

Randy Romero has two distinct Breeders' Cup memories: Personal Ensign's final victory and Go for Wand's demise.

"The best day of my life was Personal Ensign, and the saddest day of my life was Go for Wand," Romero said.

# 17

# Fleet Feet

## Arazi

*T*he Breeders' Cup Juvenile is more than just a race for two-year-old colts and geldings; it is supposed to be a preview of the Kentucky Derby the following May. The fact that the 1991 Breeders' Cup was run at Churchill Downs, site of the Run for the Roses, gave horsemen an opportunity to not only run their horses in the most prestigious race for juveniles, but also to test them over the course. With that in mind, American owner Allen Paulson and his partner, Sheikh Mohammed bin Rashid al Maktoum of the United Arab Emirates, brought over their sensational young horse Arazi for a trip over the track. It would prove to be a run for the ages.

Bred in Kentucky by Ralph Wilson and foaled on March 4, 1989, Arazi sold as a weanling at the Keeneland November sale for $350,000. Paulson had major interests in aviation and named the horse Arazi after a pilot's checkpoint in Arizona. The following July, Paulson consigned the colt to the Keeneland Summer Select yearling sale, but brought him home when the bidding reached only $300,000, well below the reserve of $700,000. Paulson, who had many horses racing in Europe, sent the colt to France to be trained by Francois Boutin, who had saddled Miesque for Greek shipping magnate Stavros Niarchos to back-to-back victories in the Breeders' Cup Mile in 1987 and '88. Boutin was regarded as one of the best conditioners in the world. Arazi debuted in May 1991 and ran second in a five-furlong race in which he led for most of the way. It would mark his last loss of the season. He rattled off six consecutive victories with ease. Words like "going away," "cantering" and "easily" described his triumphs. He concluded his European season by winning the Group One Grand Criterium at Longchamp on October 5, the day of the Prix de l'Arc de Triomphe, the most important race for older horses in Europe. The Grand Criterium may have been on the undercard, but Arazi underscored his reputation as a superstar.

So enthralled was Sheikh Mohammed by Arazi's efforts that he bought a half-interest from Paulson for a reported $9 million, an unbelievable sum, but one considered an investment in the colt's future stallion potential. Anthony Stroud, race manager for Sheikh Mohammed's Darley Stud Management, said his employer became attracted to the horse in the summer and originally wanted to buy him outright.

The challenge of the Breeders' Cup loomed as an enticing target for Paulson. A fiercely competitive individual whose love for America is reflected in his patriotic stars and stripes silks of red, white and blue, Paulson wanted the opportunity to showcase his horse at home. It was not unusual for a European invader to run in the Juvenile, but none had ever had the credentials of Arazi. He was the real deal. The Europeans regarded him as not only their best two-year-old, but the best anywhere. The North American racing public, which had heard of Arazi but had not seen him run in person, needed convincing. What better place to showcase a star than in Kentucky at Churchill Downs?

Stroud said Sheikh Mohammed supported the Breeders' Cup move, calling it a joint decision between the two owners and the trainer. As part of the partnership, Arazi would run in the U.S. with an American jockey, and in Europe with English-based American jockey Steve Cauthen. Pat Valenzuela, a talented California rider who had won the Kentucky Derby in 1989 with Sunday Silence but whose career had been pockmarked afterward by drug-use problems, received the coveted mount in the U.S. Boutin had tempered enthusiasm about running Arazi in America. Boutin's wife, Lucy, said her husband knew Arazi would do well, but he worried about the strenuous year the colt was having and what affect it would have on his three-year-old season.

"He was a fantastic two-year-old and (Francois) knew what he had," Lucy Boutin said. "Francois knew everything he had in his hands. It was like an artist painting a tableau. I've never been that close to someone who was so magical in that sense. It's like being married to a great painter or a great artist. He was artistic with his horses."

Paulson's wife Madeleine described Arazi's arrival at Churchill Downs as "like the Pope coming to America." Perhaps she overdramatized it, but Arazi certainly captured the crowd in his morning tours to the track. The European journalists followed him like an icon, while the North American media viewed the little chestnut with the crooked white blaze with fascination. Arazi did not have outstanding size—perhaps he would grow in time—or scope. He was built more like a sprinter than a classic runner, but that was of little consequence on the track.

Arazi had never before run on dirt or on a left-handed course. Clearly his class would have to assist him in his North American debut. As if to add intrigue and difficulty to his assignment, Arazi drew the outside post in the field of 14. It was almost as if the gods of horse racing were determined to make Arazi prove himself against all odds.

Opening Verse won the Mile just before the Juvenile for Paulson at odds of 26-1 with Valenzuela aboard. It set the stage for the confrontation between Arazi and Bertrando, the California star who had been supplemented for $120,000 because his sire was not nominated to the Breeders' Cup program at the time of his conception.

The bettors made Arazi the favorite at 21-10, with Bertrando at 5-2. At exactly 2:29 p.m. on a brisk but beautiful fall day, the gates opened and the 14 juveniles took their initial steps in the mile and a sixteenth race. Arazi looked like anything but a winner early, as he broke tardily and the patient Valenzuela took his time nursing the colt over to the inside. The fleet-footed Bertrando, under Alex Solis, forged to the front and cruised on a comfortable pace of 46 3/5 seconds for a half mile. It was just after this point that Arazi, who had been running eighth, started his stunning move, remembered as probably the most incredible in Breeders' Cup history. Arazi started moving forward faster than race announcer Tom Durkin could pick him up. With his brilliant speed Arazi had caught up to Bertrando on the turn into the stretch. A head-to-head confrontation seemed imminent, but the matchup never materialized. Arazi blew by Bertrando like his rival was tethered to the quarter pole.

"And Arazi runs right by him," Durkin said in shocked disbelief. Arazi ran down the stretch in a line as skewed as his blaze, starting out in the middle and finishing near the rail, five lengths the best. Valenzuela took a hold of his mount in the final 70 yards to the wire, looking like a morning exercise rider trying to save everything for the afternoon. Only in the last couple of jumps did Arazi change to his proper lead leg.

"Here is a superstar," Durkin said, emphasizing the word super.

It had been a stunning performance. Beyond belief. Wildly electric.

"I think we were all mesmerized; it was like something out of *National Velvet*," Stroud said.

Valenzuela proclaimed Arazi the best horse he had ever ridden. The European journalists treated the race with unbridled enthusiasm: "There are rare moments in racing that defy belief and stop the clock," wrote Jonathan Powell of the *London Sunday Express*. "We witnessed one yesterday at Churchill Downs by the French-trained Arazi, in the shape of a winged assassin. . . . One moment he appeared to be struggling on an unfamiliar surface. The next he had overtaken a dozen horses. The best two-year-olds in America tried to give chase but they might as well have tried to catch the wind."

"The little European toyed with the field," Brough Scott wrote in the *Independent*. "He sliced through on the inside until the turn and then, despite coming wide and on the wrong foreleg lead, he sauntered home. The official margin was four and three-quarter lengths over the second favorite Bertrando, but the ease with which this was done was almost embarrassing."

"Arazi's victory in the Breeders' Cup Juvenile at Churchill Downs, Kentucky last night left hardened horsemen gasping in amazement," wrote Robin Gray in *News of the World*. "It doesn't matter even to the Americans who was second. Arazi was phenomenal and is now firm favourite for the Kentucky Derby here on May 2."

"Horses aren't supposed to do to each other what Arazi did to the field," wrote Paul Haigh in the *Racing Post*. "Admittedly it was not a vintage field. People had been saying all week that the two-year-olds seemed a bit weak this year and that if Arazi could handle the track etc., etc., etc. But not this. No one thought he could go past them like this, as though they were tied up, as though they were marker poles. It was that which dumbfounded the American press for a while, before they remembered, recovered themselves, rushed to their keyboards, and as one man delivered themselves of the ultimate accolade in American racing: the comparison with Secretariat."

"It had to be seen to be believed," wrote Howard Wright in the *Racing Post.* "It wasn't so much that Arazi overcame the disadvantages of a bad draw and a strange racing surface to demolish the best America could offer in the Breeders' Cup Juvenile. It was that he did it all with such contemptuous ease and blinding brilliance."

"The truth about a horse is not often found among those who shovel the muck and wash down the sweat, because the job precludes objectivity," wrote Paul Heyward in the *Independent.* "This time the staff around Arazi were merely crystallizing the judgment of a global audience who traded superlatives with the fervour of a Harrods sale. This was the finest performance by a two-year-old."

"Arazi, the knock-kneed wonder horse that nobody wanted, has got all America trembling at the knees," Tony Lewis wrote in the *Daily Star.* "The pint-sized French champion produced the most devastating performance by a two-year-old that I have ever seen to win the Breeders' Cup Juvenile at Churchill Downs, Kentucky."

American journalists joined the European scribes in showering the horse with praise.

"Just as the whole afternoon of races seemed about to turn into the dullest, most anticlimactic series in the eight-year history of the Breeders' Cup, something extraordinary happened at Churchill Downs, something so rare and close to art in this sport that 19 years of history seemed to vanish in the din, and 1972 was suddenly as new as yesterday," Bill Nack wrote in *Sports Illustrated.* "Arazi took off running, recalling no less than Secretariat on his most memorable afternoons as a two-year-old."

Many esteemed horsemen saluted the pocket-sized rocket. "Toss him all the bouquets, give him his time in the sun, he's one hell of a horse," trainer D. Wayne Lukas was quoted in *Sporting Life.* "He's a monster, the best since Swaps and Secretariat," Bertrando's trainer Bruce Headley said.

Senior Jockey Club handicapper Geoffrey Gibbs told English journalists: "It's the best performance from a two-year-old I have ever seen—and I'll never see it bettered. To beat the Americans first time on the dirt was something special in itself, but the acceleration shown by Arazi was simply breathtaking."

One horseman remained dubious of Arazi's run. Ian Jory, an Englishman training in California, had watched the race at home on TV and provided commentary to one of the horse's connections, who was listening on a phone. In Jory's opinion, Arazi had started to bolt around the far turn. Jory maintained that impression after watching the race on tape three or four more times and still felt the same way when discussing the race with a journalist in 1995.

"It looked to me like it was blind panic, the horse just bolted," Jory said. "I didn't think he was going to make the turn. If you look at it, he went wide around the turn anyway. It looked to me like Patrick was just trying to steer him around the turn rather than anything else."

American journalists did not have a chance to ascertain Boutin's feelings after the race because he did not attend the post-race interview session. While Paulson sang the praises of his superhorse, Boutin quietly returned to the barn. In doing so, he may have caused a rift with the North American media, which never truly understood him. He rarely spoke in English and did not communicate with the bold bravado of a D. Wayne Lukas or the flair or wit of England's Henry Cecil. He was a proud and dignified man.

"There was no reason for him not to go (to the interview room), but he didn't feel at ease speaking English," Lucy Boutin said. "He was so happy that he won the race, he just wanted to go back to see his horse. I think the press resented that and I think they're probably right to have, but he didn't realize how important it was. He felt they could talk to him any time and he was always accessible to the press, but he did not speak English and he was misquoted and mistranslated."

Arazi's victory did not come without cost. He required surgery in his knees four days after the victory to remove bone chips. Renowned Kentucky veterinarian Dr. Larry Bramlage performed the operation, which Boutin did not want done according to his wife. Lucy Boutin said her husband wanted to bring the colt back to France and let the American vets come there and operate if necessary.

"They have different philosophies over in Europe than we do," Paulson said. "I'm a believer (that) when you've got chips and they're irritating a horse, an operation is successful most times."

*Racing Post* writer Desmond Stoneham, who was a friend of Boutin, saw the trainer at Saint-Cloud in France two days after the operation and said he was not in a good mood.

"Basically, Boutin was not in favor of Arazi having the knee chip operations done," Stoneham said. "He certainly wanted the horse to come back home. Having accepted the fact it (the operation) was done, he never wanted to train the horse for the Kentucky Derby because he knew the horse was going to stand for six to eight weeks in his (stall) doing nothing after those knee chip operations. He was going to face an impossible rushed preparation."

Paulson said were it not for Boutin, in whom he had so much confidence, Arazi would have stayed in the U.S. to prepare for the Derby. En route back to France, Arazi suffered a lung infection. All things combined, Boutin had a tough task ahead of him. Clearly, it would take a superhorse to overcome all the problems.

Paulson had never won the Derby and was not about to let the surgery impact on his dream. He had the superhorse and now he wanted to win the greatest race in America. The 2,000 Guineas would be run the same day in England and Arazi would have been favored to win it, but that became only secondary.

Lucy Boutin, born in the U.S. and the daughter of prominent Kentucky breeder/owner W. T. Young, said she understood Paulson's all-American desire to run in the Derby. Her father had that dream and fulfilled it by winning the race in 1996 with Grindstone, but her late husband didn't share that burning Derby passion, particularly under the circumstances surrounding Arazi in 1992.

"He would go to America with horses and he did very well with them, but it was sort of a spot-on thing," Lucy said. "He did it with Miesque and she was probably the biggest thing he ever had, but her career was based in Europe. She went over for the Breeders' Cup twice and she won twice but her whole career was European, it wasn't aiming for an early spring race in America. Francois was classic European."

The Arazi bandwagon, which had a host of European supporters before the Juvenile, picked up passengers literally from all parts of the globe immediately after. Everyone suddenly became a fan of the little horse with the big reputation.

The management of Pimlico Race Course in Baltimore built an auxiliary press box to accommodate the added media expected to watch Arazi race in the Preakness Stakes—second leg of the American Triple Crown—after what would presumably be a romp in the Derby.

American newspapers dispatched reporters to France to watch the horse prepare for his seasonal debut.

"The media coming over (to France) before the Kentucky Derby put a tremendous amount of pressure on Francois," Lucy Boutin said. "It was a nightmare. It was like a circus. What does one do?"

On April 7, less than a month before the Derby, Arazi made his three-year-old debut in France in the Group Two Prix Omnium and won by five lengths. He then headed for the U.S. amid major questions about his ability to duplicate his feat of the previous fall.

"When you're training a horse in France and you're trying to run in the Kentucky Derby, of course it's catch-up, it's not really the ideal preparation," Stroud said. "And, it's not the ideal preparation to be off as long as he was."

Arazi returned to Kentucky with the media falling at his feet and the industry pulling for him to duplicate his performance of the fall. Extra spin was added by the presence of European runners Dr. Devious and Thyer. The race had taken on epic proportions. As Hall of Fame trainer Leroy Jolley said: "It's more like the World Derby than the Kentucky Derby." Notwithstanding the other two Europeans—and all the others in the race—the one horse everyone had come to see was Arazi.

"I don't know how they can get the saddle over Arazi's wings," Jolley, who came with long shot Conte Di Savoya, said in mock admiration. Not everyone considered the horse a cinch to wear the garland of roses. "They should erect a monument to him if he wins," said trainer Sonny Hine, who came armed with Florida star Technology. "To undergo what he's gone through, my hat's off to him."

"I'm not saying he ain't a superstar, but he ain't won the race yet," said Craig Perret, the jockey of Pine Bluff. "I don't think he's going to come around nine horses and beat the field he's going to be hooking. If he does that, then he deserves all the billing he's got. You can talk and try to scare the whole field off, but they ain't scaring nobody."

Canadian-based trainer Jim Day, who had won the Breeders' Cup Distaff on the same card on which Arazi won the Juvenile, did not like the horse's program off only one race. Moreover, he did not particularly like the horse's build. "He looks like a flyweight with heavyweights," Day said. Indeed, the horse everyone called the next Secretariat was a lot more Little Red than Big Red. He had grown in media stature, but not in size or scope.

Boutin did not have the sanctuary of the quarantine area where European horses are stabled during the Breeders' Cup. This time his horse had a stall in one of the regular barns and the media had much easier access, even with security personnel acting as human barricades. Still, it looked like a swarm of bees on a honeycomb. Boutin was provided a translator by Churchill Downs, but she lacked horse knowledge.

"It was my fault, too, because at that point I was very shy—and still am to a great degree—about talking to the press or about talking in public," Lucy Boutin said. "I should have been translating for him because practically everything he said—or quite a lot of it—was mistranslated and it was infuriating for him and for me."

Arazi drew post 18 in the field of 19, but Paulson did not fret, saying the colt had plenty of time to gain position in the long race. Two days before the race, Arazi was headed to the track for a workout when he pitched Valenzuela after he climbed aboard, something the horse had done the previous fall in his first trip to Churchill. It was suggested by some that Arazi was intelligent enough to remember he had been at Churchill, a place that produced a stunning victory but also a painful injury. Arazi worked five-eighths of a mile in a pedestrian 1:03 1/5 after the incident, but picked it up in the final quarter of a mile.

"He finished very well, very easily," Valenzuela said. "He picked it up very smoothly. He's a better horse than he was last year. I think everyone else is running for second. He has an unbelievable turn of foot. He accelerates like you're pushing a button for a rocket." Arazi went off the 9-10 favorite in the field of 18—reduced by one prominent starter when A. P. Indy had to be scratched the morning of the race because of a bruised foot. A. P. Indy would have his day in history at season's end in the Breeders' Cup Classic, but on this day he rested and his handlers had to accept the painful card they'd been dealt.

Arazi trailed the field early and then started to make the same scintillating run as he had in the Breeders' Cup. The thrill was short-lived, however, as he flattened out by the top of the stretch and ran eighth, more than eight lengths behind outsider Lil E. Tee. After many frustrating misses, jockey Pat Day had finally won the Kentucky Derby, but the racing world had only passing interest. Lil E. Tee could have been Lil Abner for all they cared. Arazi had lost and that was the big story. In fact, his finish was the worst in Derby history for an odds-on favorite.

"Going into the turn, I thought we were going to gallop away with the race," Valenzuela said. "I asked him a little bit at the quarter pole to get by Dance Floor and he couldn't do it. He just didn't respond the way he did (in the Breeders' Cup)."

"We were sort of stuck for time," Boutin said through the interpreter. "As soon as I saw the horse go past the grandstand (the first time), I knew right away he would lose. He was too (sharp). He was too bright for this course."

"He made a good move, it looked like he was going to win it," Paulson said. "I think with the extra distance, he just didn't have it. It looked like he ran the same mile and a sixteenth race that he did in the Breeders' Cup. He was going like gangbusters, but he didn't have the stamina to finish the race."

"Sometimes horses are better at two than three; he was a very mature horse and possibly (there) were problems with the surgery, there could be any number (of reasons)," Stroud said. "This business of getting him ready for America, flying there, bringing him back, maybe that contributed to it. I don't know the answer to that question."

Stoneham said Boutin did the best he could in the limited time he had. "Arazi was as fit as a horse could get," Stoneham said. "He had to put a lot of work into him in too quick a time frame. He had to train that horse in a way he didn't want to train it because of the insistence of the strange duopoly of ownership between Paulson and Sheikh Mohammed. You never ever heard Boutin issue a word of complaint or criticism about the owners and what he was being asked to do."

Arazi returned to Europe and ran a month later in the Group One St. James's Palace Stakes, where he was fifth. He was then given time to recuperate.

Arazi returned in the fall and ran in the Group One Prix du Prince d'Orange Stakes, finishing third behind a horse named Arcangues, who the following year would record the biggest upset in Breeders' Cup history. Arazi reasserted himself by winning the Group One Prix du Rond-Point by four lengths in his next start, giving hope that the little big horse was on his way back to his old form.

After some debate as to which race would be selected for Arazi, Boutin announced a week before the 1992 Breeders' Cup that Arazi would contest the Mile instead of the Classic at Gulfstream Park.

"I spoke to the owners, considered the options and have decided to definitely go for the Mile. Arazi has been in great form," Boutin said publicly. Lucy Boutin said her husband approached the race hoping for the best with Arazi but knew he did not have the same horse that had run the previous fall. The public made Arazi the favorite, swayed perhaps by his previous start, his reputation and his trainer's record in the Mile. Once again, they watched the fading superstar run a disappointing race. He saved ground the whole way, running closer to the pace than in his previous American races, but never fired when it mattered. He finished 11th behind a horse named Lure, whose star was just rising. Originally it was feared Arazi bled internally during the race, but that proved not the case. He simply didn't have it, in what would be his final career race.

"I have a lot of enthusiasm for Arazi," Paulson said. "I still think he's the greatest. I don't know why he didn't fire."

On November 20, Sheikh Mohammed announced the colt's retirement and the plan to stand him in England as part of the original agreement with Paulson.

"We contemplated keeping him in training, but we purchased into the horse to breed because of his blistering speed and talent and at this stage we feel retirement is the best way to go," Stroud told the *Daily Racing Form*. "It's always difficult when you know a horse has so much potential but doesn't realize it on the racecourse as a three-year-old. It's much like an artist not being recognized. It has been very frustrating, but it's more frustration for the horse than anyone else."

"I know this was a disappointing year for Arazi, but as a two-year-old he should be remembered as a legend," Paulson said in the story. Sheikh Mohammed acquired full interest in the colt for an undisclosed sum, which some industry analysts suggest must have been significant.

Because of an agreement with Sheikh Mohammed, Paulson didn't reveal any details of the deal.

"It's horse trading," Stroud said. "We gave a price and they thought it was a good price. I wouldn't say any more than that."

The *Daily Racing Form* did a chronology of Arazi's life and entitled it, "The Best or a Bust?" Clearly, compelling arguments could be made either way.

Lucy Boutin said she and her husband talked about Arazi after his career ended, but not about the negative aspects. Lucy kept a scrapbook of Arazi's press clippings, something she had never done for any other horse.

"I did it because I thought he was such a fantastic horse and it was an opportunity to do something for Francois that I had never done before, to concentrate on one horse from the beginning to the end," she said.

Allen Paulson found another horse to replace the glory of Arazi when Cigar emerged as a superstar late in 1994 and eventually became the top money-winning runner in history and author of a lengthy win streak.

Sheikh Mohammed developed a galaxy of stars, including Lammtarra, who retired undefeated after winning the Prix de l'Arc de Triomphe in 1995.

Francois Boutin died of cancer in 1995. Lucy Boutin said the career of Arazi was the greatest tragedy of her husband's life as a horseman.

For one brief moment, Arazi caused all the sporting world to take notice of something special and to dream a little. It could be said Arazi was the little horse who could once, but not twice. But, oh how he did it that once!

"It absolutely just took your breath away," English racing broadcaster John McCririck said. "I was broadcasting for Channel Four at the time and we were doing it live and you couldn't find the adjectives to tell what you had seen. You knew you had seen one of the great sights of racing. That day was one of the magic days to see a racehorse."

# 18

# Smokin'

## Cigar

$\mathcal{T}$he world of horse racing is filled with four-legged mercurial stars, shining bright in a workout or a run against rivals, drawing stares from onlookers and dreams of greatness. Some of these stars are able to maintain their ability over a brief period of time, some a little longer, but few are able to do it for a prolonged period, carrying not only the weight of their riders but the expectations of the world. And for a few years, the world of horse racing—and the world of sports—witnessed one of these special racehorses. His name was Cigar and, befitting his name, he really lit it up on the racetrack.

Bred by Allen Paulson and owned by his wife, Madeleine, Cigar did not race at age two after requiring knee surgery to remove bone chips. He started nine times at three, winning twice and finishing in the money in four others, earning $88,375. At age four, Madeleine took the horse away from trainer Alex Hassinger and gave him to Bill Mott, who had won the Breeders' Cup Turf for her in 1992 with Fraise and had become one of the top trainers in the interim. But few could have predicted that even given his talent and skill, Mott would transform Cigar into a dominant horse mentioned in the same breath as such legends as Kelso, Citation, Dr. Fager and Forego.

In his first four 1994 starts, all on grass, Cigar could do no better than two thirds. Clearly at this point not even Mott had found the key to unlock the horse's talents. Two changes, however, made all the difference in the world: Mott had the horse medicated to treat an ulcer, and switched him to the dirt. Cigar had broken his maiden on that surface in his second start as a three-year-old, but was switched to turf because of his pedigree and to reduce the wear and tear on his knees. Cigar had always trained like a titan on the dirt, so the switch back to that surface could hardly be classified as rocket science. But it was that change—and Mott paying attention to detail—that spelled success.

On October 28, at Belmont Park, Cigar won an allowance race by eight lengths and the racing world barely noticed. After all, more than one horse had used the turf-to-dirt angle to run a big race. Mott pointed Cigar to the Grade One NYRA Mile for his next race. Twelve horses, headed by multiple Grade One winner Devil His Due, who had run poorly in the Breeders' Cup Classic the previous month, went postward. Those who liked Cigar received generous odds at 8.90-1. Cigar lit up the track that day, winning by seven lengths in one of his best races.

An all-in-the-family deal saw Allen become Cigar's owner at the start of the 1995 season. Madeleine wanted Eliza, the 1992 Breeders' Cup Juvenile Fillies winner, but she also wanted to lift the spirits of her husband. They made the deal, with Allen adding a free breeding to 1987 Breeders' Cup Turf winner Theatrical. Madeleine thought Cigar could become a major horse and help her husband recapture the emotion he had lost after the retirement of his pride and joy, Arazi, two years before. She was right—Cigar boosted Allen's enthusiasm—but if she had known just how good Cigar would become, it's likely she would have asked for considerably more in return. As horse trades go, that one turned out to be a real steal for Allen.

Cigar made his five-year-old debut at Gulfstream Park on January 22, comfortably winning a mile and a sixteenth allowance race. Paulson ambitiously targeted the Donn Handicap on February 11 as Cigar's next race, even though he would have to face 1994 Horse of the Year Holy Bull. That four-year-old colt had become the darling of the North American racing world. Holy Bull had it all—a catchy name and tremendous talent. Built like a heavyweight boxer and blessed with blinding speed, the big grey drew a host of admirers at a time when the sport badly needed a publicity boost.

Trained and owned by Warren (Jimmy) Croll, who had inherited the colt after the death of owner-breeder Rachel Carpenter, Holy Bull overcame a sluggish performance in the 1994 Kentucky Derby to win his next six starts with authority and brilliance, sealing his Horse of the Year title. The North American racing world became absolutely bullish about the Bull early in 1995. Memorabilia with his name drew brisk sales throughout the U.S. Visitors made daily trips to Croll's barn at Gulfstream Park to visit the horse. Croll accommodated them and so did the charismatic Bull.

After a facile win in the Olympic Handicap at Gulfstream to start the season, Holy Bull was pointed to the Donn. Cigar and the other seven horses in the race were expected to be running for second-place money against the Bull. To be sure, it was a horse race and the old adage that anything could happen gave rival trainers reason to run, but did anyone really expect the big horse to lose? Not really. However, Paulson had historically relished the opportunity to race his good horses regardless of the competition or the race, so he, for one, did not see the Bull as a mortal lock.

Holy Bull went postward as the odds-on choice. Cigar was 4-1, the last time he would go off at such a fat price. Jockey Jerry Bailey took an early lead with Cigar in the mile and an eighth race, and the matchup with Holy Bull developed in the run around the clubhouse turn. But the anticipated duel ended quickly as Mike Smith took a hard hold of the Bull and pulled him up on the backstretch. Cigar rolled on to a 5½-length win, but few really noticed. All attention focused on the injured hero, Holy Bull, the star racing had been needing. Holy Bull suffered a ligament injury that forced his retirement and left the racing industry disheartened. How would it go forward without the Bull?

As Mott would tell reporters the day before the 1995 Breeders' Cup, it was as if the baton of stardom was passed from Holy Bull to Cigar on that fateful day in February. Like Holy Bull, Cigar would win easy and often, compiling a 10-race victory streak on the year and 12 overall dating back to 1994. Equally important, he had charisma, character, confidence and intelligence. Cigar had the total package.

Managed aggressively by Paulson and trained superbly by Mott, Cigar traveled the country to take on all comers. Racetracks did all they could to attract the horse by either raising the purses if he ran or by weighting him conservatively. Cigar won the Gulfstream Park Handicap in March, then traveled to Arkansas for the Oaklawn Handicap and then to Baltimore for the Pimlico Special, none of the races proving much of a challenge. Paulson then sent him to Suffolk Downs to run in the Massachusetts Handicap, which did not have graded status but had its purse increased by $500,000 to attract him. Once again, Cigar smoked.

Most observers assumed he would now be rested. Paulson had other plans. He lived in California and wanted to run Cigar at Hollywood Park against the best of the west. The pot for the Gold Cup had been upgraded to $1 million and the field included some crack California runners, but it mattered little as Cigar toyed with his competitors.

Cigar earned a much-deserved rest and it would be 10 weeks before he returned to the races, running in the Woodward Stakes at Belmont Park in New York. Despite the layoff and the fact that Mott had not fully cranked him up, the bettors made Cigar the 1-10 favorite for the prestigious mile and an eighth Woodward. Cigar ran as if he had never been away, winning by nearly three lengths with plenty left in reserve.

Three weeks later, Cigar was back in the Jockey Club Gold Cup. Many Breeders' Cup prospects ran that day in the final major preview to the Cup, but the focus this day was on Cigar and Thunder Gulch, who had won the Kentucky Derby, Belmont and Travers Stakes. Trainer D. Wayne Lukas decided the time was right to try his colt against the older horse with the big reputation. Lukas liked a challenge as much as Paulson and when asked why he was running, the trainer replied: "There's a nationwide movement to ban smoking. We're just trying to do our part." If Lukas ever wanted to learn something about Cigar this was the time. One thing was for sure: Thunder Gulch had displayed too much courage to surrender without giving Cigar a battle. And so once again Cigar would have to prove himself, although this time the public respected him enough to make him the 7-20 favorite.

Just like in the Donn, the match race failed to materialize. Thunder Gulch finished fourth to Cigar, suffering a career-ending injury in the race in which he attended the early pace but failed to fire with his customary tenacity in the stretch. Post-race X-rays revealed a leg fracture that could heal in time and Lukas wanted to run him again. Owner Michael Tabor had other ideas. He had bought the colt for a reported $500,000 the year before and seen his investment soar in the interim, so he opted for the conservative route and announced the colt's retirement. Thunder Gulch owed no apologies for his sudden departure from the racing scene. He had given his all, showing the class and grit that earned him respect from everyone who watched him run. But like Holy Bull and others who had limped off the battlefield against Cigar, for him there would be no tomorrows.

After Cigar put away Thunder Gulch early in the stretch, Bailey said it was almost as though his horse relaxed and took it easy, knowing he had dispensed with the only horse who had a chance to beat him. Cigar won by only a length, staving off a challenge from a younger rival named Unaccounted For.

Some analysts, looking for a chink in Cigar's armor, pointed to the Gold Cup as a sign of vulnerability. They suggested that maybe the hard campaign had caught up to him and he had tired at the end—regardless of Bailey's comments to the contrary—or that the off track had limited his effectiveness. With a $3 million purse, owners and trainers were willing to take a shot at beating the invincible horse in the Breeders' Cup Classic.

In the days leading up to the race, the media camped out at Mott's barn for daily discussions. Every morning at 10:30, Mott made himself available for interviews. And there were many—newspaper, radio and TV. Despite the onslaught, Mott handled the chore with aplomb and wit. One reporter called his answers "bon Motts."

Heading out to the track on his pony at 7 a.m. to supervise Cigar's last major workout three days before the Classic, Mott talked with *New York Post* racing writer David Grening. Mott laughed at the paint job of a barn he passed along the way. If Mott was feeling the pressure, he certainly didn't show it. Neither did his horse. Cigar worked five-eighths of a mile in one minute and four-fifths, deceiving onlookers who thought he did it slower. Clearly Mott didn't want to squeeze all the juice out of his horse who could have gone much faster if asked.

Back at the barn, Mott joked with a handful of reporters, some of whom introduced themselves as being from Europe. "Hi, I'm Bill Mott from South Dakota," he replied with a good-natured grin. The mood was light. Despite the pressure, Mott felt comfortable with his horse and the people around him.

"I feel like we'll get him over there and Cigar will take care of the rest," he said. "There's a lot that has to do with fate. If it's meant to be, it will happen—we'll get there and he'll win and he'll be considered the great horse that he really is."

The day before the race, the media hovered around Mott's barn for the last chance to scoop up a story. Paulson, who had arrived the day before and who had been dancing up a storm with his wife at the annual Breeders' Cup party, had to fetch Mott for his final morning gabfest. Taken away from tending to his horses, a task that seemed more a labor of love than a chore for him, Mott emerged from his barn dressed in jeans, chaps, cowboy boots, denim shirt and down jacket. Mott did not favor the corporate look. He had worked his way up the ladder on small circuits, sleeping in tack rooms and scraping by with little money. Although he had long since left those days behind, he never lost that blue-collar work ethic and did not feel the need to make any fashion statements.

"Good morning," Mott said almost apologetically as he addressed the media troops. The primary subject that morning was the weather, which was expected to produce showers later that day and certainly the day of the race. The exact amount expected differed, some forecasting an inch, others talking about a storm that might even threaten the running of the whole day's card. Given Cigar's last race, a possible off track became the axis on which to hang the race-day story. If Cigar, who had already been burdened with post 10 in the field of 11, was to be beaten, an off track could be a key factor.

Mott said he would give some consideration to using mud calks to allow Cigar better traction in the race, but added he would talk to his blacksmith, Jim Bayes, about it in the morning. "We'll decide together, we won't kick out the idea," Mott said. A day later, Cigar's shoes would become an even bigger topic than Imelda Marcos', but on this day footwear didn't seem such a big deal.

Mott also quashed any suggestion the horse would be scratched if the track came up sloppy. "We're running, we're here to play," he said confidently. "It's a nice day today. It might be a rainy, bad day tomorrow, but we're here to run and we're going to take it as it comes up. At this point, we're not afraid of anything. If we get beat, we get beat. We're not going to start whining about anything now and making excuses. Hopefully, we won't have to make any tomorrow."

Mott had supreme confidence in his horse. He respected all the others in the race, but feared no one. There would be no trash-talking or cocky arrogance. Mott liked his chances and felt no need to insult any trainers or owners or, more importantly, their horses. Mott had too much class.

As Mott closed out the gab session he talked about growing up and knowing he wanted to train horses, but never imagining one day having the favorite for the Classic. Born in 1953, Mott learned about horses following around his father on his calls as a veterinarian of farm animals. At age 15, Mott won his first race at a bush track in South Dakota with a cheap mare called My Assets. He subsequently used his purse earnings and savings to buy a $2,000 horse named Kosmic Tour, who won the South Dakota Futurity. He left South Dakota the day after graduation from high school to train full-time, living like a pauper.

After losing the last horse he owned in a claiming race, he gathered his equipment and his humility and apprenticed for Bob Irwin for three years. Irwin had worked for the legendary Hall of Famer Marion Van Berg, who led the nation in wins 14 times, and Mott couldn't have picked a better professor. He received the greatest equine education of his life, working with many different horses and learning how to make adjustments with each one. After three years with Irwin, he worked for Marion's son, Jack, another Hall of Famer, before going out on his own in 1978. Two years later he began a run as Churchill Downs' leading trainer for nine meetings through the fall of 1986. That year he was named the private trainer for Bert and Diana Firestone, and his horses earned more than $4 million. A year later, he saddled Allen Paulson's Theatrical for victory in the 1987 Breeders' Cup Turf and the Eclipse Award as top male turf horse. Several other wealthy clients gravitated to Mott, who won the Breeders' Cup Turf with Fraise in 1992 and the 1994 Eclipse Award for top male turf horse with Paradise Creek. Throughout his rise up the ranks, Mott never lost sight of who he was or from where he had come. He remained a humble human being and horseman.

Mott said the experience with Cigar had not changed his life and that he expected his family and clients to still support him regardless of the outcome of the

Classic. "Last year at this time I had the favorite for the Breeders' Cup Turf (Paradise Creek) and I must say it was an extremely disappointing day not to win that," he said. "I don't think I could even express how low I was right after the race. But we got up the next day, went after it again and now we've got Cigar. So, there's always hope. Winning is great. It's what we want to do, but there are other things that are important, too, and win, lose or draw, we're going to make it."

At about 5:30 a.m. on Breeders' Cup day, the rains, which had begun the night before, fell with greater force. Track superintendent Don Orlando and his crew had prepared for the onslaught by sealing—packing down—the main track. This is a common procedure to allow the rain to fall off to the sides, rather than penetrating the top surface and causing the lower layers to turn into a thick, gooey mess. In addition, training was restricted to the training track to allow the maintenance crew to work on the main track. Five years earlier at the same track on Breeders' Cup day, the brilliant filly Go for Wand had tragically broken down in the Distaff. Two horses had fallen in the Sprint earlier in the card. Those incidents, plus some breakdowns earlier in the week, had resulted in criticism of the track and its safety. Rightly or wrongly, Orlando's crew would be under intense scrutiny this time.

At about 7:30, Cigar headed to the track for his final training before the Classic. On a surface some believed would be a great equalizer, if not his downfall, Cigar showed no hesitation, putting his feet down confidently, striding out in his jogging and indicating a willingness to break into a gallop, but heeding the cautionary words of his exercise rider, Fonda Albertrani.

"He was doing what she told him, but he knew he had more to do and he was saving himself," said George Williams, a onetime groom for Hall of Famers Charlie Whittingham, Woody Stephens and Allen Jerkens and later a trainer himself. The 20-year racetracker, who worked charting races for the *Daily Racing Form* at Assiniboia Downs in Winnipeg, came to New York to do a story on Cigar for the *Thoroughbred Times*. "It was all part of the psyching process that you could see developing over the week (with Cigar)," Williams added. "A horse goes out there in the slop and he'll pin his ears and he won't want to go and he'll just look sluggish and you can see it in his eyes and his ears and his body language. Cigar showed none of those signs. Nothing. If anything, he looked better in the slop than he did on the fast track. He was wound up as far as you could get him without breaking the coil."

Cigar returned to the barn and, after a grooming, stood in his stall and hung his head over the webbing and fell asleep, like an athlete resting hours before a game. Mott had bottled up the horse's energy to just the right level and a few hours later Cigar would be given the opportunity to unleash his powerful run in front of an eager audience at Belmont Park and millions more watching on TV and at simulcasting outlets around the world. Clearly, this would be more than just a race for money or Horse of the Year honors. This would effectively be Cigar's moment to announce himself to the sporting world as something truly special.

While the racing world knew and appreciated him—although some prominent racing writers and handicappers picked other horses to win the Classic—Cigar largely remained anonymous to the general population. Because he had not run two years earlier in the Triple Crown, which allows racing to capture the sporting spotlight for a couple of months of the year, Cigar lacked public recognition. Racing may have anointed him the second coming of Spectacular Bid—the last major older male horse to go through a season undefeated—but you could mention Cigar's name in cabs, hotels and bars and the people generally didn't know who he was or what he had done. In fact, in New York, where racing had lost much of its luster and only 15,000 had attended the Breeders' Cup Preview Day three weeks before, some people didn't even know it was Breeders' Cup week. The airports offered little suggestion of the event. If it had been Kentucky, the horse-mad population would have been walking and talking about Cigar. In New York, if you mentioned Cigar, you might elicit a response like, "No, thanks, don't much care for them."

Paulson had but one dream: that Cigar would be able to go one step beyond greatness by winning the Classic. "I think this would really make him and I still think he'd be Horse of the Year whether he wins it or not," Paulson said. "Hopefully he wins it. We'll cross our fingers."

To accommodate NBC, which had a commitment to televise a Notre Dame–Boston College football game at 3:30 p.m. eastern time, the Breeders' Cup had an early post time of 11:55 a.m. A crowd of 37,246 settled in on the overcast, damp and unseasonably warm day—temperature in the 60s—to await the seven-race, $10-million extravaganza.

The day progressed quickly, and the weather changed suddenly just after the Distaff with the appearance of a rainbow that caused the crowd to roar in approval. By the time of the Classic, the excitement level had risen significantly.

The moment of truth arrived, and the horse of the hour began his procession to the paddock—minus his trainer. Mott attended to a horse stuck in its stall and, despite the magnitude of Cigar's race, could not leave unfinished business in his barn. If this didn't say enough about Mott's care and love for his horses, nothing did. Another trainer might have worried about the problem later and let an assistant tend to it in the meantime, but not Mott. Once he had the problem in order, Mott ran over to Cigar, who was heading toward the tunnel. "Boy, that would have been the shits if I had to miss the Classic," he said, out of breath from running.

Unlike in the morning, when he displayed keenness and sharpness in his actions on and off the track, Cigar appeared calm and collected as he headed to the paddock. Photographers and cameramen followed him like they were chasing a prizefighter heading from his dressing room to the ring. The Classic had not had a runner of this magnitude since Alysheba in 1988. Easy Goer and Sunday Silence made a great duo in 1989, but only because of their yearlong rivalry. Cigar had no one even remotely close in the attention he commanded in the race. Had Thunder Gulch been saved for the Classic instead of running in the Jockey Club Gold Cup three weeks before, the race might have had a little more drama. Instead, Cigar had the stage to himself and the opportunity to deliver a soliloquy.

In the paddock, a controversy arose over the horse's shoes. A rival trainer, later identified as Bobby Frankel, the conditioner of Tinners Way, lodged a complaint over what he believed were turndown shoes, which were illegal. Turned-down slightly at an angle at the heel of the shoe, the alteration gave the horse a better grip of the track, much like cleats. While turndowns were the rage in the early '90s, especially in New York, they were banned in all major racing jurisdictions because of their danger. Mott seemed unaware of any problem when asked about it by NBC's Trevor Denman. What seemed like a scoop looked more like much ado about nothing as Mott cold-watered the controversy.

As Cigar and Bailey made their way to the track, the money poured in on the horse, although the odds board suggested he was by no means a shoo-in to win. He hovered around 4-5, nowhere close to the Breeders' Cup record of 1-5 by Meadow Star in the 1990 Juvenile Fillies. As Cigar galloped by the grandstand in his warmup, the crowd lining the apron clapped appreciatively. They recognized the moment as something special and took advantage of the opportunity to witness a superstar athlete limbering up before a big contest. At one point, Bailey gave his horse a relaxing pat on the neck, but Cigar cranked his neck sideways as if to say. "Leave me alone." Cigar had his game face on for the biggest game of his career.

In addition to the wet track, Cigar had to overcome his wide post. Starting from the 10 hole in the field of 11 on a track that starts its mile and a quarter races on the clubhouse turn, Cigar had an obstacle to overcome at the beginning. He would likely have to contend with mud thrown back in his face from the inside runners. The fact that he had tactical speed, which Bailey could exploit to hustle him out early and gain good position, would be an asset. Five years earlier, Kentucky Derby winner Unbridled, starting widest of all in the field of 14, was given little chance to win by some purely because of his post. It took a heady ride by Pat Day, who guided his horse over to the rail early and used a ground-saving trip, to win the Classic.

At precisely 3:10 p.m., the 1995 Classic began and one minute, 59 and two-fifths seconds later it ended with a stakes-record victory by Cigar. In between, the sports world watched a superstar do his thing. The speedy Star Standard predictably pounced on the early lead from the middle of the pack, tracked by 51-1 L'Carriere. Cigar, who went off at 7-10, maintained a close-up position in third after Bailey let him roll early to establish position. Bailey then clamped down to harness the horse's energy. The jockey would later say he felt the tips of his fingers going numb as the eager Cigar choked the feeling out of them. Chris McCarron set sleepy fractions aboard Star Standard, a half-mile in 48 1/5 seconds, three-quarters in 1:12 1/5. Cigar must have felt like he was in downtown Manhattan during rush hour.

With about three-eighths of a mile to the wire, Bailey put his horse into another gear, and he exploded like a Formula One car. After a mile in 1:35 3/5, Cigar rambled home with a final quarter of a mile in 23 4/5 to post a final time of 1:59 2/5, the fastest Classic in Breeders' Cup history. Originally, the mile had been reported as 1:36 3/5, which would have meant he sped home in an unbelievable 22 4/5—a Secretariat-like time. Even with the correction, Cigar's performance could not be diminished in any way. He overcame a poor post, a muddy track and even a little controversy. Cigar had distinguished himself as the Legend of the Fall Classic. A few strides past the wire, Bailey pointed his index finger to indicate his horse was number one. Who could argue with him?

The scene after the race resembled the Papal appearance at Aqueduct three weeks before. The crowd of photographers and cameramen who had greeted Cigar before the race had seemed to swell in the interval. They practically blocked off the track as Bailey brought his mount back. A swarm of people gathered around the winner's circle, lustily cheering the horse who was about to be proudly led over by Paulson.

"He's the greatest, isn't he, the best in the world?" Paulson said in awe of his horse.

Nearby Sheikh Mohammed bin Rashid al Maktoum, who had raced 1991 Breeders' Cup Juvenile winner Arazi in partnership with Paulson, watched the proceedings while talking to some members of the media, the majority of them from Europe. Halling, who raced as part of Sheikh Mohammed's Godolphin Stable, ran last and was eased at the wire by jockey Walter Swinburn. It was said afterward the horse did not handle the track, but like many great horses who faced Cigar, he simply didn't deliver.

In the media interview room after the race, Bailey proudly displayed an unlit cigarillo given to him by a member of the crowd.

"I don't want to light it up," Bailey said apologetically.

"You better be careful what's in it," Mott joked.

"I'm glad you didn't (smoke) it before the race," added Paulson.

Mott expressed little surprise at Cigar's latest victory. He had simply done his job. Again.

"He's gone over there 10 times this year, the last 12 in a row, and done it and looked like he did it with an amazing amount of effortlessness," Mott said. "He was as fluid as ever. The track was sloppy. He overcame the 10 hole. Once again, they brought the absolute best they had to offer and you saw the outcome yourself. I don't think there's any way to deny him now."

Mott answered the shoe question, explaining Cigar ran in a trailer, which is a half-inch longer than a normal shoe and protrudes out behind the heel. Mott said Cigar had worn them all year and several other horses, including some of his own, had them on earlier in the card.

"I think there was a trainer who was trying to claim foul and being a crybaby, I guess," Mott said. "He was taking a shot like a jock claiming foul in a race and knows he has no business claiming foul but they do it anyway."

Bailey said it was appropriate Cigar had set the record for the fastest Classic.

"Some people probably would disagree with me, but I think he's the greatest horse I've seen," Bailey said. "I never rode against Secretariat, so I can't really judge him, but (Cigar) is the greatest horse I've ever been around."

In 1995, Cigar had come to racing's rescue, fittingly in a year cigars enjoyed a resurgence in popularity. And just like those fine Cuban blends, this American-bred had an air of class and distinction about him. When asked if he planned to promote his horse in any cigar commercials or endorsements, which he had been reluctant to do during the season for fear it would be a jinx, Paulson said he would give it some consideration.

"But, I really think the horse is for the racing public, not to commercialize him," Paulson said. "I think he's going to do a lot for racing, this horse. You always need a superstar and I think we've got one here."

Of that there was little doubt. One year to the day after he began his amazing run on the dirt, Cigar had lifted the racing world on his broad shoulders.

Mott had a wealth of objectives for the horse in 1996. Sheikh Mohammed was putting together a $4 million race in March on his home court in Dubai. If he could run in it and win, Cigar could surpass Alysheba's all-time career earnings of $6,679,242. He had $5,089,015 at the end of '95 after setting a single-season record for earnings with $4,819,800. Mott hoped to have his horse run in the 1996 Breeders' Cup, which would be held for the first time outside of the U.S. at Woodbine. Secretariat had closed out his campaign there in 1973, and the anticipation of Cigar ending his racing career at Woodbine seemed almost too good to be true.

In 1996, Cigar literally became a horse of the world as he raced in three different countries, showcasing himself to admirers. The prospect of running in the inaugural Dubai World Cup, a $4 million race which Sheikh Mohammed had created to attract a superstar such as Cigar, posed a unique challenge. Cigar would have to run a mile and a quarter on a dirt track built in the desert, a daunting task considering trainer Bill Mott would have no past experience from which to draw. Even a veteran horseman such as Mott, who had just guided the veteran horse through a taxing season, would have to rely on all his savvy to pull off this challenge. He and breeder/owner Allen Paulson plotted a racing path to bring the horse to Dubai in peak physical form. The campaign began with the Grade One Donn Handicap in Florida, February 10, followed by the Santa Anita Handicap, March 2, in California. Cigar won the first race, beating a field of seven competitors by two lengths, easily the best, according to the *Daily Racing Form*'s trackman's description of the race. Plans to run in the second race went awry because of an abscess in his right front foot, which forced him to miss 12 days of training. At that point, the Dubai race was in doubt. Mott outfitted his horse with bar shoes to reduce the pressure on the ailing part of the foot. Cigar returned to the track and did a light jog and was pronounced safe to train again, 24 days away from the Dubai Cup.

After an unspectacular six-furlong workout in the mud on March 16, Cigar returned to the track three days later and rattled over seven-eighths of a mile in 1:23, the kind of time that is considered brilliant for a morning exercise. He was sent off to Dubai afterward for his next challenge. Without the benefit of the diuretic Lasix, which is not allowed in Dubai, and arguably not at 100% physically following his interrupted training program, Cigar would be put to the test. He faced a field of 10 others and Cigar prevailed, beating California invader Soul of the Matter, owned by singing icon Burt Bacharach, by half a length following an eyeball-to-eyeball stretch duel in the desert night. Cigar had upped his consecutive win streak to 14 in the process, only two back of Citation's record set between 1948 and 1950.

Cigar received time off to recuperate from the shipping and the race, which would prove to be taxing in years to come for even the toughest and classiest horses. Some, in fact, never quite recovered, mentally or physically or both. Cigar's next challenge was almost nine weeks later in the Massachusetts Handicap at Suffolk Downs. Cigar had traveled to the track the year before and won the race by four comfortable lengths. The management had given the Cigar camp the royal treatment by expanding the purse for his appearance and repeated the gesture. This time, though, he would have to carry 130 pounds, six more than he did the year before, and the most he had ever had to tote. A crowd of 22,196, the largest at Suffolk Downs in 30 years, came to see Cigar, some dressed in T-shirts with the words "The Second Coming." Cigar coasted to a 2¼-length win over a field of five nondescript runners.

Cigar's foot problems flared up again, necessitating another break in training. He returned almost six weeks later for the Arlington Citation Challenge. A crowd of 34,223 packed the suburban Chicago track where Cigar, again carrying 130 pounds, prevailed by 3½ lengths to tie Citation's record.

A month later, Cigar went for the record in the $1 million Pacific Classic, August 10, at Del Mar. Some 200 media representatives from various parts of the world came to the seaside track to witness history and report on it. The crowd numbered 44,181, some 10,000 more than the record set two years before. Speedball Siphon blasted to the lead like a bullet, tracked closely by Cigar, following the game plan drawn up by Mott and Bailey. Siphon set a blistering pace, and by the time Cigar had taken over with three-eighths of a mile to the wire, the pace had been electrifying. With a quarter mile to the wire, the teletimer showed a time of 1:33 4/5, unbelievably fast for a race, let alone one with a quarter mile to go. Cigar's lead did not last, though, because Dare and Go, an aptly named horse as it turned out, dared to go by the superstar. Cigar tried his best to repel the challenge but could not do so on this day. Dare and Go, dismissed at more than 39-1, went on to win by 3½ lengths, stamping his place in history instead of the horse whose name had become synonymous with winning for 655 days.

"We absolutely, positively, have no excuses other than maybe we went too fast and we can't blame Cigar for that," Mott said. "The fact we finished second is history now, but this is still a great, great race horse, one of the best of all time. No one can take that from him."

Bailey felt the fractions took a toll on Cigar.

"I could hear the other horse coming, but I just didn't have enough horse left," Bailey lamented. "I certainly am not putting the blame on Cigar. I'll take it because I was the one who made the decision."

Trainer Richard Mandella, whose horse Soul of the Matter had run second to Cigar in Dubai and who had also saddled Siphon, offered up an interesting quote when asked how he felt about ruining the Cigar parade.

"I felt bad for about half a second," he confessed. "Very seldom in racing are we going to find horses with 16 wins in a row; that's why beating him is so important."

Cigar resembled a beaten warrior after the race and with the streak over he was given time to regroup for the fall. Some time after that, a Japanese breeder offered Paulson $30 million, but he rejected the offer. Cigar rebounded from his loss to win the Woodward Stakes at Belmont Park on September 14 by four lengths, coming from off the pace rather than attacking it early. Three weeks later, Cigar ran in the Jockey Club Gold Cup as the 2-5 favorite. He faced five others, including an emerging star named Skip Away. Put to the challenge by his trainer, Sonny Hine, who ran the colt in his wife Carolyn's name, Skip Away had just won the Molson Million at Woodbine the day after Cigar's victory at Belmont. Bailey employed similar racing tactics again, but this time Cigar fell short, finishing second by a head to Skip Away while drifting out due to Bailey giving him some left-handed cracks.

Sonny Hine had been hospitalized with kidney stones after the Gold Cup, so he and his wife opted to pass on the Classic and gear up their horse for the next season.

"I wish Skip Away was racing," Bailey said. "Just for the mere fact I don't think it's fair to Cigar for anyone to have any doubt who was the best horse. I defy anyone to tell me Skip Away is a better horse. . . . The race I'm going to ride in the Breeders' Cup is going to be much easier than the last few. I feel I have to ride him to win rather than not to lose. I rode him to stay out of trouble, which is what you have to do when you are riding a horse that is so much superior. Maybe it's my turn to help him out. He's carried me around there 16 times without me doing much.

"There were extenuating circumstances at Del Mar that weren't Cigar's fault," Bailey added. "There was one jockey (Corey Nakatani) in there who felt his job was to get the favorite beat even though it sacrificed any chance his horse had. But I can replay the second race and say if I would have ridden a little different, I could have won. I'll be honest, had Del Mar not happened, maybe I wouldn't have raced like that. I was a little more reluctant to have him get caught in a hot pace. To me this is very important that he wins this. I want the public to remember him for what I know he really is—a great horse."

Cigar drew post seven for the Classic and was set as the 4-5 morning-line favorite.

"Cigar has been going in his races at odds much lower than 4-5, but I think there's a general consensus that he's a vulnerable horse right now because he's lost two of his last three races," oddsmaker Jim Bannon said. "You want to make sure he is odds-on, which is below even money. I thought 3-5 would be a little bit too low at this stage."

Even with Skip Away out of the picture, Cigar faced 12 others, whose owners clearly had no fear of the horse. His reputation diminished by defeat, Cigar still came to Canada as if his winning streak had remained intact. The Ontario Jockey Club (now known as Woodbine Entertainment Group) arranged for a Royal Canadian Mounted Police escort to lead the horse van carrying Cigar from the airport to his temporary lodging at Woodbine in Barn 14. He arrived three days before the race and the media descended upon him and his handlers.

"One of the biggest thrills I ever had in racing was when Cigar arrived," recalled John Whitson, Woodbine Entertainment Group's general manager of thoroughbred racing at the time. "I've never seen anything like it in my life. When his van arrived at the barn I've never seen so many people. It was like Elvis arriving or Frank Sinatra arriving at Madison Square Garden."

Two days before the race, Mott expressed optimism.

"We've been vulnerable before and you might say he's a little vulnerable here as well," Mott said. "As of right now, the foot is fine. All indications are he is in good health."

Cigar was taken to the Woodbine paddock to acclimatize him to the surroundings. He trained solidly the next day and appeared to come into the race ready.

The crowd still believed in him and bet him down to .65-1, or slightly more than 3-5. Atticus, one of two horses sent postward by trainer Richard Mandella, set the pace for the first three-quarters of a mile in a brisk 1:10 4/5. Bailey had Cigar in sixth, about 3½ lengths in arrears. Bailey began to make a five-wide move, inching to within a length of Canadian contender Mt. Sassafras, a 101-1 shot who had taken the lead with a quarter mile to the wire. California invader Alphabet Soup, who had won his last race but was disqualified and placed in third, grabbed the lead late in the stretch, while New York invader Louis Quatorze made a bid on the inside. Cigar, the old warhorse, raced almost in a line with the other two in a fantastic finish. In the end, Alphabet Soup prevailed by a nose over Louis Quatorze, a head in front of Cigar.

"He went down, but he went down battling," Mott said. "He kept fighting and I think people respect him for that. If you want to be a realist, you know that it just can't go on. He's just flesh and blood and he's wearing down. When he was at his very, very, very, best, he would shoot by and open up. Probably he shows the evidence of four years of hard racing and a lot of travel."

Jerry Bailey had arguably made a wrong move by going wide, although he claimed he couldn't go inside.

"I wanted to stay on the inside, but there were so many horses there, so yes, I was wide," Bailey said. "But I still thought I had a good chance coming from home."

There had been talk of a $10 million match race against Prix de l'Arc de Triomphe winner Helissio in Japan, but in the end Cigar was retired.

"It looks like he's backed up to where he's an equal with the rest of the division," Mott said. "Before, he was well beyond the rest of the division."

Six days after he ran in the Breeders' Cup, Cigar was officially retired, but he was given a couple of sendoffs. He was paraded at the National Horse Show inside Madison Square Garden in New York. On November 9 he stepped on a racetrack for the final time, galloping down the stretch at historic Churchill Downs— ironically, one of the few tracks where he had never run in his celebrated career— serenaded by a band and with Jerry Bailey aboard. Thousands of fans braved cold temperatures and flurries just to catch a glimpse of the great horse about to embark on a stud career. Allen Paulson sold a 75% interest in the stallion to Ireland's Coolmore Stud, a commercial breeding operation with divisions in the U.S., Ireland and Australia. Overall, the horse had been valued at $25 million. Plans called for Cigar to stand at Ashford Stud, Coolmore's American division situated next to Paulson's Brookside Farm in Versailles, for a breeding fee of $75,000 in his first season.

By March of the following year, when his stallion career had been underway, stories surfaced that Cigar might be infertile. The first nine mares he serviced failed to become pregnant and headline writers, who months before had had a field day with Cigar's name, referred to the celebrated stud as a dud.

"Cigar has only started to cover mares and this is not an unusual problem with a first-year stallion," Ashford Stud said in a press release.

But after failing to impregnate his first 34, it became apparent Cigar had indeed been sterile. A $25 million insurance policy, underwritten by Assicurazioni Generali, stipulated that Cigar had to get in foal at least 60 percent of the first 20 mares he covered. Under terms of the policy, Coolmore received $18.75 million of the settlement and Paulson $6.25 million. Assicurazioni Generali retained ownership of the horse, but publicity rights (i.e., use of the name for marketing and commercial purposes) stayed with Paulson.

"Cigar is the first horse we have dealt with where publicity rights are involved," a spokesperson for the firm said. "We want to make sure no one comes to us later and says they have the rights to market Cigar shirts or caps."

After paying out the settlement in May, Assicurazioni Generali announced plans to move Cigar from Ashford Stud and treat the horse with fertility drugs. Despite numerous attempts to make Cigar potent as a stallion, he simply could not impregnate a mare, so in May of 1999 the insurance company sent him to the Kentucky Horse Park with the proviso that if he ever became fertile he would be moved to a stallion operation.

"I was so looking forward to his babies," Madeleine Paulson said in reflection. "I think I took it harder than anybody, but then I sort of picked myself up and said, 'What are you worried about? How much can you expect from one animal?' He gave us—and the world—the greatest exhibition of horse racing. Perhaps it was too much to expect everything. I've always said, and I'll be quoted forever, that God gave us the greatest racehorse of all time. The one thing He said was, 'You may never recreate him.' And when we tried, He made sure we couldn't. That was the rule of that game. When you reflect back, you always reflect back on the positive and look at what he did. He was a phenomenal horse. He gave us all a good ride— the public, the racing world, everybody—so I'll always be grateful for that. He's got this wonderful group of people taking care of him and in particular one girl, Tammy Siters, and she writes to me. I had her come with me to Saratoga when Cigar was inducted into the Hall of Fame and presented her to everybody so they could see what wonderful care he was going to get for the rest of his life. This is a woman who adores him.

"I make him birthday cakes and fuss all over him and he's totally, utterly spoiled. Every time he thinks there's a filly coming by, he would probably like to mount her, but those days are over."

# · 19 ·

# The Blunder Horse

## Ricks Natural Star

$\mathcal{H}$is name is Ricks Natural Star and he was anything but a star in his racing career, more like a natural disaster, but for one year and one day in particular he became as celebrated as the great Cigar. The difference was Cigar was the wonder horse, while Ricks Natural Star was the blunder horse—and how he came to be in the Breeders' Cup is the stuff of which legends are made, although not necessarily for the right reasons.

The late Dub Rice and his wife Carolyn, longtime breeders based in eastern New Mexico, bred their mare Malaysian Star to the sire Natural Native and the product of the two became a chestnut colt born in 1989. The Rices named the colt, who would eventually be gelded, Ricks Natural Star in honor of their son Ricky and nominated the horse to the Breeders' Cup. The Rices nominated all their horses to the Breeders' Cup program. Although the Rices never had one of their horses run in any of the championship races in their silks, it just made good business sense to nominate. The Breeders Cup Ltd. runs a series of stakes races throughout the year leading up to the championship day of racing, and there are financial rewards for breeders who have paid into the program by nominating their foals or stallions.

And, hey, you just never know when a horse can up and run a big race and suddenly find itself in the Breeders' Cup. It saves the owner supplementary payments—between 9 and 12 percent of the purse—if the horse is not nominated to the program. In the case of Ricks Natural Star he never would have been entered in the Breeders' Cup if he hadn't been nominated as a foal because of the exorbitant cost of supplementing—between $180,000 and $240,000.

Ricks Natural Star grew into a big, strapping horse, standing some 17 hands high from the withers (or shoulders) to the ground, the equivalent of a human standing slightly less than six feet tall. But who would have thought this lanky runner would ever make it to the Breeders' Cup? Certainly not the people who conditioned him early in his career, that's for sure.

The Rices sent the colt to O. Dwain Grissom, who trained for them at Turf Paradise in Arizona. It didn't take long for Grissom and his wife, Bobbie, who galloped the colt, to deduce Ricks Natural Star didn't have much talent or speed.

"He couldn't go," Bobbie Grissom recalled. "He was just slow. He probably got up to working a half a mile but he just didn't show too much."

"They were going to give him some time (at the farm), hoping he would change," Dwain recalled. "I said 'You can give him all the time you want, this horse isn't going to change.' He was slow. He had no talent. Mentally, the horse was okay, he'd give you a hundred percent, but a hundred percent wasn't much.'"

The Grissoms told the Rices they were wasting their money and recommended selling the colt. The Rices put him in a registered horse sale in New Mexico and he fetched some $1,200. And that was the end of that deal. Or so it seemed.

Ricks Natural Star did, indeed, make it to the races for his new owner. Gail Richardson, who operated an insecticide business called The Bug Man in Artesia, New Mexico, turned Ricks Natural Star over to trainer Ralph (Bino) Black Jr. The veteran trainer had won several stakes and handicaps in his career, although Ricks Natural Star wouldn't be among his elite runners. Ricks Natural Star debuted as a three-year-old, but didn't win his first career race until his seventh start, June 25, 1993, at Ruidoso Downs in New Mexico. It took eight more starts before Ricks Natural Star won again, this time on October 27 at Sunland Park in New Mexico, in a $5,000 claiming race limited to non-winners of two lifetime. Ricks Natural Star won by six lengths, but that became the last time he would be photographed in victory. Overall between 1992 and 1995, he ran 23 times, posting two wins, five seconds and two thirds and earnings of only $6,093.

When Gail Richardson died, his estate took over the horse, but there was a period when Ricks Natural Star was turned out without any plans to race him again. He was eventually sold for $1,000 to Robert Hnulik, who had known Richardson all his life growing up in Artesia. Hnulik, who had a quarter horse stallion to whom Richardson bred some of his mares, had a long history as a breeder and racehorse owner in the New Mexico circuit. Ricks Natural Star appealed to Hnulik because he was a big, strapping horse. Hnulik thought he could develop the horse into a hunter jumper and sell him for a profit, but first he had to condition the horse to make him appealing to a seller, so he put the horse on a feed and training program.

And it just so happened an interested purchaser lived next door.

Dr. William Livingston was a 67-year-old veterinarian who graduated from Colorado State University in 1959, practiced for a year in Mississippi, then moved to Artesia, New Mexico, and set up a practice on one acre of Hnulik's 40-acre property. Livingston had fancied Ricks Natural Star ever since deworming him as a two-year-old. Livingston had been friends with Gail Richardson and wanted to go partners with his estate on ownership of the horse, whom he would treat for free.

Livingston now had a chance to buy the horse outright and made Hnulik an unusual offer to purchase Ricks Natural Star. He put a letter in his neighbor's mailbox essentially saying he would give Hnulik $100,000 from 10% of the horse's earnings until the horse was completely paid off or retired. In the absence of that, Livingston offered $3,000 straight up.

"I kind of took it as a joke," Hnulik recalled. "I went by and told him, 'Doc,

I'm going to let you screw me out of $97,000. Just give me the cash.' I thought I'd have to train the horse for a year before I sold him. He'd have brought that much ($3,000) or more if he turned out, but you never know. There's a lot of ifs. But I get a chance to get that much cash, I didn't mind selling him."

And Hnulik did just that, taking Livingston's $3,000. Hnulik had only had the horse for some six months and had made a tidy profit. Livingston, meanwhile, had himself a racehorse.

Livingston had gone into racehorse ownership before, hoping to make some money, although he'd had nothing but bad luck, or so he claimed. The first horse died of a twisted intestine. A second one, which he raised and had under the care of a trainer, died after running onto a highway and getting killed by a pickup truck. A third horse broke its neck.

Livingston treated Ricks Natural Star twice within a month for navicular disease using a vaccine he developed in 1970. Navicular disease causes lameness in the front feet, producing a short, choppy stride, and can become chronic, effectively forcing a horse to retire. In the December 1981 issue of *The Quarter Horse Journal*, Livingston was featured in an article headlined "Navicular: A Cure." He claimed to have treated 100 horses within a 14-month period and to have had an 87% success rate. He had hoped to make his vaccine available on a commercial basis, but failed to receive federal approval. The authorities rejected his research because it had not been evaluated by an independent veterinarian, although Livingston had horsemen who swore by his results then and still do.

In fact, one of the best examples of his work is a onetime rodeo horse called Pixie Scoot, owned and ridden by acclaimed horsewoman Lari Dee Guy. The Abilene, Texas, resident won numerous championships with the mare, purchased for a mere $67, in the American Junior Rodeo Association between 1979 and 1988. However, in 1985, the horse showed signs of navicular disease, and Guy thought she'd have to retire her champion. By word of mouth, Guy's father, Larry, heard of Livingston and arranged to have the horse treated. The horse responded to the treatments and was able to compete for another few years, ultimately having to retire because of her age.

Livingston noticed immediate improvement in the stride of Ricks Natural Star after two vaccinations in a month's time. He started training the horse, albeit in an unconventional way, on the five-eighths of a mile oval on Hnulik's property. While driving his pickup truck with one hand, Livingston had a hold of the lead shank attached to the horse. Hnulik had seen Livingston's training method and didn't consider it all that unusual. In fact, he said he has done that himself on occasion with horses, albeit limiting the speed so that the horse is galloping slowly beside the truck. And, if you talk to enough horsemen you'll probably hear about training variations similar to what Livingston did, although probably not to the extreme which he claimed. He said he drove three times around the oval at about 30 miles per hour, and then made a clucking sound to encourage the horse to go faster and gauge his stamina. Livingston said the horse picked up his speed significantly and started running at about 45 miles per hour, about 10–15 miles per hour faster than thoroughbred horses running full out. In Hnulik's opinion, it is highly doubtful the horse had been travelling as quickly as Livingston claimed, but that's when Livingston started to dream about running his horse in a race.

He began training the horse harder—or so he claimed—for about two months afterward, logging 12 miles overall in two sessions a day, using a lunge line. He thought the horse had the ability to run a distance of a mile and a half and wanted to run him in an allowance race—the competitive division in between the meat-and-potatoes claiming level and the high-end stakes set—but the horse didn't meet the qualifying standards. However, because Ricks Natural Star had been nominated to the Breeders' Cup, which was indicated on his registration papers, Livingston decided to take a shot in the ultimate competition. If the horse ran well, Livingston could make a case for his navicular vaccine and also collect some purse money.

Livingston set his sights on the $2 Million Turf, a mile and a half race on the grass, even though the horse had never run on that surface in any of his previous lifetime starts. The horse hadn't raced in 14 months, had last run in a $3,500 claiming race for non-winners of three lifetime and hadn't won in three years. Tackling seasoned horses, many of whom had been running against the best in the world in their division, Ricks Natural Star appeared unqualified and insufficiently conditioned to meet the challenge.

Livingston told Hnulik about his plan and his neighbor couldn't believe it. In his opinion, the horse "couldn't run to pay his own way" in races restricted to New Mexico–breds. Now Livingston was talking about going to the Olympics of horse racing off a lengthy layoff.

"I thought nobody but Doc would do it," Hnulik said. "Doc is a little eccentric. It was kind of a once-in-a-lifetime shot."

It would cost Livingston $20,000 to pre-enter the horse and a further $20,000 to enter. He didn't have the second amount, so he went to a bank and secured a personal loan using his practice as collateral.

Livingston applied for and received a trainer's license granted by the New Mexico Racing Commission. Though details are somewhat sketchy, at some point the Racing Commission called up the Breeders' Cup Ltd. seeking to know if a license in New Mexico would be honored in Canada. For the first time in the history of the event, the Breeders' Cup would be conducted outside of the U.S. When the Breeders' Cup Ltd. first had a hint Livingston might pre-enter his horse, a search was done of its last five races, a background-checking process that is common for all starters, particularly useful for those with unfamiliar backgrounds. When the Breeders' Cup Ltd. did its research it basically dismissed the horse as a possible pre-entry for the Turf. Certainly, it never expected to see an owner put up a total of $40,000 to run a horse that appeared hopelessly unqualified.

When, in fact, Livingston arranged to pre-enter the horse, Pam Blatz-Murff, the Breeders' Cup Ltd. senior vice-president of operations, helped him to coordinate the process. On October 14, well before the noon deadline closed to pre-enter horses for the 1996 Breeders' Cup, Livingston FedExed his $20,000 payment. Sixteen horses were pre-entered, two more than the maximum number that could start, and the Breeders' Cup Ltd. indicated to Livingston his horse ranked last in the order of preference. The field-selection system is based on a point system from top-three results in American graded stakes races combined with the judgment of a panel of racing experts. The first seven horses are ranked solely on the graded stakes criteria; the remaining pre-entered horses are ranked by the panel using its own criteria. Essentially, the latter selection process is designed to include horses that have run outside of North America.

There was virtually nothing within the rules of the Breeders' Cup to automatically prevent Livingston from pre-entering his horse, but if the two horses ranked ahead didn't drop out Ricks Natural Star could not enter into the body of the race. The Breeders' Cup Ltd. also told him he needed to qualify the horse in at least one workout according to acceptable standards of the host track, in this case Woodbine, which was supervised under the aegis of the Ontario Racing Commission. In every racing jurisdiction there are house rules and racing commission rules to protect the betting public and ensure the safety of the horses. In this case, because Ricks Natural Star had been absent from the races for so long and hadn't had a published timed workout at a racetrack or training center, there was little information for the public to gauge his fitness.

In addition, the horse had to pass strict fitness and soundness inspections by veterinarians assigned by the host track and the Breeders' Cup Ltd., a process instituted a few years before. On October 16, 10 days before the races were run, the Breeders' Cup Ltd. announced the pre-entries. Ricks Natural Star received scant media attention, but that was about to change in the days, weeks and even months to follow.

With no guarantee his horse would enter into the race, Livingston headed off to Woodbine—some 2,400 miles away—taking a long—and bizarre—journey. While most horsemen facing a similar distance would have flown their horse via an equine air carrier, Livingston did not have the money to cover the expense. The cost of pre-entering had practically tapped him out.

So, Livingston decided to van his horse. After loaning a trailer from Hnulik, Livingston commenced his journey, accompanied by Javier Chavez, who had worked with the veterinarian, and blacksmith Gene Pitzer, who lived about 15 miles north of Artesia in Lake Arthur. Collectively this was like the Beverly Hillbillies loading up the truck and going off to Beverly. Pitzer and Chavez drove Livingston's pickup truck hitched up to the horse van, while Livingston drove a van because he had to make a separate stop during the journey to vaccinate a couple of horses in Kansas for navicular disease. After driving some 500 miles, the trio stopped off at Remington Park in Oklahoma to work the horse the next day three-quarters of a mile, half the distance of a mile and a half race.

The appearance of the horse created a buzz at the modest track, which rarely has one of its own runners or a local connection in the Breeders' Cup. Jockey Sally Williams, who had ridden for about four years at that point, happened to be standing in the receiving barn with her helmet on and Livingston asked her if she wouldn't mind working his horse. He didn't have any tack, which is unusual to say the least for a horseman heading off to a race, let alone something as prestigious as the Breeders' Cup, so Williams borrowed some equipment from a trainer. Williams thought the horse resembled somebody's pony because of his thick coat of hair that lacked color and sheen. Livingston told Williams he'd been training the horse next to his truck, which Williams didn't consider abnormal at all. She'd ridden many horses that had been exercised that way.

The horse acted kind and gentle on the track as Williams prepared to put him to work. It became apparent to Williams a quarter of a mile into the timed exercise that the horse lacked speed, so she cracked him with the whip after another eighth of a mile, but Ricks Natural Star failed to accelerate. She hit him a few more times—including switching the stick to the opposite hand and whipping at different points of contact to rouse the horse—but it didn't matter. Ricks Natural Star didn't react, galloping along at the same pedestrian clip.

He was clocked in a turtle-like time of 1:21 2/5 seconds, the slowest of four times at that distance on the day at Remington, and almost too slow to be recorded as an official workout. Michelle Gass, who had been a clocker for some two years at the time, timed the workout.

"It's so hard to forget, it was so sad," she recalled.

Dale Day, the track's director of marketing/publicity, conducted an interview with Livingston to air in-house, while members of the media who happened upon the scene had separate chats with him.

"No one could believe what was going on anyway," Day said. "Everybody realized this horse didn't belong. The guy said he was chasing a dream and that's fine, but everybody knew realistically that nothing great would come from that as far as the horse was concerned."

Williams was quoted as saying the horse was "big and fuzzy and not ready" and claims she tried to convey that to Livingston.

"I tried to tell him in a really nice way (the horse) was slow, but he wasn't in that mind frame to hear that," Williams said.

Livingston chalked up the slow work to the horse feeling fatigued from the long van ride.

Williams said Livingston did not have help available to cool out the horse after the work and she had to do it herself.

Williams figured the horse had been three or four works away from running in a race—a cheap claiming race.

Livingston asked Williams if she wanted to ride the horse in the race, but he couldn't pay for her expenses, an obligation that is part and parcel of flying in a jockey. With a full slate of rides at Remington Park on Breeders' Cup day, coupled with the cost of air fare, hotel accommodation and any sundry expenses, Williams simply couldn't afford to make the trip—particularly when she knew Ricks Natural Star had no shot. And yet, she'd have done it if Livingston had paid her way.

"I'd have done it," she said. "I'd have run and I didn't care just because I wanted to see (superstar horse) Cigar and it would have been something I remembered for the rest of my life."

Williams' remarks about the horse, published in an article in the *Daily Racing Form*, alarmed the Ontario Racing Commission stewards, who were concerned about the horse's soundness and fitness, and they contacted her.

The Breeders' Cup Ltd. management, many stationed at Woodbine in temporary headquarters, watched from afar. Pam Blatz-Murff said the Breeders' Cup Ltd. tried to help Livingston, advising him to reconsider his plan because of the toll on the horse.

"I should have done that, but I didn't," Livingston said. "When the horse got up to 45 miles per hour, that's what got me in trouble. I just got excited about a horse that could run that fast and I got carried away. It just progressed and I stayed with it and I shouldn't have. I should have done something else with the horse. It just snowballed on me."

After the workout, the trio left, accompanied by a fourth person—an individual known only as Fuzzy whom Livingston recruited for driving purposes. Livingston stopped off in Kansas, while Pitzer and Chavez carried on with the horse. The parties later hooked up in Missouri.

By this point, the epic journey of Ricks Natural Star had started to pick up national attention—and outrage. One fan e-mailed the United States Humane Society expressing concern about perceived exploitation of Ricks Natural Star by Livingston, the safety of all the other entrants in the race and the inability of Breeders' Cup officials to automatically withdraw the horse for fear of a lawsuit.

"This is a serious matter and presents an historic opportunity for the racing industry and the Humane Society to work together toward a common goal," the e-mailer, who did not include a name, wrote.

The e-mailer also sent a message to the Breeders' Cup.

"One of the reasons I love thoroughbred racing is that horses and humans share the same goals in racing," the e-mail began. "Horses naturally thrill to the race and delight in their own speed and in the shoulder-to-shoulder effort to reach a specific spot first. But in the case of Ricks Natural Star, I believe that running him could be very detrimental to the horse. This is a horse who has not run in over a year, who had three years off before his three 1995 efforts, who has not fared well against very low-level claimers, etc., etc. To exploit him by running him so far over his head is an overtly egotistical move . . . and cannot be anything but detrimental to the horse.

"One would have thought that rules to prevent a failed $3,500 claimer from being tested in the Breeders' Cup would not have been necessary; however, this event proves that rules are necessary even for the most unlikely situation. I am sure that appropriate revisions will be made in your policies for future years. All the foregoing assumes that Ricks Natural Star and the others reach the finish line safely. A horse who is so mismatched with the competition adds a dangerous element to an already dangerous sport.

"I have heard that your appeals to the connections of Ricks Natural Star to withdraw have not been successful. Therefore, I appeal to you to establish an important precedent by disqualifying him by executive order on humane grounds."

Pam Blatz-Murff responded to the e-mail.

"First a point to make. Although we strongly discouraged Mr. Livingston from pre-entering the horse because of the danger to himself and to others, we are unable to deny the horse entry because we want to. The stewards of the racing jurisdiction that is hosting the event is the final authority. The stewards of the

Ontario Jockey Club have declined to take a stand, (so) we have asked for them to establish the following: The horse must be inspected prior to a workout on the grounds. We would like for him to work a mile on the turf. He has to have a gate card. We have established an international veterinary inspection team that has to inspect every horse on the grounds. They have a physical inspection and have to observe the horse moving. We would like blood drawn after his work. Now provided he has passed all the above, we cannot deny him entry. We have no non-competitive rule on the books nor does the OJC. It simply has never come up before."

The journey literally came to a halt when Livingston lacked the necessary horse documentation to cross into Canada. Because of an outbreak in the U.S. southwest of vesicular stomatitis—an equine disease that resembles foot-and-mouth disease in cattle—border officials had concerns about the horse's health and could not allow Livingston and Ricks Natural Star entry into Canada. He took up temporary residence at a motel in Detroit and lodged his horse outside, setting up a temporary corral with ropes. He worked towards straightening out the horse's health papers, along with the help of the Breeders' Cup Ltd., which was trying to facilitate the process.

In an article in *The Blood-Horse*, Breeders' Cup president Ted Bassett addressed the delicate situation of Ricks Natural Star.

"I don't want to chastise this fellow (Livingston) like he's some sort of nefarious character because he hasn't done anything wrong," Bassett said. "But we have to be concerned about (the horse) being competitive and about the safety of the rest of the field. This is just a very strange set of circumstances and we will be going to great lengths to determine the horse's fitness and soundness."

Livingston finally arrived on late Monday night, six days before the races and two days before the final entries. By this time, two other pre-entered horses had been withdrawn, so the horse had a chance to run, pending inspection from veterinarians and passing a qualifying test from the gate on the main track and a separate qualifying test on the grass.

Livingston didn't bring any practical equipment with him—even rudimentary things such as a water bucket, feed tub, saddle or brush—only a five-gallon bucket and a ratty old halter. He was like a rank-amateur golfer going into the Masters without a bag and only a club or two. Mike Keogh, a trainer situated at the opposite end of the barn where Ricks Natural Star had been stabled, and others provided the visiting horseman with some temporary equipment. It's not uncommon for one horseman to help out another, particularly one arriving on a temporary basis from another track, but it's quite another thing to arrive with next to no equipment.

Early the following morning, journeyman jockey/journalist Tom Wolski visited Livingston. Born in the U.S., but residing in Vancouver, British Columbia, Canada, Wolski writes a horse racing column for the *Vancouver Province* and hosts a cable television show on horse racing. He also co-hosts International Racing Tours, which annually takes a group of horse racing fans to the Breeders' Cup. Every year, Wolski looks for an underdog story in the Cup to write about in his column. When he heard about Ricks Natural Star, he pegged that as the horse he would follow. When Wolski first arrived at Livingston's barn well before the majority of the media, the owner/trainer had been looking for someone to gallop his horse, claiming his exercise rider hadn't shown up for the assignment. Livingston sized up Wolski, figured he was a jockey and asked him if he wanted to gallop the horse, but Wolski declined. Livingston took it one step further and asked him if he wanted to ride the horse in the race.

"He didn't know me from a hole in the wall and he wanted to ride me," Wolski recalled. "The last thing I wanted to do was ride a horse a mile and a half that was going to be gasping for air and the (television) cameras were going to be focusing on him. I would have been in shape. I was fit to ride, but I just didn't want to do it. It was a case of where I didn't want to embarrass myself. . . . I said to myself, 'Imagine turning down a Breeders' Cup mount.' How many jocks that aren't a star rider turn down a horse in the Breeders' Cup? Good riders can do that, but the average jockey isn't going to get to ride in the Breeders' Cup. You dream about that and the Kentucky Derby, but under those circumstances I didn't think that was my turn to make my debut. I thought I'd be a laughingstock. I didn't want to be the butt of the jokes."

He did, however, ask Livingston if he could sit on the horse while doing an interview.

"Here I'm a jockey and I'm on a Breeders' Cup horse and I'm doing a column," Wolski recalled. "In my own thinking, this is kind of cool, especially when the guy said the horse is kind—and he was."

When the media came by, Livingston regaled them with his life story, his inventions and his dream of running a horse in the Breeders' Cup. Livingston added to the sideshow when he allowed a broadcast journalist to sit on his horse, whom he claimed was kind and gentle. In retrospect, he claimed it was only "a joke thing," something he never intended to be publicized. Standing off to the side witnessing the whole spectacle was local jockey Lisa McFarland.

McFarland, who had been riding for two years but had still been classified as an apprentice because she hadn't won 45 career races, hung around for close to an hour, watching the media and Livingston interact. Then she approached him, offering to gallop the horse. When McFarland's boyfriend (and future husband) Tommy Schell first read about Livingston's plans to run Ricks Natural Star, he told McFarland that would be her Breeders' Cup mount. He figured no one would want to ride the horse, so she figured galloping the horse might give her a shot to ride Ricks Natural Star in the race. Livingston accepted McFarland's offer to gallop the horse and they arranged a time for the following morning. She asked him if he had any tack, not even sure if he knew what that meant, and said she'd bring along a saddle.

Later that night, Livingston returned to the hotel near the track where he had been staying. He came into the bar where a group of horsemen were sitting around having a few beers and watching the local news, which happened to be broadcasting a story about Livingston. One of the horsemen, Tom Bowden, watched the item and thought it was a joke, possibly part of a movie. Then he spotted Livingston standing behind him and they engaged in a conversation. Livingston showed Bowden and the other horsemen photos of himself training the horse with his pickup truck. Bowden had heard of this method employed by harness horsemen but never with thoroughbreds. As he listened to Livingston, the open-minded Bowden considered him a "knowledgeable" man but "not off the wall."

What struck Bowden immediately was that Livingston had no money, and he wondered if Livingston's plan to run in the race had been nothing more than a gaffe by some people gambling to see if he could actually do it.

The following morning, Ricks Natural Star and Lisa McFarland made their way from the barn for their initial training exercise, but the journey stalled when Ricks Natural Star refused to go into the tunnel connecting the backstretch to the main track. That is not an unusual thing for a horse in a new surrounding. Bowden happened to be there on his pony and helped escort the horse and rider. Tommy Schell joined McFarland to look out for her safety. Livingston missed the morning exercise because the stewards wanted to talk to him about his horse's fitness and the help he had brought with him.

The horse reared up on the track and attempted to unseat McFarland, but Schell saved her from an unceremonious fall, keeping a taut hold on the lead shank and yanking it down.

"This sucker, he'd still be in the air right now if Tommy hadn't got me," McFarland recalled. "I'm thinking, 'Oh my God, what the hell have I gotten myself into?'"

McFarland guided Ricks Natural Star over to the starting gate, from which he needed to break cleanly to satisfy the starter, given that he hadn't raced in a long time. The horse broke from the gate, took about 10 steps and then stopped. Then he started running backwards, hit the rail and commenced running sideways. McFarland knew that kind of performance wouldn't satisfy the starter, so she returned to the gate for a second time. She lowered the stirrups to reduce the possibility of being thrown off, and thought to herself she resembled John Wayne sitting long and tall in the saddle. She broke from the gate a second time and let the horse run freely, and this time Ricks Natural Star ran without incident.

Later that morning the Breeders' Cup Ltd. conducted the ceremonial post-position draw and morning line. Jim Bannon, an experienced horseman and handicapper who did the morning line used on the Woodbine circuit, established the horse off at 99-1, the highest odds on the tote board and the highest odds ever for a Breeders' Cup horse.

"In the newspaper and the results charts in the *Racing Form*, you will see the actual odds, which no doubt will be 300 or 400 to one," he predicted.

Meanwhile, Ontario Racing Commission supervisor Ed Hall addressed a query by the media about Ricks Natural Star.

"This is a highly unusual incident," Hall said. "It is one of the strangest things to come to light."

The stewards could scratch a horse because of a concern for its safety, but Livingston had paid his money to run and provided enough evidence of the horse's physical soundness to allow Ricks Natural Star to run. Moreover, the stewards had concerns that if they scratched the horse it could result in a possible lawsuit.

On Wednesday night, McFarland had a mount on the Woodbine card, and when she entered the jockeys' room she found herself "totally ostracized" by the other riders because she had been named by Livingston to ride Ricks Natural Star.

"I wanted the mount. I definitely wanted to ride him," she said. "A lot of the riders got annoyed with me. They didn't think the horse should run. They were trying to gang up against the man and the horse."

The following morning, she took the horse out for his first exercise on the grass. The turf course, normally closed for training to preserve it for the races, had been opened for Breeders' Cup horses only. Although she can't remember who gave her the instruction, McFarland was told to work the horse three-eighths of a mile, but Ricks Natural Star ran off in pursuit of another horse well before he reached the designated point to start the timed exercise. It basically amounted to the equivalent of a three-quarters of a mile workout, although the clockers never recorded it and few people really knew about it.

McFarland discovered something amazing in that exercise: the horse's stride improved significantly, reaching out in a dramatically different way than on the dirt. McFarland began to think that, maybe, Ricks Natural Star might have a chance. What if, she wondered, Ricks Natural Star could pull off the unthinkable, albeit stepping up into a stratospheric class level?

It is not uncommon for horses to respond differently to a different surface. Cigar reached his superstar status when moved from grass races as an older horse to strictly dirt races, although he had inherent class far superior to Ricks Natural Star and significantly better training to help him achieve his talent level.

McFarland recalled a horse called Beau Fasa who had run a few years back at Woodbine and had graduated from a cheap claimer on the dirt into a multiple stakes winner on the grass.

Livingston had missed the exercise while in conference with the stewards. Later that morning, McFarland was called in by the stewards after Livingston had told them he wanted to switch riders because he believed she wouldn't do a good job. McFarland said a rumor had circulated that she didn't want to ride the horse, talk she claims had been circulated by two riders based at Fort Erie, the province's B-circuit track located about 90 miles south of Woodbine and where she rode primarily. McFarland said the riders, whom she would not name, started the talk because they wanted to ride the horse. McFarland squelched the rumors and the stewards backed her. They told Livingston they would not allow a rider change because they felt McFarland was familiar with the horse and was capable of handling her riding assignment.

McFarland said the only Woodbine-based rider who gave her any credit before the race and was genuinely happy to see her receive a chance was Sandy Hawley, the legendary Canadian who was aboard local hopeful Chief Bearhart in the Turf.

Opinions in the media on the relative merits of the horse and his chances varied significantly. Some people were happy to see the horse receive a chance, but many were disgusted and angered.

In an article picked up by the *New York Times*, writer Bill Gallo approached the Ricks Natural Star story lightheartedly.

"Think Ross Perot is a long shot to win the White House a week from Tuesday? How about the Green Party candidate for president? Or the Libertarian? How about Mrs. Grundy of the Civic Purity League?

"How is it that a rude peasant in tatters has gained entry to the palace? How has the ultimate scruffy underdog pushed his way into the turf club, where the rich folk are spooning up Beluga and sipping Dom Perignon?

"The answer is Dr. Livingston, I presume."

Gallo attempted to contact Livingston, who was in transit with his horse from Oklahoma at the time, but talked to the veterinarian's receptionist, Johnnie Coor, who gave a background of her boss.

"He's a very smart man with good ideas, but sometimes people laugh," she was quoted as saying. "He can go off on a tangent and get very excited about it. He's very excited about that horse right now. He can barely sit down and talk."

Gallo wondered if Dr. Livingston would be the kind of man who "enjoys tweaking the bulb-nose of authority? In the form, say, of certain Breeders' Cup pooh-bahs decked out in silk suits and $85 neckties? . . . While we wait, trust the powers that be in the Sport of Kings to ignore a good story when they don't see one and to grind a dream, regardless of origin or motive, under the heels of their handmade shoes. They don't want a cheap claiming horse from New Mexico that hasn't won in three years in the Breeders' Cup Turf—not our crowd, darling—but they should want it with all their hearts. This sport's in trouble, folks. It needs underdogs and dreamers and those who would burst the bubble of its pretension.

"Certainly, racing needs a bracing slap of reality aside from the ones already administered by casino gambling, state lotteries and the rise of beach volleyball.

"Whether or not Dr. Livingston and Ricks Natural Star, a pair of worthies running gallantly uphill, will actually reach the starting gate at the Breeders' Cup is a matter of some conjecture and a lot of luck. But, as Hemingway once asked, isn't it pretty to think so? If the age of miracles has not passed and they do get to race, here's hoping both of them have first."

In a column headlined "Unqualified Nag Not Funny, Just Disgrace," the late *Toronto Star* writer Jim Proudfoot, one of the deans of journalism in Canada and a national newspaper award winner for a series he once did on horse racing, took Livingston to task.

"Everyone roots for the underdog, the little guy who deflates the stuffed shirts. So naturally Toronto is madly in love with William Livingston . . . but you need to know this is outrageous nonsense and by no means a heartwarming adventure. Also, it's insulting to the genuine underdogs who abound on the backstretch of any track.

"Some people find this situation funny and yes it would be hilarious if somebody like Sheikh Mohammed bin Rashid al Maktoum lost to a beetle like this. But this could only happen if Livingston had developed a horse truly capable of an upset. Then his cheek would be admirable. He deserves no applause for degrading something excellent, especially for the motives he has mentioned. Would you clap if somebody wandered onstage during a Toronto Symphony concert and started playing a kazoo?

"Ricks Natural Star will be a hazard to himself, obviously, and he'll imperil the others at the very outset and shortly afterward, when opponents begin zooming by him. This is no laughing matter. It's a disgrace, really. The only good news is Breeders' Cup authorities will belatedly invoke minimum standards to make sure there'll be no encore."

Veteran trainer D. Wayne Lukas, who would be saddling Michael Tabor's Grade One winner Marlin in the race, was quoted as saying the Ricks Natural Star story would last all of 30 yards. Bill Mott, the trainer of Cigar, said people would be cheering at the start for the horse and cheering at the end, suggesting he would finish last. The *Daily Racing Form* prognisticator, who evaluated the horses in every race and offered comments, said: "Every principle of handicapping said this seven-year-old is hideously overmatched here."

On race day, McFarland walked around the track with her mother after they had secured all-access passes. She reported to the clerk of scales in the jockeys room at the prescribed deadline, two hours before her race. Then she went to the trailer next door reserved for female riders and watched the races on the television.

"There was absolutely no pressure on me," she said. "I had nothing to prove. It was a real highlight for me. Everyone expected the horse to finish last, so who was I going to let down? It wasn't like I was riding the favorite."

NBC, which televised the races, provided detailed coverage of Ricks Natural Star leading up to the race. And, in many ways, it became apparent that the network and its horse racing correspondents would not treat this story lightly. It showed footage of the journalist struggling to climb aboard the horse earlier in the week and aired a pre-taped interview conducted by race announcer Tom Durkin:

"I think it's the best thing that can happen to the Breeders' Cup . . . to take a chance and realize a dream (is) what racing's all about," Livingston said.

In a voice-over, Durkin said some journalists had put Ricks Natural Star among the lovable losers in sports, notably Eddie (The Eagle) Edwards, the laughable British ski jumper who flopped in the 1988 Winter Olympics, and the Jamaican Bobsled Team.

"If we get out front and widen our lead, he's going to win," Livingston said.

Livingston noted his unusual training method with the pickup track.

"Don't you think that's dangerous (training) for the horse?" Durkin asked.

"He's not going to kick anybody (in the race)," Livingston said. "He's going to race. (The jockey Lisa McFarland) is not going to hold him back like I was. She's going to let him run."

"But the training itself, isn't that dangerous?" Durkin asked.

"Yeah, it's dangerous, but we survived," Livingston said.

"This is a horse that has had only one workout in three years," Durkin said. "This defies everything that has ever been done in preparing horses for thoroughbred racing, probably since the breed was founded in 1765."

"Well, it's a little unusual," Livingston said. "I would like to have done it a little different, but that's the way it worked out. That's the only thing I can do."

Just after the horse was led from his stall to make the long walk over to the paddock, trainer Tom Bowden, who did his best to help Livingston, ordered the handlers of the horse to give it a sound brushing due to its unkempt appearance. He also assigned one of his grooms, Jackie Whalen, to lead the horse over to the paddock, while another local horseman, Ian Ross, helped. Bowden said the three people who had accompanied Livingston were "like the three stooges. One of them was on a drunk somewhere."

Once the horse arrived there, two valets were assigned by the Ontario Racing Commission to put the saddle on Ricks Natural Star. Livingston had never saddled a horse for a race, and he stood idly by dressed in a suit and a garishly colored baseball cap, smiling proudly. In some ways, he looked as if he had crashed the Breeders' Cup ball.

The early wagering had Ricks Natural Star at 29-1. Situated in his perch high above the track, Durkin suggested the people at Woodbine "love an underdog. I suppose they like a Don Quixote tilting at windmills. There's been a lot of resentment from the people working with horses at Woodbine, not about the vast publicity that the horse has gotten this week but because Dr. Livingston violated the first rule of a good horseman. He put his own self-interests ahead of the well-being and health of this animal. And that's why there's been this resentment. It's not something a good horseman would do and entering a preposterous horse like this in this race is not something even Don Quixote would do."

Host Tom Hammond said at 29-1, there are some "incurable romantics" at Woodbine.

"Believe me, folks, this horse has no chance, no chance of winning. It would be like me racing Michael Johnson and Donovan Bailey. It won't happen. This whole thing would be hilarious if there weren't that element of danger."

Analyst John Veitch noted the great element of danger because the horse would be stressed greatly in the race.

"He's really not been conditioned for this . . . almost anything can happen," Veitch said. "We're not talking just about one horse or one jockey and that in itself is enough to be concerned about and in some situations enough to put a stop to, but we're talking about every horse in this field. When they open that gate this horse could do anything. He could go right, he could go left, knocking the horses down on either side of him. He could prop (up) and wheel and possibly run off the wrong way if he could get through the gate. There are (infinite) things that can happen in this race and there is enough reason for danger and enough chance for grievous injury with horses that are fully conditioned. I think Tom really put his finger on it: Here's a person who put their personal agenda over the well-being of a very noble beast."

"We'll hope for the best," Hammond said. "Let's hope it goes on without incident."

With 10 minutes to post time, Ricks Natural Star had odds of 36-1. Hammond said he thought the horse would be 200-1, although it would only be reflected as 99-1 on the tote board.

NBC analyst Gregg McCarron, who followed the horses to the track on his horse, noted Ricks Natural Star caused a commotion en route from the saddling enclosure, alternately freezing, lunging away from his handler and almost pitching off McFarland.

"The horse went ballistic in the tunnel," McFarland said in recollection. "He started running backwards. He hit the wall with his rear end and lunged forward. He was traumatized. He was scared. He didn't know where he was. He wasn't paying attention to me. The pony guy grabbed him, the tongue tie comes off (the horse) and all this in the course of a minute."

Behind her some of the other riders were asking her to have the horse scratched, but she carried on with her assignment.

Once Ricks Natural Star reached the track accompanied by a pony escort— something that is almost standard in North American racing and designed to help the racehorse relax in the period leading up to the race—they separated quickly from the rest of the field, avoiding the traditional post-parade introduction. Away from the crowd, Ricks Natural Star settled down.

"Let's just hope he finishes before the Classic," Hammond said on the broadcast.

"I really thought they were going to announce that Ricks Natural Star was going to be scratched," NBC handicapper Mike Battaglia said. "I honestly believe Gregg McCarron and his lead pony would have a better chance than Ricks Natural Star in this race."

Fellow handicapper Bob Neumeier said $30,000 had been bet on the horse, enough money to put a kid through an Ivy League college.

"Tom said the people are romantics, I say they're suckers. I just hope this horse doesn't influence this race. It would be a disgrace and an embarrassment to the Breeders' Cup if he does."

The gate crew attempted to load the horse first to avoid problems with the other runners, but Ricks Natural Star balked, so other horses were then loaded. Some members of the gate crew were able to push the horse into his starting stall, which elicited a tremendous roar from the crowd.

"He didn't want to walk in, but that's kind of common (in horse racing)," McFarland said. "He was fine (once in the gate) and he stood there perfectly. There were 10 more horses (to be loaded) and he was fine. That was encouraging."

At that point he was 50-1.

"I think people wanted a souvenir and they were hoping for a dream result," said Tommy Wolski, the jockey who turned down the mount. "That was the Cinderella horse."

Watching from Arizona, Dwain Grissom, the horse's original trainer, knew Ricks Natural Star had no shot, not even with a "trainload of angels." He was more concerned about the horse causing an accident.

The Rices were in Las Vegas vacationing and watching and betting on the Breeders' Cup races, but had no intention of betting on Ricks Natural Star.

"For him to be there (in the race) was a fiasco," Carolyn Rice said. "We were embarrassed for our little horse, how (Livingston) treated and trained him."

Ricks Natural Star went postward at more than 56-1 odds—high by most standards but extremely low in this case given the horse's history. Almost $61,000 had been wagered on him.

McFarland said Livingston did not give her any pre-race instructions, so she had to rely on her own judgment and instincts.

"He never told me to go to the lead or take the horse back," she said. "I frankly thought he didn't know anything about horse racing."

McFarland had concerns what would happen in the first 10 steps out of the gate, recalling the initial incident when she first rode the horse. It turned out to be a needless worry. Ricks Natural Star broke straight and true and didn't act up after the first 10 steps. At that point, McFarland had reason to be optimistic. She tracked pacesetter Diplomatic Jet on his outside flank through the opening quarter of a mile. Ricks Natural Star briefly overtook Diplomatic Jet after about another eighth of a mile as the crowd roared wildly, but by the opening half mile the hapless horse started losing track with the leaders and moved to the outside, away from the other runners. At least that's the way it appeared to most people. In Livingston's opinion, McFarland had "pulled" the horse, deliberately holding him back. He began fading badly, some 15 lengths behind leader Diplomatic Jet after three-quarters of a mile. McFarland wondered whether the horse would finish the race or become mentally unhinged in front of the raucous crowd and make a sudden turn left or right.

Ricks Natural Star did not do anything untoward, however, galloping along at a slow pace and crossing the line some 30 seconds after the rest of the field while the crowd roared deliriously. Officially, the *Daily Racing Form* listed him as distanced—at least 25 lengths back of the second-to-last horse Marlin, who ran 21 lengths in arrears of the winner.

After McFarland dismounted and weighed out, Neumeier interviewed her.

"Most people in racing, myself included, thought this was a joke of the highest proportion," Neumeier said. "I'm wondering whether you thought this was a joke?"

"No, I figured if the man had enough money or enough credibility or enough confidence in this horse, he must think he's got a chance," McFarland said. "Nobody knew about his training methods, but he swore his horse is fit enough and he'd match with this type. I'm just here to ride races and if he needed a rider, I was open to ride the horse and give it my best shot."

"I think you had more responsibility on your shoulders than even you would know," Neumeier said. "A problem in the tunnel and then early on. A pretty good break and then you were up there with the leaders and then the inevitable."

"Yes, but it's not a question of whether the horse has the speed to do it all the time, it's a matter of whether they're outclassed," McFarland said. "Even an $8,000 horse can be outclassed if it's got tons of speed going against horses for $50,000. It's just a question of whether the horse knew what company he was running with."

"Were you concerned about the horse finishing the race, the danger factor either to you, this horse or maybe even other riders or horses in this prestigious race?"

"No, I wasn't concerned because I've been on this horse and know his little antics and I get along fairly well with the horse," she said. "I warned the rider in the gate beside me, 'If he's going to come out, he's going to come out sideways to the right' but he didn't. The key was just to turn his head loose and let him run his race."

"It seemed that other riders were kind of eyeballing you as you went around the first turn," Neumeier said. "Were you aware that they were looking around, almost to suggest, Lisa, that there was a loose horse involved in this situation?"

"Well, I guess you could judge that by the crowd, too," McFarland said.

"All right, the odyssey is over," Neumeier said.

"I'm grateful to have had this opportunity," McFarland said. "I couldn't have imagined all the publicity I would have got, along with the horse. Of course, I have Doc Livingston to thank for the mount."

"I know a lot of people were thankful that there were no incidents. Good luck." Neumeier concluded.

It took McFarland half an hour to walk back to the jockeys' room because people kept stopping her and asking for an autograph, including Laurie Gulas, a locally based rider. Upon arriving in the jockeys' room and dumping her silks in the laundry basket, McFarland received a hero's welcome from the riders.

"The jockeys all told her she did a great job," recalled Tommy Wolski, who was present in the room. "It was as if she won a race."

In Wolski's opinion—and likely that of almost anybody who witnessed the race—McFarland rode perfectly. In Wolski's opinion, the horse "ran off" with McFarland and then tired. He said in situations such as that, the worst place a jockey can be is on the rail taking up space.

"She was cool. She didn't bother anyone," Wolski said.

"After all that was said and done, I stayed away (from the field) and they went on without me," McFarland said. "I guess they figured I did a great job."

Livingston couldn't understand what had happened. He could accept the horse tiring after a mile, but not after only half a mile.

While the world laughed off the Ricks Natural Star fiasco, Ricks Natural Star returned to his stall and reportedly bled profusely from his nostrils, physically exhausted—and quite possibly mentally, too—from the strain of the race and his antics en route to the track after he was saddled. He had suffered exercise induced pulmonary hemorrhaging, not entirely uncommon in horse racing and usually caused by excess stress. Ricks Natural Star was not medicated with Lasix, a diuretic given to some horses to flush fluids out of their system before they race and help limit the pressure on their systems. Lasix is not a totally preventive measure and some horses bleed through it anyway. Ricks Natural Star had run on Lasix in his previous races, but had not been required to stay on it—as is the case in some jurisdictions—because he had been absent for some time and had shown no visible signs of bleeding.

Groom Jackie Whelan called Bowden's assistant, Pam Dunslow, and told her about the bleeding. Dunslow instructed Whelan to keep the horse's head up to try and limit the flow of blood. She subsequently called a veterinarian, who later arrived and began treating the horse to stop the bleeding and reduce inflammation. The veterinarian was aghast that neither Livingston nor anyone associated with the horse attended to it after the race. Livingston said any suggestion that the horse bled is a "crock of shit" and that he had come back to the barn 10 minutes after the race.

"I got to the stall before the horse did," he said. "That's more of what (the conspirators) put out."

Amid concerns that Livingston might attempt legal action alleging Ricks Natural Star was deliberately held back in the race, McFarland was called in by the stewards and asked if anyone told her to "stiff" the horse. She insisted she didn't do any such thing.

McFarland claims when the horse switched to his right lead leg in the run up the backstretch, he moved out at least two paths and all she did was to keep him straight and out of everybody's way to avoid any accident.

"The horse did that on his own," she said. "The horse was the one that altered course, it wasn't the rider. He was beat. He had not shot at all. He was outclassed and he knew it."

She made a verbal statement, which was recorded by an employee of the commission and notarized.

Upon his return home, Livingston filed a complaint with the Ontario Racing Commission, accusing jockey Lisa McFarland of deliberately holding back the horse after the first half mile, and pointing accusatory fingers at the commission. In an Associated Press story carried by many newspapers, McFarland offered her version of the race.

"He was more comfortable being off the rail," McFarland said. "When horses come eye to eye, they have a way of communicating. He obviously felt he was outclassed in that field."

The Ontario Racing Commission, in turn, investigated complaints Ricks Natural Star bled and Livingston had been negligent in his care, including not returning to check on his horse for hours.

On November 15, Ricks Natural Star ran at Los Alamitos in California in a starter allowance race for thoroughbreds and quarter horses which in 1995–96 had started for a claiming price of $12,500 or less. The length of the dash would be 870 yards, a quarter of a mile. The track's owner, Dr. Ed Allred, offered Livingston a $5,000 appearance fee to race his horse and a $40,000 bonus—to cover Livingston's pre-entry and entry costs in the Breeders' Cup race—if Ricks Natural Star won the race, which had seven entrants.

The appearance of Ricks Natural Star and the publicity that followed increased the turnstile count by about a 1,000 or so for the racing card. Ricks Natural Star, sent postward at 10.50-1, ran last most of the way and placed sixth by some nine lengths, 2¼ lengths ahead of the second choice in the field.

After the Los Alamitos experience, Livingston drove the horse to Turf Paradise in Arizona and turned him over to veteran trainer Casey Jones, a friend and associate of John Hudman, who oversaw the horse's training for his quarter horse race. Jones, a veteran of more than 25 years at the time, suddenly found himself besieged by publicity he hadn't anticipated or wanted. He had 18 horses at the track and more on the farm, but his phone started ringing off the hook from the media, including a call from as far away as Australia. Meanwhile, people started coming by his barn to look at the horse.

On November 21, Terry Stone, the deputy director of racing in Ontario, sent a memorandum to his superior, Jean Major, in which it was indicated that Ed Hall, the supervisor of thoroughbred racing, had completed the investigation into the allegations made by Livingston. The memo stated that the information collected showed the complaints by Livingston were "unfounded and some of the statements are out and out lies."

Documents of the case are available to the public under the Canadian Freedom To Information Act, although some names and evidence are blacked out. In a November 14 letter he wrote to Stone, Hall provided a synopsis of the race involving Ricks Natural Star. Hall wrote that Ricks Natural Star loaded into the starting gate with "mild resistence . . . broke good and raced up to be in second position . . . a position maintained for the first three-eighths of a mile through the first turn to the backstretch. . . . Approximately five-eighths of a mile into the race, the balance of the field raced past Ricks Natural Star on the inside and the outside without incident. At this point, Ricks Natural Star had become non-competitive and continued to drop back to trail the field in last position. After racing three-quarters of a mile, Ricks Natural Star became hopelessly distanced and at the finish of the race galloped past the finish wire approximately a quarter of a mile behind the rest of the horses in what appeared to be a fatigued state."

In a letter written to Ed Hall, ORC commission veterinarian Dr. Greg Taylor stated Ricks Natural Star was examined by the Breeders' Cup veterinary panel on three occasions prior to his race and that he was observed by the panel on the two occasions he was on the turf course.

"We were of the opinion that the horse was sound and exhibited no physical problems on examination that would exclude him from racing," Taylor wrote. "We felt that he would be able to make the turf course; however, we did have reservations about his competitiveness."

It was also stated the progress of the horse was monitored during the race by fellow commission veterinarian Dr. Ed Fritsch, who also observed the horse while he was being unsaddled.

In a letter he sent to Hall, Fritsch wrote that Ricks Natural Star started to fall back from the rest of the horses during the run down the backstretch and "seemed to be laboring" coming into the home stretch. Fritsch wrote that he made a note to see if the horse showed any signs of exhaustion or bleeding from the nostrils when he came to the unsaddling area.

"There was no evidence of epistaxis (nose bleeding) at the time, the horse was breathing rapidly and frequently and other than that did not appear in any distress, so was allowed to proceed back to his stabling area to be cooled out," Fritsch wrote.

The letter was in a response to a report by a person—whose identity is blacked out—who "observed and treated an episode of epistaxis in a post-race scenario that occurred while the horse was being cooled out."

In a letter written to Hall by Nelson Ham, the senior commission steward, it was indicated that the stewards spoke with Livingston, whose name is blacked out, on two occasions prior to the race. The first time stemmed from an examination of the horse's past performances and a need to be satisfied about the "fitness of the horse or be privy to the training regimen that had been followed." It was indicated the stewards spoke with Sally Williams, whose name is blacked out, who informed them about the six-furlong workout at Remington Park. After talking to Williams, the stewards, according to the letter, "doubted (Livingston's) methods and did not believe that the horse would be competitive. We did not feel that we would receive any support from the Commission or the Veterinarians if we chose not to let him run." The second meeting addressed Livingston's desire to change riders and the stewards' decision to allow McFarland to stay on the horse.

In a memorandum he sent to Terry Stone on November 16, Ed Hall commented on various issues in the investigation following material gathered from various sources.

"It was evident that Ricks Natural Star was not fit to race three-quarters of a mile, let alone one and a half miles," Hall began.

It was further stated by Hall that Livingston (whose name is blacked out) should not have been approved a (license) for the sole purpose of coming to the Breeders' Cup because he had never been licensed in any capacity and had no previous racetrack experience. It was further stated Livingston brought only a five-gallon plastic pail and a worn-out bridle and was supplied with equipment, feed and bedding by other horsemen.

"Due to safety reasons, two valets were required to put the tack on the horse on race day, as (Livingston) had never saddled a horse for a race. Because of the inexperienced help (Livingston) brought with him, employees of trainer (Tom Bowden, whose name is blacked out) offered to take the horse to the paddock on race day.

"Ricks Natural Star bleeding after the race in his stall is not uncommon. Neither Ontario Racing Commission or official veterinarians observed or received a report of bleeding after the race and there is insufficient evidence to take any further action.

"After reviewing all occurrences that happened during the events leading up to the race as well as after the race, (Livingston's) ability as a trainer is in question. Should he return to Ontario, (Livingston) will be required to appear before the supervisor of racing regarding his credentials. Rules 6.30.1 and 6.30.2 should be reviewed to stop a horse from qualifying under one workout, regardless of the time elapsed between races."

On November 26, the ORC issued a letter to Livingston indicating concerns about his pre-race and post-race care of the horse.

"These events pose some concerns with your ability to meet the requisite standards of a licensed trainer in Ontario. You will be required to meet with the supervisor of thoroughbred racing as a pre-condition to entering any race in Ontario."

Livingston had 10 days to appeal the ORC's decision.

On December 5, trainer Casey Jones worked Ricks Natural Star five-eighths of a mile at Turf Paradise, and the horse stopped the timer in a solid 59 4/5 seconds handily. The clockers determined the jockey urged the horse—hence the term handily—as opposed to the horse doing it comfortably on his own—what is known as breezing. In either case, the horse had shown progress.

Coincidentally, Livingston had addressed the ORC that day concerning its letter to him.

"I'm just in the process of writing a letter now saying that as far as I'm concerned this is finished," Major told the *Daily Racing Form*. "If he wants to pursue the matter, he'll have to do it through another avenue."

Major said the complaint by Livingston that he has not been able to view the stewards' videotapes did not constitute an appeal.

On January 6, Jones worked Ricks Natural Star half a mile in 48 seconds handily. Jones had him ready to run; it was just a question of picking the appropriate race. He and Hudman thought the horse could win for a claiming tag of $3,000–$3,500 for non-winners of three lifetime—roughly where the horse had been running in 1995—and turn the story around in a positive way. However, Livingston, who had been calling Jones regularly at home, had his own ideas. He believed the horse would be claimed for $3,000–$3,500 and should be run in a non-winners of three lifetime for a claiming price of $7,500. Hudman, whom Livingston had also talked to, didn't think anybody would claim the horse.

The horse was entered for a 6½-furlong race on January 12. It would be his last race ever, although only a few people knew that. Larry Weber, who specialized in buying companies and turning them around, including a vitamin business in which he had done well, perceived the Ricks Natural Star story as nothing more than a circus and wanted to put an end to it. He planned to claim the horse and retire it because in his opinion the whole thing reflected poorly not only on Ricks Natural Star but the reputations of other trainers in general.

"There's always a problem child, whether in the horse racing business or the vitamin business, but the big issue was the embarrassment to the horse," Weber said.

He had been a fan of horse racing his whole life but had never been in a position to be an owner, although he had promised himself that at some point in his life he'd do it. He began buying and racing horses early in the 1990s under the name Run for the Roses Stable, but was largely an unknown figure in the sport.

Weber was living in Arizona when Ricks Natural Star had been shipped to the track. When he read the horse was entered in a race, he began a rapid-fire plan to claim the horse. Weber called Brian Mayberry, who trained for him in California, to make the trip to Arizona to claim the horse. Mayberry could not make it there that quickly and an associate who had been sought to do the job was in Florida and unavailable to go. Mayberry called Turf Paradise racing secretary Mike Harlow, whom he had known, and asked if they could find a trainer to claim a horse for an owner. There was no mention of the identity of the owner or the horse scheduled to be claimed. As fate would have it, Harlow called Dwain Grissom—the original trainer of Ricks Natural Star—who happened to be a friend. Grissom had not planned to go to the races the day Ricks Natural Star had been entered to run, but that changed when he received the call from Harlow. He told him to hurry to the track because an owner wanted to claim a horse and he was being recommended as the trainer.

After Weber met Grissom in Harlow's office, he asked Harlow to leave. In a closed-door meeting, Weber asked Grissom to claim Ricks Natural Star because he wanted to stop the madness.

"I said, 'Larry, I will claim the horse to stop it for you, but I will never run the horse,'" he recalled. "'If you have any intention of doing anything else with this horse, you will need a new trainer because I will not do it. I will not race this horse.' I said, 'After everything that's gone on with that horse, I do not want any kind of that publicity.'"

Grissom told Weber about the horse's early history, including the fact that he had trained him, and that he had advised the original owners to sell him. Weber had had no idea about Grissom's previous association with Ricks Natural Star.

Grissom told Weber he didn't need to spend the $7,500 to claim the horse because he probably wouldn't collect a check in the race and would be running for a lesser price next time out.

"I was just trying to save the guy some money," Grissom said. "He said, 'I don't care what it costs, I'm stopping it.' I said, 'Okay, Mr. Weber, if that's the way you feel, I'm with you.'"

Sent off at 12.50-1 odds, Ricks Natural Star plodded along and finished eighth in the field of 10 by $12\frac{1}{4}$ lengths and shortly thereafter it was announced the horse had been claimed. Jones was not completely surprised because he'd heard by that time somebody planned to take the horse. When he found out the horse had been claimed to be retired, Hudman thought it was a "publicity thing" for the owner to look good.

Weber, who really hadn't sought any publicity but was besieged by people in the media seeking to talk to him, released a statement outlining an owner's obligations.

"When these responsibilities are not fulfilled, the horse suffers in some fashion," Weber said. "There is no intention to pass judgment on the horse's connections. That is a role for racing officials and other qualified professionals. However, recent events and the publicity surrounding Ricks Natural Star have been an embarrassment to the horse and other thoroughbred conditioners and the sport of racing."

Livingston had no idea why someone would claim the horse, but he was happy nonetheless because he needed the money back from his original investment of $40,000 to run the horse in the Cup.

Ricks Natural Star stayed in Grissom's care for about a week before he was sent to Sunnyside Farm in Paris, Kentucky, owned and managed by trainer Jeff Thornbury and prominent veterinarian Dr. Robert W. Copelan.

Weber had done business with the farm and asked Thornbury if he'd consider helping with the boarding of the horse. Thornbury considered Weber's plan a great idea and happily obliged to house the horse. When it became publicized where Ricks Natural Star had been sent, the farm started receiving letters and, in some instances, small amounts of money—usually about $5—by kind-hearted people wanting to buy the horse carrots. Some people even visited the farm to see the horse.

In late April of that year, just a few days before the Kentucky Derby, Larry Weber received the prestigious Coman Humanitarian Award from the Kentucky Thoroughbred Association for claiming Ricks Natural Star and retiring him. The award has been given out almost annually since its inception in 1983, its recipients a who's-who of international horsemen.

Livingston is not surprised somebody won an award.

"The Breeders' Cup is prominent," he said. "I should get the award for working on navicular disease on horses. If they had let him run, maybe I would have got the award."

Livingston continued his pursuit of what he believed to be wrongdoing by both the Breeders' Cup Ltd. and NBC, which he thought had slandered him. He contacted Tommy Wolski, the journalist/jockey whom he met the week of the Breeders' Cup and asked to ride his horse, to provide an affidavit. Wolski declined.

Some two years after he lodged his complaint with the Ontario Racing Commission, Livingston attempted legal action in the state of New Mexico against the Breeders' Cup Ltd., seeking $100 million in punitive damages. He also attempted to sue NBC for slander. Livingston represented himself, but failed to make any headway. The district court claimed it did not have the jurisdictional authority to rule on the matter against the Breeders' Cup Ltd. and advised him to pursue it elsewhere. The court dismissed his action against NBC, judging him to be a public figure. He subsequently dropped his grievances against both the Breeders' Cup Ltd. and NBC because of a lack of money.

While it seems William Livingston is a bitter man and truly odd, it's worth noting he has enough people who will vouch for his credibility.

"I think he's a misunderstood genius," said horse owner Kathleen Krook. "He's really smart and has a very high intellect, but he can talk to people on a personal level, too. No, I wouldn't say he's odd."

"He's the darndest guy you've ever seen, he's a nice doctor," said Larry Guy, the father of champion rodeo rider Lari Dee Guy, whose champion mare Livingston rehabilitated with his navicular vaccine. "I could just go on about the guy forever. He's just one amazing kind of human being. There isn't anybody in the U.S. that has ever tried to expand (on his navicular disease cure) to any degree. I know it."

Livingston professes himself to be an "observor who finds out facts and follows them up." He has also developed a miracle crop fertilizer, an anti-aging formula and an extract to reduce arthritis, all of which have some legitimacy according to people who have used his treatments. But in the world of horse racing and in the opinion of seasoned horsemen, he will forever be known as the individual who ran a hapless horse in the biggest thoroughbred event in the world with absolutely no shot.

"I didn't have the experience to go and do what I did," he said. "Under the circumstances, I'd probably do it again. If they had been fair to me I'd have had a good chance to win the race and, at the very least, get my money back. He was a good horse. After I started treating him, he went 2½ to five feet further every stride. . . . The Breeders' Cup should treat everybody equally, which they certainly didn't do with me. . . . This is what happens when somebody does something different and gets up with the big boys. If you're not there to start with, it's a tough row to hoe. It would have been the best thing if I had placed (in the money) in the Breeders' Cup, then everybody would want to have a horse in the Breeders' Cup. If they would have allowed him to run, which they didn't, it would have been beautiful for racing and my navicular treatment."

Ricks Natural Star and his owner/trainer forced the Breeders' Cup to change its qualifying standards. Any horse age three and older who won its first race for a claiming tag of $15,000 or less and has not won for a $20,000 price or more in its previous two years is now ineligible to run in the Cup. And any horses age three and up who are winless in their career—what are known in racing as maidens—are also ineligible. It's all designed to prevent the embarrassment of another Ricks Natural Star fiasco.

"(Livingston) felt, obviously very strongly to put up $40,000, that he had found some miracle that was going to bring back older horses that had all these particular ailments," Pam Blatz-Murff, the Breeders' Cup vice-president of operations, said. "If somehow, someway it had actually worked and the horse had won the Breeders' Cup, I would imagine the $40,000 would have been a hell of an investment. He would have sold a lot of products, he probably would have had a movie deal. He could have made a big bunch of money. It wasn't to be and the jock he put on the horse did a marvelous job of keeping him out of trouble and not interfering with the other horses that were behind him and in front of him and beside him. The thing's that's very shocking (was all the money bet on the horse), just on the pure speculation that, maybe, this was the one.

"Horse racing is made up of people with dreams and you hear about the stories about the horse on the back of the farm that's been out training under the darkness of night and is going to come in and win the Kentucky Derby. You never really know if the horse is sound and he has his gate card and he has everything in order; you hate to discourage anybody from trying.

"Then there's a point where you have to be a little realistic about this whole thing. This is Grade One competition and this is the best of the best, especially in the Turf, where you're talking about horses from around the world, and horses are just not made in people's back yards. They need a tremendous amount of training and they need to show their class and their stamina on the track with other horses. It isn't something where you're going to pull an old nag out of the back yard, give him some supplements and say he can run with the best in the world."

"I'm glad to hear the horse is being taken care of, he's a nice horse," Livingston said. "I never mistreated the horse. I may have hauled the horse a little further than I should have (taking him to Toronto), but I never mistreated the horse."

People associated with the horse before, during and after the Breeders' Cup, have their own thoughts about what Livingston did.

"Strange things have happened in horse racing," said trainer Tom Bowden, who tried to help Livingston during the Breeders' Cup. "If that horse would have popped up and won, what would have happened? They would have made a movie out of it."

Livingston's neighbor, Robert Hnulik, said: "My opinion is Doc is very intelligent, but he gets off base and carried away and does what I would call stupid things and the Breeders' Cup was one of them. He's kind of a dreamer."

# · 20 ·

# That's the Ticket

## The Pick 6 Score

*T*he media is supposed to report the news, not make it, but every once in a while something strange happens, creating a story all of its own. This is one of those stories, one so fascinating it is almost unbelievable. It's about a group of people who pooled their money together and cashed the biggest ticket in Breeders' Cup history. But that in itself isn't the story. It's the fact that many of these people actually worked for the Breeders' Cup at the time in a newsmaking capacity.

The details leading up to this are like dominoes that fell together in a beautiful and symmetrical sequence, but you have to go back in time—a way back in time—to a gentleman named Gardner DeCoursey—or simply G.D. to most everyone who knows him—Hieronymus. G.D. was born in 1959 in Lexington, Kentucky, and returned there some 19 years later after growing up in Somerset, about 80 miles south, to enroll in communications at the University of Kentucky. Some of his roommates attended the races and he'd join them occasionally, enjoying the experiences but viewing horse racing with a curious skepticism. In his sophomore year, he began working at the NBC Lexington affiliate, WLEX, in a production capacity, some of his assignments involving horse races or breeding farms, and that's when he really started becoming interested in the sport.

During his tenure at the station, he met Tom Hammond, who worked as the sports director. Hammond began producing videos for the horse farms using the station's equipment and employed G.D. to videotape yearlings running through the field. That was about 1979 and '80, and in '81 Hammond started Hammond Productions with another partner, Ron Mossotti, a police officer who had his own video company specializing in saddlebreds and who had also employed G.D. When Hammond and Mossotti began their company, G.D. became their first full-time employee and did all kinds of production and direction, eventually becoming vice-president of production.

Some time around 1986 or '87, G.D. began putting together groups for the Breeders' Cup Pick 7, an exotic wager in which the bettor has to pick seven consecutive races to win, although there is a consolation prize for selecting six or, in some cases, only five. G.D. and his friends never spent wildly on the bet, nowhere near the thousands of dollars of the big-time gamblers, either individuals or groups known as syndicates. It costs a minimum of $2 to play the ticket, if you are only using one horse in each race, but the odds of winning it by playing in that way are miniscule. Using more than one horse in a race multiplies the bet incrementally (i.e., using three horses in the first race triples the wager, adding four horses in the second race quadruples it, etc.). In 1993, G.D.'s group had five of seven winners—one short of the consolation payout—but he profited handsomely on the final race, in which Arcangues won the Classic at odds of more than 133-1, the highest-priced winner in Breeders' Cup history. G.D. ran into his brother, John, at the mutuel windows before the race and was advised to take a shot on Arcangues. G.D. had not used the horse on his Pick 7 ticket. John liked the horse after reading that Arcangues had outworked all the horses trainer Andre Fabre had matched him up against on the dirt. John figured that Fabre, one of the top trainers in Europe, had principally grass horses, but some of them would have ability on the dirt. John also reasoned that if Fabre planned to send the colt to run in the biggest race of the year on the dirt, he would give the colt some consideration. He told his brother to take a shot on the horse because of the "ridiculous" odds. G.D. plunked down $5 across the board and collected about $900 in the process. John bet a similar amount and also keyed Arcangues with five other horses in the Breeders' Cup National Trifecta, combining the trifecta bets from all tracks in the U.S. into a common pool. John had been losing largely on the day and playing on "scared money" by the time of the Classic. He figured with a 99-1 shot (the highest odds on the tote board but conceivably higher in the actual mutuel price), he might have a shot to make a $10,000 score. John hit the trifecta and flew back to Kentucky thinking he'd "just won the moon" because even though a 6-5 shot had finished second, nobody would have used a 99-1 shot on top.

"I'm thinking I just bought a house and might make my first five years of payment on this thing with this one hit," John recalled. "They didn't have the pay-off until the following morning, so I didn't find out what I'd won until we were flying back. I think we were in Pittsburgh and some guy picked up the paper and said, 'You're not going to believe what the tri paid' and it paid something like $1,100 (for a $2 wager) and I was like, 'You've got to be kidding.' The thing that was the most disappointing about Arcangues was that the betting lines (at the pari-mutuel windows) were horrendous. I spent probably 20 minutes in line prior to the Classic to get my bets down. I'd gotten back to our seats and I was telling the guys, 'You've got to bet this horse.' When I'd gone to bet him, he was something like 60-1. Three minutes before post time he was 99-1 and I said, 'Well, I'm not going to go back because I'll never get my other bet down.' If the Breeders' Cup had been anywhere where they could have managed the crowd that year, I could have got all of my buddies to go back down. One of my friends was having a great day. He wouldn't have had any problem at all putting down $100 across the board. That's one of those woulda-coulda-shouldas, I guess, that you get a horse like that and you've got an opportunity for a life-changing score and you kind of mess it up somehow."

It would be six years later that G.D. would be able to proclaim himself as King of the Pick 6 World. After receiving varying amounts from a total of 19 people from Hammond Productions and the Breeders' Cup Newsfeed team, he had about $240, of which he contributed $25. In years past, he and a few others had put together a Pick 6 ticket, but never with as many people and usually spending about a couple of hundred dollars.

As part of his Breeders' Cup job, he shot daily footage made available to news stations during Breeders' Cup week. At the end of each day, he'd pick one of the races for the big day and spend time handicapping, eliminating horses he felt didn't belong and finding ones that did appeal.

The Breeders' Cup Ltd. had changed the Pick 7 to a Pick 6 earlier that year when the Filly & Mare Turf race was added, and instead of beginning the wager with the first race, it commenced with the third one. The Breeders' Cup Ltd. also switched up the order of the races, beginning with the Distaff, followed by the Juvenile Fillies, Mile, Sprint, Filly & Mare Turf, Juvenile, Turf and Classic. The previous year it had been the Juvenile, Juvenile Fillies, Sprint, Mile, Distaff, Turf, Classic. The Breeders' Cup Ltd. offered a guaranteed payout of the pot, including consolation money if there failed to be one or more tickets with all the winners.

The night before the races, a group of Breeders' Cup Newsfeed employees gathered together for dinner at a Greek restaurant and G.D. asked if any of them wanted to contribute to the pool. A sheet of paper was passed around and anyone could join. G.D. knew some money would be coming from Hammond Productions employees. Production manager Angie Poole sent out a blanket e-mail to the 20 or so employees at Hammond. Coincidentally, Hammond had been commissioned by the Breeders' Cup Ltd. to do a special DVD of the 1999 Breeders' Cup prep races, some 80 in all. Craig Miller, vice-president of interactive media for Hammond, had been in charge of putting the DVD together and had contributed to the pool. Rachel O'Neill, who worked as an administrative assistant, contributed $20 from her lunch money. It was a chunk of cash for her because she was basically supporting herself and her husband. They had just graduated from college—she had studied journalism at Southern Methodist University—and he had opened up a chiropractic clinic.

Angie Poole took all the money, including one check, and gave it to Susan Hanvey, the accountant, who placed the contents in an envelope and then in a locked box.

Alex Morra, a soundman who worked with G.D. during the week, anted up $10. Morra worked for the parent company of Hammond and "drew the unlucky straw" to go to the Breeders' Cup, the first horse racing event in which he had been employed, working principally in video and film productions.

"I couldn't have told you the first thing about what a Pick 6 was," Morra said. "I knew basic stuff, but I didn't know how much the ticket cost. When G.D. asked me if I wanted to put any money on the bet I said, 'How much are people giving?' He said 'about $10 or $20.' It's like a lottery ticket. I'd hate if somebody won the Powerball and they'd asked me 10 minutes before they won it if I wanted any part of it and I said no. That's the only reason I was involved with it."

TV reporter Jeff Piecoro, who had pooled money together with G.D. and others in previous Pick 6 bets for several years, contributed $20. The group had usually spent between $150 and $200 each year on their ticket. G.D. would usually contribute a quarter to a third of that total.

"There had always been four of five of us, it just so happened that that year was the year everybody and their brother got in on it," Piecoro said.

Stan Starks, a horseplayer of almost 30 years who worked in an editing capacity for the Newfeed team, contributed $10, but only because he was "kind of goaded" by Cathy Bruce, another editor. They had worked for the fledgling Military Channel, which had ceased operations the previous August. She had routinely beaten him on basketball bets and liked to tease him about it, so he figured he had to make a contribution or face the consequences. He figured there was no chance the group would win. He had handicapped the races since the past-performance lines had come out 10 days in advance of Breeders' Cup day and it looked impossible to him to win the bet.

The morning of the races, G.D. and his brother John conversed, something they routinely did the night before or the day or the Cup, and identified "live horses" as opposed to playing the Pick 6. The conversation lasted about an hour, but it proved to be significant. John recommended Cat Thief, a long shot that G.D. hadn't planned to use. Cat Thief had run in some of the biggest races of the season, but had only one win in 10 starts. He had lost his last three, including finishing third in the Grade Two, $400,000 Kentucky Cup Classic Handicap at Turfway Park six weeks before. Neither the winner, Da Devil, nor the runnerup, Social Charter, had distinguished themselves as horses of any great importance.

To the naked eye, the race offered nothing of significance, but John had taken notice. He regularly attends the races and often sits with a professional horseplayer who pays keen attention to track bias, which takes into account whether horses are winning on the inside or the outside of the track on a daily basis and whether or not their speed holds up. John had noticed that in the Kentucky race, Cat Thief had run on the inside part of the track, which didn't play in his favor, and fought gamely in defeat.

"I knew right then you could throw that race out or you could look at it a little closer," John said. "On a fair track, he probably would have won the race and ran (considerably faster), which would have been competitive in the Breeders' Cup Classic. Another reason I liked Cat Thief is we had played the Friday card at Gulfstream the day before the Breeders' Cup and it seemed like speed and rail were playing really good. I knew that Cat Thief, especially with Pat Day up, had enough speed to get a good position on the track. He would have had what I would have considered the second-best speed in the race. Old Trieste was the only other speed in the race and he was more of a sprinter. Old Trieste had drawn outside of Cat Thief, so Day could just let the horse go. He could just track basically from the rail and make his move whenever he wanted. I saw that as how I thought the race was going to shape up and I said that turning for home, Day's going to be in front. Anybody who knows horse racing knows that Day is somebody who always saves a lot of horse for the stretch run. I said to G.D., 'You put Pat Day in front with Cat Thief in a race that doesn't have other than Behrens a tremendous amount of talent in it, he's as live as anybody to win that race.'"

G.D. planned to use two horses, Behrens, the logical favorite, and General Challenge, but he wasn't really sold on that horse, whom he didn't consider a good shipper. To add General Challenge would have required more money than the syndicate had collected, so G.D. settled on Cat Thief.

John had not been among the syndicate members and can't recall if he'd ever pooled together with his brother on the bet. If they had done it, it likely only occurred when the Breeders' took place at Churchill Downs and the brothers had time to huddle together.

The Pick 6 ticket looked like this: Mile: Silic and Hawksley Hill; Sprint: Artax, Successful Appeal, and Affirmed Success; Filly & Mare Turf: Soaring Softly and Spanish Fern; Juvenile: Anees and Forest Camp; Turf: Daylami and Yagli; Classic: Behrens and Cat Thief. Most of the horses were favorites in the morning line or choices under 15-1, but Anees and Cat Thief principally stood out. Anees had a win and a third in three lifetime starts, but he had impressed G.D. and Piecoro with his daily training leading up to the race.

"It was horrible that week, it rained just every day and we shot every Breeders' Cup horse that works out," Piecoro said. "Horses were having a tough time and there was this one horse who's just going. I mean he's running like he's on a treadmill. He's just flying. You say, 'Who, who the heck is that?' I couldn't make out the name. I had never heard of him. The next day the same thing happened. This horse is out there on the track and he's running unbelievably. I'm like 'I don't know who that is.' We said, 'We've got to use this guy, he's unbelievable.' I think that was the one that knocked a lot of people out of the Pick 6, that and Cat Thief."

Anees was ridden by Gary Stevens, who in his autobiography *The Perfect Ride*, wrote about Anees' final workout.

"The track was muddy the day we ran; there were not many horses working on it," he said. "Anees went six furlongs in one minute, thirteen seconds, a very good workout . . . but somehow the clockers managed to miss that performance. They recorded Anees's time as having been two seconds slower. The next day's *Daily Racing Form* contained an article stating that the colt had been unimpressive in his workout and advising handicappers to toss him out of their betting—the colt had no chance. I had actually phoned a reporter to say how well Anees had worked. Right after the *Racing Form* article appeared I received an anxious phone call from (the colt's racing manager Richard Mulhall) questioning Anees's workout. I assured the boss that the colt had indeed worked very well and I expected him to run well in the Breeders' Cup. I couldn't predict that we would win, but I guaranteed him that we would get a piece of the million-dollar purse. This wasn't just idle talk. From every sign Anees was showing me, I felt that he would perform well in the Juvenile."

Cat Thief hadn't won a race since the Swaps Stakes in July and had come into the Breeders' Cup following a third-place finish in a Grade Two race at Turfway Park six weeks before. But trainer Wayne Lukas had been touting the colt, who had been running in fairly tough company all season and usually placed second or third.

G.D. made his individual bets and the Pick 6 for the syndicate well ahead of the races and stashed the tickets in his wallet. He called Angie Poole and quickly gave her the numbers of the horses he used in the individual races, and she headed out to buy a *Daily Racing Form* to find out the names of the horses.

G.D. scurried around shooting footage in the paddock, track and winner's enclosure. He had barely enough time to catch his breath in between races or make any sudden bets.

In the Juvenile, the race before the Pick 6 commenced, Cash Run—a great name if ever there was one—grabbed the cash at more than 32-1 odds. G.D. hadn't fancied the horse. But it's better to be wrong in the race that doesn't matter.

In the first leg of the Pick 6, the bettors liked Hawksley Hill, instilling him as the post-time favorite in the Mile at 3.70-1. Silic went postward as the fourth choice at 7.20-1. Hawksley Hill had won his last race, but was disqualified and placed fourth. Silic had also come into the race off a win, albeit one that stood up. Silic prevailed in the Mile by a neck, coming from almost last to first, running down another late-runner, Tuzla, who had odds of 13.70-1. Hawksley Hill finished strongly but placed fifth, beaten by less than a length. Next came the Sprint, in which Artax was the slight second choice at 3.70-1, marginally behind Forestry, who had the same odds but had slightly more money wagered on him. Successful Appeal had odds of 16.40-1 and Affirmed Success 13.50-1. Artax and Successful Appeal had won their last races, while Affirmed Success placed second. The Sprint is traditionally the race that eliminates most players because it rarely runs to form, usually because some horses are eliminated at the start or incur traffic problems and find themselves lacking running room. Artax broke well and tracked the pacesetter before taking over after half a mile and prevailing by a half-length. Successful Appeal ran fifth and Affirmed Success 12th.

In the inaugural running of the Filly & Mare Turf, the public made Soaring Softly the favorite at 3.60-1, while Spanish Firm became the co-second choice at 4-1. Both horses came into the race off wins, and Soaring Softly continued her victorious ways, running from near the back and soaring down the stretch to win by three-quarters of a length. Spanish Fern never made a serious move and finished last.

While busy doing his job, G.D. had reason to celebrate because he had already won the first Pick 3, in which bettors are required to pick the winners of three designated races. Next came the Juvenile and few people gave Anees a shot, sending him off 30.30-1 off his third-place finish in his last race, in which Forest Camp had placed second. The public made Forest Camp the 2.70-1 favorite. Forest Camp ran sixth after leading comfortably by two lengths following three-quarters of a mile then fading quickly. But Anees, who started off last in the 14-horse field, didn't really get hold of the track until slightly more than half a mile from the wire, about 15 lengths off the lead. Stevens said he gave the colt a tap on the shoulder with the whip, encouraging the colt to lengthen his stride. Anees started passing horses but was still seventh, about eight lengths from the lead; however, Stevens thought he might finish fourth. Once the colt had straightened out in the stretch, Stevens hit him right-handed and Anees exploded again.

"I was flying by other horses," Stevens wrote in his book. "By the eighth pole,

I knew I was going to win. A sixteenth of a mile from the wire, I was in front. Suddenly Anees's ears went straight up in the air and he started looking at the grandstands. To keep his attention, I hit him left-handed, and he ducked out, away from the whip. I thought to myself, 'Don't blow this, Stevens. Don't do anything stupid. Right now, you've got the race in the bag.'"

Anees won by 2½ lengths, although Stevens said his horse ran hard for only about fifty yards. In any case, Anees knocked countless people out of the Pick 6.

Craig Miller had been outside his house raking leaves and would go inside every half hour to watch a race and would then telephone Angie Poole. After Anees won, Craig stopped raking and began pacing back and forth as dreams of a large payoff began dancing in his head.

In the winner's circle, Piecoro, who had been doing interviews with the winning connections, told NBC announcer Mike Battaglia he had Anees and was still alive on the group's ticket. Piecoro knew Battaglia from having worked with him for years on Turfway Park's racing shows and filling in occasionally at Keeneland's.

Piecoro also informed some of the people working in the Newsfeed central office, but at least one person didn't believe him. Cathy Bruce, who had contributed $10 to the syndicate's pool and convinced fellow editor Stan Starks to pitch in with a similar amount, had worked with Piecoro at the fledgling Military Channel. She knew him to be an inveterate practical joker.

"He just pulls your leg all the time," Bruce said. "All around me everyone is believing it and I'm like, 'Jeff is pulling our leg. He's getting them good.'"

Meanwhile back in Lexington, Angie Poole and Craig Miller, vice-president of interactive for Hammond, had been telephoning one another regularly as the races unfolded, in total disbelief of what was happening.

G.D. told Morra they might have a chance to win, particularly because he considered Daylami practically unbeatable. Daylami had won three Group One races in Europe before running ninth by 23½ lengths on soggy ground in the Prix de l'Arc de Triomphe, but he had trained solidly for the Turf and the public made him the 8-5 favorite. Yagli, the fourth choice in the wagering at odds of 7.30-1, had run fourth in his last race. Daylami ran in the middle of the pack, but moved up to second by only a head to pacesetter and defending champion Buck's Boy at the head of the stretch and then took control inside an eighth of a mile to the wire to win by 2½ lengths.

With only one race to go, G.D., Morra and Piecoro felt good about their chances. They had worked on a story about Behrens earlier in the week and expected that horse to win the Classic. If Behrens won, he would have likely keyed several winning tickets. The mutuel departments at all racetracks know how many tickets are live on exotic wagers because of scanning equipment that provides that information.

Emotions were running high in the Newsfeed central office.

"Everyone is completely into it. They're happy, they're pulling for Cat Thief and I'm going, 'Man, I hope Jeff's not pulling our leg,'" Cathy Bruce said.

Behrens had placed second in his last start, but never really became a factor in the Classic, placing seventh. Cat Thief, dismissed at 19.60-1, tracked pacesetter

Old Trieste for the opening three-quarters of a mile, then took over and won by 1¼ lengths.

"When Anees won the race, that's when I started thinking we've got a shot at this thing because Daylami was the superstar of the day if you ask me," G.D. recalled. "That horse ran so smooth you could have saddled him and he might have won the Classic. He was really the best horse of the day. I thought we had a lock there and then I thought Behrens was pretty solid. Obviously he didn't show up, but thank goodness Cat Thief did."

"I'll never forget Battaglia asked, 'Who do you have in the last one?'" Piecoro recalled. "He said, 'Why did you take Cat Thief?' Sure enough that was the difference. When they turned for home, G.D. is trying to shoot, so he has to keep his composure. Battaglia starts yelling, 'You guys are going to win the Pick 6.' That was the neatest part to be around the guys like that."

The total amount of the Pick 6 hadn't been posted at that point, let alone that there was only one winning ticket. G.D. and Morra congratulated one another and a photographer from *The Blood-Horse* snapped a shot of the two, who at that time were unaware of the magnitude of their windfall.

In the Newsfeed office, most of the members who had invested in the syndicate celebrated the win, although Cathy Bruce remained unconvinced.

"I'm going, 'Boy, if this is a practical joke, this is like the best one yet. He's got us,'" she recalled. "I even expressed that to a couple people. 'Boy, you know how Piecoro likes to fool around. I hope he's not messing with us.' Everyone's saying, 'No, no, it's in.'"

Some of the syndicate members approached one of their fellow employees, Richard Eng, who hadn't invested in the ticket, and asked what he thought their winning ticket would be worth. Eng figured there would be several winning tickets, each worth between $400,000 and $500,000.

The Pick 6 had a total pot of $5,436,691, of which three-quarters went to winning tickets—or in this case one ticket—before the application of 25% in state taxes. Consolation tickets for picking five of six selections in the Pick 6 were worth $5,996.20 apiece. That amounted to $3,058,138.60.

Piecoro told G.D. they had the only winning ticket, but G.D. thought Piecoro had misread the tote board and kept repeating that.

Just as quickly as G.D. started celebrating, he came to a sudden and startling realization.

"It's dark and the racetrack's closing down and you don't know how many people have seen you celebrating and what you're celebrating about, so I grabbed a security guard in the winner's circle and said 'Just take me to the press elevator,'" he said. "The security guard was receptive. I didn't really tell him (the full extent) why I needed him. I just felt uneasy. I just didn't really want to walk around. You just don't walk over to a mutuel line and say, 'Hey, by the way I've got the Pick 6 ticket.' First of all, I wanted to go to the head of the mutuels and the security guard had no clue where it was, so I said just take me to the press elevator for the press box. I told him I had a quite a bit of money in tickets. Nonetheless, I think I gave him a $100 bill for doing that."

NBC's Breeders' Cup host Tom Hammond, the same person whom G.D. had met many years ago at WLEX-TV and who later hired him to work for his production company and taught him to read the *Daily Racing Form*, found out after the broadcast G.D. and his group had won. Hammond had regularly participated in the office pools, but hadn't ever been part of G.D.'s syndicates because he'd always departed for the Cup well before the group pooled its money. Hammond had been "flabbergasted" by the group's score, particularly that it had picked Cat Thief.

"There were a lot of people there that didn't really follow horses so much—that were betting on faith and just to have some action—that got back tremendous amounts of money," Hammond said. "I was so happy for them. Things of good fortune like that rarely happen to me, so I was happy for them and happy I didn't bet along with them and jinx 'em. It was quite a treat to see (G.D.) win, but very ironic because of our connection. I had basically brought him into the horse business."

While G.D. departed to take care of business, Morra remained behind to take care of the video equipment, still totally unsure of the magnitude of the moment. Meanwhile, Piecoro, who still had to do some voice-over work, and others returned to the Newsfeed central office. They had a deadline to send out the feeds later that evening. Some members of the syndicate talked about buying cars, houses or horses.

"I'm shaking because we're millionaires basically or thousandaires or whatever you want to call it," Piecoro said. "Actually, work was kind of easy because we know we've won some money, but Tammy (Joslyn) was the levelheaded one."

Tammy, one of the on-line producers, and her husband, Jim, one of the videographers, had contributed $20 to the syndicate's pool.

"We had to get a nine o'clock (video news release) feed, basically all the races, plus sound bites, the whole day's events needed to be ready to go just a few hours later," Tammy said. "We were all pretty cool about it, excited. It was really exciting (winning), but the other thing was that not everybody was in on the pool. Everybody had an opportunity but some chose not to, so it was somewhat awkward. It would have been fun if everybody had put into the pool."

One of the unfortunate people included Richard Eng, who had regularly anted up in years past and had given input on the horses G.D. picked. But this time he didn't participate in the syndicate.

"For some stupid reason I didn't put my name down and the ticket went without me," Eng said. "The way the ticket was put together wasn't the most unaffordable, especially when cut up among so many people. I didn't put my name down, but many other people did, fortunately for them. Life deals you funny cards. It was one of those things that cost me (a lot of money). But I was really happy for the people I worked with because I had worked with them for six or seven years and I was probably more of a horse player and a horse person than some of the others in the group. Some of the others were TV people or technicians or cameramen. They weren't into horse racing as maybe myself, G.D. or some of the others."

After taking the elevator to the press box, G.D. approached Karl Schmitt, the senior vice-president of communications for Churchill Downs at the time and the person overseeing the Gulfstream press box that day. G.D. told Schmitt he needed a place to sit down and talk. Schmitt said he could tell something had happened to G.D. because he had "eyes as big as silver dollars." G.D. told Schmitt he had hit the Pick 6 and asked to go into Schmitt's office.

"I was not cheering. I was in a daze," G.D. said. "I'd been working my tail off all day long and I was begging for a cold beer, actually. I said, 'Carl, I've got the Pick 6 ticket.' He was pretty stunned as well and I've got a big stack of tickets and I said, 'Here's the ticket, double check it for me.' He did. He was very, very helpful."

Upon checking the results, Schmitt confirmed he'd won. He asked G.D. what he wanted to do and he told him he wanted to call his brother.

"He was wired and he was sort of out of breath but he knew the one thing he wanted to do was call his brother," Schmitt said. "That's the mark of a true horse-player. He wanted to call the guy who gave him the horse that got him over the hump."

Driving home from Keeneland, John began to wonder if his brother had been the winner, knowing his selections. It had been 15 minutes to half an hour after he'd returned home when the phone rang.

"He said, 'We did it, we hit the Pick 6. I threw Cat Thief in,'" John recalled. "He was obviously scrambling around. There was a lot of noise in the background. He said he couldn't talk long, but he was just overcome with emotion, as you could imagine."

John had had a disappointing day at the races. He put $100 into a Pick 6 ticket with some friends who collectively spent between $2,000 and $2,500. They didn't have Soaring Softly, whom John wanted to use but was voted out by the syndicate, and Anees. He also didn't play Cat Thief to win.

"Handicapping the horses is only half of the game," he said. "The other half is knowing how to bet. I consider myself a great handicapper but a poor bettor. My tickets on Cat Thief were primarily exacta and trifecta wagers. I liked Cat Thief and I loved Behrens. I thought there was no way that Behrens would miss hitting the board in that race. If Behrens had run anywhere in the top four, I would have (won various exotic bets). That's my downfall—not playing straight money, a lot of wins bets or Pick 3s. Obviously that would have been a good spot for a Pick 3. I want to say I did play one Pick 3, but didn't use Anees."

After talking to his brother, G.D. asked to be taken to the mutuel department, whereupon Schmitt called down to mutuel director Patrick Mahony. By this time, the word had filtered through the press box and Schmitt asked G.D. what he wanted to do. Schmitt felt it important to at least pass the information to a member of the notes team providing quotes and/or information for the media. G.D. did not want to engage in that just yet. He didn't know at the time of his win who had anted up at Hammond.

"There was going to be a lot of questions I couldn't answer," he said. "I didn't know how many people had signed up and at what increments. If people in the media were going to ask questions, such as how many people were in the pool, at that time I couldn't have told you there was 19. There could have been 30. There were too many questions I really couldn't answer regarding that."

Two reporters, Mary-Jean Wall of the *Lexington Herald-Leader*, and Marty McGee of the *Daily Racing Form*, joined G.D. on his journey to the pari-mutuel office, peppering him with questions along the way.

The Gulfstream Park pari-mutuel department would have known the exact location where the winning tickets—or ticket—were sold, although not necessarily whether there would be an immediate claim. At the request of the mutuel department, a county trooper went up to the press box and joined G.D. and the uniformed security person to collect his winnings.

"We had an escort bring him down because he wouldn't have known how to find the location where we wanted to process the ticket," Mahony said. "It's not customary, but if he has in his possession a piece of paper worth $3 million we felt the prudent thing to do was to provide him with a security escort. He has to come in behind a secured area and we sat him in a supervisor's room and then we processed the ticket. We looked at all his identification and then we issued him a check. If a customer asks for a security escort we'll do it, but that's when a cash payment is made. Certainly not in the range of $3 million. I had been working as director of mutuels at Gulfstream since 1983 and had never experienced a ticket of that amount. It's certainly not an everyday experience. First, the fact we're hosting a Breeders' Cup is unusual. It was the third time we had done it but that's a major sporting event and the handle levels are of far greater magnitude than we would typically see, not only on-track but the network totals are far greater than we would normally experience. Because it was a guaranteed Pick that stimulates the amount bet into that pool and there's such great quality of racing comprising the six races that make up that Pick 6, it's a great deal of money bet into the pool and you always have this possibility you could wind up with a single winner and a payout like that. We'd had Pick 6s, but hadn't paid out anything close to that obviously, so the emotion of it was certainly extraordinary."

In addition, the mutuel department had to deal with some other unbelievable payoffs. Cat Thief keyed an exacta with 26.50-1 shot Budroyale that paid a whopping $1,209.60. The trifecta with 75.30-1 Golden Missile paid $39,031.20. The superfecta with fourth-place finisher Chester House, a 63.60-1 shot, returned $692,907. Any and all of those figures—less the applicable taxes—are staggering. The ticketholder of the superfecta came to Gulfstream to collect his winnings the following day, although his identity has never been publicized.

"There's no way I would have ever had the exacta, the tri or the super in that race," G.D. said. "It was incredible. That super was $692,907. Now you tell me that's not a score!"

When the winning odds exceed 300-1, there is also a federal withholding tax, which was 28% at the time of the gross payout after the removal of state taxes from the overall pool. It can only be claimed in the U.S. for tax purposes if the ticketholder files detailed records of winning amounts and losses. That is common for major horseplayers. Overall, the group shared a net amount of more than $2.2 million, a North American record for that particular wager and possibly a world record, too.

G.D. kept the check in the envelope presented to him by the mutuel department and buttoned it in his pants pocket. By this time, Morra, Jeff Piecoro and Jim Joslyn, who had done most of his videography during the week and had ample free time on race day, had joined him.

"Who thought we were going to hit it?" Jim Joslyn said. "If I had known we were going to win and I was shooting, I don't know if my heart could have taken it. I don't know how G.D. shot the stretch run."

After G.D. finished with the mutuel department, he and the three other Newsfeed employees walked over to their car in the parking lot, escorted by a security guard. When they returned to the hotel and the conference room where the Newsfeed team worked in two editing suites, G.D. received a hero's welcome. He generously gave everyone from the Newsfeed group who did not participate $100 from his own winnings of bets other than the Pick 6. Back in his hotel room, the phone started ringing nonstop with requests for interviews.

"There was about two or three stations in Miami that wanted me to come down and do interviews and I wish that I would have but I just didn't want to," he said. "I belong behind the camera. I didn't really want to get out there."

Sometime shortly before midnight, after the Breeders' Cup Newsfeed people had finished sending out feeds and had put away all their equipment they gathered together for dinner at Tony Romas.

"The look on everybody's face . . . that's one thing I'll always take with me," said Richard Eng. "It was like a glow on everybody's face who had a winning ticket. As far as myself, obviously I regret not being part of it, but it was my choice. Nobody pushed me one way or another. It was a very democratic process."

G.D. couldn't reach his wife Laura, to whom he been married 12 years, until the following morning.

"She was on a shopping trip with her sister and some friends, something they do every fall in Nashville," he said. "She was pretty calm about it. Things like that don't really affect her."

On Sunday morning, Angie Poole's husband, Larry, called Ron Mossotti and asked him if he had seen the paper. When Mossotti told him he hadn't, Larry Poole told him about the windfall.

"He just started laughing," Angie said. "He couldn't believe it. Who could? You think about it, it's like winning the lottery. What are the odds of that happening?"

Angie called her sister, who she talked to the night before, and was asked if she had passed on the news to their grandfather, Lyle Haws, who was an important figure in their lives. Angie had been reluctant at first.

"I didn't want him to think I'm a gambler because I'm not," she said. "It was just an office pool."

The victory brought to mind Chris Schulte, a 10-year Hammond employee who worked in a variety of capacities and regularly organized the office pools. He died in 1993 after an 18-month battle with cancer. In his honor, Ron Mossotti created a scholarship in Chris Schulte's name in the communications department of his alma mater, Eastern Kentucky. Students selected for the scholarship in their fourth year of the program received $1,000 to help pay for their tuition and an internship at Hammond. One of the interns, Jesse Kelsey, was subsequently hired full-time and, in this particular instance, had been a contributor to the syndicate.

Rachel O'Neill, who had gone to her hometown in Ohio for the weekend, awoke late that day having forgotten about the pool. She was reminded of it when she saw a copy of the Lexington paper, which her stepfather had purchased, and the story of G.D.'s score. Rachel started screaming like crazy and then phoned the club where her husband was playing golf and asked to speak to him. She said it was an emergency, that she had just won the Pick Six. But the message that was delivered to him was that his wife had just won the lottery. He knew she didn't play the lottery and didn't heed the call.

G.D. returned home Sunday morning aboard a plane chartered by Taylor Made Farm, a commercial breeding/sales operation, to take people to Lexington for the Keeneland horse sales. Several Hammond employees, including Angie Poole and her son Larry, Ron Mossotti, Craig Miller and Kelly Gordon, a producer, made the trek to the airport to greet G.D. and congratulate him. He headed to Keeneland to work at the November Breeding Stock Sale for a client that was having a dispersal, then returned home. John visited him later that day and helped him work out the percentages of each of the contributors. Because of the partners involved, the pari-mutuel department required individual forms, noting the social security numbers of each of the winners and other pertinent information. G.D. had an attorney prepare a legal document—and he had all the people involved in the win sign it and notarize it—that whatever happened with the portion of the money that he gave them he would never be liable.

The score caught the attention of many people, including noted handicapping authority Andy Beyer of the *Washington Post*, who wrote a column that appeared in the *Daily Racing Form*.

"After poring over these races for hours I concluded that I can't play the Pick Six because it's too tough," he wrote. "I'd be willing to offer anybody this proposition: Make out an imaginary $25,000 ticket for the Pick Six, and I'll wager that you don't hit it."

G.D. fired off a response to Beyer, but never received a reply. John felt offended by Beyer's column, feeling he didn't give his brother credit. Richard Eng, who writes a weekly column for the *Las Vegas Review-Journal*, did a story about the Pick 6 score, offering his opinion about Beyer's suggestions and some personal thoughts. Eng had four of the five winners going into the Classic among the top two selections he provided for the *Review-Journal*. He tabbed Lemon Drop Kid and Ecton Park, neither of whom figured in the finish, as his preferred picks going into the last race.

"Beyer is a pre-eminent turf writer and handicapper . . . I respect his opinion immensely," Eng wrote. He added that Beyer's thoughts are "sage advice for those consumed by the (exotic bet). . . . Normal people don't win a bet like this. Big syndicate players betting thousands of dollars might . . . Beyer's advice was correct for 99.9 percent of the players in the Pick Six. All except for G.D. G.D. and friends."

A couple weeks after the score, G.D. organized a get-together at Hammond Productions for all the syndicate members—the ones who couldn't make it were represented by others—for a group photo and to disperse the winnings. G.D. has never disclosed publicly how much he made on the score, but it didn't exceed $250,000, including the money he made from his other successful wagers. G.D. never divulged how much the other syndicate members profited individually and he's inclined to keep it that way, and, for the most part, all of the winners didn't want to disclose that information, either. Suffice to say, a small investment earned each of them one heck of a return.

"It changed a lot of lives and it really did some good," G.D. said. "For several of the freelancers that were working the Breeders' Cup Newsfeed I was able to give them a check that would amount to what they would make in two or three years. That was the best thing about it. I don't really want to get into any names, but that was really special to know that it's really helped them a whole lot."

Morra was 26 at the time and a month away from marriage.

"If you gave me $15 for $10 I'd be happy," Morra said. "I'd only been out of college for a few years and for $10 to get me that was pretty exciting. It's a good way to have something to invest for the future for yourself and your family. You can't retire off that money obviously, but it doesn't hurt. The year before that I was working on a job in Puerto Rico and I'd won a lot of money on the slot machines, not that much but a lot. It's funny how I had a few years of my life where I had won money just being in the right place at the right time. It's probably my only claim to fame that I'm ever going to have in my life."

For Cathy Bruce, the money helped her through a rough financial and emotional period. She had been working on a freelance basis after her full-time employment with the Military Channel ended in mid-August, though the company had ceased paying employees eight weeks before. The money also gave her the financial wherewithal to help pay for the tombstone of her four-month-old great-nephew, Cameron, who died of sudden infant death syndrome five days before the Breeders' Cup. Bruce flew home for the funeral two days before the Breeders' Cup and returned the following day.

"That Monday when I got the phone call (Cameron died) to that Saturday it was being about as low as you can be to probably one of the highlights, at least financially, so far in my life, hope they'll be more," she said. "It went from very low to very high in a matter of days. It was very emotional because I'm close to my nieces. They are more like my kids to me. When I got pregnant with my first child, I was like 'I couldn't possibly love anyone more than my nieces. I don't need to have children, I have my nieces.' Watching my niece, Takeisha Brents, go through the grief . . . that was tough. It was just so horrible watching someone I've taken care of and loved all my life seeing her killed with grief. Most of the funeral arrangements were done while I was out of town. After we won on Saturday and I got back on Sunday and touched base with everyone and found out what still needed to be done and where I could help out, that was [the priority]. I just said, 'Hey, don't even worry about it, I got it.'"

Stan Starks used some of his money to go on a planned trip with his wife to Las Vegas.

"I went in style," he said with a hearty laugh. "Before that, we used to go about two or three times a year anyway, but we would have to be on a pretty tight budget. Now we could go and splurge. I could bet more. That was the main thing. It didn't matter so much if I won or lost. I could play like I wanted to, so that was great. I didn't anticipate it happening. It was like a windfall, so I could take a shot at something. After we got the money and could afford to go to Las Vegas we started winning big."

He won $8,000 on the first trip. His wife won a $10,000 jackpot on the slots on their next trip after only investing $20. Stan won $12,000 several times after that playing craps.

About a month after the score, Jeff Piecoro, who was 35, and his wife, bought their second house, using his winnings as a down payment. The earnings allowed them the opportunity to buy a better house than originally considered for them and their two children, Nicholas, who was five, and Olivia, two.

"I'm in a neighborhood I would have never been able to afford had I not won that money," Piecoro said. "I would have never been able to put that amount of down payment down. The other thing that is really neat about it is that I have an autistic child. My son, Nicholas, was five at the time, and it enabled us to do a lot more with him in terms of the therapies that he gets. We have girls that come to the house and work with him. Obviously with that windfall of money I was able to do a lot more with an occupational physical therapist coming to the house and things like that before we may have not been able to give. It changed my life hugely."

Tammy and Jim Joslyn put their winnings into mutual funds to use for college educations for their three children.

"It happened at the end of October 1999 and, gee, look at the stock market," Tammy said with a laugh. "Only the Joslyns can invest in safe mutual funds and not be real thrilled with the outcome right now. We've tried to keep the money we invested in those college funds. We invested all the money in one lump sum at the same time. That was at the peak of the market. Since November of 1999 it continues to decline. We have tried not to touch that money so that we could at least built it back up to what we invested. In other words, we keep laughingly saying 'We really should have just bought a damn racehorse' but we were trying to do the prudent thing. We saw this as a great opportunity to provide an education for our kids. We may not be out of the woods yet."

One of their children is attending Carnegie Mellon University in Pittsburgh, which has one of the top Bachelor of Fine Arts programs in the U.S.

"We're really hoping she'll pay us back—and then we can get that racehorse," Tammy said with a hearty laugh.

Rachel O'Neill, who put her lunch money into the pot, used the winnings to help her husband Chuck pay off his student loans and to purchase equipment for the chiropractic clinic he'd just opened. Rachel also bought herself a brand new BMW.

"It was beautiful," she said. "It was the only frivolous thing I did (with the money)."

She left Hammond about a month after the Pick Six score to help her husband with his new clinic.

Susan Hanvey, the accountant at Hammond, used some of her winnings to build a house.

Angie Poole used some money to buy a house, but put most of the cash away for her children's education.

Craig Miller used some of his winnings to pay off some debts, donate to charity and invest in the stock market. But it is his recollection of the day that is his greatest reward.

"That day was just a day you can't describe," he said. "It was a crazy day, a wild day, just pretty cool."

He also wrote about the Pick Six in a writing contest sponsored by Winstar Farm in Versailles, Kentucky. This is Craig's story, published for the first time.

"Although retired to stud, my favorite winner will always be Anees. Against steep odds, the bay colt won the 1999 Breeders' Cup Juvenile, defeating favorites High Yield, Captain Steve, Chief Seattle, Forest Camp and Dixie Union. Many tickets hit the floor that day after Anees crossed the finish line, but not all; there was at least one ticket still alive! Anxious because of the improbable perfect start of four wins in a row, I began to imagine the unimaginable of winning the Pick Six. As I watched Anees get bumped near the gate and then come from behind to win by $2\frac{1}{2}$ lengths, my sunny autumn afternoon quickly became surreal. First Silic, then Artax, then Soaring Softly, now the improbable Anees, oh-my! Surely the favorite Daylami and the iron horse Behrens could keep the dream alive. After Daylami defeated Royal Anthem in the Turf, my adrenaline was soaring and my mind wondering, 'Why the hell did we pick Cat Thief over Lemon Drop Kid?' And, 'Why in the hell is there 30 minutes between races?' Oh well, Behrens is the favorite and has a great post position and after the Anees win I believed this day is meant to be. It is fate, Behrens will win the Classic—so I thought.

"The final race begins and out of the gate Cat Thief sprints toward the lead and never looks back. Obviously Cat Thief going nearly wire to wire would be my second choice for the winning horse category and perhaps is the choice of many of my Pick Six colleagues. However, Anees going off at more than 15-1 and winning clearly is the reason no other Pick Six ticket was cashed that day and at least one-sixth responsible for the highest single pari-mutuel payoff in racing history."

John received a winning share from his brother.

"G.D., being the honest man that he is, said on the phone, 'Some of this money is yours,'" John recalled. "I said, 'Hey, I'm happy for you. Don't worry about me. If something comes out of it, fine. If it doesn't, life goes on.' G.D. tipped me a nice amount and two (people) I don't know from Adam and have never met in my life sent me checks in the mail for at least $3,000 each. Of course, I sent them thank-you notes and told them how happy I was for them."

One of the checks came from the Joslyns.

"We said all along we wouldn't have had any of this if it wasn't for him," Jim Joslyn said.

G.D. also sent Carl Schmitt a gift and a thank-you note.

"It was very thoughtful for a guy to be mindful enough to do that," Schmitt said. "I'd known him for a long time. It was a thrill, and the biggest thrill for me was being the guy that verified the ticket for him and looked back at him and said, 'You're the man.' It was just one of those nights where you kind of go, 'Wow.'"

The irony or coincidence, depending on your interpretation, is that somebody so close to the Breeders' Cup—an actual employee—wound up with the only winning ticket and actually orchestrated it.

"Some people would probably see that, but I'm a player and you can find me at the simulcasts," G.D. reasoned. "There was really no inside information, if you will. The best thing about it is probably being on the track every single morning of the week and watching these horses. That's the first time I saw Daylami. I saw him every morning out there."

Stan Starks had been so overjoyed by the score he wanted to tell everybody, but had been cautioned by one of the Newsfeed supervisors not to talk to the media because of concerns about how it would be perceived by the public.

"I'm like, what the heck, why do I care?" Starks said. "He was afraid it might look like an inside job, since we all worked for the Breeders' Cup and were out there every day."

G.D. said the news didn't really affect his two daughters Kelly, nine at the time, and Lindsay, three years younger, but some of their school friends noticed because of a story that appeared in the *Herald-Leader*.

"Then you'd go to the school functions and they'd say, 'You won a million dollars.' You know how those kids are."

In January of the following year, G.D. produced the annual Eclipse Awards and encountered Ted Mudge, the president at the time of Amtote, the company that processed the betting system used at Gulfstream. Mudge was in awe of what had happened and G.D. told him he didn't have a chance to keep the winning ticket. Mudge worked at Gulfstream Park and, after G.D. gave him the winning numbers, printed a facsimile ticket for him on Breeders' Cup paper as a memento.

In July 2000, G.D. left Hammond Productions to take a job with Keeneland, where he works as director of broadcast services. Nick Nicholson, who took over as president of Keeneland in January 2000, had worked with G.D. for many years at the Jockey Club and their families know one another.

A year later, Keeneland sent out a press release heralding the launching of a new interactive digital race replay system that allows fans to watch replays of Keeneland races in addition to races throughout North America. G.D. spearheaded Keeneland's efforts to introduce this technology.

In the overall pantheon of sports wagering—certainly in the Breeders' Cup, anyway—the Pick 6 may be his most significant achievement.

"You work pretty hard in the industry and I feel like I've done a lot of good productions for everybody from horse farms, racetracks, the Breeders' Cup to the

Jockey Club," he said. "Believe me, I've gotten good gigs, producing the Eclipse Awards and still a lot of my peers recognize that, but a lot of people recognize me as the Pick 6 guy. I don't want to be recognized as that. My brother is a great handicapper, he's better than I am. I wish I was as good as he is."

John once had 20% of a Pick 6 ticket worth $75,000 and he's had other scores. He just wished he had his brother's intuition and luck.

"Maybe G.D. seeing me hit Pick 6 tickets got him inspired, I don't know," he said. "I guess that's where I was lucky, playing small tickets and having good scores, but he played a little larger ticket and had that big score.

"G.D. has a friend, Cecil Watts, the best man at his wedding, and we used to go to the Red Mile harness track on a Friday night, four or five of us, and have a couple beers. G.D. would always seem to hit a trifecta for something that was like $1,000, just boxing three horses or something. Cecil would always kid G.D. about his luck. He'd say, 'G.D. wins $1,000 and all I got out of it was a cheap Red Mile hat.' Every time Cecil would see G.D. after the Breeders' Cup hit, he'd say, 'There he is, the guy that hit the $84 million Pick 6 and I got a hat out of it.' One time G.D. went to Lake Tahoe for a skiing vacation after an Eclipse Awards show in San Francisco and he stepped off the plane and went to a video poker machine and put in four quarters and won about $1,200. Yeah, he's walking around lucky at times."

G.D. has a simple thought about his Breeders' Cup score: "It's one of those days that'll never (happen again)."

That was something Stan Starks, the longtime horseplayer, tried to convey to one of the people who lucked out on the score and hadn't had any experience playing the horses. "They don't realize how lucky they were, not only to be part of a Pick 6 win but for there to be only one ticket," Starks said.

That's why G.D. and his friends had reason to party like it was 1999. They had just made the score of the century.

# 21

# The Fix Six

## The Pick 6 Scandal

There's an old adage that crime doesn't pay, and if you need a perfect example, then consider the case of the Fix Six, the greatest scandal in the history of the Breeders' Cup and one of the most notorious in the annals of sports. Three wise guys thought they could beat the game, only to find out there's no such thing as a sure thing.

The three anti-heroes are Chris Harn, Glen DaSilva and Derrick Davis, who entered Drexel University in the early '90s. Founded in 1891 by financier Anthony J. Drexel in the west end of Philadelphia, Pennsylvania, Drexel was originally established as an institute of technology but became reclassified as a university some 81 years later. Drexel developed a reputation for its computer sciences program, attracting students seeking to enhance their skills and their minds.

Harn, DaSilva and Davis each possessed computer skills, but they had different personalities and backgrounds. Davis came from Maryland, had engineering smarts and athletic skills that he showcased in high-school soccer. He had good looks, a sense of humor and an eye for fashion. Harn, who grew up in both California and Kentucky and later moved to Maryland to live with his mother after she divorced, had a string-bean physique, long hair he occasionally wore in a ponytail and a penchant for baggy clothes. He also had a pronounced stuttering problem, although he reduced the severity of it by developing confidence in social situations. He read a lot and dazzled opponents who dared to play him in computer video games. DaSilva, who had grown up in New Jersey, had a flair for fashion and style, both in the clothes he wore and the way he coifed his hair. He also had a black cat that he kept with him, but which frequently liked to roam.

DaSilva and Harn had been assigned to a residence upon admission, but in the spring of their freshman year they moved into the frat house known as Tau Kappa Epsilon. Popular with business, engineering and information technology students, Tau Kappa Epsilon was unlike the other dozen or so frat houses on the campus. It stood out because of its beautiful exterior and well-kept interior. It housed about 50 people—including Davis, who lived across the hall from DaSilva and Harn—all of whom had responsibilities. DaSilva served as the secretary—an elected position—for a period of time. The other two worked as house managers, in a kind of superintendent capacity. All three liked to drink and party and go nightclubbing.

None of the three graduated. Davis attended Drexel for 16 months, but never declared a major. Both Harn and DaSilva had six-year stays at Drexel (Harn majoring in information systems and DaSilva majoring in business administration and marketing), but each fell a few credits short. It was not unusual, however, for students to last as long in the program as Harn and DaSilva and not graduate, according to a TKE frat brother who knew the other two.

There was nothing to suggest these three would become the most infamous trio to ever pass through Drexel's doors or that they would reconvene years later for the greatest technological scam in thoroughbred horse racing history.

After leaving Drexel, Davis returned to his home in Baltimore, Maryland, and began a business, Utopian Networks Inc. It specialized in computer installation and service for companies that didn't have their own computer staffs. He also married.

Harn found employment shortly after leaving Drexel as a computer programmer in Delaware with Autotote, the leading North American provider of hardware, software, networks and services to watch and wager on races. More than 100 North American racing and wagering operations are powered by Autotote equipment, including 10 of the top 15 thoroughbred horse racing tracks and 10 of the 12 largest OTB networks. Harn began as a software engineer in March 1997, impressing his superiors with his mind and skills. During a business trip to Peru, he met and later married a local woman and together they began a family. He left Autotote in February 2001 to take a job with a company based in San Diego. But the job entailed travel and it impacted on his family, so he called Autotote and asked for his old job. Not only did Autotote agree to rehire him and pay for his relocation costs, he was given a new job, working as a senior software engineer in research and development. His responsibilities included troubleshooting and providing technical assistance for all of Autotote's systems, including the telephone voice recognition systems enabling bettors to place wagers from anywhere to pari-mutuel facilities. He was among only a handful of technicians who had the password to access the systems.

DaSilva moved to Manhattan after leaving Drexel and lived with his girlfriend, to whom he later became engaged, in an apartment. He began working in a marketing job with Arthur Andersen, an accounting and consulting firm, but left a year later to join an internet company called Medscape, which specialized in providing clinical information for doctors. He lasted a couple years before leaving to take another job with a digital company but was laid off less than a year later. By this time, he and his girlfriend had parted and he was living alone. After the experience with the digital company, he found some employment with Andersen Consulting, but was laid off once again and collected unemployment insurance. He built up a web page called DaSilva Digital and advertised his company as a "provider of creative technology-enabled solutions that help companies capture value from the internet and other emerging technologies."

But he had little success with his company. He had also developed a cocaine dependency and was charged and convicted at one point for drug possession and placed on probation.

Though Harn, Davis and DaSilva participated in some of the football pools at their frat house, none of the three were known as gamblers, but all that was about to change early in the year 2001. Harn had some ideas how to make some money quickly, and even though the means to do it were illegal he considered them foolproof. He grafted the bar codes of uncashed winning tickets onto tickets Auto-tote used for test purposes. It is not uncommon for some bettors to forget, lose or throw away winning tickets, and without any proof of purchase there is no way of collecting; hence untold sums of money annually go uncollected like uncashed lottery tickets.

When Harn tried out the grafted tickets and they worked, he discovered a license for printing money, albeit using a plan. And the plan involved the other two, though DaSilva and Davis didn't find out until a year later of each other's involvement. Harn began with DaSilva, shortly after his arrest for drug possession, by telephoning him and seeking to meet him in New York. They had maintained a relationship since leaving Drexel and Harn occasionally stayed with DaSilva during trips to Manhattan. Harn told DaSilva about his grafting scam and they tested out some of the tickets at Aqueduct one day. Following a few bets, they cashed about $2,000 in winnings and celebrated later that night. Harn gave DaSilva some tickets and instructed him to use them to avoid drawing attention and suspicion. DaSilva was to use the tickets at one track, only twice a month and on weekends when it was crowded. They would split the winnings evenly and when DaSilva exhausted his supply of tickets Harn would provide him with an an additional batch. After almost a year, they had collected nearly $50,000 apiece in winnings.

Early in October 2002, Harn instructed DaSilva to open a touch-tone telephone account with the Catskill Off-Track Betting Corporation in Poughkeepsie, New York, using an internet site called InterBets.com to access it, and to deposit $1,400 from their winnings. DaSilva followed the instructions and gave Harn the account number. Though not completely sure of Harn's intentions, DaSilva dutifully followed his former college roommate's plan and was rewarded when they won $1,757. Harn had correctly picked the designated four consecutive winners of the Pick Four bet at Balmoral Park, a harness-racing track in Illinois. Harn told DaSilva he won by calling in the bet, then changed the numbers of the horses midway through the Pick Four. Harn, along with some other employees at Autotote, knew the password to access the computers of racetracks hooked up to Autotote's system. A couple of days later, they played a Pick Six—in which the bettor is required to pick the winners of six designated races—at Belmont Park in New York. Several winners nailed the Pick Six, which was worth more than $80,000 after taxes. Harn called DaSilva after the races and told them of their latest windfall. By this time, DaSilva had been living the good life, spending his winnings on drugs and women, in trips to various parts of the U.S., while returning to New York for his monthly meetings with his probation officer.

While Harn was working in partnership with DaSilva, he also had been scheming with Davis, although DaSilva didn't know it. Harn had shown Davis how to make money using the fraudulent tickets during a trip to Delaware Park. They had made about $11,000 apiece in five months.

Harn knew he couldn't continue to collect large amounts with DaSilva, lest it arouse suspicion, so he called Davis and told him about his success with DaSilva. Harn had his eyes on the Breeders' Cup Pick 6, scheduled to originate from Arlington Park in suburban Chicago on October 26. Harn instructed Davis to open an account at the same Catskill OTB location in upstate New York, accessing it by the InterBets.com carrier. Davis made separate deposits totaling $2,250 and gave Harn the account number. Some 20 minutes before the start of the Ultra Pick Six on the Breeders' Cup, Harn played the bet using various combinations. On one ticket, he employed all of the horses in the first two races and singled horses in the final four races, collectively costing $364. On his second bet, he singled four horses on the first four races and used all of the horses in the final two races, which collectively cost $192. But playing a $12 ticket, or the equivalent of multiplying the bet six times, it cost $1,152 overall.

That same day, Harn came to work, even though he hadn't been scheduled for a shift. During the running of the Pick Six races, Harn and Davis communicated via phone.

The first race began with a stunning result in which 4-5 favorite Rock of Gibraltar, the European invader with a five-for-five record on the season, finished second, beaten by 26-1 shot Domedriver. Countless Pick Six players who had singled (or in betting parlance "keyed") Rock of Gibraltar probably knew then and there they had lost any hope of winning the bet. At best, they could only hope to collect the consolation payoff by picking at least five of six winners. The second leg saw Orientate, the 27-10 favorite, win. Starine, a 13-1 shot, won the third leg, sending further pangs of despair among Pick Six players. Vindication, the second choice at slightly more than 4-1, won the fourth leg. At this point, the computer system used for the Pick Six sent data from all simulcast outlets pooling into the host track. The system, as it was set up then, could not accommodate all the permutations and computations of the multiple-race bet until after the completion of the fourth leg of the Pick Six. Technically, tickets could be tampered or altered by changing the losing numbers of the first four races to winning numbers, which coupled with using all the numbers for the final two races ensured a guaranteed payoff. All it took was the capability and know-how of the system to manipulate the numbers—and Harn had the ability to make the changes by accessing the system.

High Chaparral, the 9-10 favorite, won the fifth leg, leading up to the sixth and last leg. Medaglia d'Oro went postward as the 27-10 favorite and had the lead with only a quarter mile to go, but Volponi, the longest shot in the race at more than 43-1 odds, secured the lead and registered a stunning victory. It also ended most people's Pick-Six dreams.

It was announced shortly afterward that the Pick Six, which accumulated a total pool of $4,569,515 from the host track and simulcast outlets, produced six winners, each worth a return of $428,392 before taxes. Moreover, those winning tickets counted among the consolation payoffs for picking five of six winners, the financial returns each worth $4,606.20.

When it was also announced that the six winning tickets had been purchased at the same location—a Catskill, New York OTB outlet—more than a few people began to wonder. In fact, *New York Times* horse racing writer Joe Drape said to a fellow New York reporter: "That is really weird."

Harn knew immediately he and his conspirators were in trouble, even though Davis and DaSilva wouldn't truly comprehend the total gravity of their misdeeds for a few days.

Arlington Park pari-mutuel officials contacted the Catskill OTB hub seeking a report of the results—such data is readily available to racetracks combining in the common pool—curious that all the winning tickets originated from the same location. At that point, Arlington did not suspect any wrongdoing. All that changed the following morning because of a New York Racing Association official who caught the faint scent of a scandal. Bill Nader, a senior vice-president with NYRA and an employee in the racetrack business for more than 20 years, had talked to Glen Mathes, NYRA's director of public and media relations, and sensed something unrealistic, if not a bit suspicious, about six winners emanating from one location. The fact there happened to be a New York connection had little to do with Nader's curiosity. If it had happened at any location, he'd have felt the same way because of the uncommon occurrence. Nader called Jim Gallagher, NYRA's vice-president of pari-mutuel operations, and asked if he could obtain the data of the bet at the Catskill OTB. When the information revealed the same ticket had been repeated six times and had an unusual betting pattern, Nader strongly suspected wrongdoing. Each of the tickets showed only one horse had been selected in the first four legs of the Pick Six, followed by all eight horses in the fifth leg and all 12 in the final leg, amounting to $192 for each ticket. In 1999, a similar amount had been spent on what became the only winning ticket that year in the Breeders' Cup Ultra Pick Six, albeit the methodology of selecting the horses had been radically different. The 1999 winning ticket featured two horses in five of the six races and three in the other. Moreover, most of the picks included the betting favorites, along with some long shots that fortuitously prevailed in two of the six races. There had been nothing unusual or untoward about the system employed in that wager.

Upon inspection of the tickets and the system employed in the latest Pick Six score, Nader could not believe some of the betting strategy. In particular, Rock of Gibraltar had not been used in his race but Domedriver had. In fact, Domedriver had been singled. Furthermore, High Chaparral, the kind of prohibitive favorite that would likely be singled, had been used with all the horses in his race. In Nader's opinion, it just didn't add up.

"It was really an adrenalin rush because when I saw the configuration of the bet, I was just totally blown away," he recalled. "I think I said 'This is very wrong' about six times in a row. If somebody said there were six winning tickets at any track it was worthy of a full investigation. The key point here was that it was highly improbable that there would have been one winner, never mind six winners, from one site. When you looked at the percentage of handle that Catskill represented in the Pick Six pool on that day it was miniscule. Then step two was to find out that the six tickets were the same tickets. It was really a $12 ticket. It's almost like saying I'm going to play the lottery for $12, but I'm going to play the same numbers. Nobody would do that. Rock of Gibraltar came with big credentials. It was impossible not to put him on a play of that magnitude, and then in the High Chaparral race you were using every horse on each of the six tickets? It just made no sense at all. It just looked like cheating. From the first second we looked at it, it was wrongdoing and there was no way anybody could convince me it was a valid ticket."

At that point Nader began calling and e-mailing key people in the industry. He notified Gil Carmichael, Arlington Park's director of operations and wagering services, to make sure his company did not pay off the bet, and Ken Kirchner, the Breeders' Cup senior vice-president of product development. Nader subsequently sent e-mails to additional executives at the National Thoroughbred Racing Association—the partner of the Breeders' Cup—Arlington Park and the Thoroughbred Racing Protective Bureau. The New York State Racing and Wagering Board had been closed for the day, but Nader had the cell number of Joe Lynch, the chief of racing operations for the board, and had Gallagher, who formerly worked for the organization, call him. A call was also placed to an official of Autotote to inform the company it might have had an interior problem. Nader then removed himself from the situation.

"We weren't the host track and we weren't the receiving track, although we had an interest because we could have had many horse players who had five of six winners and they were being cheated or money was being stolen from them in this type of illegal activity," Nader said. "We did have an interest, but at that point it became a full-blown investigation. That's one good thing about the computer. You can alert a lot of people in a hurry, so I plastered out an e-mail and made the phone calls. I don't want to give myself too much credit because it really wasn't that complicated. Once we got the information that we needed, it was pretty black and white. The one thing we did that really helped was made sure there wasn't a money-wire transfer on Monday morning because then the chase would have been on to get the money back."

Carmichael had just returned to his office following the Breeders' Cup breakfast toasting the winners of the previous day when he received the call from Nader, indicating his concerns and plans to do some further investigation. Arlington had just received the Catskill OTB printout, which according to Carmichael looked "clean," albeit unusual. Coinciding with Nader's call, Arlington notified Keith Peterson, the state auditor for the Illinois Racing Board, who had been at the track, which had a scheduled day of racing. It is common on live race days for the racing board to have an auditor physically on-track to watch and monitor the wagering. The executives of Arlington Park and Churchill Downs Inc., which is a partner in the track, also began an internal investigation. At that point Arlington had no real concern from a financial standpoint because it still had possession of all the money from the Pick Six pool, which technically did not have to be wire transferred until the following day. But as the information of possible wrongdoing began to emerge, Arlington put a freeze on the processing of the payments. The Illinois Racing

Board gave the track a similar directive. About that time, Carmichael received an e-mail from Nader indicating a serious problem in the Pick Six wagering based on NYRA's preliminary investigation. From that sprung a whole series of dialogues among officials from Arlington and officials from the Breeders' Cup and National Thoroughbred Racing Association. All parties sought further information on the separate systems which processed the bets in New York (Autotote) and Chicago (Amtote). Each tote system has different features but are designed to dialogue with one other.

While the Pick Six situation became a legal issue for the state of Illinois, from an industry standpoint it involved a security problem. If, in fact, something unscrupulous had happened, it had the potential to bring the business to its knees. In 2001, more than $14 billion had been wagered on thoroughbreds, most of the money bet at off-track simulcast locations. Clearly, the problem had to be addressed rapidly and methodically, lest the betting public lose its faith and trust. Coincidentally, two years before, IBM had done a review of the industry and recommended major changes in the computer technology, which it deemed to be antiquated. Concerns about cost precluded the implementation of the changes.

Now the proverbial horse was out of the barn and the door was wide open.

Two days after its signature event, the Breeders' Cup Ltd./National Thoroughbred Racing Association sent a letter to New York State Racing and Wagering Board chairman Michael Hoblock noting the unusual nature of the Pick Six wagers and seeking a thorough review.

And shortly thereafter a media release was issued alerting the sporting world of a possible scandal.

"Our obligation in this case clearly is to protect the customer and the integrity of the process," Breeders' Cup president D. G. Van Clief said in a media release. "We are simply asking for a complete and rapid investigation by the proper authorities to determine the facts and to maintain confidence in all aspects of our competition."

Breeders' Cup officials noted their concerns related to possible electronic manipulation of wagering data and not in any way to the racing competition itself. Furthermore, the Breeders' Cup confirmed Arlington Park had withheld payment of the Pick Six winning tickets to the Catskill off-track betting outlet pending the results of the investigation.

Later that day the *Daily Racing Form*—the industry's bible—posted a story by industry writer Matt Hegarty providing additional information about the probe. The story indicated the board had been investigating a bettor, an unnamed 29-year-old Maryland resident, but did not know whether the bettor had acted alone or as part of a group. Moreover, the investigation would examine the computer security information, which records the times at which bets are placed, to determine if there was anything altered.

Hegarty quoted Donald Groth, the chairman of Catskill OTB, who indicated the winning bettor wanted to remain anonymous. Groth also dismissed any suggestion of wrongdoing, telling Hegarty "there is nothing to indicate that this was anything but a very good day for our customer. I know why you're suspicious, but that's not my job. I'm familiar enough with the customer that I believe this is legitimate."

Groth told Hegarty he had personally checked the time stamps for the telephone calls and the information indicated the bets had been placed well before the start of the first leg of the Pick Six, which commenced at 2:37 eastern standard time. Autotote president Brooks Pierce told Hegarty the company had been "100% certain" the pools had closed and that the bettor in question had made his wager 20 minutes before the first race of the Pick Six.

The *Thoroughbred Times*, posting a story the same day written by Bill Heller, also quoted Groth, who said: "We do not think there's anything suspect, so we welcome those who have greater knowledge to explore it to ensure the integrity of the races. It was a lucky day for a lucky fan. We believe that's what it was. We hope that's what it was."

In the *Times* story, it quoted the bettor in question, identified only as Derrick, who claimed he had made a mistake in the dollar-value of the bets but found out it was too late to cancel it.

"I kind of screwed up with their phone system," Derrick told the *Times*, adding he was unaware of the investigation.

"No money has been paid out and it might not until the investigation is complete," he said. "This is kind of ridiculous. I'm still in a state of shock. The fact that there's an investigation going on, what am I going to do?"

Davis said he knew he had the Pick Six after the first four races because he had the entire fields in the final two races.

"Vindication, I thought, was pretty much a lock," he said. "Orientate was a favorite. Domedriver and Starine were the only two long shots I had. I liked Domedriver. I did a lot of research. I liked Starine. I was trying to play it a couple different ways.

"I got divorced at the beginning of the year," he said. "It's been a crappy year up to now."

The following day, *New York Times* racing writer Joe Drape identified Derrick as Derrick Davis. Drape quoted Ed Martin, the executive director of the New York Racing and Wagering Board, who said: "It could be as simple as someone getting lucky or there were some shenanigans involved. We'll see what happens as the review continues."

Pierce said company records indicated Davis made the two bets a minute apart, more than 20 minutes before the Pick Six pools closed.

"We've done the autopsy and do not have any question about the veracity of the bets," Pierce told Drape. "I can understand how skeptics can look at a pool of this size and only one winner—especially with those four singles—and have concerns. But I also would like to think we have a pretty good story about a guy who didn't bet much and made a lot of money. I believe that is good for racing as well."

In a follow-up story by the *Daily Racing Form*, Hegarty revealed that the New York Racing Association, which operates Aqueduct, Belmont, and Saratoga, requested the New York State Racing and Wagering Board investigate two other Pick Six wagers the previous August at Saratoga. The first payoff on August 4 paid

$330,389; the second one on August 17 paid $421,988; and both were placed through the New York City OTB Corporation.

Hegarty pointed out the vulnerability of the Pick Six to computer manipulation because of the way data is transmitted from many different sources into commingled pari-mutuel pools. In particular, he revealed that although the information regarding the amounts of Pick Six wagers is sent immediately, the actual structure of the bet, including the specific horses that are being used, is not transmitted until after the fifth race is run in the Pick Six sequence. The reason, Hegarty explained, is because Pick Six wagers include so many potential combinations that the size of the computer files could create traffic problems in the tote network that links tracks across the country and continually updates wagering information. He also indicated that according to some racing officials, the difference creates a window of opportunity—sometimes lasting up to 2½ hours—in which data is being stored and when a computer expert or someone with access to the pools could manipulate specific bets.

He quoted an unnamed official close to the investigation, who said: "According to all the scam theorists I've talked to, the money would go in at the right time, but the horses would not get selected until after the fourth leg has been run. That's exactly what we saw here."

The *Thoroughbred Times'* Bill Heller did a follow-up story with quotes from Davis, but still identified him only as Derrick.

"I didn't past-post anything," Derrick said. "I do computer work, but I'm not a hacker." Because he did not want to go to the track on Breeders' Cup day, Derrick told Heller he went to the internet to look for an online betting service.

"If you go to Yahoo and do a search for horse betting, the first web site name that popped up is InterBets, so I clicked on it, made a call and set up an account," he said. "I didn't do anything wrong. I'm the guy who won this, but I'm the last person to find out what's going on. It's ridiculous. If I would have hit the lottery, I don't think it would be this tough with everything going on."

In an interview with the *New York Post*, Davis reasserted his innocence.

"If they got proof that I did something wrong, then show it to me, if not give me my money," he said.

Heller quoted Martin about the New York State Racing and Wagering Board's investigation into the big Pick Six payoffs at Saratoga.

"There could be nothing wrong; there could be everything wrong," Martin said. "If it's found that there's a problem with Pick Six wagering, my board would have to reconsider Pick Six wagering."

Five days after the Cup, Autotote, through its parent company Scientific Games Corporation of New York, conducted a conference call for media and stock analysts and announced the firing of an employee who had exploited a weakness in its system. Lorne Weil, the chairman of Scientific Games, described the employee as a "rogue software engineer" but did not reveal his identity. By day's end reporters identified the employee as Harn and linked his connection to Davis from their days at Drexel.

Weil said upon further review of the initial investigation, Autotote determined the fired employee had taken advantage of a weakness in its system, specifically the ability to alter the bet after the running of the first four races of the Pick Six.

Scientific Games had its trading on Nasdaq suspended during the announcement the employee had been fired.

"I think people see this for what it is—a rogue individual bound and determined to exploit the only weak link we see in the system so far," Weil said.

Later that day when the *New York Times'* editors gathered to discuss the top stories, they decided to move the Pick Six developments from the sports page to the front page of the paper. The *Times* staffed the Triple Crown, the Saratoga meet and the Breeders' Cup and ran occasional feature stories, but didn't follow horse racing on a daily basis similar to the tabloids. But something about this story triggered an interest at the *Times*, which viewed the scandal as a great caper and had Drape delve into it vigorously. He began covering horse racing in 1996 after following news and national affairs prior to that at some other newspapers. He was instructed to report the character and flavor of the story and not write it as a police story, so Drape started making numerous phone calls, along with freelance Bill Finley, and things started to fall into place.

The following day, in a story headlined "Worker Dismissed as Inquiry Widens into Big Racing Bet," Drape detailed the firing of the employee, whom he identified, and other salient information.

"He is caught in the middle of a maelstrom," Davis' lawyer, Steven A. Allen, told Drape. "As far as he's concerned, he made a legitimate bet. The race was run and he won and he should have received his payoff and that should have been the end of it. Now, instead, there's an investigation, people are making a variety of wild accusations and his reputation is being sullied for no good reason."

Drape quoted Davis' father Thomas, who said: "I just think it's like the equivalent of his hitting the lottery. I know in the bottom of my heart that it's a legitimate bet."

Harn declined comment when contacted by Hegarty, referring questions to his New York–based lawyer Daniel Conti, who refused to respond to specific questions.

"The past 24 hours have been very difficult for Chris and his family," Conti said in a statement. "He's been fired from his job, and he now finds himself the target of a criminal investigation. Suppositions abound, yet no one has referred to a single shred of legally recognizable evidence that Chris has done anything wrong."

Neither Davis nor Harn were charged at that point.

Hegarty quoted two former Autotote employees, who described Harn as a quiet and somewhat shy individual. They said he knew the system intricately. One of the former employees said Harn often worked on weekends as an on-call technician, sometimes with the entire office to himself.

"It's not like there's a guard at the building or anything and it's locked down," one of the coworkers told Hegarty. "You go in there, you're on call, and it's like being the Maytag salesman. Ninety-nine percent of the time, you sit there with absolutely nothing to do."

One of the former coworkers recalled that Harn could "get on a computer anywhere he was and dial into the system and do whatever he wanted to do."

Hegarty said tote experts indicated a properly trained technician, working from Autotote's headquarters in Delaware, could have retrieved the Pick Six wager by entering the company's system and searching through a Catskill computer file containing the Pick Six bets, which are identified by serial number.

Ted Mudge, an executive with multi-track operator Magna Entertainment and a former president of Autotote, provided an interesting perspective on Davis' bet in an interview with Eric Mitchell of *The Blood-Horse*.

"Every big player in the country knows that was not a normal bet and that something happened here," he said. "People who bet Pick Sixes make a primary bet and then make variations on that primary bet."

Mudge said if Davis didn't have the only winning ticket or the payoff had not been so large, the incident might have passed unnoticed.

"Instead of holding six of 30 tickets and disappearing into the woodwork, Volponi came rolling in and left him naked," Mudge told Mitchell.

Weil said if fraud had been committed it would have been detected regardless of the number of winning tickets, although possibly not as quickly.

*Washington Post* horse racing writer Andy Beyer, who is also a popular figure in the sport for his handicapping expertise, took issue with Weil's comments in the conference call. The conference call had been viewed by some as nothing more than an attempt to talk to stock analysts, many of whom had little or no knowledge of horse racing or the intricacies of betting and therefore could not vigorously question Weil.

"I worry that my fellow bettors and I have been the ongoing victims of cheaters within the pari-mutuel business," Beyer said in a column he wrote for his paper and reprinted in the *Daily Racing Form*. "The question I wanted to ask Weil in the conference call was this: 'How do you know this hasn't been going on for years?' If he responded with assurances that Autotote's detection systems would have caught the wrongdoer, I had my follow-up question ready: 'Are you saying, Lorne, that this rogue employee knew all of the weak links in the processing of Pick Six bets? He knew how to crack into the system. He knew how to alter a bet that was already placed—something the tote companies had claimed was impossible. And yet he didn't know you had a detection system guaranteeing that he would be caught?' Maybe I am just a typical, cynical gambler, but I doubt that the tote company would have detected any wrongdoing unless the crooked Pick Six play had already become a national scandal. The whole tenor of (the) conference call was to reassure analysts and investors and thus protect Scientific Games' stock price. But if Autotote's brass believe that no damage has been done, they are totally out of touch with the business for which they process billions of dollars of wagers. I do not know a single horseplayer who thinks the Breeders' Cup scandal was an isolated incident of a sort that has never happened before and will never happen again. Most think this is the tip of an iceberg."

By week's end, the NTRA announced the formation of a wagering technology working group to review computer security in connection with wagering on horse racing and to work with other industry groups to ensure customer confidence. The working group would identify and retain outside expertise in technology and security to advise the racing industry. Nine days after the Cup, the NTRA announced developments of its wagering technology working group and some planned future steps.

"The incidents now under investigation represent a wakeup call to which our industry is responding vigorously," NTRA commissioner Tim Smith said. "We are committed to identifying and implementing all reforms necessary to assure the integrity of racing's wagering systems. The wagering technology working group established by the NTRA is a vital part of this effort. It will move forward aggressively and operate in a manner designed to assure our customers that the pari-mutuel system is protected from abuse."

The NTRA subsequently announced it had retained Ernst & Young LLP, a leading security services provider, to coordinate its efforts with tracks, tote companies and the Thoroughbred Racing Protective Bureau.

"Every industry involved in these kinds of financial transactions faces similar issues," Ernst & Young said in a press release. "We look forward to helping the horseracing industry determine both short-term and longer-term steps to address wagering security and enhanced public confidence."

On November 6, 11 days after the Cup, Drape and Finley co-authored a story revealing a third person had been snared in the Pick Six dragnet. The story detailed the Drexel and Tau Kappa Epsilon connection to Davis and Harn, that the third person had a telephone betting account at the Catskill OTB shop, and that officials were examining several winning tickets with substantial payoffs that he cashed before the Breeders' Cup. The third person would be identified the next day as Glen DaSilva.

To this point, authorities had yet to charge any of the individuals.

In the *Daily Racing Form*, Hegarty revealed the specific bets at Balmoral Park on October 3 and October 5 at Belmont Park in which DaSilva had come under investigation. The betting strategy for the Pick Six at Belmont Park resembled the same pattern employed in the Breeders' Cup Pick Six by Davis. DaSilva spent $784 on his Belmont Pick Six ticket, betting eight separate $2 tickets that paid $13,070 apiece. In addition, DaSilva also had 96 consolation tickets, worth $113 each, running the total payoff to $115,408 before taxes.

DaSilva cashed one $2 ticket on the Pick Six at Balmoral, using single horses in the first two legs and every horse in the final two legs.

On November 8, the scandal reached new heights when the United States Department of Justice took over the investigation with assistance from the New York State Police and the Federal Bureau of Investigation. The same day the NTRA, through its wagering technology working group, announced it had called for three steps to improve electronic wagering security and increase customer confidence. The steps, made in conjunction with the major racetrack operators and totalizator companies, included: the installation of software to scan all pools in multi-race wagers after each race; software to record telephone account wagers; and a review of any winning simulcast wager involving multiple-leg bets.

"Longer-term changes and improvements also clearly are necessary, but these are important first steps," NTRA commissioner Tim Smith said.

Churchill Downs Inc., one of the three largest multi-track operators in the U.S., announced betting at its tracks would be closed one minute before the horses are loaded into the starting gate. Tom Meeker, CDI's chief executive officer, said the early closing would allow the company's tracks to post the final odds on its races before the horses leave the gate. Many tracks had odds changing during the running of the races due to the computer technology.

On November 11, the *Daily Racing Form* reported Davis, DaSilva and Harn would surrender to the United States attorney's office in the Southern District of New York, facing possible felony fraud and conspiracy charges.

The *New York Daily News* reported DaSilva planned to surrender, but would not plead guilty.

"They made bets," DaSilva's attorney, Ed Hayes, told the *Daily News*. "They won. These are very risky bets. They have very high payouts. Can the government show the bets they placed are different than the bets they won? I don't think so."

A day later, nearly three weeks after the Breeders' Cup, the saga of the most notorious scandal in horse racing history turned into the homestretch when Davis, DaSilva and Harn surrendered to authorities. They resembled young executives dressed in suits, but the apparent sins of their deeds were evident with handcuffs. They were arrested and named in a criminal complaint accusing them of conspiring to commit wire fraud. Davis and DaSilva failed drug tests that showed evidence of cocaine in their urine. They later appeared in front of U.S. Magistrate Judge Mark D. Fox, who released them after they posted $200,000 each in bail. The prosecutors had a deadline of December 17 to issue an indictment and planned to pursue various fraud and conspiracy charges upon the presentation of evidence to a grand jury.

Later that week, the racing commissions in Illinois and Canada took the first steps in temporarily banning some multi-race wagers in their respective jurisdictions. The Canadian Pari-Mutuel Agency banned the Pick Six, Pick Four and Superfecta, which requires picking the first four finishers in a race. The CPMA cited concerns about how the data is transmitted. The Illinois Racing Board temporarily banned Pick Six and Pick Four wagers, pending a review of the tote systems at tracks and OTB shops in the state.

The decision by the CPMA angered officials at the Woodbine Entertainment Group, which operates the biggest thoroughbred and harness tracks in Canada. Officials from Woodbine and other Canadian tracks planned to make presentations to the CPMA to amend the decision, concerned about the impact on the daily handle. The CPMA partially amended its decision after listening to presentations by the racetrack officials and reinstated Superfecta wagering.

That same week Autotote sent a letter to racetracks indicating plans to install a system to monitor the activities of people with access to its betting network. The system, designed by a Canadian firm, had already been in place at some Canadian-based tracks.

Also, the New York Racing Association announced a change in its Pick Six policy. Instead of allowing players to make an alternate selection because of a late scratch, they would automatically receive the betting favorite, a policy in place at some tracks.

On November 19, the NTRA planned a significant announcement for the following day: the hiring of Giuliani Partners, headed by former New York city mayor Rudy Giuliani, to help in implementing security controls. The Breeders' Cup management team knew some of the employees from Giuliani's firm from experiences relating to the 2001 Breeders' Cup at Belmont Park and had retained the company for its consulting services. Given Giuliani's background as a former state attorney and his track record of systematically addressing problems during his tenure as mayor of New York City and his strong national stature, the Breeders' Cup considered him a great choice to help it through its greatest crisis.

The announcement came the same day Harn appeared in the United States District Court and pleaded guilty to one count of conspiracy to commit wire fraud and one count of money laundering. And the *New York Times* provided a sneak preview of what was to unfold in a front-page story by Joe Drape. Not only did Drape outline Harn's planned pleas, but also the method he and his conspirators used to make money using uncashed betting tickets. Harn provided testimony how he used his work computer to rig three sets of bets, the other offences relating to DaSilva's wagers on the Pick Six bet at Balmoral Park and the Pick Six bet at Belmont that collectively totaled more than $100,000 in winnings.

It was also revealed in Harn's testimony that the day before the Breeders' Cup he sent DaSilva an e-mail asking him to send checks totalling $31,500 to his personal creditors.

"This morning, by pleading guilty, Chris has accepted fully the responsibility for the crimes he has committed," Harn's lawyer Daniel Conti said.

U.S. Magistrate Judge Lisa Margaret Smith revealed Harn could face up to 25 years in prison, although it would likely be reduced substantially because of his confession.

Davis' lawyer, Steven A. Allen, said his client would continue to fight the charges, while DaSilva's lawyer, Ed Hayes, said his client might seek a plea bargain.

"Everybody has to do what they have to do, but just so people know, the prosecutors went to Mr. DaSilva first and he said, 'I can't testify against a guy I've been friends with and has a two-year-old daughter,'" Hayes revealed. He also said he addressed Harn's lawyer and said they should go in together so "nobody had to be the rat. But Harn decided to go in alone. I guess it was too much to expect that the three TKE's could resist not ratting out each other. This would never happen if it were Sigma Pi's or Theta Chi's involved."

Former frat brothers of the three accused suddenly found themselves contacted by reporters seeking background information. Some of the TKE brothers willingly talked, but some maintained a code of honor and declined.

Meanwhile in Manhattan the NTRA announced its alliance with Giuliani Partners to manage and oversee the horse racing industry's review of its electronic wagering systems. Additionally, the NTRA announced the launching of a "systematic examination" of multi-race wagers for the entire year to identify whether additional security measures were required.

"This step is a logical expansion of the aggressive process being undertaken by the technology working group," NTRA commissioner Tim Smith said in a press release. "It responds to the concerns of fans and may well provide additional information helpful in strengthening security systems. We are determined to learn everything necessary to assure the pari-mutuel system's integrity and protect our customers' interests. . . . The addition of Giuliani Partners to the team will help in a variety of ways. Clearly, Rudolph Giuliani brings independence and credibility both to our review of past wagers and our commitment to future improvements."

"Thousands of fans wager everyday on horse racing across the country and should be confident with the knowledge that their wagers are being handled in a secure fashion in an honest system," Giuliani said in the release. "The NTRA should be applauded for its immediate response in rallying racing leaders to review the security of electronic wagering systems and to maintain the confidence of its consumers. I look forward to working with the leaders of the racing industry to develop new safeguards for one of America's most popular sports."

In an interview with Drape, Giuliani explained the scam as an example of the "pig factor."

"Very often . . . somebody goes too far and it becomes obvious, and then below that surface can often be other situations," Giuliani said.

The following day, in an announcement that fell through the cracks, the New York Racing Association named Patrick Mahony vice-president of pari-mutuels, replacing Vince Hogan, who would be retiring at the end of the year. Mahony had been head of the pari-mutuel department at Gulfstream Park in 1999—the year the Breeders' Cup instituted the Ultra Pick 6, which was legitimately won by a group of 19 people. Mahony handled the paperwork for the wager when G. D. Hieronymus, who had purchased the ticket, came to pick up the group's winnings. Mahony had a wealth of experience in racetrack administration—specifically in pari-mutuel wagering—and the NTRA drew upon it as part of its many task forces assembled after the Pick Six scam.

On November 22, the New York Racing Association announced plans to prohibit its mutuel clerks from canceling tickets immediately after the start of a race. NYRA clerks had previously been allowed up to 15 seconds to cancel bets made at their computer terminals. Most tracks employed a similar practice to protect clerks from last-second errors and to prevent someone from placing a major wager and then refusing to pay after the ticket has been entered into the mutuel machine.

In another interesting development, the *Thoroughbred Times* reported that officials from the three major tote companies backed out of a question-and-answer period scheduled for the following week at the annual University of Arizona Symposium on Racing. The officials, who initially agreed to appear and answer questions about the Pick Six scandal, canceled on the advice of legal counsel.

And in yet another interesting happening, the California law firm of Lisoni and Lisoni filed a class-action lawsuit against Autotote on behalf of California handicapper Jimmy (the Hat) Allard. He charged Autotote with negligence and alleged the betting public "may have been cheated out of countless millions of dollars the past eight years, with the Breeders' Cup fraud being the first time it has been discovered."

"No matter how good you are, there are 1,000 ways to lose a horse race and only one way to win," Allard said at a media conference at the National Press Club in Washington, D.C., a day later. "Now there are 1,001 ways to lose."

On December 11, DaSilva pleaded guilty to wire fraud, computer fraud and money laundering, facing a maximum penalty of 25 years in prison and fines of up to $750,000, although both would likely be reduced considerably.

"He's going to take responsibility for what he did," DaSilva's attorney Ed Hayes said. "He got involved in something he shouldn't have done. He's going to take his medicine, which isn't going to be fun."

The following day, Davis pled guilty to one count of wire fraud and computer fraud, facing a maximum penalty of five years and a maximum fine of $250,000. He would also face reductions in both time and money because of his decision to waive his right to a jury trial.

"I'm truly sorry and regret my involvement in this entire wrongdoing and am throwing myself on the mercy of the court," Davis said. "I take full responsibility for my acts." All three were released on bail.

On December 13 at the 29th annual Symposium on Racing in Tucson, Arizona, the NTRA presented an update on some of the programs implemented to enhance electronic wagering systems security. Meanwhile, in an interview with the *Thoroughbred Times*, an official with the Illinois Racing Board said the suspended Breeders' Cup Pick Six payout could not be distributed to holders of consolation tickets until federal officials in New York lifted a freeze on the money.

The pool had 78 consolation tickets worth $4,606.20 apiece but now worth some 10 times that amount because of the corrections in the payoffs.

In a follow-up article four days later, Hegarty reported the United States attorney prosecuting the Breeders' Cup Pick Six case decided to treat the winnings of the bet as "criminal proceeds," thus causing a further delay to rightful ticket holders. Breeders' Cup president D. G. Van Clief said officials from his organization planned to meet with the Illinois Racing Board and officials from Arlington Park to discuss steps in distributing the money.

On December 27, the NTRA announced that *New York Times* racing writer Joe Drape had won the Media Eclipse Award for writing in the news/commentary category for his series of articles on the Pick Six scandal.

"Truthfully, this is the only award I've ever wanted to win, partly because I don't count covering the people involved with horse racing as work," Drape said in an NTRA release. "As the man said: A bad day at the track is better than a good day anywhere else. I'm also honored to be on the same roster with folks who have won the award in previous years. It's hard not to smile when you see Red Smith's name on the list. He cared about the game and was the greatest of them all."

When interviewed for this book, the veteran reporter was asked why his newspaper took such an interest in the Pick Six story. He said the *Times* had many people in senior management who followed horse racing and viewed the Pick Six story as a scandal that crossed several cultural and economic divides. "It had all the makings of a good yarn and it picked up momentum incredibly in the office."

The scandal also provided an example of a journalist digging hard and of competition in media outlets, where the old adage is be first, be fast and be correct. In this case, as one of the most prominent newspapers in the country, the *New York Times* had a chance to really make its presence felt and Drape took full advantage of the opportunity.

"Once you get ahead, you keep driving," Drape said. "It becomes a part of you. You want to keep on top. You don't want to get beat. I've got to give (freelancer) Bill Finley his due. I had sources and he had sources."

In the middle of January, Hegarty reported Harn's hearing would not be heard until after Davis and DaSilva's. The delay would allow U.S. District Court Judge Mark Bryant to consider the sentences for Davis and DaSilva before deciding on Harn's punishment.

"That's how it is done in these cases," an official told Hegarty, speaking on the condition of anonymity. "The guy who goes first is sentenced last. There's no way Harn gets sentenced on Feb. 19, and it probably won't be done until a month after Davis and DaSilva get sentenced."

The government recommended that Davis face a sentence of 36 to 47 months in prison. DaSilva, who did not admit to a role in altering the Breeders' Cup Pick Six ticket, faced a recommended sentence of 21 to 27 months in prison.

Towards the end of January 2003, almost three months after the Breeders' Cup, the National Thoroughbred Racing Association and Churchill Downs Inc., which is a partner in Arlington Park, filed a petition in United States District Court in New York. The two organizations sought a legal attempt to free up the $3.1 million in Pick Six winnings held up by the Illinois Racing Board and release it to the rightful consolation winners.

While racing continued before and after the sentencing of the three Pick Six offenders, the fallout could be felt everywhere. A breach in security had changed horse racing forevermore, providing a significant wake-up call for industry officials.

"This incident is going to change this industry, at least in the way in the way it processes its wagers, I'm sure," Breeders' Cup president D. G. Van Clief said. "With a little luck—and at this point we're all a lot more relaxed about it than we were before—the industry comes out of this particular incident considerably stronger than it went in. I think we end up with better technology and a higher level of consumer confidence eventually and a much sounder dialogue with some of our key customers, the bettors. You could say the year ended with an unpleasant bang. It could have been catastrophic. I think we're going to be able to look back and say it wasn't a catastrophe, it was a near catastrophe."

In its March 2003 edition, *Vanity Fair* devoted nine pages to the story of the Fix Six, providing a comprehensive portrait of Harn, Davis and DaSilva and how they came together to participate in their crime. In the article titled "Winner Lose All," acclaimed writer Bryan Burrough, who is considered one of the leading business journalists in the U.S., noted that DaSilva had no idea that Harn had been working with Davis on the bet that exposed all three.

The article also noted that not only did Harn take advantage of the deal to receive a lesser punishment in exchange for cooperating with the prosecutors, he and his attorney "seemed so anxious, on the edge of their seats" to explain the whole plot.

"We had heard they were bringing in something new. So after the (prosecutors) laid down the ground rules, the procedural stuff, Chris couldn't wait to tell us about the ticket-cashing scheme," New York State Police officer Charles Sullivan said in the article. "He went on to explain that. I don't know why. It was a way he had beaten the system. He was almost bragging."

According to the article, Harn's admission was the first investigators heard of the bogus-ticket scheme, and he talked nonstop, filling in several blanks. Burrough wrote that as Harn spoke, the investigators couldn't help but like him. He seemed utterly without guile and proud of what he had done.

Burrough wrote that Harn's attitude may have reflected a failure to grasp the seriousness of the situation, particularly when he asked his interrogators when he would receive his computer back because he wanted to send his resume to a head-hunter. Sullivan and his investigators were stunned by Harn's remarks.

"We all looked at each other like, 'What are you thinking? You're going to jail,'" Sullivan said in the article. "Afterward, I remember we all asked, 'What was that all about?'"

On March 10, the law firm representing Autotote sent a letter to United States District Judge Charles L. Brieant, who would be handing down the sentences to DaSilva, Davis and Harn. The letter was intended to apprise the court of the "severe harm to Autotote, to its employees and to the pari-mutuel industry" that resulted from the criminal conduct engaged in by the three accused. Furthermore, the letter stated Harn's betrayal of Autotote's trust caused "industry-wide upheaval, the effects of which linger today and threatened Autotote with irreparable financial losses. . . . That Autotote has successfully overcome the crisis that resulted from Harn's criminal conduct is a great credit to the professionalism of Autotote's employees and in no way diminishes the egregious nature of Harn's disloyalty."

The letter said Autotote conducted its own internal investigation after regulatory authorities notified the company of the suspicious wagering on the Breeders' Cup Pick Six. Additionally, the letter said Harn "facilitated" the cover-up of his crime by falsely explaining why he had accessed the Catskill computer system and by providing an "innocent" explanation for erasing any record of changes he made to the system. This suggested Autotote had no definitive record of what Harn had done. The letter said Autotote gave Harn another opportunity to cooperate with the company in the presence of his counsel.

"Rather than reveal what he knew about the Breeders' Cup Pick Six conspiracy, the other altered wagers, as well as the altered winning tickets, Harn chose to keep this information from Autotote. Harn's decision to refuse to co-operate with Autotote further exacerbated the harmful consequences of his unprecedented act of betrayal."

The letter added that in order to restore bettor and track owner confidence after Harn's acts, Autotote was "compelled to demonstrate the continuing integrity of its systems." It indicated Autotote had to purchase a new software application at a cost of nearly $1 million and had to pay almost another million in attorney and public relations fees. The letter concluded that Harn's betrayal of the trust Autotote placed in him affected an entire industry.

"Were it not for quick action by industry regulators, law enforcement agents and Autotote personnel, the disruption to this industry would have been far greater," the letter concluded.

What the letter did not indicate—if such a thing was possible—was what type of sentencing Autotote considered appropriate, particularly when it had been speculated Harn would likely receive the lightest sentence of all because of his cooperation with government investigators instead of Autotote officials. In effect, Harn doublecrossed Autotote.

On March 20, 2003, almost five months after the infamous Breeders' Cup Ultra Pick 6 scandal became public, Harn, Davis and DaSilva appeared in a federal court in White Plains, New York, for sentencing. Davis received three years and one month for wire fraud conspiracy. DaSilva, who pleaded guilty to fraud and money laundering, received a two-year sentence. DaSilva and Davis faced the possibility of reduced sentences for successfully completing drug-rehabilitation programs during their incarceration. Harn followed the other two and was given one year and one day for fraud and money laundering. The additional day allowed for a deliberate reduction in his sentence for good behavior, possibly commuting his jail time to only a few months.

The judge, Charles Brieant, said Harn could have received up to 7¼ years had he not agreed to help authorities. Brieant told prosecuting attorneys that "except for the improbability of the bet," he did not see how the government could have made its case without Harn's cooperation. That, however, was disputed by the prosecuting attorney for the U.S. Southern District of New York, who said Harn's cooperation assisted the government "a great deal."

Harn acknowledged he had hurt "a great number of people. Forgiveness is earned, not granted, and I hope to pay my debt to society not with words but by my future actions." The fact that Harn, who had engaged the other two to carry out his plan, received the lightest term of all surprised even his fellow conspirators.

The three were allowed to serve their sentences at minimum-security institutions near their family members. Harn's wife and young daughter returned to Peru.

Burrough found some character similarities in the Fix Six trio to the two principal figures in the movie *The Falcon and The Snowman*. Starring Timothy Hutton and Sean Penn, the movie portrayed the real-life story of Christopher Boyce and Andrew Daulton Lee, who were sentenced for selling classified government information to the Soviets in the late '70s. Boyce, who deciphered the information while working as an entry-level clerk at a U.S. defense institution, received a 40-year term, while Lee was slapped with a life sentence, his punishment harsher because of previous drug convictions.

But unlike Christopher Boyce and Andrew Daulton Lee, the perpetrators of the Fix Six didn't sell off government secrets to other countries—they only ripped off the racing industry and the people who entrusted it by betting money.

Their sentences received scant coverage in the major dailies compared to when the scandal first started to spark and became horse racing's version of Watergate. The U.S. military attack on Iraq had just been waged when the three were sentenced and the implications of an American exercise to liberate a country ruled by a savage dictator had far more importance in world affairs. Besides, this was just a betting scandal in a sport that was literally pushed to the back pages of most newspapers and mentioned only occasionally in broadcasts.

The sentencing cleared the way for the holders of the 78 consolation tickets that correctly picked five of the six winners to be paid in full. In addition to the $4,606.20 that had already been paid, an additional $39,580.88, which included interest, was forwarded.

The whole scandal may be made into a movie. Robert Wuhl, the creator and star of the onetime television show *Arli$$*, is scheduled to cowrite, direct and produce a television movie for Home Box Office about the Fix Six. The movie will be based on the articles written by Joe Drape of the *New York Times*.

"I see this as a story about growing up—the scam story is only part of it," Wuhl told the *Hollywood Reporter*. "They pulled a scam that worked, but it worked too well. They left a lot of tracks and they got caught."

In a sport in which the favorite wins roughly 33% of the time, they were beaten by a long shot. Then again, perhaps it was only a matter of time before they were caught, if you believe in Rudy Giuliani's so-called "pig factor." Maybe it's as simple as the words of another famous U.S. politician, Abe Lincoln, who once said: "It is true that you may fool all the people some of the time; you can even fool some of the people all the time; but you cannot fool all of the people all the time."

Or maybe it just proves that crime doesn't pay.

# 22

# The First Family of Racing

## The Paulsons

*H*e was an aircraft builder and she was a onetime stewardess and together they flew high as the most dynamic husband and wife team in racing. And even when he died, his empire did not crumble, although it did splinter because of a family feud. Through it all, one thing remained the same: the success of the Paulson name in the Breeders' Cup.

Allen E. Paulson grew up on a farm in Iowa during the Depression, but had a love for flying that he developed in his teens and still maintained well into his later years, piloting his planes around the world at record speeds. He once set 35 international records in two around-the-world flights in eight months. In the August 30, 1986, issue of *The Blood-Horse*, Paulson attributed his success to hard work, the willingness to assume risk and decisiveness. "There's no such thing as a lazy, lucky guy," he said.

Allen dabbled in the horse business in the 1960s, when he owned some claimers, yet it wasn't until the '80s that his interest changed from a passing fancy to a serious commitment. In 1982, he bought seven two-year-olds at the California Thoroughbred Breeders' Sale at Hollywood Park for $1,335,000. The following year, he paid $2.5 million for Savannah Dancer (equaling the record for the most expensive yearling filly sold at auction). In 1985, he paid $4.5 million—the highest price ever paid for a horse in training—for Estrapade at Keeneland's November breeding stock sale. All together, he spent more than $14 million in his first few years in racing, buying not only racehorses but future breeding prospects for personal and commercial purposes. At one time he had 180 broodmares, but by 1995 had scaled back to about 120, spread over various farms he owned throughout the U.S.

Paulson had a horse in the initial Breeders' Cup in 1984, when Savannah Dancer raced in his red, white and blue silks with the letters AP on the back in the Juvenile Fillies. Trained by Ron McAnally, she finished fifth, but was elevated to fourth on the disqualification of Fran's Valentine, who was ridden by Pat Valenzuela. In later years, the Paulsons and Valenzuela teamed up for some memorable Breeders' Cup wins. Paulson had a strong stable running in Europe during those years and shipped Committed to run in the 1985 Breeders' Cup Sprint. It cost

337

$200,000 to supplement the horse, whose sire was not nominated to the Breeders' Cup program. Committed failed to earn a check, finishing seventh in the Cup with the legendary Steve Cauthen aboard. Another Paulson European invader, Palace Music, who in later years would become renowned as the sire of Cigar, ran second in the Mile.

In 1986, Paulson had a big contingent: Prankstress in the Juvenile; Palace Music (in partnership with Nelson Bunker Hunt) in the Mile; and Turf candidates Theatrical (in partnership with Bert Firestone) and Estrapade. He collected two seconds and a third overall. Palace Music ran second by a head, while Theatrical lost by the same margin.

As they say at the racetrack, Paulson was sitting on a victory. His first winner came in 1987, when he had Le Belvedere in the Mile and Theatrical in the Turf. Le Belvedere ran an unspectacular ninth in the race won by the great European invader Miesque. Theatrical won the Turf, but not before one of the greatest controversies among owners in Breeders' Cup history. Paulson owned 50 percent of the horse, the other half belonging to a group that included the breeder Firestone. Paulson wanted to race Theatrical in his colors in the Breeders' Cup, but Firestone refused to acquiesce. Their squabbling became public, and rather than become involved in a long, drawn-out fight, Paulson resolved the disagreement by buying out Firestone and his partners. Lawyers hammered out an agreement the night before the race. An Irish-bred son of Nureyev, Theatrical was making his third start in the Breeders' Cup. Trained by Dermot Weld, Theatrical made his first appearance in the 1985 Turf, in which he ran 11th. The following year, after moving to the U.S., he ran second for trainer Bobby Frankel. In 1987, Bill Mott, a young conditioner from South Dakota, whom the Firestones hired in 1986 to work privately for them, finally made Theatrical a winner. And what a race it was, a fitting finale to the Great Silk Squabble the previous night. Theatrical and Prix de l'Arc de Triomphe winner Trempolino, owned by Bruce McNall and Paul deMoussac, engaged in a thrilling stretch duel. Theatrical had the lead after a mile, then held on by a half-length as the French invader, ridden by Pat Eddery, rallied strongly from well back and gave the American horse a run for the money. Pat Day, on the inside, pumped furiously on Theatrical, determined to finally win the Breeders' Cup after a near miss the year before.

Theatrical displayed the grit and desire that would make him a champion. At season's end, he won the Eclipse Award as best male turf horse, but lost to Breeders' Cup Classic winner Ferdinand in Horse of the Year balloting. Paulson felt the horse had been robbed of a just honor. For the next three editions of the Breeders' Cup, Paulson had a total of five starters, but only one, Tagel, who ran third in the 1988 Juvenile, collected a check.

But the '90s would prove to be Paulson's decade. Actually, Paulsons is more accurate, given the impact of his second wife, Madeleine, the onetime airline stewardess who shared his love for breeding and racing. In Madeleine, he had the perfect partner.

"I'm a female who thinks she's a male," she once said. "I think as a mother, the eternal mother. I think of (the horses') well-being, I love them passionately, just like a mother. I'm very competitive. It's a loving sport. You can't be in the sport and not love the animals. But I think women love them more."

Allen ran only one horse in the 1990 Breeders' Cup—Opening Verse, who placed seventh in the Classic. Opening Verse returned in 1991 to win the Mile with Valenzuela aboard at 26-1. Race caller Tom Durkin understandably called it a "shocker."

Paulson barely had time to savor the Mile victory before his next runner, Arazi, started in the Juvenile. Arazi went postward at 21-10, a slight favorite over California invader Bertrando. Starting from farthest out in the field of 14, Arazi put on a burst of speed around the turn that carried him from last to first and had all in attendance gasping in awe. Including the Paulsons.

Allen Paulson had one more runner that day in Cudas, who ran in the Classic. Cudas, like Arazi, had come from France, but unlike Arazi there had been no advance hype about him and there would be no hype about him afterward. Cudas earned no kudos for his performance, running last by 27 lengths. Then again, Cudas went postward at odds of more than 76-1, so it wasn't unexpected.

Paulson had done marvelously well that day. He could afford a humble ending. The following July, Paulson surprisingly fired trainer Dick Lundy, who had been his exclusive American trainer for more than three years and the man who saddled Opening Verse to victory. On the surface it seemed simple enough. Paulson assessed his slumbering stable and opted for a switch, perhaps like an owner of a sports franchise firing the manager or coach to change his luck. In a July 13 *Los Angeles Times* article written by Bill Christine, Paulson was quoted as saying: "I've got to do something to get my two-year-olds going. A trainer can concentrate on the super horses and forget all the rest." Paulson had a variety of American trainers he employed, including Bill Mott, who saddled Theatrical to a Breeders' Cup victory, but he gave the young horses to Alex Hassinger. The 29-year-old had rich bloodlines—he is the nephew of Breeders' Cup founder John Gaines—and had worked on one of Paulson's farms. "This is a great experience, it's a great day for me," Hassinger told Bill Christine. "The split is a shock to everybody. I enjoyed working with Dick. He is my friend and we talked on the phone. I wish him all the luck in the world."

Eight days after his original article on the split, Christine wrote a subsequent story indicating the real reason for the dismissal. Paulson was suing Lundy, alleging improprieties in the sale and purchases of horses in the United States and Europe. Paulson accused Lundy and bloodstock agent Stephen Grod of conspiracy to defraud. According to the suit, Paulson said he lost more than $1.1 million in various sales with Lundy and Grod as agents. Lundy could not be reached for comment, but Grod called the lawsuit "ridiculous." Paulson eventually won a $1.7 million judgment in August 1995 when Los Angeles Superior Court Judge Avivak Bobb ruled that Lundy and Grod "conspired to defraud and defrauded Paulson and (William) Condren and (Joseph) Cornacchia 1992 Partnership."

Led by Arazi, Paulson had his strongest contingent ever in 1992 for the Breeders' Cup. Actually, this time both Paulsons would be represented as Madeleine had her first Breeders' Cup starter in Fraise. Allen was so sure of his horses, he promised Pat Valenzuela a Rolls-Royce if he won the four races—kind of like hitting for the cycle in baseball. The day started off strongly as Eliza, the brilliantly fast lass who had been called the female version of Arazi, won the Juvenile Fillies as the 6-5 favorite. Next came the Distaff, but Fowda, an 8-1 proposition, ran ninth, beaten by nine lengths. Both of the horses were trained by Hassinger. About an hour later, the Paulsons' despair turned to strawberry fields forever. Madeleine Paulson's Fraise—French for strawberry—won the Turf at 14-1 by a nose over 9-10 favorite Sky Classic.

Madeleine dressed in a strawberry suit that day to fashionably announce her support for her first Breeders' Cup horse. Madeleine had acquired the four-year-old colt on a bet—with Allen—the year before. The Paulsons had been looking to spice up a game of golf one day, so they decided to bet horses. Madeleine offered her half-interest in a two-year-old named El Roblar, whom the Paulsons considered to be another Dinard, the 1991 Santa Anita Derby winner. Allen put up Fraise as his side of the wager. Fraise had not distinguished himself at the time, but became a Breeders' Cup winner the following year while El Roblar never lived up to his potential.

"It was destined; I fell in love with the horse before," Madeleine said. "I saw the program he was on and I was possessed with that horse. I had to have him. I played well that day. I gave (Allen) two strokes a hole. No foot wedges, nothing, just straight golf. And Allen couldn't have any mulligans. He was quite a gentleman after the game."

Madeleine liked her chances with Fraise, even if the public didn't.

"The television people put a microphone on Allen for his other races, when Eliza won and when Arazi ran in the Mile," Madeleine told writer Jay Hovdey. "The Fraise race came and there was no microphone. I remember thinking, 'It's their mistake. We're going to win.' I couldn't see Fraise for most of the race. It was so crowded. I finally saw him when he made the lead. And then Sky Classic was there, but he did it. Pat Valenzuela's ride was brilliant. But you know what? I don't care how brilliant the rider is. You still have to have the horse. Fraise won fair and square."

The day ended with A. P. Indy, the well-bred colt who had missed the Derby because of a foot problem, winning the Classic. Coupled with his other big victories that year, A. P. Indy earned Horse of the Year honors.

The Paulsons collectively won more money that day than any owner ever had before in the Cup. They had posed in the winner's circle with presenters such as Merv Griffin and Eva Gabor. But, their big star was gone. Arazi's flame flickered, then blew out.

The Paulsons' two-year Breeders' Cup run came to a halt in 1993. They sent only two horses—Fraise in the Turf and Diazo in the Classic—and neither finished in the top three. Fraise's fourth-place effort earned $112,000. In 1994, the Paulsons ran four horses, two each for Allen and Madeleine—but again they had a bad day at the races. For all the money they had invested, the Paulsons simply did not have good enough stock to compete in the Breeders' Cup that year. Miss Dominique, named for Madeleine's daughter from a previous marriage, ran third in the Distaff at 77-1, the longest-priced horse in the race, and collected $120,000. Fraise, running for the third year in a row but only a shadow of his former self, ran 11th in the field of 14. Stablemate Dahlia's Dreamer, whom Allen had given Madeleine as a birthday present, finished 12th. Flag Down, a grass horse running on dirt in the Classic, ran 12th in the field of 14.

Following the 1994 Breeders' Cup, there was an interesting development that not only regenerated Allen's racing spirit, but also gave the industry a badly needed star in 1995. Cigar, a four-year-old by Palace Music out of the dam Solar Slew, was bred by Allen but owned by Madeleine. Cigar became an emerging star when his new trainer, Bill Mott, put the colt on medication to help with an ulcer and moved him full-time to the dirt from the turf.

Madeleine had seen greatness in Cigar and, more importantly, sensed an opportunity to revitalize her husband's spirits, which had dwindled after the Breeders' Cup.

"After Arazi's retirement, Allen started to lose a little bit of interest," Madeleine said. "I said, 'What's wrong?' and he said, 'After you've had an Arazi, it's pretty hard to get excited.' I remember saying, 'Well, something will happen.' Sure enough, there was Cigar. If you wait long enough and the right conditions come along . . . I don't know, I believe in fate. Why does it all work out? And it couldn't have worked out for two better people: my husband and Billy."

Madeleine proposed a deal to her husband. She would be willing to trade Cigar in exchange for Eliza, who by that time had been retired to the breeding shed. Allen gave it a lot of thought. Eliza was a champion and a valuable mare, but Cigar had possibilities. Allen agreed to the trade and sweetened his end by giving up a free breeding to Theatrical. It turned out to be a steal of a deal for Allen, even after he gave some valuable horses to Madeleine, when Cigar's profile rose with each magnificent win. Not that Madeleine really minded. She still mourned selling Fraise to the Japanese as a stallion prospect after his racing career ended following the 1994 Breeders' Cup.

"I sold him to Japan because he really was well-suited to them and I've cried ever since," she said. "I really miss him. I miss the memories. We had a bond. I felt very, very close to him. I cried and cried and I still cry. I can't believe I sold him. But I would never have been able to give him the number of mares he's had—75 his first season—and so why should I deny him a good future? And I realized then I never wanted to go through a situation where you fall in love with your horse and then you've got to think of their future and he's got to move away from you. I said, 'If I get broodmares, then I can have them at Brookside (Farm in Kentucky) and can go and visit them and love them and I get to see their progeny and race them.' At the time I thought, 'I have a chance to get Eliza, but he has a chance to have a beautiful dirt horse.' And I explained to him that this horse would be able to compete with Holy Bull and all the greats and at the end of the year he would have the opportunity to race him in the Breeders' Cup. It all sounded exciting to him and the dream came true. And ever since I've been saying, 'Gimme back my horse. I want him back.' But I couldn't have coped with the pressure. I couldn't have done what (Allen) did."

Paulson took the Cigar on an amazing journey, showcasing him all across America en route to the Breeders' Cup. Two nights before the Cup, the Paulsons appeared at the annual Breeders' Cup party. They danced like they didn't have a care in the world. Madeleine strummed a toy guitar. Allen played with a yo-yo. The excitement was electric that evening and the Paulsons were a couple of live wires. If they felt any nervousness about Cigar, they certainly didn't show it. The following day, while a crowd milled around Mott's barn, Paulson fielded questions, including what it felt like to own Cigar.

"I think it's one of the biggest thrills you could ever have to get a horse like Cigar," Paulson said. "Personally, I don't know of any horse I've ever known in my lifetime that's better than Cigar."

A stone's throw away from where Allen talked, Madeleine walked her beloved dog, Oliver, whom she vowed not to trade—not even for Cigar.

The following day, Cigar lived up to everything that had been said and written about him by winning the Classic in record time. After 11 years of running horses in the Breeders' Cup, Allen Paulson, with the help of his wife, had won the big one.

In 1996, Allen Paulson piloted Cigar's career like he did one of his airplanes, picking out races like checkpoints. Hopes of a final flourish to the season—and likely his career—came in the Breeders' Cup, but the horse had a tough trip under Jerry Bailey. The old warhorse ran third, beaten only a neck by Alphabet Soup and a head by Louis Quatorze.

Even without Cigar, the Paulson camp had other stars to follow in 1997. The three-year-old filly Ajina won the Coaching Club American Oaks and the Mother Goose Stakes, the final two legs of the New York Triple Tiara Series, at Belmont Park in the summer. Ajina placed third by 7¼ lengths in the opening leg, the Acorn Stakes. Geri returned to the races in June and in his third start off the layoff won the Atto Mile at Woodbine in September. The seven-year-old Flag Down won a race at Saratoga in August.

The Paulsons came to the 1997 Breeders' Cup without a superstar along the lines of Cigar but with a strong contingent: Ajina and Ascena in the Distaff; Geri in the Mile; Flag Down in the Turf; and Dowty in the Classic. Ajina, coupled with Ascena, went postward at 4.80-1, third choice overall behind even-money favorite Sharp Cat and 17-10 second-choice Hidden Lake. Sharp Cat, under Alex Solis, gained the early lead but surrendered it to Ajina in the stretch, and the daughter of Strawberry Road went on to win by two lengths under Mike Smith. Entrymate Escena finished third by 5½ lengths. In the Mile, Geri made a gallant run after bouncing around between rivals entering the first turn, finishing second by two lengths to European invader Spinning World. Flag Down ran third by only 1¼ lengths to 19-10 favorite Chief Bearhart in the Turf. Dowty, co-owned by Allen and Madeleine, ran fourth in the Classic but was elevated to third after Whiskey Whisdom bumped him in midstretch. Overall, Team Paulson had a win, a second and two thirds.

Ajina was voted the champion in the three-year-old filly division at the Eclipse Awards.

In 1998, the Paulsons had only two representatives at the Breeders' Cup, but this was a classic case of quality instead of quantity. Escena ran in the Distaff and led all the way, nosing out 4-5 favorite Banshee Breeze, who had broken her maiden in her first start of the season and only her second lifetime race. She developed into a rock-solid sophomore, rattling off successive victories in the Coaching Club American Oaks, Alabama and Spinster Stakes by a combined 18 lengths. She had a solid finishing kick, but was the victim of a slow pace in the Distaff, as jockey Gary Stevens, who picked up the mount when Jerry Bailey stuck with Banshee Breeze, set moderate fractions and had enough in reserve to hold off the favorite. Escena concluded a decent season, blemished only by her sixth-place finish in a race at Saratoga two months before. She had begun the season with victories in the Grade One Apple Blossom Handicap Stakes at Oaklawn Park and the Grade One Vanity Handicap at Hollywood Park. She ran second two months later at Saratoga in the Grade One Go For Wand Handicap Stakes, then came up flat in the Grade One Personal Ensign Handicap almost four weeks later. She was then given time off and trained up to the Breeders' Cup, where she showed her class off the layoff.

Yagli followed up one race later in the Turf and ran second, beaten by the front-running Buck's Boy. Yagli came into the race practically overlooked by the bettors, who sent off the five-year-old at more than 19-1. He had run second a month before at Belmont Park, preceded by a victory almost two months before that.

The following July, Allen Paulson made a special visit to the Kentucky Horse Park to see Cigar, who had been pensioned to the retirement home for horse racing legends after he failed as a stallion prospect because of fertility problems.

It would be the last time Allen Paulson saw Cigar.

The Paulsons did not have a banner Breeders' Cup in 1999. They had only two runners—Garbu in the Mile and Yagli in the Turf. Garbu, a 21-1 shot, showed early speed then faded to second-last. Yagli, one of the contenders in the Turf, ran fourth.

On July 19, 2000, Allen Paulson died of prostate cancer at age 78, six years after he was diagnosed with the disease.

"He was absolutely amazing, he just was incredible," Madeleine said. "He was a wonderful man and I was blessed to have him as my husband. We were in racing together, we were a team, and we enjoyed it. It was a lifestyle for us."

Tributes poured in from around the world for the man who had given so much to the game by sharing his horse, the great Cigar, with millions of admirers. His racing empire continued under the name Allen Paulson Living Trust, although there was a stipulation in his will to disperse the racing and breeding stock.

In November, the Breeders' Cup took place at Churchill Downs and Jay Privman paid tribute to the patriarch of the Paulson dynasty in the official Breeders' Cup magazine.

"A drive not just to be the best but to do the best is what propelled Allen Paulson throughout his life," the article began. "He was not ostentatious, but he was proud. So whether it was developing engine parts for airplanes, building corporate jets, setting round-the-world records for airplane flight or racing and breeding thoroughbred racehorses, Paulson strived for excellence. . . . His racing and breeding operation supported one of the great stables of the 1980s and 1990s. Nowhere did Paulson's influence in racing have more of an impact than on the Breeders' Cup. When Paulson passed away in July, he left behind a record-setting legacy of his commitment to racing and breeding."

Heading into the 2000 Breeders' Cup, Paulson had been represented by a record 32 runners in the event's history, plus four more in partnership, either with his wife or Sheikh Mohammed. Paulson won a record six races as an owner and bred five winners.

"He was a pretty special guy," trainer Bill Mott was quoted in Privman's article. "He was one of the toughest competitors I'd ever known. He was never afraid to take a little chance. He was always willing to go for the big one. One of the things he once told me is, 'You measure the risk by the size of the reward.' That kind of stuck with me. . . . He was excited with the big races, sure, but when it was over, it was on to the next one. He enjoyed the wins, but he always was looking forward. There were more mountains to conquer."

The Allen E. Paulson Living Trust had one representative in the 2000 Breeders', a four-year-old colt called Hap. Unfortunately, there would be no storybook finish for Hap, who placed ninth by more than four lengths in the Mile. He was regarded as a long shot at 20-1.

Early in 2001, Madeleine Paulson created a new stable, Action Racing, with Ernest Moody, who owned Action Gaming, a slot machine business. He owned horses with his companion, Mercedes, the stable name under which their horses raced. A mutual friend introduced Madeleine to Ernest Moody and the idea of forming a partnership to breed and race appealed to him because of Madeleine's premium bloodstock. They adopted silks colored red, white and black and with the faces of four aces, and employed Simon Bray as their trainer. He had been Allen Paulson's west coast trainer until dismissed by Paulson's son, Michael, one of the trustees of his father's estate. Michael Paulson moved 10 horses, including the three-year-old colt Startac, who had just won the Grade One Secretariat Stakes, from Bray's shedrow to the barn of Laura de Seroux. An exercise rider for 15 years for the late Charlie Whittingham, one of the greatest trainers in the history of the game, de Seroux took out her trainer's license in August 1999. She stabled her horses at San Luis Rey Downs training center, about 35 miles northeast of Del Mar. Michael Paulson indicated in a press release that the moves were being made in the best interests of the horses and the estate.

"It was observations and just kind of a gut instinct after discussing our horse operation with several very knowledgeable people," he said in an interview for this book. "It was more of a gut instinct that it was the proper thing to do."

The next day Michael Paulson moved prominent stallions Theatrical and Jade Hunter and some broodmares and foals to Hill 'n Dale Farm in Lexington, Kentucky, from nearby Diamond A Farm in Versailles.

The following January, Madeleine Paulson filed suit in a superior court in San Diego County to have Michael Paulson removed as a co-trustee of the Living Trust. The suit alleged that Michael Paulson "breached fiduciary duties" related to the trust. The suit called for him to be held responsible for any damages suffered by the trust. The suit also claimed Michael Paulson failed to follow the trust's requirement to promptly disperse the thoroughbred stock.

"As a trustee, I thought it was my obligation to keep the horse operation intact for an indeterminate amount of time based on the economy of the whole horse industry," he said. "As a result of 9-11 and even before that the drop in the economy, horse sales dropped off a fair amount and also our racing operation was so successful. We were generating quite a bit of cash that the Trust needed. It was more of a fiduciary role . . . of maintaining the horse operation further than just dispersing, which would have damaged the value that they'd entrust. We had a business plan. We were waiting for the economy to return. We were fortunate to have a lot of well-bred horses. Upper pedigrees saw a drop of anywhere from thirty percent to fifty percent in value starting late in 2001 and into 2002, so we didn't see the value of selling our top-pedigree horses at fifty cents on the dollar. The original intentions when my father passed away was to disperse the horses. In fact, we sold literally half the horses in the first four months after he passed away, but that's when the dramatic change happened in the economy and horse sales went with it. During that period we slimmed down our horse operations and got it operating very profitably, so it just made sense in a down economy to keep the horse operation going because we're generating needed cash."

The Paulson empire raised its successful head in the months that followed the court battles when the four-year-old filly Azeri, a daughter of Jade Hunter, started to develop into one of the top distaffers in the country. Azeri, named after an airport checkpoint in Turkey, had been put up for sale as a yearling, along with Startac, without a reserve but Allen Paulson had bought both back on the recommendation of Madeleine.

Azeri impressed Bray with her potential, but she was moved from his barn before he had a chance to saddle her in a race. Azeri debuted on November 1, 2001, at Santa Anita in a six-furlong race on the main track. With Mike Smith aboard, Azeri won by six lengths at odds of more than 17-1. She returned almost six weeks later at Hollywood Park and won a 6½-furlong race by three lengths. She raced again almost a month later in January and won a mile race by three lengths. A month later she placed second in the Grade Two La Canada Stakes, her first added-money event. From that point forward, she rattled off six consecutive victories, four of them with Grade One classification. First came the San Margarita at Santa Anita, followed by the Apple Blossom at Oaklawn Park, the Milady Breeders' Cup Handicap at Hollywood Park, and then the Vanity Handicap a month later at the same track. In her next start two months later, she took the Clement Hirsch Handicap at Del Mar and then the Lady's Secret Breeders' Cup Handicap at Santa Anita almost two months later. Her next start would be the Breeders' Cup Distaff at Arlington Park.

The day before the race, Michael Paulson indicated he planned to keep the filly racing as a five-year-old.

"To get a mare like her, I've got to keep her going," he said. "It would be a shame to retire her."

Azeri kicked off the first of the eight Breeders' races and displayed her most dynamic run of the season, forging to the front under Mike Smith and romping to a five-length tally. It gave de Seroux her first Breeders' Cup victory with her first starter. She paid tribute to both Allen Paulson and Charlie Whittingham for helping her career.

Michael Paulson said it was a "very emotional day" winning the race.

"I wish my dad were here," he said.

He then paid tribute to Azeri.

"She's in a league of her own, a world of her own, and she's a super horse," he said. "It's a gift left by my dad."

Madeleine Paulson attended the event but was not part of the victory presentation.

Azeri's victory immediately placed her in the forefront for Horse of the Year honors.

Some six weeks after the Breeders' Cup, the Paulson family feud took a new twist when it was revealed the parties had reached a settlement in their dispute. The entire racing holdings would be dispersed without a reserve in four separate sales, beginning in March. Michael Paulson had attempted to change the terms of the trust by allowing Azeri to continue training and racing. Under terms of the settlement, the racehorses under the care of Laura de Seroux would stay with her until five days before shipped for sale.

In late January 2003, Azeri received the Horse of the Year Award, only the second time a filly or mare had received the honor since the start of the Eclipses.

Early in February, the Paulsons' impasse reached a resolution when they agreed on a settlement that would keep Azeri in training with Laura de Seroux and racing for the Living Trust. Several two-year-olds in training would also be excluded from a scheduled sale. As part of the agreement, Madeleine Paulson would not be involved in the Trust's horses, but would retain control of the Del Mar Country Club.

"The press made it more bitter than it was," Michael Paulson said. "Behind the scenes, it wasn't bitter from my side. I was doing what I thought was best for the Trust's beneficiaries. I guess other people thought otherwise, but the facts prove we're running a very successful horse operation and generating cash for the Trust's estate, which benefits all the beneficiaries. That was my primary focus at the time. All the litigation and the press, that wasn't from me. I don't know who was out there trying to dirty the water up."

Michael Paulson said the Living Trust, which would be operated by him and his brothers, would keep 40–60 horses—subject to change, based on the economy and other things—including breeding stock and yearlings.

Madeleine Paulson is reluctant to engage in a war of words with her stepson, but offered some interesting thoughts nonetheless.

"It's resolved now, our lives go on," Madeleine said. "I wish the boys well. I had a great life with my husband. It should be left like that. Without Azeri would they have settled? I don't know. The fact of the matter is we all owned a leg. It's not Michael Paulson that owned a leg or owned the horse. It's the Living Trust and that's where you've got to be very careful not to start thinking you own everything. We were all equal owners of Azeri, but the Trust held the horse. It's been resolved, I'm happy with the settlement and now they can go and see what else they can do in racing."

Madeleine Paulson and Ernest Moody had more than 50 horses, including racehorses and weanlings, by the middle of 2003.

"I feel confident enough with what I have that somewhere along the line I'm going to have some very nice horses," she said.

Madeleine said her late husband left her with a legacy, pointing to the bloodlines he gave her.

"We used to always talk about the bloodlines," she said. "Racing isn't always about racing, it's about breeding, too. You've got to realize we bred most of our champions. We bred Azeri. We bred Cigar. That's a big thrill for a lot of us."

Michael Paulson said his father would be extremely proud of his sons' accomplishments with the horses he left behind.

"I know my father wouldn't want to mandate the sale of a Horse of the Year from the Paulson family. I definitely know that," he said. "Knowing my father the 45 years I had the privilege of being his son, I know he'd be very proud of what we did with the horses. It's icing on the cake to see my dad's AP silks still flying high, keeping his memory and his legacy alive."

# 23

# Heard around the Rail

## Twenty Interesting Stories

$\mathcal{O}$ne of the great things about horse racing, at least from a personal perspective as a writer, is the stories related to the individuals involved in the sport. Whether it's about the owner, trainer, rider, stablehand or, simply the horse, there are always stories to be told—and they're not always restricted to the winners, either.

Sometimes, the stories tell themselves, but often you have to go beyond the surface. And sometimes the stories don't become apparent or truly important until the passage of time.

It is with this in mind that I've gone through every Breeders' Cup race and assembled a list of some of the more interesting ones. Some are sad and some are bad and some are just plain funny.

Because I couldn't narrow it down to 10 choices, I decided to go with 20—after all, this book is all about a celebration of the 20th edition. Here they are, then, in no particular order:

## ALEX SCOTT

When Hilal Salem's Sheikh Albadou won the 1991 Breeders' Cup Sprint—at odds of more than 26-1—he gave trainer Alex Scott his first Breeders' Cup win with his first starter.

The win was big news for the Europeans—and the English in particular. The year before in the same race, England's dynamic sprinter Dayjur, trained by the legendary Major Dick Hern, for whom Scott worked as an assistant from 1985 to 1987, appeared to have the Sprint won until he jumped a shadow 40 yards from the finish and lost by a neck.

Sheikh Albadou returned the following year to defend his title but ran fourth in what proved to be the last starter for Scott in the Cup.

On September 30, 1994, Scott was murdered at his farmhouse estate in the village of Cheveley, Cambridgeshire, eight miles from the Newmarket yard where he trained his stable. A disgruntled employee, William O'Brien, who had worked for eight years on the estate property Scott had purchased two years before, shot

Scott in the chest. O'Brien was charged and sentenced 10 months later to life imprisonment.

Scott had only been 34 when he died. At the time of his murder, he had been regarded as a fast-rising trainer, whose clients included the powerful Maktoum brothers, members of the ruling family of the United Arab Emirates and the most prominent owner/breeders in England. Scott's future appeared bright indeed.

Among the horses Scott trained for the Maktoums was an unraced two-year-old Nijinsky colt called Lammtarra. Scott liked the horse's future even before he debuted and made a futures bet of 1,000 pounds (or the equivalent of about $2,000) at odds of 33-1 on Lammtarra to win the Epsom Derby the following June. Lammtarra won his only start at two and then went to trainer Saeed bin Suroor, a relative unknown at the time, after Scott's untimely passing.

Lammtarra went on to win the Epsom Derby, then won his second Group One race in the King George VI and Queen Elizabeth Stakes almost two months later. Coincidentally at that exact time, O'Brien received his life sentence. Lammtarra completed his brilliant season winning the Prix de l'Arc de Triomphe and was retired thereafter.

Saeed bin Suroor has gone to become one of the top trainers in the world and has won several Breeders' Cup races.

Alex Scott has been remembered with an annual race in his name at Newmarket racecourse. His widow, Julia, has helped set up a memorial fund in his name and a scholarship to assist young trainers to travel abroad.

"The subsequent success of Lammtarra (after the Epsom Derby) not only confirmed (Scott's) judgment but showed how close (he) had been to making the all-important breakthrough into the top echelons of his profession," the *Times of London*'s Michael Horsnell and Richard Evans cowrote in a story the day after O'Brien's sentencing. "Mr. Scott trained 164 winners in Britain before he was robbed of the opportunity to fulfill his undoubted potential. The achievements of Lammtarra . . . are his poignant epitaph."


## MICHAEL DICKENSON


Trainer Michael Dickenson has been described in a variety of ways—odd, eccentric, weird—but brilliant may be an appropriate adjective after what he did to win the Breeders' Cup Mile twice with Da Hoss.

In 1996, Dickenson gave jockey Gary Stevens a detailed description of how to ride the horse and on which part of the course—and the strategy worked to perfection. However, Da Hoss suffered a tendon injury, the type of thing that could permanently end a horse's career.

As a gelding, Da Hoss had no residual breeding value, so Dickenson worked hard to bring the horse back to the races. Two years after winning the Mile, Dickenson figured he could win it again. He trained the horse on his farm/training center, which he meticulously built, and pointed him to a race one month before the Cup. Da Hoss won the race, though he didn't beat any horses of consequence, but Dickenson figured he had Da Hoss tight and ready for the challenge.

Few people believed him—including Stevens, who turned down the mount, which went to John Velazquez—but Dickenson proved smartest of all when the horse repeated in the Mile. Dickenson also collected $2,500 after betting Stevens' agent, Ron Anderson, that Da Hoss could win the race.

Incidentally, Da Hoss prepped for the Cup at Colonial Downs in Virginia. The track opened in 1997 and has had an interesting and at times controversial history because of disputes over race dates, but it worked wonders for Da Hoss. He is the only horse to have prepped there for a Breeders' Cup race.

## BLACK TIE AFFAIR

He won the Breeders' Cup Classic in 1991 and went on to be named Horse of the Year, but this horse just didn't get any respect—at least from Dave Feldman.

Feldman was known as the King of the Turf in Chicago because of his long history in the Windy City as a race announcer, owner, trainer, president of the Illinois Horsemen's and Protective Association and racing writer with the *Chicago Sun-Times*. He authored the epic book *Woulda, Coulda, Shouda: Handicapping Tips for Anyone Who Ever Bet on a Horse Race or Wanted To*. He wore outlandish clothes and made bold predictions and proclamations, some of which attacked the quality of Black Tie Affair.

Feldman did not believe Black Tie Affair had a chance to win the Classic, even after winning five consecutive races at five different tracks leading up to the Breeders' Cup, and said so in the *Sun-Times*. Moreover, Feldman brazenly said he'd buy ice cream cones for everyone in the grandstand if the horse won, but later reduced it to the first 200 people.

Feldman's comments didn't sit well with trainer Ernie Poulos. They had a long and bitter history—a kind of Hatfield and McCoy feud—and had, in fact, trained in the same barn at one time.

As fate would have it, Poulos happened to be sitting beside Feldman on the flight from Chicago to Louisville, Kentucky, for the Cup. Poulos, being a gentleman, helped Feldman, who had a heart condition, transport some of his carry-on luggage from the overhead area after the plane landed. Poulos wasn't in the best physical health himself, having had both of his knees replaced. While acknowledging in the paper Poulos' assistance, Feldman still ripped the horse.

Black Tie Affair led all the way in winning the Classic, ridden by Jerry Bailey, who recorded his initial Breeders' Cup victory. Bailey picked up the mount because Pat Day had been committed to Summer Squall, who ran ninth in the field of 11. Shane Sellers had ridden Black Tie Affair for the first time in the horse's last race, the Washington Park Handicap, winning by 7½ lengths, and was available for the Classic. But Poulos was upset that Sellers whipped the horse repeatedly in the stretch drive of the race.

The day after the Breeders' Cup, Poulos was back in Chicago to run a horse at Sportsman's Park, where Feldman had been the track announcer for 32 years in one of his previous jobs. Poulos and Black Tie Affair's owner, Jeffrey Sullivan, stood first in line for the free ice cream cones courtesy of Feldman. Instead of cones, Feldman bought ice cream bars, but it made for an interesting story and photo the following day in the paper.

On March 30, 1997, Ernie Poulos died.

"One of the first people to call me was Dave Feldman and, in fact, he did a really nice article on me that I tried to continue on with Ernie's legacy, and I found that kind of interesting that he did that," Poulos' widow Dee said. "I think he missed the action after that."

Dave Feldman died on April 30, 2001. A stakes race was subsequently run in his honor at Florida's Gulfstream Park. It is not a black-tie affair.


## ARTAX

The authoritative winner of the 1999 Sprint had himself an eventful year.

Racing as the heavy 4-5 favorite on the undercard of the Preakness Stakes almost six months before, Artax broke slowly and then was impeded by a crazed individual. He ran on to the track from the infield by cutting his way through the fencing and avoiding security and took a swing at the horse an eighth of a mile from the wire.

Jockey Jorge (Chop Chop) Chavez did his best to avoid the individual, who took a swipe at the horse but hit the jockey on the boot. Artax ran a distant fifth in the field of eight and the stewards refunded all money bet on the horse. The winner of the race, the Maryland Breeders' Cup, which is part of the yearlong Breeders' Cup series, was named Yes It's True—an appropriate name for the unbelievable incident that happened.

Artax went on a five-race losing streak after that, but regrouped to win two races, including breaking a 22-year-old track record in his start before the Breeders' Cup. In both races, Chavez was aboard after an absence of four races.

Artax won the Sprint in a sizzling time of 1:07.89, tying the 26-year-old Gulfstream Park track record set by Mr. Prospector and setting a Breeders' Cup Sprint record. Chavez' win followed a victory aboard Beautiful Pleasure earlier in the card in the Distaff. Chavez had been 0-for-19 in Breeders' Cup races up to that point. Trainer Louis Albertrani, who did a splendid job with the colt, recorded his first win with his first—and only—starter to date.


## THAD ACKEL

It proved to be a bittersweet year for 33-year-old trainer Thad Ackel when he won the Breeders' Cup Turf with Great Communicator in 1988. Earlier in the year, Ackel's father, George, who was admittedly his best friend, had died suddenly at the age of 66. He died while undergoing an electrocardiogram after apparently suffering a heart attack the day before. George Ackel had a majority interest in the six-year-old gelding with partners who were collectively known as Class Act Stable.

Thad Ackel had a minority interest—and really earned his keep. He unlocked the secret that turned the gelding from a onetime claimer into a world-class grass horse. After replacing the exercise rider, Ackel discovered his hot-tempered horse responded better to daily galloping when allowed to run freely with only a slight hold.

In 1987, Ackel moved his modest stable in Louisiana to California to try and crack that tough circuit. He won two of his first three races there with Great Communicator, but it was in his 14th start of the season, in the D.C. International in Maryland, that Great Communicator signaled his future brilliance. He ran second by a neck in the prestigious race, giving Ackel and the horse's connections the confidence to try the Breeders' Cup Turf.

With Angel Cordero Jr. aboard, Great Communicator flashed his customary speed, opening up a significant lead; however he faded with a quarter mile to go when the real running began, placing a distant 12th by 13¼ lengths in the field of 14.

Ackel was furious with the ride and subsequently hired Ray Sibille, a transplanted Cajun like himself. Great Communicator ran fourth by 2½ lengths in his next start, but then won two consecutive races and four of six, including the Grade One San Juan Capistrano Stakes. In the two losses, Great Communicator posted a second and a third.

Great Communicator came into the 1988 Breeders' Cup off three consecutive losses, albeit two consecutive seconds, but Ackel had high hopes.

"I've been really looking forward to it all year, that's been my major goal," he indicated in a comment that was included in the Breeders' Cup biography book of the horses and their owners, trainers and breeders. "I can't wait to get back. My motto is 'I'm lucky in Kentucky.' I've always had winning meets there. I have a lot of friends in Louisville, so I'm real anxious to get back there."

Sent postward at 12-1, Great Communicator rushed to the front, dropped back by less than a length after a mile and a quarter, but regained the lead and held off Sunshine Forever, who was voted the champion male turf horse at the end of the year.

Great Communicator won his next start after the Breeders' Cup, then was given a brief respite. He returned two months later and won a stakes race, then finished second in his next start. After a sixth-place finish after that, he won the Grade One Hollywood Turf Cup.

He went off form in four consecutive starts. Various tests were done to try to determine why Great Communicator appeared to be fading in the finish—usually the sign of a bleeding problem that affects the air passage—but the results didn't yield any answers. After a distant eighth-place finish in the Oak Tree Invitational in which he'd finished second the year before leading up to the Cup, Great Communicator was given a lengthy six-month rest from the races.

In his first four races after the return he still continued to struggle, but an examination finally revealed why. He had a displacement of the soft palate, which affected his breathing. A minor surgical procedure called a myectomy corrected the problem and Great Communicator returned solidly his first time back, winning the Henry P. Russell Handicap in a brilliant time of 1:58 flat for the 1¼-mile race. The win happened 10 days before the Breeders' Cup. The jubilation was short-lived because Great Communicator broke a hind leg in his next start and had to be humanely destroyed.

Although he wanted to continue training, Ackel had to return to Louisiana to oversee his father's real-estate holdings. When he whittled down the remainder of his racing stable, Ackel returned home. He has since dabbled the odd time in training and/or owning horses.

Great Communicator was the only horse Thad Ackel ran in the Breeders' Cup.

Sibille's victory in 1988 represented his first and only ride to date in the Cup. There has been no other rider to hold that perfect distinction.


## KONA GOLD

There's something to be said about trying again and again. Take Kona Gold, a warhorse as good as gold.

In 1998, trainer Bruce Headley, who owned Kona Gold with Irwin and Andrea Molasky, brought the four-year-old gelding to run in the Sprint. He ran third that year. In 1999, Kona Gold came back and finished second, only a half-length back of Artax after an awkward beginning. Finally, on the third try in the same race, he won—and mighty impressively, too, stopping the clock in 1:07.77, the fastest six furlongs in Churchill Downs history and bettering the Breeders' Cup mark set by Artax.

It also ended a brutal losing streak for jockey Alex Solis, who began the card with an 0-for-31 record in the Breeders' Cup.

"Thank God I got the monkey off my back," he said after the win. "It's been aggravating and sad."

Solis had been aboard the horse for all of his career races with the exception of the initial start.

Kona Gold, who won the Eclipse Award as the top sprinter in 2000, ran again in 2001 and finished seventh, beaten about 3½ lengths. In 2002, he ran a credible fourth, beaten only 3¼ lengths.

There has never been another horse that has run in the same race five times in a row, but there has been one who has run in the same one four times in a row. El Senor ran in the Turf from 1988 to 1991 but never won.


## BRUCE MCNALL

At one time he was one of the most influential sports tycoons, parlaying his coin collection into all kinds of enterprises, including horse racing.

McNall, who operated his horse racing empire under the name Summa Stable, had six starters in the Breeders' Cup between 1985 and 1990. In 1985, his initial starter, Eastland, did not finish in the Distaff, while Bob Back ran 12th in the Turf. In 1986, Dahar ran fifth in the Turf. McNall came close to winning the '87 Turf with Trempolino, the Prix de l'Arc de Triomphe winner he owned in partnership with Paul deMoussac. Trempolino ran second by a half-length to 8-5 favorite Theatrical. The following year, McNall's starter Frankly Perfect failed to finish in the Turf.

In 1990, McNall was looking to run Golden Pheasant, whom he owned in partnership with his Los Angeles Kings' star player Wayne Gretzky. Golden Pheasant certified himself as a star runner when he won the Arlington Million in late August, but an injury prevented him from running in the Breeders' Cup.

Saumarez proved to be a capable backup. A four-year-old maiden at the start of the season, Saumarez came into his own, winning several races, including the Arc, so McNall entered the horse in the Turf. But Saumarez, the second betting choice in the race at 27-10 odds, ran fifth by 11 lengths.

That was the last Breeders' Cup starter for McNall. McNall's financial empire fell apart in the following years. In March 1997, he was sentenced to 70 months in prison after pleading guilty to two counts of bank fraud, one charge of wire fraud and one count of conspiracy.

## COUNTESS DIANA

In 1997, a two-year-old filly emerged as a star in the making. Countess Diana won two of her first three races and then recorded her first Grade One victory in the Spinaway Stakes on August 29. Two days later, Diana, The Princess of Wales, died. Countess Diana won two more races that year, including the Juvenile Fillies.

While the world mourned Diana the princess, the racing world celebrated Diana the countess, who was voted the champion in her division.

## DAVID MILCH

As one of the top writers/producers in Hollywood of cop shows such as *NYPD Blue* and *Hill Street Blues*, David Milch is no stranger to success—and he certainly has had a fair share of it in horse racing.

Milch, in partnership with Jack and Mark Silverman, won the 1992 Juvenile Stakes with Gilded Time. It was Milch's first runner in the Cup. The undefeated colt subsequently was named the Eclipse Award winner in his division. The following year, Gilded Time ran third in the Sprint, his first race since the victory a year before, the long layoff due to an injury. Milch returned to the Cup in 1999 with Caffe Latte in the Filly & Mare Turf race. Milch had to pay a $90,000 supplementary fee—the equivalent of 9% of the $1 million purse, as opposed to only 2% for nominated horses—to run the three-year-old who hadn't been nominated at birth. Caffe Latte ran fourth, collecting $59,920.

Milch returned to the winner's circle when Val Royal won the 2001 Mile at Belmont in course-record and Breeders' Cup–record time.

Milch purchased Val Royal for $1 million two years before the Mile following a string of victories in France. The colt won his North American debut in the Del Mar Derby, but injured a tendon in the process and did not return to the races for 18 months because trainer Julio Canani wanted to take his time. Val Royal ran second in his return, but developed a quarter crack and was sidelined for an additional seven months.

Less than three weeks before the Breeders' Cup, Val Royal ran in the Oak Tree Breeders' Cup Mile and won impressively. Similar to Caffe Latte, Val Royal hadn't been nominated to the Breeders' Cup and it would cost 9% of the $1 million purse to run him. Milch had enough confidence in Canani to pay the supplementary fee and Val Royal won, earning $592,800, more than doubling his lifetime earnings to that point.

Milch missed the race, staying behind in California while nursing a cold.

The victory was the first for jockey Jose Valdivia Jr. in only his second Breeders' Cup ride. Valdivia's uncle, Fernando Toro, won the inaugural Mile in 1984 aboard Royal Heroine. The horse's sire, Royal Anthem, won the Mile at Belmont in 1990. Valdivia won his inaugural North American race at Belmont on July 17, 1994.

Recurring tendon problems forced Val Royal's retirement early the following year, and he was subsequently sold to South African interests as a stallion prospect. Milch's 2002 Breeders' Cup representative, Disturbingthepeace, whom the TV producer owned in partnership with his wife Rita, ran a nonthreatening seventh in the Sprint following a win at Del Mar two months before. The four-year-old had won six of eight races prior to the Cup, including six in a row, the last three Grade Two races.

## AFFIRMED SUCCESS

From 1998 to 2001, Affirmed Success ran in the Breeders' and documented one of the most interesting patterns of any horse to ever run in the event.

He ran in the Sprint the first year with Jorge Chavez aboard and placed sixth. The next year he ran in the Sprint again, this time with Jerry Bailey, and ran 12th. The next year he ran in the Mile, with Chavez aboard, and placed fourth. The following year, he ran in the Mile again, this time with Bailey, and placed 11th. He was the betting favorite the first time and a long shot the next two times, but in his fourth try, this time as a seven-year-old, he drew considerable support.

## BILL SHOEMAKER

For all he had done in his illustrious career, Bill Shoemaker was practically snake-bitten in the Breeders' Cup.

It took him 14 races before he finally snapped the losing streak, winning aboard Ferdinand at age 56. Earlier in the card, he appeared to be in a great position to win, but Jeanne Jones, who took a six-length lead into the stretch in the Juvenile Fillies, swerved slightly in deep stretch and lost by a nose. Trainer Charlie Whittingham insisted the filly was spooked by a cameraman, causing her to swerve and costing her the win.

The Shoe's win with Ferdinand proved to be his final ride in the Breeders' Cup as a rider. He went on to a career in training afterward.

## MISS ALLEGED

When this four-year-old filly won the 1991 Turf, she pulled off one of the biggest upsets in Cup history—at odds of more than 42-1 and in an impressive time.

Winless in seven starts on the year coming into the Cup that year at Churchill Downs, she had been grouped with two other nondistinguished horses in the mutuel field because the tote board could only accommodate 12 betting interests. She rallied from eighth after a mile to mow down the field in front of her in the final quarter of a mile.

The victory was the first for breeder/owner Issam Fares, trainer Pascal Bary and jockey Eric Legrix. Miss Alleged subsequently followed up her victory by winning the Hollywood Turf Cup a few weeks later en route to being named the Eclipse Award as the champion female turf horse that year.

## ONE DREAMER

Breeder/owner Leonard Lavin was seemingly dreaming when he entered this six-year-old mare in the 1994 Distaff.

She appeared to have no shot and was the second highest-priced horse in the field at odds of more than 47-1. She paid a whopping $96.20 to win. The exacta with Heavenly Prize, the 2-1 third favorite in the field, paid $340.80. The trifecta paid a juicy $5,843.80 because the long shot in the field, 77-1 Miss Dominique, ran third.

The highlight of the race, at least from a visual point of view, was the reaction by the horse's ponytailed exercise rider Pete Garrett. As he escorted the winning horse away after the victory presentation, the happy horseman received generous applause from the crowd. He promptly removed his fedora and bowed triumphantly.

Trainer Tom Proctor could have taken a bow, too. He had never started a horse in the Cup before. He hasn't made it back to the Cup since.

## DAYLAMI

When Daylami won the 1999 Turf, much was made of the victory by jockey Frankie Dettori, who had been criticized every which way for his ride aboard Swain the year before in the Classic. But the win also ended a lengthy drought for European horses at Gulfstream Park. They came into the event 0-for-20.

"European horses, which begin growing winter coats in the cool of early autumn, have tended to look flat in the sun's Miami vise," *Sports Illustrated*'s Bill Nack wrote in a summation of the '99 Cup. "To lure the reluctant Europeans, Cup officials this year promised to expand housing from two to four barns—to minimize crowding and, consequently, body heat—and install air-conditioning units. Despite all that—and a cool front that blew through—the Europeans were 0-20 by the time Dettori climbed aboard Daylami."

The list of previous high-profile European losers included Zilzal (even-money favorite 1989 Mile) and Arazi (3-2 favorite '92 Mile).

## PLEASANT TAP

This horse has the distinction of running four years in a row in four separate races—and not winning once.

He began in 1989 in the Juvenile and ran sixth. The following year he ran in the Turf and placed eighth. He continued in the Sprint in his third try and ran second. And he finished off his final attempt in the Classic, running second.

Chris Speckert saddled the horse in the first, third and fourth runnings, while Ross Pearce did it the other time.

Incidentally, Speckert won with Pleasant Stage in the 1991 Juvenile Fillies.

In 1993, the year after Pleasant Tap concluded his streak, Pleasant Tango ran in the Classic and finished fifth. All of the Pleasant horses were owned and bred by Buckland Farms, the stable name for racing patriarch Thomas Mellon Evans. His horse Pleasant Colony won the first two legs of the 1981 Triple Crown. Pleasant Colony is the sire of the pleasantly named horses.

## VOLPONI

Everybody knows this is the horse who won the 2002 Classic at 43-1 odds, but how many people know the horse is named after Paul Volponi, who is the features writer for the *American Turf Monthly*, racing editor of the *Gambling Times* and a correspondent for *The Blood-Horse*?

Volponi had been compiling his year-end awards in 1998 for the now-defunct *New York Thoroughbred Observor* and wanted to make special note of Michael Dickenson's job on Da Hoss. But Volponi didn't feel he could select Dickenson for trainer of the year off that one result, so he created the Volponi Awards for various categories. Volponi translates to sly, old fox in Italian, and Volponi received some positive feedback from readers for his creative awards.

The next year Volponi gave the Volponi trainer award to Hall of Famer Phil Johnson for his job in winning a number of races with horses off layoffs. Volponi said that among fans Johnson is the "Rodney Dangerfield of trainers, getting no respect and taking little money at the windows. That probably makes his barn workers and owners very happy."

Volponi had never met Johnson and was a little concerned that the trainer might think he was being called a "put-over artist." When the trainer's daughter, Karen, who writes for the *Daily Racing Form*, approached Volponi after the article had been published, he was preparing himself for the worst. Instead, Karen Johnson told Volponi how much her father enjoyed the article and that he should come by the barn and introduce himself. It touched Volponi that Johnson, who had plenty written about him in his celebrated career, would be so heartened by a single paragraph heralding his horsemanship.

Johnson subsequently renamed an unstarted two-year-old horse, in whom he had an interest as a part-owner, Volponi. The writer called the trainer, who invited him and his wife and daughter to drop by the barn and see the horse. In an article in *The Blood-Horse* after the Classic victory, Volponi the journalist recalled his first meeting with the trainer and their subsequent relationship.

"It didn't take long for me to realize that the best part about a racehorse named Volponi was that P. G. Johnson and his family were behind him," Volponi said in the article. "The horse could have run backwards, and I would not have been the least bit upset. The real honor was shaking P. G. Johnson's hand in the paddock before a race and telling him, 'Good luck.'

"The first time Volponi raced, he disappointed a lot of fans at 3-5. A railbird called out to him repeatedly, 'Volponi, you suck.' I was severely tempted to go over and show that knucklehead my driver's license. When he started running in stakes, the name Volponi was spelled out on his saddlecloth. I covered a few of those events. And when he won, it was like writing a review of a dinner party I had hosted."

Volponi the journalist used his namesake in his Breeders' Cup Pick Three bet and cashed more than $1,400 off a $2 bet. He also bet the horse to show, which paid out $12.40.

"I knew he was really going to run well," Volponi said. "He seemed like the greatest show horse ever."

Volponi liked his namesake because he didn't think the horse would be caught up in speed duels, would move up on an off track being by the sire Cryptoclearance, and would improve with blinkers, having won a race with them by 13½ lengths earlier in his career.

"At the end of the day, Johnson proved to the racing world that he truly was the sly, old fox, lulling them all to sleep while he stole away with a $4-million hen house. When I sat down at a keyboard to give P. G. Johnson the Volponi Award, I didn't realize just how right I had gotten it.

"To have a relationship with (Johnson) far outweighed having a horse named Volponi, and as a coincidence the horse got good. I've enjoyed the horse and I've enjoyed that P. G. Johnson is so happy with him. Johnson is back on top. At the end of the year, he had one of the top-three horses in the world. It's super for him. I love him. I love his family."

As an aside, the journalist had had a heavy heart the previous year on Breeders'

Cup day. His father's funeral was the morning of the races, which were at Belmont Park. After finishing with the funeral and everything else, Volponi went to Belmont Park later that day to witness the Cup in person and caught the Classic. It was a sombre time for Volponi, then, but it was a completely different mood for him and his family a year later.

"I watched the race from home on TV. When Volponi split horses at the head of the stretch, my entire family rocketed to their feet, raising their voices. Our two German Shepherds began barking wildly. After that, (race announcer) Tom Durkin's call never stood a chance of being heard in my house."

The *New York Thoroughbred Observer* ceased publication after 1999, so there won't be any more Volponi awards unless Volponi the journalist resurrects them.

The journalist has written a book called *A Day At The Races*, based on May 8, 2002, the opening day of the 2002 Belmont meet. As a matter of coincidence, Volponi the horse raced that day in his season-opener and won.

One more thing: Volponi's victory gave his sire Cryptoclearance his first Breeders' Cup winner with only his second starter. His only other starter, Victory Gallop, ran fourth in the 1998 Classic.

Cryptoclearance made three consecutive starts in the Classic between 1987 and 1989—and in each case finished fifth and with a different rider on his back. Pat Day was aboard the first time, followed by Craig Perret and then Jose Santos. The winning rider on Volponi in the Classic? Jose Santos.


## BEST PAL


He has the distinction of being the only Breeders' Cup horse to run three times for three different trainers.

He made his debut for Ian Jory running in the 1990 Juvenile and placed sixth. He returned three years later for trainer Gary Jones and ran 10th in the Classic. A year later, he ran in the Classic again, this time with Richard Mandella as trainer.

Not only did he have different trainers, but different riders, too. Pat Valenzuela was aboard the first time, Corey Black the second time and Chris McCarron the last time.

John Mabee, who bred the horse, remained the owner throughout.


## YUTAKA TAKE


Hopes were high for Japanese fans when this Japanese sensation rode for the first time in the Breeders' Cup in 1994. He was aboard Erin Bird in the Distaff and Ski Paradise in the Mile. Neither horse finished in the top three.

Six years later, Take returned to the Breeders' Cup—his fame in his homeland considerably bigger than the previous time he came to America—and rode Agnes World in the Sprint and Maltese Superb in the Filly & Mare Turf. Both horses had come from races at Kyoto Racecourse, one of the Japanese Racing Association's major tracks, but neither of the starters fared well in their respective races.

## FLAT FLEET FEET

She might have had the all-time best tongue-twisting name in Breeders' Cup history. Imagine race caller Tom Durkin saying it for a mile and a sixteenth when this horse ran in the 1995 Juvenile Fillies. Fortunately, the field only had eight horses and Flat Fleet Feet did not live up to her name. Although she did show some fleetness for half a mile, she finished second-last. The horse that ran last in the race was named Gastronomical. You might say she lacked gas after trailing the field the entire way.

## APELIA

It was said that the meaner this filly became the better she ran. In 1993, she developed quite a mean streak and had herself quite a season.

In the days leading up to the 1993 Sprint, she exacted her nastiness on unsuspecting Canadian horse racing writer Ted Labanowich by biting his forearm and leaving him with a welt. Labanowich took it as a sign of good luck and wrote about it and then placed a few bucks on the filly. Well, Apelia couldn't take a bite out of her opponents and finished last.

While Apelia's story may not have been as compelling as some of the others listed here, she certainly left her mark on Ted Labanowich.

# · 24 ·

# The Best of the Best

## The Greatest Races

*W*hat is the greatest race in Breeders' Cup history? I asked racing fans via the Internet to offer their opinions about the greatest race. One of the replies, from Richard Perloff, said it best: "You don't ask the easy questions, do you? This one is nearly impossible to answer."

Another reply, this one from Carol Sinclair, offered this opinion: "When the best horses in the world gather to compete against each other, every race is special in its own way." Sinclair offered a top-10 list, but added an 11th choice and then said: "But I really could go on and on and . . ."

Racing fan Michelle Brown could not separate the inaugural Breeders' Cup Classic—"that finish is what racing is all about"—and the 1988 Distaff, saying Personal Ensign "looked hopelessly beaten and kept coming for one of the gutsiest finishes I've ever seen by either sex." She added: "These are the two races I automatically think of when I think great Breeders' Cup races. I can't imagine anyone who could watch these two races and not be (or become) a fan of the sport."

Brown's response is characteristic of racing fans. They are an opinionated lot, and they put their money where their mouths are every time they make a bet. But asking anybody to pick the greatest Breeders' Cup race is hard, maybe even impossible, because like art it is a matter of taste. Some races produced high drama, others were run predictably, while some became great only when viewed in hindsight.

Given my choice, I'd pick the 1989 Classic featuring Sunday Silence and Easy Goer because I really came to admire Sunday Silence. He was the near-black stallion who had overcome adversity early in his life and developed into a legend under the direction of Charlie Whittingham. For a second choice I'd pick Personal Ensign's win in the 1988 Distaff. How could you not admire a filly capping off her undefeated career by digging deep within her competitive belly to beat a gallant Kentucky Derby winner, on an off-track at that? Were it not for the bias I have towards Sunday Silence, there would be no question that Personal Ensign's race would stand up as the best, in my opinion. Thirdly, I'd go with the 2001 Classic. That was true grit by both horses, yet somehow Tiznow managed to find that something extra needed to win. Rounding out my superfecta of super races is the

1984 Classic. Man, if that was a harbinger of what was to follow in years to come it surely did the job.

But enough about my choices. Here are the people's choices for the greatest races of all time in chronological order:

## 1985 TURF

"It just impressed me, a bunch of little things, and it was soon after I started really paying attention to all aspects of horse racing. Like the name Pebbles, too. If I saw it again I'm sure I could tell you more."

—Josh Kuperman

## 1986 TURF

"I got sick and tired of hearing how unbeatable Dancing Brave was. I noted this colt had a tough time on courses where the stretch was not long and wide.

"Knowing that no one in their right mind would try to overhaul Estrapade early in the race and her rider would no doubt slow down the pace, this deep closer would have both the tight turns and the short stretch of Santa Anita to contend with as well as the pace.

"I had a shirt printed up 'Dancing Brave, how do you like our turns?' and wore it all day through the crowd, yelling: 'Manila . . . Manila.' Many thought I was balmy. I then stationed myself near the paddock to wave the shirt in the face of both (owner) Prince Khalid Abdullah and (jockey) Pat Eddery. I made sure that both saw my comments.

"As the race unfolded I was really excited. The only bigger excitement was in all the people who wanted to take the 'balmy' guy's photograph after the race. Too bad I was too chicken to walk up to (NBC's) Susan Smith before the races to see if I could have gotten on the tube.

"Fortunately, my sister and many of the friends back home (in British Columbia, Canada) made a major score on that race. I still carry a picture of one of the shortest-priced favorites to lose in the history of the Breeders' Cup in my wallet."

—Tim Yatcak

## 1987 CLASSIC

"The set-up was out of a script from Hollywood, exactly where it was run.

"The two top contenders (Ferdinand and Alysheba) each were winners of a Kentucky Derby and both came into the race in top form. This was a legitimate one-on-one faceoff, much more substantive than the '89 match between Easy Goer and Sunday Silence.

"The stretch run ranks as the best of the bunch and the crowd was raising the rafters all the while. (Tom) Durkin's call couldn't have been better. The two Derby winners hit the wire together in a dramatic finish to the world's richest horserace! And the Shoe finally got his Breeders' Cup win. Good show."

—Warren L. Clark

"The perfect ride by the Shoe, the determination of Alysheba and the oh so close finish. This was the Breeders' Cup at its best."

—Jerry Stone

## 1988 DISTAFF

"While I know that everyone has his or her own opinion, I cannot imagine that anyone who has attended every Breeders' Cup in person—as I have—could answer anything but Personal Ensign's final race of her career.

"On a dark, dreary, cold day at Churchill Downs, the undefeated filly looked every bit a loser just a stride or two from the wire. She never took hold of the wet track, was climbing terribly around the turns and really didn't want any part of racing that day. Nevertheless, Randy Romero called on every bit of her heart, class and courage to get up in the last jump to beat Kentucky Derby heroine Winning Colors by a scant nose.

"I can still remember to this day the exact place where I was standing on the third floor of Churchill's old wooden clubhouse. And I can still remember that Personal Ensign wore saddle cloth No. 6 and Winning Colors No. 2. At the time I was still living in Los Angeles. Next to witnessing Secretariat's 1973 Belmont Stakes win in person and Native Diver's third straight Hollywood Gold Cup win in 1967, no moment in thoroughbred racing has so moved me. The hair was literally standing up on the back of my neck—and not from the cold chill of the air."

—Ron Hale

"I was at the Derby in 1988 cheering on Winning Colors. It was my first Derby and I had picked the winner. I was hoping for great things for her. I knew of Personal Ensign's achievements and was thoroughly impressed. I wanted to see her retire undefeated.

"I got stuck in a traffic jam and had to watch the race on TV. It looked like Winning Colors would take it—out in front, the rest of the field beaten. There I was, cheering her on again—and then Personal Ensign began to run. It looked impossible, but she was flying. I stared in awe, then found myself screaming, first for Personal Ensign, then for Winning Colors, then just screaming.

"How did she do it? I still don't know. Too much class to get beat? Too much talent? Too much heart? In any event, it was the performance of a true champion and the race of a lifetime to me."

—Mary Schott

"It figured on paper to be an excellent race. No one could have written a script with a more heart-pounding finish. In one last, desperate lunge, Personal Ensign prevailed. Wildly cheering strangers embraced, cried and generally lost themselves in joyous frenzy. No one waited for the official order of finish to be posted. In our hearts, Personal Ensign had done the impossible. For that moment, she belonged to each and every one of us. She was our brave champion.

"In my hand, crushed beyond all hope of ever going through any kind of totalizator, was a $2 straight trifecta ticket. It came home with me, along with memories of one of the most incredible horse races of all time. The mental image of that last, desperate lunge will always stay with me, as will undying gratitude for being able to see the best the sport had to offer at their very best."

—Melissa Pappas

"Personal Ensign's stretch run on Winning Colors was thrilling to behold. Everything on the line for the undefeated filly and she gets up on the wire to beat an unpopular winner of the Kentucky Derby by a nose to close out a fairytale career. This was a race now etched in the memory of horse players everywhere."

—Larry Loonin

"Personal Ensign looked hopelessly beaten and her undefeated record in doubt when she made a dramatic run down the stretch to catch Winning Colors by a nostril at the wire.

"She displayed pure class and determination in willing a win out of a most certain defeat. That is what makes greatness—and she was great."

—Alex Boguslav

## 1988 CLASSIC

"I had a terrible day betting, absolutely couldn't beg or borrow a winner. I had blown my entire stake except for an extra $50 I always keep stashed away. Alysheba had been my hero all year and I went to play a small exacta with Alysheba/Seeking the Gold and to put a few bucks on his nose.

"It was raining and he wasn't supposed to like an off track, so he was around 8-5 instead of odds-on. I waited too long to make the bet, though—I was at Churchill Downs—and when I tried to find a window there were long lines. The only window I could get my bet in was the $50 window. With about 10 seconds to post I ran up to the window and in total desperation, out of time, bet a $50 exacta Alysheba/Seeking the Gold. It was by far the biggest bet of my life.

"The rest is history—it came in and paid $28.40—a tremendous overlay—and I slowly and carefully counted out the entire winning amount of over $700 in front of my sister-in-law, who had been saying all day that Alysheba would not win. He came through for me and allowed me to believe I was a handicapper after all and, of course, hooked me on the sport forever."

—Virginia Cox

"It was so dramatic, being run in near darkness at famous Churchill Downs, on an off track. Knowing that Alysheba was so close to being the top money earner of all time added to the effect. Seeking the Gold flying at the end made the race all the more exciting. Tom Durkin's call was moving, especially when he called Alysheba 'America's Horse' after the finish. Maybe a little soppy, but it sounded spontaneous.

"I didn't get to see this race while it was being run. I had to attend a stupid wedding and missed the Turf and the Classic and had to watch the taped versions. It was killing me during the ceremony knowing that those races were being run and I wasn't watching. If I'm ever in that situation again, I'll get my priorities straight."

—Ruth Ann Schmidt

"Run in near darkness, the Midnight Classic was the setting for Alysheba's greatest victory. He had run third in the Juvenile in 1986 and second by a short head in the 1987 Classic as a three-year-old. As a four-year-old, he proved himself the best on a muddy track he hated. The vision of him racing into the lights at the wire beneath the Twin Spires at Churchill Downs with his ears pricking as the call rang out—'Alysheba with a short lead is unyielding, Seeking the Gold a final move, as they come to the wire and Alysheba, America's Horse, has done it'—never fails to give me goosebumps and bring tears to my eyes. Alysheba was a very special racehorse and this was his most glorious moment."

—Carol M. Sinclair

## 1989 CLASSIC

"I have been to eight Breeders' Cup races but never felt the sense of anticipation I did before the Classic, the final rematch of Easy Goer and Sunday Silence. This was east vs. west, fullback vs. halfback, royally bred vs. cheap yearling. It was like a heavyweight championship bout from the 1970s, when two fighters were at their absolute physical and mental peak . . . and it delivered.

"I will never forget the roar of the crowd as the race went off with Easy Goer settling into the back of the pack and Sunday Silence stalking the leaders. As they turned for home, Blushing John (no slouch) assumed command with Sunday Silence breathing down his neck. At this point Easy Goer kicks into gear but he is five lengths behind and Tom Durkin utters what I feel is his most memorable phrase: 'Sunday Silence prepares for the oncoming power of Easy Goer.'

"Blushing John starts tiring as Pat Day flails away at Easy Goer, who is gobbling up ground down the middle of the track but falls short by a quickly diminishing head. As the race ended Sunday Silence fans were high-fiving and hugging while Easy Goer fans felt distraught and some had a tear in their eye.

"It is a race I will never forget and have played on videotape numerous times."

—Howard Schmidt

## 1990 DISTAFF

"This great moment is a very sad moment. Go for Wand. Equine athlete. Trying with every ounce of courage against champion Bayakoa. She tried so hard that she ran beyond her ability and it cost her her life. Even in breaking down she got up. She just did not want to get beat. I am not sure I have ever seen a more determined effort, be it human or animal, in my life. Go for Wand's courage is what was great in this race."

—John Van Der Laarse

## 1991 DISTAFF

"I followed Dance Smartly's entire career. There had been some doubt as to how well she would do against the fillies from the U.S., even though she had already won against the boys many times.

"I watched the race by myself and during the whole buildup to the race itself, I paced the room. I talked to her through the entire race, willing her to get up front. When she came across the finish line first, I was jumping up and down and yelling and screaming. I bought the Fred Stone print of her winning that race and it hangs in my family room."

—Cathy Cleverley

## 1991 JUVENILE

"I just watched it again on videotape and I think this may the single most impressive performance by a thoroughbred I've ever witnessed. I remember being down at the Del Mar satellite wagering facility that day and, when Arazi made his move, the room got eerily quiet. Then the whispering began and every couple of seconds you could distinctly hear someone say, softly, 'Secretariat.' It was as though we had no other way to measure the greatness of the race we'd just seen except by comparing it with the greatest horse of our lifetime.

"Arazi's race was awesome from first to last. He broke from post 14 and Pat Valenzuela choked him back right out of the gate, lost all the ground and angled him over to the rail. He was last or next to last, as the field straightened away down the backstretch. Then the magic started. Arazi started a move up the rail. But about the five-sixteenths pole, Valenzuela had to angle him outside. He was literally passing a horse with every stride and the jockey had enough sense to get him out where his momentum wouldn't be impeded.

"Arazi's move on the far turn is, to this day, the single most amazing turn of foot I've ever witnessed. The little colt was moving so fast that Valenzuela couldn't even keep him in a straight line. He turned into the stretch at least five or six wide. But, by that point, it didn't matter. He blew by Bertrando (no slouch on the lead) like that one was standing still. In the space of a couple dozen strides, Arazi had put daylight between himself and the rest of the two-year-olds in the world. Valenzuela was gearing him down from there to the wire."

—Richard Perloff

"The race was phenomenal. I noted how Arazi had a poor start and was left behind. Then in the turn to see this horse literally zooming past all the others was unbelievable. I have enjoyed the race over and over again, which is a sign of brilliance."

—Richard Bochonko

### 1994 JUVENILE FILLIES

"I was completely disgusted with racing after the disastrous Go for Wand (race) and hadn't watched a race since then. I was flipping through the channels one Saturday afternoon and happened upon the stretch run of Flanders and Serena's Song. I'm not an advocate of racing two-year-olds, but couldn't take my eyes off those two fillies who had so much heart. Of course, it happened again—a breakdown— but unlike Go for Wand, Flanders didn't have to be put down. Those two beautiful fillies gave me back my love for racing. I am one of Serena's most ardent fans and look forward to Flanders' babies."

—Monika Edelle

"To me, the race that epitomizes the thrill for the spectator and the indomitable will of the racehorse is Flanders vs. Serena's Song. Two wonderful fillies battling down the stretch, neither giving an inch, with Flanders' extraordinary courage in finishing on three legs while refusing to lose. This is the drama, the tragedy, the thrill of horseracing at its best. Serena's Song has proven what a wonderful racehorse she is. How good then was Flanders? They run their hearts out for us, sometimes they give their lives for us."

—Joan Ludlow

### 1994 MILE

"Early in that summer I had fallen for one of the most futile animals ever, Johann Quatz. I mean this horse never won. Yet he was always entered in the marquee races and always tried his heart out. His effort in that year's Eddie Read would have netted me a small fortune had his nose been about three inches longer and beaten Fastness for second. But with Johann it never happened.

"One day in late August I was milling over a future book odds sheet that had Johann Quatz listed in both the Turf and the Mile. In the former, he was 60-1, in the latter 75-1. The previous year, Johann Quatz had run in the Mile at Santa Anita and he had never won past nine furlongs. Plus trainer Ron McAnally had always put him in the toughies, so I figured there was no reason for him to start now. I was 100% sure that if the horse was alive at the time, he would be entered in the '94 Mile, so I took the 75-1.

"That year I travelled to Lexington to meet my friend and we had a great week going to different local tracks and playing the races. Being in Louisville that year, though, we went to Churchill Downs to see the Breeders' Cup. A generous scalper sold us some wonderful seats near the three-sixteenths pole and the day was incredible. JQ was indeed entered in the Mile that day and, befitting his current losing streak, was put in the mutuel field, which represented a pretty fair estimate of his chances. But, I had 75-1 on him if for some reason he was able to pull it off.

"As they loaded in the gate, my friend and I laughed about my chances while also discussing Lure's shot to win his third straight Mile. As the gates opened, JQ found his usual spot at the back of the pack about 15 lengths off the early pace. I smiled as they went around the clubhouse turn. He looked helplessly beaten, even at that point.

"As they went down the backstretch he maintained his distant position, but as they entered the far turn he unleashed his rally. And I had never seen the horse run harder. Midway around the turn he was picking off horses left and right. 'C'mon, Johann,' I screamed. But, as I looked back at the front pack, a horse was beginning to take dead and powerful aim on the leaders.

"Straightening into the lane, Johann was eight wide but still flying. He was probably still nine to 10 lengths beaten, but still had a chance. As I peered back to the front, that horse had now gotten the lead and was looking very strong. I screamed again, 'C'mon, Johann,' but it was becoming evident that Barathea was to be the Mile winner. Approaching the sixteenth pole, Lanfranco Dettori had pulled Barathea well clear and I knew it wasn't to be. But, Johann was still flying. And, in that one brief moment, my stomach turned to knots. The s.o.b. was going to run his eyeballs out for me on a day when I could have won a fortune on him, but he ran second. 'No, Johann . . . nooooo.' Sure enough, Alex Solis caught Unfinished Symph right near the wire to get up for second.

"Johann Quatz was probably the longest shot in the race to win, but on my first trip to Kentucky and first trip to Churchill Downs, one of my favorite days at the races ever, he ran second for me when I could have won a fortune. God, I had to pick the biggest loser ever to fall for.

"I bet that horse in every race he ran from the '94 Eddie Read to his last race which was the day after the '95 Breeders' Cup at Belmont (he was actually pre-entered in the Mile but didn't draw in) and he never won for me."

—James Campbell

## 1995 JUVENILE FILLIES

"On a wet track she didn't like, My Flag looked hopelessly beaten at the top of the stretch, just like her dam Personal Ensign did in the 1988 Breeders' Cup Distaff. But also like her dam, her courage and will to win brought her to the wire first, beating a gray filly on the rail trained by D. Wayne Lukas. Just like her mama did when she caught Winning Colors in the '88 Distaff. It was deja vu all over again!"

—Louis Margarite

## 1995 JUVENILE

"I was very excited about the Juvenile. I had been following Unbridled's Song like so many other people. I was disappointed in his loss in the Champagne, but he had shown tremendous early speed and I felt with rating that he would be a winner. So, that is what happened in the Breeders' Cup. I had a winning bet on him."

—Joel Schiff

## 1995 CLASSIC

"With the Breeders' Cup being the showcase of class it is, almost all the races have been notable in one way or another. I think, though, that from the standpoint of pure excitement of the thoroughbred in action, Cigar's classic victory has to top them all.

"From the first furlong, the horse showed his desire to go to the front, but he also demonstrated his ability and willingness to be rated. The move he made at the top of the stretch was so powerful it was breathtaking. From start to finish this fine horse proved his professionalism and mastery of the game . . . an ability commonly referred to by saying the horse 'knows how to win.' What more could you ask?"

—Lynn Cronin

## 1998 MILE

"Da Hoss, trained by Michael Dickenson, enters the Breeders Cup Mile off of only one race since his dramatic win in the same race two years earlier. The agent for Gary Stevens decides not to take the mount on Da Hoss and chooses Among Men instead. John Velazquez picks up the mount on Da Hoss, who needed a horse to withdraw to just get into the race.

"Da Hoss turns for home just behind the leaders. Da Hoss hits the front early in the stretch only to lose the lead to Hawksley Hill. Da Hoss would not be denied as he battled back in a thrilling stretch drive that did not deserve a loser.

"Da Hoss prevailed by a nose and forever etched his name into the greatest Breeders' Cup champions."

—Andrew Willnus

## 2001 CLASSIC

"As soon as I found out the Breeders' Cup would return to Belmont Park in 2001, I started to make plans. With my grandfather still going strong at his house in Queens, the accommodations were a cinch. Transportation was no problem either. My family had run the gauntlet that is the New York–Washington corridor many times. Leaving mid-day on Friday would allow my dad and I to arrive in Queens early evening while missing most of the traffic.

"Why my dad was coming along was something of a mystery all weekend. The $75 per person we shelled out for clubhouse seats probably wasn't it. Visiting his dad and aunts probably wasn't it either. He didn't have to go to the Breeders' Cup with me to go to New York. He could have driven up with me and then allowed me to fulfill my horsey passions alone. Yet my whole life Dad has attended the horse events with me and my sister—we're involved in dressage—including all the shows, vet visits, clinics, smiles, and tears despite his ambivalence towards the equine participants.

"Mostly, Dad was coming because the Breeders' Cup was meaningful to me and Dad likes to be there for those moments. So we showed up Breeders' Cup morning with our tickets and our heavy jackets because boy was it cold! We quickly determined that our seats, prone to the wind and no sun, were not the best place to sit around waiting for the races to start.

"Since I was the Belmont Park expert, having visited it once before on Woodward Stakes day in 2001, I showed my dad around. The track, the winner's circle, the paddock, the grandstand and the betting windows. He was really impressed by the $500 minimum windows. Go figure.

"The pre-Breeders' Cup races began and we watched those two along the rail. I wanted my dad to experience the rush of being right up next to the track and seeing the horses come closer and closer before blowing by like locomotives. I'm not sure he was impressed.

"Once the Breeders' Cup races got underway, I made dashes between the paddock right after each race was over so I could get a front seat to see the saddling and walking of the horses. No need to stand in the long lines at the windows; I had made all my bets in the morning and did not yet have the need to cash one. After the horses exited the paddock, I then made the mad dash back to my seat to catch the post parade and not miss any of the action. My dad, on the other hand, usually tailed after me, arriving at the paddock several minutes after me and then heading back to the seats before the horses had left for the track. I think he just wanted to leave time to meander by the $500 window.

"As the day wore on I got tired of the fight through the crowds to get to the paddock so I hunkered down at my seats to withstand the wind and cold and watched the Juvenile, Turf and Classic. After European horses won the Juvenile and Turf and my only cashed ticket was a $2 show on Milan in the Turf, which paid only $4.50, I was eager for the Classic and some redemption.

"In 2000 I watched the Breeders' Cup for the first time as a true racing fan. I'd seen it several times before in passing, because I was always a horse person, but I'd never been a racing fan. I became enraptured with Red Bullet in the Preakness and became hooked. While everyone was touting super horse Fusaichi Pegasus in the 2000 Classic, I thought a dark California horse would be his undoing and thus picked my first Breeders' Cup Classic winner. The winner, of course, was Tiznow.

"The year 2001 had been a tough one for Tiznow. A promising Santa Anita Handicap win was followed by back problems and two lackluster Breeders' Cup preps and a puzzling refusal to train. But something about the bay from the west coast kept tickling me. I'd been a huge supporter of him since the previous summer and knew that he always ran his best race in the third off the layoff, which the Breeders' Cup was going to be. I also knew that Tiznow had a fighter's heart and if someone took the race to him, eye to eye, he would win. So I had $2 to win on Tiznow sitting in my pocket. Yes, I'm a $2 bettor. I don't make enough money to bet more than that!

"My dad, who didn't really see the need for seats at all since we watched the race on the giant TV, was taking the big race in stride. The same calm, relaxed look on his face as he was probably scanning the crowd trying to figure out which of them liked to visit the $500 window.

"When the gates opened for the race, we were all on our feet. Tiznow with his wonderful speed and tractability took up a stalking position in third. As the soon-to-be re-born sprinter Orientate faded and Albert The Great took over the lead, Tiznow still seemed primed for take-off. But as they rounded the turn and approached the top of the stretch, he never punched in or took off like he did at Santa Anita earlier in the year. Instead, he seemed to be plugging along. Tiznow seemed to have little fight as Sakhee, the great Arc de Triomphe winner, ranged up on his outside and took a half-length lead.

"But when Tiznow suddenly sprang into gear, my heart leaped. I started screaming as he fought back against Sakhee and began to close the distance between the two. The wire was close and Tiznow was back in contention and when race announcer Tom Durkin called 'Tiznow wins it for America' I absolutely lost it. This was a colt I had loved from afar for over a year, whom people had doubted and wondered if he was a worthy Breeders' Cup Classic winner, a worthy Horse of the Year. I had faith all year even when he ran a dull third in the Woodward, which I attended to see his return to the races.

"Faith and love mean a lot more than money and I was jumping up and down and screaming like I scored big on the Pick Six. When I finally noticed the photo sign flashing to indicate the race was not official and the stewards were looking at the photo of the finish, my heart skipped a beat as I wondered if it was possible that Durkin had called the finish wrong. The replays showed it close, so close. And when they finally put Tiznow's number on top, I lost it again. I grabbed my dad's arm and cheered and screamed as the great bay returned to the grandstand to get his purple and yellow blanket for the winner's circle celebration.

"By this time, everyone around me in the clubhouse probably thought I was insane and I doubt my dad was an exception. But there was a smile on his face and a glimmer in his eye when he declared that the whole trip was worth it just to see my reaction. That's how wonderful my dad is; he had a great time because I had a great time. I hardly wanted to leave, hoping to glimpse Tiznow on his way back to the stable or to bask in the glow of a victory that in reality meant just over $14 for me.

"Despite my pre-race intention to keep the ticket as a memento if he won, I was too excited that I actually had a ticket or two to cash to remember to save it. But it was truly special to my heart. As for my dad, I'm not real sure how he felt about the experience. He does have some residual effects. As holders of clubhouse tickets we were given nifty orange strings to attach to our ticket and wear around our necks. The orange shoelace-type strings had Breeders' Cup 2001 written all along them in white lettering. My dad now uses this to hold his badge for one of the offices he visits for work. Once at a meeting, a co-worker of Dad's was extremely impressed with the string and demanded to know where Dad got it. Dad had a blast relaying the story to me of how jealous the co-worker was that Dad attended the Breeders' Cup.

"The 2001 Classic was not the fastest or the flashiest renewal. But it will always be the best in my eyes as a courageous (and under appreciated) colt fought back to make history and again capture my heart, and my dad and I shared a day that only a father and daughter can."

—Catherine Conk

"So many moments: Personal Ensign winning the 1988 Distaff like she was supposed to, but letting Winning Colors help her make a show of it; Sunday Silence taking his revenge on Easy Goer in the 1989 Classic and nailing Horse of the Year; the red flash of Arazi in the 1991 Juvenile. But in the end the glamour of blazing talent won't do it, and even the hard-fought victory of a low-priced favorite falls short. We want a hero; someone we can look up to; someone who fights against the odds and adversity and guts out a win in the face of failure.

"I went to New York for the Breeders' Cup in October 2001 and found the city still reeling [from 9-11]. Downtown smelled like death. And winter came early that year. October 27 rose with a cold, hard wind. Out at Belmont I was ducking into my seat for the races, then back indoors until the next batch of horses were in the gate.

"The day started with tragedy when Exogenous reared up en route to the track and suffered multiple injuries which proved to be so serious she had to be humanely destroyed six days later. While it seemed like there was nowhere to go but up from that first race incident, it remained a cold, hard day without too many thrills. I lost most of my bankroll and shivered through the day.

"When it came time for the Classic, it appeared to be a wide-open race. In the absence of the retired Point Given, the favorite's role had fallen to Aptitude, a respectable, uninspiring sort who had flashed a big speed figure in his last. Maybe he had turned a corner, but no one I know was excited about him. There was also a lot of talk about Godolphin's Sakhee, brilliantly entered in the Classic rather than the Turf in the face of conventional wisdom. Sakhee's stablemate Fantastic Light had just dominated the Turf, and Godolphin were looking to complete the late double with a horse who was, at that point, the best in the world.

"Entered, but a relatively forgotten fourth choice at almost 7-1, was defending champion and 2000 Horse of the Year, Tiznow. He had followed up his championship year with a successful spring campaign in his native California, but a back injury kept him out of the races for several months afterward. Tiznow had been having a hard time coming back, having prepped for the Classic with two disappointing third place finishes in the Woodward and the Goodwood, the second as an even-money favorite. There were rumors of continued back problems and of troubled, willful behavior. He fussed, he balked, he had to be galloped going the wrong way. He just did what he wanted to do, and no one knew what he would want to do in the Classic. I didn't care. I loved him anyway.

"New Yorker Albert The Great, happy at home, got off to his usual fast start, and after a half mile chasing future sprint champion Orientate, Albert was leading the way, as he had the year before, with Tiznow right behind him. Then, as before, Tiznow leaped ahead. The replay was made complete when a European in blue loomed on the outside. But where Giant's Causeway never did get a head in front of Tiznow in the 2000 Classic, Sakhee did. Albert was hanging tough, fading slowly, and Tiznow was battling on. But it was Sakhee in front by half a length at the stretch call and it looked like he would win the race. And why not? Majestically bred, racing in the colors of Europe's leading owner, Sakhee had come to America after establishing his supremacy on the European turf with a six-length victory in the Arc. He was a serious racehorse.

"I sadly figured Tiznow was beat. Everyone did. Except Tiznow. He would not lose because what he wanted that day was to win, and he wanted it very badly. Inch by inch in those last few yards, Tiznow's pink colors crept up inside the blue, till Tiznow was in the lead again. Sakhee tried valiantly to hang on, but had no further response. He was beat. He was every bit as fast and fit as Tiznow, and racetrack royalty to boot, no California outsider.

"But Tiznow simply wanted it more, wanted it all the way. Did he know it was the big race, that this was the one? How could he? He's a horse. Yet horses seem to pick up on things sometimes, that they couldn't possibly know, and maybe he knew something was up. But he didn't know about the World Trade Center or Sheikh Mohammed and the intricacies of the political world. He couldn't suspect that in the coming months the New England Patriots of the National Football League would use his victory as inspiration for their own championship season. And he for sure didn't know that I had a bet on him that would restore my decimated bankroll. He didn't win for the football team or for me, and he didn't win for America. He won for Tiznow. And that was enough."

—Lynelle White